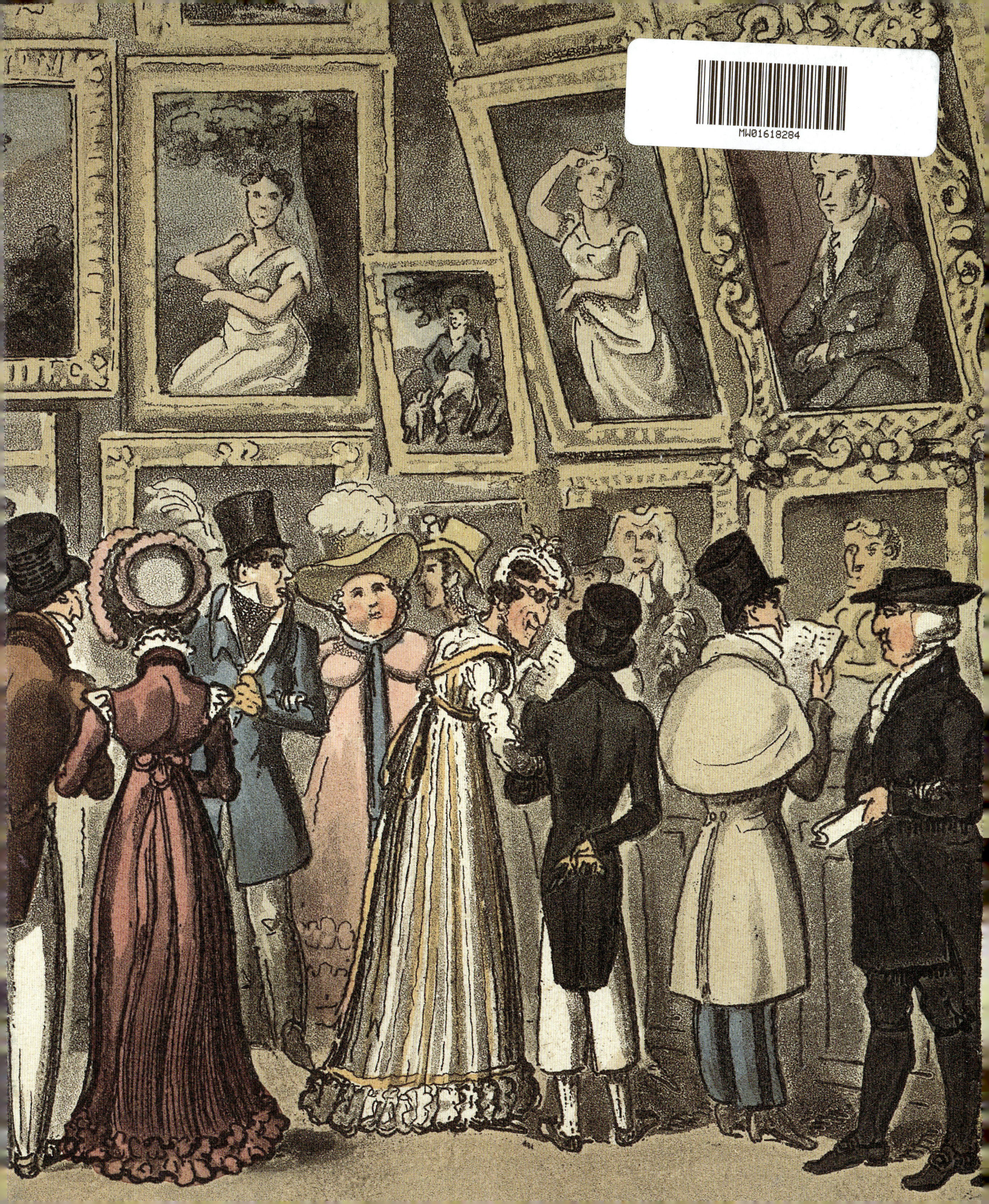

ART ON THE LINE

The Royal Academy Exhibitions at Somerset House
1780–1836

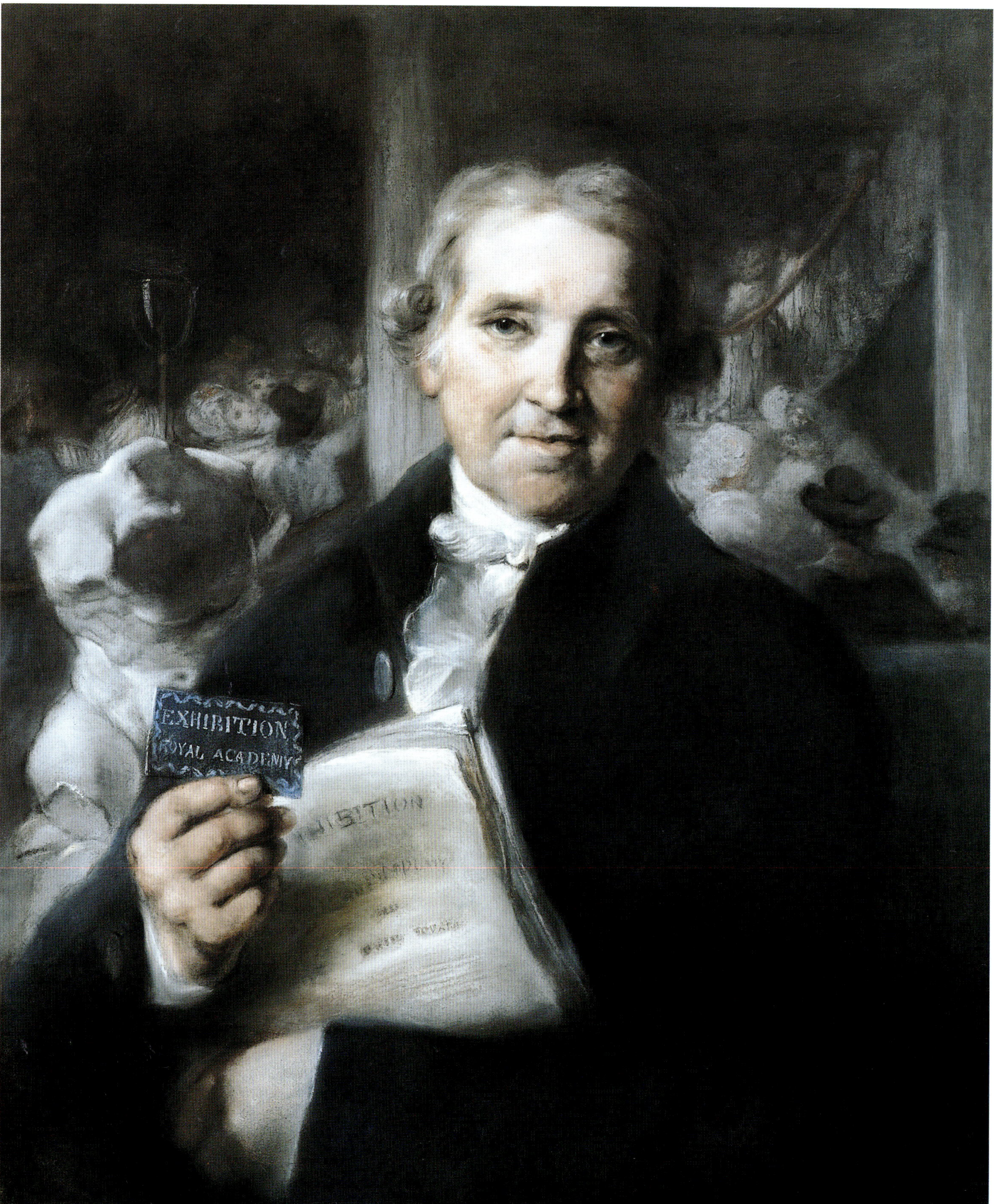
EXHIBITION
ROYAL ACADEMY

ART ON THE LINE

The Royal Academy Exhibitions at Somerset House
1780–1836

Edited by

DAVID H. SOLKIN

Published for
THE PAUL MELLON CENTRE
FOR STUDIES IN BRITISH ART
and
THE COURTAULD INSTITUTE GALLERY
by
YALE UNIVERSITY PRESS
New Haven and London

Designed by Gillian Malpass

Printed in Singapore

Library of Congress Cataloging-in-Publication Data

Art on the line: the Royal Academy exhibitions at Somerset House,
1780–1836 / edited by David H. Solkin.
p. cm.
Includes bibliographical references and index.
ISBN 0-300-09091-9 (cloth: alk. paper)
1. Art–Exhibitions. 2. Royal Academy of Arts (Great Britain)
3. Art, British–18th century.
4. Art, British–19th century. 5. Somerset House (London, England)
6. Art and society–England–London. I. Solkin, David H.
N5054 .A78 2002
709′.41′07442132–dc21

2001026307

A catalogue record for this book is available from
The British Library

ILLUSTRATIONS: Works reproduced are in oil on canvas,
unless otherwise indicated.

FRONTISPIECE: John Russell, *A Porter at the Royal Academy*, RA 1792, pastel.
The Courtauld Institute Gallery.

Contents

Foreword

THIS BOOK, TOGETHER WITH THE EXHIBITION that it accompanies, examines the history of the Royal Academy exhibitions that took place annually in Somerset House between 1780 and 1836. These years were in many ways the crucial period for British art, a period spanning the last phase of Gainsborough's career, the *Discourses* of Sir Joshua Reynolds and the flowering of the genius of Turner and Constable. At every annual exhibition, painters struggled to secure the best places for their works in the Great Room, as near as possible to the famous 'Line', the wooden moulding that still runs around the walls at a distance of some eight feet from the floor. Ambitious pictures of historical subjects, executed in the 'grand manner', and boldly coloured portraits of famous sitters by leading Academicians were usually to be found in the most privileged positions, with their frames resting 'on the Line' itself. Meanwhile, paintings with delicate or highly wrought surfaces tended to be shown beneath, at eye-level or even lower. Other works were 'skied' – hung almost invisibly in the ceiling cove. A worse fate was to be left out of the Great Room altogether and to be consigned to a space of much lesser prestige. Historians have long thought that it was the nature of such annual exhibitions, the crowded, intensely emulative conditions under which artists showed their work, that motivated many of the developments in European art at the beginning of the modern period. The present project sets out to test these ideas in practice, by presenting the actual pictures in the very space in which they were first seen by the public and where artists annually placed their reputations 'on the line', in the eyes of their rivals, of critics and connoisseurs, and of the public at large.

* * *

We have been honoured and delighted to receive the Patronage of her Majesty the Queen in this undertaking, and to have received the active support of the Trustees and staff of the Royal Collection Trust through loans of paintings for the exhibition. From the beginning, the project has been developed in partnership with the Paul Mellon Centre for Studies in British Art and has been strongly supported by all the principal public and private collections of British art throughout the country. We have received also the generous support of the Samuel H. Kress Foundation, the Rose Foundation, the Deborah Loeb Brice Foundation, White Public Relations and the group of Courtauld Exhibition Patrons, including especially Mr Danny Katz and Nicholas and Judith Goodison. To them, and to another warm supporter of our work who wishes to remain anonymous, I should like to express our thanks.

* * *

As the exhibition opens, it will effectively launch a season in which, with the opening of the new Tate Britain and the British Galleries at the Victoria and Albert Museum, and other major events in Europe and North America, the achievements of artists working in Britain will be the focus of international celebration. It is fitting that the season should begin in Sir William Chambers's Great Room at Somerset House, now happily again becoming familiar to Londoners as one of the capital's leading exhibition spaces.

John Murdoch
Director
Courtauld Institute Gallery

Acknowledgements

THIS BOOK WAS WRITTEN to complement a major exhibition at the Courtauld Institute Gallery, which took up residence in Somerset House in 1990. For a variety of reasons – but mainly because the Gallery's project focused on the Royal Academy exhibitions and not on the individual works that they contained – the decision was made at an early stage to produce a volume of essays dealing with the salient aspects of the topic as a whole, as opposed to a catalogue of the objects we just happened to be able to put on display. The complexities of this enterprise were such as to necessitate the involvement of a large team of authors, and it is to them that I owe my principal debt of thanks. Not only have they adhered to the highest standards of professionalism, but each has also stuck closely to her or his brief in an admirable demonstration of intellectual commitment to the common good; even more heroically, they put up with the badgering of an editor who was rarely capable of leaving well enough alone. I can hope only that they share my pride and pleasure in the results.

If I had to single out one of my contributors for service above and beyond the call of duty, this would have to be Anne Puetz. Under the aegis of a Curatorial Research Fellowship provided by the Paul Mellon Centre for Studies in British Art, Anne has selflessly devoted three years of unremitting toil to *Art on The Line* in its various aspects. Although most of her labour has been in service of the exhibition, she has also played an absolutely essential part in the genesis of this book. It is almost entirely thanks to her efforts that the Courtauld Institute library has been able to put together the largest single archive of contemporary press reviews of the early Royal Academy shows – a mine of information that provided vital support for much of the research underpinning the following chapters. Anne has come to know this material better than anyone else and has willingly shared her knowledge with the rest of us; directly or indirectly, we all owe her a great deal.

So, too, do we to Professor Hamish Miles, who allowed us to borrow and photocopy his extensive personal collection of review materials, painstakingly compiled during the many years that he has been researching the works of David Wilkie. This was a scholarly act of truly exceptional faith and generosity. The archive has also benefited from the crucial help provided by Susan Palmer of Sir John Soane's Museum and by Mark Pomeroy of the Royal Academy of Arts; in addition, significant contributions have come from Dr Holger Hoock of Corpus Christi College, Oxford, and from another of our authors, Greg Smith. I should also like to express my gratitude to Dr Sue Price, the Courtauld Institute Librarian, for doing her utmost to ensure that the materials we assembled could be put to the best possible use by our team of researchers and by the scholarly community at large.

Elsewhere in the Institute, a heartfelt vote of thanks is due to its Director, Professor Eric Fernie, for his unswerving support for *Art on The Line* from the moment of its inception. I am grateful also to the Courtauld Research Committee for its help with funding, and in particular for enabling me to avail myself of the services of Dr Sibylle Beck, who has carried out the difficult task of picture research in so exemplary a fashion. A further word of appreciation is due to John Murdoch, the Director of the Courtauld Institute Gallery, for persuading me that this was a project worth doing and for playing such an instrumental role in carrying it through. But neither the exhibition nor the book could ever have got off the ground without the active encouragement of the Paul Mellon Centre for Studies in British Art and of its Director, Dr Brian Allen. What Brian and his colleagues recognized from the outset in *Art on The Line* was a unique opportunity to involve university- and museum-based scholars in a project of exceptional significance for everyone interested in the history of British art. The Centre has done everything in its power to turn this idea into a reality, and for this I can say only 'thank you very much'.

David H. Solkin

Contributors

Ann Bermingham is Professor of Art History and Women's Studies at the University of California, Santa Barbara

Mark Hallett is Lecturer in History of Art at the University of York

Sarah Hyde is Interpretation Curator at Tate Britain

K. Dian Kriz is Associate Professor of Art History at Brown University

C. S. Matheson is an Associate Professor in the Department of English at the University of Windsor, Ontario

John Murdoch is Director of the Courtauld Institute Gallery

Martin Myrone is a Curator at Tate Britain

Gill Perry is Senior Lecturer in History of Art at the Open University

Marcia Pointon is Pilkington Professor in History of Art at the University of Manchester

Anne Puetz is Paul Mellon Centre Curatorial Research Fellow at the Courtauld Institute Gallery

Michael Rosenthal teaches at the University of Warwick

Nicholas Savage is Librarian of the Royal Academy of Arts, London

Greg Smith is an independent scholar based in London

David H. Solkin is Reader in History of Art at the Courtauld Institute of Art, University of London

John Sunderland is Witt Librarian at the Courtauld Institute of Art, University of London

William Vaughan is Professor of History of Art at Birkbeck College, University of London

Alison Yarrington is Professor of Art History at the University of Leicester

Preface

'The Exhibition'

DAVID H. SOLKIN

THE YEAR 1780 MARKED THE BEGINNING OF an important new chapter in the history of England's Royal Academy of Arts, founded in December 1768. For the first eleven years of its existence the Academy had held its annual exhibitions in rented premises in Pall Mall, while conducting its pedagogical and administrative operations in a run-down suite of rooms in Old Somerset House on the Strand. But the replacement of this former royal palace with a grand new building designed by William Chambers provided the RA with an interior large enough to contain its school, library and collection of casts, together with the 'Great Room', a top-floor gallery purpose-built for the display of works of art. Here, and in the rooms immediately adjacent and below, the latest products of the nation's artists were placed on public view every spring and early summer between 1780 and 1836, when the Academy moved westward to cohabit with the National Gallery in Trafalgar Square. Throughout this span of fifty-seven years Somerset House effectively defined the centre of the London art world; during an era when a remarkable variety of visual spectacles proliferated in a seemingly endless array for the delectation of the capital's inhabitants and visitors, the display at the RA was known simply as 'The Exhibition', in implicit acknowledgement of its uniquely important status.

This derived in large part from the Academy's links with royalty and from its privileged location within a magnificent building provided at the public expense. Although contemporary art could be found in numerous other venues, there was only one official showcase for the achievements of modern British painters, sculptors and architects; so it is hardly surprising that each year's offerings at Somerset House came under especially intense scrutiny. Even if they had to pay to gain access, contemporary viewers none the less regarded these events as their own public property and as valuable barometers of the country's progress and well-being. The Exhibition also provided a glamorous social occasion, where everyone who was anyone had to see and be seen. In a period of profound and disturbing social change, the Royal Academy's visitors found a fashionable refuge under the aegis of high visual art, but also a place where the aesthetic went hand in hand with a remarkably broad spectrum of topical concerns.

For the nation's artists, meanwhile, the establishment of Somerset House as their premier display space represented the fulfilment of a long-held ambition, that their efforts should find a state-supported arena at the very heart of British life. On so grandiose a stage the Academicians could confidently project themselves as dignified and disinterested arbiters of taste, even if such claims proved easier to make in theory than to sustain in practice. The Great Room may have been designed to show pictures of such elevated intellectual ambition as to transcend the particular circumstances of their production; but instead the RA supplied its audience with highly individualistic demonstrations of theatricality and novelty, fundamentally in tune with the intensely competitive spirit of contemporary entrepreneurial capitalism. The fight for attention and for custom that took place without fail every spring – in an age before the rise of dealers in modern art – produced a small number of winners, and a host of losers, the vast majority of whom have since been virtually forgotten. In retrospect by far the most important triumph, however, was almost certainly that of the profession as a whole. For the annual jousting on the Strand sharpened the skills of a phalanx of great exhibition performers – Reynolds, Lawrence, Turner and Wilkie among them – whose achievements distinguish the Somerset House period as a defining moment in the history of British art. It is a moment we shall find well worth revisiting.

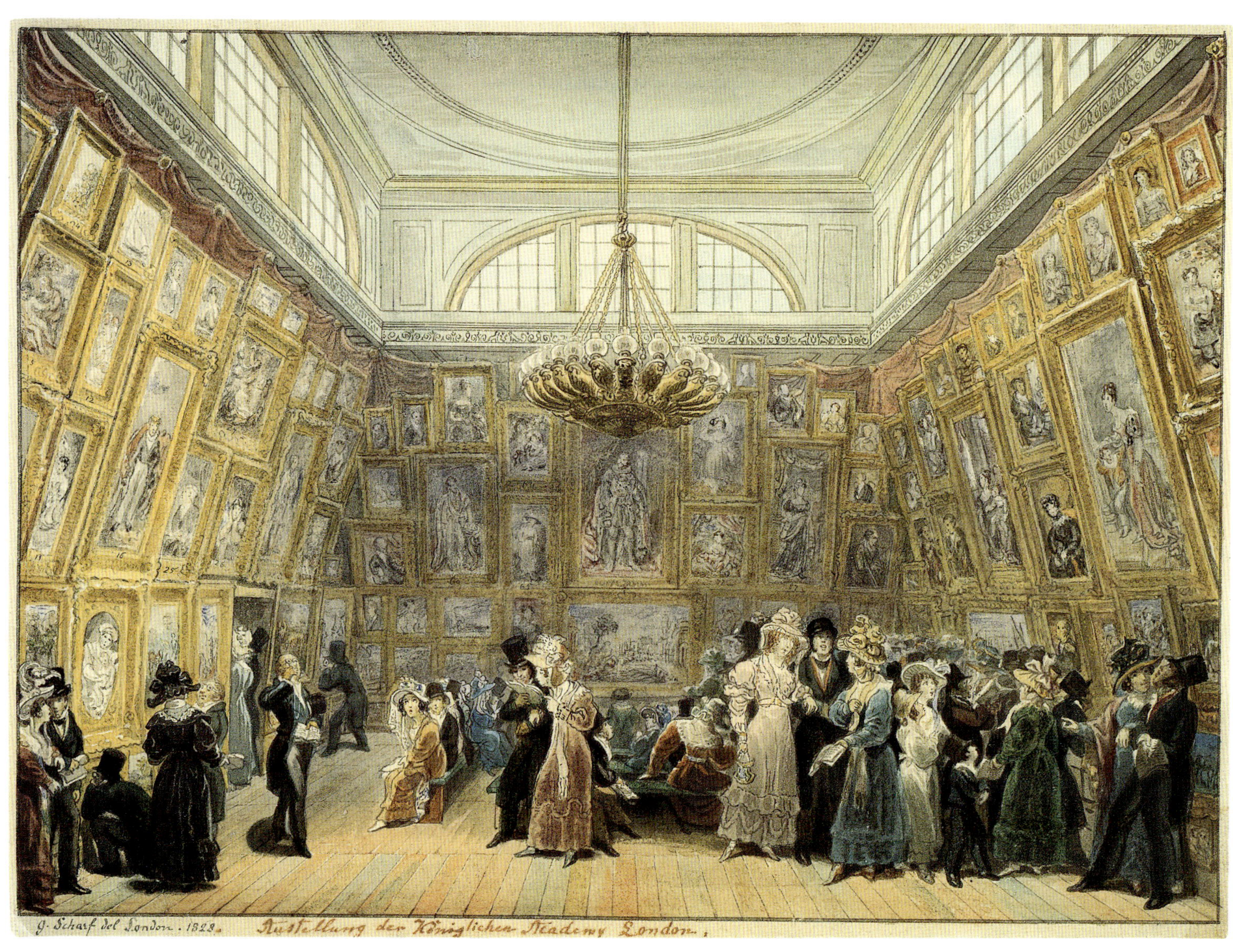

1 George Scharf, *The Royal Academy Exhibition of 1828*, watercolour. Museum of London.

Introduction

'This Great Mart of Genius': The Royal Academy Exhibitions at Somerset House, 1780–1836

DAVID H. SOLKIN

At the first Royal Academy exhibition to be held in Somerset House, few works generated more curiosity than Johann Zoffany's view of the Tribuna of the Uffizi (fig. 2), the opulent hexagonal gallery built to hold the Medicis' most treasured works of art. What the London audience of 1780 especially admired were Zoffany's amazingly precise reproductions in miniature of a score of canonical masterpieces of European painting – among them five major compositions by Raphael (his *St John* dominates the central wall), three by Guido Reni, an Annibale Carracci, two Rubenses, a Holbein, a Correggio and Titian's *Venus of Urbino*.[1] Though the Grand Duke of Tuscany's collection of pictures ranked among the world's finest, his antique sculptures constituted an even more impressive ensemble. One of the principal reasons why so many art lovers travelled to Florence was to see the Arrotino, Cupid and Psyche, the Dancing Faun, the Wrestlers, and the Venus de' Medici, all of which feature prominently in Zoffany's design. Its other main point of interest is provided by a series of more than twenty portraits of suitably distinguished admirers, formed mainly of British Grand Tourists and *cognoscenti*; the company includes at least five present and future earls, several knights and baronets, as well as the artist himself (the fourth standing figure from the left). Commissioned some eight years previously by Queen Charlotte, the *Tribuna* went on public exhibition under conditions that could hardly have been better designed to maximize its impact: for as part of the initial display in the Royal Academy's magnificent new Great Room, Zoffany's image of Europe's most famous cabinet was bound to strike a particularly resonant chord in circumstances where his viewers were unusually aware of the gallery space they occupied, and of their own behaviour in front of works of art.

A reviewer (George Cumberland?) writing under the pseudonym of 'Candid' was quick to link the figures shown within the painting to those examining it from without:

> This picture, which is a minute copy of a part of the great gallery at Florence, at the same time that it is an amazing monument of imitative talents, is a striking instance of laborious industry: wherever the eye fixes, we are struck with the likeness of the thing we look upon; and considering the nature of the subject, it is astonishing how so much effect could be preserved amongst such a croud of objects, living, marble, and on canvas: – the consequence is, that this accurate picture has the same effect on the spectator which the gallery itself [i.e., the Great Room] has on first entering it; the multitude of excellencies contained in it, dissipate our ideas, and it requires some time to arrange them before we can coolly examine the merit of any individual piece; – but the result is the same in both cases; we assign to every piece its deserved praise, and bestow our tribute of admiration on that friend to the arts whose skill discerned, and whose zeal provided these admirable relicts for our entertainment.[2]

Though the attempt to draw a parallel between the Uffizi and Somerset House may have been little more than wishful thinking on the critic's part, surely at the time many spectators would have been struck by the several obvious ways in which Zoffany's scene corresponded to their own experience of the Great Room, where most of them were standing for the very first time. Like the Tribuna, the principal gallery in the 'superb and stately mansion'[3] designed by William Chambers was closely hung with paintings from below eye level to a considerable

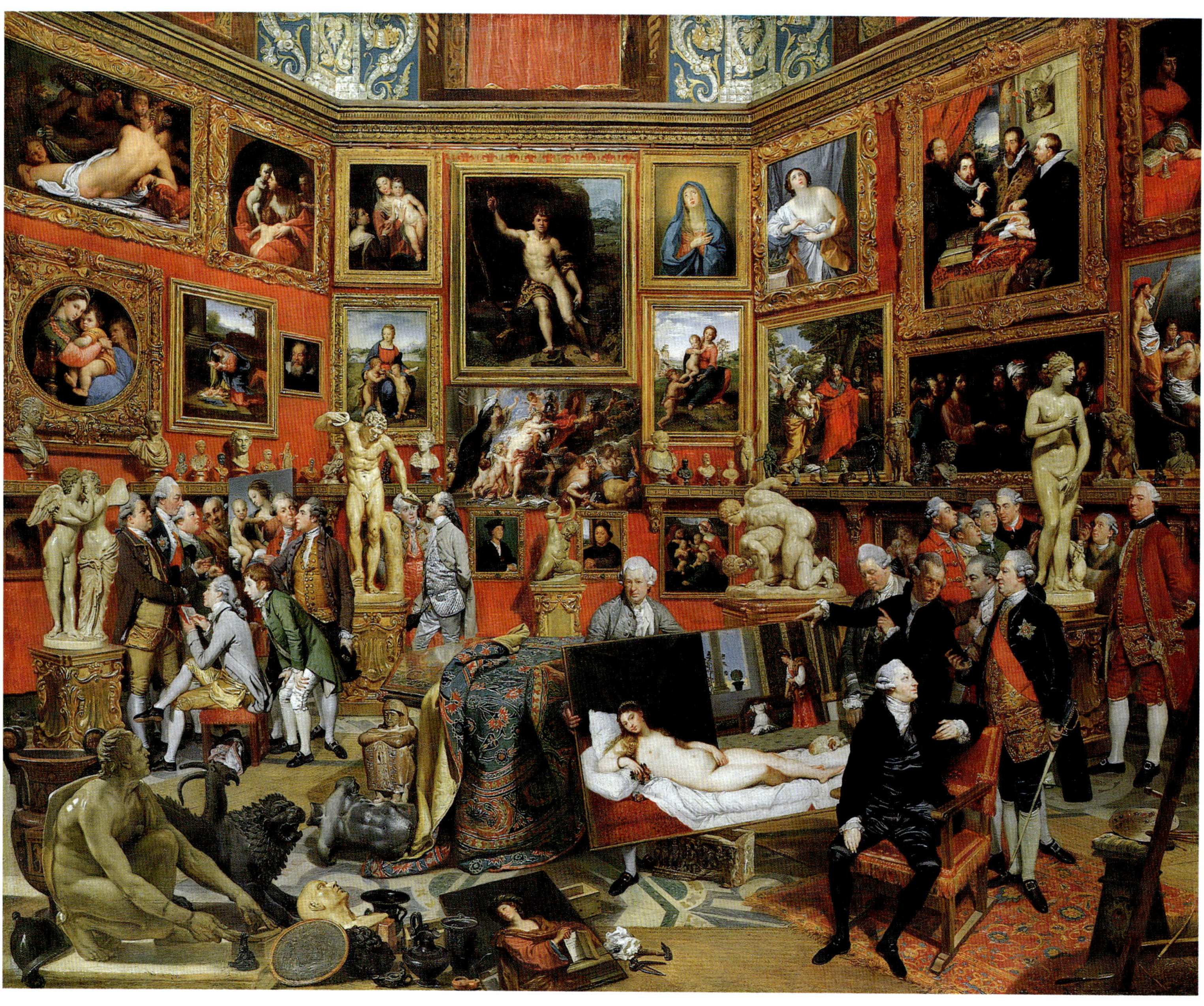

2 Johann Zoffany, *The Tribuna of the Uffizi*, RA 1780. The Royal Collection © 2001 Her Majesty Queen Elizabeth II.

height above the floor (see fig. 33); in both spaces, too, the larger pictures were placed above the smaller ones in two horizontal zones, divided by a more or less continuous shelf in the case of the Uffizi, and by 'the line' at Somerset House. These fundamental points of resemblance may have reminded exhibition-goers in 1780 that the conventions followed by the Academy for arranging its annual displays had a long and illustrious history, as did the viewing practices that the Great Room invited its visitors to adopt.

The idea of hanging pictures frame to frame, in a mosaic-like pattern up and down the walls, would have seemed perfectly natural to European viewers and collectors at any time between the late sixteenth and the earlier part of the twentieth century. Although occasionally encountered even today (something quite like it can still be found at the Royal Academy's summer exhibitions), within the past hundred years or so this form of display has fallen out of favour, to the point where many have begun to wonder how its usage could ever have been sanctioned in the first place. 'What perceptual law could justify (to our eyes) such a barbarity?' the artist and critic Brian O'Doherty has recently demanded, implicitly claiming the sparse distribution of paintings throughout the 'pure' white spaces of the modernist art gallery as a triumph of twentieth-century civilization. The only explanation he can offer for the unforgivably misguided behaviour of an earlier era comes down to its belief in pictorial illusionism. Thus,

Each picture was seen as a self-contained entity, totally isolated from its slum-close neighbour by a heavy frame around and a complete perspective system within.[4]

If perspective operates as the law within this system, giving order to the world evoked by each individual picture, the frame acts as the policeman, by setting the illusion it contains within secure limits, and ensuring that there is no overstepping of spatial bounds. For O'Doherty, 'The classic package of perspective enclosed by the Beaux-Arts frame makes it possible for pictures to hang like sardines'.[5]

While this explanation may help us understand what made such arrangements possible, clearly it falls far short of explaining what made them desirable, or in any event acceptable, for a span of three centuries and more. Perhaps perspective can help us solve this conundrum, or at least point us in the right direction; but only, I would suggest, if we recognize certain important disjunctions between its rules and what it was actually like to look at pictures in a space like the Great Room at Somerset House.

Here we might usefully invite Zoffany's *Tribuna* to serve as our initial guide. One would be hard pressed to imagine a more accomplished demonstration of the laws of linear perspective than this *tour de force* of pictorial illusionism; down to the most minute detail, every feature in the composition participates in the same all-embracing geometric and optical order – a coherent system for reproducing the three-dimensional world on a two-dimensional surface, which operates in the manner of a window on to a reality beyond. What makes the illusion work is the consistency with which Zoffany has adhered to the schema first codified by the Italian art theorist Alberti in the fifteenth century, which requires that all objects be arranged along orthogonal lines that converge on a single vanishing point, in the centre of the horizon (in this case, just to the left of the head of the central figure, who happens to have been the custodian of the gallery). This construction presupposes that the artist has portrayed the scene as if from a single fixed position, which the viewer must in turn occupy if he or she wishes to appreciate the full impact of the representation. In the words of one utterly typical eighteenth-century English theorist of perspective, 'a Picture cannot appear strictly true, unless the Eye be placed exactly in the Point of Sight for which it was drawn: It follows, that a Picture ought always to be placed in such a Position, that it may be viewed from that Point'.[6]

As Peter de Bolla has pointed out, there is an authoritarian politics of vision at work here, which legislates the placement of both image and spectator; yet as he has also noted, even if pictures were always meant to be hung in obedience to the laws of perspective, in eighteenth-century Britain this rule was often broken in practice, and perhaps nowhere more dramatically than in the Great Room at Somerset House. Here not only were many of the exhibits impossible to see from the correct 'Point of Sight' – because they were too high or too low, or at the wrong angle to the floor – but the physical process of moving through and within this interior necessarily created an endless and constantly shifting multiplicity of viewpoints, from which the paintings could be discerned clearly, badly or not at all. Contemporary artists and critics often complained when pictures were 'skied' or otherwise placed where they were difficult to see, and it is hard to find anyone actively voicing their approval of the overall approach or the results it achieved. None the less I would argue that viewers derived certain significant advantages from this mode of display, even if these benefits were achieved at a cost which nowadays we might consider too high.

What happens when we cannot look at a perspectival illusion from its proper vantage-point? According to certain eighteenth-century writers on perspective, the image will appear distorted, even incomprehensible, offering an unpleasantly deformed version of the truth it seeks to convey. But other commentators, more sensitive to the conditions in which pictures were presented, believed that this was an obstacle which the combined efforts of artists and viewers should be able to overcome. In a treatise of 1738 John Hamilton recommended that,

> as Pictures are generally, if not always placed in such Positions, that they may be viewed from several different Situations; they ought to be so drawn, that in any of those Situations, fronting them, they may appear as little disagreeable to the Eye as may be; and if nothing in the Picture in these Views, appear remarkably deformed, the Eye will overlook little Variations from the strict Appearance the Objects ought to have, and the Imagination will be ready to supply the Defect.[7]

Here the final clause contains what is, for us, the crucial observation: that once viewers, by virtue of the physical positions they take in relation to a given image, are no longer subject to the 'strict' laws of linear perspective, they are free to use their imaginative faculties, making spectatorship less an experience controlled entirely from without than a mental process orchestrated at least partially from within. One obvious consequence of this shift is to make it possible, and probably inevitable, for individual viewers to exercise their imaginations in different ways, each coming to his or her own conclusions about what it is that they are seeing. Others may choose not to look at all, and to follow their 'fancy' in different directions. Just as importantly, it also follows that when a group of people confront a single picture, they will have different experiences, depending not only on their varying physical vantage-points but also on who they are – on the psychological perspective that each member of the audience brings into play.

Questioning the notion that the only proper place from which to regard a painted image is that projected by the artist, an anonymous mid-eighteenth-century commentator insisted that

> a large portion of the charms and value of a good picture consists in the fact that, when placed in a good light – it may be contemplated and enjoyed by a company or party of many persons at the same moment. Each seeing it from a different

point. Each taking his distance according to the length of his vision – This notion of a propriety in the view of a picture, being taken, from '*the true point of sight' is confounded*.[8]

What this passage makes clear is that viewing should be understood as a *social* experience, mediated by one's place within a 'company or party', as well as by individual subjectivities which have in turn been socially produced; that instead of being just one, there are many equally proper 'points of sight', that these will necessarily give rise to a variety of opinions, and that pleasure will arise from their expression and exchange. Although the theory of perspective may dictate that we all perceive the same correctly designed image in one uniform manner, in common eighteenth-century practice viewing generated a plurality of responses, which first entered into circulation through the medium of conversation.

Zoffany's *Tribuna* incorporates several devices which seem deliberately designed to highlight this disjunction. At first glance his picture emphatically proclaims its obedience to the laws of perspective, and to their insistence on the validity of only one 'point of sight', which is both the artist's and the spectator's. But then we notice that Zoffany has given himself at least three discrete viewpoints (and these are only the most obvious ones): aside from the central position outside the scene from which he imagines himself (and us) surveying its contents, there is the place he occupies within the image, where he is shown presenting the Raphael *Madonna* he had recently sold to Lord Cowper to this nobleman and several other Grand Tourists; more tellingly, perhaps, in the lower right-hand corner we discover the artist's palette and brushes resting on an easel, presumably holding the *Tribuna* itself, which we therefore see and cannot see. By assigning himself these multiple viewpoints, Zoffany suggests that his very identity as a sentient being and an artist, and hence the truth of his representation, is anchored in a vision that is not fixed but mobile, and in a consciousness shaped by the flux of social experience. This mobility of vision is further registered in Zoffany's portraits of the living figures in the room, each resplendent in his own individuality, and all assuming different stances in relation to the works of art which temporarily occupy their attention. Or which do not, in certain obvious cases: for if the *Tribuna* offers a meticulously rendered visual catalogue of a great art collection, and models the performance of the connoisseurial gaze, it also suggests another order of cultural priorities, that of polite social discourse.

One of the more remarkable features of Zoffany's composition is that it shows no one looking at the pictures on the walls – the main *raison d'être* for Queen Charlotte's original commission. Instead the actors in his scene gather around paintings and sculptures that rest on easels and pedestals respectively, where they can be surrounded as objects of shared and sociable interest. Significantly, the only two paintings that anyone bothers to consider – Lord Cowper's Raphael and the *Venus of Urbino* – appear without their frames, as if to indicate their permeability, their openness to an interplay of conversational trajectories which seem to find a more natural focus in the three-dimensional medium of sculpture. Ranged in their serried ranks on the walls of the Tribuna, the Grand Duke's paintings form a magnificent display, but one that signally fails to compel the attention of the assembled company. While a picture seen in relative isolation may command the gaze with relative ease, an ensemble of compositions hung one above the other and frame to frame can, apparently, be ignored. What Zoffany seems to have appreciated – and this might help to explain why he departed from the terms of his commission by including many more living figures than his royal patron had envisioned or desired – is that paintings displayed in this fashion cannot exert the regulatory power ascribed to the laws of perspective, no matter how obediently these may be followed within each individual design. If a hang makes it difficult or impossible to view works from their 'proper' positions, and presents the spectator with an infinite number of different points of sight, then the paintings that constitute the ensemble must suffer a loss of autonomy and authority.

But it may be misleadingly anachronistic to speak in terms of suffering or loss; for something of considerable value has been gained, in the way of imaginative liberty for the audience, and of opportunities for its members to pursue agendas of their own. In such circumstances, viewing works of art could and did become more of a broadly social, and less of a purely 'aesthetic' experience than we have become accustomed to expect. Eighteenth- and early nineteenth-century Englishmen and women went to galleries and exhibitions to look at the pictures on the walls, but for much else besides: to see other people, to be seen by them and to talk with one another. While we cannot be certain what they spoke about, the period's evident fondness for satires on connoisseurship suggests that a considerable proportion of the Royal Academy's audience (by contrast with the Uffizi's more select public, no doubt) possessed only a limited tolerance for a narrow concentration on the finer points of art. Instead there was a general expectation, to the despair of certain professional critics, that conversations in front of paintings should range freely over a wide spectrum of issues, exploiting the latitude that was implicit in the very nature of the hang.

In the presence of so many paintings, with their rich colours and gilt frames, the viewer's attention could hardly help but be dispersed over the ensemble, which took on different aspects as his or her eyes moved round the room; no wonder that one early nineteenth-century critic compared the exhibitions with a 'kaleidoscope'.[9] The effect of a 'gaudy chaos'[10] was heightened by the sheer variety of the works on display – in marked contrast to those we find in the *Tribuna*. The pictures represented there consist principally of history paintings, along with a much smaller number of portraits; these two branches of the art ranked first and second respectively in order of importance, according to the academic doctrine of the hierarchy of genres. Furthermore, Zoffany's viewers would have recognized that all but a few of the pieces he had so scrupulously copied could be described as examples of the most 'noble' manner: what Sir Joshua Reynolds referred to as the 'great style' or the '*gusto grande*',[11] representing the idealizing tradition of classical art which was understood to have originated in ancient Greece and Rome, and to have been re-established in sixteenth- and seventeenth-century Italy. Most of the *Tribuna*'s paintings and sculptures play by the same basic rules, in other words: they also adhere to a broadly uniform standard of taste, which has informed their acquisition and effectively determines how they are meant to be judged. But there was nothing even remotely like this coherence at the Royal Academy's annual exhibitions. Despite all the efforts by Sir Joshua Reynolds and others to encourage the production of an art elevated above the quotidian – that, in emulation of the most revered old masters, dealt in general rather than particular truths – the great majority of British painters (and sculptors, to a somewhat lesser extent) recognized that there was little call for history painting, or the grand style, and they modified their aims accordingly. Although in theory a great deal of lip-service may have been paid to the idealist doctrines of the Academy, and to its belief in the supremacy of historical art, in fact production was ruled by the practicalities of the market-place, which was anything but consistent or uniform in its demands. The twin pressures of fashion and competition for patronage placed a premium on innovation and individuation, as the exhibitions proved in no uncertain terms. One important consequence of the absence of any dominant aesthetic was that viewers were encouraged to respond to the presence of enormous numbers of remarkably diverse works in an equally wide variety of ways.

We might use the same adjectives to describe the exhibition audience. Each year Somerset House received visitors in their tens of thousands (61,381 in 1780, rising unsteadily to 91,827 by 1822 and declining slightly thereafter), during the period that the show was open to the public – for five weeks during the 1780s, increasing gradually to twice that length by the 1830s. Unlike Zoffany's gathering of Grand Tourists, and equally in contrast to the select company who attended the Academy's annual dinners, the throngs of paying customers constituted what the *Edinburgh Review* described as a 'motley multitude'[12] of both sexes, which encompassed everyone from great aristocrats to the lowest ranks of the urban middle class. Judging from the size and character of the crowds attending the RA in 1822, 'one might imagine that all Cockney-land was peopled with connoisseurs',[13] sneered a commentator in the *Literary Gazette*. But even among the more fashionable visitors, few were probably inclined to dwell at length upon the subtleties of a single composition, or to try and unravel its thematic complexities. In part this was because the overall arrangement of the works discouraged close attention to individual examples, even when their authors had gone to enormous lengths in an attempt to capture the notice of the crowd; but as Andrew Hemingway has drily observed, it is also 'likely that most of those who visited exhibitions approached the display with an attitude neither reflective nor profound'.[14] Instead of engaging in the cool and measured judgements that 'Candid' had recommended – we recall that it was the figures in Zoffany's *Tribuna* whose example he had in mind – they came simply to be entertained.

What brought most people back to Somerset House from one year to the next was the opportunity to see something new, as many contemporary observers more or less ruefully acknowledged. The pursuit of novelty for commercial gain, or so it was often argued, had not only destroyed the high ambitions of the British School, but also helped to explain why the Royal Academy had taken on the character and appearance of a shop filled to overflowing with second-rate goods. An article published in *Fraser's Magazine* in July of 1832 articulates this point with particular reference to the *form* of the yearly shows:

> Annual exhibitions are quite as much calculated to create a hankering after mere novelty, and to give rise to a habit of hasty and superficial examination, as to induce attentive study of what is most deserving. More particularly will such be the case when no line is drawn – no standard of eligibility established, but it is considered indispensable to cover the walls from top to bottom – array them *en cap-à-pié* – if possible with good paintings, if not, with such as are to be had. Nothing like margin is allowed; for, it should seem, an exhibition is expected to be a dense crowd of frames and canvasses, wedged together as their forms and dimensions will best permit, without any regard to arrangement, except that certain places are provided for the privileged and for some of the stars; whilst the rest are looked upon as so many ciphers, valueless in themselves, yet adding importance to the significant figures – a very fallacious kind of arithmetic, because, in such cases, the ciphers are not only useless, but actually depreciating. Rather does the majority of inferior works tend to 'swamp' the entire assemblage, and to leave an impression of disappointment on the spectator, in spite of the satisfaction he has derived from such as are really meritorious. To be contemplated as it deserves, a picture requires its own atmosphere – to be viewed apart from other subjects. This is quite out of the question in a place where it is almost impossible to look at any one piece from a proper distance, without taking in a glimpse of some half-dozen others. . . . Unless it be very conspicuous, from its size or situation, in order to obtain notice in the exhibition-room, a picture must have something that will catch the eye at once, no matter whether that quality be attained by the sacrifice of more valuable ones or not. Even those spectators who do possess discrimination do not always exercise it, their attention being distracted by such a multiplicity of objects; while those, likewise, who are really attached to art for its own sake, are apt to feel palled and sated by over-abundance, unless they check their curiosity, and examine only a few pieces at each visit.[15]

Here what *Fraser's* is bemoaning is the collapse of distinctions between works of art – and viewers – of different classes; the minority of truly discriminating spectators cannot exercise or demonstrate their superior judgement in circumstances such as these. To do so they must remove themselves to the exclusive confines of the private cabinet or gallery, where pictures of real value can be seen in isolation, away from the mass of inferior productions (and from the vulgar crowd). Needless to say, this hardly qualifies as an objective account. Published in a leading high Tory magazine just a month after the passage of the Great Reform Bill, *Fraser's* 'Royal-Academical Lounge' voiced the deep anxieties of the established political elite when confronted by the prospect of something that to them looked suspiciously like democracy. Later on in the same review, this fear of the popular will comes out into the open:

> now-a-days every thing must be for 'the people' – the million. Considered in itself, this might seem rather a matter for congratulation than the contrary; but, unfortunately, instead of educating themselves up to the level of literature and art, the people demand that both sink down to the level of their taste and comprehension; . . . Let us not be reminded of the examples of ancient Greece, and comparatively speaking, we may almost add ancient Italy, where art was at once popular and dignified. There, patriotic and religious feeling – not the patriotism of modern reformers, of whose religious feelings it would be mere irony to speak – conspired to elevate the minds even of the least-educated classes, and rendered them open to the impressions of loftier nature. Then there was reverence for the elevated, the noble. Our modern reformers, on the contrary, of all classes, reverence nothing – not even themselves. No sympathy have they with aught that is generous in feeling or dignified in sentiment; . . . Unless something occur to interpose a timely check to our present unnatural position, the million will, ere long, be the principal if not the sole arbiters in all matters of taste.[16]

The noble template offered by Zoffany's *Tribuna* seems to have been entirely forgotten. Although expressed with greatest urgency at moments of social crisis, the general tenor of such sentiments was anything but new; exactly fifty years earlier Sir Joshua Reynolds (who was not being particularly original either) had warned the students of the Royal Academy not to 'degrade [their] style' by attempting to cater to popular taste. 'I MENTION this', he said, 'because our Exhibitions, while they produce such admirable effects, have also a mischievous tendency, by seducing the Painter to an ambition of pleasing indiscriminately the mixed multitude of people who resort to them'.[17] For Reynolds the hallmark of this 'degraded style' was a preoccupation with the precise imitation of minute particularities – just as we find, paradoxically enough, in Johann Zoffany's *Tribuna*.

Recognizing the 'mixed multitude' as a potential threat to its dignity from the very outset, the Academy took practical steps to try and ensure that only properly qualified visitors – those able to spare a shilling for their own refined entertainment – gained access to its annual displays. These were expected to be well-mannered affairs – not only because they were restricted to the wealthier ranks of society, but also because the audiences included such a high proportion of women. The sociable and studious roles which George Scharf assigns to female visitors in his Great Room view of 1828 (fig. 1) instantiates the widely held belief that the mixing of the sexes was essential to the modern civilizing process; yet there was always the danger, especially in places of public assembly, that this mixture could stimulate improper sexual desires. The gentlemen whom Zoffany describes peering at the Venus de' Medici may represent the triumph of the aesthetic over the erotic, or at least some sort of balance between the two. At the Somerset House exhibitions, however, it was unclear whether the average male visitor devoted more of his attention to the beauties of fashionable nature than he did to those of elevated art. In a discussion of the proposal that the Academy hang paintings on the staircase to allow for more works to be shown, a journalist commented that 'The fair Amateurs, with ancles turned, not less delicate than those of the Venus de Medicis, may be mortified at the eyes of the visitors being drawn to *the walls*',[18] instead of to themselves. That Somerset House offered rich opportunities to indulge in such voyeuristic pleasure was widely acknowledged, and hardly prompted the raising of a critical eyebrow.

The most dramatic instance of an exhibition-goer following the promptings of desire well beyond the limits of what was socially acceptable took place in 1781, at only the second of the Academy's displays in its new headquarters. Curiously enough, this episode involved the son of a prominent aristocrat – precisely the sort of person whom we might expect to find in Zoffany's *Tribuna*. On 2 May 1781, the Honourable Edward Onslow, second son of George, 1st Earl of Onslow, 'in the public rooms of the exhibition of paintings in Somerset House, at mid-day and in a crowded company of both sexes', turned away from 'talking with two or three beautiful young women, the honourable Miss Keppels',[19] to make insistent sexual advances to a gentleman by the name of Felix McCarthy. Unfortunately for Onslow, the object of his attentions proved anything but receptive: McCarthy responded with angry shouts followed by a slap across Onslow's face, at which point the 'honourable aggressor was obliged to run out of the house, with the execrations of the whole company'.[20] Through the press and word of mouth the affair quickly became public knowledge, and after a brief but fruitless campaign to save his reputation, Edward fled the country in disgrace. As Karen Stanworth has noted, what made his behaviour particularly reprehensible (not to mention incomprehensible) in contemporary eyes was the setting in which he had chosen to act upon his 'unnatural' desires: a public art exhibition, in broad daylight, and in the company of women as well as men.[21] But we might also choose to draw a rather different conclusion: that no less than the efforts by men to look up women's skirts as they traipsed up the 'stare case' to the Great

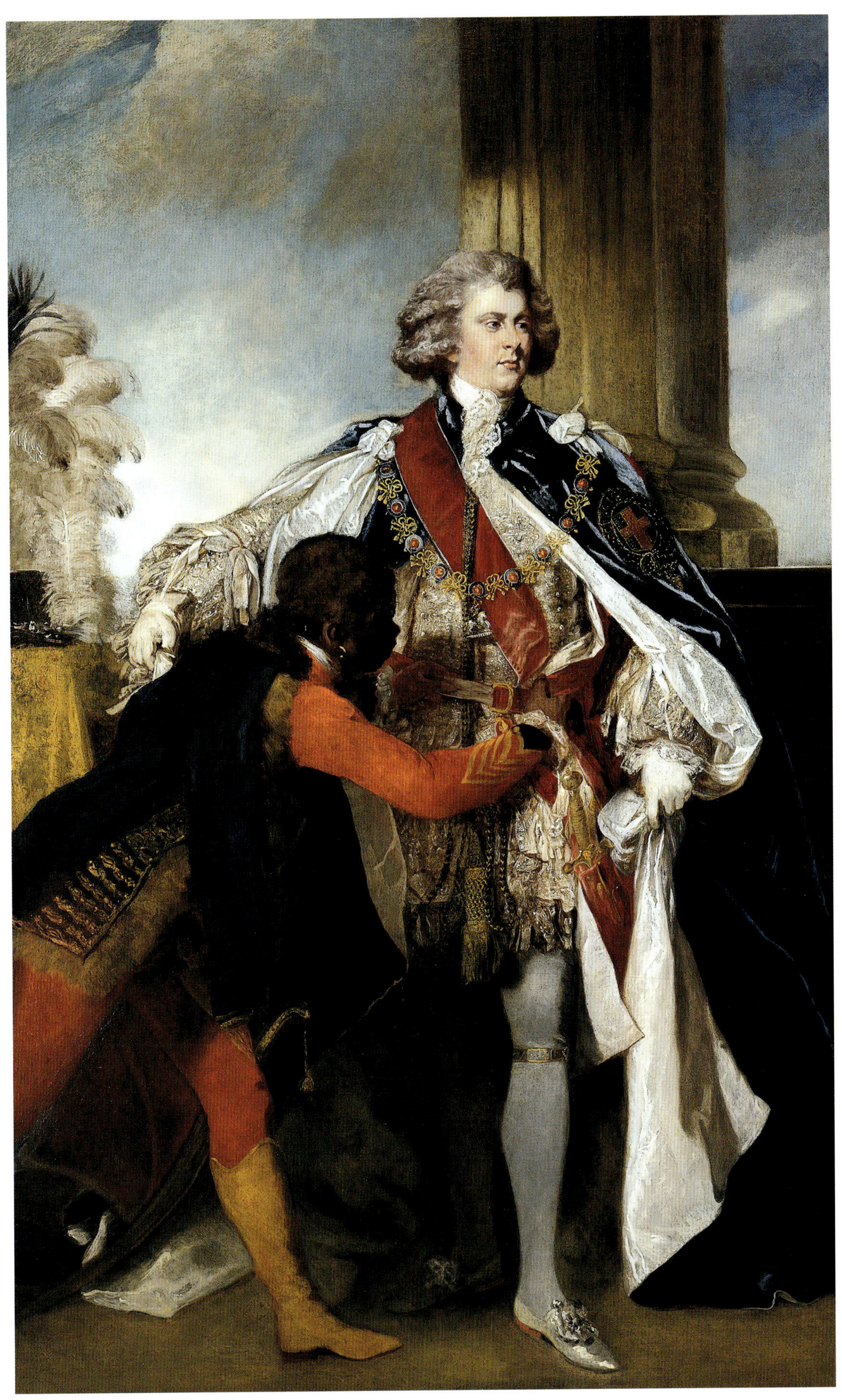

3 Sir Joshua Reynolds, *HRH George, Prince of Wales with a Black Servant*, RA 1787. The Duke of Norfolk, Arundel Castle. Reproduced by kind permission of His Grace The Duke of Norfolk.

Room, or the fantasies that we know were stimulated there by portraits of women of dubious repute (and by works like Henry Fuseli's *Nightmare*, RA 1782; see fig. 53), Onslow's transgressive actions were entirely consistent with the highly sexualized atmosphere of the Somerset House displays, at least in their first decades. This episode also has a great deal in common with several notorious instances of scandalous behaviour that had occurred at Vauxhall Gardens, one of the most widely publicized as recently as 1773.[22] Vauxhall was another forum for the display of modern art, and a place where fashionable men and women gathered in large numbers; that crowds encouraged the licence traditionally associated with carnival is something worth keeping in mind, too, not just in regard to the Onslow affair but for the exhibition experience as a whole. Presumably the Academy had good reasons for its yearly expenditure on Bow Street constables, whose attendance was required to 'Keep the Peace'.[23]

The constant presence of a rowdy crowd, and its reputation for sexually indecorous behaviour, were not the only characteristics that linked the temple of the muses at Somerset House to the centuries-old world of carnival.[24] Another was the humour, mildly subversive in tone and intent, which so frequently found an outlet in exhibition satires and reviews; witness, as one small example, the following comment on Reynolds's grand full-length portrait of the Prince of Wales (fig. 3), one of the highlights of the Great Room in 1787:

> At first sight, some singularities start out – that catch immediately. Amongst these – is one of a *black robing the Prince of Wales* – on a supposition, we suppose, that from his humbled state he has no *white servant* left. His highness seems to take it very patiently, and the black is pushing him about as he pleases.[25]

One can easily imagine this joke, at both the prince's and Sir Joshua's expense, being repeated and elaborated upon by the Royal Academy's public. Although occasionally the exhibitions provoked quite serious social commentaries, like the article in *Fraser's Magazine* that was examined above, the impulse to lampoon the pretensions of the 'great' – and of art itself – was never very far from the surface. As an arena intended for the diversion of the public, Somerset House proved far more conducive to laughter and playful flirtation than to considered aesthetic or political debate.

If the exhibitions generated a multiplicity of critical responses, which ran the whole gamut from the flippant to the grave, this was in part because these annual events generated such deeply contradictory meanings. While the host institution may have been royal in name, in fact it was run by artists and paid for by the 'motley multitude' who thronged into the annual shows. An 'Academy' it may have been, dedicated to the pursuit of higher, transcendent truths; but the yearly display of its achievements only brought confirmation of its failure to live up to this mandate, and of its slavish subservience to the transient gods of vanity and fashion. Ostensibly designed as a showcase for the laudable achievements of the British School, and as an engine for the edification and improvement of society at large, the exhibitions were – all denials to the contrary – a doubly commercial enterprise, operating as both a highly profitable spectacle and a marketplace for expensive luxury goods. In 'this great mart of genius',[26] as the *Literary Gazette* called it in 1822, the pretensions of artists to disinterested liberality came into open conflict time and again with the fiercely competitive nature of their trade. And as we have seen, the character of the audience was no less unstable: both an elevated public and a vulgar crowd, and united only by an insatiable taste for novelty, it fluctuated constantly between the classical and the grotesque.

More than all this topsy-turvydom, however, it was the excessive nature of the Academy exhibitions that secured them most firmly within the orbit of the carnivalesque. Although contemporary observers may have justifiably complained that the setting made it impossible to give individual works of art the close attention they deserved, one suspects that most viewers found this a small price to pay in return for so richly various an entertainment. For the inconsequential cost of one shilling, visitors to Somerset House could always count on receiving far more than they could possibly handle: an overabundance of works; of styles, themes and 'points of sight'; and a surfeit of artists, critics and other spectators, all in numbers that grew ever more overwhelming as time went on. The following essays will attempt to bring this 'gaudy chaos' into order.

I

Architecture and Experience: The Visitor and the Spaces of Somerset House, 1780–1796

John Murdoch

New Somerset House was a building with a programme. At a practical level it was intended primarily for the housing of public offices, the need for which was the result of a growth in the machinery of government characteristic of modernizing states in the later seventeenth and eighteenth centuries, a process perhaps particularly advanced in England. The most important of these offices were for the administration of the Navy and for various branches of the Excise. Since their accommodation required the demolition of the old royal palace of Somerset House, it was necessary also to rehouse the Royal Academy, for the library, administration and teaching rooms of the youngest of Britain's learned societies had since 1771 occupied part of the northern courtyard. At the same time, the Royal Society, which was squeezed into inadequate and inglorious premises in Crane Court off Fleet Street, was in need of a suitable headquarters. The decision to include in the project these two learned institutions, to which the Society of Antiquaries was added in early 1776, and the fact that it was their part of the new building which opened first, reinforced the perceived significance of Somerset House as proclaiming the civilization of the British state, as well as its power. Edmund Burke 'and various other Men of taste in Parliament, having suggested the propriety of making so vast and expensive a design at once an object of national splendour as well as convenience, it was resolved, not only to execute the Work with the strictest attention to the business of the Public Offices; but likewise with an eye to the Ornament of the Metropolis; and as a Monument of the taste and elegance of His Majesty's Reign'.[1]

Accordingly, the building was provided with sculptural ornament which expressed the nature of the state and its governance. On the front facing the Strand (fig. 4) the head of 'Ocean', surrounded by heads representing the principal navigable rivers of England, established the maritime theme which was to be continued throughout the rest of the building. In the centre of the *piano nobile* appeared medallions of the King, Queen and Prince of Wales; above, at the attic, were four figures bearing the emblems of Justice, Prudence, Valour and Moderation, 'qualities by which Dominion can alone be maintained'.[2] Surmounting the whole were the arms of the British empire, supported on either side by the Genius of England and by Fame. Carried out by craftsmen-contractors to the extremely high standards of workmanship which the architect William Chambers was accustomed to demand, and ornamented by allegorical paintings and sculptures by the founding members of the Academy, the building represented all that was best in British art, craft and industry: by its learned deployment of the forms of classical architecture, it served publicly to endow the modern British *imperium* with a legitimizing sense of inheritance from the empires of the past.

Architecturally, the form of the building, with its explicit references to buildings which Chambers had studied as a young man in Italy, revealed and emphasized his conception of modern classical architecture as an emanation of the Palladian tradition. Chambers's own analysis of the Strand block stressed its formal reliance on Italian models. He described it as 'an attempt to unite the chastity and order of the Venetian Masters with the majestick grandeur of the Roman. The great proportions are such, as have been observed by Palladio in the Tieni, Porti and other of his Palaces in and about Vicenza; and the detail, with regard to form, disposition, and measure, chiefly collected from the same Palladio, from Vignola, from Raphael, from Baldassar Peruzzi . . .'.[3]

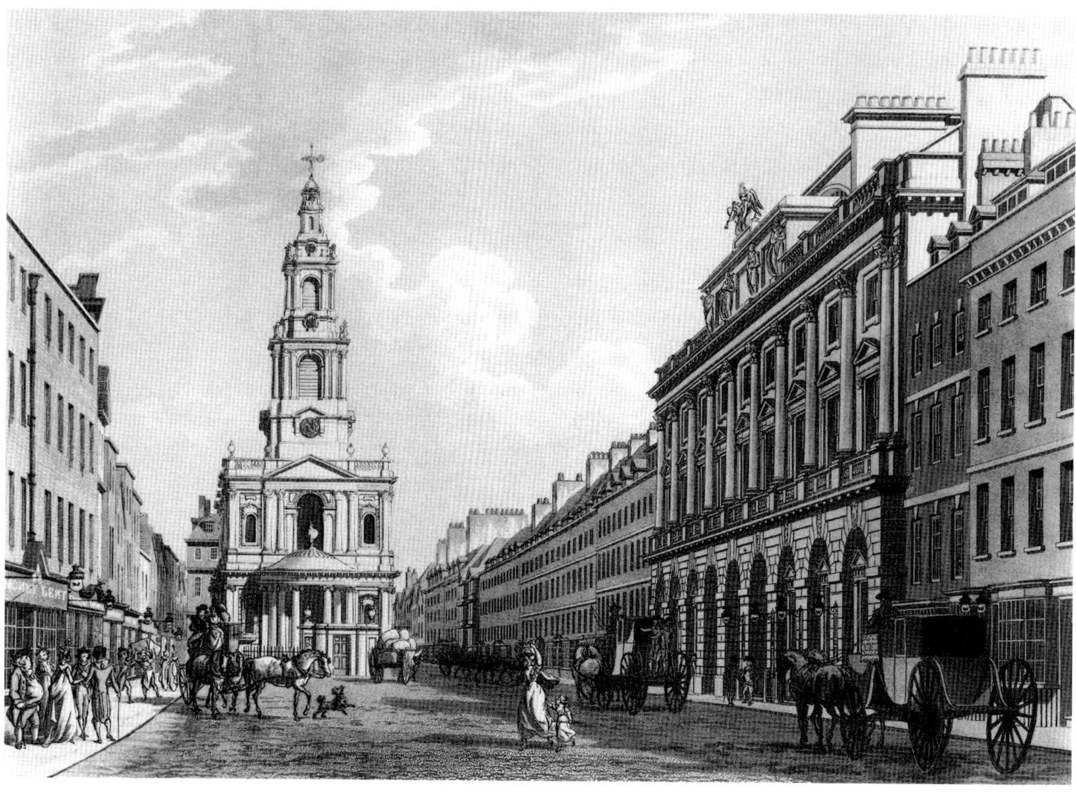

4 Thomas Malton the Younger, 'St. Mary's Church and Somerset House in the Strand', aquatint from *A Picturesque Tour through the Cities of London and Westminster* (1792–1800). By permission of The British Library.

There were similar references to the antique architecture of Rome, perhaps most directly in the vaulted brick basements, which recall the stripped structural brickwork of the ruined imperial baths, the aqueducts, and the subterranean terracing of the imperial palace. They, and the light wells around the courtyard of Somerset House, provide a sense of the visual drama inherent in the exploration of excavated buildings in Rome in the mid-eighteenth century, and disclose in Chambers a sensibility obviously educated by his familiar contact, as a young man in Rome, with Piranesi.[4]

Inside, the presence of casts of the greatest sculptures known from antiquity acknowledged the inescapable centrality of the Roman antique in the academic curriculum. Joseph Baretti, in the guidebook to the Royal Academy rooms which he published when the building opened, was insistent that without knowledge of the sculptures represented by the casts, the visitor

> who enters, not knowing what to expect, gazes a while about him, a stranger among strangers, and goes out, not knowing what he has seen. The subsequent Lists of the Casts of the Academy, with some kind of explanation to each, may therefore be useful to those that love the Arts, and desire not to love them blindly.[5]

Immediately, in the hall, the visitor encountered the Apollo Belvedere and the Belvedere Torso: straight ahead at the foot of the stairs was 'a very elegant group' of the Medici Vase and the Furietti Centaurs, with 'a Basso-relievo representing a Triumph, which is in the Capitol at Rome'.[6] In the Life Academy on the ground floor, and in the two rooms of the Academy of the Antique on the first floor, the principal canonical statues were placed, more casts of the Apollo Belvedere and the Torso, the Antinous figures from the Belvedere and the Campidoglio, the Arrotino, Camillus, Cincinnatus, Cupid and Psyche, the Dancing Faun, the Borghese Gladiator, the Dying Gladiator, the Laocoön, several figures from the Niobe group, Meleager, Mercury, Zingara, and the various Venus figures – Callipygian, Caelestis, Medici – and so on.[7] These famous sculptures formed the object of lifelong study for students and Academicians alike, gave them their vocabulary of human posture and expression for use in the painting of their most important pictures and, like the whole of the new building, declared their belief in a permanent and universal system of values in art.

As pervasive as the intellectual dominance of Italy was the willing acknowledgement of the example of France. Chambers, like Edward Gibbon, was one of the educated Englishmen of the last days of the *ancien régime* who exchanged ideas freely across the frontiers of a Europe largely formed in the image of French cultural hegemony. Intellectually, the defining experience of his early career was the year 1749–50 which he had spent as a student in Paris at J. F. Blondel's new and progressive Ecole des

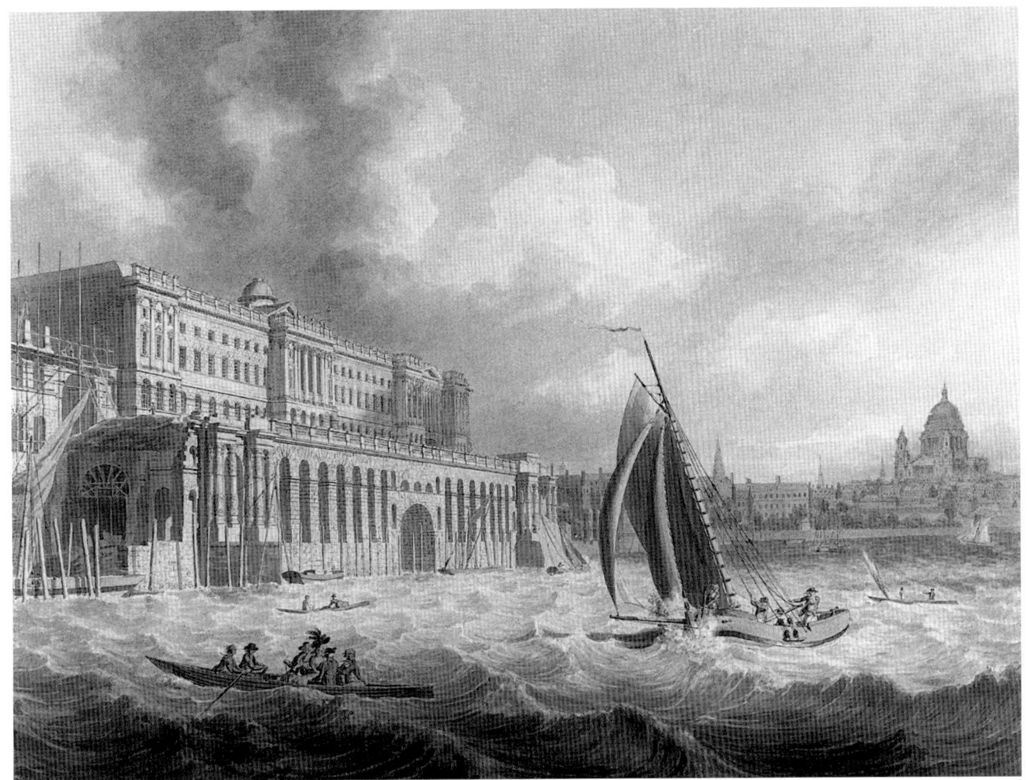

5 Edward Dayes, *Somerset House, London*, 1788, watercolour. The Courtauld Institute Gallery, Spooner Collection.

Arts. There he had laid the foundation of lifelong friendships with the rising generation of French neoclassical painters and architects, completing his studies alongside them at the French Academy in Rome.[8] As a product himself of this royalist academic tradition, Chambers naturally assumed an instrumental role in establishing a new Academy in London under royal patronage,[9] drafting its constitution and planning its structure of officers and professors, partly on the model of the académies of painting and of architecture in Paris, and partly as an improvement on them. In 1774, in the hope or expectation of receiving the commission for the design of Somerset House, Chambers set off again to France 'to examine with care and make proper remarks upon . . . [the] many great things' that had been built there recently.[10] In particular he looked with close attention at Ange-Jacques Gabriel's Place Louis XV[11] and Jacques-Denis Antoine's Hôtel des Monnaies, both then nearing completion. Like Somerset House (fig. 5), the Monnaies was a building designed to house key apparatus of the modern state, set out palatially with an extremely extended riverside façade sheltering a complex of courts behind it, and a central pavilion which, revolutionarily, dispensed with a pediment over the order, substituting an attic storey fronted by statues representing virtuous attributes of the state (fig. 6).[12] This fresh experience of the latest neoclassical public architecture, and the organization of urban space in Paris, had a major effect on the overall block planning

6 Hôtel des Monnaies, Paris, from the river.

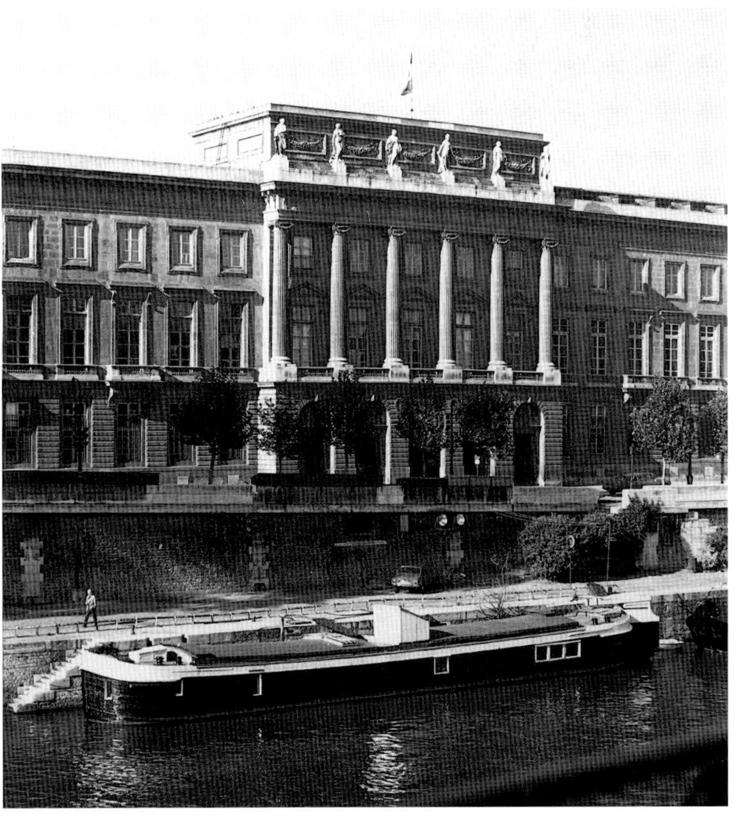

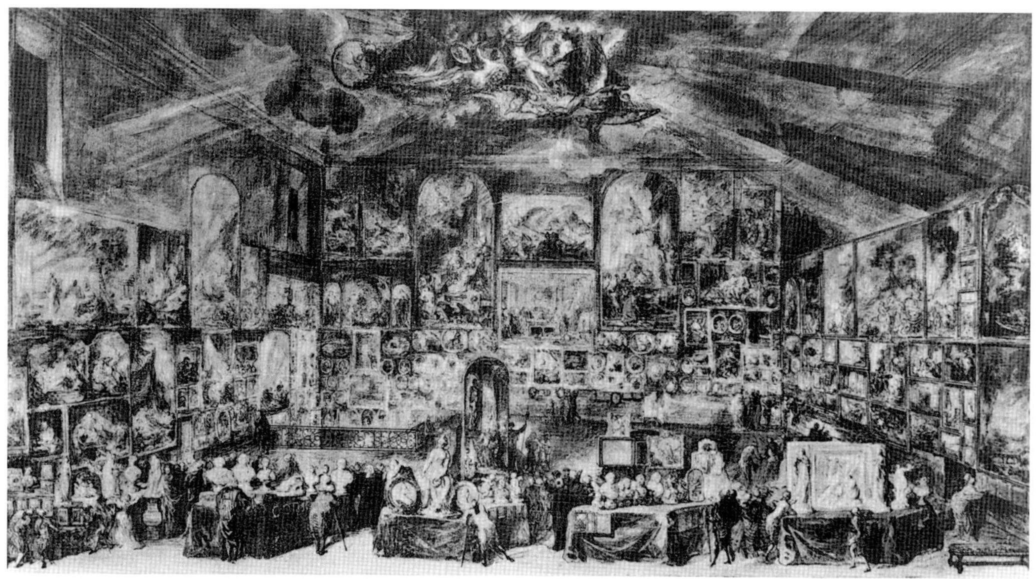

7 Gabriel de Saint-Aubin, *Salon de 1767*, pen and ink, watercolour, heightened with gouache. Private collection.

and appearance of Somerset House, which remains still the most overtly 'Parisian' building in London.[13]

For the arrangement of the Strand block, where the Royal Academy would be accommodated, Chambers looked also to those older Paris buildings which were directly associated with the business in hand.[14] Principal among these was naturally the Louvre, the eastern entry to the courtyard of which, conceived by Louis Le Vau, was surely among the unacknowledged sources for the entry vestibule on the Strand (fig. 8). And for the Royal Academy's exhibitions, there could be no more appropriate exemplar than the site of the biennial Salons of the Académie

8 François Denis Née after Meunier, *Le guichet du Louvre*, date unknown, engraving. Musée Carnavalet, Paris.

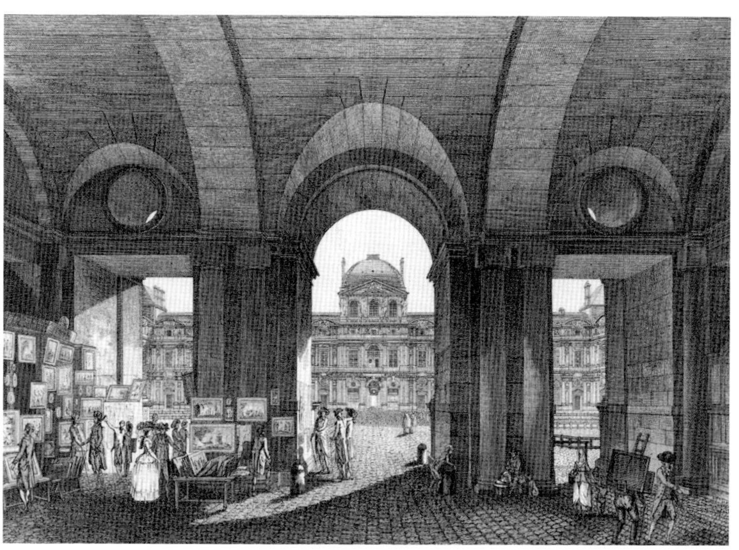

de Peinture et Sculpture, held in Le Vau's Salon Carré of the Louvre (fig. 7).[15] It was this room which gave Chambers the architectural idea which he transferred to London, the defining form which he set out to improve on but not fundamentally change, either in its architectonics or its underlying character as a seventeenth-century princely art gallery redolent of the centralized monarchical system which produced it.

It would surely be wrong to suppose that Chambers took lightly any of his decisions about the form of the accommodation for the Academy's exhibitions, or that they were not profoundly a function of his own mentality. Believing that a rational architecture should reveal itself clearly and immediately to the visitor, he would have consciously applauded an exhibition layout that similarly could be apprehended in a single circuit of the eye. Walking through the Salon Carré in the summer of 1774 – it was not an exhibition year – Chambers might also have reflected on the sensation of being a very small figure in a very large space, conspicuous, and therefore self-consciously exposed to the view of others. He would have known that the Salon exhibitions since 1737 had established themselves as an important part of the public life of Paris, the space itself giving its name to the very notion of academic exhibitions and becoming the accepted 'theatre' within which the public ritual of the exhibition took place. Standing within the Salon, with that feeling of intense, conspicuous self-consciousness sharply upon him, Chambers may have realized that, architectonically, the floor space occupied by the individuals who made up the public was as important a part of the room as the wall space; and, by extension, that in such a theatre the public for art had become as significant a part of the performance as the art itself. His adoption of the form and display strategy of the Salon signified the trans-

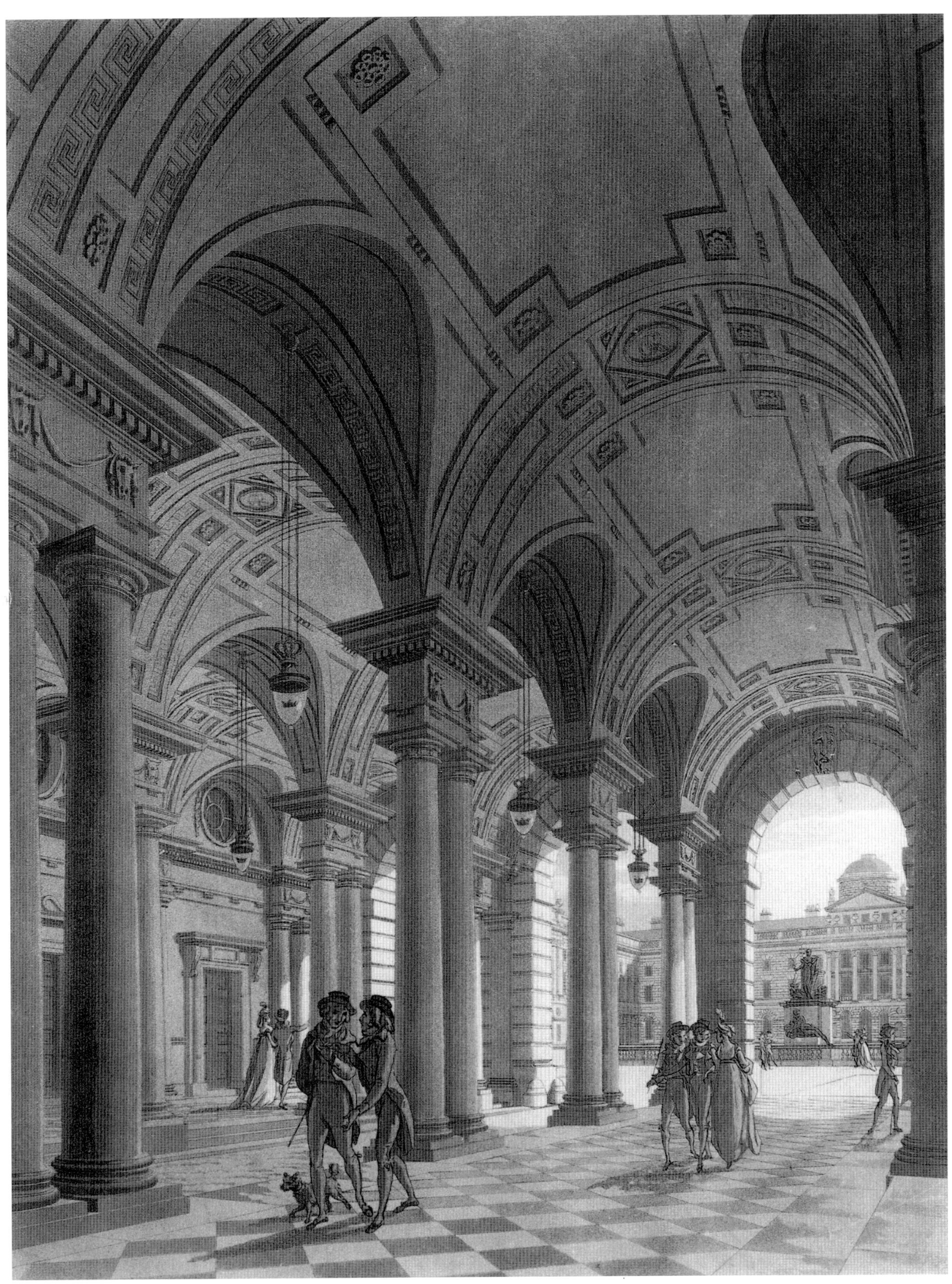

9 Thomas Malton the Younger, 'Vestibule, Somerset Place', aquatint from *A Picturesque Tour through the Cities of London and Westminster* (1792–1800). Inland Revenue Art Collection, London.

11 Somerset House, west-wing staircase, looking up.

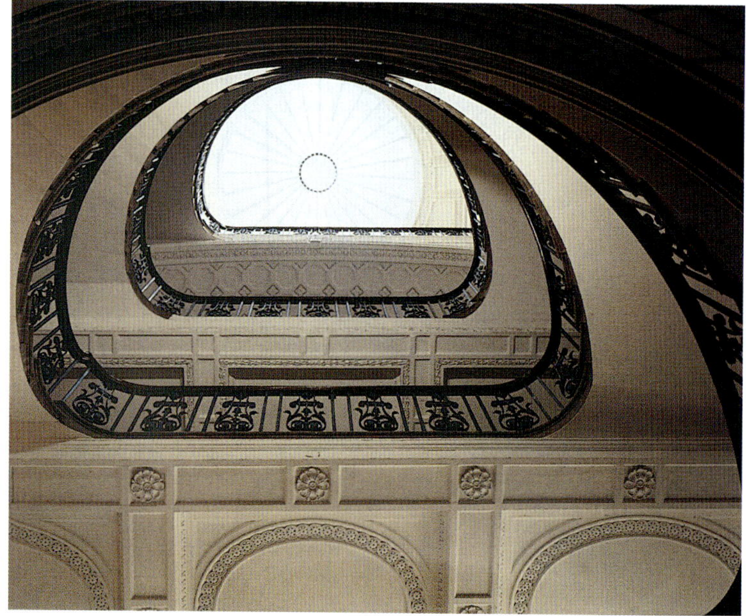

10 Somerset House, the Great Room, looking north-west.

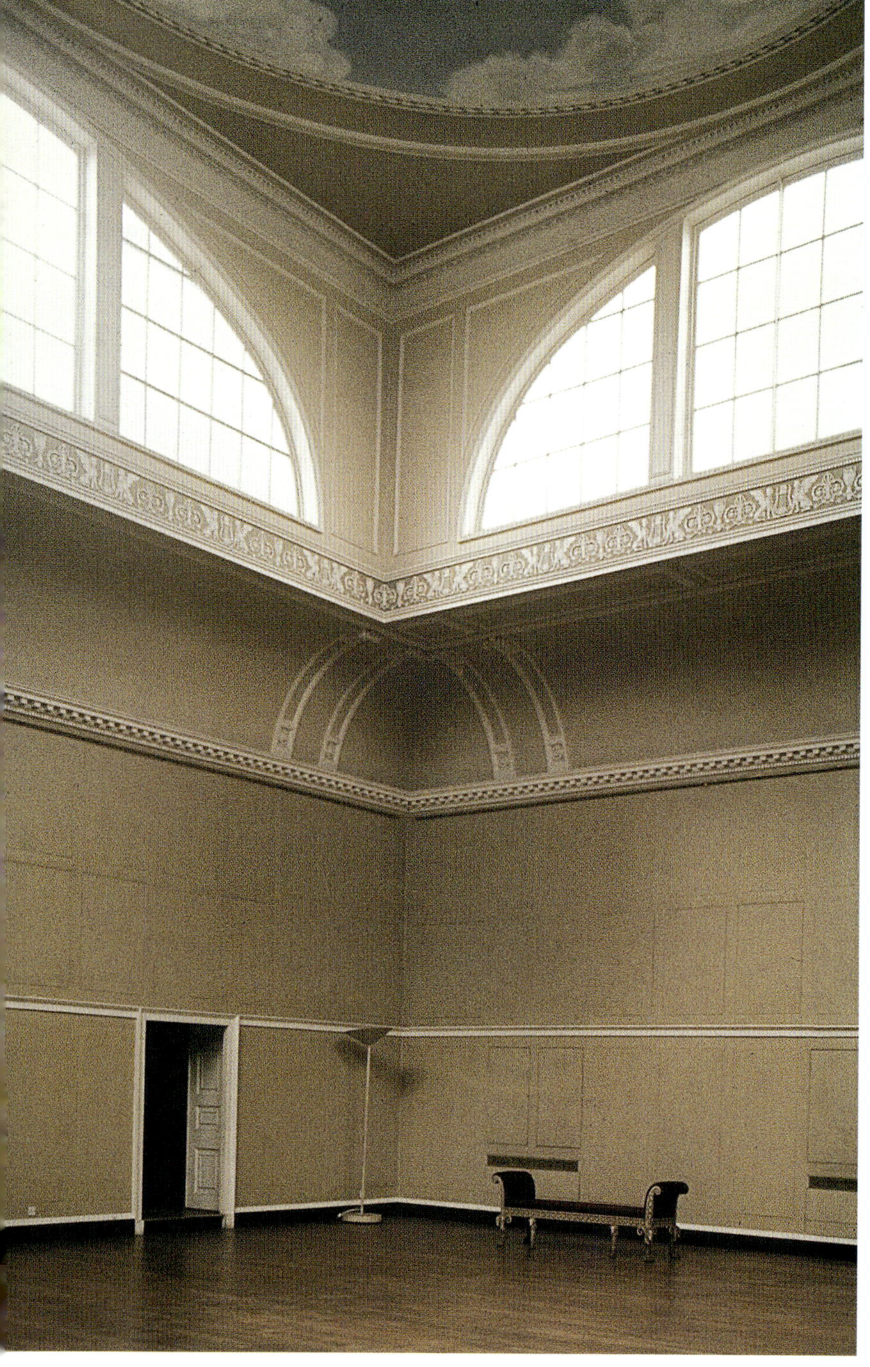

fer to England of one of the principal stages on which the metropolitan elite of *ancien régime* France had constituted itself as a critical public, free and occasionally threatening in its independence, but none the less, in that space, the recipient of the cultural goods provided under the aegis of a monarch who proved his kingly benevolence by the benefits he conferred on his people.

Although the Salon was Chambers's starting point for considering the form of the new arrangements in London, he certainly did not regard his model uncritically. In various ways he set out to surpass it in efficiency, elegance and dramatic force. For example, instead of the haphazard public approach to the Salon, he attempted to provide an orderly, carefully framed and deliberately allegorical approach.

From the street, the visitor to the Academy would pass through a series of artfully changing levels, signalled by steps constituting a series of plinths for each successive architectural composition. From the vestibule, presided over by Joseph Wilton's busts of Newton and Michelangelo, the view of the rest of the building across the courtyard was laid out (fig. 9). From the hall, presided over by Apollo,[16] the staircase curved away: framed by its Doric screen, and combining commodiousness with magnificence,[17] it rose from comparative dimness at the bottom to a blaze of light at the top (fig. 11), forming an allegory of enlightenment suitable for an educational institution, and functioning both literally and symbolically as the *gradus ad Parnassum*, the steps which lead within the Academy from the aspirant student's first faltering efforts in the drawing schools below, to a fulfilling appearance as an exhibitor in the Great Room at the top (fig. 10). The message was declared by the iconography of the staircase itself, which rises through four of the architectural orders from Doric at the base, through Ionic at the mezzanine and Roman at the first floor to Corinthian, the

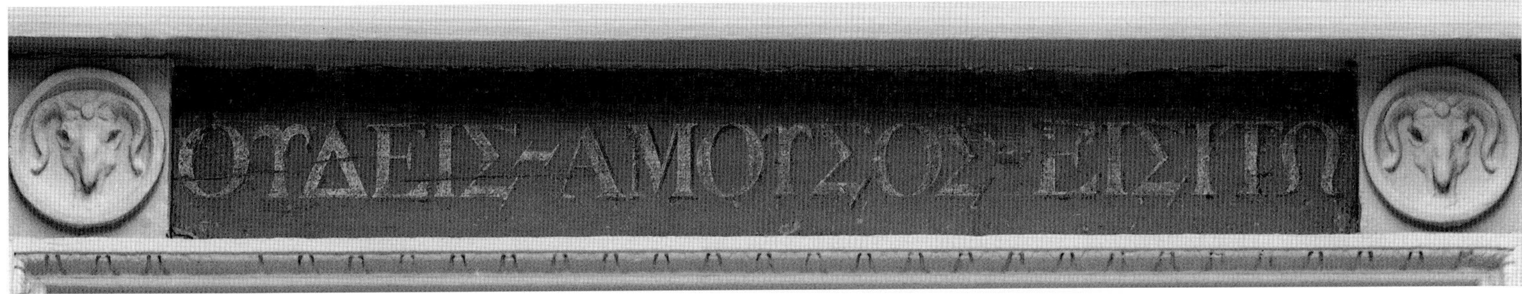

12 Somerset House, inscription above the entrance to the Great Room.

highest of the orders according to Chambers, at the top. On the mezzanine landing – contrived, as Baretti tells us, to provide a pause in the ascent – a panel by Cipriani in chiaroscuro showed 'several Genii employed in the study of Painting, Sculpture, Architecture, Geometry, and Mechanicks'. At the 'half-space' on the final flight of steps, another Cipriani composition showed *Minerva Visiting the Muses on Mount Parnassus*: 'Nothing more apposite could be thought of for the place; and the application of that subject to it is quite obvious, that Artists will rise to excellence in proportion to the extension and variety of their knowledge, whereof Minerva and the Muses are the symbol'.[18]

At the top, under the skylight, the visitor passed across the landing and through the Corinthian screen into the Ante-room, the decoration of which by Rigaud confirmed the theme of the whole ascent, with a *Sacrifice to Minerva* on one side and a *Marriage of Cupid and Psyche* on the other – 'an emblem', says Baretti, 'of the mental and executive faculties requisite to constitute a perfect Artist'.[19] Over the door to the Great Exhibition Room appeared the motto 'ουδεις αμουσος εισιτω' – 'Let no one [literally] without the Muses enter' (fig. 12). The warning, on which Samuel Johnson must have advised,[20] was aimed primarily at imperfect artists, at the unattuned public, and perhaps most feelingly at critics without taste. Finally the visitor entered the Great Room itself, the very temple of art, the roof of which, as if it were that of the Pantheon in Rome, was fictively open at its centre. Here

> as the Pictures of the Exhibition were to be the great ornament . . . very few decorations are introduced on any part of the Room, that the attention of the Beholders might not be called off from the main object. A few however have been bestowed round the foot of the Lantern and in the ceiling, at the four Angles of which are painted in chiaroscuro Groups of Boys employed in the Arts of Painting, Sculpture, Architecture, and Geometry, that fill the Spandrels of a large oval foliage-frame, surrounding a space supposed to be open in the centre, through which is seen a very well executed sky, much more properly introduced there, than the finest Picture would have been, for the alledged [*sic*] reason. This whole performance came from the masterly hand of Mr. Catton.[21]

For the future design of picture galleries, Chambers's most influential innovation here was indeed the roof, not so much for its iconography as for its structural virtuosity, and for the fact that it provided the principal source of light in the room, from four semicircular ('Diocletian') windows in the lantern providing an even wash of light across the walls. The Academy exhibitions had previously enjoyed the benefits of top-lighting in the gallery on Pall Mall (see fig. 31), though in a very much smaller room, where the central lantern was a simple structure similar to those traditionally used to light stairwells. In the Great Room, the construction of the lantern stretched the inherent capabilities of carpentry in oak to the limits, and involved the most skilful concealment of 'very strong trusses in the coves of the Room and in the divisions of the four Diocletian Windows'.[22] By achieving top light from a single, large lantern in a space of this size,[23] Chambers surpassed the only comparable exhibition room in London, that designed by James Paine in 1772 for the Society of Artists. In Paris, his French colleagues, simultaneously engaged in a vigorous professional debate about the introduction of top-lighting in the Louvre, must have been as intrigued by news of the building in London as Chambers had been inspired originally by the arrangements at the Salon.[24] But top-lighting was not achieved in the Louvre until 1789, when a lantern similar in structure to Chambers's was introduced as a prototype for the lighting of the Grande Galerie.

Other aspects of the Salon Carré were also altered. The first of these was the staircase. Though it was made to look quite grand in Gabriel de Saint-Aubin's well-known etching of it in 1753 (fig. 13),[25] the 1720s staircase was actually very small, and though pretty with its low wrought-iron railing, it was clearly inadequate for the numbers of visitors to the exhibitions. The stairwell also impeded the view of the pictures hung on the walls above it, and generally failed to communicate any sense of ceremony or grandeur to the moment of the visitor's arrival in the room. According to 'L'Espion anglais' in 1777, it was in short, 'a kind of pitfall, almost always choked'.[26] By 1780, the year in which the new London Academy building opened, Maximilien Brébion, the Louvre house architect, in consultation with Chambers's old friend Jacques-Germain Soufflot, had produced a plan, placing in the adjoining room a new grand staircase that rose by three easy flights to a broad landing and formed a

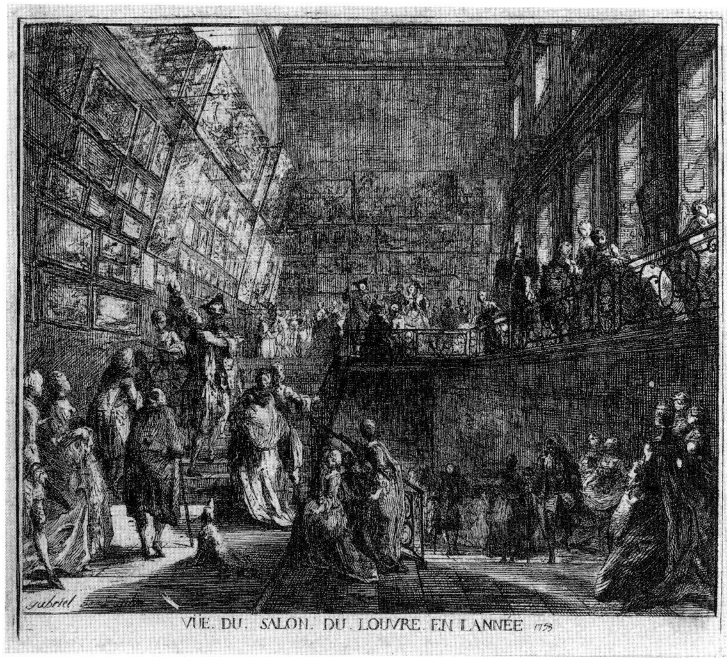

13 Gabriel de Saint-Aubin, *Vue du Salon du Louvre en l'année 1753*, etching. Kupferstichkabinett, Staatliche Museen zu Berlin–Preußischer Kulturbesitz.

'majestic vestibule' to the north door of the Salon. It was ready in time for the exhibition of 1781.

How did the hanging of the pictures at the Salon relate to that in Chambers's Great Room? 'The line', the most extraordinary of Chambers's innovations, raises many questions, but as an idea it seems to have originated, like so much else in the Great Room, from a critique of the traditional Salon arrangements. In the Salon the hanging had often been chaotic, with no pre-ordained order and with the heights of paintings varying awkwardly. The line seems primarily to have been a practical expedient to establish a common height for the largest canvases, to support their weight on their bottom rails and to provide an architectural discipline for hanging the rest of the exhibition. It gave a starting point for the work of the Committee of Arrangement, and by imposing an easily understood order, helped to establish an expectation in the Academy, and eventually in the minds of the visitors, as to where and how the most important pictures would be shown. The line also established beneath it a contained and rational space, close to the eye, for smaller pictures, where their distinctive effects might properly be appreciated. Whether above or below the line, however, paintings must have been intended originally to be hung, as they had been at the Salon, more or less directly on the wainscoted walls, hanging out no more than is natural for any picture hung against a vertical surface. The intention must also have been that everything should be fairly visible, therefore not below a decent chair-rail height, and not breaching the cornice.

In deciding the height of the line, Chambers would have had in mind the visibility of the exhibits when the room was crowded, and the angle at which light from the lantern would strike the picture surfaces, but also the architectural proprieties, and the nature of the paintings which deserved to be most prominently placed. In many ways, his placing of the line seems surprising because, as a permanent part of the articulation of the walls, it seems quite awkwardly sited, joining the architrave of the door in an unresolved way and dividing the elevation of the walls much less gracefully than would a normally placed dado rail. But as Baretti emphasized, the Great Room was a special case; like the Salon it was a gallery in the tradition of baroque picture galleries, which would appear in proper form only when fully dressed with major paintings constituting a monumental frieze around the room at high level. It was not meant to be seen naked.

Apart from the traditional Salon, the Grande Galerie in the Louvre, and perhaps more remotely the Tribuna of the Uffizi (see fig. 2), as exemplary galleries of the greatest pictures, Chambers would doubtless have had in mind his own recent experience of moving the Raphael Cartoons to Buckingham House[27] from the gallery which Sir Christopher Wren had provided for them at Hampton Court. The Cartoons, the greatest Italian Renaissance paintings in England, and the central treasures of the British state, exemplified in the eighteenth century everything the British School of painting aspired to be. They were the epitome of greatness in the art of history painting. Monumental in scale, bold in design, broad in colour and execution, the Cartoons definitively required to be seen at a height at which their great virtues would tell most strongly. Similarly, painters who wished their work to be seen at its best in the Academy exhibitions, as conceived by Chambers and Reynolds, would have to emulate Raphael in scale, design, colour and execution. The automatic application of this principle by John Inigo Richards, Matthew Peters and George Dance (the Committee of Arrangement) to a picture conceived in a different spirit, led to Gainsborough's withdrawal from the exhibition of 1784: 'Compts to the Gent of the Committee . . . he has painted his Picture of the Princesses in so tender a light, that notwithstanding *he approves very much of the established Line for Strong Effects*, he cannot possibly consent to have it placed higher than five feet & a half, because the likeness & Work of the Picture will not be seen any higher; therefore . . . will beg the rest of his Pictures back again' (my emphasis).[28] Gainsborough's picture was big enough, at 100 × 70½ in., to be on the line, and a contribution from him was important enough, but at this stage in his career he was aiming at different qualities of style from those required of paintings that would be hung so high. Later, there would be other artists who found that the honorific places on the line did not suit their work.[29]

So much for the intention, for the emulative and determining spirit in which Chambers considered the exhibition arrangements in the Salon and framed a space which would reinforce in artists the fundamental teaching of the Academy. The experience of artists and visitors in many ways lived up to intentions, but in others, as in the case of Gainsborough, the nature of the arrangements led to difficulties, and to hostile critical comment, and ultimately resulted in the Academy moving out of Somerset House altogether. Principally, as in France, the problems were created by the success of the exhibitions, the sheer volume of works of art sent in, and the large numbers of visitors.

In both of these respects, the fundamental problem was that the building was just not big enough for what it had to contain. The Great Room, though more efficient than the Salon, was smaller, and the Royal Academy exhibitions, unlike those of the French, were open to all artists who wished to 'send in'. From early on, therefore, the exhibitions spread through the whole of the building, from the Life Academy on the ground floor and through the Library, Antique Academy and Council Room on the first. Exhibitors hated being placed anywhere but in the Great Room, but the worst fate was to be in the Life Academy, probably because the fixed furniture and other equipment must have disrupted the display greatly, but also for the simple reason that the room became perceived as a place for superfluities. In 1811, the Academy tried to alleviate this feeling by reserving the Life Academy for sculpture. This was sensible, and important in that, because it was on the ground floor, it effectually opened the exhibitions to the display of large finished marble sculptures, rather than merely models. But within a year or two, the exhibition reviewers were again commenting on the unsatisfactory arrangements. Similar attempts to create an uninvidious allocation of particular media to particular places led to architectural drawings, watercolours and prints being placed in the three Fine Rooms on the first floor, but this principle of allocation literally reinforced the sense that work in other media was on a different level from the paintings above. Even there, painters were extremely disappointed to be put in the Ante-room, partly because of the poor light, but presumably also because the architecture very clearly told visitors at that point that they were just about to arrive at the principal gallery.

In the Great Room itself, Chambers's attempt to create orderly spaces for works of different scale and rhetorical power worked better, but soon the smaller pictures were reaching down to skirting level, and being hung inside the fireplace; worse still, small pictures, usually head and shoulders portraits, were being squeezed in above the large pictures above cornice level. The problem is already visible in the Burney watercolours, which show the hang in 1784 (see figs 17–19). Such overcrowding and poor viewing conditions may have been related to peculiar difficulties faced by each Committee of Arrangement, but partly the problem was inherent.

Another factor may well have been that the lantern lighting may not have worked as well as expected even for the best-placed paintings. The geometrical principle of good lighting is so simple that it is inconceivable that Chambers did not understand it thoroughly, but the fact is that light from each of the Diocletian windows strikes the surface of paintings hung nearly vertically on the line at an angle that produces reflections for the spectator standing at a 'natural' viewing distance on the floor. Obviously this effect can be alleviated by canting the top of each canvas outwards; but if, at the same time, there is a demand that more pictures should be admitted into the exhibition and more of the height of the room be used, it is equally obvious that the upper part of the wall has to be built out in some way to provide a surface on which the topmost register of pictures can be hung. The print by Earlom after Brandoin (see fig. 31) shows that this was already done in the early exhibitions at Pall Mall; the Burney watercolours reveal that by 1784 it was also necessary in the new premises. They show that the upper register of paintings on the north and east walls rose in a single inclined plane from the line, well outside the cove and extending into the lantern. This cannot have been possible without a carpentry framework of some sort, and whatever it was, it was evidently quite simple – certainly nothing like the 'investment' that was later required for the re-usable 'établissement' at the Salon.[30] In any case, a massive structure should not have been necessary, given the presence of the line as a permanent support, the fact that the windows below the line were already provided with wainscot covers, and that the main, upper wall spaces were not interrupted by large windows, as they were in the Salon.

The cost of the annual works appears to have been minimal. Several large jumps in expenses, for example in 1784 and 1792, were caused by increases in the really heavy items of expenditure, especially the cost of printing the catalogue. The only year for which invoices survive is 1788, and these show the costs of carpentry and upholstery in that year, and almost certainly indicate the recurrent cost. As detailed in the following chapter, the total joinery cost of the exhibition in 1788, including 106 man-days of labour putting up and taking down the pictures, was £21 6s. 1d. Of this £7 8 1 was for lengths of narrow studding, laths, screws and eyes, and cord – evidently the sort of material required to construct the temporary framework shown in Thomas Sandby's diagram of the structure in 1792 (fig. 14).[31] Another invoice from 1788 shows that re-usable green baize for the walls and floor, and to cover plinths for sculpture and the admission desk, cost only £5 6s, with another £2 6s for insurance. The prints of 1787 and 1788 by Martini after Ramberg (see figs 35 and 37) show the effect of this room dressing, and indicate its sumptuousness.

Beyond vapidly patriotic journalistic praise in 1780, history does not record what either the Academicians or critical visitors thought of the technical installation of 'The Exhibition' in its new home. Probably because of the Pall Mall precedent, journalists found basically what they expected, but were pleased that it was much grander, and worthier of the nation, than it

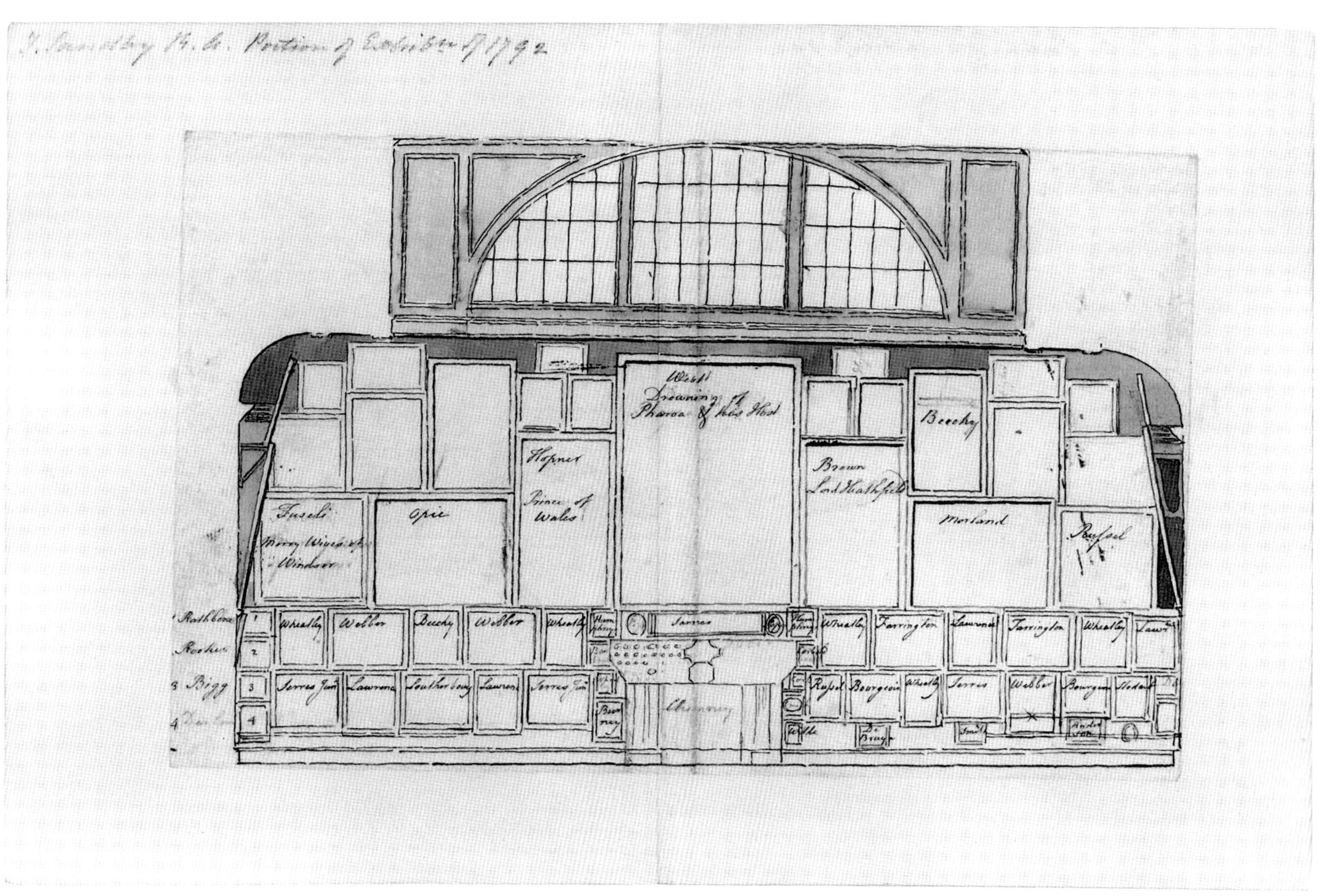

14 Thomas Sandby, *The Royal Academy Exhibition of 1792: The Great Room, East Wall*, pen and wash. Royal Academy of Arts, London.

had been before. None the less, expenditure was occurring every year, and, it could have been pointed out, the brand new exhibition room did not answer fully the practical needs of the Committee of Arrangement. Inside the Academy in the 1780s, Chambers's administrative dominance, his control of the purse, and the fact that he was the architect of a building that was still in course of construction, meant that no one else was really in a position to ask why a special setting for the exhibition, even such a cheap one, was needed every year. Had he been asked, Chambers could have answered that the need arose from the very success which the move to the new premises had brought; he would have said that no one could have anticipated the increase in the numbers of pictures sent in, nor the clamorous disappointment of those whose pictures were rejected: the sums of money spent on carpentry were anyway negligible relative to the costs of printing, advertising and dining. Finally and unanswerably, he would have pointed out that, with the tremendous success of the exhibitions, the annual deficits in the Academy accounts were transformed into strong annual surpluses, and there was no need to call on the King's Privy Purse.[32] Nevertheless, in 1791 we hear what may be the echo of incipient murmuring on the Council as Chambers sought the publication in the catalogue of a letter attesting that all his work on the building has been done in a proper manner 'in order to remove the most distant suspicion respecting the strength of the Building, and the Safety of those who visit the Exhibition'.[33] While the old wolf remained fit, almost no Academicians dared challenge him; when they finally did, when he was too sick to attend Council during the winter and spring of 1794–95, it was for deficiencies in his bookkeeping rather than the qualities of the building that the hounds went after him.

Some aspects of the building were, none the less, the subject of open professional debate. Anticipating criticism of the new edifice, Chambers and Baretti had referred in 1780 to the fundamental problems of the site, the fact that on the Strand the building had to be squeezed into a frontage of only 135 feet between rows of existing terraced houses and shops. Yet the decision to turn what had been the barbican and entrance range of Old Somerset House into one of the new building's principal public spaces could only have been Chambers's own, whatever administrative pressures he was under. Technically, it was a decision fraught with problems. Combining the need for a principal entrance to the whole complex at street level, capable of taking high vehicles, with a suite of formal rooms on the *piano nobile*, and then seeking to place on top of the whole a room with the proportions of the Salon Carré, was perhaps quixotic. Chambers's fellow architects were critical, and after the building opened, the 'correction' of the north elevation of Somerset House, eliminating the Great Room, was one of the ways in which the young John Soane publicly twisted the tail of his illustrious senior (fig. 15).[34] To make the building work at all, Chambers had to use the utmost ingenuity – externally, for example, by disguising the disproportionate height of the lantern with the attic storey of sculpted royal virtues by Carlini and Ceracci, and by covering the view of the windows and flat timber roof with the arms of the British empire by Bacon. Internally, the problem of bringing the visitor up through the building – overcoming the height of the entrance vestibule first, and then that of the fine rooms on the first floor, within a site plan that did not allow for ample stairwells – similarly forced Chambers into ingenious solutions, including, as we have seen on the Academy side, the use of the ascent for Cipriani's unfolding allegory of education as a distraction. Despite these 'entertainments' to provide pauses at which visitors could catch their breath, the climb was severe. The final flight was relieved by only one small landing, on which it was impossible to rest when the building was open to the public. Curving up around the drum of the stairwell, each stone step apparently held in place only by having one end cantilevered from the wall, this final flight looks not only steep but dangerous. Visitors passing one another on the stairs, who peer over the slender banister down into the indistinct gloom of the basement far below, experience a real twinge of vertigo, and fear of falling. This may have been one of the factors underlying the 'distant suspicion' that the building was not safe for exhibition visitors. But Chambers must have intended there to be such a *frisson*, noting we may imagine in conversation with Edmund Burke how the emotion of fear would have produced the sense of the sublime in his architecture. Perhaps everyone enjoyed it – the stairs are, after all, extremely safe, since they work, not as a series of cantilevers, but by being fitted closely together, with the load serving to tighten the joints and transmit the thrust round the curve of the walls to each landing below. Rowlandson's famous etching of *The Exhibition Stare Case* (see fig. 44) is in that respect good-natured, picking up the fear of falling and turning it to comic effect. But this image should lead us also to reflect how different the public

15 Office of Sir John Soane, *The Strand Front of Somerset House. Soane Lecture Diagram*, date unknown, graphite, pen and wash. The Trustees of Sir John Soane's Museum, London.

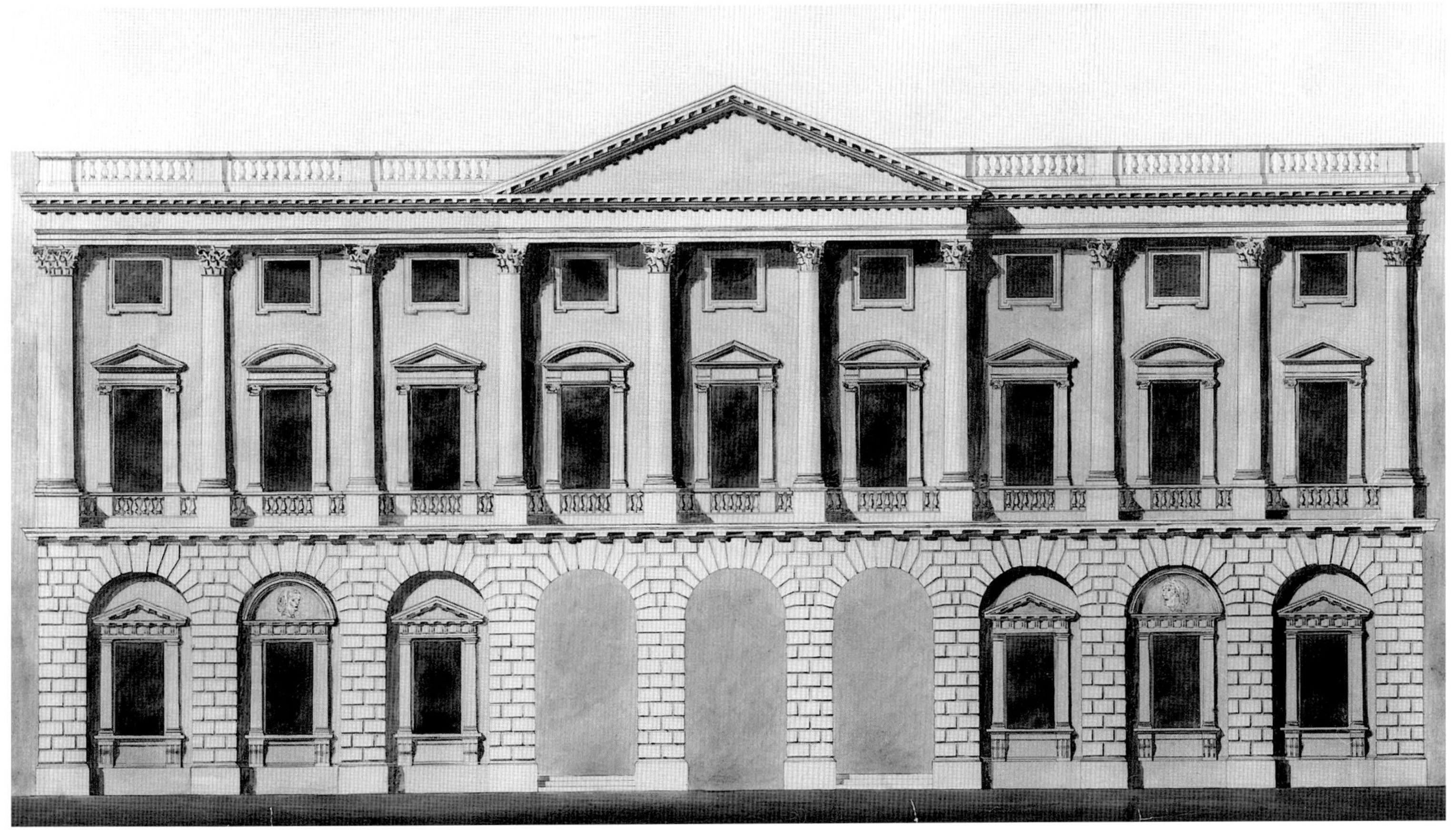

perception of tumbling disorder in the approach to the Great Room was from anything that Chambers could have intended. Instead of Apollo or the stately Minerva, Rowlandson sees the Venus Callipygia: instead of looking at art, the connoisseurs look at ladies' bottoms: instead of an orderly public ascending the *gradus ad Parnassum*, there is 'la foule' – a mob – whose values the Academy exists to exclude: ουδεις αμουσος εισιτω.

And as with the arrangements for displaying the works of art in the exhibition, it was the numbers that exposed both the virtues and the limitations of the building from the point of view of the public. The truth is that Chambers, representing in this respect perfectly his fellow Royal Academicians, designed a building which expressed contradictory attitudes to the business of showing art to the public. On the one hand was the wish to show art, and to attract a great volume of praise; on the other was the wish to show art only to those possessing 'taste', whose response was thereby certain to be favourable. On the one hand was the wish for royal patronage, and the habitual dependence, especially for portrait painters, on commissions from the nobility; on the other was the sense that, like writers in the third quarter of the eighteenth century, painters too could create and publish their work as speculative producers in the marketplace. On the one hand was the wish to be popular, on the other was the fear of the uncontrollability of opinion and the volatility of fashion: the wish on the one hand to be open to the public, and on the other to introduce a ticket charge high enough to exclude many people. From such contradictory impulses came a building which has a very large public room as its climax, but a means of access to that room which, despite its improvement on the old corner staircase in the Salon, is still strait and narrow, which fails to provide space for an orderly public, and performs in effect the perverse feat of converting it into a tumbling mob.

Contemporary press coverage of the exhibition picked up this sense of contradictory impulses, especially as represented in what was seen as the unconvincing reason for the entrance charge. Chambers, the king's nominee as Treasurer of the Academy, must have been primarily responsible for the decision to charge, and for the unfortunate form of its public announcement:

> As the present Exhibition is a Part of the Institution of an Academy supported by Royal Munificence, the Public may naturally expect the Liberty of being admitted without any Expence.
>
> The Academicians therefore think it necessary to declare, that this was very much their desire, but that they have not been able to suggest any other Means, than that of receiving Money for Admittance, to prevent the Rooms from being filled by improper Persons, to the entire Exclusion of those for whom the Exhibition is apparently intended.[35]

Criticism came from all sides. From one perspective, through heavy irony, it was suggested that the king was too mean to stump up:

> This Academy, having . . . assumed the Form of a Royal Institution, the Members have thought proper to apologise . . . for taking a Shilling from those who are admitted to view the Paintings. The Apology is, that the Academicians could think of no other Means to prevent the Rooms from being filled by improper Persons. This would be no Reason in France, or in Prussia, where an imputation of this Nature on the Munificence of the Prince would be studiously avoided.[36]

– and, from another, probably with a good briefing from a dissident Academician who disliked the Chambersian royalism of the institution, a correspondent pointed out that it had never been the intention that the exhibition should be free, but rather that its profits should limit the dependency of the Academy on the king:

> the Success of the Spectacle has been so great, that his Majesty's Munificence has been almost unnecessary; this Year it will be entirely so; and the Academy, apparently under Royal Protection, is actually supported by the Exhibition.[37]

Other voices were evidently populist, responding to the wilful exclusionism of both the charge for entry and of the Great Room inscription, and expressing at the same time the irritation of the lay enthusiast at the whole notion of taste:

> One word more, my Cousins, and I have done. If this same Greek Inscription had in plain English been insisted on, and none but people of real taste admitted into your attic story, what figure would the sum total of your receipts have made in comparison to what it is now likely to make, from the numbers of the pretenders to taste who pay to see the Exhibition?[38]

And finally, disguised by the jocular irony of almost all art journalism at the time, there is the voice of a sovereign public, newly self-confident, and well aware of its economic power:

> In justice to the Royal Academicians and to the public, those who are in possession of the catalogue of their Exhibitors, are requested to correct the following *erratum in the advertisement*: – Instead of 'supported by Royal munificence', read 'supported by the generous encouragement of the public'.[39]

The tendency of these notices of the opening of the exhibition in its new building was thus to expose the self-deception and inner conflict of the Academy, and to claim the institution unambiguously as part of the public, as opposed to the royal, domain. Though the papers dutifully report that 'their Majesties, accompanied by their Royal Highnesses the Prince of Wales, the Bishop of Osnaburgh, Prince William, the Princess Royal, and the Princess Sophia Augusta, were at Somerset House to see the apartments of the Royal Academy and the Exhibition' (cf. fig. 16),[40] the real excitement was at the size of the crowds, and the effect that a great public event such as the opening had on the city –

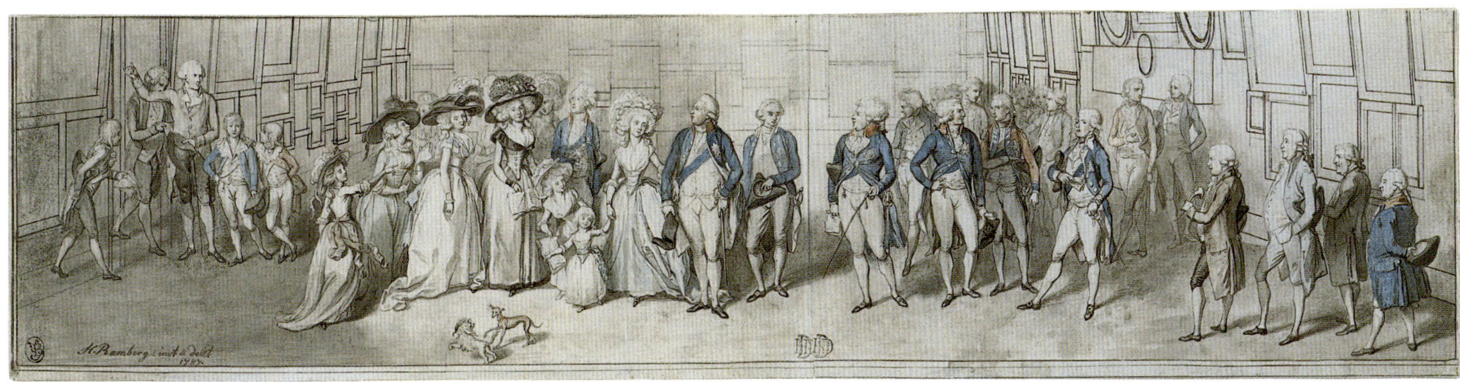

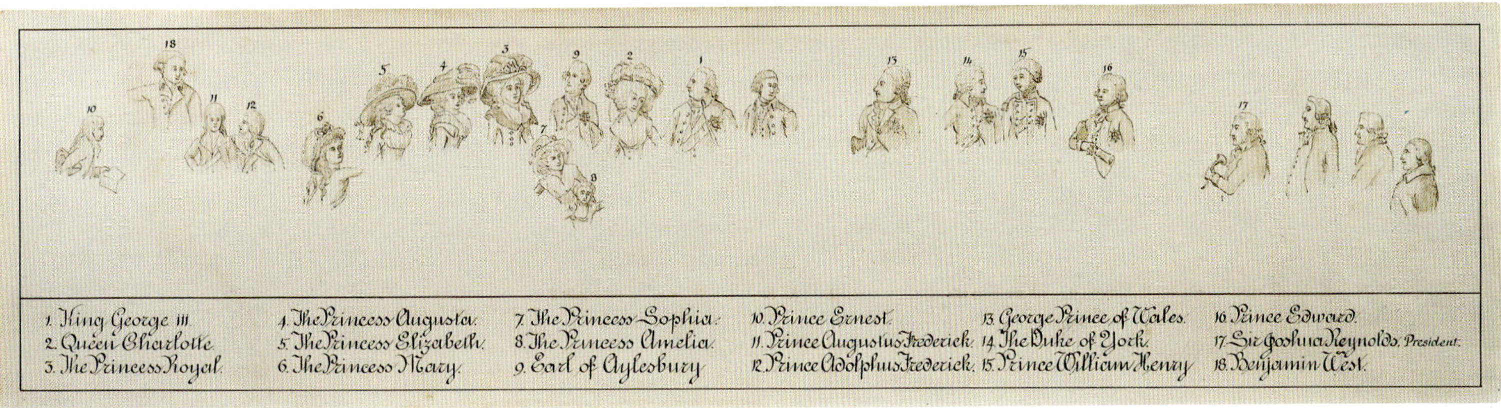

16 Johann Heinrich Ramberg, *The Royal Family at the Royal Academy* (study for *Portraits of their Majesty's and the Royal Family Viewing the Exhibition of the Royal Academy 1788*; see fig. 37), 1787, pen, ink, watercolour and graphite. The Courtauld Institute Gallery.

> The concourse of people of fashion who attended the opening of the Royal Academy exhibition yesterday was incredible; the carriages filled the whole wide space from the New Church to Exeter 'Change. It is computed that the door-keepers did not take less than 500£. yesterday from the admission of the numerous visitants of all ranks.[41]

– and on the building which was meant to cope with the crowd:

> The ground [*sic*: presumably 'grand'] exhibition room was so crowded, that it was scarcely possible to move, and intensely hot besides; and this crowd and heat were rendered more disagreeable by reflecting that they were in great measure occasioned by the architect having employed space which would have rendered the room larger, and consequently more airy and commodious, in the construction of an antichamber [*sic*] of no kind of use or beauty.[42]

The last remark makes clear the short step in perception in 1780 between seeing the exhibition as the property of its London public, and seeing the hierarchical form of the new building as an obstacle to the success of the exhibition. At this level, there was something politically inappropriate in Chambers's determination to bring to London the ethos and the architecture of Louis XIV's Louvre. Chambers's conception of civil culture as, like architecture, the product of a largely Roman-French tradition, about which it was the duty of scholars such as he to educate princes, and in turn, the duty of princes graciously to induct the people, belonged to a different world. The imagined orderly progress of the ideal visitor to the exhibition, from street to vestibule, from vestibule to staircase, and from the staircase to the Ante-room, glad in the knowledge that he was retracing the *gradus ad Parnassum*, was in 1780 an ideological figment of the architect's mind. What the public actually wanted was to see the pictures, laid out as glorious commodities for potential purchase; they wanted to see what marketing people call 'the offer'. This they wanted to do without having to struggle up 'three pair of stairs',[43] without panting at the top, and without suffering in the heat caused by the overabundance of people.

Are we then to understand from all this that the building and the exhibition experience were seen as failures? On the contrary, the evidence overwhelmingly indicates that they were a great success and one of the most influential 'inventions' of that mechanism by which, in early modern states, citizenries acquired power through their collective market dominance and their ungovernably individual, humorous, critical voices. In Britain, this part of the process was almost entirely peaceful. The contradictions, perversities and inadequacies of what the Academy offered to the public on its opening in 1780 are an index of the ambitions and anxieties of its ruling coterie, and show how the members of that group twisted and turned to find a way of accommodating contradictory impulses. The whole strategy was to hold as many such impulses as possible together, to combine everything from the need for new government offices with that for rooms for the learned societies; to merge in a single image the compulsive power of the state with its persuasive legitimacy, and the immemorial hierarchies of society with the forces that challenge them.

What better way of integrating a crowd – we may imagine it as made up of the followers of John Wilkes, libertarian tradesmen and office workers of the City of London – into the fabric of the state than by providing a space which, though unmistakably royal, they would actively choose to enter? – a space that they would occupy, without insurrection, and where they would constitute themselves as a modern public while still the *clientes* of the king? In the twentieth century, the world recognized such tactics of social assimilation as part of the strategy of governments for the retention of their leadership in the face of forces which might otherwise displace them. What we may see as a clever 'hegemonic' initiative by George III and his principal adviser in cultural policy, William Chambers, to set up the Royal Academy in 1768, was continued in the physical realization of the new spaces in 1780. With their help, strong challenges to the existing cultural order, the increasing size of the metropolitan clerisy, and changes in the relations between producers and consumers in the market economy of the arts, were accommodated and naturalized within a structure that spoke eloquently of traditional forms and values. At the level of the state, the survival of the British constitutional settlement of the seventeenth century through the European revolutions of 1789–1848 was guaranteed by the prosperity of public institutions of this kind, and of citizens who willingly enrolled themselves in such cleverly conservative manifestations of the state.

2

Staging the Spectacle

John Sunderland and David H. Solkin

Putting on the annual Royal Academy exhibitions in Somerset House proved more often than not to be a highly complicated business, dogged by practical difficulties, poor organization, and more than the occasional personal crisis. Huge numbers of exhibits were involved: the 489 works shown in 1780 had grown to 1,195 by 1797, remaining thereafter in the region of 900–1,200 until the Academy moved to the new National Gallery in 1837. The task of administering the overall process lay in the hands of the Academy's governing Council, which consisted of the President and eight elected Academicians, four of whom were replaced each year. One of the Council's tasks was to act as a jury for the exhibition, or, as one of the founding statutes put it, 'to receive or reject the several performances' submitted for their consideration;[1] this review (which works by Academicians did not have to undergo) usually took place in the first week of April. At around the same time, the job of physically preparing Somerset House for its annual invasion by art works and art lovers would have been getting under way.

In particular, readying the Great Room for each exhibition required the employment of a small army of manual labourers, principally carpenters and upholsterers. The carpenters' main job was to construct the wooden armature that joined the 'line' – the narrow moulding running around the room at a level of eight feet from the floor – to the edge of the cove above; all the pictures above the line were secured to this structure, so that they confronted the visitors at an angle of some 17 degrees from the perpendicular. As John Murdoch has observed (in Chapter 1 of in this volume), hanging paintings on an incline had several advantages: this not only allowed for more works to be shown, but it also enhanced their visibility by cutting down on both reflections and shadows. Though we are still not sure exactly how the armature was designed or constructed, several documents in the Royal Academy archives provide a wealth of revealing clues.

For the exhibition of 1788 (and unfortunately for this year alone) there survives a file of invoices detailing a variety of costs, including a bill of £21 6s. 1d. from the carpenter George Neale. Since 1788 is not an exceptional year, the Academy's expenses being slightly lower than in 1787 and slightly higher than for 1789, it is possible to infer that no major expenditure on carpentry was taking place, or that carpentry at this level did not cost enough for the Council to bother about. Even so, Neale's invoice specifies quite a considerable amount of structural-sounding wood:

To 4–12 ft 1/4 inch white deals at 2s 4d	0-9-4
To 2–10 ft 1/4 inch ditto at 2s 1d	0-4-2
To 2–10 ft 1 inch ditto at 1s 7d	0-3-2
To 31–11 ft 1 inch ditto at 1s 8d	2-11-8
To 1–11 ft 1/4 inch ditto at 2s 3d	0-2-3
To 2 dozen and 6 pantile Lagths [laths?]	0-5-0
To nails and screw eyes	2-17-6
To Strand Line and Lay Cord	0-15-0
To taking down seats and taking in pictures and fixing up and taking down ditto 106 days	15-18-0

Also in April, the upholsterer George Seddon invoiced the Academy for:

Porterage of Green Baize Covers to Somerset Place	
2 Workmen laying down the Baize in Exhibition Room and Room adjoining, and covering Stand for figures & Rails in the Hall and pay place & 4 benches with new Baize & 4 Stands with ditto where the Drawings are & new Baize to a picture –	1-8-0
used tacks etc	

20 yards of Green Baize @ 2/6	2-10-0
2 Workmen taking up the Green Baize in the Exhibition Room and Room adjoining Brushing & folding up ditto	1-8-0
Warehouse room & Insurance on your Green Baize Covers Value £46 from Midsummer 1787 to Ditto 1788 @ 5 pct per Annum	2-6-0

The unique survival of the 1788 invoices is, apparently, purely a matter of chance, so we have to assume that the expenditure was more or less typical – that, in other words, it was as routine to bring in someone like Neale to construct a framework on which to hang the pictures as to employ Seddon to instal the green baize, or (another invoice) Charles Catton to put summer clouding on the north and west windows of the Great Room,[2] and, from time to time, to repair and clean the Corinthian columns at the top of the stairs. The standards of presentation at each exhibition were high, and having carpenters on site to hang the pictures was inevitable. The Martini prints after Ramberg of 1787 and 1788 (see figs 34 and 36) show the results at their most sumptuous. And from Thomas Sandby's careful studies of 1792 (see figs 25–7), we get some idea of how it all worked underneath. The line was employed to support the lower end of a framework in the form of a scaffold, which was attached at its upper end to the wall beneath the cornice, and braced. Then the upper horizontal member was used to support the weight of a lighter extension up into the cove, the latter being presumably tied back on to the cornice, or through the cove into the main structural carpentry of the roof. It is exactly the sort of lightweight deal armature that we should imagine from Neale's list of materials. The paintings, with screw eyes in their frames, would have been lashed on at the appropriate angle with cord, and at the end of the exhibition, the whole would have been removed.[3]

Only after the armature had been built could the task of hanging the pictures begin. The responsibility for determining where each work went rested with the Committee of Arrangement (usually known, somewhat misleadingly, as the Hanging Committee), a group of three members of the Council chosen each year, usually in the March before the exhibition; the current Secretary and Keeper could also be members of the Committee in each year, though their role seems to have been largely administrative. The Council considered special requests from exhibitors during the first week or so of April, and from that period the appointed Committee set about arranging the exhibition space in preparation for the official opening on the first Monday in May (or sometimes the last Monday in April). Their decisions – we shall say much more about this topic below – could often make the difference between an exhibiting artist's failure or success. Of particular importance was whether a painting was hung in the Great Room or in one of the less prestigious spaces elsewhere in the building; and even within the Great Room itself, certain locations were far more advantageous than others. Each year this grandiose interior featured well over two hundred pictures (not counting miniatures, which were removed to a lower floor in 1793); and while there were few formal regulations which successive hanging committees had to follow, from what we know about their practice (and we know quite a lot) it is clear that each display was designed in accordance with a set of fundamental principles.

Actually, there were two main rules of thumb. The first was to respect the integrity of the line, as a continuous boundary between the upper and lower registers of the walls; pictures were to be hung either above or below the line, but not across it – as Thomas Gainsborough learned to his frustration in 1784, when he threatened to withdraw from the exhibition altogether unless the Council agreed to hang his large portrait of the three eldest royal princesses at a height of no more than five and a half feet (158 cm) from the floor. When the Academy refused to bow to Gainsborough's demands, because to do so would have entailed a breaking of the line, he removed all eighteen of his pictures from the show, and from this point onwards refused to exhibit with his fellow Academicians. This rather unfortunate episode helped to codify the line's authority as a matter of official policy. By contrast, the second convention followed by the Hanging Committee was more in the nature of an unspoken rule governing the organization of each wall; this was a commitment to lateral symmetry, or at least to a fairly close approximation thereof.

Perhaps the best way to learn how both these principles operated is by looking at Edward Francis Burney's remarkably precise drawings of the north, east and west walls of the 1784 exhibition (figs 17–19); about half of the hang on the Great Room's south wall can be seen in a contemporary engraving after Daniel Dodd (see fig. 34). One of the first things we notice from Burney's visual memoranda is that the largest paintings are placed in the centre of the walls. Around these works, pictures are arranged in ranks according to height, though with no great regularity. Rather there are patches of grid-like arrangements which dissolve one into another, or are interrupted by a large picture or by a work on an oval support. Across each wall there is some sense of images echoing or rhyming, reinforcing an overall impression of symmetry: portraits are arranged so that their subjects' postures mirror each other; landscapes or seascapes are paired. In general, the smallest pictures are hung low on the wall (i.e., below the line), though some are also hung quite high. The subordination of smaller to larger works supports a partial affirmation of generic and technical hierarchies, in line with academic doctrine; but since scale functioned as the key factor in determining a picture's position, those same hierarchies were easily disrupted. The same circumstances also suggest two competing orders of attention: for while the very largest pictures were given the most prominent places, the works nearest to the audience's eye were the smaller images below the line.

Looking more closely now at Burney's watercolour of the north wall, we see the pictures clustering in centrifugal fashion

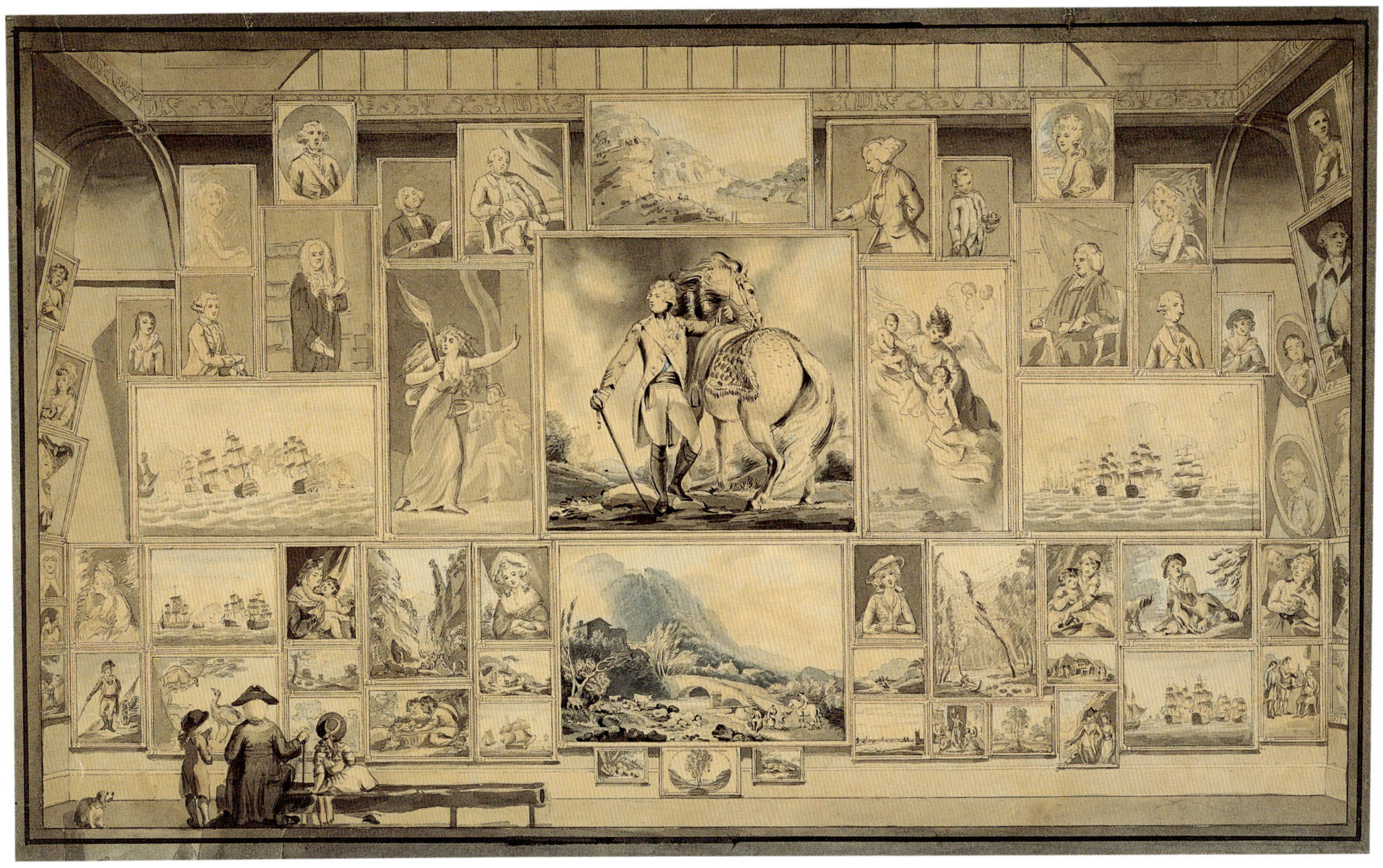

17 Edward Francis Burney, *The Royal Academy Exhibition of 1784: The Great Room, North Wall*, pen, grey ink and wash, with watercolour. By courtesy of the Trustees of the British Museum.

around Sir Joshua Reynolds's large equestrian portrait of the Prince of Wales (fig. 22), hung precisely on the central axis with its base resting on the line; full-lengths of royal sitters frequently occupied such prominent positions, as a reminder that this was, after all, a *royal* academy. To the left of the Reynolds we see Henry Fuseli's *Lady Macbeth Sleepwalking* (fig. 20), which is balanced on the other side by Benjamin West's *Apotheosis of Prince Alfred and Prince Octavius*, commissioned by the king (fig. 21). In a fashion that was standard for Great Room hangs, these three works achieve the semblance of a triptych dominating the middle of the wall; the symmetry then extends into the pair of large seascapes by Dominic Serres, which provide visual ballast on either flank, while Philippe de Loutherbourg's view of *Brother Bridge, which divides Westmoreland from Cumberland* (unlocated) adds yet more stabilizing anchorage directly beneath Reynolds's *Prince of Wales*.

The most important position in the room as a whole was that above the fireplace on the adjacent east wall, with which visitors came face to face upon entering from the Ante-room. Here each Hanging Committee tended to place an exceptionally large and ambitious work, preferably a history painting by a senior Academician; in 1784 West obliged with his outsize canvas of *Moses Receiving the Laws on Mount Sinai* (fig. 24), which must have been brought into the room either folded or rolled up, before being stretched, framed and displayed. The same process would have been reversed once the exhibition had ended, in order to get the picture out of the room and down Chambers's vertiginous staircase.

To facilitate the installation and removal of so many paintings, the exhibitors must have been encouraged to use thin frames designed for the purpose, and quite different from the more ornate surrounds usually used for displaying pictures in private houses. The use of special (and presumably re-usable) exhibition frames appears to have been standard practice at least during the first few decades of the Academy's residence in Somerset House; both the prints after Ramberg (see figs 35 and 37) and Burney's drawings show how the use of simple, flat wooden borders made it possible for the pictures to be hung directly abutting one another. The task of their arrangement was also made easier by the fact that most works came in four standard sizes: 'full-lengths' (90 × 55 in.), 'half-lengths' (40 × 50 in.), 'kit-cats' (36 × 28 in.), and 'three-quarters' (30 × 25 in.), the last of these favoured for

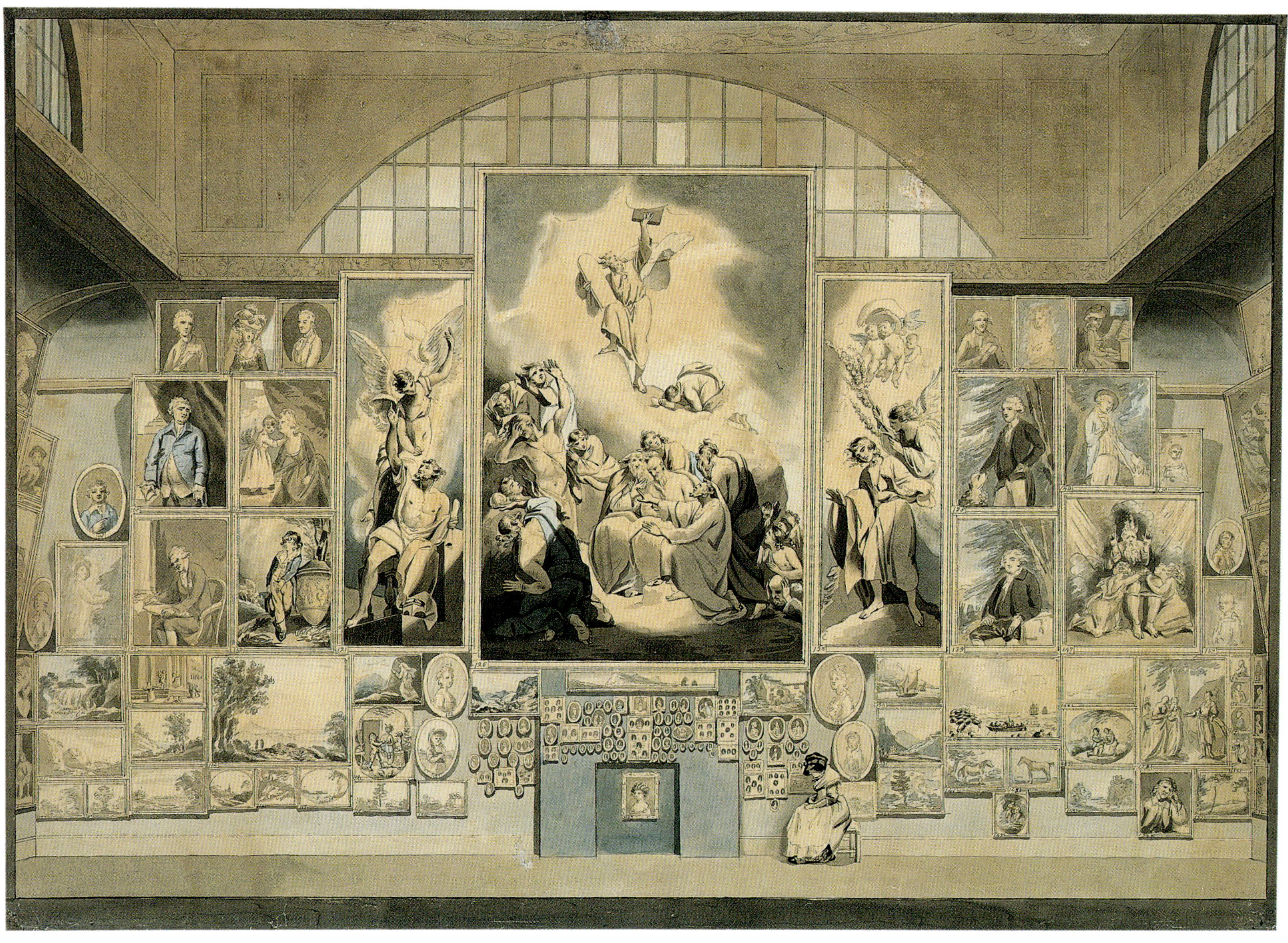

18 Edward Francis Burney, *The Royal Academy Exhibition of 1784: The Great Room, East Wall*, pen, grey ink and wash, with watercolour. By courtesy of the Trustees of the British Museum.

small head-and-bust portraits. Although these basic formats remained in use throughout our period, by the early nineteenth century, if Rowlandson's rather generalized portrayal of the Great Room (see fig. 39) is anything to go by, more varied and decorative frames had come into use, making it harder and harder to hang pictures without leaving substantial bits of wall space showing in between. This trend had become even more marked by the time George Scharf produced his watercolour in 1828 (see fig. 1); by now the special exhibition frame seems to have become a thing of the past. Over the same span of years, the pressures on artists to try and overshadow the competition prompted more and more of them to expand the scale on which they worked; here Sir Thomas Lawrence's exhibition portraits – such as his *Kemble as Coriolanus* of RA 1798 (fig. 23) – offer a well-known example. But instances of painters pursuing a 'bigger is best' strategy can also be found much earlier on, as we have already seen in the case of Benjamin West.

In 1784, West's *Moses Receiving the Laws* must have been one of those pictures which required last-minute attention to ensure that it looked its best for the exhibition audience. To enable artists to give a final touch to their performances once these had been positioned on the walls, a varnishing day was set aside just prior to the private view. To begin with this was restricted to a single day, and does not seem initially to have been regarded as an automatic right or practice. Thus on Thursday, 29 April 1802, the Council refused Thomas Lawrence's request to varnish his picture on Saturday morning, 'supposing the scent of the varnish would not be off by Dinner time'[4] – when the annual Academy dinner was scheduled to take place in the Great Room. At other times, however, the Council felt compelled to remind exhibitors of their duty to tidy up their works. On 16 April 1804 a note was sent from the Council to John Singleton Copley, James Northcote, Richard Westall, John Opie, Samuel Woodforde, John

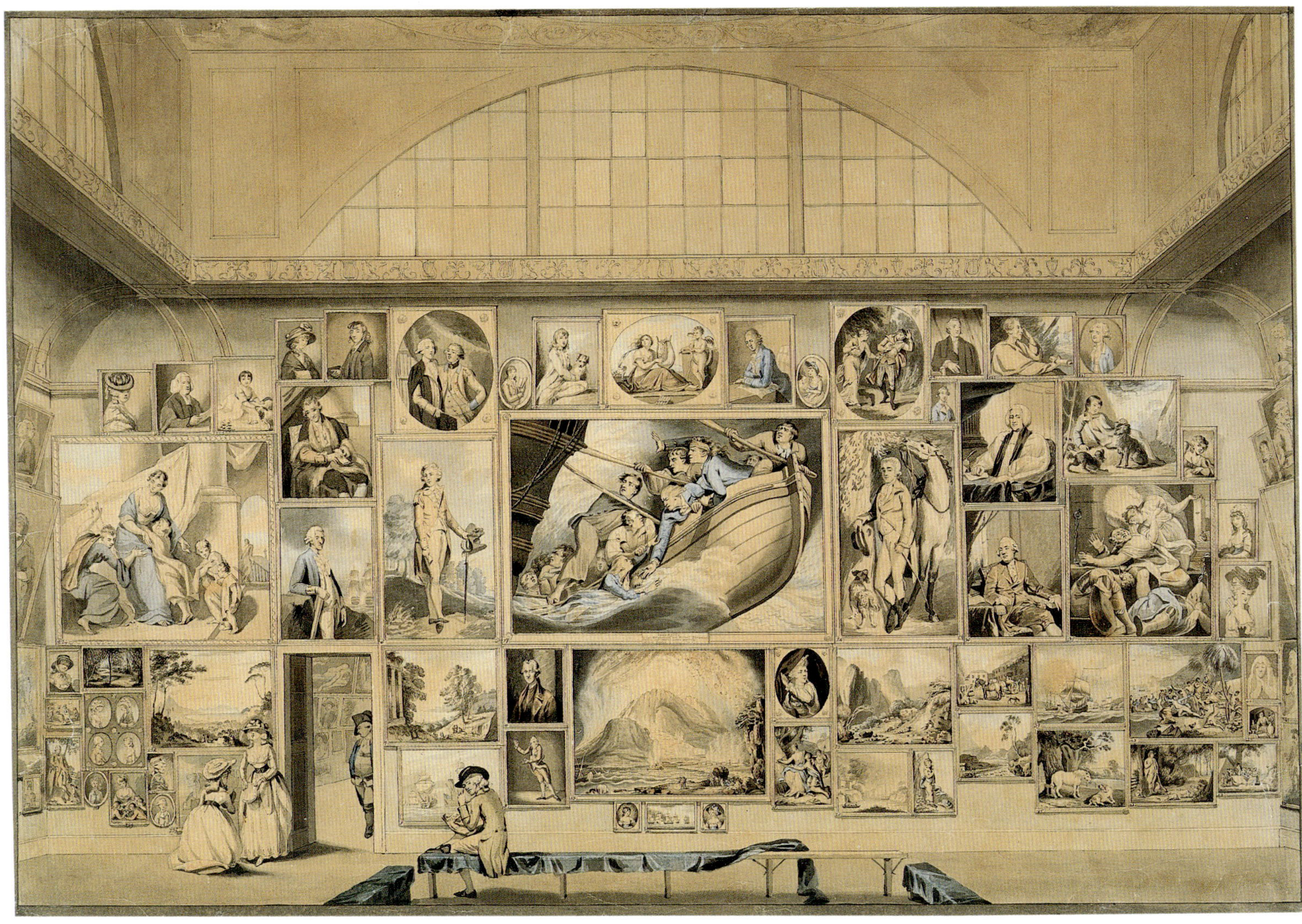

19 Edward Francis Burney, *The Royal Academy Exhibition of 1784: The Great Room, West Wall*, pen, grey ink and wash, with watercolour. By courtesy of the Trustees of the British Museum.

Hoppner, Martin Archer Shee, Henry Thomson and William Beechey, telling each of them the following:

> Sir, The Council being of opinion that your Pictures require Varnishing, I am directed to acquaint you that they have appointed Thursday next the 26th as the only day on which you can be admitted for that purpose, untill [*sic*] 4 o'clock in the afternoon.[5]

Only five years later, in 1809, did the Academy institute varnishing days for members as official policy, and they soon became a standard fixture which several artists willingly exploited as opportunities to do far more to their paintings than simply smooth out their glossy surfaces.[6] As Michael Rosenthal observes (in Chapter 10 of this volume), no one turned this occasion to better account than J. M. W. Turner, who delighted in the chance to transform his canvases in public from vague sketches into finished compositions; it must have been at least partly for Turner's benefit that the Academy resolved in 1825 to extend the number of varnishing days from one to four. Eventually, in 1852, the entire custom was abolished[7] – something which C. R. Leslie felt would have occurred much earlier had it not been for Turner. 'I believe', Leslie tells us in his *Autobiographical Recollections*, that 'had the varnishing days been abolished while Turner lived, it would almost have broken his heart. . . . He said, "You will do away with the only social meetings we have, the only occasions on which we all come together in an easy unrestrained manner. When we have no varnishing days we shall not know one another."'[8] However, in 1862 the procedure was revived with members allowed two days and non-members one day 'to varnish and retouch their pictures'.[9] With the completion of the varnishing ritual the annual exhibition was ready to be seen – first by the royal family, then by the Academicians and selected guests at the Academy dinner, and finally by the general public.

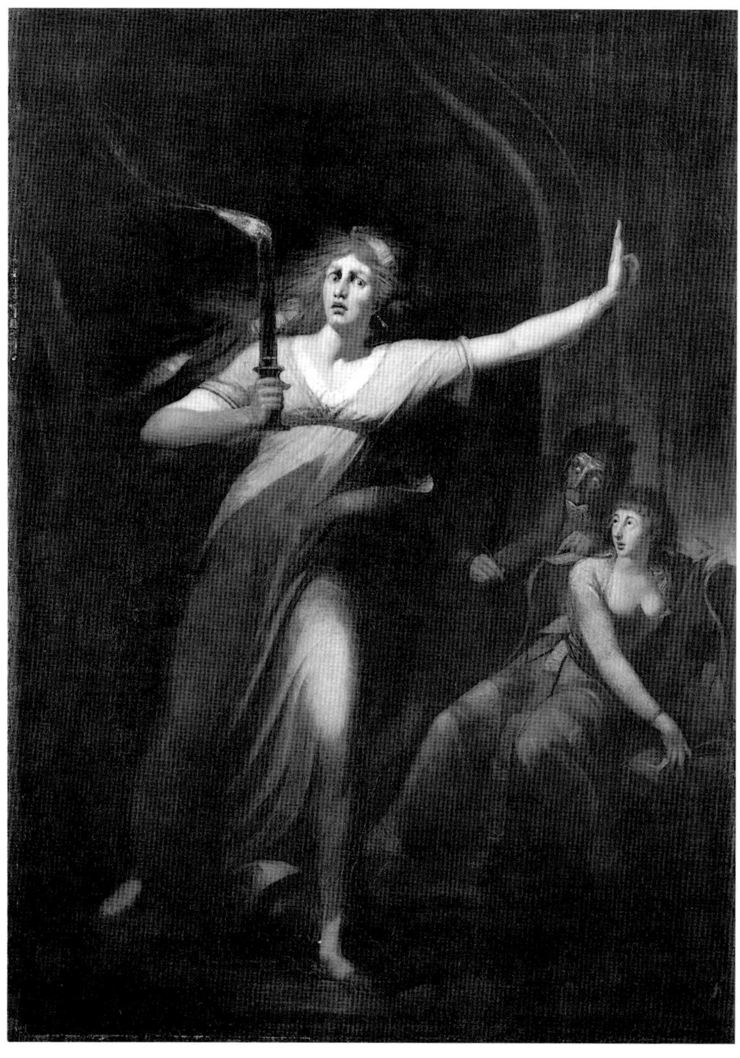

20 Henry Fuseli, *Lady Macbeth Sleepwalking*, RA 1784. Musée du Louvre, Paris.

Only after all the pictures (or at least the frames awaiting their arrival) had been hung could they be numbered, on small pieces of card usually inserted into the lower left-hand corner of the frame. Numbers were assigned to works in sequence according to their location, starting above the door leading in from the Ante-room and continuing somewhat irregularly in a clockwise direction around the walls. The same order was followed in the catalogue, which visitors were meant to consult as they moved around the show;[10] to satisfy the public's interest in individual artists, in 1783 the Academy's printers added an index of the names of all exhibitors, cross-referenced to the relevant catalogue numbers. From these numbers, and from our knowledge that there were about sixty paintings on each wall, we can often establish roughly where each picture was positioned. Here Sandby's drawings of RA 1792 (figs 25–7) can help show us how this worked: as was always the case, number 1 appears on the west wall, just above the entrance. In this year it was Thomas Lawrence's *A Lady of Fashion as La Penserosa* (fig. 28; the 'lady' in this case being Emma, Lady Hamilton). By the time viewers reached the next wall (i.e., the north: fig. 27), the numbers were in the sixties; Lawrence's central full-length of George III (fig. 29), for instance, was assigned number 65.[11] People who visited the annual exhibition on a regular basis must have known how to navigate their course around the Great Room, even without the help of the catalogue. What may strike us today as a bewildering and overcrowded patchwork of paintings would have been familiar territory for British art audiences of the eighteenth and nineteenth centuries. They would have been aware, too – thanks in part to constant reminding by the press – of the crucial role played by the Hanging Committee – though perhaps not of all the horse trading that had taken place behind the scenes.

21 Benjamin West, *The Apotheosis of Prince Alfred and Prince Octavius*, RA 1784. The Royal Collection © 2001 Her Majesty Queen Elizabeth II.

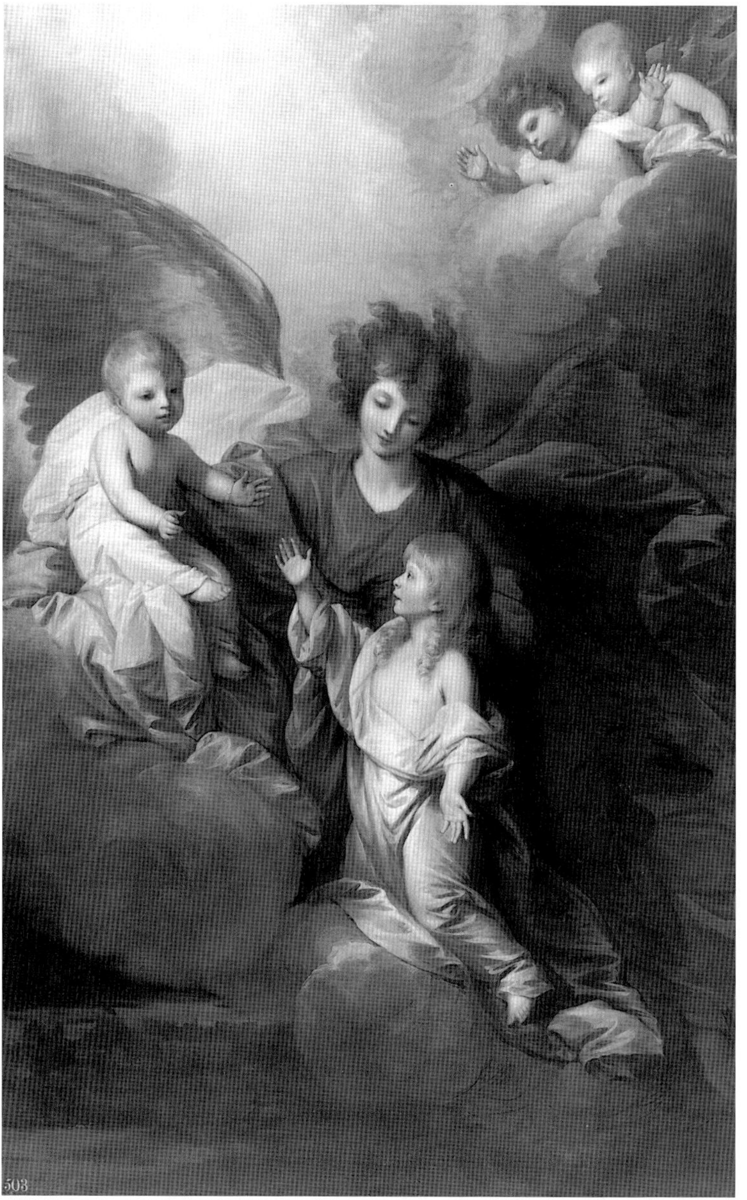

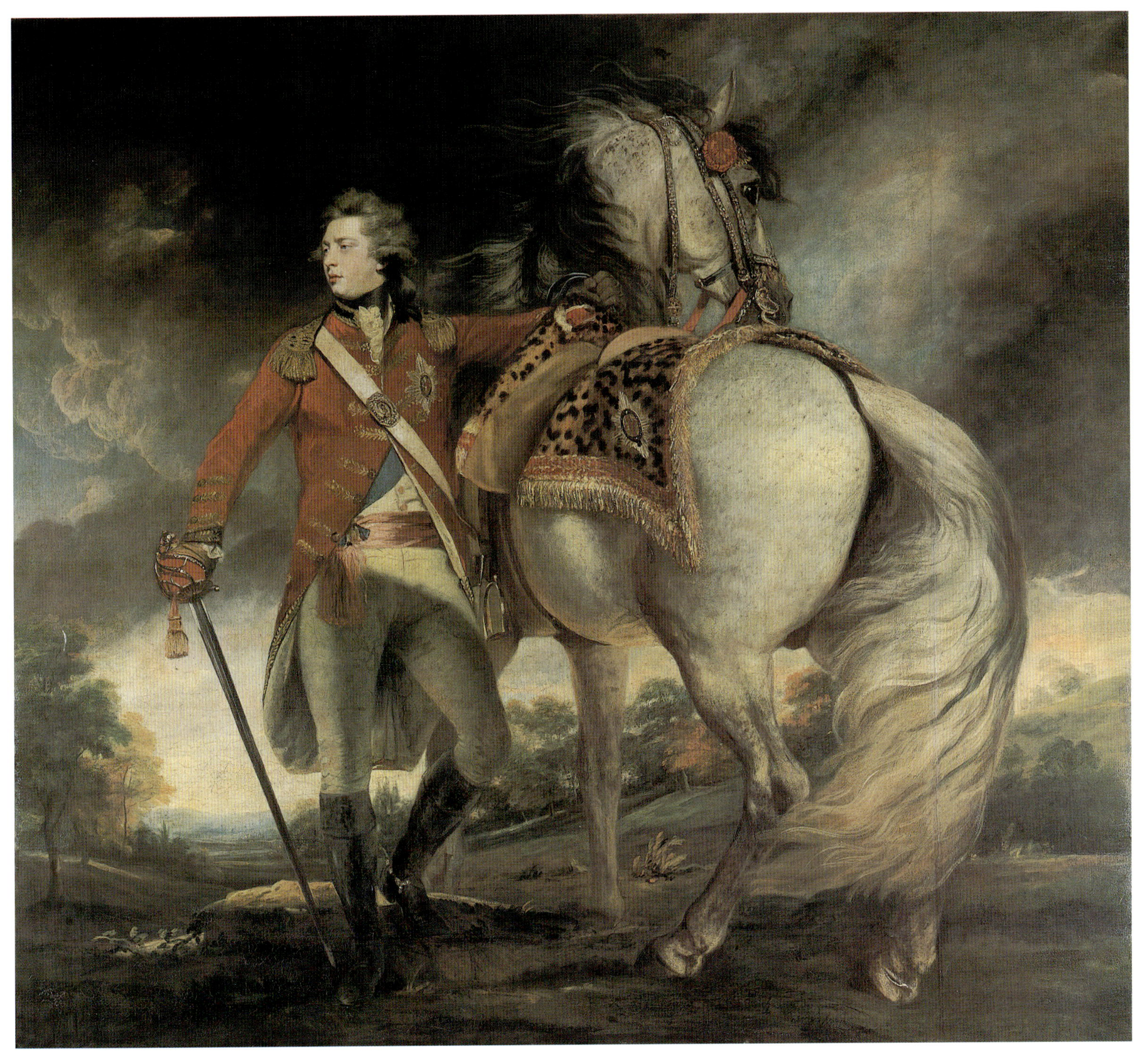

22 Sir Joshua Reynolds, *HRH George, Prince of Wales*, RA 1784. The Lloyd Webber Foundation.

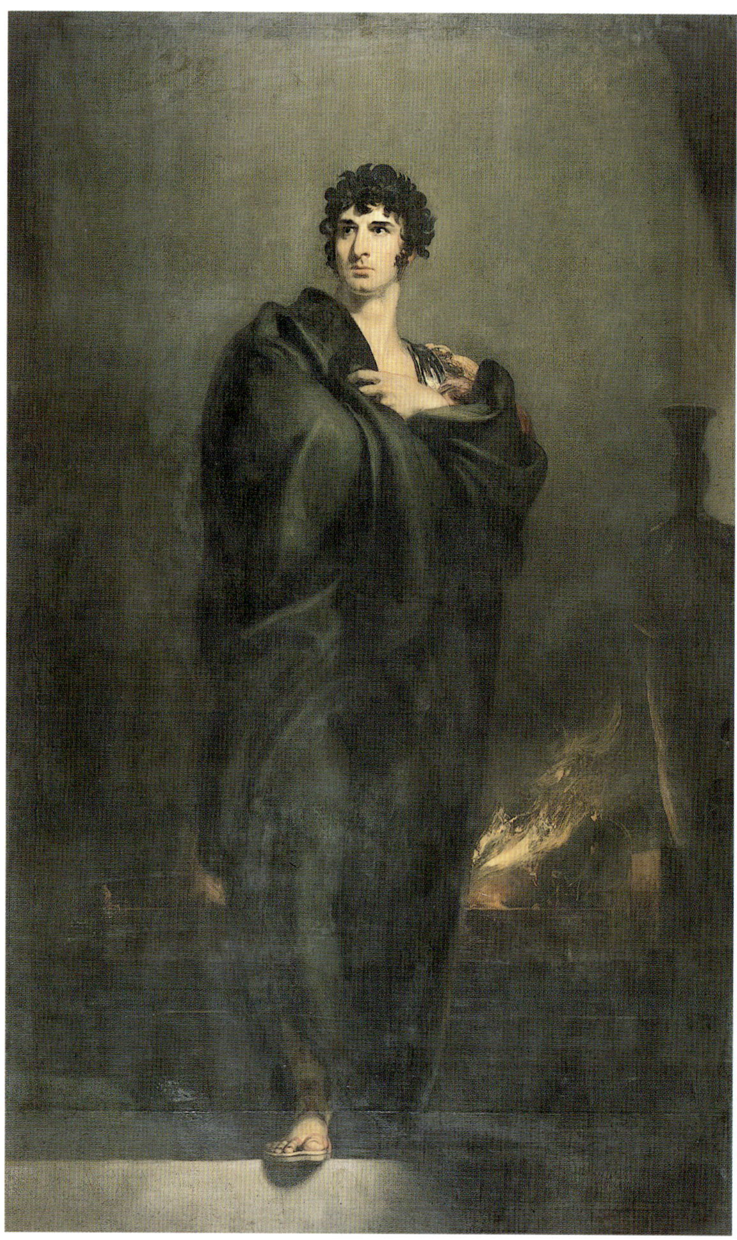

23 Thomas Lawrence, *John Philip Kemble as Coriolanus*, RA 1798. Guildhall Art Gallery, London.

For this information our best source is the landscape artist Joseph Farington RA, the consummate Academy insider and between July 1793 and December 1821 the unofficial diarist of the London art world.

An exceptionally full account of the politics of the hanging procedure can be found in Farington's diary for the spring of 1795, covering the period of his membership of the Committee of Arrangement. In that year its membership was finalized on 20 March, and the pictures examined on 4 April, two days before the task of arranging began.[12] Right from the outset the Committee was assailed with special pleading and polite persuasion aimed at influencing their decision-making. On a single day, 27 March, Farington was approached by the artist the Reverend Daniel Gardner requesting his 'interest in procuring a reception for two pictures and a drawing which He has prepared for Exhibition'; by Sir Francis Bourgeois, who asked for his portraits to be shown in a particular way; and by John Yenn, who passed on a request from his fellow architect Henry Holland that a crayon portrait of him 'might be well hung'.[13] Such petitions continued throughout the time of Farington's tenure. On 8 April the clergyman Thomas Hughes called on behalf of Richard Cooper the drawing master to try and convince Farington to 'hang his black lead pencil drawing in a particular direction'. The diarist replied that, 'as one of the Committee I wd. do all I could to oblige him'.[14] The next day it was the turn of Thomas Malton, who asked Farington to hang one of his architectural drawings in the Antique Academy.[15] Despite notices of delayed and withdrawn pictures, a provisional hang of the Great Room was completed on 13 April;[16] but two days later the final arrangements were disrupted when Thomas Banks took away the porters 'to make a frame for his model to stand on'.[17] Meanwhile, in the Great Room, thirty frames were hung up without the pictures, and matters were further complicated when

> Sir William Chambers wrote to me to request a good situation for the whole length portrait of the Turkish Ambassador by [Carl Fredrik von] Breda. – It is the opinion of the Committee it cannot be removed into the great room witht. detriment to the exhibition.[18]

After discussion, the Committee decided to stand firm on this matter, and the hang was finalized on 24 April. Farington then calculated that he, with William Tyler and George Dance, had spent a total of thirty-six days working on it.[19]

There are several things worth noting about this account. Personal attachments and institutional standing clearly played some part in the arranging of pictures. But ultimately, once the hang was established, even the request of the Academy's Treasurer, with regard to a picture of not inconsiderable diplomatic import, could be overruled. More significantly, the hanging was a protracted procedure which evidently was undertaken without a good proportion of the pictures actually being present. Instead, what Farington refers to elsewhere as a 'Skelton [i.e., skeleton] frame' could be submitted.[20] In 1776 the *Morning Chronicle* for 2 May claimed that a number of the most important pictures had still to arrive when the king attended the exhibition – that is, within a few days of the public opening; much the same thing happened again in 1795. Such instances provide further confirmation that the arrangement of the pictures must have been largely based on a knowledge of the size of the given work, no doubt supplemented in many instances by a familiarity with its basic character. This was by no means an exact procedure. From what Farington tells us, in short, we can conclude that the exhibition hang could be determined by a number of factors: personal attachments, politics, preferment and, perhaps most of all, practicability. Given the fact that the personnel responsible

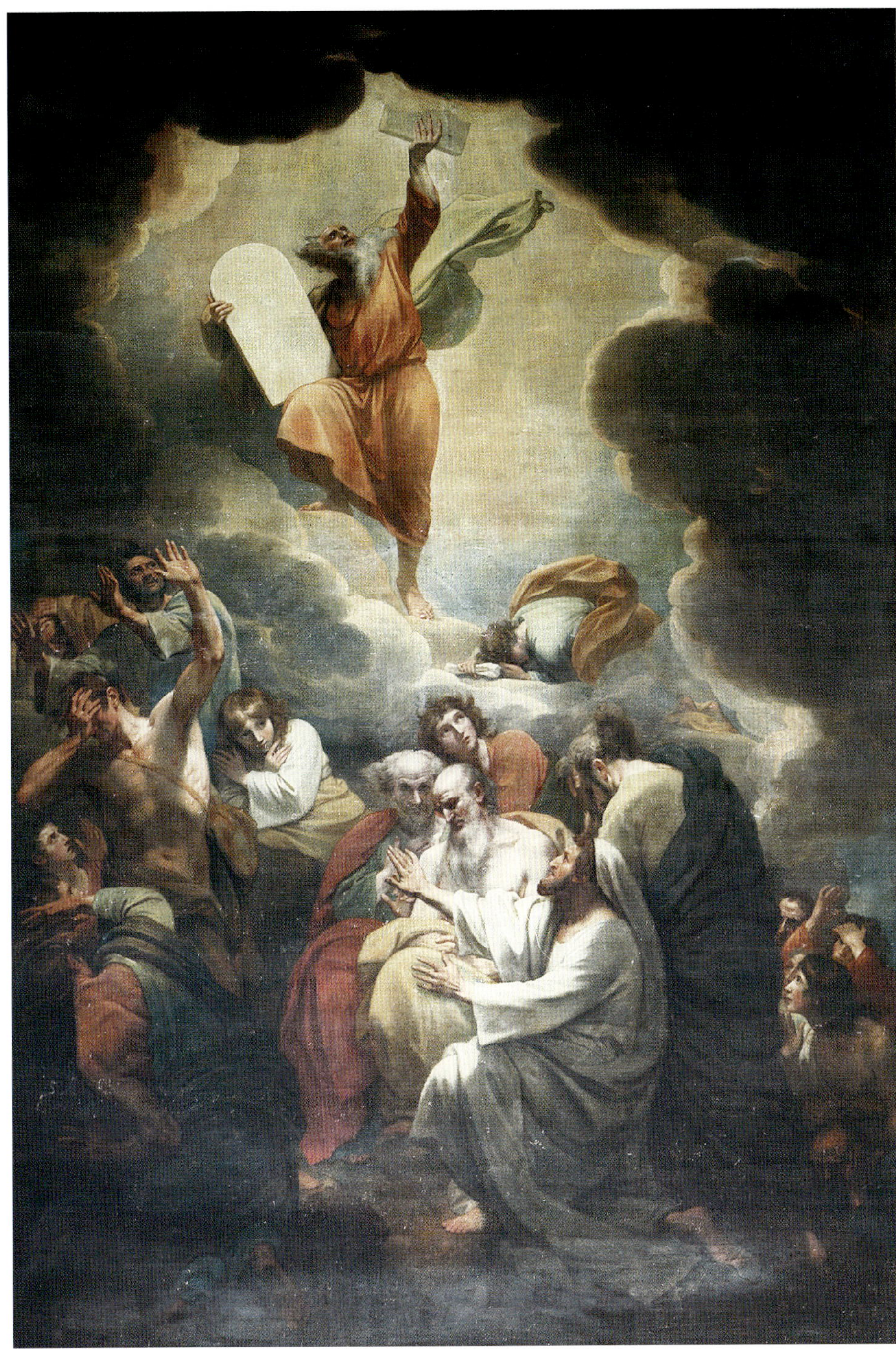

24 Benjamin West, *Moses Receiving the Laws on Mount Sinai*, RA 1784. Palace of Westminster, London.

for arranging the exhibition changed from year to year, it is hardly surprising that all of these factors were themselves in a constant state of flux, as a few additional case studies can confirm.

One incident that took place in 1809 nicely demonstrates how the planning of the exhibitions was often subject to unusual and somewhat haphazard circumstances. At the centre of this episode was a large and immensely serious picture of *The Celebrated Old Roman Tribune, Dentatus, Making his Last Desperate Effort against his own Soldiers, who Attacked and Murdered him in a Narrow Pass* (fig. 30); its author, Benjamin Robert Haydon, then just twenty-three years old, was one of the country's most ambitious young history painters. In his diary, Haydon recorded that the *Dentatus* had been given a place in the Great Room, thanks to the intervention of Fuseli, who was then a member of the Hanging Committee by virtue of the fact that he was Keeper. Subsequently, however, according to Haydon, 'Mr West [President of the Royal Academy], under pretence of doing me a service, told Fuzeli he thought he had not done me justice. Fuzeli then said, "get him a better place yourself" and went away . . .';[21]

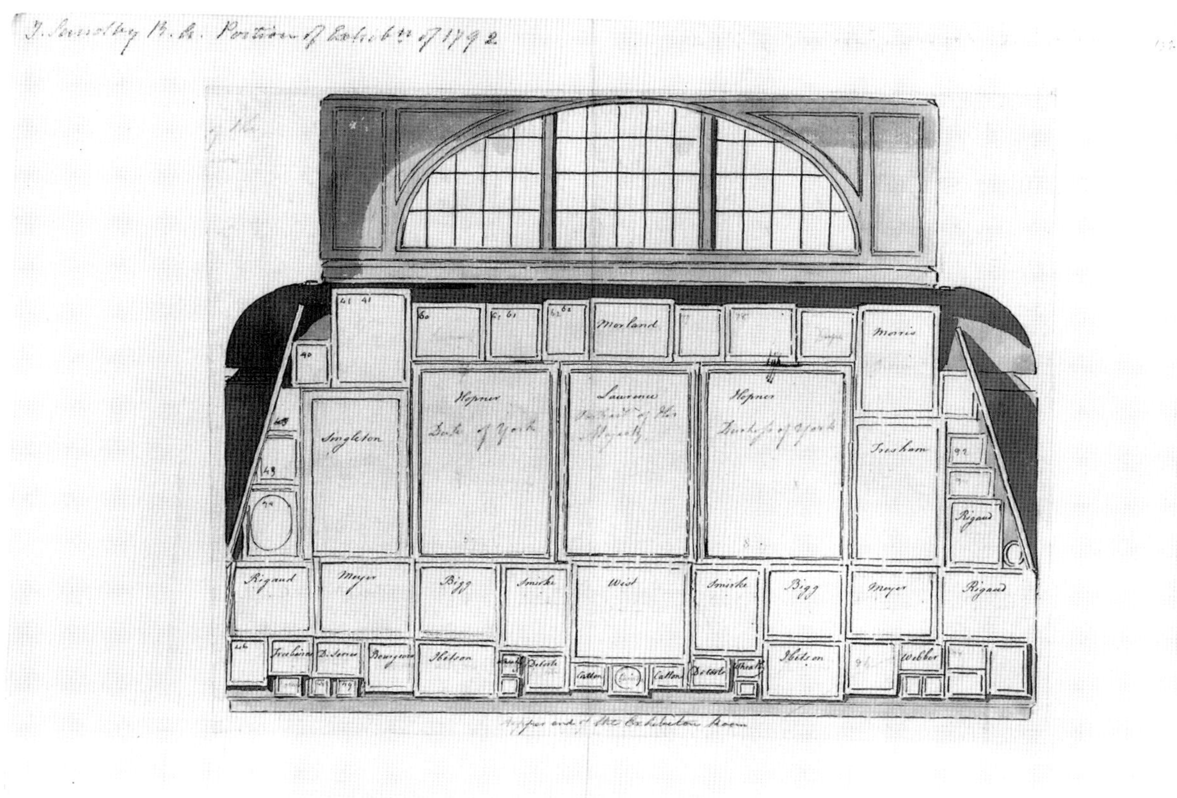

25 Thomas Sandby, *The Royal Academy Exhibition of 1792: The Great Room, North Wall*, pen and wash. Royal Academy of Arts, London.

West then had the picture moved to the Ante-room, telling Sir George Beaumont that he had hung it in the best light in all the Academy. Haydon had nothing but contempt for West's explanation, which he later dismissed as a deceitful cover-up for an utterly despicable act: 'This picture was hung in the great room . . . *and after two days it was taken down and put in the dark*, on the assertion that I occupied the place of an academician; when, instead of an academician's *picture*, a little girl in a pink sash was put there to fill the place.'[22] In later life this supposed maltreatment of Haydon's beloved *Dentatus* would enter his personal mythology as one of several pieces of evidence of the Academy's neglect of serious art in general, and of its hostility to him in particular. While his well-known tendency to paranoia may lead us to doubt the veracity of certain details of his account, it is probably true that pictures by Academicians tended to find better places on the exhibition walls than works by institutional outsiders. Haydon was not, and would never be, a member of the Academy.

In 1809 he was not without his supporters, however. The Earl of Mulgrave bought the *Dentatus* for the respectable sum of £150, and the artist's allies in the press championed his cause. In a review of the exhibition which appeared in the *Examiner* for 30 April 1809, Robert Hunt claimed that 'Haydon has added new dignity to the Historical art of his country: his picture of "the old Roman Tribune Dentatus", ought not to have been hung in the Anti-room [*sic*], but in the large room, in the best post of honour except the President'. Three weeks later, on 21 May, Hunt clarified his misgivings about the Ante-room, suggesting that it seemed 'to be considered by the Academy, as I am sure it is by the tasteful visitor, little more than a mere vestibule to the large room, and is therefore frequently hurried over with scarcely a glance'. In any case this was hardly the proper place to hang a monumental classical history painting (at 228 × 138 cm or 90 × 54 in., the *Dentatus* is on the scale of a full-length portrait) – a rare example of that type of work which more than any other deserved the RA's full support. If Haydon was right in believing that the President of the Academy had overridden a decision of the Hanging Committee – which would have been a most unusual occurrence – then he would have had good cause for feeling that his work had been deliberately, and unjustly, demoted by the powers that be. When an aspiring young artist invested so much time and effort in producing a work designed to catapult him to fame, an unfavourable placement at Somerset House could do untold damage to his career; damage from which, as in Haydon's case, he might never fully recover.

Whether or not Haydon was rightly informed about what had happened to his picture, it was one of the Academy's constant concerns to envelop the deliberations of the Hanging Committee in a veil of secrecy. At its meeting of 10 April 1820, the

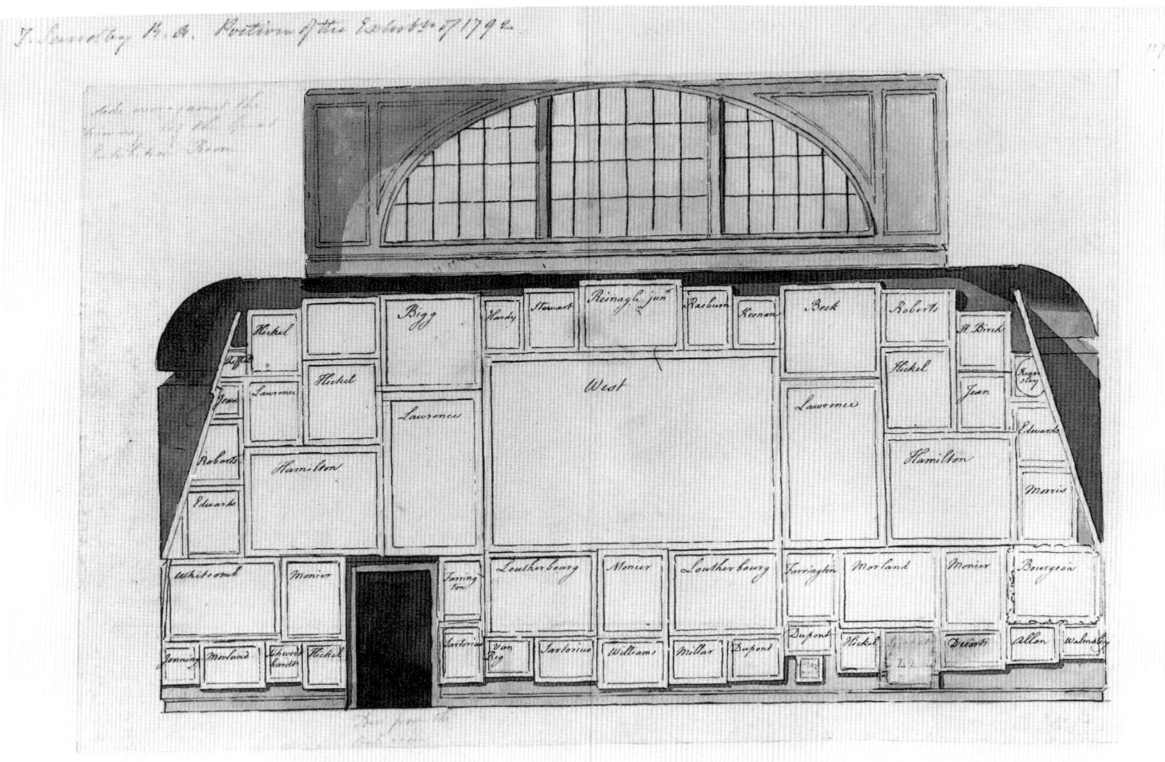

26 Thomas Sandby, *The Royal Academy Exhibition of 1792: The Great Room, West Wall*, pen and wash. Royal Academy of Arts, London.

27 Thomas Sandby, *The Royal Academy Exhibition of 1792: The Great Room, East Wall*, pen and wash. Royal Academy of Arts, London.

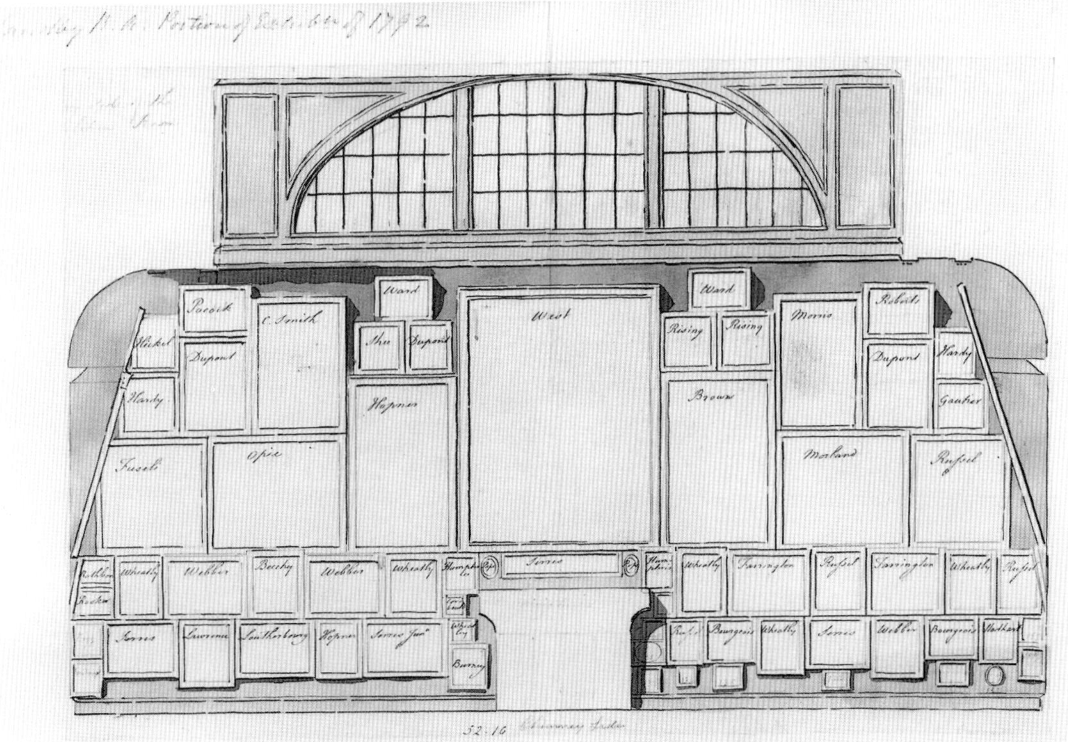

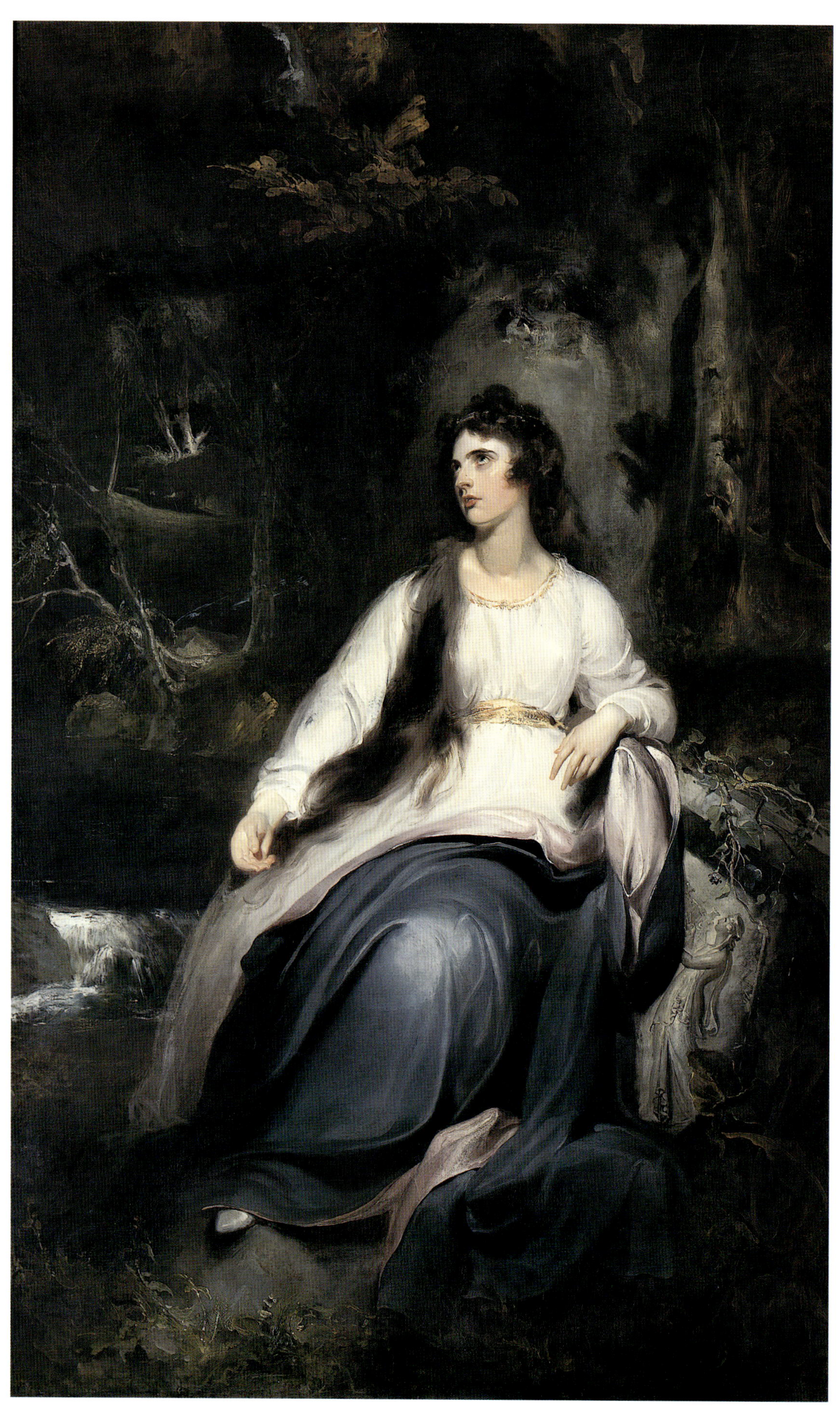

28 Thomas Lawrence, *A Lady of Fashion as 'La Penserosa'*, RA 1792. The Earl of Abercorn.

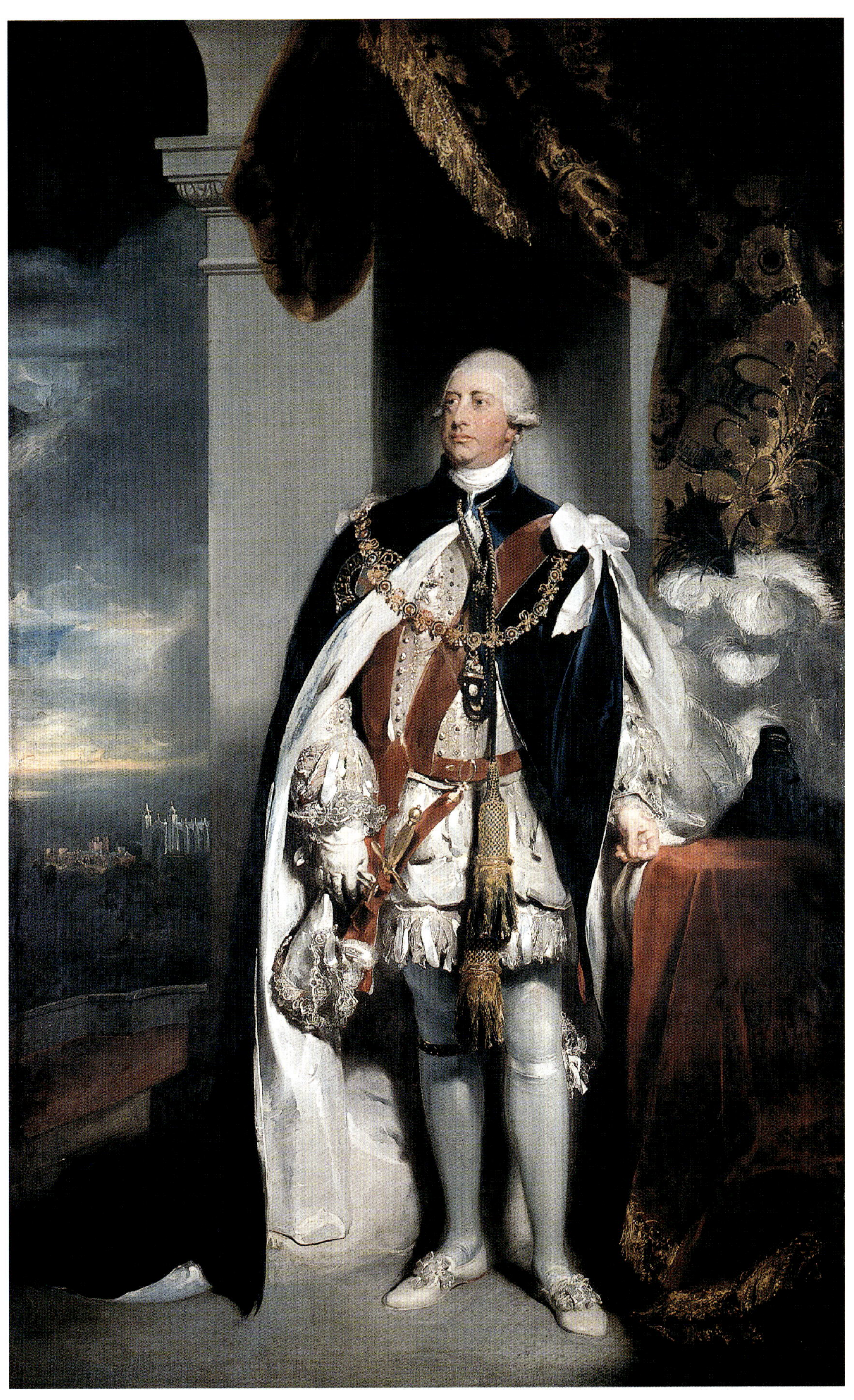

29 Thomas Lawrence, *George III*, RA 1792. Herbert Art Gallery, Coventry.

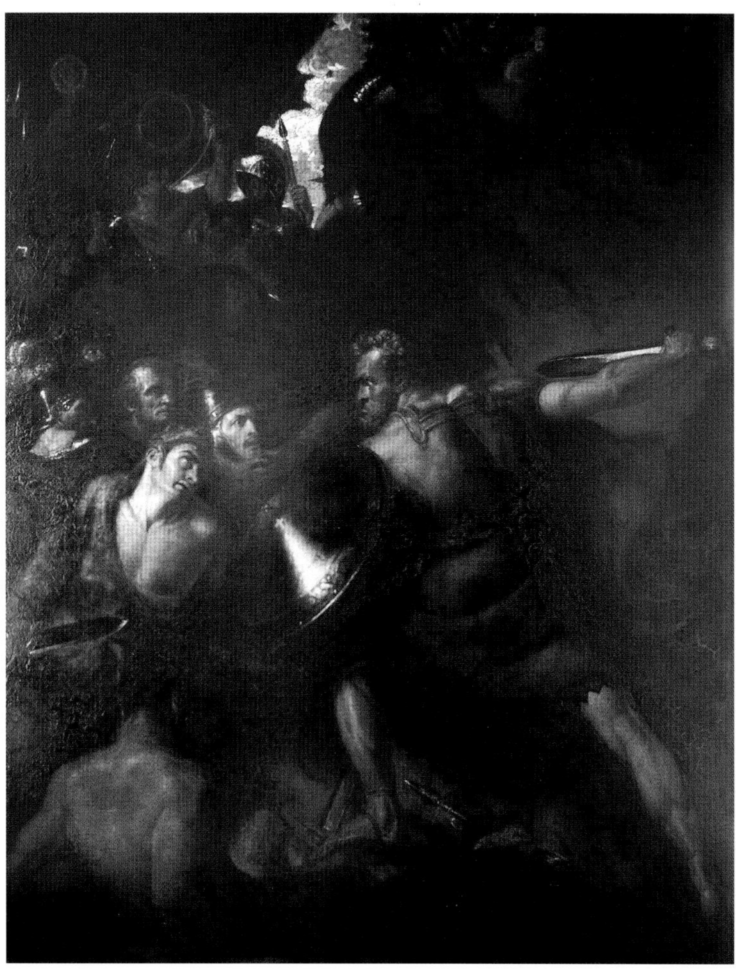

30 Benjamin Robert Haydon, *The Celebrated Old Roman Tribune, Dentatus, Making his Last Desperate Effort against his own Soldiers, who Attacked and Murdered him in a Narrow Pass*, RA 1809. Private collection.

governing Council resolved that none of its members 'shall communicate with any members of the Academy, or other Artists on the situation of their pictures during the time of arrangement for Exhibition without the consent of the majority on Council'.[23] The passage of such resolutions, and the fact that such consent was never forthcoming, none the less failed to stop crucial information from leaking out, often at the most inopportune moments.

Twelve years prior to Haydon's experience with *Dentatus*, a rather similar incident had occurred. On 20 April 1797 Farington noted in his diary that 'Bourgeois [Sir Peter Francis Bourgeois] has been at Academy to solicit Hamilton for situations for his pictures'.[24] The history painter William Hamilton was on that year's Hanging Committee. Bourgeois's solicitations seem to have produced a result opposite to what he intended, for four days later he called to tea at Farington's, 'Indignant, having been told by a Frame Maker, that His picture of Coriolanus is hung in the Anti-room. – I advised him not to make any remark to Kemble on the arrangement, which He said He thought would be most prudent'.[25] Neither Farington nor Bourgeois wished to risk upsetting John Philip Kemble (1757–1823), the most celebrated male actor of the age, whom Bourgeois had portrayed in one of his greatest Shakespearian roles; no actor desirous of publicity would have been pleased to learn that his portrait 'in character' had been positioned anywhere but in the Great Room. Thanks to his frame-maker informant, however, Bourgeois was able to marshal his connections to prevent a disaster. On the evening of 28 April Sir Francis dropped in at Farington's once again, this time to thank him 'for having been the cause of removing his picture of Coriolanus from Anti-room to great room'.[26] A senior Academician like Bourgeois clearly knew how to play the game – with far greater skill, certainly, than someone like the young and excitable Haydon.

The shifting of Bourgeois's picture also had one interesting 'knock-on' effect, since it took place after all the exhibits had been numbered for the catalogue. In the first edition of 1797, his *Coriolanus* appears as number 344, consistent with its placement in the Ante-room; but once inside the Great Room it became number 279, the number given in all subsequent editions. Meanwhile the reverse happened to the work that the Bourgeois replaced: the new number 344 which took *Coriolanus*'s place in the Ante-room was a seascape by an up and coming young painter named Joseph Mallord William Turner, whose work, now untraced, was entitled *Fishermen Coming A-shore at Sunset, Previous to a Gale*. Usually referred to as the *Mildmay Sea-piece*, this composition seems to have been well received despite its demotion from the Great Room. The critic Anthony Pasquin wrote,

> We have no knowledge of Mr. Turner, but through the medium of his works, which assuredly reflect great credit upon his endeavours; The present Picture is an undeniable proof of the possession of genius and judgement, and what is uncommon, in this age, is, that it partakes but very little of the manner of any other master: he seems to view nature and her operations with a peculiar vision, and that singularity of perception is so adroit that it enables him to give a transparency and modulation to the sea, more perfect than is usually seen on canvas.[27]

Apparently certain works of art could transcend the circumstances of their display.

Turner was later involved in one of the more curious disputes regarding the line – curious because his intervention resulted in the removal of one of his pictures from the Great Room into a space of lesser prestige. In 1812 his sublime historical landscape, *Snow Storm: Hannibal and his Army Crossing the Alps* (see fig. 113) was initially placed over the northern door on the west wall of the Great Room. Here the members of the Hanging Committee 'thought [it] was seen to great advantage', but Farington, who was on the Committee, soon discovered that Turner felt otherwise:

Calcott [Augustus Wall Callcott] came and remarked that Turner had sd. That if this picture were not placed under the line He wd. rather have it back; Calcott also thought it wd. be better seen if under the line. He went away & we took the picture down & placed it opposite to the door of entrance, the situation which Calcott mentioned. Here it appeared to the greatest disadvantage, – a scene of confusion and injuring the effect of the whole of that part of the arrangement. We therefore determined to replace it which was done.[28]

Turner remained adamant in his opinion that the *Hannibal* had to be viewed below the line, and within a few days his opinions had prevailed. By 1812 he was clearly not someone to be trifled with – not only because of his prominence as both an artist and an Academician, but also (or at least so one presumes) because by now he had established his own private exhibition gallery, where he was completely in control. Yet even if the RA may have needed Turner somewhat more than he needed them, his influence still had its limits. The Hanging Committee was not about to rearrange the entire main hang to accommodate his alpine snow scene, deciding instead to place it 'at the head of the *new room*' abutting the north side of the Ante-room and the west wall of the Great Room. Previously the Keeper's apartment, this was first used as an exhibition space in 1811; later, from 1816, it was also used as the School of Painting, with pictures for the students to copy from lent by, amongst others, the Dulwich College Collection (now the Dulwich Picture Gallery). Five days after registering his first objections Turner finally 'came and approved of the situation of His large picture provided other members shd. have pictures near it'; as a result, the decision was taken to reserve this room for oils, and to remove the drawings back 'below stairs', where they had hung until the previous year. But not all were satisfied by this change in the display. C. R. Leslie later recalled his thoughts at the time of the 1812 exhibition: 'There is a grand Landscape by Turner, representing a scene in the Alps in a snow storm, with Hannibal's army crossing; but as this picture is placed very low, I could not see it at the proper distance, owing to the crowd of people'.[29]

And as always, the crowds were almost inescapable: in 1780 there were over 61,000 visitors (averaging more than 2,000 each day); the following year, after the initial excitement had subsided, the numbers slumped to 42,824, but then bounced back to an average of close to 50,000 throughout the next decade. From the 1790s onwards the figures rose steadily, peaking at 91,827 in 1822 (thanks in part to the spectacular success of Wilkie's *Chelsea Pensioners*), and never dropping below 70,000 after 1820. The rooms were almost always crowded. More to the point, perhaps, at a shilling per visitor – and from 1798, catalogues were sold for an additional sixpence, doubling to one shilling in 1809 – the exhibitions turned a sizeable profit, more than sufficient to cover the Academy's expenses throughout the rest of the year. All that time and money spent preparing the annual displays proved an extremely sound investment. For if the Royal Academy cherished its public image as the disinterested guardian and director of English high art, it also operated its exhibitions as a highly lucrative business. And once all the behind-the-scenes negotiations had been completed, and the last pictures secured to the wall; once the final touches of varnish and gilding had been applied to the paintings, and the catalogues printed and delivered; once the carpenters and upholsterers had laid down their tools, and the annual dinner had taken place – only after weeks of careful preparation, in one of the defining moments of each London social season, did Somerset House open its doors to the public. Then it was time for the show to begin.

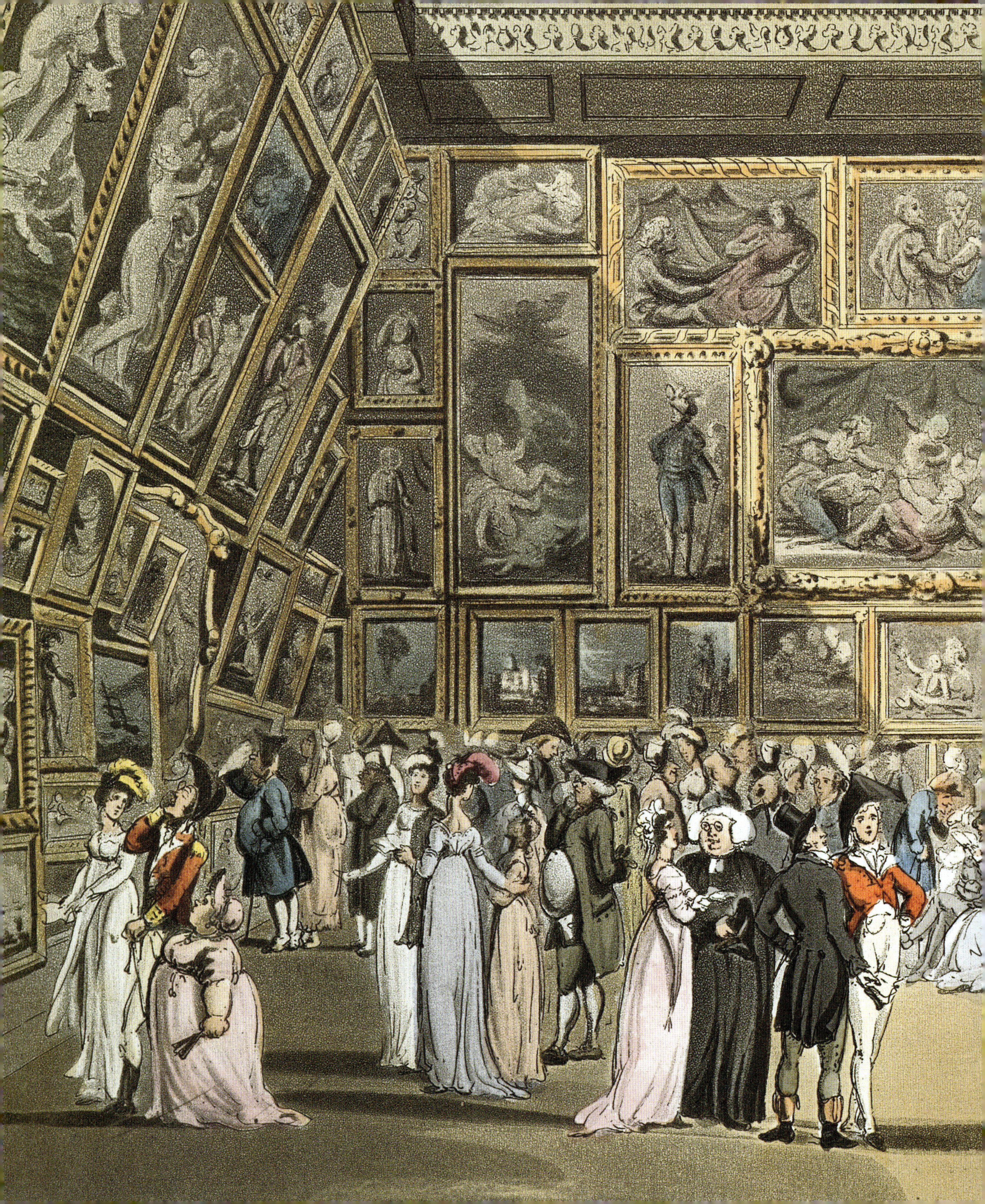

3

'A Shilling Well Laid Out': The Royal Academy's Early Public

C. S. Matheson

The advent of annual art exhibitions in England during the second half of the eighteenth century helped stimulate certain fundamental shifts in the nature of contemporary artistic production; but their impact on the development of the viewing public proved at least equally profound. Exhibitions provided their spectators with ideological and aesthetic instruction, in part by generating a range of devices which were deliberately designed to locate and define, direct and assert the composition of their audiences. Here I shall be considering two such devices: the Royal Academy's exhibition catalogues, and the principal graphic representations of its annual shows themselves.

Both the catalogue and what we might term the retrospective exhibition print constitute highly regulated modes of disseminating information about the physical arrangement of the gallery space, the art works which collectively form its display and, more obliquely, about the character, social location and deportment of spectators. Visual representations of gallery interiors and viewers, such as the works discussed below, formed part of a conscious and broadly political construction of a public for contemporary art in late Hanoverian Britain. Like the exhibition catalogue, retrospective exhibition prints are productions with a material relationship to the hierarchized, institutional space of the gallery. The first duty of the exhibition print is to record (and thus ratify) the constitution of the annual show through convincing graphic accounts of individual performances, the relation between them, and the cumulative visual impact of the ensemble. A second duty, which merges with the pedagogical mandate of an institution like the Royal Academy, is to testify to the efficacy and power of the spectacle by representing a strategic cross-section of viewer responses. Exhibition catalogues and exhibition prints simultaneously inform and regulate their audiences; their tendencies are similar while their functions, as we shall see, are complementary. Visual accounts of the annual Royal Academy show by artists as diverse as Charles Brandoin, Daniel Dodd, J. H. Ramberg and Thomas Rowlandson offer suggestive information concerning the place and deployment of printed catalogues in the Academy's main exhibition space. Furthermore, the prints suggest how catalogues directed the physical movement of spectators within the gallery, modified their gazes (especially in the case of female viewers) and shaped sociable interactions.

Given the ideological potential of the catalogue, it is not surprising that the form emerged in Britain in the midst of vigorous debates over the authority and direction of the fine arts. The catalogue began as a simple answer to a shift in the nature and scale of public art display, which occurred when an informal group of leading London artists mounted the first annual exhibition of their works, under the auspices of the Society for the Encouragement of Arts, Manufactures and Commerce, in April 1760. A simple, eight-page typographic catalogue of the works on show was produced and sold as a practical (and perhaps more genteel) alternative to collecting a sixpence admission fee at the door.[1] Initially the group seems to have regarded the catalogue as a convenient promotional supplement to the display. But if at first the catalogue bore less relation to the immediate life of the exhibition than to the commercial afterlife of the artist and his studio-cum-showroom, this situation quickly changed. The exhibition of 1760 appears almost to have collapsed under the weight of its own success, as an unexpectedly large number of visitors were attracted by the novelty of the event. Moreover, the organizers' difficulties were compounded by the fact that many visitors shared catalogues rather than purchasing their own. A

Hill after Rowlandson and Pugin, *Exhibition Room, Somerset House*. Detail of fig. 39.

subsequent letter sent from the artists to the Society complained that the rooms had been 'crowded and incommoded by the intrusion of great numbers whose stations and education made them no proper judges of painting and sculpture, and who were made idle and tumultuous by the opportunity of a shew'.[2]

The Society of Artists of Great Britain, as the main body of exhibitors officially styled themselves from 1761 onwards, attended to the physical dangers of overcrowded rooms and a troublesome breach in class distinction by doubling the price of the catalogue from sixpence to a shilling, and making its purchase mandatory for each spectator. One shilling, as Giles Waterfield notes in connection with the British Institution exhibitions early in the next century, was a price sufficient to exclude the lower orders from participation.[3] As a further measure Samuel Johnson was called upon to rationalize the admission charge in the preface of the following year's catalogue. While the Society was 'far from wishing to depreciate the sentiments of any class of the community', he writes, 'everyone knows that all cannot be judges or purchasers of works of art'.[4] Despite Johnson's insistence that the exhibition's purpose was 'not to enrich the Artists, but to advance the Art', the catalogue would always function as a discreet marketing tool. But once its purchase had become a matter of compulsion, and not choice, this ephemeral text came to dictate the social conditions of the exhibition and its public by admitting people whom the artists deemed qualified to experience their work, and keeping out those whom they did not.

Clearly then the catalogue is an expression of political impulses as well as a gesture of aesthetic facilitation; the information it dispenses evokes and extends the ideologically chartered environment of the gallery as it lists, orders and identifies the individual paintings on show. Catalogues control the public as an expression of admission policy, they can address the public authoritatively in their prefaces and eventually seek to manipulate its movement through the institutional space of the gallery. This combination of functions is captured in visual representations of gallery interiors and scenes of exhibition, particularly as the period progresses. Exhibition prints, that is to say, follow naturally from the editorial acts manifested in and enacted through the catalogue.

During the closing months of 1768, one faction of the Society of Artists seceded to form the core of the Royal Academy of Arts. This new institution opened its first exhibition the following April, in chambers on Pall Mall that had successively housed Lambe's auction rooms and Dalton's print warehouse. Following what had by now become generally accepted precedent, the Academy adopted the policy of charging its viewers a shilling each for admission; but because of their royal connection, the Academicians felt obliged to include a justifactory Advertisement in their inaugural catalogue:

> As the present Exhibition is a Part of the Institution of an Academy supported by Royal Munificence, the Public may naturally expect the Liberty of being admitted without any Expence.
>
> The Academicians therefore think it necessary to declare, that this was very much their desire, but they have not been able to suggest any other Means, than that of receiving Money for Admittance, to prevent the Room from being filled by improper Persons, to the entire Exclusion of those for whom the Exhibition is apparently intended.[5]

The qualifications of this brief preface effectively illustrate the Academy's ambivalence over the nature of its obligation to a viewing public. The 'natural' expectations and liberties of one portion of their audience must be denied as a result of the demonstrated character and behaviour of another. What is theoretically liberal and correct is sacrificed to what seems practically and socially expedient, a dilemma that apparently divides the architects of the scheme from their original conception of the exhibition, and the exhibition itself from the otherwise ostensibly liberal Academy.

Something of the ambivalence of the catalogue advertisement is captured two years later in the first visual representation of a Royal Academy exhibition, Richard Earlom's mezzotint after Charles Brandoin's *The Exhibition of the Royal Academy of Painting in the Year 1771* (fig. 31). The Academy's difficulties over admitting and vetting the body of the public find a corollary in the divided impulses that inform this image. Brandoin presents us with a range of individuals possessing dramatically varied aesthetic backgrounds and expectations (as their dress, posture and pantomimic responses to art suggest), but it is not entirely clear if a narrative or satirical account of their public conjunction is on offer here. The work is advertised in Sayer and Bennett's 1775 print catalogue as a scene featuring 'the pictures as actually placed, and a pleasing groupe of connoisseurs &c who were actually present, correctly drawn by Mr. Brandoin, and engraved in metzotinto by Richard Earlom'.[6] Although the commercial description of the print foregrounds its historicizing intent by pointedly marketing the work as delineation of 'actually placed' pictures and 'actually present' connoisseurs, there is at least a hint of drollery in Brandoin's treatment of most of the assembled spectators. The print hesitates between functions, much as the early Royal Academy catalogues suggest an institution hesitating between making provision for and regulating a viewing public.

Perhaps one of the difficulties facing Brandoin in 1771 was the lack of a clear visual precedent for representing an institutional exhibition in England. Instead he had to borrow from and adapt an existing graphic idiom for his task, a debt that appears more marked in the engraving of his design. The range of spectators in the *Exhibition*, the flat planes of images assembled in the gallery's cluttered hang, and the composition's satirical edge strongly evoke scenes of spectators before print-shop windows, a minor but distinct genre of urban representation during the second half of the eighteenth century. But drawing a visual equation between a Royal Academy show on the one hand, and an

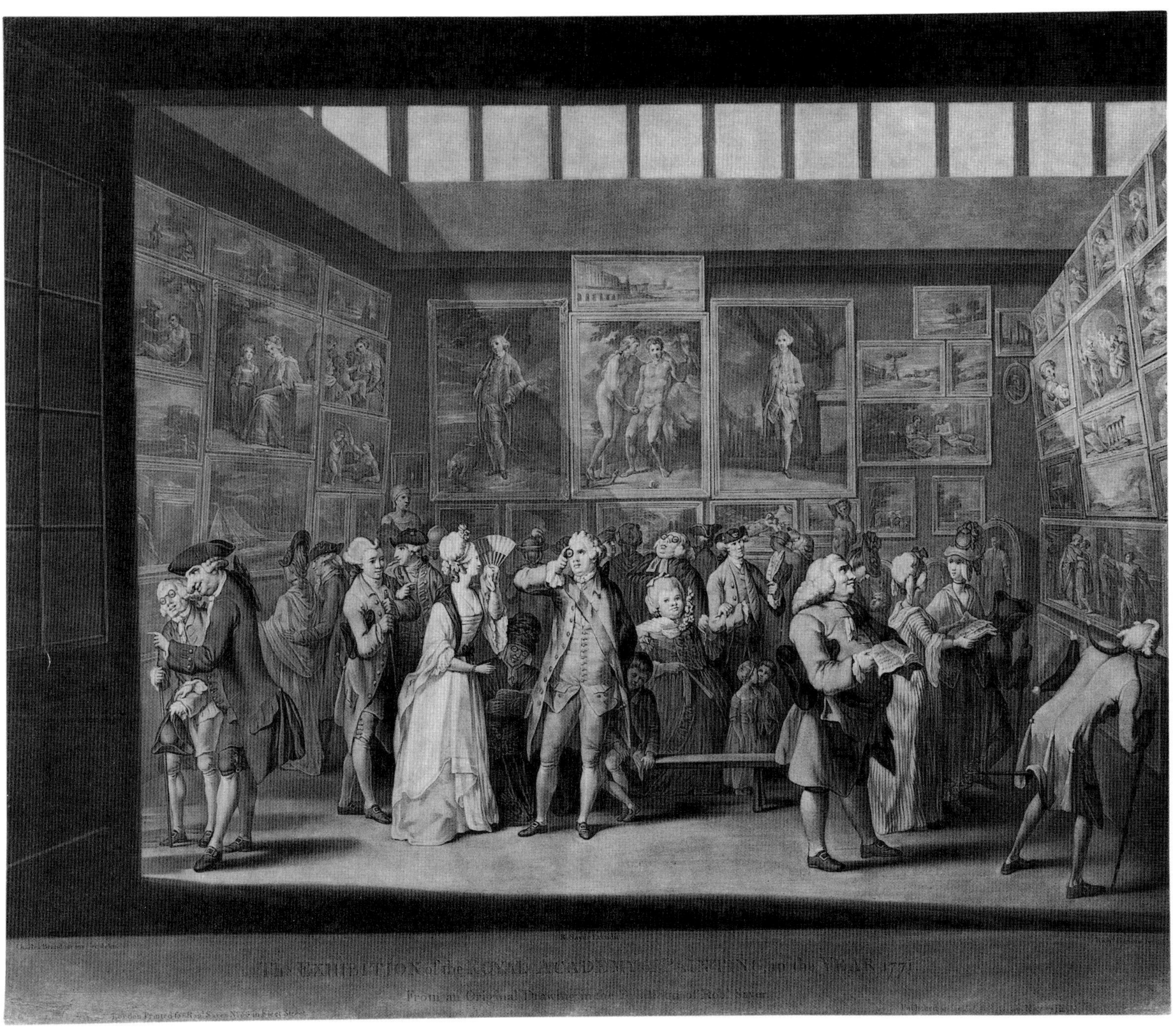

31 Richard Earlom after Charles Brandoin, *The Exhibition of the Royal Academy of Painting in the Year 1771*, mezzotint. Yale Center for British Art, Paul Mellon Collection.

unregulated and in many senses subversive exhibition venue on the other, creates tension within the composition. One priority of the work becomes the task of differentiating between the authority of different spectators, specifically between those who possess a connoisseurial background and others who do not. Since the nature of the exhibition is initially defined through one's response to the spectators and only secondarily by the art works on display, this distinction is crucial.

The *Exhibition . . . in the Year 1771* offers several visual focal points, creating a loosely knit body of male and female viewers ranked according to the nature and depth of their aesthetic contemplation. As we shall see, the exhibition catalogue is one tool for signifying the tendencies of their disparate gazes. In the left corner two of the 'pleasing groupe of connoisseurs', identifiable as an artist known as the Chevalier Manini and Dr Robert Bragge, a dealer in art and antiquities, amiably confer over paintings which lie just beyond the boundaries of our visual field.[7] Manini and Bragge were well-known figures at art auctions and related events, as their inclusion in James Bretherton's satiric print of around 1770, *Eight Heads of Artists and Amateurs*, 'drawn from ye life' attests.[8] The presence of these virtuosi at the Royal Academy strategically links its annual exhibition back to the sphere of judges and purchasers of art. Here Bragge familiarly draws Manini's attention to some aspect of a composition disregarded by other spectators and withheld from viewers of the print. The pair's situation in the gallery and their lively private exchange offer a teasingly literal definition of connoisseurship as the apprehension of qualities not apparent to the general spectator.

Compositions that attract the educated gaze of the exhibition's spectators are consistently unavailable to readers of the print. This is the case, to take another instance, with the work contemplated by a bespectacled clergyman at the rear of the gallery, who rather unprofessionally misses a painting of Adam and Eve on the back wall, and the dandified figure of a gentleman-connoisseur who claims a prominent place in the foreground. The connoisseur's critical and searching scrutiny, literally magnified by the quizzing-glass in his hand, is bluntly juxtaposed to the variously limited gazes of the women immediately before and behind him. Seated on an undecorated plank bench an elderly female viewer reads from an open exhibition catalogue while the disaffected object of her tuition droops beside her. The gaze of a more fashionable woman at the connoisseur's elbow is physically limited and decorously regulated. She purposely shields her face, either from coquettishness or a desire to examine discreetly James Barry's *Temptation of Adam*, which hangs at the rear of the gallery. Barry's composition was well received by critics, although a number of spectators found its nudity shocking. One contemporary reviewer memorably attributed this feature to the effect of Barry's recent travels: 'an insufficiency of drapery' apparently being 'a fault common to most painters immediately after the tour of Europe, on account of the difference in climate'.[9]

The cast-eyed, cock-hatted man to the right of *Adam* has been identified by Diana Donald as John Wilkes, the radical politician and MP for Middlesex.[10] Wilkes's attendance at the Academy's exhibition is logical, given both his public office and his history of involvement with the fine arts.[11] His visage can be cross-referenced with a number of other articles offered for sale in Sayer and Bennett's catalogue, including a print by Pine after Kitcherman (*sic*; presumably a misspelling for Kitchingman) listed as 'John Wilkes, The Patriot of Patriots'.[12] As a subject of frequent satiric and graphic representation, Wilkes provides a visual association between this account of the Royal Academy exhibition and the print-shop window, an intriguing point given the fact that Earlom's print was probably displayed in turn at Sayer and Bennett's busy Fleet Street shop.

While Wilkes's attendance at the exhibition evokes crucial issues of publicity and cultural property, the print registers considerable uncertainty about how to manage these associations. Brandoin mutes the radical politician's presence through a piece of low comedy, chiefly the physical contrast between the statesman (and author of a scurrilous essay on women) and his unidealized female companion. The joke is made more barbed by Brandoin's use of a painting of a reclining female nude, positioned on the wall behind Wilkes's head so that it emerges as if an embodiment of his thoughts. In spite of these innuendoes, Wilkes's physical and political position in the gallery makes his presence a significant one; occupying a recessed space between the mannered connoisseur and the stolid, John-Bull-like spectator in the foreground, he effectively bridges these stations and modes of viewing. Wilkes is not orientated towards any specific painting in the exhibition, as his posture suggests movement through the space rather than fixed contemplation of the works. His catalogue is held aloft in a manner that might swiftly become rhetorical or combative, fitting perhaps given the nature of his art activism in the years framing this composition. The catalogue that Wilkes brandishes draws the viewer's eye to the full-wigged head of the citizen-spectator in the foreground, whose apparent reliance on the institutional document suggests that he is a relative newcomer to the world of art and connoisseurship. To judge from the disparity between his dress and physique and the elegant serpentine lines of the male portraits adorning the gallery walls, 'John Bull' lacks the cultural sophistication that might prompt him to issue commissions of his own. Donald has recently commented on the satirical piquancy of thus 'picturing the inept responses of John Bull to the new pleasures of fashionable culture'.[13] Yet while he may lack the grace of an idealized masculinity signified in the portraits, or the *ton* of the dandified connoisseur, his solid attention offers an assurance for the future stability and popularity of the event.

More concerted acts of differentiation and construction of the viewing public occur after the relocation of the Academy in 1780 from Pall Mall to its grand new premises in Somerset House – a move which prompted several restatements, notably by Sir Joshua Reynolds in his ninth *Discourse*, of the institution's public and civilizing aims (as discussed by Dian Kriz and Martin Myrone elsewhere in this volume). This shift in location also seems to have prompted some re-examination of the Academy's relations with its exhibition patrons – or at least that is what is suggested by two slight but significant alterations in the content and format of the 1780 catalogue. Rather surprisingly, here the hesitant and qualified Advertisement from the inaugural publication (see p. 40 above) reappears for the first time since 1769, perhaps in response to the short-lived but intense public clamour over continuing the practice of charging an admission fee into what was now a building provided at public expense. In one sense the Academy seems to be starting over from scratch in its relations with its public, with little having altered in the twelve years since its first exhibition. However, the institution was now prepared to make new provision for a spectator moving about the gallery and observing works within its cluttered hang. Previously the Academy had followed the awkward practice of organizing its annual exhibition catalogues alphabetically by artist, with paintings listed beneath each name, and therefore out of exhibition order.[14] But in 1780 the catalogue is modified into a sequentially numbered list that follows the arrangement of

A

CATALOGUE.

☞ The PICTURES are numbered as they are placed in the Room. The Firſt Number over the Door.

The PICTURES, &c. marked (*) are to be diſpoſed of.

R. A. Royal Academician.
A. Aſſociate.
H. Honorary.

1 A Landſcape *T. Gainſborough, R.A.*
2 Portrait of a lady *T. F. Rigaud, A.*
3 Fruit & flowers, with a portrait of the Leghorn Runt. *J. Cole*
4 Maria, from Sterne. *T. Gaugain*
5 Portrait of a gentleman. *H. Robinſon*
6 The burning of the French fleet at La Hogue, 1692. *T. Mitchell, H.*
7 Portraits of their royal highneſſes, Prince William Henry, and Prince Edward. *B. Weſt, R.A.*
8 View of Mariſtow on the river Tavy, Devon. *W. Tomkins, A.*
9 A view of the Quebeck after the engagement, and Capt. Farmer taking leave of his people. *R. Paton*
10 The Quebeck blowing up, after burning four hours. *R. Paton*
11 Portrait of a gentleman. *R. Liveſay*
12 Portrait of a lady. *Sir J. Reynolds, R.A.*
13 Portrait of a Newfoundland dog. *C. Catton, jun.*
14 Portrait of a gentleman *T. Gainſborough, R.A.*
15 The troops at Warley-camp reviewed by his Majeſty, 1778. *P. J. De Loutherbourg*

32 *Catalogue of the Royal Academy, Year MDCCLXXX.*

paintings in the various galleries, beginning with the composition placed immediately over the door in the Great Room (fig. 32). From this point onwards priority is given to respecting the disposition of paintings in the display itself rather than recording an artist's work as an autonomous unit; and with this new arrangement, the catalogue symbolically folds the individual's productions into the larger spectacle.

In spite of the catalogue's reformatting, and the tentative acknowledgement of the public this change represents, some viewers continued to feel frustration with the limitations of the document. A few years later the German tourist Frederick Wendeborn sarcastically observed that the modified text 'not only informs him of the artists who have executed every production he sees before him, but also that a portrait, which attracts his attention, and of which he wants to know a little more, is that of a gentleman and not a lady; or he is told, that the animals which he sees painted before him, are horses or dogs, or that such a picture is intended for a landscape, and not a sea-piece'.[15] Evidently Wendeborn was irritated by the polite convention of excluding sitters' names from the portraits listed in the catalogue; this was a very hollow piece of humility, he reasoned, given that the subjects could be identified through newspaper reviews. Since portraits consistently formed the bulk of each year's exhibition, Wendeborn's irritation seems perfectly justified. Many others must have sympathized with Anthony Pasquin's complaints about viewers 'buzzing and fidgetting about the room . . . in the ardent wish to know who or what such a lady or gentleman is, or can be, even from those, most allied by the ties of consanguinity'.[16] Despite the inconvenience of this practice, and the fact that it drew a sharp distinction between the general body of spectators and the social network of the sitter, it continued until 1796.

The earliest published visual representation of the Academy's grand new display space is William Angus's engraving of 1784 after Daniel Dodd's *Representation of the Exhibition, of Paintings, at Somerset House* (fig. 34). During the preceding years, the novelty of the building itself, coupled with growing public interest in the annual displays, had generated a dramatic increase in visitor numbers. Samuel Johnson was one observer who could hardly contain his amazement. As he informed Mrs Thrale in early May of 1783, 'On Monday, if I am told truth, were received at the door, one hundred and ninety pounds, for the admission of three thousand eight hundred Spectators. Supposing the show open ten hours, and the Spectators staying one with another, each an hour, the rooms never had fewer than three hundred and eighty justling [*sic*] each other'.[17] On 8 May, Johnson observes that 'the exhibition prospers so much, that Sir Joshua says it will maintain the Academy: he estimates the probable amount at £3,000'.[18] The increased revenue freed the Academy from dependence on the Privy Purse for the first time in its history. It is this new status of the exhibition, a fairy godmother rather than an awkward stepchild of the Academy, that seems to be acknowledged and fictionalized in Dodd's portrayal.

Though both Johnson's and Reynolds's figures proved to be slightly over-optimistic, 55,357 paying customers passed through Somerset House during the run of the 1783 show, an astonishing number of visitors when one considers that the dimensions of the principal exhibition rooms, the Ante-room and the Great Room, were 25 × 19 and approximately 53 × 43 feet respectively.[19] This means that each visitor could claim a space roughly 2 feet 8 inches by 2 feet 8 inches, if the crowd was evenly distributed in the top-floor galleries. The spectators must have been packed shoulder to shoulder in each room, pooling more deeply in corners, in the vicinity of sensational works or in the centre of the gallery. To this physical density, surely complicated by the dimension of the women's clothing, was added the problem of crowd circulation: ingress and egress from the chambers, as well as the movement required to view both miniatures and 'skied' pictures, large history paintings such as Benjamin West's *Moses Receiving the Laws* (see fig. 24), and a host of smaller compositions lower down on the walls. Some years later Wendeborn observed that during May Somerset House was 'often so crowded with gentlemen and ladies, with pretended connoisseurs and supercilious critics, who all come to stare at the pictures that, in the middle of the day some ladies are ready to faint, on account of the heat of the rooms, and the powerful perfumes of the odiferous [*sic*] company [with] which they are filled'.[20]

Unsurprisingly, Dodd's *Representation of the Exhibition* does not allude to the physical discomforts of the event, but stresses its gentility and underlying order. Spectators in the foreground are grouped in structured pairs or clusters of three; they fall naturally into decorous attitudes on the benches; the females all appear duly attached or escorted, and even the trailing hems of their gowns are free from any imminent danger. These are bodies behaving politely, navigating the room with the measured grace of dancers in a minuet, affirming with each move the exhibition's significance, elegance and 'public benefits'. The population of the room and the population of the portraits that form the lion's share of the exhibition (over half of the 235 works in the Great Room, excluding miniatures) are virtually indistinguishable. Collectively these spectators are fit patrons, subjects and viewers of the paintings on display; their poise expresses an ideal continuity between the actions of looking, sitting to an artist and being seen as a representation.

Dodd's view resolves some of the ambiguities around the issue of audience that manifested their presence in Brandoin's mezzotint, in part by presenting a much more obviously homogeneous crowd. The earlier composition, as we have seen, turns on a series of ironic juxtapositions: noted picture dealers share space with a bumptious parson, a sturdy citizen new to the art scene rubs shoulders with an aristocratic connoisseur, a tired boy is a foil for sharp-eyed coquettes, who level gazes over fans and catalogues like sportsmen taking sightings behind a bush or tree. This is a group of disparate types brought together by the novelty of the event, rather than a coherent 'public' like that which Dodd chooses to represent. In Brandoin's work humour is generated by the inequality of the spectators, or those moments in the gallery when nature overcomes culture. The presiding geniuses of his exhibition are, after all, Adam and Eve, and not Moses – temptation, and not law.

Dodd's definition and regulation of the crowd is accomplished in several ways. In the first place, marginal forms of sociability – such as the pervasive flirting of the Pall Mall scene, or the private, superior jocularity of experts like Manini and Bragge – are suppressed or rewritten to direct attention back to the exhibition itself. Secondly, Dodd has chosen a perspective of the room that showcases the altar-like arrangement of three West submissions: *Moses Receiving the Laws on Mount Sinai, The Call of the Prophet Isaiah* and *The Call of the Prophet Jeremiah*, all works executed on commission for the Royal Chapel at Windsor Castle. Dodd's editing of the gallery space posits history painting as the dominant mode of academic production, although Reynolds's dramatic portrayal of *Mrs Siddons as the Tragic Muse* (see fig. 82) gets a look-in above the line at the extreme right. The king's patronage of the institution is metonymically signified through the presence of West's paintings – an admission of influence that we shall see treated much more literally by Ramberg a few years later. West's theologically sanctioned narratives of revealed religion give the scene a certain gravitas, implying that the gallery, like the royal chapel, is a consecrated

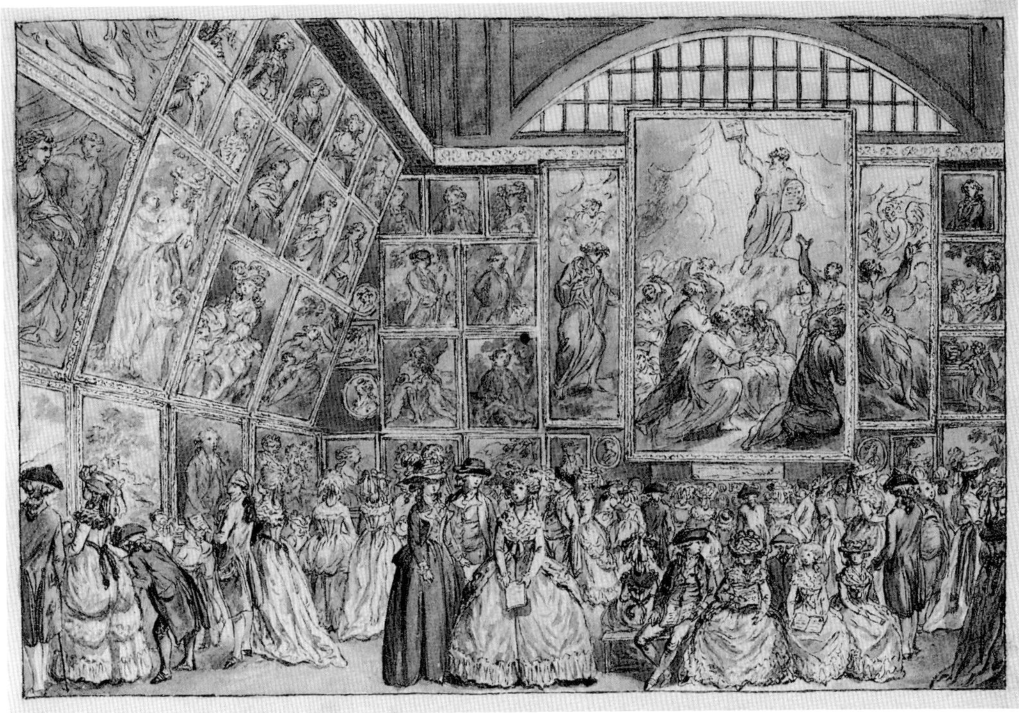

33 Daniel Dodd, preliminary study for *Representation of the Exhibition, of Paintings, at Somerset House*, 1784, pen and wash. Courtesy of the Huntington Library, Art Collections and Botanical Gardens, San Marino, California.

34 William Angus after Daniel Dodd, *Representation of the Exhibition, of Paintings, at Somerset House*, 1784, engraving.

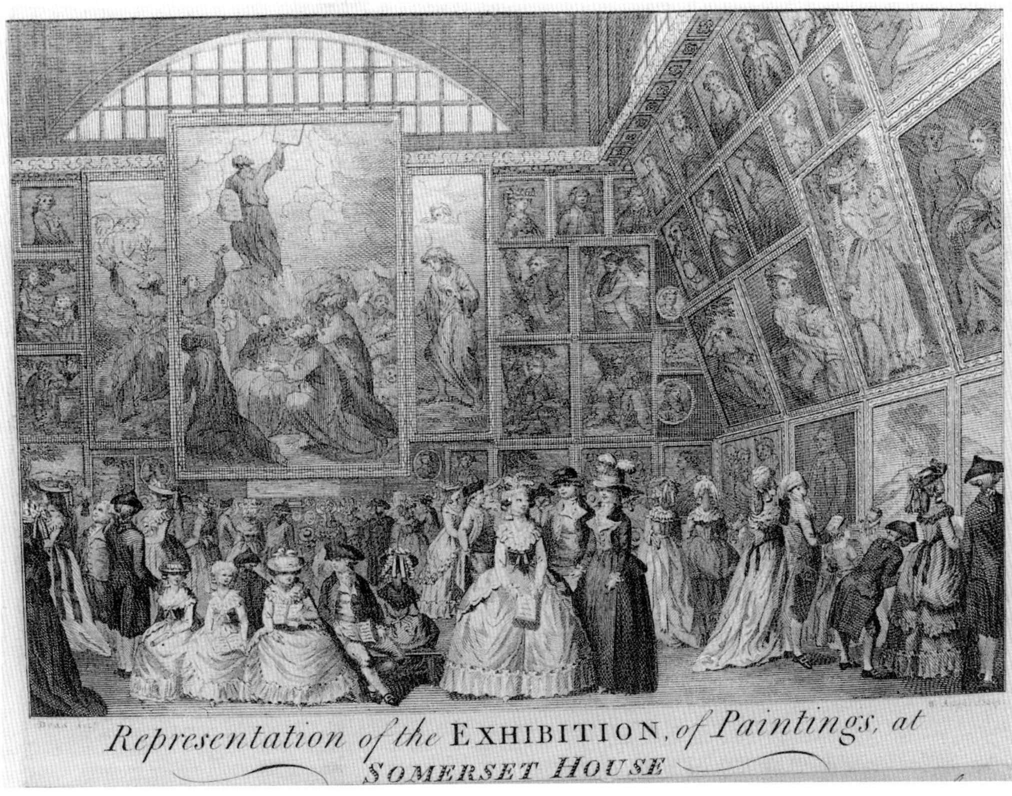

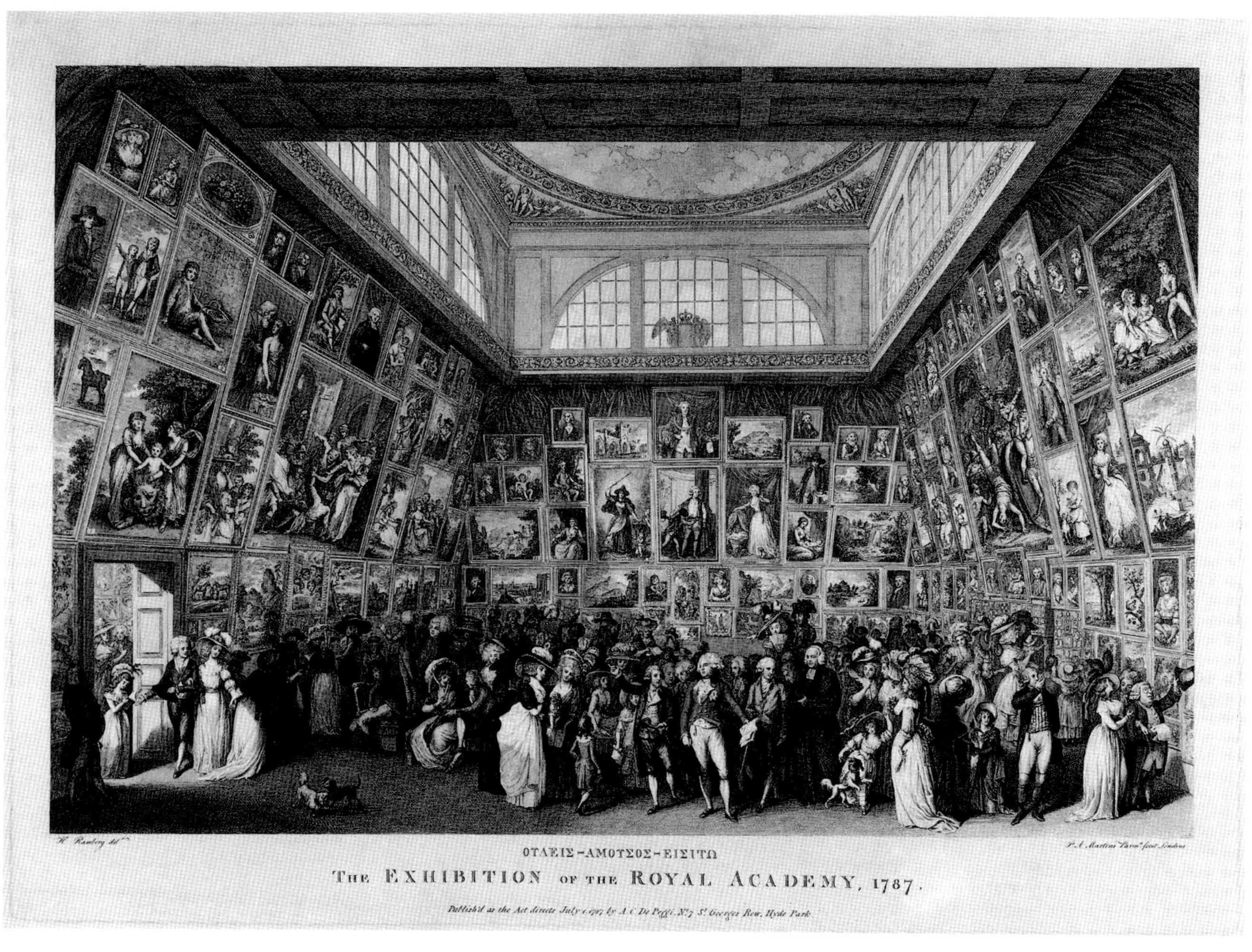

35 Pietro Martini after Johann Heinrich Ramberg, *The Exhibition of the Royal Academy, 1787*, engraving and etching. By courtesy of the Trustees of the British Museum.

space. The Israelites who cluster on the slope of Sinai in West's scene – Yahweh's public, if you like – are parallelled by the British public crowding in at the foot of the canvases. Similarly the tablets of the law, handed down to Moses from the heaven just above Somerset House, find echoes in the printed catalogues sported by spectators throughout the gallery. This conflation of divine law with academic regulation is amusing, and provides Dodd with a third strategy for crowd control. In the society of equals he represents, no spectator is actually shown reading (that is, requiring) a catalogue. The readiness of the gentleman at the right to consult his text may be explained by the fact that he is squiring a woman and female children round the show. Catalogues are most evident in the foreground, where viewers have detached themselves from the display to rest and converse. The presence of these documents seems a guarantee of good behaviour as spectators turn from the paintings and to each other, an assurance of their continuing participation in the event and of the regulation of their gaze.

Dodd's control over the image of this particular exhibition is even more striking when one considers the political lacunae of the design. The 1784 Academy show coincided with the spectacle of a highly contested Westminster election race between Sir Samuel Hood, Sir Cecil Wray and Charles James Fox. Just as a number of London's print-shops were drawn into the fray, so the Academy felt the ripples of lively partisanship; hardly surprising in a place where numbers of people gathered, in some cases wearing political insignia,[21] and where portraits of Hood (by Northcote) and Fox (by Reynolds) formed part of the display. But Dodd's picture gives not the slightest hint of this, or of the controversy sparked by Gainsborough's row with the Hanging Committee which prompted his permanent boycott of the annual show.[22] The *St James's Chronicle* took advantage of the incident to rehearse grievances about the arrangement of Chambers's 'ill-contrived and miserable Building,'[23] while the *Morning Chronicle* commiserated with Gainsborough for falling into the hands of a Hanging Committee who 'forgot that they were employed to cater for the public. Puffed up with the idea of the important theatre they were for once permitted to shift the scenes in, they imagined themselves to be the real heroes of the drama in which they performed only a part'.[24]

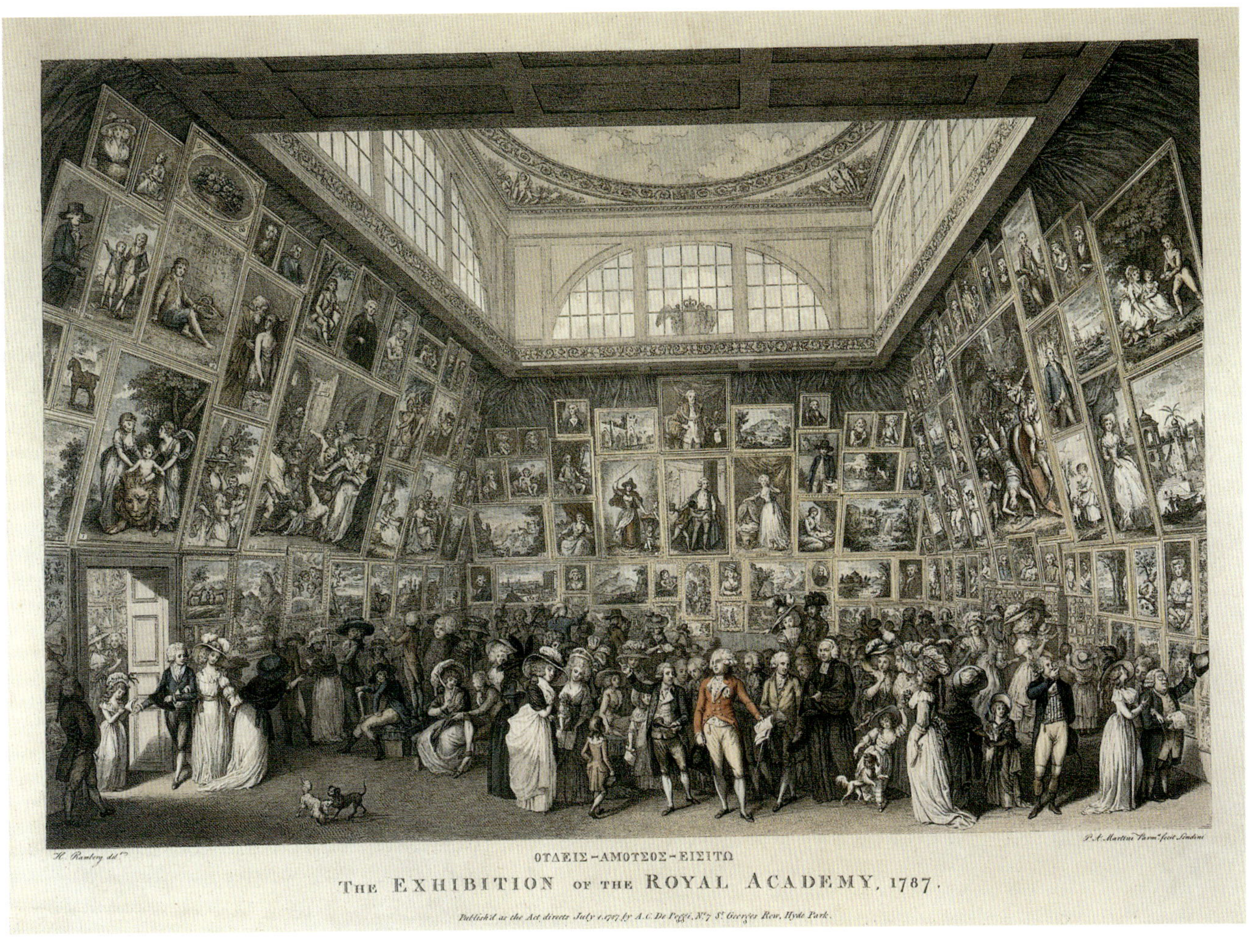

36 Pietro Martini after Johann Heinrich Ramberg, *The Exhibition of the Royal Academy, 1787*, hand-coloured engraving and etching. By courtesy of the Trustees of the British Museum.

The *Morning Chronicle*'s attack on the institution is significant on two counts: first for its articulation of a growing sense of public authority, very distinct from the image of a biddable audience offered in Dodd's design, and secondly for its explicit equation of the exhibition with theatre and the theatrical (an issue further explored by Gill Perry in Chapter 8). The *Chronicle* describes the Committee members as custodians of rooms that the artists make ready and the public brings to life. If public taste has decided in favour of Gainsborough, then the painter's exclusion represents a dereliction of duty on the part of the selectors. Publicity in this reading is the exhibition's *raison d'être*; the public are judges and witnesses, effectively sharing the bill with the artists themselves.

The print of the exhibition of 1787 drawn by Johann Heinrich Ramberg and engraved by Pietro Martini (fig. 35) retreats from this emerging sense of publicity to reaffirm the authority of the event, what Habermas calls the 'representative publicness' of the Academy as an institution.[25] The Greek phrase above the title of the print reproduces the legend that appeared over the doorway of the main exhibition room in the period. Translated as 'Let no Stranger to the Muses Enter',[26] the inscription establishes the print's position as a continuation of the material fabric of the exhibition room and therefore as a pictorial performance supportive of Academic policy. Viewers 'enter' Ramberg's print through a phrase that lyrically alludes to the institution's admission requirements, and which nominally recreates the passage of the public into the Great Room itself. In addition, the imperative inscription indicates that this graphic translation of the event is governed by the same social and political expectations as the public spectacle it describes.

The press of the crowd in this main exhibition space is eased by Ramberg's provision of a still focal point in the person of George, Prince of Wales, who is shown being guided around by Reynolds, the President of the RA. In an early(?), hand-coloured impression (fig. 36), the prince's visual pre-eminence is further emphasized by the scarlet coat he wears amidst the subfusc of his immediate circle. The disposition of the figures of Reynolds and the prince offers a persuasive illustration of the structure of patronage manifested in the Academy, as the spectators in the gallery (and the eye of the viewer of the print) are made to revolve with almost ritualistic care around a member of the royal family.[27]

Relations between the rival art societies in the decade leading up to the foundation of the Royal Academy were sufficiently fraught for Reynolds to claim in his first *Discourse* that a national academy could not have been realized without the monarch's intervention in the artists' affairs, a claim that is implicitly confirmed by the inclusion of a royal proxy in Ramberg's composition. Even the cynical anonymous author of *Observations on the Present State of the Arts, with the Characters of Living Artists* (1790) admits that royal patronage was a 'sufficient protection' for the Academy at a time of scarifying internal battles. While the same writer regarded royal patronage as useful in principle, he, along with a good number of his contemporaries, was much less certain about the Prince of Wales's role in this regard. Although the prince attended the annual Royal Academy dinners, few saw evidence that the Academy 'derived any benefit from these compliments which he has condescended to pay to the President'.[28] According to the *Observations*, the prince had been added to the list of the Academy's protectors simply because he more than once sat to Reynolds for his portrait – on one occasion for the performance that is visible on the wall behind the central group in Ramberg's print (see fig. 3).

The Prince's open catalogue in the *Exhibition of . . . 1787* advertises his participation in and compliance with one of the Academy's main rituals. His attention, flagged and advertised by the text, is pedagogically significant given the vigorous behaviour to be observed in viewers on the margins of the prince's own circle. An unflattering review of the same display speculated that a decline in the quality of exhibited work proceeded 'not from the defect of the artists, but from their unwillingness to submit their best performances to *vulgar taste*'.[29] In Ramberg's print this vulgarity makes its presence manifest in the physical deportment of a number of the spectators, especially that of a couple who have enthusiastically clambered on to a bench for a better view of the royal entourage. The man's unrefined pointing and caricatured features are contrasted to the self-conscious immobility of his female companion, whose partially lowered fan and direct gaze suggest at least a half-hearted observation of the strictures of female decorum. Their attention is directed to the prince, and channelled in turn by the royal gaze and Reynolds's outstretched arm to John Opie's large picture of the *Assassination of David Rizzio*. While these 'ordinary' viewers fail on their own accord to attend to history painting, two influential public figures provide an intermediary step that may eventually bring them (along with the viewer of the print) to a proper, edifying focus upon the grand manner. This vignette becomes an effective illustration of the process outlined in Sir Joshua's ninth *Discourse*, in which viewers' thoughts are led upwards 'through successive stages of excellence'[30] to refined taste and virtue.

Elsewhere in the gallery the exhibition catalogue assists in drawing up a typology of late eighteenth-century spectatorship. The gaze of a young woman entering the Great Room from the Ante-room is pointedly regulated by the institutional text, just as the gazes of most of the female spectators are mediated by the catalogue or through a discoursing male companion. An example of the latter is the May–December combination positioned to the right of the self-reliant figure of the connoisseur, whose presence complements that of the prince as a reference point within the overall design. In the hand-coloured print this point is more literally made, with the connoisseur wearing blue in counterpoint to the prince's red. Both figures attract the attention of naïve viewers; each embodies a distinct aspect of patrician authority and each offers a lesson that may assist in ameliorating the behaviour of the assembled spectators.

The print develops an interesting contrast between different modes of communicating information on the artists and their paintings. While negligently holding a catalogue open against his walking stick, the prince attends to Reynolds, whose gestures and commentary are directed at one of the more prominent history paintings on view. Such oral dissemination of connoisseurial information was a common practice in noble or private collections, where frequently a housekeeper, steward or other domestic attendant would be appointed to act as an animated catalogue for appropriate visitors, or the proprietor himself would elect to guide distinguished guests. Ramberg's references to the practices of the noble cabinet serve two significant political ends: in his portrayal, this mode of offering aesthetic information becomes a means of asserting and maintaining social distinction within the press of the exhibition crowd, as well as discreetly promoting contemporary British painting to an audience composed at least in part of potential patrons and collectors. However, difficulties are created by alluding to the practices of the private cabinet within the commerce of a crowded public space. Ramberg and Martini would directly address these tensions in their account of the following year's display.

Here Ramberg's prescription for diffusing the persistent unwieldiness of the crowd involves a drastic excision in the body of the public. The event he describes in *Portraits of Their Majesty's and the Royal Family Viewing the Exhibition of the Royal Academy, 1788* (fig. 37) – the title tells an important story in itself – is in fact an exclusive private view, one of the regular occasions when the Academy's royal patrons were shown around the display just prior to its official opening. Alongside them appears a tutor with a group of students. This might be read as an allusion to the educational mandate of the Academy itself, or as a reference to the relative youth of a national audience for British art; in either case far greater caution is exercised by the artist in admitting spectators into a representation of the event, as the telling detail of a *slightly* open door to the gallery indicates.

The viewer moves from this over-determined scene of instruction to the massed ranks of female royals in the foreground, a highly contrived group bound in an intricate continuum of costume, gesture and exhibition catalogue.[31] Significantly, the physical gaps between the female members of the family, and symbolically the spaces between them in years, are bridged by the open

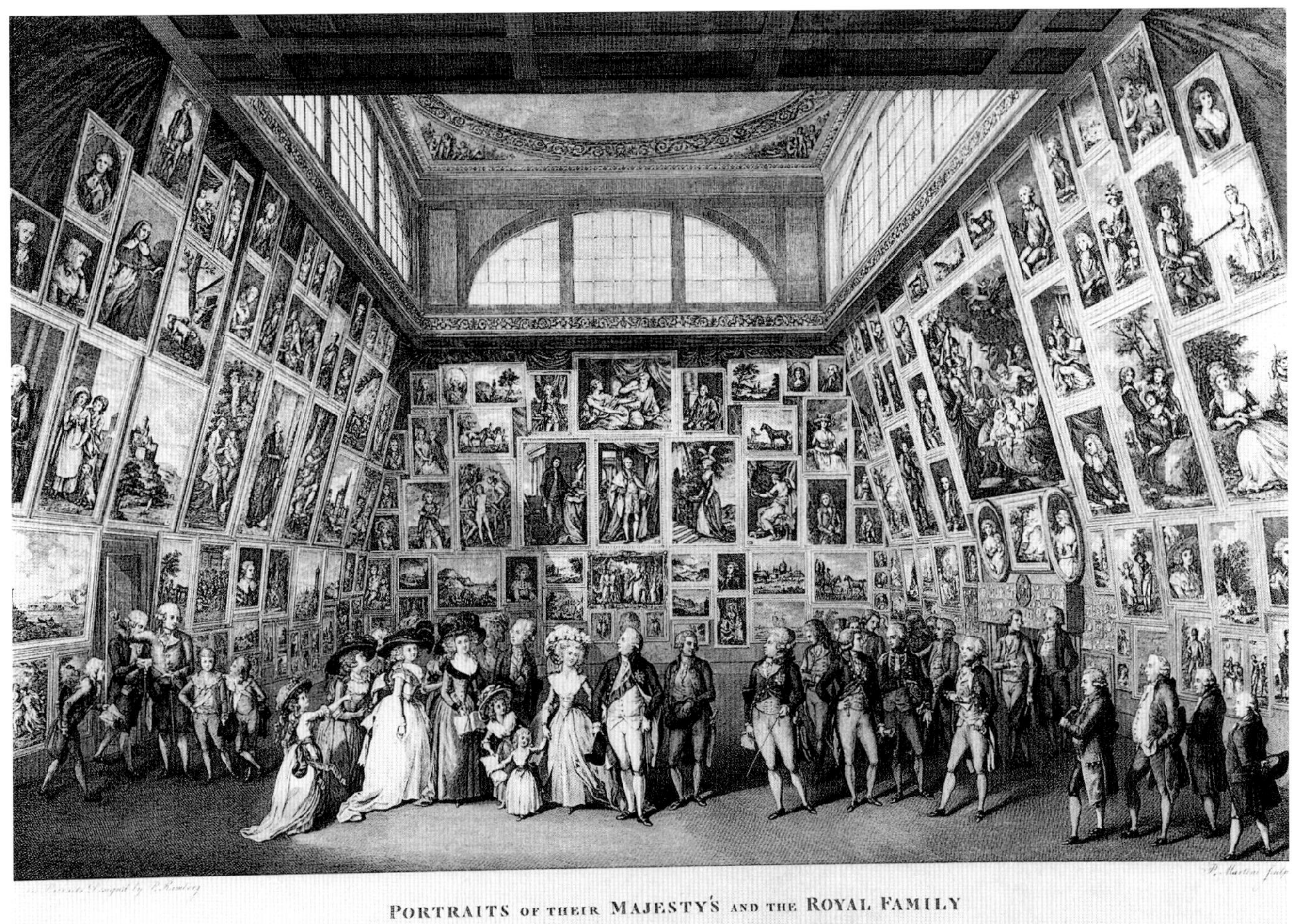

37 Pietro Martini after Johann Heinrich Ramberg, *Portraits of their Majesty's and the Royal Family Viewing the Exhibition of the Royal Academy, 1788*, engraving and etching. By courtesy of the Trustees of the British Museum.

text. Acting as a powerful ideological signifier, the catalogue serves to isolate and unify the female spectators as a group, thus qualifying their presence in the gallery by a visible assurance of the continued institutional regulation of their gaze. This regulation is extended from the smallest princess, not much larger than the catalogue her sister proffers, to a queen bodily and visually orientated towards the Academy's chief patron (he for *istoria* alone, she for *istoria* in him). By contrast the male royals, gathered in the foreground in a manner that recalls the swagger of Grand Tour portraiture, display distinct postures and relative independence from the institutional text. In most cases their catalogues are phallically rolled and held by their sides. As male spectators they exist autonomously within the public space defined by the Great Room, while their female counterparts are firmly gathered and confined within a picturesque subset of the event.

The intricate gendering of gazes in the *Portraits of Their Majesty's* . . . becomes more charged in light of the publication history of Ramberg's and Martini's performance. Their print of the exhibition of 1788 was also sold in modified form as a fan leaf, which survives in at least one unmounted specimen (fig. 38). The commodification of the Somerset House display into a fashion accessory is an obvious indication of the social location of the event, but more tellingly, the fan leaf is a form that directs this construction of Academy history and policy specifically back to female viewers. The commercial refashioning of the print reinscribes the lessons of the composition itself regarding women in the public space of an institutional gallery. As a device that can screen the eyes or deflect the gaze of others, a fan determines the extent or direction of female vision, just as the exhibition catalogue seems to do in Ramberg's later print.

Thomas Rowlandson and Augustus Pugin's *Exhibition Room, Somerset House* (fig. 39), published exactly twenty years later in Rudolph Ackermann's *Microcosm of London* (1808), displays the artist's familiarity with what had become the conventions of institutional gallery representation, as well as some significant and studied points of divergence from the genre. Although still bound to set the stage in considerable detail, Rowlandson does not portray one particular exhibition; he offers a generalized rendering, as the phrasing of his title implies. His purposes, moreover, unlike Brandoin's or Ramberg's, do not involve explaining

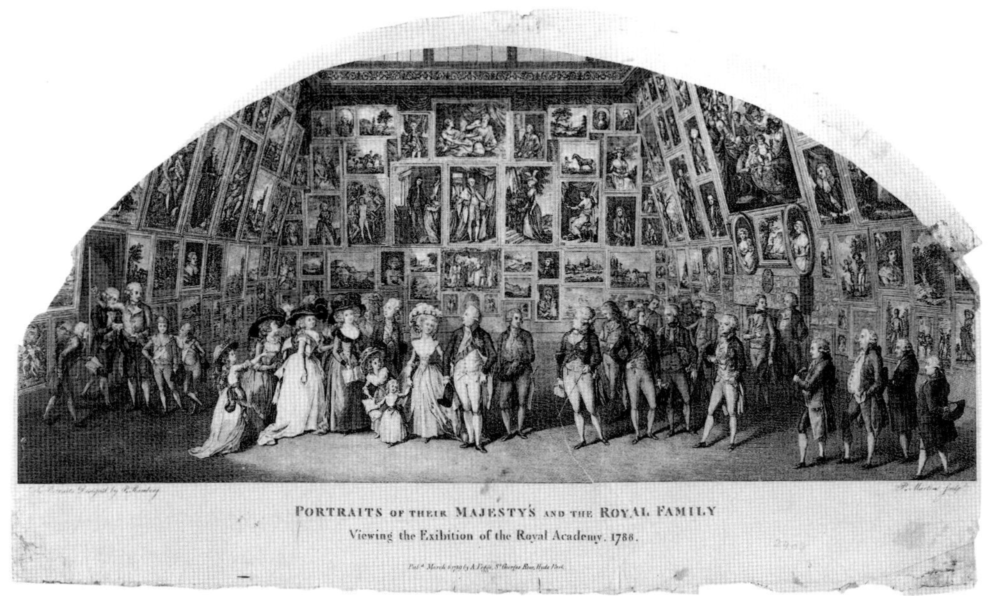

38 Pietro Martini after Johann Heinrich Ramberg, *Portraits of their Majesty's and the Royal Family Viewing the Exhibition of the Royal Academy, 1788*, engraving and etching, fan mount before letter, printed on kid. By courtesy of the Trustees of the British Museum.

the political or historical features that define the distinct nature of the spectacle, or ratifying the Academy's hanging policies in a specific instance. As indicated in the *Microcosm*'s accompanying commentary, the paintings shown on the walls are meant to be admired as examples of the draughtsman's skill – an opportunity for the artist to display 'much separate manner in the delineations . . . and such an infinite variety of small figures, contrasted with each other in a way so peculiarly happy, and marked with such appropriate character'.[32] But Rowlandson is chiefly concerned with the sociability of the gallery and its relation, as the title of Ackermann's volume implies, to equivalent sites in the capital. The *Microcosm* treats the Royal Academy alongside the Royal Exchange, the Foundling Hospital, Fleet Prison, the Bank of England and other places of public resort, and in so doing implicitly raises questions about the Academy's claim to a unique civic identity.

Rowlandson also makes light of the notion that the Great Room bears any special weight of cultural responsibility by pointedly inserting two easily legible narratives among the assemblage of imaginary paintings. At the left a group of spectators contemplates a large generic rendering of the *Rape of Europa*, while at right a spirited *St George Slaying the Dragon* is distinguished by its bright palette. Given the fact that Britain was in the midst of a difficult war with France, it is both significant and amusing that the viewing public is ranged between the mythologically and heraldically evoked constructs of Europe and England. But considered as works of art, the *Europa* and *St George* function together as a kind of comic précis of history painting, a *reductio ad absurdum* of the grand manner to one heroic and one anti-heroic prototype. It is hardly any wonder, then, that the spectators who attend to these defining compositions are the most pilloried in the scene. In the left foreground Rowlandson replaces the stock gallery figures of a discoursing man and younger female companion with a silenced male and a young woman who gestures interrogatively towards her catalogue. Perhaps because of the theme of *Europa*, her escort shows obvious signs of confusion or embarrassment, but the woman is unfazed by the work, and modesty does not prompt her to deploy the fan she carries. On the right a frail, bespectacled virtuoso leans on his cane for a nearer look at a rampant symbol of British nationhood.

Rowlandson's approach to representing and containing the crowd in this scene suggests fewer anxieties about the viewing public than Ramberg's prints had expressed two decades earlier. Although the back reaches of the Great Room contain a rather frenzied, anonymous crowd, in the foreground a group of different social and professional types – with a clergyman and officers to ensure the peace – stands out distinctly on its own. Their presence reassures us of the respectability of the event, and also of its comprehensibility, thus easing the cumulative effect of a strolling, chatting, noticing, lounging audience which lacks other clear signs of regulation. In Rowlandson's construction of the public, its members are not shown as requiring the example of an authoritative or learned viewer, or even in need of instruction from texts. Many spectators are shown grasping catalogues (significantly reduced from their actual size), but very few bother to consult them; what these texts do, more than anything else, is simply assist in the creation of comic incidents. Using the Great Room at Somerset House as a picturesque backdrop, Rowlandson mildly lampoons 'the peculiar mode by which different persons shew the earnestness with which they contemplate what they are inspecting',[33] as they go about their seriocomic business of attending to modern art.

The strategy of equating the Academy with other civic venues was pushed to an extreme some thirteen years later in Pierce Egan's illustrated novel *Life in London; or the Day and Night Scenes of Jerry Hawthorn, esq., and his Elegant Friend Corinthian Tom.* Embellished by George and Robert Cruikshank with woodcuts

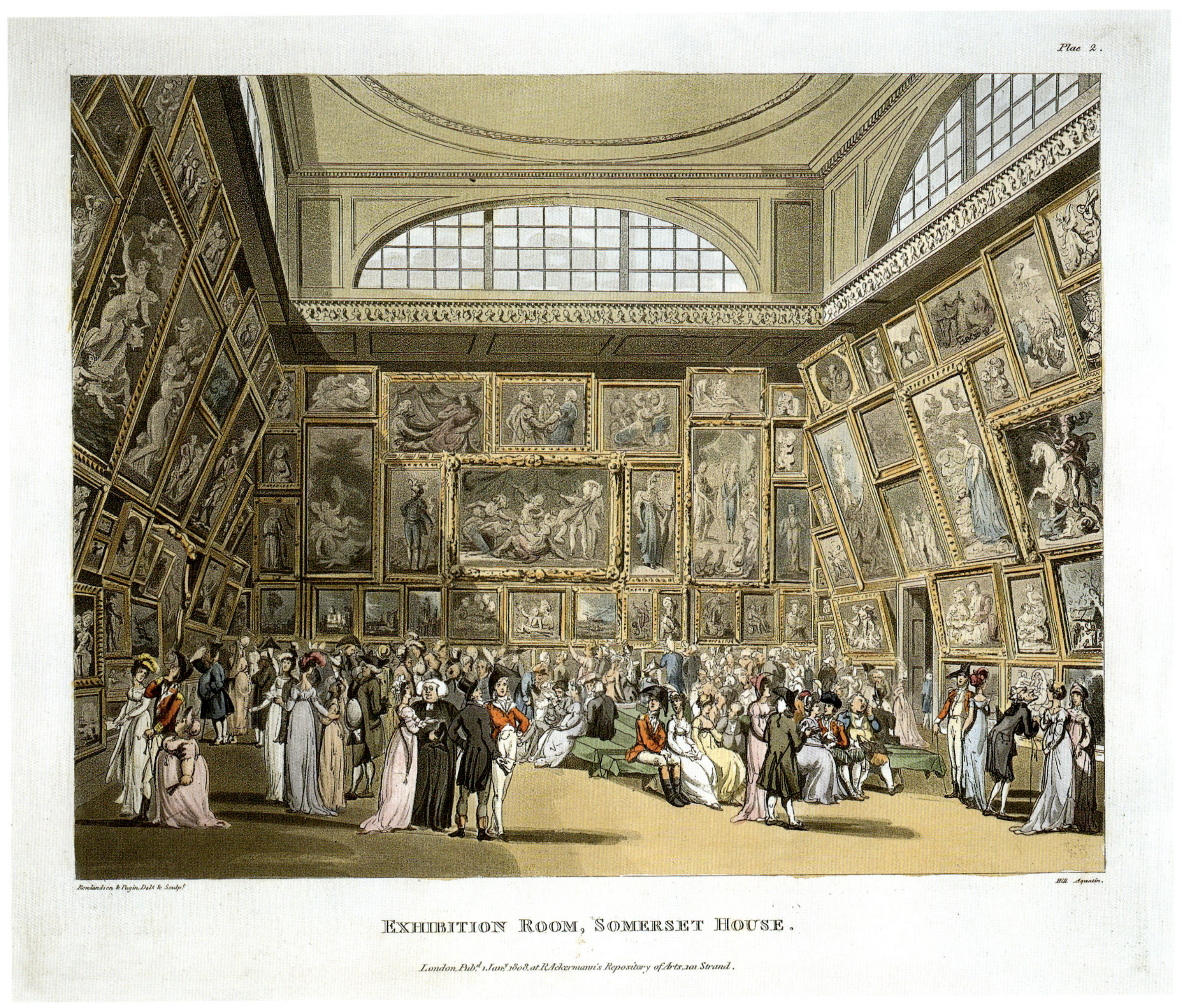

39 John Hill after Thomas Rowlandson and Augustus Pugin, *Exhibition Room, Somerset House*, hand-coloured aquatint from *The Microcosm of London* (1808).

and 'thirty-six scenes from real life' in aquatint, *Life in London* was published in weekly instalments by Sherwood, Neely and Jones from September 1820, then revised and reissued in full in 1821. So popular was the work that it was rapidly pirated, imitated, merchandised and even transformed for the stage – most successfully perhaps by W. T. Moncrieff as *Tom and Jerry; or Life in London. An Operatic Extravaganza in Three Acts.* The extent of the novel's audience, the complexity and diversity of its dissemination, and the generic fluidity of a narrative that moves between the private sphere of the portfolio and library, and the public sphere of the print-shop window and theatre, makes *Life in London*'s representation of the Royal Academy particularly significant.

Egan characterizes his episodic tale in the preface as a 'Camera Obscura' of London. The 'rambles and sprees' of the dandified Corinthian Tom, the impecunious Bob Logic, recently down from Oxford, and the sporting proto-squire Jerry Hawthorn[34] constitute a 'rough guide' to a metropolis Egan constructs dialectically, principally through contrasts between East End and West End, 'criminality' and 'respectability', the demands of survival and the dictates of fashion, the pleasures of sport and the fatigues of culture. Representative sites in one geographical or social region of this masculine city have their equivalent in the other. Tom and Jerry's visit to the Royal Academy in Chapter 7, for instance, is pointedly framed by an evening's entertainment at Vauxhall and an undercover trip to a beggar's assembly in the 'Back Slums'. The 'rational amusement' afforded by the exhibition is thus thrown into relief by the bourgeois gluttony of Vauxhall's pleasure grounds, 'where reflection is not admitted', and by the Hogarthian excesses of a gathering of drunken mendicants.[35]

When urban locations are juxtaposed in this fashion the result is both unexpected and powerful. Egan's narrative structure does not create a rigidly divided city, as one might expect, but a subversively fluid metropolis in which the *flâneur* is the only real constant. Viewed through the eyes of young protagonists in search of adventure and novelty, London is simply a vast network of subcultures, each with its particular leaders, codes, dress, rituals and dialect. Since the associations of one venue are inevitably carried into the next, the autonomy of specific sites like the Royal Academy is ruptured, often to comic effect. In this economy the Academy has no inherent superiority or significance, contrary to the message of earlier graphic representations, but is coolly evaluated in terms of its entertainment value:

> 'my Coz. and I [said Tom] intend to have a *lounge* tomorrow at the Exhibition of Pictures, at Somerset House, if you will accompany us, we shall esteem it as a favour'. 'I am sorry that a previous engagement of some importance prevents my accepting your offer, as it is a *bob* well laid out', answered the *Oxonian*. 'I agree with you, Logic', replied Tom; 'it is, I think, not only one of the cheapest but the best shilling's worth in London: and it is so truly rational and interesting, that you reflect upon it, at any period, with the greatest satisfaction and pleasure to your feelings'.[36]

This consumer-orientated approach to London's institutions and spectacles is reflected in the title of the Cruikshanks' aquatint, 'A Shilling Well Laid Out: Tom and Jerry at the Exhibition of Pictures at the Royal Academy' (fig. 40). Here the emphasis is clearly on those who have disposed of their shilling, rather than the substance of the exhibition. Accordingly the Great Room is contracted to a single corner and doorway, and the display itself to one landscape, a handful of highly contrived portraits and a single Descent from the Cross. The spacious, slightly elevated gallery perspectives favoured by Ramberg and Rowlandson – the visual equivalent of an omniscient narrative voice – are replaced by an eye-level glance towards a region of the gallery where foreground and background space are collapsed together. Nearly as many spectators are in motion as in contemplation, and while a certain social uniformity is suggested by the dress and deportment of those engaged in a morning lounge, there is no general intellectual or aesthetic consensus represented in the design. No quarter is given to that habitual figure of authority, the connoisseur; indeed the connoisseur's attempts to deploy specialized viewing aids like a quizzing-glass or telescope (as recorded at left) seem futile given the press around the doorway. But just to the left, beneath the black and the Turk engaged in deep conversation, we see a social type whom we have not encountered before, in the person of a seated figure who has achieved a moment of equipoise between the actions of reading, writing and looking. His solitariness and focused absorption, together with the sheaf of papers on his lap and his act of notation, suggest that he may very well be a critic.

Following established graphic convention, the Cruikshanks have used catalogues to indicate the nature or sophistication of a spectator's engagement with art. According to Tom, glancing at the pictures and marking one's catalogue is the first step of a multi-layered process of judging the works. His companion Jerry Hawthorn, seated on a bench with a Miss Trifle, is therefore doubly marginalized, as both his text and attention are deployed in the service of gallantry. The suggestion that the Academy might be a place of assignation (which the previous night's excursion to Vauxhall might lead us to expect) is, however, muted by the busy seriousness of their nearest neighbour. Although Tom himself stands holding an open text, he converses with a companion about a representative male portrait on the right. This vignette accompanies Tom's pronouncements in the text on the genre of portraiture, namely, that the features of someone such as a philanthropist, scholar or hero – one who has *earned* rather than *inherited* a right to public attention – are the only portraits worth examining. Tom's argument for a meritocracy in portraiture is punctuated in the print by a physical gesture – pointing his walking stick – that characterizes his ease and confidence. As the self-styled architect of his own fortune, Tom meets the portrait as an equal. This worldliness and independence mean that he is an engaged although not over-involved consumer of the scene around him, in marked contrast to the male viewer at the right, whose reliance upon the text and close proximity to a portrait may allow him to grasp one work, but certainly not the import of the genre or the exhibition as a whole. These latter tasks pass to urbane figures like Tom, who possesses an encyclopaedic knowledge of London and an accommodating gaze, and to the seated critic apparently capable of both seeing and communicating what he sees. Both men offer an alternative to what Tom calls the 'flippant *soi-disant* judges' who clutter the room.

The Cruikshanks have not produced a closed, commemorative, 'historical' print of a Somerset House exhibition. Here the Royal Academy figures as part of the warp and woof of London itself, its patrons mobile rather than obedient, and the exhibition an experience to be performed rather than internalized. What is striking about this representation, and a measure of the distance travelled by England's viewing public during the sixty years since the Academy's foundation, is the glimpse it offers of a new sense of spectatorship as a 'natural' component of urban life. In this respect the Cruikshanks' print registers the impact of the pro-

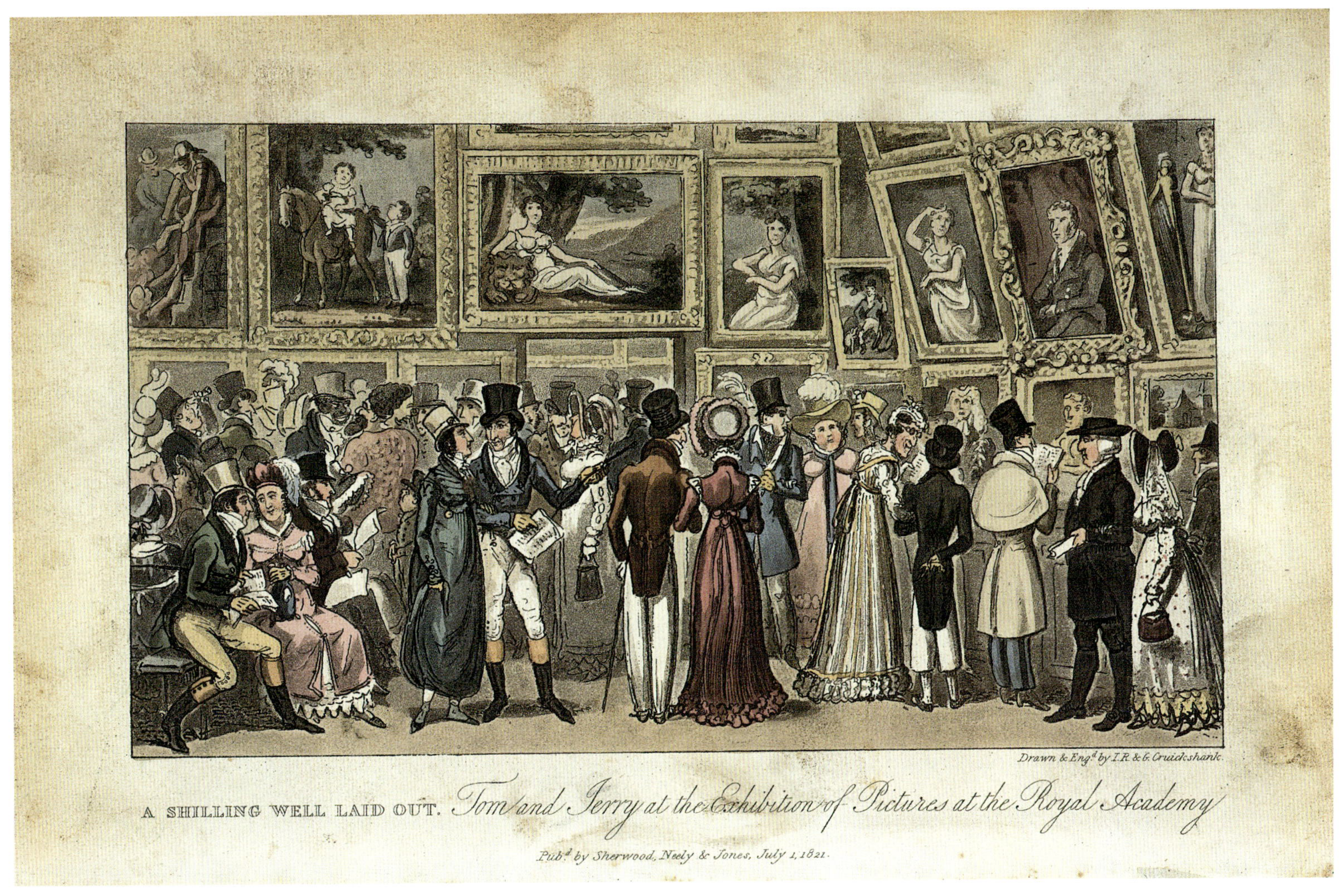

40 George and Robert Cruikshank, 'A Shilling Well Laid Out: Tom and Jerry at the Exhibition of Pictures at the Royal Academy', colour aquatint, from Pierce Egan, *Life in London; or the Day and Night Scenes of Jerry Hawthorn, Esq. and his Elegant Friend Corinthian Tom: Accompanied by Bob Logic, the Oxonian, in their Rambles and Sprees through the Metropolis* (1821).

liferation of galleries, exhibitions and institutions in the early nineteenth century, and anticipates the sea-change shortly to be effected by the founding of a national gallery.

Retrospective exhibition prints are complex devices for locating and defining an art-viewing public. Although they appear to offer a representative cross-section of the gallery population and sometimes, in tandem with the printed catalogue, a simple record of the contents of the exhibition, they are highly selective in what they choose to see and strategic in their manner of arrangement. In these various representations of the Royal Academy shows, aesthetic education is overtly joined to political instruction. Exhibition catalogues, an expression of institutional policy physically borne by viewers in the gallery, are used by graphic artists to catalogue spectators in turn. Catalogues, which regulate admission, address the public in their prefaces and influence physical movement in the exhibition space, become a visual device for establishing an aesthetic hegemony within the gallery, and an instrument for gendering the gaze. The Great Room views of the 1780s by Daniel Dodd and J. H. Ramberg offer themselves as paradigms for the constitution of future exhibitions – exemplary texts of a paternal relationship between art, its constituencies and the state. The nature of this relationship is problematized in 1808 by Rowlandson and in 1820–21 by George and Robert Cruikshank, who present Somerset House as a more secular, civic and urban venue. Then – as today – the Academy's complex, difficult and dynamic relationship with its public was played out through the bodies, eyes and minds of spectators at its annual exhibition.

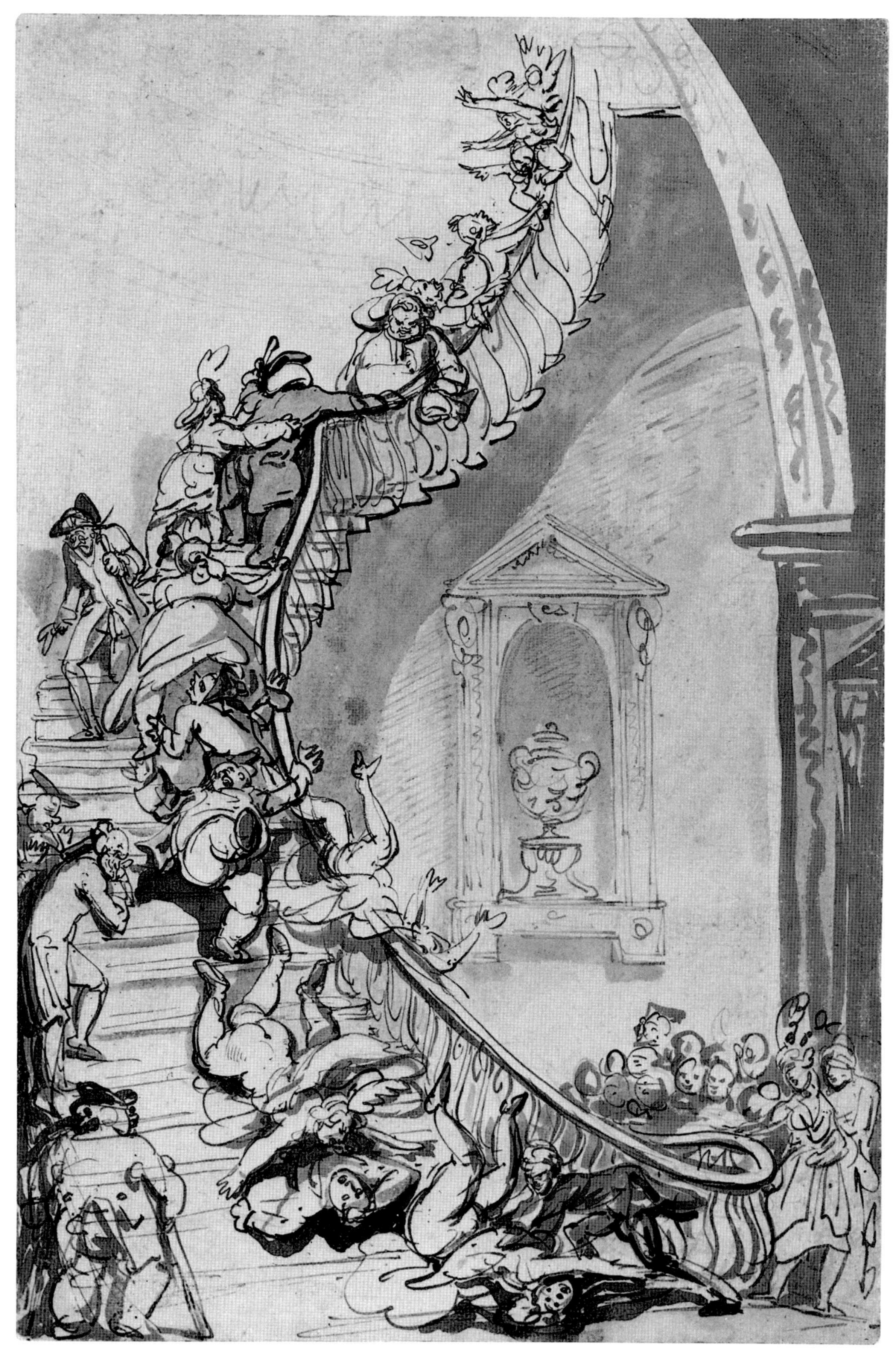

41 Thomas Rowlandson, *The Exhibition Stare Case*, *c.*1800, pen and wash. College Art Collections, University College, London.

4

'Stare Cases': Engendering the Public's Two Bodies at the Royal Academy of Arts

K. Dian Kriz

THOMAS ROWLANDSON'S DRAWING, *The Exhibition Stare Case* (*c*.1800;[1] fig. 41), is surely one of the wittiest images ever produced on the subject of Royal Academy exhibitions; and yet, unlike other renderings of these events, it includes no representations of the modern paintings and other art works that ostensibly drew crowds of fashionably dressed men and women annually to Somerset House. As the punning title indicates, the setting is not the Great Room, but the steep and spiralling stairway leading to it, where the splayed limbs and sprawling bodies of visitors form a spectacle that is bound to upstage the artistic displays in the rooms above. It is typical of Rowlandson that the comic charge of this image derives largely from the sight of male connoisseurs leering at the cascade of semi-nude female bodies strewn along the staircase in revealing and provocative poses. In this chapter I will argue that the 'exhibition' of the female visitor at the Royal Academy is more than simply a humorous trope deployed by satirists, but crucial to the construction of a viewing public for British art.

Rowlandson's portrayal of an active, if potentially unruly, viewing community of men and women exists in sharp contrast with the idea of an artistic public that the Royal Academy's President, Sir Joshua Reynolds, had evoked in his ninth *Discourse* on art, delivered at the official opening of Somerset House in October 1780. 'Gentlemen', he began, 'The Honour which the Arts acquire by being permitted to take possession of this noble habitation, is one of the most considerable of the many instances we have received of his MAJESTY's protection; and the strongest proof of his desire to make the Academy respectable'.[2] These introductory references to honour, nobility, royal favour and respectability are consistent with the central theme of this address and indeed all of the President's public pronouncements: the Academy's function was to produce an English school of art that would refine the taste of its public, which in turn would exert a beneficial influence on the country as a whole. While, as Reynolds admits, such refinement through art may not lead directly to 'purity of manners', it provides one means for 'disentangling the mind from appetite, and conducting the thoughts through successive stages of excellence . . . [that] conclude in Virtue'.[3] The success of this process of refinement was widely believed to be crucial to the well-being of the British nation, which, as a result of its defeat of France in the Seven Years War (1756–63), had consolidated its claim to be the leading commercial and military power in Europe.

According to Reynolds and a host of other contemporary writers on the arts, a flourishing commerce was essential for a nation to reach the highest stage of civilization, but it also posed a threat if the riches it provided led only to the pursuit of more wealth and the gratification of the appetites.[4] Thus the arts were charged with a crucial social function: to transform base appetite into refined taste through the production of an ideal beauty that was 'general and intellectual'.[5] And what better site to celebrate and promote such a transforming improvement of commercial society than the Academy's new quarters in Somerset House, situated between the commercial centre of the City to the east and the political centre of Westminster to the west, and between the thriving thoroughfare of the Strand to the north and, on the south, the Thames – the principal commercial conduit linking London to ports foreign and domestic.

For art to refine a nation grown rich and powerful from commerce, it had to transfigure base appetite into disinterested aesthetic appreciation. Gazing upon ideal and generalized beauty was not supposed to feed the desire to touch, taste or smell,

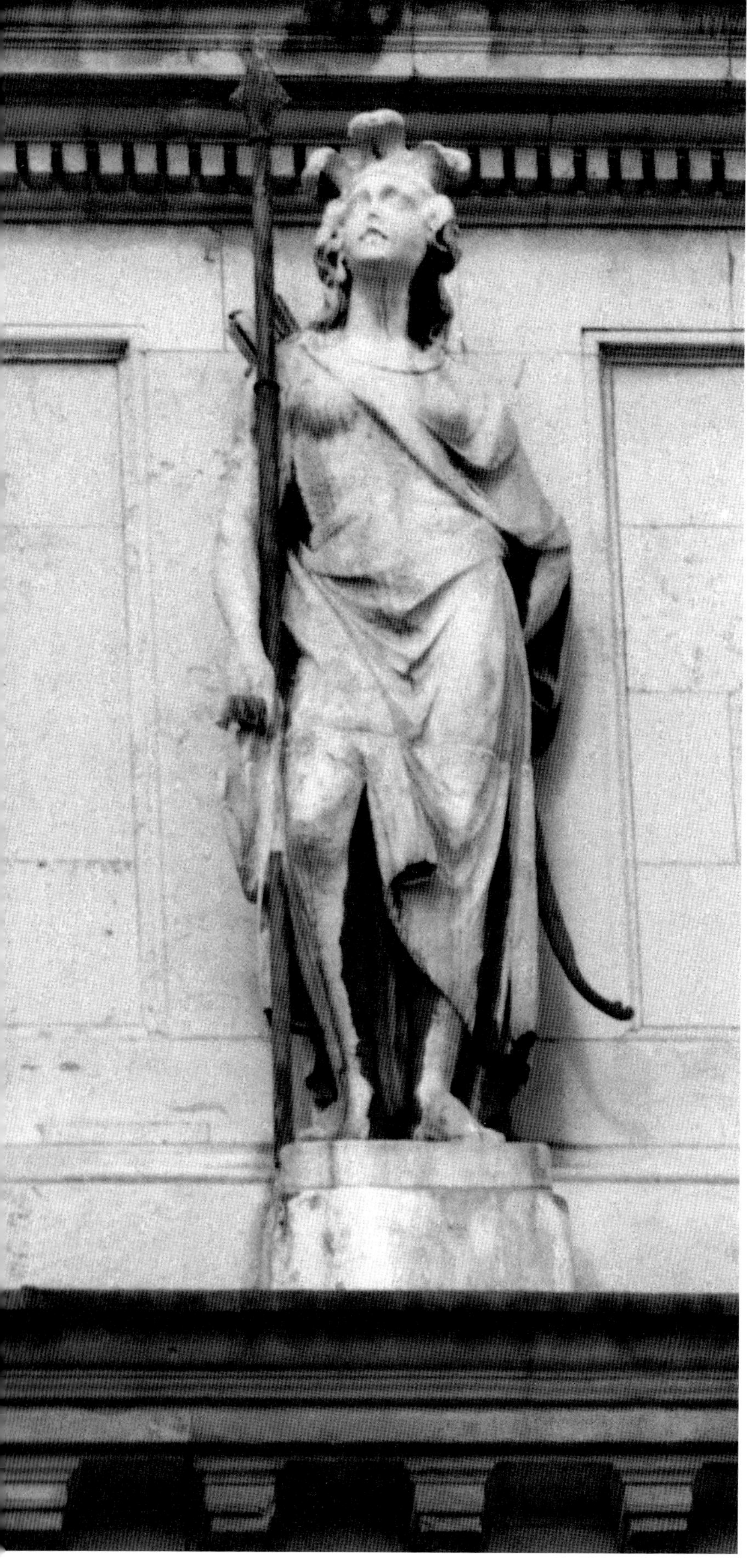

but to elevate that most abstract of human entities, the mind. The discerning eye and mind characterized a viewer who was disembodied, but did have a gender, as Sir Joshua demonstrated in addressing himself to 'Gentlemen'. While the Academy and its audience were comprised of women as well as men, within the discourse on the liberal arts propounded by Reynolds, women were deemed incapable of comprehending the highest forms of art, especially history painting, which was designed for public edification. Fully understanding such elevated art works demanded the ability to reason, to invent and to engage in abstract thought. These were characteristics that distinguished the leisured and learned gentlemen from all women, and from those men who did not have the financial means and social breeding to acquire a liberal education.[6]

Female bodies were not excluded from this masculinist discourse on fine art; they figured prominently as important subjects of painting and sculpture. In fact the ability to transform the base matter of a sensuous female body into a refined and purified image of ideal beauty was the mark of a highly accomplished liberal artist, just as the ability to judge and appreciate such an aesthetic transformation was the mark of the true connoisseur.[7] Within the physical spaces of the new Somerset House, such ideal figures of female beauty marked out both the interior and exterior of the building. Visitors to the Royal Academy who wished to conclude their outing with a promenade around the large and imposing courtyard had to pass though the main gateway, which was embellished (on the side facing the court) with female allegorical figures of the four continents executed by Joseph Wilton after designs by the building's architect, William Chambers. Appropriately for a building complex housing the Navy Office, which was so crucial to protecting and extending Britain's overseas trade, Asia, Europe and Africa are shown bearing tribute to Britain, emblematically referenced in the official arms displayed in a cartel directly above the statues. Completing the group is the figure of an Indian woman who personifies America (fig. 42); she carries no tribute, but is shown 'armed and breathing defiance', a topical reference to the escalating conflict between Britain and its American colonies.[8] The aestheticized female body of the savage, then, serves as the site where colonial conflict, localized and as yet unresolved, can be contained and naturalized within a sculptural scheme celebrating the triumph of British commerce.

Reynolds, too, depicted a female allegorical figure in his contribution to the decorative scheme of the new building: an oil painting of *Theory* (fig. 43) for the ceiling of the Royal Academy's library. The presence of the library within the Academy complex marked it as a liberal institution grounded in intellectual learning, to be distinguished from a guild or drawing school concerned mainly with the perfecting of mechanical

42 Joseph Wilton after a design by William Chambers, *The Four Continents: America*, 1780, Portland Stone. Courtyard façade of Strand block, Somerset House, London.

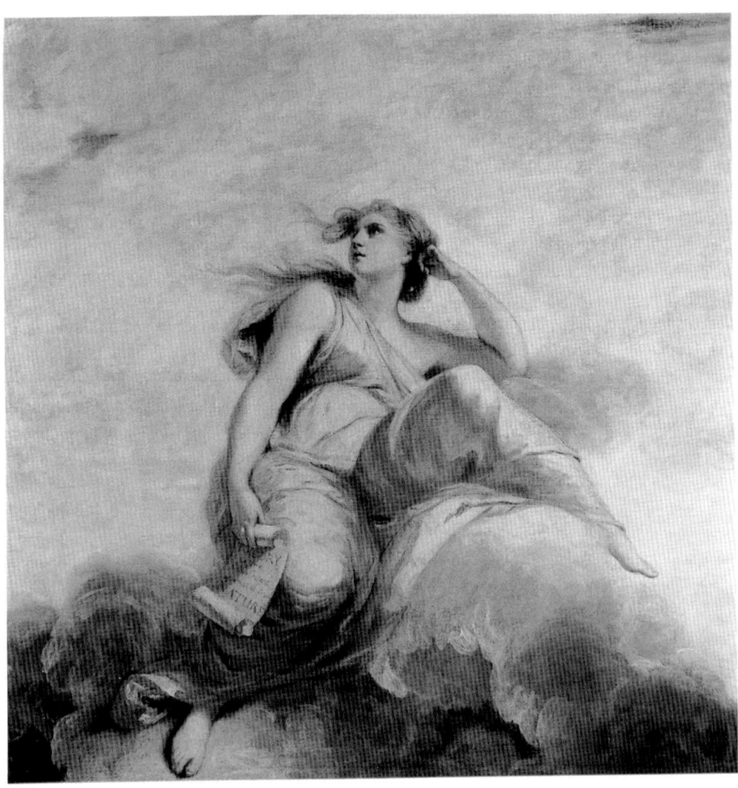

43 Sir Joshua Reynolds, *Theory*, 1780. Royal Academy of Arts, London.

skills. *Theory* embodies that distinction. Reynolds's depiction of a beautiful woman attired in light blue classical drapery, holding a scroll, followed the description of Theory found in Cesare Ripa's *Iconologia*.[9] However, in placing Theory's ample figure on a cloud, her hair gently tossed by the wind, Reynolds deviated from Ripa's description, which states that she is to be shown 'in the act of descending from the top of a stairway'.[10] Perhaps the President of the Royal Academy was concerned that Theory might stumble and fall were she to be shown descending from the sublime heights of the intellect, much as Rowlandson's beauties were to do some twenty years later. Theory's legs are modestly covered, but they are splayed as suggestively as those of Rowlandson's tumbling women. She appears in no danger of falling, however, securely ensconced on her less than ethereal cloud bank, eyes raised, her left arm supporting her head in an attitude of aesthetic contemplation. Robed in classical allegory, painted by the President of the Academy, and located within the officially consecrated spaces of Somerset House, Theory was insulated from discussion of her body as overtly sexualized. The discourse of high art provided an aesthetic alibi in which any erotic thoughts could be sublimated into a disinterested evaluation of form, composition and colour.[11]

While the library, presided over by *Theory*, served as a major repository of intellectual knowledge about the arts, it was transformed into a public arena every spring when the annual exhibition of modern art occupied not only the Great Room, but other spaces within the Academy complex in Somerset House. As visitors ascended the steep spiral staircase to the exhibition rooms, Theory descended into practice. In terms of art production, 'practice' involved those genres of painting that actually sustained artists financially: portraits (and landscapes) rather than history painting, which was the privileged object of academic theory. The conflict around history painting and portraiture will briefly concern us later. First, however, I would like to address how the divide between theory and practice affected spectatorship, especially the physical conditions under which works of art were viewed. Invariably the tensions and conflicts that the theory/practice dyad raised concerning viewing contexts turned on the unstable boundary that separated the art object from the commodity.

John Brewer has perceptively observed that one of the ways writings on taste and aesthetics attempted to insulate works of the imagination from the economic exigencies of the marketplace was to isolate the man of taste from a given social milieu, hence any particular physical space of viewing: '[The man of taste] is not part of a larger public or audience, except in the most abstract sense as a person who appreciates culture; he is certainly not placed in a public gallery, theatre or pleasure garden'.[12] The man of taste (and the gender specificity is important here) may form part of a privileged public for art that is conceptualized abstractly in terms of class, education, gender and so forth, but he does not seem to possess a body that enters into the physical spaces and social relationships involved in the actual viewing of works of art.

Visual and written commentaries on the annual exhibitions, however, could not so easily banish the physical presence of viewers within a particularized space. In fact, most were quick to acknowledge (with varying mixtures of delight and disapproval) the specific character of the site and the panoply of exchange – among the bodies, male and female, and the art objects displayed there – as Rowlandson's *Exhibition Stare Case* so wittily demonstrates. While Rowlandson's original drawing capitalized on the multiplicity of gazes among exhibition visitors, a later version which circulated as a print (*c*.1811; fig. 44) enhances the complexity and comedy of gendered visual exchange by animating the art object itself.[13] Here the urn that sits in a niche in the background of the earlier image is replaced with a statue of the Callipygian Venus. She stares aghast over her shoulder at the cascade of bodies on the stairway, while making a spectacle of herself by presenting her well-formed posterior to public view.

Twenty years before Rowlandson drew his first *Stare Case*, art critics had taken comic advantage of Somerset House's treacherous spiral stair in reviews that addressed the exhibition as a place where art and female bodies vied for the male gaze. For as Andrew Hemingway has noted, many of the press reviews were as much about the nature and motives of the visitors attending the annual exhibitions as the art on display.[14] In 1785, for example, the critic of the *Morning Post* observed: 'there are two descriptions of persons who visit the Royal Academy: – some perambulate the rooms to view the *heads* – others remain at the bottom of the stairs to contemplate the *legs*'.[15] Two years later the critic of the *World* exclaimed that it was the dual spectacle of pictures and real women (or parts thereof) on display that made the exhibition of the Royal Academy such a success:

> Exhibitions are now the rage – and though some may have more merit, yet certainly none has so much attraction as that at Somerset House; for, besides the exhibition of pictures living and inanimate, there is the *raree-show* [peep-show] of neat ancles up the stair-case – which is not less inviting.[16]

One way to understand Rowlandson's two *Stare Cases* and these playful observations is to place them in the broader context of writings and visual representations that attempt to legislate the viewing practices of exhibition-goers in a country where public art exhibitions had only recently been introduced. In the preceding chapter in this volume, C. S. Matheson reveals how official catalogues and engraved depictions of the Royal Academy exhibitions in the decades around 1800 sought to categorize and regulate the behaviour of visitors based on their competence in making aesthetic judgements. More specifically, her analysis of the prints after Ramberg, Rowlandson and others shows how these works confirmed and reinforced the gendered nature of the discourse on the liberal arts, by suggesting that women were incapable of assessing the true value of art without the guidance of a qualified male companion or text.

While there is ample evidence to suggest that Matheson is correct in her assessment of the regulatory disposition of such images, this interpretation does not exhaust the meanings that could be attached to the female exhibition-goer repeatedly invoked by contemporary discourses on the fine arts.[17] One thing is clear from this incessant repetition: for the exhibition to succeed, her presence was required. This fact is underscored in two letters published anonymously in the *Morning Post* in May 1780. The anonymous correspondent charges the Academy with being insensitive to female visitors, who, upon entering certain rooms in the Academy's new quarters, were suddenly and unexpectedly confronted with (reproductions of) classical sculptures of the male nude that, like Rowlandson's Callipygian Venus, all but threatened to come alive. The – undoubtedly male – writer ironically suggests that the Academy should warn its visitors about these works in an exhortation meant to call up the popular spectacles of the fairground: 'Apollos, Gladiators, Jupiters and Hercules all as *naked*, and as *natural* as if they were alive!!'[18] Not content to leave the threat (or appeal) posed by these unclad male figures to the reader's imagination, the writer explains that 'without the least force on reason it may fairly be deduced, that the woman who has not a *delicate fear* of those statues before her eyes, "is not afraid of what man can do unto her"'.[19] In other words, he charges the Academy with treating its respectable women visitors as though they were prostitutes – the only type of women who could be imagined not to fear the raw male sexuality manifested in these classical models.

Arguably, the critic's real anxiety, contrary to his stated concern, is that female visitors will *not* be as shocked and fearful as they should be when confronted with these statues. But I want to pursue a somewhat different line of enquiry, involving how the writer's ideas of public and private are defined through the differential access that men and women should have to various spaces within the Academy apartments. Some sense of this spatial distinction comes across in the following irate passage:

> Now in the plenitude of your discretion, my good cousins! How comes it to pass that these same statues with their *nudities* exposed, are without reserve laid open to the indiscriminate view of the female part of your visitors? Has decency totally left the direction of the institution; or has the unblushing countenance of a P[rostitute?] laughed you out of the sense of delicacy, that those figures which heretofore deterred ladies from ever entering the apartments of the Old Academy, are now drawn out in the full face of day, and obtruded on their view without the least reserve?[20]

The writer goes on to connect these sculptures, 'with their nudities exposed', to paintings that depict immoral themes such as the *Rape of Europa*, and then praises certain contemporary artists (including Reynolds and Thomas Gainsborough) because they 'are never found raking stews and brothels for subjects'.

In the context of this outburst the study rooms at the Academy housing antique casts are structurally aligned with the 'stews and brothels' that, the critic insinuates, furnished the erotic subject matter for European masterworks of the Renaissance and seventeenth century. I am not suggesting that the writer regarded the Academy's study rooms as dens of immorality, but rather that he saw them as private spaces, defined by their suitability for men only. In contradistinction to these restricted spaces is the space of the exhibition, which had to be accessible to both men and respectable women, whom the writer repeatedly invokes collectively as 'the public'.

What I wish to emphasize here is that no one definition of the 'public' could adequately describe the diverse and often conflicting interests that were invested in the Royal Academy. In this instance, the liberal notion of a disembodied 'public' of gentlemen scholars is not merely insufficient, but is almost the antithesis of the term as used by the writer to the *Morning Post*. He conceives of the Academy's 'public' as not simply constituted by both men and women who visit the exhibitions, but as determined in the final instance by respectable women.

British commentators on the fine arts deemed continental viewers, like respectable women, to be crucial constituents of a public capable of legitimizing Britain's claims to artistic ascendancy. The important role accorded to women in presenting the best, most decorous face possible to nations across the Channel, was underscored by a critic writing for the *Morning Herald* and

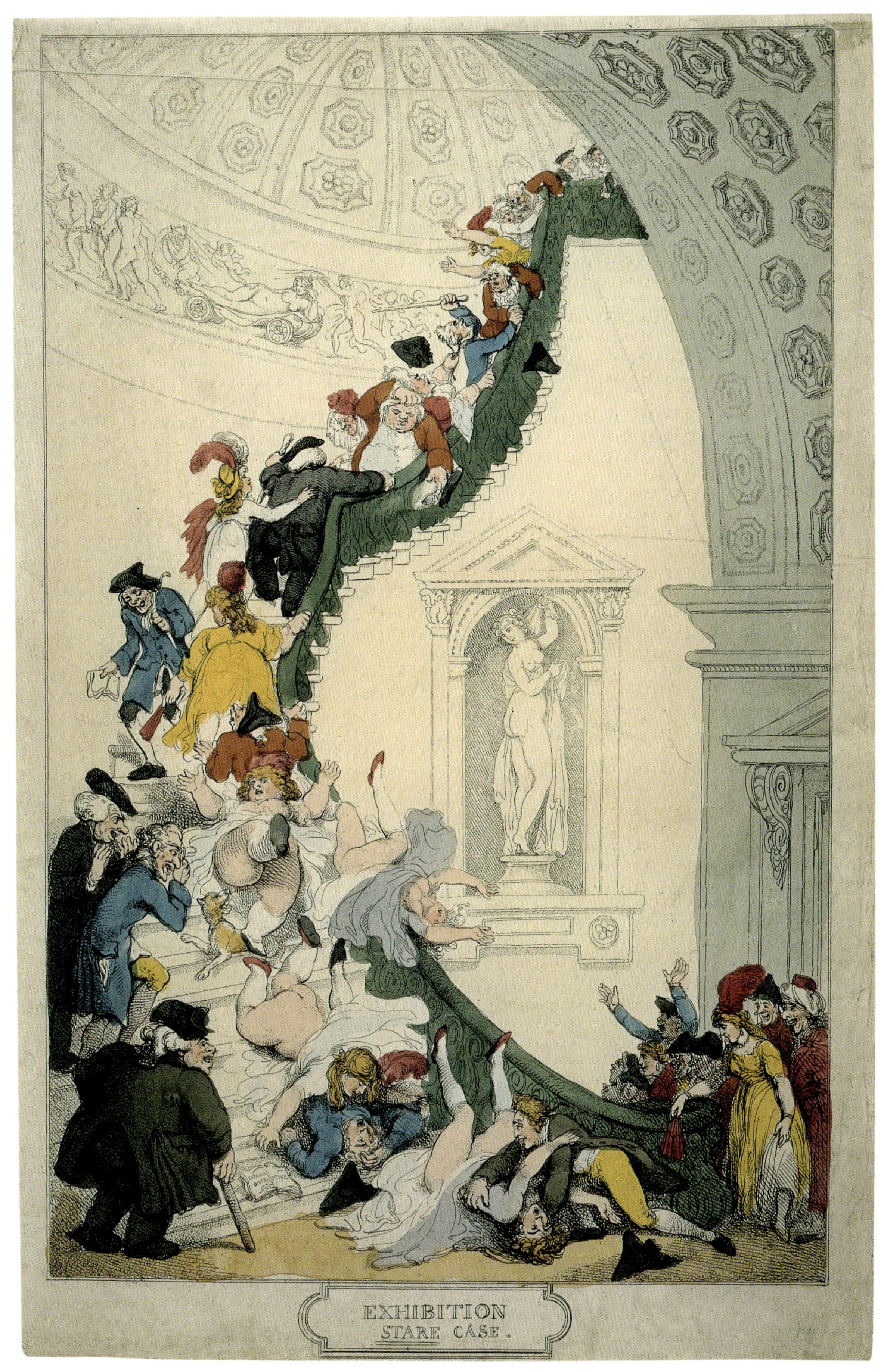

44 After Thomas Rowlandson, *The Exhibition Stare Case*, *c.*1811, hand-coloured etching. The etching, though not the colouring, may be by Rowlandson himself. By courtesy of the Trustees of the British Museum.

the *Daily Universal Register* in May 1786. 'The French who visit our exhibitions', he began, 'are shocked at the indelicacy of placing the portraits of notorious prostitutes, triumphing as it were in vice, close to the pictures of women of rank and virtue. In Paris, such portraits would on no account be admitted.'[21] The portraits in question were seen to share the same power of contamination with their living *alter egos*, by degrading (paintings of) respectable women, and by implication turning the exhibition from a public space into a brothel. Nowhere in the art criticism of the period was there a similar concern about the French (or any other foreigners) encountering paintings of dissolute English*men* on the walls of the annual exhibition.

This fixation with how Englishwomen were perceived by foreigners was perhaps most strikingly demonstrated prior to the Academy's arrival in Somerset House. In 1777 a critic began his series of articles on the exhibition not with an assessment of the art on display, but with a discussion of fashionable Englishwomen in the metropolis.[22] This reviewer, in the *St James's Chronicle*, adopts the persona of 'Gaudenzio', an Italian artist who is making his first visit to London; his observations take the form of letters sent from London to an English artist who has been studying for many years in Rome.[23] After disparaging the dress of Englishmen and their continental counterparts, and comparing their costume unfavourably to that worn by the Tahitian prince, Omai, who had recently taken London by storm, Gaudenzio turns to the 'Ladies', who

> appear to me to be the best Production of this Iland [*sic*], and the most beautiful . . . hearing that their Minds are as much superior to those of other Nations as their Features, I saw with Pleasure that their Dress is likewise elegant, which made me wish they would finish what is so well begun, and banish the Few Remains of French, Chinese, and Gothick Taste, still to be found endeavouring to shelter itself under the Protection of the other Parts of it.[24]

Lest modern readers think that this critic was only interested in celebrating the most ephemeral, feminine and commercial forms of culture, in the next letter he launches into a critique of the British nobility's failure to support a school of history painting.[25] Such critiques were consistent with Reynolds's advocacy of history painting in Britain and were to be repeated by artists and cultural commentators well into the nineteenth century. However, unlike Reynolds, who denigrated the realm of fashion, 'Gaudenzio' extolled both the fashionable English woman and history painting as 'productions' that enhanced Britain's cultural image both at home and abroad.[26]

The writers and critics cited above were not the only ones who identified women as a potent indicator of the state of a particular society. Throughout the eighteenth century a host of commentators, ranging from social philosophers to travel writers, asserted that there was an intimate connection between the condition of women in any given society and the degree of civilization it had attained.[27] In his *History of Women*, published in 1779, the Scottish physician William Alexander put the case quite clearly:

> the rank, . . . and condition, which we find women in any country, mark out to us with the greatest precision, the exact point in the scale of civil society, to which the people of such country have arrived; and were their history entirely silent on every other subject, and only mentioned the manner in which they treated their women, we would . . . be enabled to form a tolerable judgement of the barbarity, or culture of their manners.[28]

Such a gendered system of evaluation was based on a model of social evolution, now referred to as the 'four stages theory'. This model posits all human societies as emerging from a 'state of nature' to form a primitive collectivity based upon hunting and gathering; some of these societies then progressed to the pastoral stage, later evolving to the agrarian stage, and finally reached the most advanced and civilized form, the commercial stage. Gaudenzio's reference to the Tahitian Omai and to Chinese fashion in his assessment of Englishwomen underscores the point that this mode of evaluating societies served to promote Britain as a commercial power and cultural leader within a global system encompassing both ancient civilizations such as China and those complex societies emerging in the 'New World' as the result of British and European colonialism.

Writers employing the four stages theory evaluated women on the basis of two interrelated phenomena: how they were treated by men, and what type of work they performed. In primitive societies women were virtual slaves to their men, who forced them to perform arduous physical labour and to satisfy their base sexual urges. By the time the commercial stage was reached, women's function and relationship to men had been removed from the realm of fulfilling material (or purely sexual and reproductive) needs. Here this theory of civilization intersects with the associated discourse on 'civility', that is, politeness. Women are at the centre of this discursive network, or rather a particular type of woman – one who could provide those forms of sociability, especially conversation, that would soften the brutish manners of men. Only women who had considerable financial means and social standing could acquire those polite accomplishments (such as dancing, the art of conversation, and a smattering of French to embellish that conversation) necessary for the production of 'softened' and socialized males.[29]

More was at stake here than ensuring that modern Englishmen did not devolve into brutes; or at least such was the claim of the author of 'The Merits of the Fair Sex Considered', which appeared in the *Universal Magazine* in 1765. This writer was in no doubt whatsoever that 'it is the acquaintance of the ladies only, which can bestow that easiness of address, whereby the fine gentleman is distinguished from the scholar, and the man of business'.[30] It is precisely here that the function of women in the setting of the exhibition can productively be located. For in order for the Academy to maintain its institutional commitment to promoting national ideals and artistic professionalization, the annual exhibition had to be dissociated from a marketplace populated by men of business, whose judgements were based upon the exchange value of art as luxury commodity. But just as the exhibition was not to be a gathering place for men of business, neither was it to be given over solely to experts, such as the connoisseurs pictured in Brandoin's image of the exhibition of 1771 (see fig. 31). For art to signal Britain's coming of age as a nation with claims to cultural authority on a par with its military and commercial power, it had to be able to command the interest of a broader class of people than pedants indulging in debate over finer points of brushwork, composition and style. Specifically, it had to attract the same sort of refined public that marked the other, more established forms of courtly and cosmopolitan culture prevalent throughout Western Europe: the Salon in Paris, royal fêtes, aristocratic balls, opera and higher forms of theatre, etc. Modern scholars have paid scant attention to the Academy's need to display the right sort of people as well as art in order to gain the attention and the good opinion of both foreigners and Britons. That such a pressing need was foremost in the thoughts of the earliest reviewers of the Royal Academy exhibitions seems clear from their opening notices, which invariably remarked on the presence of the royal family, distinguished visitors and fashionable members of the *bon ton* before commenting on the art which was displayed there. Women were a crucial component of this process, for, as we have seen, they were the sign of and essential to the production of a polite, commercial society. Hence, the positioning of refined and sociable British woman within the space of the exhibition at Somerset House was just as important to the cultural production of Britain as the world's most civilized commercial power as the placement of her 'rude' American and African counterparts over the entry gate to the courtyard.

As a space of display, governed as much (or more) by fashionable people as fine art, the exhibition was open to the kind of criticism and praise garnered by other spaces of leisure within the metropolis, as well as to commentaries specific to a display of fine art.[31] Much critical hand-wringing centred on the predominance of portraits over history painting in the annual shows. For when theory descended into practice, the art changed as well as its public: the liberal ideals of history painting gave way to the financial realities of making art that would sell, namely portraiture above all. This line of argument was not limited to one political or social faction. Even commentators who regarded the Academy as a positive force for improving British commerce by raising the aesthetic quality of its manufactured goods, bemoaned the overabundance of portraits in the exhibitions as a sign of the 'mercantile character of our school'.[32]

The critique of portraiture focused on the vanity of sitters who preferred to surround themselves with their own likenesses rather than patronize art that embodied the public values of the nation. Women figured strongly in this critical discourse, for, if women were an index of civilization, they were also firmly associated with a commercial world of fashion that feeds on the pursuit of vain and selfish pleasures. Furthermore, within artistic discourse paintings were often associated with women, or described as though they possessed feminine attributes (wanton, chaste or seductive, for example).[33] We have seen that critics were particularly inclined to associate portraiture with the female body or body parts. Recall the *Morning Post*'s observation in 1785 that some of the visitors to the exhibition 'perambulate the rooms to view the *heads* – others remain at the bottom of the stairs to contemplate the *legs*'.

The following year, as if to alleviate the plight of the male spectator who might be tempted to run to and fro between the Great Room and the bottom of the staircase, a young woman planted herself daily under her portrait. At least so claimed the critic for the *Morning Herald*:

> If a certain *smiling belle* is determined to exhibit the *original* as well as the *semblance* to the visitors at the Royal Academy, by placing herself every day directly under her own portrait; we would advise her to desire her *cicishero* [i.e., *cicisbeo*, the term of abuse for an effeminate male guide] to whisper his *soft nonsense* in lower tones, and not to continue to expose himself to the ridicule of the company.[34]

One way of understanding this passage is to stress its regulatory aspect: women are vain, emotional creatures, and are therefore vulnerable to seduction by the wrong kind of art (portraits) and the wrong kind of men. Both art and women (and by extension, the whole of society) are degraded as a result. But this somehow misses the point, for the tone of the passage is lightly mocking, not savagely critical. The critic does not seem worried that women, the nation or the Academy will suffer great harm from the actions of this amorous couple.

Compare the tone of this passage with another, from Hannah More's *Strictures on the Modern System of Female Education* (1799), which exploits the common association of paintings with women in order to expose the threat to male authority and domestic tranquillity posed by women, like the *Herald*'s 'smiling belle', who exhibit themselves in public:

> . . . if a man select a picture for himself from among all its exhibited competitors, and bring it to his own house, the picture being passive, he is able to *fix* it there; while the wife, picked up at a public place, and accustomed to incessant display, will not, it is probable, when brought home, stick so quietly to the spot where he fixes her, but will escape to the exhibition-room again, and continue to be displayed at every subsequent exhibition, just as if she were not become private property, and had never been definitely disposed of.[35]

It would certainly be correct to argue that this passage from More's tract on female education and the newspaper account of the young woman posing below her portrait both participate in the forging of a feminine ideal that sought to fix women of the polite classes within certain (domestic) spaces. But ideologies and social meanings are produced by the forms that representations take, not just their 'content'. More's passage is admonitory and proscriptive; injecting humour into this passage that likens women to pictures would be out of place within the genre of the reformist tract. Art criticism, on the other hand, not only has a different primary function, but derives from quite a different literary tradition. As Iain Pears has observed, English art criticism was not adapted from philosophic and aesthetic discourse, but embraced lower literary forms such as satire and burlesque.[36] Samuel Johnson's roughly contemporaneous definitions of these terms associate satire with the censuring of wickedness or folly, and burlesque with a 'tendency to raise laughter by unnatural or unsuitable language'.[37] The latter definition seems an especially apt way to characterize much of the critical writing examined here, as well as Rowlandson's comic images, since they seem designed primarily to provoke laughter, or to effect censure through laughter.

One sure way to raise a laugh in the context of an official display of 'fine' art is to treat the exhibition as a form of 'low' entertainment, as did the writer disgusted at the Academy's display of fig-leafless sculptures, although another critic cited earlier promised visitors both types of spectacle: 'an exhibition of pictures living and inanimate . . . [and] the *raree-show* of neat ancles up the stair-case'.[38] Just as fine art is exemplified by the pure, rational, classical body, low entertainments are associated with its inverse: the grotesque body, characterized by protuberances, distension, disproportion, and the physical needs and pleasures associated with the lower bodily functions.[39] In his *Stare Case* Rowlandson effects just such a substitution of the grotesque for the classical body through the use of caricature, a visual form relying on exaggeration and inversion. In place of the 'beautiful people', with their sleek, decorous, fashionably adorned bodies, who supposedly constituted the exhibition-going public, the artist delivers a chaotic mass of exposed body parts: thrashing arms, swollen legs and buttocks, and faces deformed by fright and lust.

Although some of Rowlandson's fashionable visitors were brought low by their tumble on the Academy's stairs, it is not necessarily the case that the verbal and visual burlesques levelled at the exhibition between May and July served to discredit the event or the institution that sponsored it. Caricature developed as an aristocratic form, and functioned to bond together individuals within a social group: it worked as a type of in-joke, rather than censure.[40] Those viewers who actually had occasion to clamber up the Academy's steep staircase could appreciate the humour of his *Stare Case* even more fully than those who had not. Beyond serving as an in-joke, however, these visual and verbal burlesques served the important function of publicity. For an event like the exhibition to be judged a success – to be regarded as worthy of notice by foreign and domestic visitors alike – it had to maintain a high degree of visibility. Satire and burlesques, in the form of newspaper criticism and prints, were crucial vehicles for this operation. What they offered their viewers was not a testimonial for history painting over portraiture (other visual and written texts served that function). Nor did they function principally to warn their viewers about the instability of the line separating polite from impolite entertainment (exhibition as brothel) or the respectable from the disreputable woman (female exhibition-goer as *demi-mondaine*). Rather, these images and descriptions of the exhibition public, like other satires and burlesques of fashionable urban life, exploited this instability as a source of anxious pleasure and comic delight. I am not suggesting that this comic rendering of women in the exhibition was essentially radical or liberatory: the humour and success of these texts depended upon a racialized and class-based notion of civility and civilization, as well as the same oppressive ideal of femininity that was propounded by Hannah More. But they did somewhat gleefully suggest that this feminine ideal was just that – a 'theory' that refused to become the secure basis of female practice.

Further visual evidence of that 'failure' comes from a rather unexpected source: a portrait (frontispiece) in pastels of one of the Royal Academy porters, produced by John Russell and displayed in the exhibition of 1792.[41] Although the exhibition provides the context for the portrait, its central figure projects a touching intimacy that seems to have little in common with the laughter solicited by the burlesques of Rowlandson and contemporary art critics. However, keeping the burlesque at bay was not so simple when the subject involved an exhibition in progress. The porter gazes pleasantly out at the viewer, greeting him/her as a visitor about to ascend the staircase to the main exhibition rooms at Somerset House. Standing at the foot of the stair, he proffers an entry ticket in his right hand, while his left clutches a copy of the exhibition catalogue. If these texts promise the viewer access to a space where the modern art of Britain is displayed and celebrated, the picture visualizes that experience in terms of the two very different bodies that engender very different Academy 'publics'. Jostling for space behind the porter is a cast of a famous classical fragment, the Belvedere Torso, which served as an important model for the most serious and ambitious forms of history painting and sculpture. While the Torso was a sign of the Academy's commitment to the liberal arts and a public of rational, disinterested gentlemen, its cultural authority is decidedly undermined by the manner in which it is represented. Through the frontal positioning of the Torso (which renders invisible its most famous feature, the strong, well-muscled back), the introduction of cavernous shadows around the neckline and chest, and the highlighting of the ragged surface of the stumps of the left arm and right leg, Russell has emphasized its fragmentary, even mutilated character. This sense of violation is enhanced by the metal rod (holding one of the lamps set on the banisters of the hall landing) which is located behind the Torso but which appears to emerge, like a skewer, from within its neck. Headless, legless and armless, the sculpture seems to be as much about the violent loss of a masculine artistic ideal as its continuing presence. Precariously squeezed in between the edge of the picture and the porter's right arm, the Torso competes for space and attention with other body parts, those belonging to the visitors going up the staircase in the background. The presence of male visitors is indicated by two figures wearing black hats, symmetrically placed to the porter's right and left, but the bulk of the bodies are female, although 'bodies' is not really the term that best describes the indistinct mass of heads appearing just behind the sculpture. They are so tightly compressed that it is hard to imagine their possessing bodies at all. One of the female heads unaccountably turns at an impossible angle to glance back towards the viewer. Her look is too vaguely defined to read, but its very blankness unsettles the general aura of welcome generated by the porter's deferential gaze. To his left (our right) the mass of women, sketchily indicated by (headless?) figures in light-coloured gowns, continue a somewhat ghostly progress to the top of the stairway.

It probably would be a mistake to make too much of this uncanny image. Its surreal aspects – the bodiless female heads weirdly juxtaposed with a headless male torso served up *en brochette* – are probably the result of poor design rather than an attempt to turn the exhibition into a house of horrors. But perhaps Russell was on to something when he insisted on visualizing in this pastel not one but two publics. One was defined by a (crumbling) masculine ideal of civic virtue and liberality, and the other marked by an (always precarious) ideal of feminine politeness and respectability, but both were essential for the Academy and its exhibition to stage their authority and visibility before the nation and the world beyond. That this artist did not manage to synthesize these two ideal publics into a harmonious unity is perhaps not surprising, given the very different constituencies they represented and the very different symbolic systems that they relied upon. The definition of and relationship between the 'public's two bodies' would continue to be a subject of much heated debate as the Academy continued to instruct, to display and to promote the fine arts throughout the decades that it occupied Somerset House (and beyond). The terms of that conflict would change over time, but its intensity would remain a crucial element in the Academy's ability to sustain the excitement and interest of its publics.

MORNING POST, and

MONDAY, MAY 2, 1791.

, (TUESDAY)

CE.

NT,
VAL:

LIE.
f the favourite
alled
E.
ons,

n Boxes Five

x o'clock, and

x et Regina.

May 2, 1791.
spectfully ac-
) there will be
E
h Instant.

LANE.

ENTED,
ADE.

RDAN.

CK.
GARDEN.

ENTED

ROYAL ACADEMY, SOMERSET-PLACE.

THE PRESIDENT and COUNCIL give Notice,
That the EXHIBITION will Open THIS DAY, at Twelve o'Clock,
And continue Every Day, (Sundays excepted)
from Eight in the Morning till Seven in the Evening.

JOHN RICHARDS, R. A. Sec.

Admittance ONE SHILLING.
Catalogues gratis.

PROFESSIONAL CONCERT,
HANOVER-SQUARE.

THE COMMITTEE most respectfully acquaint the SUBSCRIBERS and the PUBLIC in general, that the TWELFTH PERFORMANCE will be THIS EVENING, the 2d of May.

PART I.

Overture, Haydn.—Song, Signor Lazzarini.—Sonata Piano Forte, Miss Parks.—Song, Mrs. Billington.—Overture, Double Orchestra, M. S. Bach.

PART II.

New Overture, M. S. Clementi.—Song, Signor Pacchierotti.—Concertante, Violin, Tenor, Hautboy, and Violoncello, by Messrs. Cramer, Blake, Parks, and Smith. (Rawlins, Jun.).—By particular Desire, the New Terzetto, by Signor Lazzarini, Signor Pacchierotti, and Mrs. Billington. (Haydn).—Symphony, Rosetti.

Doors to be opened, at Seven, and to begin at Eight o'clock.

Tickets transferrable as usual, Ladies' to Ladies, and Gentlemens' to Gentlemen only.

The Ladies' Tickets are blue, the Gentlemens' Brown.

No Tickets, but those of the Night, will be admitted.

The Subscribers are intreated to give particular Orders to their Coachmen to set down, and take up, at the Side Door in the street, with their horses' heads towards the Square.

The Door in the Square for Chairs only.

KING's THEATRE—HAYMARKET.
Mr. VESTRIS, Jun's. NIGHT.

ON THURSDAY next, May 5, will be gi-

RANEL
IS OPEN FOR T
On MONDAYS, WEDNES
BY DE
A MASQUERA
EVENING, M

Tickets at One Guinea each;
House, Messrs. Longman and
and at Mr. Rickman's Masque
street.

Doors to be opened at Ten o'
Dresses to be had that Eve
Ranelagh-House.

The Managers respectfully in
Rotunda, by a new Invention,
any Place of Public Entertainm

By COMMAND,
PATRONAGE of TH
And under the D
The Earl of UXBRIDGE, H
(Of the ROYAL SOCIET
HONORARY VICE
The Duke of LEE
The Earl of EXET
The Earl of SAND
Lord Viscount FIT
Lord GREY DE W
JOAH BATES, E

WILL be performed i
ABBEY, on MONDA

PART

The Coronation Anthem, "
Overture, (Esther). * Song, "
numberless," (Saul.) Chorus,
and skies," (Deborah.) * Son
despair," (Saul.) Duetto and
head shall raise," (Judas Macc.
Lord," (Anthems:) Chorus,
(Saul.)

PART
First Grand C
FIRST PART OF IS

5

'The Business of Criticism': The Press and the Royal Academy Exhibition in Eighteenth-Century London

MARK HALLETT

On Tuesday, 27 April 1784, the *Public Advertiser* joined a host of other London newspapers in announcing that 'the EXHIBITION' – by which it meant the Royal Academy exhibition – 'the most safe and gratifying of the Amusements of the Metropolis', had opened the previous day.[1] As the *Advertiser's* welcoming comments themselves suggest, the experience of visiting the Academy's yearly display was continually informed by a wide range of printed texts that circulated inside and outside Somerset House. Within the building, most obviously, the official catalogue provided an essential and surprisingly substantial intermediary between spectator and spectacle, as C. S. Matheson's chapter in this volume confirms. In 1784, for instance, this booklet ran to thirty pages, included the names and addresses of all the participating artists, and listed the 539 exhibited works in the order of their appearance along a route that began above the doorway into the Great Room, and ended in the 'Exhibition Room of Sculpture and Drawings' two floors beneath. Meanwhile, other texts geared for consumption beyond the Academy's walls provided a more varied and critical commentary. These writings were most commonly found in London's many newspapers, which carried a veritable flood of responses to the Academy's annual offerings, ranging from prolonged discussions of individual paintings and painters to paragraphs of rapid-fire gossip and fragments of satire directed at the shows and their clientele. During the last decades of the century additional coverage often came in the form of ephemeral pamphlets – some rhapsodic, others quite scabrous in tone – and from Britain's first dedicated art magazine, which incorporated Royal Academy critiques alongside a host of essays on related topics. An analysis of these three modes of cultural journalism suggests that the late eighteenth-century exhibition review was a discursive form torn between two seemingly contradictory imperatives. On the one hand, such writings promoted and indeed embodied an inclusive, consensual and decorous engagement with the Academy display on the part of a new 'polite' public for art; on the other, they dramatized the repressed tensions and conflicts that seethed under the show's smooth surfaces, reconfiguring the exhibition at Somerset House as a potent symbol of a wider pattern of political corruption, institutional autocracy and cultural decline.[2]

* * *

In the late eighteenth century, the London presses poured forth a multitude of daily, bi-weekly and tri-weekly newspapers (19 in 1783, 23 in 1790). Costing around fourpence per issue, and normally in a four-page broadsheet format, these papers served primarily as vehicles for advertising: as one press historian has observed, 'the dissemination of news was not [their] primary purpose; less than half the sixteen short columns of a newspaper were usually devoted to news items. Advertisements were of much greater importance, and from them newspapers derived the greater part of their revenue'.[3] The front page of the *Morning Post, and Daily Advertiser* of 2 May 1791 (fig. 45) reveals the mass of commercial promotions typically encountered by readers when they turned to their daily paper's front page, in this case ranging from an advertisement for an evening performance of *La Bella Pescatrice* at the King's Theatre to an announcement of

Morning Post, and Daily Advertiser. Detail of fig. 45.

THE MORNING POST, and Daily Advertiser.

No. 5621.] MONDAY, MAY 2, 1791. [Price 4d.

KING's THEATRE, PANTHEON.

TO-MORROW EVENING, (Tuesday) May 3, will be presented, LA BELLA PESCATRICE.

End of the First Act, A NEW DIVERTISSEMENT, Composed by Monf. D'Auberval, called LA TRIUMPHE DE LA FOLLIE.

End of the Opera, the 2d representation of the favourite Pantomime and Comic Ballet, called LA FILLE MAL GARDEE. With new Scenes and Decorations, By Monf. [illegible].

Pit Half-a-Guinea—Gallery and Green Boxes Five Shillings.

No money to be returned.

The doors to be opened at Half past Six o'clock, and to begin at Half past Seven precisely.

Vivant Rex et Regina.

KING's THEATRE.

PANTHEON, May 2, 1791.

THE Nobility and Gentry are respectfully acquainted, that, (by particular desire) there will be A GRAND MASQUERADE at this Place, on THURSDAY the 19th Instant.

THEATRE ROYAL, DRURY-LANE.

THIS EVENING WILL BE PRESENTED, THE SIEGE OF BELGRADE.

To which will be added, THE SPOIL'D CHILD.

Little Pickle (with Songs), Mrs. JORDAN.

For the BENEFIT of Mr. QUICK.

THEATRE ROYAL—COVENT-GARDEN.

THIS EVENING WILL BE PRESENTED, A Comedy, called, THE BROTHERS.

Written by R. CUMBERLAND, Esq.

Captain Ironsides, (1st time) Mr. WILSON; Young Belfield, Mr. FARREN; Elder Belfield, Mr. DAVIES; Old Goodwin, Mr. HULL; Paterson, Mr. MACREADY; And Sir Benjamin Dove, Mr. QUICK. Lady Dove, Mrs. WEBB; Violetta, Mrs. WELLS; And Sophia, Mrs. POPE.

End of Act II. by particular desire, A SONG by Mr. INCLEDON.

End of the Play, a DANCE of JOCKIES.

After which will be revived a Grand Burlesque Tragedy, in Two Acts, called, ALEXANDER THE LITTLE; Or, THE RIVAL QUEANS.

Written by Colley Cibber, with capital Additions by Fielding, Dean Swift, G. A. Stevens, &c. &c. &c.

Alexander, Mr. QUICK; Clytus, Mr. WILSON; Cassander, Mr. MUNDEN. The Princess Statira, Mrs. WEBB; And Roxana, Mrs. MARTYR.

The Tragedy will be interspersed with Airs, Duets, Glees, &c. composed by Arne, Arnold, Fischer, Dibdin, &c. with A GRAND OVERTURE, and A FINALE, in a style entirely new, composed by Mr. Shield. And the Triumphal Entry of ALEXANDER.

Tickets may be had of Mr. Quick, Broad-court, Bow-street; and of Mr. Brandon, at the Theatre, where Places may be taken.

SONS of the CLERGY.

THE REHEARSAL of the MUSIC, to be performed at the Anniversary Meeting of this CHARITY, will be in the Cathedral Church of St. Paul, on Tuesday the 10th, and the Feast on Thursday the 12th of May.

STEWARDS.

The Right Rev. the Lord Bishop of Gloucester,
Rt. Hon. Henry Addington, Speaker of the House of Commons.
Right Hon. the Lord Mayor.
Rev. John Lynch, D. D. Archdeacon of Canterbury,
Rev. Richard Farmer, D. D. F. R. S. and S. A.
George Byng, Esq. M. P.
Rev. Septimus Collinson, M. A. Fellow of Queen's College,
Charles Abbot, Esq.
William Garrow, Esq.
John Keysall, Esq.
William Dent, Esq.
Thomas Cadell, Esq.

The Music will consist of the Overture of Esther, Mr. Handel's Dettingen Te Deum, and Jubilate, with the Chorus from the Messiah, "Hallelujah, for the Lord God Omnipotent reigneth," an Anthem composed on purpose for this Charity by Dr. Boyce, and Mr. Handel's Grand Coronation Anthem. The Music to be conducted by Dr. Hayes.

Tickets will be timely distributed for the Rehearsal and Feast Days; and it is to be hoped, that no Person will be desirous of being admitted without first contributing to this Charity. The greatest care will be taken, that those who contribute liberally shall be seated commodiously; a circumstance that cannot fail to be agreeable. By this means the Stewards hope they shall considerably augment the Collection; the whole of which (as well at the Church as the Hall) is appropriated for apprenticing the Sons and Daughters of necessitous Clergymen, and all the Expences of the Rehearsal and Feast Days are paid by the Stewards.

The Doors of the Cathedral will not be opened before Ten o'clock. The Choir and Aisles will be carefully matted.

Benefactions to this Charity will be thankfully received by John Bacon, Esq. at the First-Fruits-Office, in the Temple, Secretary to the Stewards.

LAST WEEK of the EXHIBITION.

EUROPEAN MUSEUM, KING-STREET, ST. JAMES'S SQUARE.

THE MANAGERS appointed to conduct the Sale by Private Contract of PICTURES, DRAWINGS, and VALUABLES of every Description, as above, give Notice that the present Exhibition will finally close on Saturday next, the 7th Instant; and the Purchasers are desired to take Notice that the Pictures and painted Glass will be delivered on the Monday and Tuesday following; and the Subscribers and others, who intend to exhibit and sell by Private Contract Pictures, Drawings, Curiosities and Valuables in the next Exhibition, which will commence about the 16th Instant, are requested to send an Account of the same, in Writing, to Mr. Wilson, the acting Manager of the European Museum, on or before Saturday next, as, after that Day, no Subscription for the Second Exhibition can be received.—The Sale by Private Contract will continue, and the present magnificent Assemblage of Pictures, painted Glass, &c. may be publicly viewed until Saturday the 7th Inst. when the European Museum must be cleared to make Room for a new Arrangement.

Admission One Shilling, descriptive Catalogues included.

Subscriptions for the ensuing Exhibition will be received all this Week, at Baron Dimsdale, Sons, and Barnard's; Sir Robert Herries and Co.; Sir Herbert Mackworth and Co.; and by Mr. Wilson, at the European Museum, where Proposals may be had gratis.

ROYAL ACADEMY, SOMERSET-PLACE.

THE PRESIDENT and COUNCIL give Notice,

That the EXHIBITION will Open THIS DAY, at Twelve o'Clock,

And continue Every Day, (Sundays excepted) from Eight in the Morning till Seven in the Evening.

JOHN RICHARDS, R. A. Sec.

Admittance One Shilling.

Catalogues gratis.

PROFESSIONAL CONCERT, Hanover-Square.

THE COMMITTEE most respectfully acquaint the SUBSCRIBERS and the PUBLIC in general, that the TWELFTH PERFORMANCE will be THIS EVENING, the 2d of May.

PART I.

Overture, Haydn.—Song, Signor Lazzarini.—Sonata Piano Forte, Miss Parks.—Song, Mrs. Billington.—Overture, Double Orchestra, M. S. Bach.

PART II.

New Overture, M. S. Clementi.—Song, Signor Pacchierotti.—Concertante, Violin, Tenor, Hautboy, and Violoncello, by Messrs. Cramer, Blake, Parks, and Smith. (Rawlins, Jun.)—By particular Desire, the New Terzetto, by Signor Lazzarini, Signor Pacchierotti, and Mrs. Billington. (Haydn).—Symphony, Rosetti.

Doors to be opened, at Seven, and to begin at Eight o'clock.

Tickets transferable as usual, Ladies' to Ladies, and Gentlemens' to Gentlemen only.

The Ladies' Tickets are blue, the Gentlemens' Brown. No Tickets, but those of the Night, will be admitted.

The Subscribers are intreated to give particular Orders to their Coachmen to set down, and take up, at the Side Door in the street, with their horses' heads towards the Square.

The Door in the Square for Chairs only.

KING's THEATRE—HAYMARKET.

Mr. VESTRIS, Jun's. NIGHT.

ON THURSDAY next, May 5, will be given, a new Collection of SERIOUS and COMIC MUSIC.

The Vocal Parts by Signor Albertarelli, Signora Cappelletti, Signora Sestini, Signor Tajana, And Signor David.

At the end of the First Part, LA MORT D'HERCULE, and his APOTHEOSIS. The Part of Hercule by Mr. VESTRIS, Sen.

At the end of the Second Part will be exhibited, a new Historical Dance, called, L'AMADRIADE; OU LA NIMPHE DES BOIS. BALLET PANTOMIME.

Pherusse Amadriade, Madle. Hilligsberg, Hilas Berger Thesalien, Amant d'Amadriade, Mr. Vestris.

In which Mr. Vestris, Sen. (for that Night only) will dance LA MINUET DE LA COUR.

Tickets and Boxes to be had of Mr. Vestris, No. 9, Haymarket; or at Mr. Jewell's Office, No. 79, Haymarket.

Those Ladies and Gentlemen who wish to retain their Boxes, are requested to send their commands before to-morrow evening, as after that time those Boxes not retained will, on account of the numerous applications, be disposed of.

Mr. GIORNOVICHI's CONCERT.

HANOVER SQUARE ROOMS

ON WEDNESDAY next, the 4th Instant.

FIRST PART.

Overture, HAYDN; Concerto, French Horn, Mr. PIELTAIN; Song, Signor PACCHIEROTTI; Concerto Violin, Mr. GIORNOVICHI.

SECOND PART.

Overture, GIROVETZ; Concerto Piano Forte, Mr. DUSSEC; Song, Mrs. BILLINGTON; Concerto Violin, Mr. GIORNOVICHI; Duetto, Sig. PACCHIEROTTI, and Mrs. BILLINGTON.

SIMPHONIE.

Doors to be opened at Seven, and to begin at Eight o'Clock.

Tickets 10s. 6d. each, to be had of Mr. Giornovichi, No. 20, Pall-Mall, and of Messrs. Longman and Broderip, Cheapside and Haymarket.

Mr. CRAMER's BENEFIT.

At Willis's Rooms, King's-street, St. James's.

ON FRIDAY next, the 6th of May, will be A CONCERT.

Part I.

Overture, Haydn.—Glee.—Song, Signor Lazzarini.—Concerto Violin, Master Charles Cramer (aged Six Years and a Half).—Song, Mrs. Billington.—Concerto Violin, Mr Cramer.

Part II.

Concertante, for Violin, Tenor, Hautboy, and Violoncello, by Messrs. Cramer, Blake, Park, Smith, and (Rawlins, Jun.)—Song, Signor Pacchierotti.—Sonata Piano Forte, Mr. Cramer, Jun.—Song, Mrs. Billington.—New Overture, M. S. Clementi.

Doors to open at Seven and to begin at Eight o'clock.

Tickets Ten Shillings and Sixpence, to be had of Mr. Cramer, No. 7, Newman-street; and at Messrs. Longman and Broderip's, Haymarket, and Cheapside; and at Mr. Dale's Music Shop, Hollis-street, Cavendish-square.

N. B. The Tickets delivered for the 29th of April will be admitted.

FANTOCCINI—SAVILLE-ROW.

THIS PRESENT MONDAY, May 2, will be presented, the musical piece of L'AMORE DISCORDE.

After which the Comedy of LES PETITES AFFICHES.

And the Comedy of L'ERREUR DU MOMENT; OU, LA SUITE DES TROIS RECETTES.

In which the Flight of Harlequin, and the Eating and Drinking Scene, will be introduced.

End of the First Piece, A FAVOURITE HORNPIPE.

End of the Second Piece, the Pantomimic Scene of THE TURK.

The Whole to conclude with a Solo on the Mandolin, accompanied with the Violin, and the favorite PAS DE DEUX.

Admission Five Shillings.

Doors to be opened at Half past Seven, and to begin at Eight o'clock.

Places for the Boxes to be taken of Mr. White, at the Theatre.

The Nobility and Gentry are intreated to order their Coachmen to set down and take up with their Horses' heads towards Boyle-street.

THEATRE ROYAL, HAYMARKET.

EIDOURANION; or, LARGE TRANSPARENT ORRERY.

On this elaborate and splendid Machine, which is 20 Feet Diameter, Mr. WALKER, Jun. Will Deliver his ASTRONOMICAL LECTURE, On Wednesday Evening, the 4th of May next, at Seven o'Clock.

Tickets and Books of the Lecture to be had at the Theatre Box Office; and of Mr. Rice, in the Week of Exhibition.

RANELAGH

Is Open for the Season

On MONDAYS, WEDNESDAYS, and FRIDAYS.

By Desire;

A MASQUERADE will be THIS EVENING, May 2, 1791.

Tickets at One Guinea each, to be had at Ranelagh-House, Messrs. Longman and Broderip's Music Shops, and at Mr. Rickman's Masquerade Warehouse, Oxford-street.

Doors to be opened at Ten o'Clock.

Dresses to be had that Evening of Mr. Rickman, at Ranelagh-House.

Vivant Rex et Regina!

The Managers respectfully inform the Public, that the Rotunda, by a new Invention, is rendered as warm as any Place of Public Entertainment.

By COMMAND, and under the PATRONAGE of THEIR MAJESTIES

And under the Direction of

The Earl of UXBRIDGE, Honorary President.

(Of the Royal Society of Musicians),

Honorary Vice Presidents,

The Duke of LEEDS,
The Earl of EXETER
The Earl of SANDWICH,
Lord Viscount FITZWILLIAM,
Lord GREY DE WILTON,
JOAH BATES, Esq.

WILL be performed in WESTMINSTER-ABBEY, on MONDAY the 23d, of May, 1791.

PART I.

The Coronation Anthem, "Zadock the Priest."—Overture, (Esther). * Song, "O Lord whose mercies numberless," (Saul.) Chorus, "Immortal Lord of earth and skies," (Deborah.) * Song, "Fell rage and black despair," (Saul.) Duetto and Chorus, "Sion now her head shall raise," (Judas Macc.) Song, "O magnify the Lord," (Anthems.) Chorus, "Gird on thy sword," (Saul.)

PART II.

First Grand Concerto.

FIRST PART OF ISRAEL IN EGYPT.

PART III.

SECOND PART OF ISRAEL IN EGYPT.

On THURSDAY the 26th of May,

A GRAND SELECTION.

PART I.

Overture and Dead March in Saul.—The Funeral Anthem, part of it never performed in the Abbey. "Glory be to the Father," (Jubilate.)

PART II.

Fifth Grand Concerto. Song, "Every day will I give thanks," (Anthems.) * Chorus, "Your harps and cymbals sound," (Saul.) * Song, "Come divine inspirer," (Joseph.) Chorus, "The mighty power in whom we trust," (Athalia.) * Song, "His mighty arm with sudden blow," (Jephtha.) Duet and Chorus, "O never bow we down," (Judas Macc.) * Song, "Let the righteous be glad." * Chorus, "Praised be the Lord, Hallelujah," (Anthems.)

PART III.

Second Hautboy Concerto. * Recit. "It must be so," (Jephtha.) * Song, "Pour forth no more," (Jephtha.) Chorus, "No more to Ammon's God," (Jephtha.) Song, "Awful pleasing Being say," (Joshua.) Chorus, "When his loud voice in thunder spoke," (Jephtha.) Recit. "Ye sacred priests," (Jephtha.) Song, "Farewel ye limpid springs," (Jephtha.) * "My heart is inditing," (Anthems.)

On SATURDAY the 28th of May.

PART I.

* Overture to the Occasional Oratorio. * Song, "Waft her angels" (Jephtha.) * Chorus, "Fall'n is the foe," (Judas Macc.) * Song, "Father of Heaven," (Judas Macc.) * Air and Chorus, "In sweetest harmony," (Saul.) * Song, "Sin not, O King," (Saul.) Chorus, "Fix'd in his everlasting seat," (Samson.)

PART II.

OVERTURE, JOSEPH,

FIRST PART OF ISRAEL IN EGYPT.

PART III.

SECOND PART OF ISRAEL IN EGYPT.

On WEDNESDAY the 1st of June,

THE MESSIAH.

The Band will be as Numerous, and the whole conducted on the same Grand Scale as on the preceding years

The following is a list of the principal Vocal Performers, who have generously offered their assistance at the several Performances:

Madame MARA,
Mrs. CROUCH, and Signora STORACE;
Signor PACCHIEROTTI,
And Signor DAVID,
Mr. KELLY, Mr. SAVILLE, Mr. SALE,
Mr. NIELD, Mr. KNYVETT, Mr. BARTLEMAN,
Mr. CHAMPNESS, Mr. MATHEWS,
Mr. RENNOLDSON, Mr. GOSS,
Mr. BELLAMY, jun. &c. &c. &c.

In the list of Instrumental Performers are Messrs. Cramer, Mara, Sarjant, Ashley and Sons, Baumgarten, Parkinson, J. and W. Park, Holmes, Hogg, Lyon, Florio, Potter, Foster, Dance, Blake, Mountain, Soderini, Boyce, Messrs. Gresbachs, Howard, Franki, Leffler, Flack, Shaw, Ely, Hackwood, C. Evans, Scola, Waterhouse, Rawlings, Napier, Wagner, Shield, Miller, Neibour, Patria, Kellners, Cantelo, Leanders, Asbridge, &c. &c.

The Profits will be applied to the Use of the Fund for decayed Musicians, Sons of the Clergy, and the Middlesex Hospital.

The Office at the St. Alban's Tavern, St. Alban's-street, is open every Day, from Ten in the Morning till Six in the Evening, for delivering Tickets, at One Guinea each; and at Messrs. Longman and Broderip's Music Shops, in Cheapside and the Haymarket.

N. B. The First Rehearsal will be on Thursday the 19th, the Second on Saturday the 21st, and the Third on Tuesday the 24th of May.

[The Pieces marked thus * were never before performed in the Abbey.]

By Order of the Directors,

JOHN ASHLEY.

SCHEME of the IRISH STATE-LOTTERY,

For the Year 1791.

No. of Prizes.		Value of each.		Total Value.
1	of	£ 20,000	is	£ 20,000
1	—	10,000	—	10,000
2	—	5,000	—	10,000
4	—	2,000	—	8,000
8	—	1,000	—	8,000
10	—	500	—	5,000
40	—	100	—	4,000
100	—	50	—	5,000
160	—	25	—	4,000
250	—	20	—	5,000
400	—	15	—	6,000
11,400	—	10	—	114,000
12,376	Prizes.			£ 199,000
	First drawn Ticket		—	500
	Last drawn	—	—	500
27,624	Blanks.			
40,000	Tickets.			£ 200,000

The Drawing to commence on Friday the 11th Day of November next, and the Prizes to be payable from and after the 1st Day of June, 1792, without Discount of any Kind.

Signed, by Order of the Managers and Directors,

CHRISTOPHER and ROBERT DEEY,

Secretaries.

MR. COSWAY's COLLECTION of PICTURES will be Open for the Inspection of the PUBLIC, at his House in Pall-Mall, This Day, 2d of May.

Admittance One Shilling.

Descriptive Catalogues, with a beautiful Engraving designed by Mr. Cosway, and engraved by Condi, Price Two Shillings.

MONEY MATTERS.

To those who have MONEY—and to those who want it.

MR. SANGSTER, No. 21, Duke-street, Westminster, continues to advance Money on Bills, Notes of Hand, Annuities (redeemable at Pleasure), and on all Kinds of Real or Personal Security; and in Cases of Emergency Part of the Money may be had on the first Application.

Persons who have Money to lay out will constantly find at this Office a Variety of unexceptionable Securities, by which they may make Twelve or Thirteen per Cent. safely and legally.

Applications to be made personally, or by addressing a line (Post paid).

Those who wish to consult Mr. Sangster at their own Houses, may be waited on at the shortest Notice.

Ladies of Character may be supplied with the strictest Secrecy.

This day is published, Price 2s. 6d.

ANOTHER SKETCH of the REIGN of GEORGE III from the Year 1780 to 1790, being an ANSWER to the SKETCH, &c. &c. PART I.

Printed for J. Ridgway, York-street, St. James's-square; Messrs. Baldwin, and Bell, and H. D. Symonds, Pater-noster-row; Mr. M. Sewell, Cornhill; and Mr. Westby, opposite, St. Clement's Church, Strand.

This Day is published;

Price One Shilling,

A COMPARATIVE REVIEW of the ADMINISTRATION of Mr. HASTINGS and Mr. DUNDAS, in War and in Peace.

By RALPH BROOM, Esq.

Author of The Elucidation of the Articles of Impeachment, &c.

Printed for John Stockdale, Piccadilly.

This Day is published,

In Two Volumes 8vo. price 12s. in boards,

With the Original Plates,

THE ORLANDO OF ARIOSTO, reduced to XXIV Books; the Narrative connected, and the Stories disposed in a regular Series.

By JOHN HOOLE,

Translator of the Original Work,

In Forty-six Books.

The Translator hopes he shall not be deemed reprehensible by the warmest admirers of this Poet, for having adopted the only plan that seemed wanting to make the powers of his Poetry more universally felt and acknowledged.

Printed for J. Dodsley, in Pall-Mall.

Where may be had,

The Complete Translation of the Orlando Furioso, in 5 vols.

Also, Mr. Hoole's Translation of Tasso's Jerusalem, 2 Vols. 8vo.

This Day is published;

In One large Volume Quarto, price 1l. 1s. in Boards,

AN EXPOSITION of the NEW TESTAMENT: Intended as an Introduction to the Study of the Scriptures, by pointing out the leading Sense, and Connection of the sacred Writers.

By WILLIAM GILPIN, M. A.

Prebendary of Salisbury, and Vicar of Boldre, in New Forest, near Lymington.

Printed for R. Blamire, Strand; sold by B. Law, Ave-Maria Lane, and Messrs. Rivingtons, St. Paul's Church-yard.

Speedily will be published,

In Two Volumes 8vo.

With PRINTS in Imitation of Drawings,

REMARKS on FOREST SCENERY, and other WOODLAND VIEWS (relative chiefly to picturesque Beauty) illustrated by the Scenes of NEW-FOREST, in Hampshire.

By WILLIAM GILPIN, M. A.

Prebendary of Salisbury, and Vicar of Boldre, in New Forest.

Printed for R. Blamire, No. 5, Strand.

LAKES in CUMBERLAND and WESTMORELAND

Proposals for publishing by Subscription,

TWENTY VIEWS of the LAKES in CUMBERLAND and WESTMORELAND, to be engraved from the Original Drawings made on the Spot in the Year 1788, by John Smith, for John Christian Curwen, Esq. under whose particular Patronage the Work is undertaken.

The Plates will be executed in a high-finished Manner.

CONDITIONS.

I. The Work to be published in Numbers, each containing Four Prints: the Size of the Print Fifteen Inches and a Half by Ten Inches. Price to Subscribers, One Guinea; Non-Subscribers, One Pound Six Shillings each Number.

II. Subscription Money not required until the Delivery.

The First Number, containing the Four following Views, viz.

1. View on the Great Island in Windermere.
2. Elter Water.
3. Buttermere Water.
4. Wyburn or Leathes Water.

Will be ready for Delivery in May, and the Four following Numbers with as much expedition as the nature of the Work will admit of.

The Subscribers, and the Public in general are respectfully informed, that every possible care and attention has and will be given to the execution of the whole, in order to render this Work deserving of patronage.

Subscribers' names received at R. Blamire's, No. 5, Strand; and at J. Smith's, No. 23, Bryanston-street, Portman-square, where some of the Prints may be seen.

PARLIAMENTARY REGISTER.

This day is published, price 1s.

NUMBER VIII. of the present Session,

THE PARLIAMENTARY REGISTER;

or,

HISTORY of the PROCEEDINGS and DEBATES in the HOUSES of LORDS and COMMONS during the present Session.

Revised and collated with the Notes of several Members.

*** At the desire of several persons of distinguished abilities and rank, this Work was undertaken. The favourable reception it has met with during the three last Parliaments, not only demands the most grateful acknowledgments of the Editors, but encourages them to prosecute a continuation of the same, during the present Parliament. For this purpose, and to prevent misrepresentation, they beg leave again to solicit the assistance of all their former Friends, and every other Gentleman. A strict attention will be paid to all their commands and favours; nor will any assiduity or care be wanting to preserve that truth and accuracy for which this Work has hitherto been distinguished.

Printed for J. Debrett, opposite Burlington-house, Piccadilly; and sold also by R. Baldwin and J. Bew, in Paternoster-row; and J. Sewell, in Cornwall,

Of whom may be had,

The Parliamentary Register of the Present Session.

The Parliamentary Register from 1780 to 1784, in 14 volumes, price 3l. 3s. half bound and lettered.

The Parliamentary Register from 1784 to 1791, in 13 volumes, price 6l. 11s. half bound and lettered.

45 *Morning Post, and Daily Advertiser*, 2 May 1791, front page. By permission of The British Library.

the publication of the latest volume of *The Parliamentary Register*. Perusing the *Morning Post*'s columns at greater length also demonstrates how many events and publications relating to the visual arts were being advertised in the London newspapers. Scattered across the page we find notices flagging the last week of an exhibition at the European Museum in St James's Square, a one-man display of paintings by the Royal Academician Richard Cosway, and a scheme to engrave 'TWENTY VIEWS of the LAKES in CUMBERLAND and WESTMORELAND'. Meanwhile, at the head of the second column we find an advertisement announcing the opening of the Royal Academy exhibition itself: 'The PRESIDENT and COUNCIL, give Notice, That the EXHIBITION will Open THIS DAY, at Twelve o'clock, And continue Every Day, (Sundays excepted) from Eight in the Morning till Seven in the Evening . . . Admission ONE SHILLING'. Versions of this advertisement continued to appear in the *Post* for the duration of the show, and – as was the case each year – appeared in a number of other broadsheets. This confirms the extent to which the London newspapers' advertisement pages functioned as crucial sites of publicity for the annual parade of paintings at Somerset House, continually alerting readers to the exhibition's existence within what was evidently a highly competitive cultural and artistic marketplace.

Alongside their swathe of advertisements, the late eighteenth-century London papers carried a mass of other materials, including political and military news from home and abroad, information and gossip about the royal family and members of the English aristocracy, notices of public appointments and promotions, crime stories, articles and letters dealing with contemporary theatre, literature and music, and commentaries of various sorts on the art world, including reviews of the exhibitions at Somerset House. The authors of these brief articles tended to be anonymous or (more infrequently) pseudonymous, a mix of hack journalists and unpaid correspondents, whose efforts were co-ordinated by notoriously authoritarian editors. These men served a range of different interests, both acknowledged and secret. Newspapers, for instance, were often stuffed full of notices and reports that, masquerading as journalism, were in reality paid 'puffs' for various products or events. Many newspapers, moreover, received subsidies from either the government or opposition groupings, and were blatantly partisan in their politics. In sum, the paper provided an environment for the exhibition review that, while strikingly inert in its overall structure and layout – to the inexperienced eye, a 1790s newspaper will look very similar to one published thirty years earlier – was, in its contents and preoccupations, a fluid site of different voices. The reviews of the Royal Academy exhibitions published in the London papers reflected this duality, simultaneously maintaining long-established conventions of format and rhetoric whilst continuously mutating in response to the changing character of the exhibitions they described, and to the shifting political and cultural agendas of the newspapers themselves.

The newspaper reviews tended to appear very soon after 'the Exhibition' began, in late April or early May, though – largely, no doubt, because of pressures on column space – they were often broken up into different instalments or parts, 'to be continued' over several issues. In whichever paper they appeared, the reviews were normally found on an inside page, where they would often be juxtaposed with discussions of other cultural events, such as plays and concerts, or extracts from recently issued books and romantic or topical poetry. Partitioned off by the thin white borders of the column space and a perfunctory headline – 'Royal Academy' is the most common – exhibition critiques took a limited number of forms. Typically they began with an introductory paragraph or two discussing the show's overall quality, and what this suggested about the state of British art more generally. One of several directions might then be pursued. Certain writers, for instance, would focus in detail on examples of the most prestigious pictorial genres – history paintings and grand portraits – before providing shorter discussions of a selection of more modest works. Alternatively, and far more commonly, there would be an initial concentration on the most prominent exhibitors, whose works would be dealt with as a group, before pieces by secondary masters would enter into consideration. From the mid-1780s onwards, we also find other critics regularly proceeding in yet another fashion, in which they discuss the exhibits in catalogue order. In the words of the *Morning Post, and Daily Advertiser* of 28 April 1784, 'we shall not adhere to the usual mode of commenting separately on the works of the several artists, but shall begin with the first number, and proceed in regular succession to the last, omitting such alone, as we may not think worthy of our attention'.[4] This method of review, even when made up of short fragments of commentary, could be made to extend over many issues of the newspaper. Thus, the *Post*'s coverage of the 1784 show, having reached painting number 29 on the first day of criticism, takes until the middle of the following month to complete. Over the next decade, this type of criticism itself gradually turns into something rather different, in which the newspaper review, while still adhering to a roughly numerical order, takes the form of a series of more extended responses to far smaller groupings of works, extracted by the critic from the exhibition display as a whole.

As well as adopting a variety of formats, exhibition reviews were also characterized by different types of rhetoric. To begin with there were certain critics who, taking their cue from the discourse of art theory, wrote in the elevated and abstracted tones associated with texts such as Jonathan Richardson's *Essay on the Art of Criticism* (1719), still respected as a layman's guide to art appreciation, and the annually published *Discourses* of the Academy's President, Sir Joshua Reynolds. This approach was bound to privilege the most culturally elevated works on show, such as the painting of *Moses Receiving the Laws* by Benjamin West that can be seen in the background of Dodd's engraving of the 1784 exhibition (see figs 24 and 34). The *Public Advertiser* for 28 April, for instance, praised West's enormous canvas in a language that assumes a learned and meditative perspective on the part of artist, reader and viewer:

> The composition of this Picture appears to have been considered with great Judgement: the group which fills the lower part of the piece, consists of the Elders, who accompanied Moses to the top of the Mount, where he and Joshua ascended to the upper summit where the law was delivered to him. The figure of Moses is extremely striking, sublime and original, and does infinite credit to the invention of Mr West. Moses is represented standing, holding one table, not written upon, in his right hand; whilst the left, which sustains the second table, is extended into the cloud over his head, where the finger of the Deity is supposed to inscribe on that table a part of the law. Several of the Italian Masters, as well as the French and the Flemings, have ventured to delineate the figure of the Deity. The attempt is, perhaps, more deserving of censure than of praise; as it is aiming at something beyond the reach of human conception. Mr West has, with great judgement and propriety, endeavoured to convey an idea of the presence of the Almighty, by the sublimity, the grandeur, and the awful solemnity of the scene, with the striking effects it produces on all who are present, leaving to every spectator to form in his own mind an idea of the Godhead.[5]

Significantly, the *Public Advertiser* prefaced its analysis with a vigorous promotion of history painting as 'the most elevated department of the art'. This kind of writing, offering a self-consciously cerebral perspective on painting and its purposes, not only complemented the first format of criticism noted earlier, in which history paintings and grand portraits were given pride of place, but also reinforced the pictorial hierarchies expressed in the exhibition hang itself, where examples of the higher, more 'public' genres of painting were typically found in prominent positions within the Great Room, and were clearly designed to catch the viewer's first glance, while more humble pictures were given progressively more marginal positions on the walls. This rhetoric, when positively applied, reinforced the Academy's own aspirations as a sponsor of an art that would stand comparison in its seriousness and ambition with that produced by continental artists, both past and present.

Yet things are a little more complicated than this. The *Public Advertiser's* writer finishes his review of *Moses Receiving the Laws* by declaring that 'In this great work, Mr West seems to have exerted his utmost art: the masses of light and shadow, the expressive characteristic of the heads, the ample folding of the draperies, the distribution of colours, with the ease and freedom of execution of this picture, justly entitle it to rank with the first class of the Italian schools.'[6] In concentrating so closely on matters of form and style in his concluding remarks, the *Advertiser's* correspondent draws as much upon the themes and technical jargon found in the discourse of connoisseurship as upon those found in art-theoretical treatises of the period. This discourse, it is important to note, was traditionally linked to the figure of the aristocratic art collector; hence the fusion of vocabularies found in the review as a whole works to link the high-minded goals of an Academy designed to sponsor history painting, and made up of professional artists seeking cultural and social respectability, with the rules and preoccupations associated with patrician taste, and with the elite connoisseur in particular. But the fact that the connoisseur was often satirized as a pretentious and short-sighted creature, driven by unwholesome desires, enables us to appreciate that the linguistic alliance being attempted here was not necessarily an easy or sustainable one. Rather, the *Public Advertiser's* seemingly confident rhetoric does no more than mask the irreconcilable contradictions between the supposedly public ethos of the Academy exhibition and the private interests and sensual pleasures that were frequently attributed to the aristocratic aesthete.[7]

The *Public Advertiser's* review also suggests how often critical writing focused on the individual qualities of the most well known exhibitors, who were regularly singled out in order to be showered with extravagant commendation. While during the eighties the most obvious target of such treatment was the illustrious Sir Joshua Reynolds, he and West were not the only artists to be spotlit by the beam of flattery. In 1784, for instance, the landscape painter Philippe de Loutherbourg basked in a blaze of journalistic hyperbole. The *Morning Post* declared that it was 'impossible to say too much in praise of [his] works', and that 'wherever the master throws his pencil, we are enchanted by his magic';[8] the *Public Advertiser* suggested that he was 'an enchanting master' who had 'given us this year several fresh proofs of his unrivalled Abilities in the Line of Landscape';[9] whereas the *Morning Chronicle* called all of his paintings 'capital pieces',[10] which 'are spoken of with rapture by all who have seen them'.[11] This form of writing sharpened the focus on the show's 'star' artists encouraged by the second review format noted earlier (which began with all the works by each of the leading exhibitors in turn), and linked a newspaper's exhibition commentaries with its nearby theatrical and musical reviews, which similarly concentrated on the best-known performers of stage and concert hall. In this process, the exhibition became filtered through an emergent journalistic rhetoric of artistic celebrity, in which critical debate on the works on display at Somerset House was subordinated to the praise of individual contributors.

The vocabulary employed on such occasions carried close – and to some observers disgraceful – echoes of the language of the paid newspaper advertisement, and raised suspicions (sometimes justified) that this was no more than 'puffing' – that is, commercial promotion masquerading as disinterested analysis. While journalists and editors were castigated for encouraging and participating in this notorious practice, certain commentators laid the blame squarely at the door of the artists themselves; on one occasion they were publicly urged to stop inserting 'paragraphs enumerating their own merits, for which they pay half-guineas, and guineas: it is now no secret'.[12] Another commentator similarly bemoaned the 'general reliance on the force of puffing in the newspapers of the metropolis, among our little artists, as well as our little authors', declaring that it was 'indicative only of feebleness in both, and ought to be much regretted, as the system is now so methodically pursued, that the application of a few guineas to paragraph writers, will make any wretched dolt conspicuous for talents which he does not possess'.[13]

Whatever the extent of such puffery, the prevailing sense that it was widespread must have helped give rise to the self-professed 'plain speaking' critic, whose discussion was ostensibly unclouded by the high-minded language of theory, the social pretensions of the connoisseur, the gross superlatives of celebrity criticism and – most importantly of all – the secret interests of the 'puff'. Numerous late eighteenth-century art critiques began or concluded by claiming such an objective, commonsensical perspective. In a typical formulation, the *General Advertiser*'s art reviewer in 1785 spoke of how much he prided himself on his 'plain English', and the fact that he had not 'perplexed' the reader's understanding by the 'introduction of the technical terms of *relief*, and *in-drawing*, and *fore-shortening*, and *back-ground*, and *bringing out*, &c. &c. &c. &c.'[14] Flaunting their refusal to accept the authority of either traditional pictorial hierarchies or artistic reputations, such writers felt free to court controversy by puncturing overblown reputations, and to enliven their irreverent commentaries with shafts of low wit and satiric humour. Their entire approach dovetailed nicely with the third review format noted above, in which each work on display – however grand or lowly – was discussed in catalogue order, and assessed on its own merits. Invariably certain works fared much better than others. Thus while the *Morning Post* of 14 May 1784 had high praise for the paintings of Fuseli and de Loutherbourg, it peppered other exhibits with jokey, dismissive comments, even deliberately misspelling the names of individual artists: '44. Portrait of a Nun, by F. RENALDY, – She has not even charms enough to warm a Friar, and that is saying a great deal. 45. The Death of Captain Cook, by J. H. RHOMBERG [*sic*]. – We fancy this picture has met with an accident, from some washerwoman's emptying her blue-bag on it.' In a rather more restrained appeal to basic common sense, the *Morning Herald*'s critic of the same year declared of West's altarpiece that 'One or two of the principal figures, though marked with the wrinkles of age, have faces as fair as if they used *cosmetics!*'[15]

The playful iconoclasm of such comments frequently mixed with more hard-edged and politically resonant forms of criticism, often from an anti-establishment or Whig viewpoint. Though sometimes targeted at individual exhibited works, such barbs were more regularly directed at the Academy itself, as a despotic and faction-ridden institution whose leaders suppressed merit, privileged certain artists and ran what was supposedly an enlightened public body according to the dictates of greed and envy. Thus a writer in the *St James's Chronicle* in 1782, reviewing the annual exhibition, noted that 'all corporate bodies become soon oppressive and iniquitous, and they generally ruin the Purposes they were meant to serve'.[16] Although attacks on the Royal Academy's integrity did not always come from the opposition press, they undoubtedly tapped into the demand for political reform that played such an important role in defining the ideological positions of the capital's newspapers in the last decades of the eighteenth century.[17] For those unhappy with the status quo, the Academy offered itself as a prime example of a public body ruined by the machinations of a ruling clique, and hence as an obvious surrogate for those political institutions and spaces – whether the court, the ministry or Parliament – that were widely believed to have been similarly corrupted by the workings of faction and self-interest. This explained, suggested many critics, why the annual exhibitions had descended into a parade of the hackneyed and the incompetent: amongst 'the little dirty paltry aristocracy of the Royal Academy', thundered the pro-opposition *Morning Post* on 16 May 1794, 'the jaundiced eye of envy never ceases to crush rising merit'. As a result, nothing but 'daubings' were to be found occupying 'the place of better pictures, in the present Exhibition at Somerset House'.

Whether party-political or art-theoretical, none of the rhetorical approaches used by late eighteenth-century art reviewers was ever consistently or rigidly applied. On the contrary, the fact that different critical strategies may have contradicted one another did not stop them from frequently intermingling within the space of the same review. To confirm this, we might usefully glance at the third page of the *Morning Chronicle* of Thursday, 8 May 1794 (fig. 46). Here, at the head of the second column, and jostling alongside reports about the war with France and advertisements for Thomas Appleby's Vegetable Tea, we find a discussion of seven pictures in the Academy exhibition. The review begins with fifteen lines on picture number 28, Julius Caesar Ibbetson's *Distant View of Anglesea*, then moves on to a history painting, two portraits and another landscape, before ending with six lines on Anna Tonelli's *Ariadne* (no. 348). In flitting from one image to the next, the *Chronicle*'s commentator not only roves across a variety of pictorial genres, but also deploys a variety of interpretive approaches. At times he confidently dons the mantle of the connoisseur, by invoking seventeenth-century artists like Ruisdael and Claude, or demonstrating his awareness of touch and form as issues to be judged; elsewhere he offers his opinions of various contemporary practitioners, whose achievements he relates to the physical, moral and political character of the British nation, often in a highly charged way: 'the shield of Eneas, a soldier of *these degenerate days* could not lift'. Aside from privileging the critic's own free-wheeling tastes, this compilation of responses to a few selected works makes certain assumptions about the cultural habits of readers of newspapers: namely, that they are catholic in their modes of artistic appreciation and prepared to slide between very different sets of criteria when reading about art.

REVOLUTION IN POLAND.

FRONTIERS OF POLAND, APRIL 22.

The Patriots on the 17th instant, after having rendered themselves Masters of the grand Arsenal at Warsaw, obliged the Russian Garrison, consisting of 3,000 troops, to evacuate the town. Baron Igelstrohm, the Russian Ambassador, was obliged to take refuge with the Prussian army under General Wolky, encamped a league's distance from that Capital. His Majesty the King of Poland is retained as an hostage by the Patriots. Some reports state, that his Majesty escaped into a Convent under escort of 500 Russians.

The Ambassador of a neighbouring Power *(probably the Prussian)* has also been retained as an Hostage.

The Insurgents have established a Revolutionary Tribunal; and several persons are said to have already suffered death.

Lithuania, according to the latest accounts, is likewise in a state of Insurrection.

General Kosciusko is very active in fortifying the town of Cracow; he ordered a declaration to be published, by which those Citizens who do not wish to remain in the town, in case of a siege, are permitted to quit it within eight days time; in consequence of which declaration, a great number of rich Merchants, with their goods, together with a great number of women and children, have passed the Bridge over the Vistula, in order to settle in the village of Podgorze, belonging to Gallicia.

We likewise learn that General Kosciusko has ordered the Bridge to be broken down, and a number of boats which were on this side of the Vistula, to be rowed into a place of security. The three complete Polish regiments, Lubomirsky, Czapsky, and Ozarowsky, have joined his standard.

APRIL 22.

The 17th of this month proved a dreadful day to Warsaw. General Igelstrohm, a few days before, had given orders to the whole of the Russian cavalry, in garrison there, to march from Warsaw to join the troops which had been previously detached, in order to act against the army under General Kosciusko.

When the insurrection took place on the 17th in the morning, General Igelstrohm ordered the only three battalions of Russian infantry who remained in the garrison, to take up arms; at the same time he sent a message to the King, informing his Majesty of the event. The King sent him word, that he had already been informed of what had happened; that his Majesty had only to add a request of the General to send all his troops out of the Capital, in order to prevent bloodshed, until the minds of the people should in some measure be pacified.

General Igelstrohm, in the mean time, had sent General Bauer, at the head of a detachment to protect the Arsenal; but this was too late. The Patriots had already rendered themselves masters of all the artillery contained in that building; and the latter General, with his detachment, on their arrival, were forced to lay down their arms, and to surrender prisoners of war. The Patriots afterwards, provided with arms from the Arsenal, formed themselves in order of battle, and marched against a battalion of the Russian infantry, whom they drove out of the town.

General Igelstrohm, however, placed himself at the head of the two other battalions, and took post in Catherine-street, where he was determined to defend himself; these battalions were fired upon with great violence from every window; and, after an engagement which lasted thirty-three hours without intermission, the Russians retreated from Warsaw, with the loss of half their number, almost all killed. Thus Generals Igelstrohm, Apraxin, and Subow, at the head of the remaining Russian infantry, joined the Prussian corps, under General Wolky, stationed in the neighbourhood of that Capital. The people of Warsaw were obliged to set several houses on fire, where the Russian soldiers had posted themselves during the engagement.

The houses and palaces, which had been inhabited by the Russian officers and their adherents, were plundered by the mob; particularly the baggage of the Russian Generals fell a prey to the rapacious part of the lower order of the people.

A number of the Russian soldiers, who kept themselves concealed during the engagement, were afterwards massacred as soon as they appeared in the streets.

The Magistrates had assembled during the tumult; but all their endeavours to restore tranquillity proved ineffectual.

The Patriots have since sent an account of this Revolution to General Kosciusko, at Cracow; at the same time inviting that General to come to their assistance.

WARSAW, APRIL 22.

The Polish Patriots are now masters of this Capital. The Russian troops have been forced to retreat to Zacroczim, where they are united with the Prussian body of troops, under General Wolky. General Igelstrohm is likewise at Zacroczim, together with the other Russian Generals, who, sword in hand, were obliged to fight their way through the avenues of Warsaw, and through the ranks of the armed Polish Patriots. We are in great anxiety on account of M. Von. Buchholtz, whose fate is yet unknown.

BANKS OF THE VISTULA, APRIL 25.

The Revolution in Poland is at the highest pitch. The Patriots have constituted themselves into a Revolutionary body. They are masters of Warsaw, and all the Polish artillery contained in the Arsenal of that Capital. The King is in their hands, as also the Prussian Ambassador, Mr. Von Buchholtz, and Baron Von Asch, the Russian Resident.

General Igelstrohm, with the other Russian Generals Apraxin, Pistor, and Count Nicolas Subow, with 1,200 Russians; the remainder of 3,000 men, who garrisoned Warsaw, have joined the Prussians at Zacroczim.

The Patriots are fortifying Cracow, and are levying a great number of new corps.

Prince Adam Czartorinsky is said to have arrived at Cracow, in order to take an active part in the Revolution.

To the EDITOR of the MORNING CHRONICLE.

SIR,

It is remarkable that none of the leaders at the different periods of the French Revolution have been at all similar to each other in those qualities by which their several characters have been essentially distinguished. Strongly marked characters they have all been—as will ever prove the case in times of political convulsion, where ability, being alone useful, gets the start of all feebler claims to popular respect;—but their characters seem to have been as distinct from each other as they were from those of the common herd of men. The good intentions and sedate prudence of NECKAR, half-compliant with popular wishes, yet startled at the efforts of popular indignation, present to our conception a very different picture from the enthusiasm for liberty, tempered and restrained by somewhat, perhaps, too much for the times, of loyal and soldier-like feelings of FAYETTE. From these characters, that of BRISSOT is widely different—the mild and liberal philosophy of whose mind again forms a striking contrast to the decisive and daring spirit of DANTON; and this decisive and daring spirit is equally distinct from the wily caution and the provident policy that appear to constitute the character of ROBESPIERRE.

OLD BAILEY.

SIXTH DAY.

Mary Butler was tried for robbing Thomas Bolt, near Temple Bar, in the Strand, of two guineas and a half and some silver.

It appeared in evidence, that the prisoner, after she had picked the pocket of the prosecutor, put the money into her mouth and swallowed it.

The Jury found her guilty.

The Common Serjeant (before whom the prisoner was tried) said it had of late become a common practice for the prostitutes who infested the Strand to plunder gentlemen who passed that way, and put the money in their mouth and swallow it. He sentenced the prisoner to be transported to Botany Bay for the term of seven years, as a warning to women of a similar description.

The same day the session ended.

This Week all the Beauty and Fashion in this vast Metropolis, will view the Empress of Germany's wonderful VANHUYSUMS, valued at One Thousand Guineas, previous to their removal from the European Museum, St. James's-square.

To the true Lovers of Painting, who visit MONSIEUR DE CALONNE'S COLLECTION, Spring Gardens, we would recommend an early hour, as the Rooms are generally filled about One o'clock, when the study of the Fine Cabinet Pictures, which for want of room, we must confess are hung too low, is too much interrupted by the Company.

The admirable style in which Godfrey has built that elegant little Pleasure-boat that is rowed with so much success at the New Theatre, must occasion him to have a greater demand than ever for those beautiful articles. Indeed when personages of fashion sojourn at their country villas, what can be a greater addition to their happiness than to have one of these pleasurable appendages in which they may solace themselves and company either on the river or the lake.

BIRTH.

Last night Mrs. Davison, of Harpur-street, was safely delivered of a Daughter.

MARRIED.

Saturday last, at Hammersmith, Mr. Thomas Clarke, of Sadlers'-hall, Attorney at Law, to Miss Bowyer, only daughter of the late Samuel Bowyer, Esq. of the Exchequer-office, Inner Temple.

DIED.

Sunday last, at his grandfather's house at Kensington, Master Alexander Baxter Allardyce, aged seven years, the son of Alexander Allardyce, Esq. M. P. for Aberdeen, &c.

A few days since at his family seat of Kinnaird, near Falkirk, James Bruce, Esq. the celebrated Abyssinian Traveller. Mr Bruce, after having encountered so many perils in distant regions, received his death from a fall down his own stair case.

STOCK EXCHANGE.

Bank Stock 168¼	Ditto Ann.
3 per Cent. red. 70⅞ ¾ ½	India Bonds 9s 10s dis.
3 per Cent. Con. 71 70⅞	New Ditto
Ditto Scrip. 72¼	New Navy 1¼ ¾ dis.
4 Cent Con. 84¼ ⅞	Exchequer Bills 10s. 11s pre.
Navy 5 per Cent Ann 103¼ ⅞	Lot. Tick.
Bank L.A. 20 3-16½	Irish ditto
Ditto short 1778 & 17 9 9¼	4 per Cent Scrip 88
India Stock 208	Omnium 6
Ditto Scrip	Light L. A. 21

ERRAT.—In the second Advertisement in the Last Page of Monday's Paper, for SUTTON Colts, read SURTON Colts.

NOTICE.

BY virtue of orders from the Magistrates of Ostend, bearing date the 28th February, and 3d April, 1794, the under-signed Assignees for the time being, do give notice to the Creditors of Messrs. Mendes Fonteyne and Co. late Merchants in Ostend, bankrupts, that a General Meeting of the said Creditors will be held at the said Bankrupts' House, in this City, on Thursday the 15th of May next, in the afternoon, to deliberate finally respecting the affairs of the estate.

Each Creditor is requested to attend, as the resolutions of the meeting will be equally binding on absentees (if any) as on those present.

The said Magistrates of Ostend do further ordain, that all the Creditors of the said Estate, do deliver in their pretensions duly authenticated and affirmed on oath, in the space of three times six weeks from the date hereof, either to the underwritten, or to those who may have succeeded them in the said office of assignees to the estate of Mendes Fonteyne and Co. on pain of being totally excluded, as no later claims will be admitted; but the funds of the estate will then be divided among the Creditors who shall have given in their pretentions agreeable to the above orders of the Magistrates.

Ostend, 3d April, 1794.

Signed, J. DE CONINCK. GEO. BELL. H. F. BELLIROCHE.

A true Copy, GEORGE BELL.

SALES BY AUCTION.

By Messrs. JAQUES and SON,
TO-MORROW, the 8th, at 11 o'clock, on the Premises,

THE genteel HOUSEHOLD FURNITURE and CHINA of

Mrs. LAWSON,

at No. 26, NEW NORTH-STREET, Red Lion-square; comprising several prime goose beds, and bedding; four-post bedsteads, and fine cotton hangings; excellent cabinet work, in a variety of drawers, tables and chairs; large pier glasses, carpets, stoves, kitchen requisites, &c.

To be viewed the day preceding, and the morning of Sale.—Catalogues may then be had on the Premises; and of Messrs. Jaques and Son, Hatton-garden.

TO SADLERS, HARNESS-MAKERS, &c.
By Mr. GIBBONS,
On the Premises, the corner of Chancery-lane, TO-MORROW, May 8, 1794, at eleven o'clock,

THE entire and valuable Stock in Trade, of Mr. HESTER,

Sadler and Harness-maker, retiring from business: Comprising a general assortment of plated and polished Bridles, silver and plated mounted Whips, plated Bitts, Stirrups, Spurs, Buckles, Horse-Rugs, Collars, a great variety of hunting shaft, plain and welted Saddles, some Harness, a quantity of second-hand Saddles, Tools and various other Effects.

To be viewed Wednesday to the sale, when Catalogues may be had, and of Mr. Gibbons, Bucklersbury, Cheapside.

SALES BY AUCTION.

ST. JAMES'S STREET AND PICCADILLY.
TO BE SOLD BY AUCTION, by Mr. WILLOCK,
On the Premises, in a few days,

THE VALUABLE LEASE of the SPACIOUS and ELEGANT SHOP AND HOUSE most eligibly and desirably situate at the corner of St James's street and Piccadilly, in the occupation of MESSRS SCHAEFFER AND CO. LINEN DRAPERS AND MILLINERS, together with the LARGE AND VALUABLE STOCK IN TRADE, consisting of printed and white Callicoes, corded, India and muslin Dimities; Muslins of all descriptions, Irish Linens, diaper table Cloths, furniture Prints, long Lawns and Sheetings, Sattins, Silks, Modes, Gauzes, Ribbands, Feathers and Flowers; also made up Caps, Hats, Bonnets, Gowns, Muffs, Tippets, &c. &c.

Particulars and Catalogues of all which are preparing, and may soon be had on the Premises; at the Rainbow Coffee-house, Cornhill; Baptist Coffee-house, Chancery-lane; and of Mr. Willock, No. 25, Golden square.

VILLA and FURNITURE,
WESTBOURN GREEN, PADDINGTON.
By Mr. WILLOCK,
On the Premises, on Thursday the 22d instant, at one o'clock,

A COMPACT and very desirable MODERN BUILT COPYHOLD VILLA, most delightfully situate at Westbourn Green, ONLY ONE MILE AND A HALF from GROSVENOR and PORTMAN-SQUARE; and within TEN MINUTES WALK of KENSINGTON GARDENS, containing four Cheerful Bedchambers, two Dressing Rooms and Servants' Chambers, an Entrance Hall, Bow Drawing Room, Dining and Breakfast Parlours, and all requisite Domestic Offices for the accommodation of a genteel Family, a DETACHED LANDRY, Coach-house, and four stall Stable, with Loft and Coachman's Room over, a NEAT PLEASURE GROUND and KITCHEN GARDEN, walled round and abundantly cropped and planted with the CHOICEST FRUIT TREES, in great perfection.

The Premises possessing all the advantages of their CONTIGUITY TO TOWN, are nevertheless apparently as retired as if they were at a great distance, and are situate within the MOST DELIGHTFUL VIEWS of the rich surrounding country, and were late in the occupation of Sir JOHN BERNEY, Bart. Immediate possession may be had, and the Purchaser may be accommodated with the FURNITURE at a VALUATION or not, at his option.

To be viewed ten days preceding the Sale, and particulars may then be had at the house, at the Rainbow Coffee-house, Cornhill; Baptist Coffee-house, Chancery-lane; and of Mr. Willock, No. 25, Golden-square.

LEASEHOLD ESTATES.
By Mr. WALDRON,
At the King's Arms, Holborn, near Southampton-street, THIS DAY, at twelve o'clock, in eleven lots.—Judd Place, East, in front of the New Road, Sommer's Town,

No. 10, A SUBSTANTIAL well-built LEASEHOLD HOUSE, with entrance and hall in a wing, attached to the body of the House, with garden, vaults, &c.

No. 13, A House upon a similar plan, and convenience.

No. 14, A ditto.

Judd Place, West.—The second House from West-street, a genteel well planned House, with garden, vaults, &c. Also two other Houses, unfinished, one the corner of West street, the other the next door to the sign of the Crown and Anchor.

Warren-street, Fitzroy-square.—No. 5, A good substantial well-built House, with a front and garden, in the New Road, vaults, &c.

No. 10, A House upon a similar plan and convenience.—Also one unfinished House, the second from the corner of Fitzroy-square.

Tottenham Place, Tottenham Court Road.—No. 30, A substantial well planned House, with ten rooms, vaults, &c.

No. 17, A House upon the same plan, unfinished. The whole in the parish of St. Pancrass, the taxes therefore very low. Term, Ninety-six years, at low ground rents.

To be viewed and particulars may be had at the place of Sale; the Southampton Arms, Tottenham Court Road; and of Mr. Waldron, No. 19, Catherine-street, Strand.

PLATE, JEWELLERY, FRENCH CHINA, &c.
By Mr. BROWN,
By order of the Proprietor, TO-MORROW, at Tom's Coffee-house, opposite the Royal Exchange, Cornhill, at eleven o'clock,

THE remaining part of the genuine Stock in Trade of a Jeweller and Silversmith, retired from business; consisting of three hundred ounces of plate, gold seals, fancy and other rings, rich gold-mounted bracelets, lockets, snuff boxes, etwee cases, trinkets, shoe and knee buckles, seals, tea caddies, coffee urns, waiters, bottle stands, stock buckles, sleeve buttons, gold studs, ear rings, tureens and ladles, bottle stands, and a variety of other articles in that line of business. To which is added, by permission, some elegant French Desert and Tea Services, and several pair of beautiful jars and ornaments. Japan soy, and preserved Nutmegs, the property of a CHINA DEALER, deceased. The whole of which will be sold without reserve.

To be viewed one day preceding the sale, when catalogues may be had at the place of sale, and of the Auctioneer, No. 65, Cannon street.

SUPERB HOUSHOLD FURNITURE, LINEN, CHINA, PRINTS, CARPETS, &c.
By Mr. WEBBE,
At the Great Rooms, Dean-street, Soho, late Christie's, THIS and the 4 following Days, precisely at 12 o'Clock,

ALL the elegant HOUSEHOLD FURNITURE, Linen, China, beautiful Prints, &c. of Capt. AUGUSTUS NEVILLE, gone abroad.

Comprising a drawing suit in blue damask, large pier glasses, superb 4 post and field bedsteads, with rich chintz cotton dimity furnitures, most capital down goose beds, large fine blankets and counterpanes, beautiful carpets, of various dimensions, two of which is 21 feet long, mahogany secretaries and bookcases, ditto wardrobes, sideboards, with cellerets, tambour fronts, double chests of drawers, ladies inlaid dressing tables, elegant inlaid card and Pembroke tables, commodes and single chests of drawers, two sets of mahogany dining tables, card and Pembroke ditto, drawing chairs, in red and green leather, with sofas to match, parlour chairs, in satin hair cloth, and sofas, two table services, containing 150 pieces each, deserts to match, beautiful tea and coffee equipages, a wardrobe of table and bed linen, an iron chest, a large well chosen collection of elegant prints, in high finished burnished gold frames, black and gold, glasses, &c.

The whole in excellent preservation, and well worth the attention of those who wish to furnish elegantly.

May be viewed, and Catalogues had.

LEASEHOLD CARCASS OF A HOUSE AND LAND, STOCKWELL.
By Messrs. GRIFFITHS and Co.
At Garraway's, Cornhill, on Monday, 12 May, 1794, at 12 o'Clock, in one Lot,

THE CARCASS of a HOUSE planned for five Bed-chambers, a Drawing-room, two Parlours, two Kitchens, &c. very desirably situated, facing the late Mr. Angell's Park at Stockwell, in the high road leading to Croydon, and near to the White Horse. The rooms are of good dimensions, is well timbered, the brick work substantial, and the materials of the best. The roof is covered with slate, and the lead gutters are laid; the spring water is remarkably good. The situation is an agreeable distance from the high road, on an eminence commanding pleasing prospects, which cannot for a number of years be interrupted by buildings. There is a good depth of ground behind the premises, in addition to which is one acre of fine meadow land, parallel and immediately adjoining, the house to be held for upwards of 90 years, the land 38 years. The whole subject to a pepper corn rent.—May be viewed, and descriptive particulars had at the White Horse, near the Premises; at Garraway's; the Horns, Kennington; and of Messrs. Griffith and Co. Blackman-street, Southwark.

CAPITAL WINE VAULTS AND PUBLIC HOUSE.
TO DISTILLERS, BREWERS, PUBLICANS, &c.
By Mr. LANGDON,
By order of the Proprietors, on the Premises, Little Newport-street, Long Acre, on Friday next, precisely at three o'clock in the afternoon,

THE valuable LEASE and TRADE of that compact substantial House, known by the ROSE AND CROWN WINE VAULTS. The premises contain five bed-rooms, neatly finished, club-room, parlour, cheerful bar, and yard behind ditto—on the basement, kitchen, good cellarage, &c. &c.

The above premises are held for an unexpired term of eight years from Midsummer next, and fitted up with every convenience to facilitate trade; its point of situation undeniable, being the leading street to Covent Garden, and the East end of the town, which will, with other local advantages, render it an enviable situation, and such as must insure success.

The household furniture and small stock in trade, to be taken as usual, by appraisement.

To be viewed To-morrow, when particulars may be had, and of Mr. Langdon, Sworn Broker, Old Baily.

SALES BY AUCTION.

CHOBHAM, in SURRY.
By Mr. RAINE,
On Friday next, the 9th inst. at the Rainbow Coffee House, in Cornhill, at 12 o'clock, IN TWO LOTS,

TWO FREEHOLD FARMS, with Possession of each at MICHAELMAS next, situated in the Parishes of CHOBHAM and WINDLESHAM, in the County of SURRY, now in the occupation of Mr. James Martin.

Lot I. HALE BOURN FARM, with a Dwelling House two Barns, and other Outbuildings, and SIXTEEN contiguous INCLOSURES of FERTILE MEADOW and ARABLE LAND, containing about SIXTY ACRES, Fifteen of which are Meadow and nearly TITHE FREE; and also an INCLOSURE of PASTURE and WOOD LAND, a distance from the Dwelling, called SLADE INHAMS, containing about FOURTEEN ACRES.

Lot II. A very complete and TITHE FREE ESTATE, called HEAME's FARM, situated on WESTERLY GREEN, within a ring fence, with a Dwelling House, Barn, Stable, Yard and Garden, and Ten Inclosures of Meadow and Arable LAND, containing upwards of

THIRTY-FOUR ACRES.

The above Estates are entitled to an extensive Common Right; and they have been for many years in the occupation of Mr. Martin and his Family, at an old low rent; and being situated within Four Miles of Bagshot, and Seven of Chertsey, are capable of immediate and very considerable Improvements.

To be viewed by leave of Mr. Martin until the Sale, of whom printed Particulars may be had; also at the King's Arms, Bagshot; Sun, at Chobham; Swan, at Chertsey; Bush, at Staines; at the Rainbow Coffee House; and of Mr. Raine, land-surveyor, Charlotte-street, Bloomsbury; where correct Plans may be seen.

MIDDLESEX and ESSEX.
By Mr. RAINE,
On Friday next, the 9th inst. at the Rainbow Coffee House, in Cornhill, at 12 o'clock, IN TWO LOTS,

A LEASEHOLD BRICK HOUSE, very pleasantly situated at BULL's CROSS, near ENFIELD, in MIDDLESEX, commanding extensive Views over a rich country intersected by the New River, which runs in front of the Premises; a Coach House, Stall Stabling, Offices, Garden, and Orchard, well planted and in good condition; and an INCLOSURE of RICH MEADOW LAND, the whole about THREE ACRES; late the Residence of

JOHN WHITEHEAD, Esq.

Term unexpired 24 Years, at the extreme low Rent of Twenty-five Pounds per Annum.

A LEASEHOLD ESTATE, consisting of Six Houses and Gardens, situated in and near to Church-street, WESTHAM, in ESSEX, in the occupation of John Green, and others, at several Rents amounting to Thirty three Guineas per Annum.

Term, unexpired, Ten Years, at a Rent of 2l. 7s. 4d. per Annum.

To be viewed till the Sale; and printed Particulars may be had of the Tenants; at the Swan, at Stratford; and Waltham Cross; George, Enfield Town; Ship, at Tottenham; at the Rainbow Coffee House; and of Mr. Raine, in Charlotte-street, Bloomsbury.

HAMPSHIRE.
By Mr. RAINE,
On Friday next, the 9th Inst. at the Rainbow Coffee House, in Cornhill, at 12 o'clock, IN THREE LOTS,

A VALUABLE FREEHOLD ESTATE, consisting of a very neat, and principally new built Brick Dwelling House, in the Cottage Style, which appears to be situated in a small Park near the entrance of the Village of Eversley, within two miles of Hartford Bridge, in HAMPSHIRE, and nine from Reading, in BERKSHIRE; together with offices, excellent three stalled stable, coach house, barn, gardens, cottage, and other out buildings; mellon ground, garden, and orchard, inclosed in part by brick walls and lofty pales; together with Three Rich Inclosures of Meadow Land, bounded in part by the River Loddon, which divides the Counties of Hampshire and Berkshire; the whole in most excellent Repair, Order and Condition, and contain upwards of seventeen Acres, the late residence of

THOMAS LEWIS, Esq.

Also the REVERSION, after the MARRIAGE or DEATH of a LADY, aged 75, to three Inclosures of FREEHOLD ARABLE LAND, containing about Eight Acres, near the above.

The Purchaser may be accommodated with part of the Household Furniture, Meadow Hay, and Effects, or they will be sold by auction.

Printed Particulars may be had at the House; also at Demezy's, at Hartford Bridge; Dunning's, Blackwater; King's Arms, Bagshot; Bush, Staines; Crown, Reading; at the Rainbow Coffee House; and of Mr. Raine, land-surveyor, in Charlotte-street, Bloomsbury, London; where a correct Plan may be seen.

TO BUILDERS AND OTHERS.—FREEHOLD.
By Mr. RAINE,
On Friday next, the 9th instant, at the Rainbow Coffee-house, in Cornhill, at twelve o'clock,
IN EIGHT LOTS,

EIGHT Substantial and well built FREEHOLD BRICK HOUSES, wholly covered in, seven of which contain two rooms on each floor, and the eighth, a Centre House, four rooms on a floor; the whole carried up four Stories above the Basement Floor; with ground for a Fore Court and Garden to each. The Estate forms nearly the whole of

St MATTHEW'S PLACE, HACKNEY ROAD,

and commands pleasing and uninterrupted prospects from each front.

Particulars may be had at the Nag's-head, opposite the Premises; at the Rainbow Coffee-house, and of Mr. Raine, in Charlotte-street, Bloomsbury.

At the White Hart Tavern in Holborn, on Monday, the 9th day of June, 1794, at 5 o'Clock in the afternoon,

AN exceeding good LEASEHOLD MESSUAGE or DWELLING HOUSE, being No. 39, in Great Ormond-street, in the Parish of St. George the Martyr, in the county of Middlesex, for an unexpired Term of 37 years and an half from Michaelmas 1794, subject to the Annual Ground Rent of 6l. and now in the possession of Anthony Vandam, Esq. who quits the Premises at Michaelmas, 1794.

Particulars and Conditions of Sale to be had of Mr. Maxwell, Fletton, near Stilton, Huntingdonshire, and at the Office of Messrs. Wilmot, Dunn, and Lancaster, Lincoln's-Inn, New Square.

LEASEHOLD, POTTER'S FIELD.
To be Sold by Private Contract, and Immediate possession given,
By Messrs. SKINNER and DYKE,

A COMMODIOUS DWELLING HOUSE, with all convenient Offices, four stall stable, coach-house, court-yard and garden, situate in the best part of Potter's-field, Tooley-street, a small distance from the river. The Premises are well built, exceedingly well fitted up, and in perfect repair, fit for the immediate reception of any family, whose business is near the river.

Held for upwards of 20 years, at a rent of only 4l. per annum.

For further particulars apply to Messrs. Skinner and Dyke, Aldersgate street.

VALUABLE ESTATE, HANTS.
TO BE SOLD BY PRIVATE CONTRACT,
By Messrs. SKINNER and DYKE,

A CAPITAL and very VALUABLE FREEHOLD ESTATE, delightfully situate on an eminence, at an agreeable distance from the Sea, two miles from Christchurch, and nine from Lymington, call'd HIGHCLIFFE, late the property and residence of the Right Hon. the EARL of BUTE, deceased;

Consisting of a spacious and elegant Mansion House replete with Offices suited to every purpose, excellent Pleasure and Kitchen Gardens of great extent, fully cropped and planted, screened by lofty walls, clothed with a choice selection of the best fruit trees, a large Ice-house, a handsome Conservatory, beautiful Temples, Pleasure Grounds, Lawns, Shrubberies, and Plantations, laid out with great taste, and in complete order, and Three Hundred and Twenty-five Acres, or thereabouts, of Meadow, Pasture, and Arable Land, in a high state of cultivation. A large and commodious Gallery in the Parish Church. The Mansion House is an elegant and substantial Structure, erected on a judicious plan, with several suits of apartments, superbly finished. The Situation truly desirable, being placed on a beautiful elevated spot, commanding extensive Marine Views, enriched by pleasing prospects of the Isle of Wight, and the verdant scenery of the New Forest, so truly picturesque, that description must fall short of its beauty and variety. The whole is in excellent repair, and well adapted for the Seat of a Family of the first distinction.

Particulars and Tickets for viewing may be had of Messrs. Skinner and Dyke, Aldersgate-street, who are authorized to treat for the same.

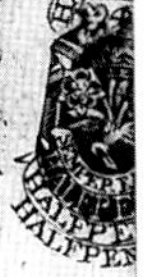

46 *Morning Chronicle*, 8 May 1794, p. 3. The Bodleian Library, University of Oxford.

How did reviews such as this contribute to the broader workings of the Georgian newspaper? 'High culture', as John Brewer has recently written, 'is less a set of discrete works of art than a phenomenon shaped by circles of conversation and criticism formed by its creators, distributors and consumers'.[18] In the eighteenth century, London's newspapers – which were widely read in the public spaces of the coffee-house and the tavern as well as in the private environs of the home – provided a crucial, and highly visible, means of generating and sustaining these 'circles' amongst the disparate individuals and communities who made up 'polite' urban society. One of the most important ways in which this social formation came to define its own collective identity was by what we might call its aesthetic literacy – by the ability of its members to look at, to read about and to talk about the visual arts – a literacy ritualistically confirmed and played out by the annual visit to Somerset House. In newspaper exhibition reviews, we can now suggest, the members of a new, largely bourgeois public for art found a model for their own responses to the works on show, and a variety of tools which they could use to fashion their own identities as informed spectators and consumers of painting, sculpture and drawing: not just certain points of interest and paths of viewing, but most importantly of all, perhaps, a working lexicon of phrases and terms with which to analyse the Academy shows and the visual arts more generally.

Yet the same reviews were comprised of a range of competing vocabularies that do not always easily mesh. Incorporating different attitudes to both viewing and interpreting works of art, and addressed to a variety of imagined reading subjects, press accounts of 'the Exhibition' could easily be used to expose the institutional injustices and political conflicts of the art world and, more indirectly, of contemporary culture as a whole. Here, then, the language of art criticism became available to its readers not only as a badge of their membership of the 'class of the polite', but as an instrument whose forms and uses could equally well express aesthetic conflict, political discontent and cultural degeneration. This becomes even clearer when we turn to our second category of journalistic response to the Academy displays: the pamphlet review.[19]

* * *

If the *Morning Chronicle* commentary I have just been examining appeared to contain a multiplicity of perspectives, their presence can partly be explained by the fact that this account was patched together from at least two sources. More specifically, five of its seven commentaries on individual exhibits are closely based on those found in a contemporary pamphlet: *A Liberal Critique on the Exhibition for 1794*, written by John Williams under the pseudonym of Anthony Pasquin. The other two responses – to pictures by Richard Westall and William Redmore Bigg – express sentiments entirely at odds with Pasquin's far more negative conclusions. Whereas the *Chronicle* praises Westall's self-portrait as 'not a mere map of the face, but a picture of the mind', the *Liberal Critique* states that 'it is said to be a coarse and unfavourable likeness'.[20] The contrast between their respective attitudes to Bigg's work is if anything even greater: lauded in the *Chronicle* for his 'peculiar attention to nature, simplicity and truth', Bigg is roundly castigated by Pasquin for his palpable lack of ambition: 'any professor who is satisfied with accompanying half-measures, is a being with half a soul'.[21] These differences help make the *Chronicle*'s account of the exhibition the more generous of the two; later on we shall see that the *Liberal Critique* mounted a sustained and vitriolic attack on the Academy display as a whole. Looking at the two publications together, however, offers a useful reminder of the overlaps that existed between different genres of exhibition commentary, and the extent to which the London newspapers drew upon what had become an influential and controversial site of art criticism.

Pamphlet commentaries on the Academy displays began as early as 1771, when Robert Baker's *Observations on the Pictures Now on Exhibition*, which covered three concurrently running displays, included nine pages on the RA. Baker suggests that 'such observations as these may not perhaps interest the generality of spectators, of whom the greatest part never descend into minutiae in looking at a picture, and not a few go to these exhibitions only for the sake of saying they have been there'.[22] While clearly directed to a select minority of art enthusiasts within the wider exhibition audience, there was enough demand for pamphlet commentaries to become an increasingly familiar presence in the London art world. Typically some thirty pages or so in length, they varied in format and character, at times mimicking the layout of the exhibition catalogue, at others taking the form of extended poems or pieces of prose, and ranging in their tone from polite appreciation to vicious satire.

Given their portability and focus, it seems plausible to suggest that, unlike the newspaper reviews of the period, pamphlet commentaries would often have been taken around the exhibition itself, and been treated as a supplementary guide. This appears especially likely in cases where a pamphlet's layout was similar to that of the catalogue, with the critic's responses to individual exhibits being printed underneath the work's number, title and the name of its producer. As two pages from *A Candid Review of the Exhibition (Being the Twelfth) of the Royal Academy* (1780; fig. 47) immediately make clear, this type of pamphlet typically contained observations of widely varying lengths, and highlighted certain pictures at the expense of others. If visitors walked around Somerset House clutching texts like this in the manner of a vade-mecum – and there seems no reason to imagine that they did not – they would have been encouraged to follow a highly circumscribed tour of the show, stopping to peruse certain paintings at length, while glancing at others and ignoring many works altogether. But what kinds of journey did such pamphlet reviews offer, and what perspectives did they espouse?

To begin answering these questions, it is necessary to look a little more closely at the *Candid Review* itself. The title page

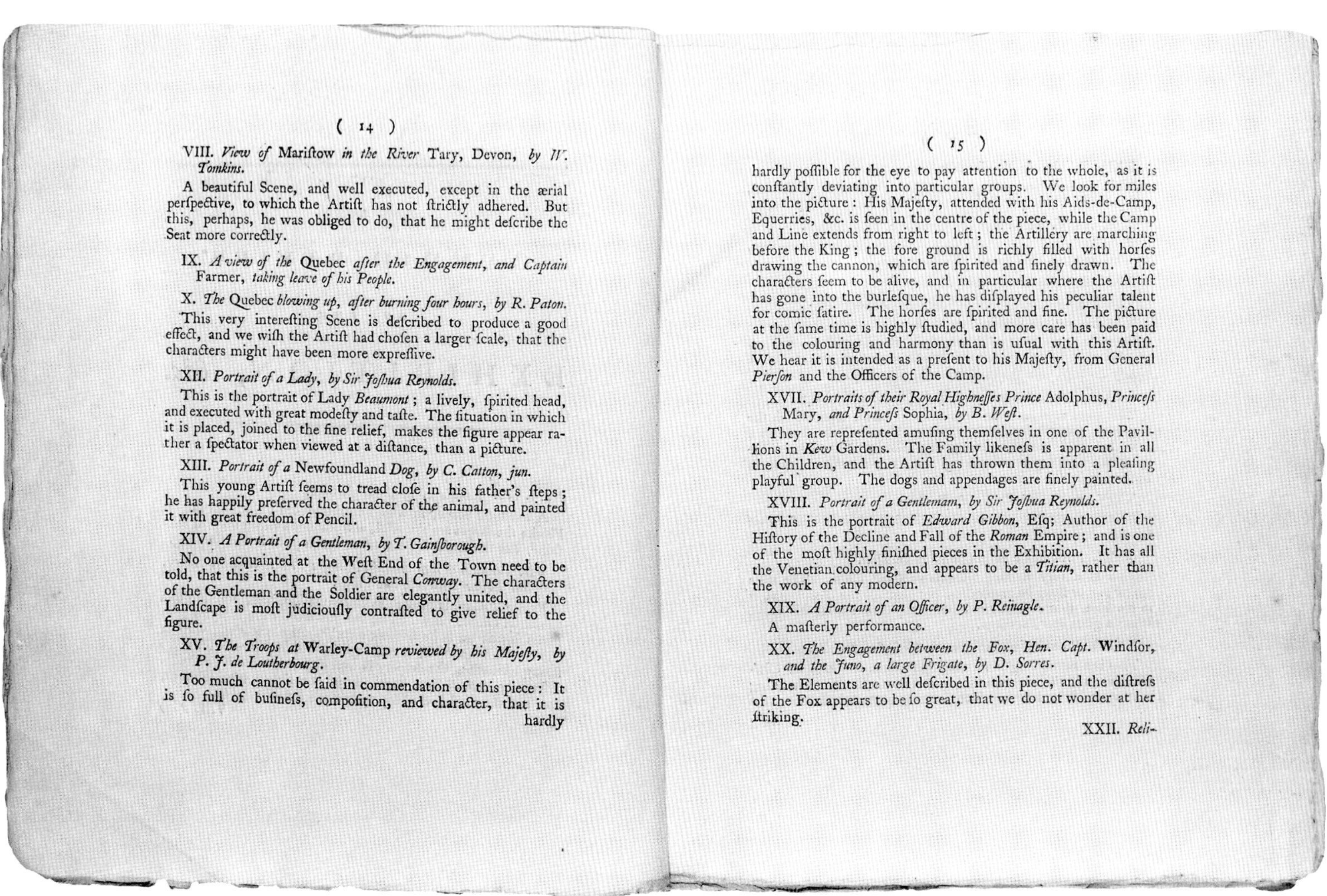

(14)

VIII. *View of* Mariſtow *in the River* Tary, Devon, *by W. Tomkins.*

A beautiful Scene, and well executed, except in the ærial perſpective, to which the Artiſt has not ſtrictly adhered. But this, perhaps, he was obliged to do, that he might deſcribe the Seat more correctly.

IX. *A view of the* Quebec *after the Engagement, and Captain* Farmer, *taking leave of his People.*

X. *The* Quebec *blowing up, after burning four hours, by R. Paton.*

This very intereſting Scene is deſcribed to produce a good effect, and we wiſh the Artiſt had choſen a larger ſcale, that the characters might have been more expreſſive.

XII. *Portrait of a Lady, by Sir Joſhua Reynolds.*

This is the portrait of Lady *Beaumont* ; a lively, ſpirited head, and executed with great modeſty and taſte. The ſituation in which it is placed, joined to the fine relief, makes the figure appear rather a ſpectator when viewed at a diſtance, than a picture.

XIII. *Portrait of a* Newfoundland *Dog, by C. Catton, jun.*

This young Artiſt ſeems to tread cloſe in his father's ſteps ; he has happily preſerved the character of the animal, and painted it with great freedom of Pencil.

XIV. *A Portrait of a Gentleman, by T. Gainſborough.*

No one acquainted at the Weſt End of the Town need to be told, that this is the portrait of General *Conway*. The characters of the Gentleman and the Soldier are elegantly united, and the Landſcape is moſt judiciouſly contraſted to give relief to the figure.

XV. *The Troops at* Warley-Camp *reviewed by his Majeſty, by P. J. de Loutherbourg.*

Too much cannot be ſaid in commendation of this piece : It is ſo full of buſineſs, compoſition, and character, that it is hardly

(15)

hardly poſſible for the eye to pay attention to the whole, as it is conſtantly deviating into particular groups. We look for miles into the picture : His Majeſty, attended with his Aids-de-Camp, Equerries, &c. is ſeen in the centre of the piece, while the Camp and Line extends from right to left ; the Artillery are marching before the King ; the fore ground is richly filled with horſes drawing the cannon, which are ſpirited and finely drawn. The characters ſeem to be alive, and in particular where the Artiſt has gone into the burleſque, he has diſplayed his peculiar talent for comic ſatire. The horſes are ſpirited and fine. The picture at the ſame time is highly ſtudied, and more care has been paid to the colouring and harmony than is uſual with this Artiſt. We hear it is intended as a preſent to his Majeſty, from General *Pierſon* and the Officers of the Camp.

XVII. *Portraits of their Royal Highneſſes Prince* Adolphus, *Princeſs* Mary, *and Princeſs* Sophia, *by B. Weſt.*

They are repreſented amuſing themſelves in one of the Pavilions in *Kew* Gardens. The Family likeneſs is apparent in all the Children, and the Artiſt has thrown them into a pleaſing playful group. The dogs and appendages are finely painted.

XVIII. *Portrait of a Gentlemam, by Sir Joſhua Reynolds.*

This is the portrait of *Edward Gibbon*, Eſq; Author of the Hiſtory of the Decline and Fall of the *Roman* Empire ; and is one of the moſt highly finiſhed pieces in the Exhibition. It has all the Venetian colouring, and appears to be a *Titian*, rather than the work of any modern.

XIX. *A Portrait of an Officer, by P. Reinagle.*

A maſterly performance.

XX. *The Engagement between the Fox, Hen. Capt.* Windſor, *and the Juno, a large Frigate, by D. Sorres.*

The Elements are well deſcribed in this piece, and the diſtreſs of the Fox appears to be ſo great, that we do not wonder at her ſtriking.

XXII. *Reli-*

47 *A Candid Review of the Exhibition (Being the Twelfth) of the Royal Academy*, London 1780, pp. 14–15. By permission of the Syndics of Cambridge University Library.

declares that the pamphlet is dedicated to the king, costs 1s. 6d., has run into two editions and is written by someone named only as 'an artist'. In addition, an eight-page preface reveals the motive for publication as a desire to exploit the interest generated by the Royal Academy's recent move to Somerset House. This preface takes the form of a rhapsodic tour that begins by describing the building's exterior as seen from the Strand. It continues by detailing the contents of the various rooms that visitors would encounter as they proceeded to the exhibition, and it ends with an account of the Great Room itself: 'the grand Exhibition-Room is noble and spacious, measuring about sixty feet by fifty [the writer exaggerates; the actual dimensions are 53 × 43]. It is very judiciously lighted by four arched windows, which distribute an equal light over the whole; the ceiling is painted with a tender Sky, and has a very good effect'.[23] And then, without further notice, the reader is taken through the exhibition itself, beginning with the first catalogued painting, a landscape by Thomas Gainsborough. Continuing onwards, the reader quickly becomes aware of the relentlessly positive tone of the reviewer, and of his tendency to concentrate on the works of the leading Academicians. Even when he dares to criticize adversely an individual painter, his comments are always tentative and polite: '*View of Maristow in the River Tary, Devon, by W. Tomkins.* A beautiful scene, and well executed, except in the aerial perspective, to which the Artist has not strictly adhered. But this, perhaps, he was obliged to do, that he might describe the seat more correctly'. The writer concludes by asserting that he 'has endeavoured to point the Spectator to the features that principally struck him, without descending to minute faults; and if the Review can serve to rescue the Artists from ignorant and uncandid criticism, it will have answered the intention of the Author'.[24] This final admission, together with the effusive paragraphs that precede it, suggests that the *Candid Review* functioned as part of what we might call the Academy's publicity apparatus. Its production may well have been sanctioned by certain senior Academicians, in order to pre-empt anticipated attacks in the press on the institution and its display. A 'review' this may have been, but 'candid' it was not.

It was not long before this puff on behalf of the RA came under satirical attack. The following year saw the appearance of a radically different piece of art criticism in pamphlet form, entitled *The Ear-Wig; or, An Old Woman's Remarks on the Present Exhibition of Pictures of the Royal Academy*. Anonymously published to coincide with the exhibition's opening in 1781, in all probability this was composed by the frustrated history painter Mauritius Lowe, who enjoyed a notoriously troubled and embittered relationship with the Academy even while he exhibited within it, and whose own contribution to this year's display was limited to a pair of drawings on biblical themes.[25] Unsurprisingly, given this context, Lowe's commentary mixed selective praise for certain exhibitors with vicious denunciations of others, and included, as the title page declares, 'observations on the causes of the Decline of the Arts'. Significantly, *The Ear-Wig* ends with a 'description of the Buildings of Somerset House' that is taken almost verbatim from the previous year's *Candid Review*; but here this text functions as an ironic postscript to an extended narrative of artistic in-fighting and dissipation, beginning with a comic and libellous tale about the contemporary painter Johann Zoffany, before the 'Old Woman' lays down the principal theme of her critique. The exhibition, she complains, offers 'the most sterile field for observation I ever beheld, where so many objects glare on the sight, and tawdry yellow vies with dirty red. – I have paid my shilling at the door, I am under no compliment to any of the displayers, so have at them!'[26] After several comments on the failings of modern artists, and on 'the partial, illiberal conduct of the Academicians' that has so 'disgusted' artists like himself, Lowe moves rapidly through the works on display, again beginning with the first of the numbered exhibits, and more often than not condemning their inferior quality in acidic terms: '*2. Gipsey Boy and Girl – W. Burgess*. – A bad black thing – the Devil all over!'[27] is one brief example. Even though certain pictures and certain artists – such as Gainsborough – escape this kind of censure and are described in highly positive ways, overall *The Ear-Wig* is a highly combative, punchy text that questions not only the quality of the exhibition, but also the decorous treatment of the Royal Academy which the *Candid Review* had tried to encourage. Where the earlier pamphlet had constructed an elegant continuum embracing the visitor's passage from the exterior of Somerset House up and into the Great Room, Lowe's aggressive, sceptical and often self-consciously crude running commentary follows the same path to an entirely antithetical conclusion, leaving his readers in no doubt of a shocking shortfall between the grandeur of the spaces without and the aesthetic degradation of those within.

Over the next two decades, the satirical pamphlet review became ever more elaborate and condemnatory, developing into a recognized journalistic genre, and frequently taking the form of verse commentaries on the Academy's contents. From 1782 onwards, the radical polemicist John Wolcot, writing under the name Peter Pindar, produced an innovative series of poetic send-ups of the exhibitions, issued annually under the running title of *Lyric Odes to the Royal Academicians*. Pindar's efforts proved a runaway success, with a collected, enlarged set of the *Odes* reaching a seventh edition by 1787. Other satirists soon followed his example, including 'Anthony Pasquin', whom we have already encountered as the author of *A Liberal Critique on the Present Exhibition of the Royal Academy* from 1794. When we read this text as a whole, rather than the extracts published in the *Morning Chronicle*, we find that it offers a highly politicized condemnation of the Academy exhibition, of its organizers and even of its patron. Stating that his pamphlet has been written to combat 'Tyranny and Corruption' and to 'rescue merit from Oppression', Pasquin makes no bones about the bankruptcy of the current display:

> if the primary places in the exhibition were occupied by works of great and genuine merit, the candid critic would be satisfied, but to behold eternally the most despicable daubings obtruding themselves upon the gazer's eye, and, as it were, saying 'damn you shall look at me', is extremely painful to all those, who would generously prefer talent to stupidity and modesty to impudence . . . how lamentable it is, that there is no precise way of amending this abuse of power.

He then goes on to extend his criticism to no less a figure than George III: 'with the richest monarch in Europe for their patron, the arts of England are literally kept from destruction by the votive shillings of a motley public, who pay the salaries of the professors, and find oil for the lamps in the plaister and living schools, though the king arrogates the character of being the high supporter of the system. But it is a provident assumption of dignity, unaccompanied with either risk, anxiety or expense!'[28] Though hardly a call for revolutionary change, such charges gave voice to a widespread dissatisfaction with the status quo that went far beyond the confines of the art world. In an echo of contemporary developments in and around the Paris Salons, the London exhibition review – whether in newspaper or, even more pointedly and extensively, in pamphlet form – became an instrument of political opposition, implicating the Academy in that broader pattern of corrupt behaviour which contemporary reformists and radicals identified with the governing ministry and the court.[29]

In response, conservative pamphleteers utilized precisely the same satiric strategies to defend the Academy and its officers. Perhaps the most remarkable product of this rearguard action was *The Exhibition* of 1793 by the self-styled 'Timothy Tar-Barrel', who defended the Academic establishment on the grounds that its authority was needed to control the notoriously competitive mass of exhibitors. 'Tar-Barrel' conjures up a grotesque vision of quarrelling painters, engaged in constant combat as they try to hang their pictures in the absence of any Committee of Arrangement: 'Each flew to the place he deemed the best, vociferously asserted his claim, and prepared with violence to defend it. No sooner did one attain the object of his wishes, than he was shouldered from it by another, who in his turn gave way to a third, who in like manner yielded his post to the first, who was again tumbled down by a fourth, and a fifth in endless succession'.[30] Then, as the furore increased in intensity, the artists who had lost their places

> broke, tore and destroyed, whatever was within their reach. And now pictures encountered pictures, and frames engaged frames, and bustos, and marble fragments, flew about like hail-stones, and cast a horrid gloom on the scene of action, while the crash of broken mouldings, and tumbling statues, the cries of the wounded, and the shouts of the victors, united in a noise most tremendous. This multifarious room, which was lately adorned with such an assemblage of art as the whole world beside could not equal, in less than an hour exhibited nothing but ragged canvas, and tattered galliguskins; and a crowd of men, whom genius, with pride and pleasure, called his children, were transformed into a regiment of *Sans Culottes*, fighting for slops in Rag Fair.[31]

Here 'Tar-Barrel' brilliantly and cruelly exposes the aggression and paranoia generated amongst the army of exhibitors by the process of arranging their works.[32] But this apocalyptic vision of disorder also underlines the need for authority and control within the Royal Academy, so as to protect it from the greed and selfishness of individual artists, and – as the final line makes clear – against the wider forces of chaos, destruction and democracy which contemporaries associated with the French Revolution.

The Exhibition was far from being the only text to take sides with the Academy against those pamphleteers and other writers who sought to undermine its institutional and ideological authority. The year 1788, for instance, saw the publication of *The Bee; or, the Exhibition Exhibited in a New Light*, which according to its anonymous author was designed 'to rescue the Arts and their Professors from . . . malevolent influences'.[33] And here it is also worth remembering that Reynolds's annual Discourses to the Academy, which provided a sophisticated theoretical rationale for the institution and its activities, were also published in pamphlet form throughout this period. With so many participants on opposing sides of the debate, the Royal Academy became an important ideological battleground towards the end of the eighteenth century, taking its place among the many sites of cultural confrontation that were, in Terry Eagleton's words, making the 'space of the public sphere . . . much less one of bland consensus than of ferocious contention'.[34]

* * *

One of Anthony Pasquin's many targets in *A Liberal Critique* were his fellow writers on art, who, he claimed, 'know little or nothing about the subject!' It is because of this, or at least so he suggests, that 'our periodical works [are] filled with absurd and destructive criticism'.[35] Although Pasquin's complaint may have been largely justified, he might have been prepared to make an exception for the *Artist's Repository and Drawing Magazine, Exhibiting the Principles of the Polite Arts in their Various Branches*, which the writer and engraver Charles Taylor launched in 1784. Published in instalments over the next decade, and gathered together in a five-volume compilation in 1794, the *Repository* offered its readers a miscellany of textual and visual materials relating to the arts. Its pages contain such things as a guide to drawing, treatises on perspective and architecture, a dictionary of artistic terms, and – most pertinently for us – a mass of essays and reviews. These include a piece entitled 'Hints on Criticism', pocket biographies of famous artists such as Sir Godfrey Kneller and Sir James Thornhill, an 'Essay on Landscape Painting', attacks on 'puffing' and, finally, a series of articles on the Royal Academy and its exhibitions. Perusing its contents, we quickly realize that Taylor's periodical can justifiably be called Britain's first specialist art magazine, addressed to a 'middling' public of readers eager to learn how to look at and discuss the visual arts. At the same time, its pages betray the dialectic that we have identified as structuring the journalistic art criticism of this period, in which reviews of the Academy exhibitions espoused cultural consensus and improvement on the one hand, and betrayed the anxieties and tensions of a fragmenting cultural sphere on the other.

As a publication devoted to providing its audience with a varied knowledge of the visual arts for use in polite conversation, the *Artist's Repository* provided a rather different context for commentaries on the Somerset House displays from either the newspaper or the pamphlet. Here the reviews were framed by historical accounts that located the Academy shows within that civilizing process of which the *Repository* saw itself as a part, and to which its urban readership of art lovers was confidently assumed to subscribe. With the onset of regular exhibitions, Taylor suggests, 'connoisseurs, and picture-dealers, no longer bore their former sway in raising, or in ruining an artist's reputation, and future; their interference was discarded: the public sought after those masters whose labours had most interested their regard. A visible improvement in every department of art, was the consequence of this encouragement; and each succeeding exhibition demonstrated the talents of the British artists, and their grateful returns to the fostering care of a discerning public'. He goes on to argue that 'Exhibitions have contributed greatly to the cultivation of a national taste among us, which is apparent, from our improvements on former productions, and in the spread of judgement and attention to the arts among genteel society'. If shows of modern art had helped foster a sense of social collectivity by their promotion of an aesthetic literacy that was both English and genteel, Taylor no doubt saw his own publication as contributing to the same agenda. To succeed in this venture, he proposes, requires a careful avoidance of that politicized and belligerent language which marked so much contemporary art-criticism: approaching the subject of the Academy exhibition, he explains that, 'as our intention is not to raise one artist by depreciating another, or to serve the purpose of party of any kind, or in any instance, we shall steer clear of many disagreeable circumstances which the critics of the day are involved in'.

Yet when it comes to reviewing the shows themselves, we discover the magazine using precisely that fraught language of corruption, alienation and abuse that Taylor seems so firmly to reject. For the *Repository* interweaves its praise of the exhibition as a phenomenon with a far darker account of the schisms and dissension that have characterized the Royal Academy's recent history, and that threaten to undermine the continuing legitimacy of its annual displays as a central forum of artistic display and polite taste. In 1785, for instance, the magazine proclaims its sympathy with the current unhappiness with the Academy felt by such leading painters as Thomas Gainsborough, Joseph Wright of Derby and John Singleton Copley; 'these artists,' it is noted, 'in conjunction with Mr Stubbs and others, are said to meditate a severe revenge'. The *Repository*'s critic – presumably Taylor himself – then proceeds to offer a scathing review of the works that are on view, commenting that there are 'very few excellent performances', and concludes by lamenting that the British School has broken down into a multiplicity of warring factions. Like some of the reformist critics I have cited above, Taylor lays the blame for this on the Academy's corrupt leadership, and its refusal to further the careers of those outside its own charmed ranks: 'O for a liberal, a public spirit, which should reward *merit* not men: which by healing breaches, by soothing the offended, by concord, by affection, by esteem, should attract, and unite, as it were, in one resplendent form, the merit and abilities of British artists!'[36] The following year, after noting that 'out of Forty academicians only fifteen exhibit', and questioning whether the results can properly be called an Academy exhibition at all, he again exclaims 'O! For a recipe to restore harmony among British Artists!'[37]

In observing that even the most avowedly polite, didactic and culturally inclusive periodical could not resist engaging with the political and personal conflicts in the contemporary art world, we find final confirmation of the two contradictory impulses that informed the writing of exhibition reviews: a desire to promote the annual presentation of the latest British art as the means of forging an expanding art public into a consensual community of taste; and a compulsion to reveal the stark discrepancy between the audience's desires *as* a public and the lack of 'public' spirit on the part of the Academy itself. Yet the *Repository*'s plaintive cries for help also suggest a response to the Academy exhibition that is deeply pessimistic in a way that we have not yet encountered. For Taylor, the experience of walking around the Great Room and gazing at its laden walls, rather than being eloquent of that shared artistic and cultural enterprise suggested at first sight by the massed ranks of canvases on display, served, ironically enough, to suggest the *absence* of those paintings and painters whose works might have provided a more intellectually and emotionally satisfying focus for the visitor's gaze. On this reading, the sheer optical excess of the spectacle generated not so much a reassuring sense of artistic, aesthetic and cultural plenitude – although this is the utopian vision it might seem to hold up – but rather a profound sense of lack and of disappointment, and a powerful awareness of what was missing. Here, surely, we can recognize not only a specific grievance about the politics and the products of the late eighteenth-century art world, but also the beginnings of a distinctively modern suspicion of the spectacle in urban, commercialized society, and of the spurious promises it makes to the uninformed eye.

* * *

On 30 May 1794, a writer in the *Morning Post*, reviewing the Academy exhibition, bemoaned the current state of art criticism itself:

> The business of Criticism seems in the present day not a little perverted and disguised; its original office must have been the calm, and candid discussion of the claims of genius and assiduity to public favour and protection. Liberality held, with even hand, the balance of judgement. . . . It has now almost universally degenerated into fulsome and ignorant panegyric, and rancorous and undistinguishing abuse. The modern Critic is a malignant being, prompt to wound, and unprepared to judge. He covers his ignorance under the cloak of general censure, and struts in all the pedantry of misapplied technicals and hackneyed remarks. To feel the beauties of a Work of Art, and hold them up to fame, requires an enlightened and liberal mind – an Ass can bray forth abuse.[38]

These words eloquently suggest the continuing desire of late eighteenth-century English art critics to encourage a virtuous traffic of ideas and values among painters, spectators and readers that is magically uninfected by either hyperbole or vituperation, and so help to fabricate and maintain a consensual public sphere. Yet, of course, the writer's nostalgic yearning for a lost golden age of criticism, and his castigation of other modern critics, suggests quite how unrealizable this ideal had come to seem; for by now the spaces of artistic display and critical discussion had instead become a battlefield of deeply polarized interests. Though Somerset House may have tried to project the image of a peaceful temple to 'enlightened and liberal' values, it could not stand above the fray of an ideologically fractured and politically antagonistic visual and literary culture.

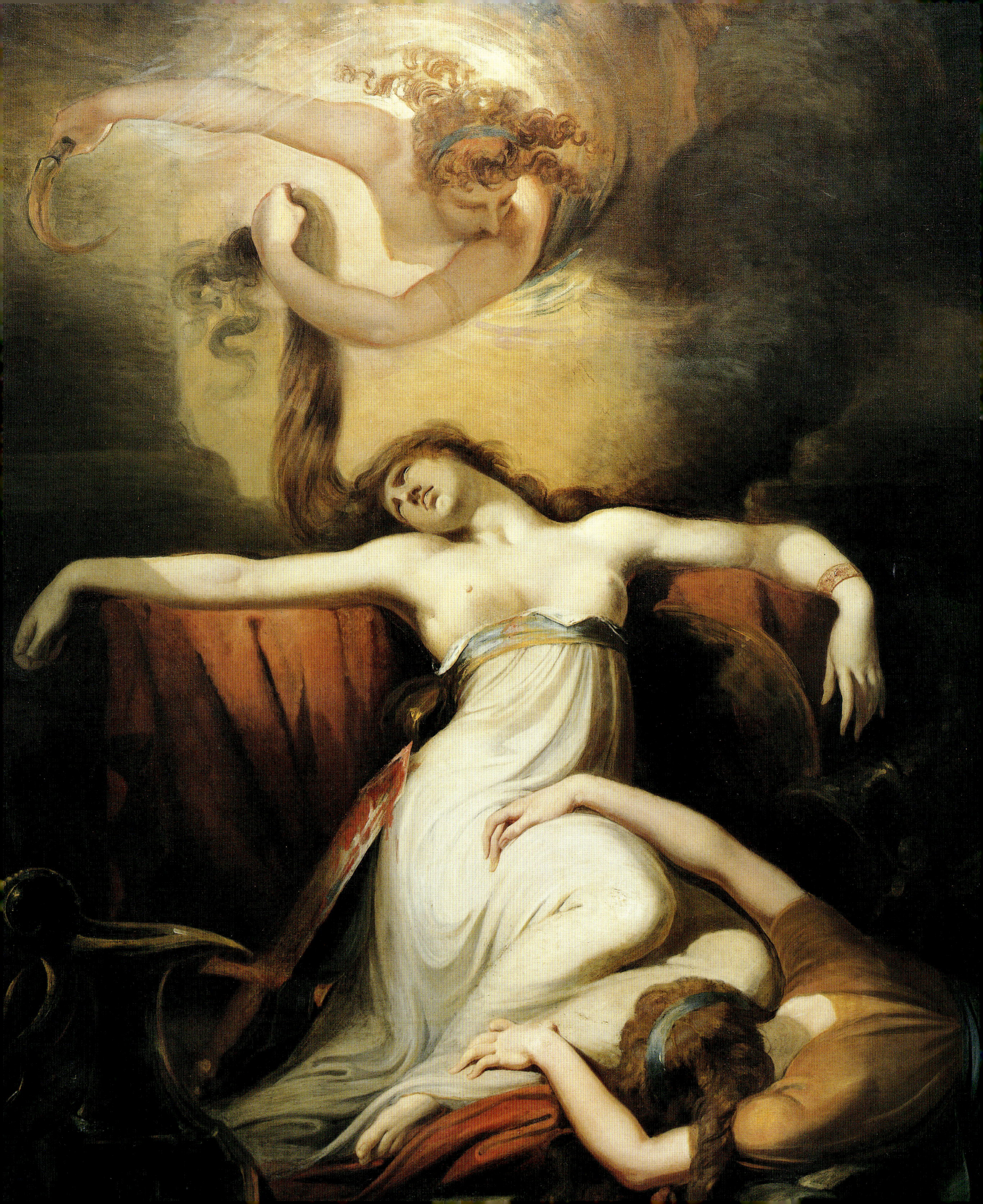

6

The Sublime as Spectacle: The Transformation of Ideal Art at Somerset House

MARTIN MYRONE

THE OPENING OF THE NEW ROYAL ACADEMY at Somerset House in 1780 can be seen as a moment of triumph for officially ordained high culture in Britain. With its exuberant and sophisticated use of the classical orders, the building itself constituted an exultant proclamation of the Academy's privileged relationship with the elevated cultural traditions of ancient Greece and Rome, Renaissance Italy and seventeenth-century France. Inside, this new building provided an ennobling setting for the institution's rather ramshackle collection of casts after antique masterpieces, while the decorations by Academicians referred to and celebrated the conventions of idealized art. The Academy's teaching rooms would, it was hoped, be the breeding ground of a new generation of high-minded artists, steeped in the best traditions, while the new Great Room was to be a forum for their best achievements. The visitors who made the arduous journey up the great spiralling staircase were forcibly, even physically, made aware that this was a journey upwards towards the heights of culture, and still then warned by the inscription at the end of the ascent: 'Let No Stranger to the Muses Enter'.

The ideas of permanence, trans-historical cultural value and intellectual progress given physical form by William Chambers at Somerset House were at the heart of the Academy's pedagogic programme, expressed in the lectures of the various professors, its procedural teaching, and of course in Sir Joshua Reynolds's *Discourses*. During the eighteenth century at least, the Academy's official spokesmen all subscribed in their different ways to the notion that there was an ideal in art, which could be achieved by emulating the examples provided by antiquity and the Renaissance. If, in historical perspective and with a critical eye, we can recognize that this ideal was far from assured, and was rather unstable, incoherent and politically loaded, it was nevertheless a persistent presence in Academic thinking. The Academy was founded and operated on the basis that the ideal in art was achievable; this possibility had to exist for the institution to make sense. As Reynolds asserted in his third *Discourse*, delivered in 1770, the ideal had a substantive presence that was unaffected by the vagaries of culture and language:

> The Moderns are not less convinced than the Ancients of this superior power existing in the art; nor less sensible of its effects. Every language has adopted terms expressive of this excellence. The *gusto grande* of the Italians, the *beau ideal* [*sic*] of the French, and the *grand style*, *genius*, and *taste* among the English, are but different appellations of the same thing.[1]

Reynolds was acutely conscious that his own writing emerged from a tradition of literature on ideal art, stemming from sixteenth-century Italy but most influentially codified by the French Académie in the late seventeenth century. Implicated in this conception of a trans-cultural ideal of the *grand style* is a strict systemization of the various branches of visual art that Sir Joshua himself, for very significant reasons, skirts around. That different kinds of art could be ranked in a hierarchy of genres had been stated most forcibly by the Secretary of the Académie, André Félibien:

> he who paints fine landskips, is above him who paints Fruits, Flowers, or Shells: He who paints after Life is more to be regarded than he who only represents still Life; and as the Figure of a Man is the most perfect Work of God upon Earth, it is also certain that he who imitates God in painting human Figures, is by far more excellent than all others. Moreover

Fuseli, *The Death of Dido*. Detail of fig. 56.

though it be no small Matter to make the Picture of a Man appear as if it was alive, and to give the Appearance of Motion to that which has none; one who can only draw portraits, has not as yet attained to this high Perfection of Art, and cannot pretend to the same Honour with abler Painters. He must for that end advance from Painting one single Figure, to draw several together; he must paint History and Fable; he must represent great Actions like an Historian, or agreeable ones as the Poets. And soaring yet higher, he must by allegorical Compositions, know how to hide under the Vail [*sic*] of Fable the Virtues of great Men, and the most sublime Mysteries. He is esteemed a great Painter who acquits himself well in Enterprizes of this Kind.[2]

By this measure the Great Room should annually have been filled with the most ennobling kinds of art works: grandly conceived allegorical, historical and literary works conveying their narrative content with the incisive lucidity of the poet or historian. Yet while Félibien and his forebears were writing in the context of monarchical, courtly or religious authority, Reynolds and his contemporaries were operating in a quite different setting. Despite the Royal nomenclature, the Academy did not have the legislative, authoritarian backing of the French and other continental academies. Moreover, where ideal art had previously, in principle and principally, been addressed to an elite minority who claimed the authority of representing the 'public', England's Royal Academy existed in a period of rapid commercialization, in which art was increasingly seen as a commodity and addressed to a large, anonymous, multitude of consumers. Neither state nor Church nor king provided much in the way of regular work for artists. As was frequently noted, the Great Room, far from being a site for the exclusive exercise of taste by a narrow elite acquainted with 'the Muses', was more like a shop window for artists scrabbling, often frantically, for public attention, acclaim and therefore business. The annual exhibitions and the surrounding critical discourse, maintained by gossip, scandal and trashy journalism as much as by the Academicians themselves, became, therefore, a space for cultural conflict and aggression. Ideal art, by definition privileged and precious, was subjected simultaneously to a variety of agendas, motivated by commercial, aesthetic and political imperatives.

The Academy's relocation to Somerset House provided the occasion for Reynolds to restate the supreme value of the great style in a special Discourse delivered, not as usual at the prize-giving ceremony for the students, but separately on the official opening of the Academy's new rooms on 16 October 1780.[3] Here Somerset House is represented as a monumental statement of cultural ambition, founded upon, but not to be identified with, commercial enterprise. While Reynolds acknowledges that 'Trade and its consequential riches' provide the material wealth that underwrites high culture, he insists that the most supreme artistic achievements be addressed to the intellect, rather than the senses. Commercial activity provides man with sensual comforts, raises him above his natural, primitive state, but does not certainly lead on to 'purity of manners'. Rather, all enlightened members of society share a moral responsibility to go beyond mere comfort to attain a higher, intellectual, state of 'Virtue'. In art this path leads to the ideal, which requires the exercise of severe and self-sacrificing moral faculties.

Why should Reynolds have been so concerned with this theme at the opening of the Academy at Somerset House? First, and foremost, his speech reiterates the moral centrality of the artist in national life. While art, as Sir Joshua points out, has a peculiar capacity to feed the senses, it also has the capacity for moral instruction, and to be the source of national pride. Indeed, it is the very susceptibility of art to consumerist desires that puts so great a burden on the artist – at least the artist who operates under the aegis of the Academy. Reynolds's ninth *Discourse* is not so much an abstract statement of the ideal as a pertinent warning to his students and colleagues about the dangers of allowing their art to be too consumed with sensuality – a theme taken up and greatly elaborated with reference to the topic of sculpture in his next discourse, delivered at the prize-giving ceremony two months later.

In a typical sign of compromise, Reynolds does not identify this ideal of art with a particular genre, unlike his French predecessors and many of his British contemporaries. Both James Barry and Henry Fuseli, in their lectures as Professors of Painting, emphatically reasserted the supremacy of history painting, as did many reviewers of the Academy's exhibitions, albeit more indirectly, as Mark Hallett has shown in the previous chapter. Even well into the nineteenth century, when the absence of ideal art in the annual shows elicited perennial complaints, reporters would sometimes open their accounts by literally counting up the number of idealizing images on display.[4] But even this ostensibly simple task proved anything but straightforward, given the presence of so many hybrid works on the Academy's walls. If the pursuit of higher, universal truths often had to be blended with a concern for the particular appearances of more 'common' nature, this was simply because in modern Britain practical support was lacking for the type of art conventionally identified with the ideal: large-scale paintings of subjects taken from elevated literary sources or the most important events from history.

Since the foundation of the Academy, it had become painfully obvious that the material encouragement necessary for the expensive and time-consuming production of history paintings was not going to appear. Following the failure of a scheme to decorate St Paul's Cathedral with religious paintings in 1772, Reynolds acknowledged in private that the aim of making 'historical painters' was almost bound to be frustrated.[5] Similarly, two years later, Chambers was drily warning that it would soon be necessary to create a 'hospital' to care for the young artists whose hopes were raised by the Academy, but who were finding little employment in the higher forms of artistic practice.[6] Even as the Academy moved into the most grandiose public building in London, even as the institution gained financial stability, and even as the Academy's institutional supremacy was confirmed, its own President could not bring himself publicly and explicitly to state that contemporary painters should be producing history paintings.

Indeed, the move to Somerset House served only to draw even greater attention to the Academy's failure to catalyse the material support needed for the production of high art. If intended as an exemplification of the Academy's leading role in the cultural progress of the nation, as a public exhibition space Somerset House soon acquired a host of negative associations. Conveniently close to the fashionable West End, the Royal Academy was only one place to go alongside the miscellany of displays and events available during the London season, and it was criticized for encouraging blatant idiosyncrasy among both the public and the participating artists. In traditional art theory, artistic competition and emulation were essential in order to maintain the continuity of the great style. Although the Great Room offered a space where that kind of competition could take place, it was sometimes remarked that the presence of a motley and undiscriminating crowd encouraged artists to adopt aggressive strategies which went beyond the bounds of laudable improvement. In a pamphlet called *The Ear-Wig*, prompted by the exhibition of 1781, the failed history painter Mauritius Lowe made this fear explicit:

> The desire of Distinction, which is one of the most laudable and most efficacious motives in the progress of the Polite arts, may perhaps be also one of the causes most prejudicial to their glory and preservation . . . all have not the genius and abilities necessary to obtain their end: but those, in some measure, by their intrigues, and by their singularity, procure the attention of the spectators; they comply with the cry of the multitude, who require novelty: and at length, by a blameable complaisance, procure admirers and patrons.[7]

A similar point of view can be found in a letter written two years later by Andrew Skiddy of Chelsea to John Strange, the British diplomatic resident at Venice, himself a congenial host to a number of artists and a keen collector of old masters. Skiddy provides a vivid characterization of the exhibition as the site of fashionable display:

> there is a fashionable Rage which seems to prevail here for some late years, which is gratified at the moderate Expence of a Shilling a Visit. I mean the different Exhibitions of the Works of English Artists. . . . To these Places of Publick Resort, do People Flock in a forenoon to saunter about gazing at each other as at any other kind of Route, and now and then perhaps look with admiration on an *Outré* Piece, that on account of its staring Colours and sharp unnatural Angles would *attrappe* their Notice sooner than the most chaste and most classical piece in your Collection.[8]

In much the same vein, in 1780 the novelist Henry Mackenzie published an extended attack on contemporary 'figure-making' that encompassed pictorial production:

> the garish light of some paintings, the unnatural *chiaro scuro* of others . . . in short, all those sins against nature and simplicity, which artists of inferior merit are glad to practice, in order to extort the notice of the public, and to make a figure by surprise and singularity.[9]

Especially after its removal to Somerset House, the Academy was frequently projected as a site of social play and display that promoted a collapse, into a single all-embracing spectacle, of the distinctions between fashionable social practice and artistic practice. As early reports of the exhibitions testify, the very heat and noise and crush of the crowd, combined with the overbearing impression of pictorial profusion on the walls, sometimes created conditions of extreme discomfort. The Great Room could present an experience of unity, but not the abstract unity of form and narrative, spectatorial subjectivity and objectified virtue, projected by the discourse on ideal art; here contemporaries encountered a disorienting, modernistic blurring of the senses, a veritable maelstrom that sacrificed academic principles to a regime of competing visual sensations.

Even as Reynolds in the ninth *Discourse* strives to assert the values of the ideal, he obliquely acknowledges this potential disruption of cultural order. Recognizing the destructuring of artistic hierarchy encouraged by the market and the exhibitions, he shies away from prescription with regard to the genres and asserts instead that the ideal is essentially no more than a matter of form, a way of making pictures that denies the sensual. At the same time, the index of value that Félibien and other earlier commentators assigned to the hierarchy of genres is transferred by Reynolds to a more elusive and imprecise framework of moral responsibilities. Instead of proactively attending to an ordained, structured route to the ideal, as Reynolds presents it the modern artist should be more concerned to react to the threats of the sensual 'appetite', and strive against them to approach higher truths. The Great Room, which simultaneously asserted the authority of the Academy and offered a forum for the experience of sensual delight, forced artists to confront this challenge.

Much art presented at the Somerset House exhibitions conformed in fairly unequivocal ways to the most stringent definition of the ideal. With the right kinds of material support (royal patronage above all), Benjamin West in particular was able to produce paintings on religious and literary themes that were assured reiterations of the form and content of an authoritarian great style (e.g., figs 24 and 48). On the other hand, there was still more, much more, art that could not be said by any means to conform to this ideal – fashionable portraits, landscapes and comic genre pieces, for instance. But it would be a mistake to suggest a simple, sharp opposition between the rare instances of ideal art proper and a mass of market-led imagery (although this

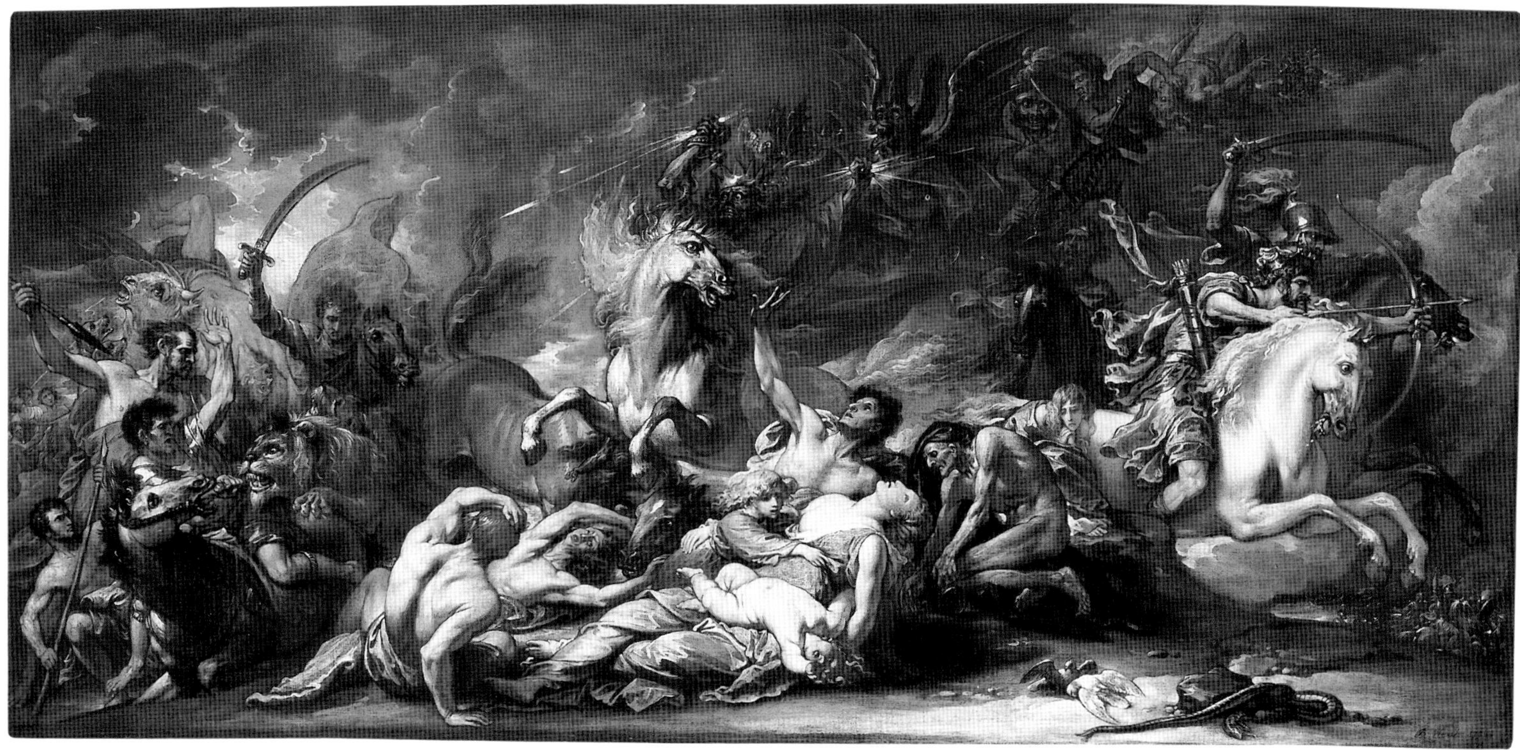

48 Benjamin West, *Death on the Pale Horse*, RA 1796. The Detroit Institute of Arts, Founders Society Purchase, Robert H. Tannahill Foundation Fund.

was often how it was described at the time). For Reynolds himself, the genre of allegorical or 'grand manner' portraits allowed for the production of paintings that mimicked the formal appearance of historical paintings while also attending to the financial imperatives of portraiture (e.g., fig. 49). During this period, portraiture became aggrandized and even occasionally put on a par by critics with ideal art more traditionally defined. Reynolds's own concern with the formal (rather than content-based) qualities of the ideal provided theoretical licence for this development. Modern-life scenes from West's *Death of Wolfe* (1770; exhibited RA 1771; fig. 50) onwards provided elevated subject matter that was understood by a broad audience much less familiar with the ancient literary and historical themes that were posited as the most appropriate basis for ideal painting. Likewise encompassing both portraiture and a narrative element, theatrical subjects also provided a means of producing a high-minded art that was none the less responsive to the peculiarities of contemporary public taste. While it would be a valuable undertaking to survey the transformation of the high genres of art under the influence of the Academy exhibitions, here I am concerned with a much more specific issue: the emergence of works intended for public exhibition which both conformed to an elevated conception of narrative art and, through their use of sensational, supernatural or horrific imagery, addressed a consumer society concerned primarily with painting and sculpture as sophisticated forms of visual entertainment.

The reality of commercial spectacle and sensation was accommodated to a revised notion of ideal art through the eighteenth-century notion of the sublime, the aesthetic celebration of danger, grandeur and horror for its stimulating effects. As defined most famously by Edmund Burke – though his voice was only one of many – the sublime was an aesthetic which represented and articulated a profoundly felt anxiety about uncertainty and change. By the late eighteenth century the term had become commonplace in the improvised, informal and often half-baked writing that then passed as art criticism, where it typically functioned as a 'buzzword' that had a certain currency without being fully theorized. As far as artistic practice was concerned, the sublime can probably best be described as a certain kind of effect which had more to do with manipulating public and critical response than with attending to some pre-ordained theoretical prescription.

The task of investigating this sensationalist, sublime idealizing art requires reference to specific examples. To that end, I want to consider three cases of artists who deliberately produced 'sublime' works to further their own ambitions, and who in so doing dramatized the operations of late eighteenth- and early nineteenth-century exhibition culture. The names of two of these individuals, James Northcote and Henry Fuseli, are still relatively familiar today. My final example, the sculptor Thomas Procter, is now virtually unknown; but his career as an exhibitor presents an especially pertinent instance of the transformations of ideal art in the context of the Great Room at Somerset House.

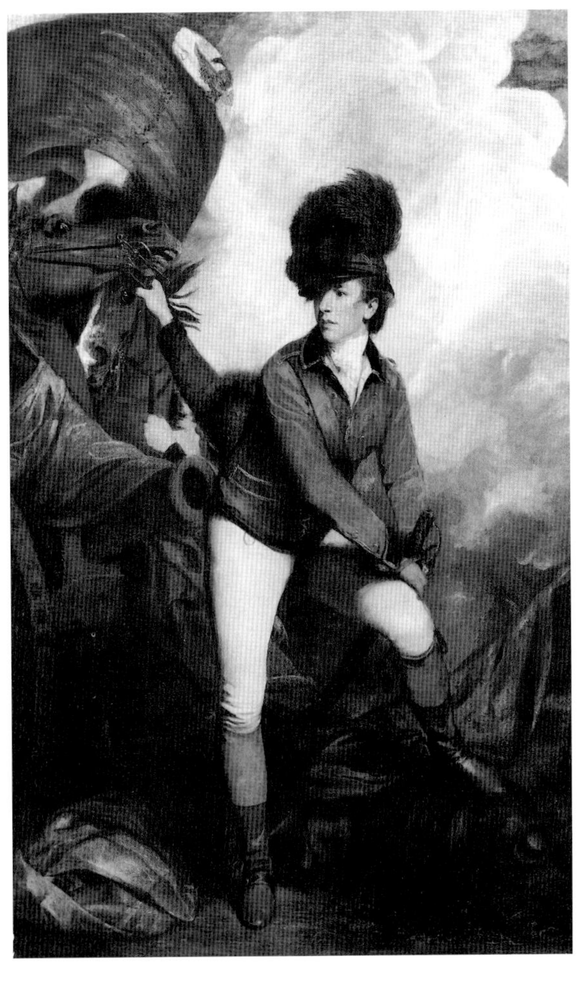

The career of James Northcote in many ways encapsulates the history of the British art scene during the reign of George III. Reaching artistic maturity at the end of the 1760s, Northcote studied at the Academy, trained under Reynolds himself (whose Discourses he transcribed into good copies for his master), and like many of his generation, buoyed up by the promise of the Academy, went to Italy in 1777 with the intention of becoming a history painter in an idealized mode. He was not alone in finding that ambition thwarted in practice. After three years studying in Rome, Northcote returned home in 1780 and set about relaunching his career. In an extensive memoir drawn up later in life, he described his financial situation at that crucial juncture:

> James so managed his expences during the time he was out of England that at his return to his native country he was without money having spent the whole of what he acquired before by his industry previous to his travels, as none of his time when abroad had been employed to the purpose of getting money but solely in the way which he thought would promote his improvement in his Art and literally he had not two Guineas left at his return.[10]

Back in England Northcote, now aged thirty-three, first re-used the strategy which had served him so well in the mid-1770s: he

49 *(left)* Sir Joshua Reynolds, *Lieutenant-Colonel Bannastre Tarleton*, RA 1782. National Gallery, London.

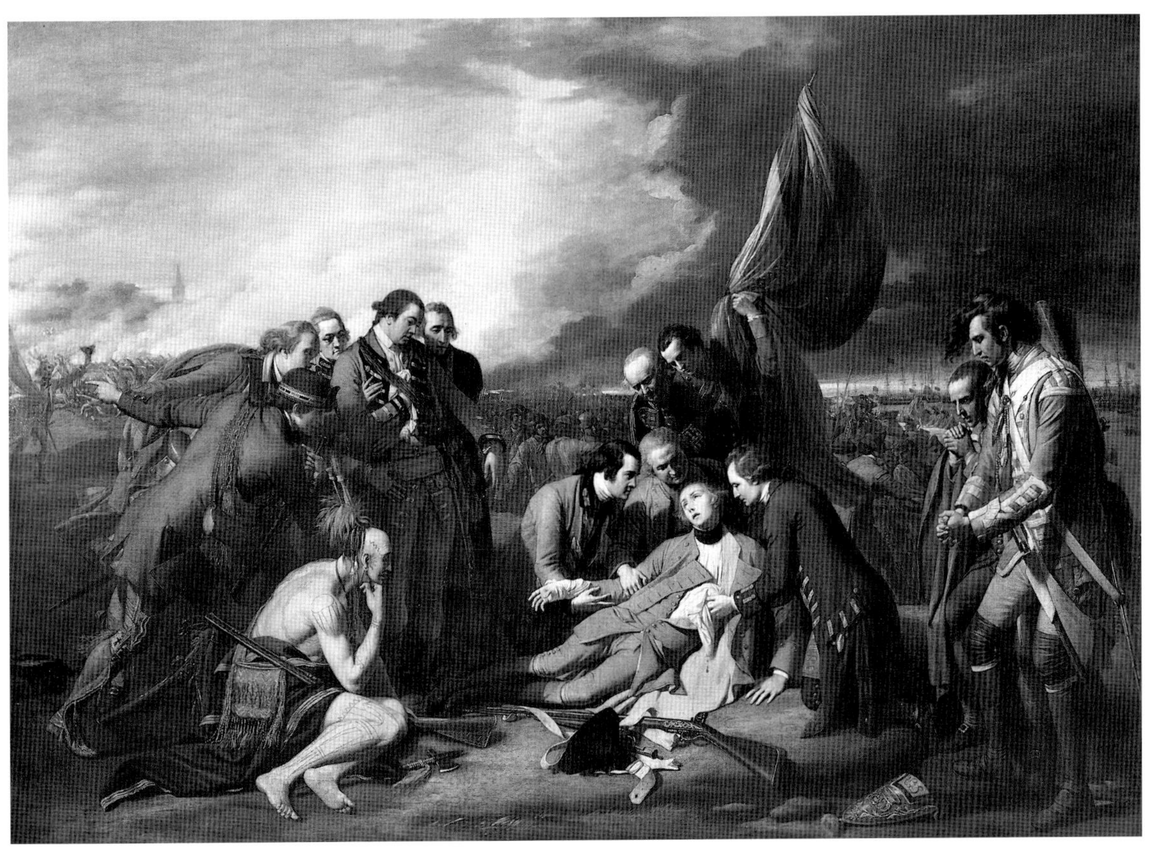

50 Benjamin West, *The Death of General Wolfe*, 1770, RA 1771. National Gallery of Canada, Ottawa. Transfer from the Canadian War Memorials, 1921 (Gift of the 2nd Duke of Westminster, Eaton Hall, Cheshire, 1918).

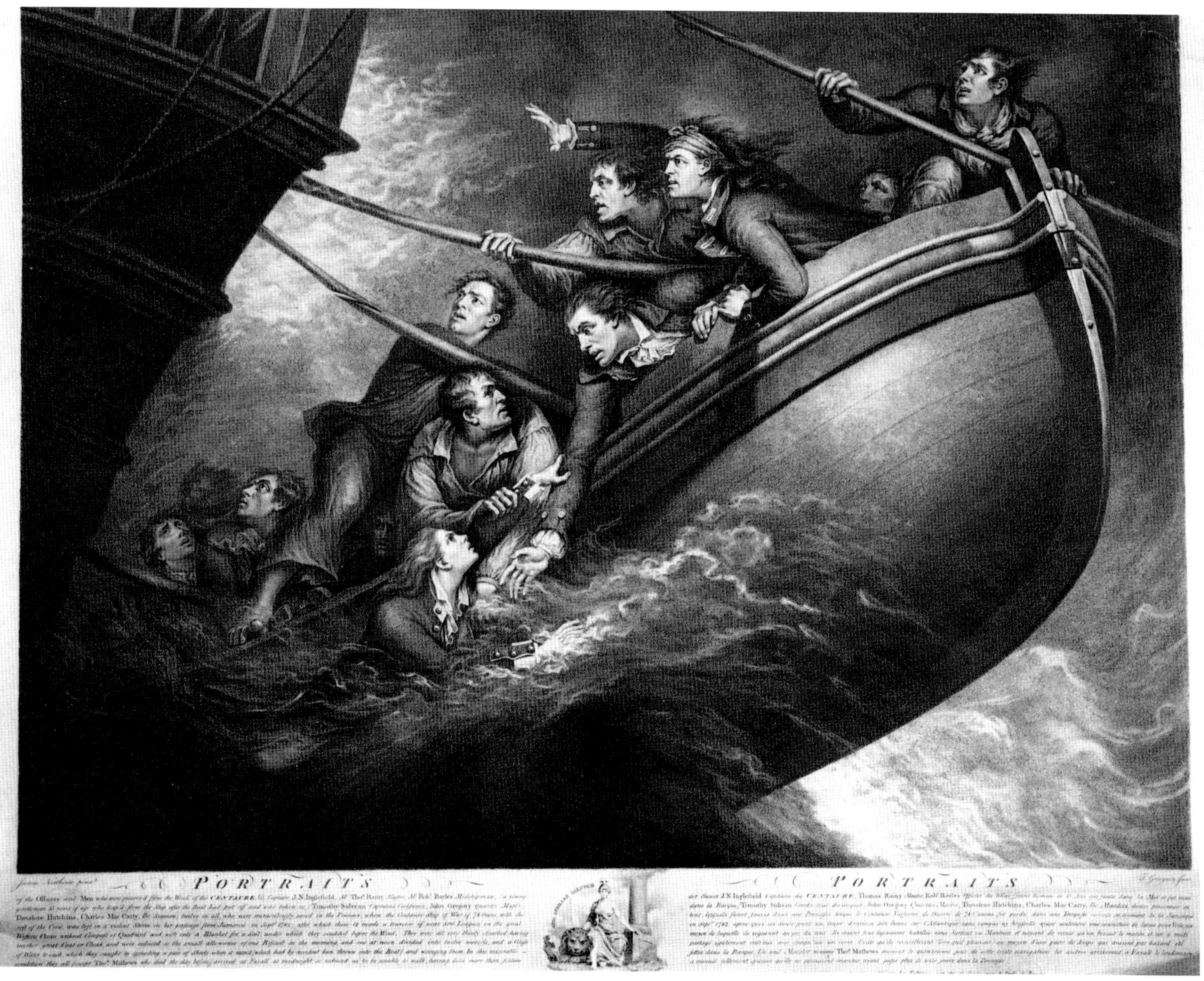

51 Thomas Gaugain after James Northcote, *Portraits Painted from Life, Representing Capt. Englefield with Eleven of his Crew Saving Themselves in the Pinnace, from the Wreck of the Centaur, of 74 Guns, Lost Sept. 1782*, stipple of 1784 after lost original exhibited RA 1784. The caption notes that 'The Size of the Picture is 12 Feet by 8 Feet 5 inches'.

returned to his native Devon and painted portraits of the local gentry. Such a provincial career did not, however, bring great rewards in terms of money or social status, so Northcote went again to London. There he faced apparently insurmountable challenges in the portrait market. Reynolds, Gainsborough and George Romney dominated high-class portraiture, and John Opie was on the rise, aided and abetted by the critic John Wolcot ('Peter Pindar') – who had, just to make things worse, turned against Northcote. In his memoir, the latter wrote:

> James being in the awkward state before described and deprived of all resource in the line of portrait painting, betook himself from necessity to painting small historical and fancy subjects from the most popular authours [*sic*] of the day, as such subjects are sure sale amongst the minor print dealers.[11]

Here he refers to an underworld of small-scale art business, rather than the public arena of the exhibitions; this was work undertaken, he goes on to say, only for want of 'higher employment'. The artist's solution to this problematic situation was to paint a 'large composition which should demand the attention of the publick at the Exhibition of the Royal Academy'.[12] The work he conceived was the large painting he exhibited in 1784 under the title *Portraits Painted from Life, Representing Capt. Englefield with Eleven of his Crew Saving Themselves in the Pinnace, from the Wreck of the Centaur, of 74 Guns, Lost Sept. 1782* (fig. 51).

As E. F. Burney's visual record of the exhibition suggests, this canvas must have dominated the exhibition space (see fig. 19). The sheer scale of the image meant that it had to be hung on the line in the middle of one of the walls of the Great Room; here, given the hanging procedures, it would be the central work around which all the others were arranged. In terms of subject matter, the picture made an equally insistent call upon the public's attention. Captain Englefield was a celebrity; in 1782 he had been crossing the Atlantic in the *Centaur* loaded with booty won in war when the ship was struck by a hurricane. Englefield and eleven of his crew escaped, and though he faced a court-martial on his return, he was cleared and proclaimed a hero – and thus an appropriate subject for the most noble form of art.

This episode is notable in a number of respects. Despite the ambitions that had taken him to Rome, the evidence is that the production of this large-scale painting on a heroic theme was for Northcote more a career tactic than a vocational choice. Faced with a lack of patronage the artist turned directly to the public at large, with a work calculated to occupy an important position in the Academy's Great Room and so to attract the notice of visitors. On that level, Northcote certainly succeeded. Press reviews were generally favourable, and the painter was on a number of occasions pronounced a 'rising star'.[13] But instead of undertaking this project in the high-minded spirit proposed by his mentor Reynolds, he had quite self-consciously endeavoured to 'demand the attention of the publick'. The scale of the work, its knowing references to the grand manner (for instance, the pose of Michelangelo's Sistine Chapel *Jonah* is here reversed and recast in the third figure from the left), and its dramatic narrative all served to situate Northcote in relation to a tradition of elevated picture-making. His theme, however, was a modern subject taken from contemporary news reports, and its realization entailed the significant employment of the conventions of portraiture. Northcote himself seems to have attached an explanatory plaque headed 'Portraits' to the picture frame, as this is visible in Burney's drawing and reproduced in the engraving. By representing actual individuals, rather than invented literary characters or historical personages of established significance, Northcote was compromising the ideal of history painting as abstracting and paradigmatic. There were obvious precedents for this hybrid manner in the recent works of West and Copley among others, and discussion about the propriety of depicting elevated narratives in contemporary dress was current in the period. More peculiar to the *Capt. Englefield* is its sensationalism. The extraordinary, quite ludicrous tilt of the lifeboat, the dramatic gestures and expressions of the figures, and the bold simplicity of the composition as a whole all contrived to give the image a striking presence in the midst of the portraits, landscapes and figure subjects arranged on the wall around it. The same elements also conformed to the emerging taste for the sublime, so often expressed in reference to storms and the overwhelming effects of nature. Hence this picture, which Northcote felt had established his reputation in London, was made to operate simultaneously on a number of different fronts: it tapped into popular interest in a recent news event, and cast that event as a sublime phenomenon; and aside from exploiting the recently established vogue for elevated modern-life painting, it engineered an extremely dramatic visual presence in the Great Room. In his memoirs, Northcote presented the production of *Capt. Englefield* as an effort to release himself from the market for less elevated kinds of portraiture. Yet if it did ensure his release (and after 1784 Northcote secured a number of important commissions for historical compositions) the work itself is surely the kind of *outré* piece that Andrew Skiddy must have had in mind.

Northcote went on to produce a number of similarly ambitious canvases on literary and historical themes, particularly for John Boydell. His *Murder of Wat Tyler* (fig. 52), almost equal to *Capt. Englefield* in terms of Baroque excess, was clearly a dominant presence in the 1787 exhibition, to judge from Martini's engraving (see fig. 35). But Northcote's primary occupation remained that of a portrait painter. In this respect he was typical of most artists of his generation who, whatever the Academy might have led them to believe, all too rarely had the chance to practise in the highest genre.

One of Northcote's close contemporaries did, however, work almost entirely in the field of literary and imaginative narrative painting: the Swiss-born Henry Fuseli. Whereas Northcote undertook a conventional training in art, both at the Academy and with a leading London master, Fuseli was what one might call a 'surprise invader', an artist 'alien' to the metropolitan art world and its institutions, who was welcomed as an invigorating force by the establishment.[14] Fuseli did not have any formal art training, and after coming to England in the 1760s first established himself as a translator and writer. He then left for Italy where he spent most of the 1770s; here he did little in the way of serious art study but a great deal in the way of self-promotion, before launching himself as a painter in London at the precise moment when the Academy took up its new quarters at Somerset House. From 1780 until his death in 1825 Fuseli was a constant presence at the annual exhibitions, quickly becoming and remaining one of the most talked-about of artists, with every exhibit drawing acclaim and criticism in roughly equal measure. Soon he became virtually a brand-name, to the extent that other artists were regularly identified as purveyors of the 'Fusilesque'.[15] Fuseli was identified above all with supernatural and horrific subjects, most famously with the *Nightmare* (RA 1782; fig. 53), but also with the picturing of obscure and sublime scenes from Shakespeare, Milton and the classics; he also drew on even more arcane themes from medieval literature or legend, such as *Percival Delivering Belisane from the Enchantment of Urma* (RA 1783; fig. 54). Critics came to expect each exhibition to contain works imitating the Swiss painter, one commentator in 1819 remarking with a sense of surprise that he could see only one 'Fuseli looking picture' at that year's show.[16]

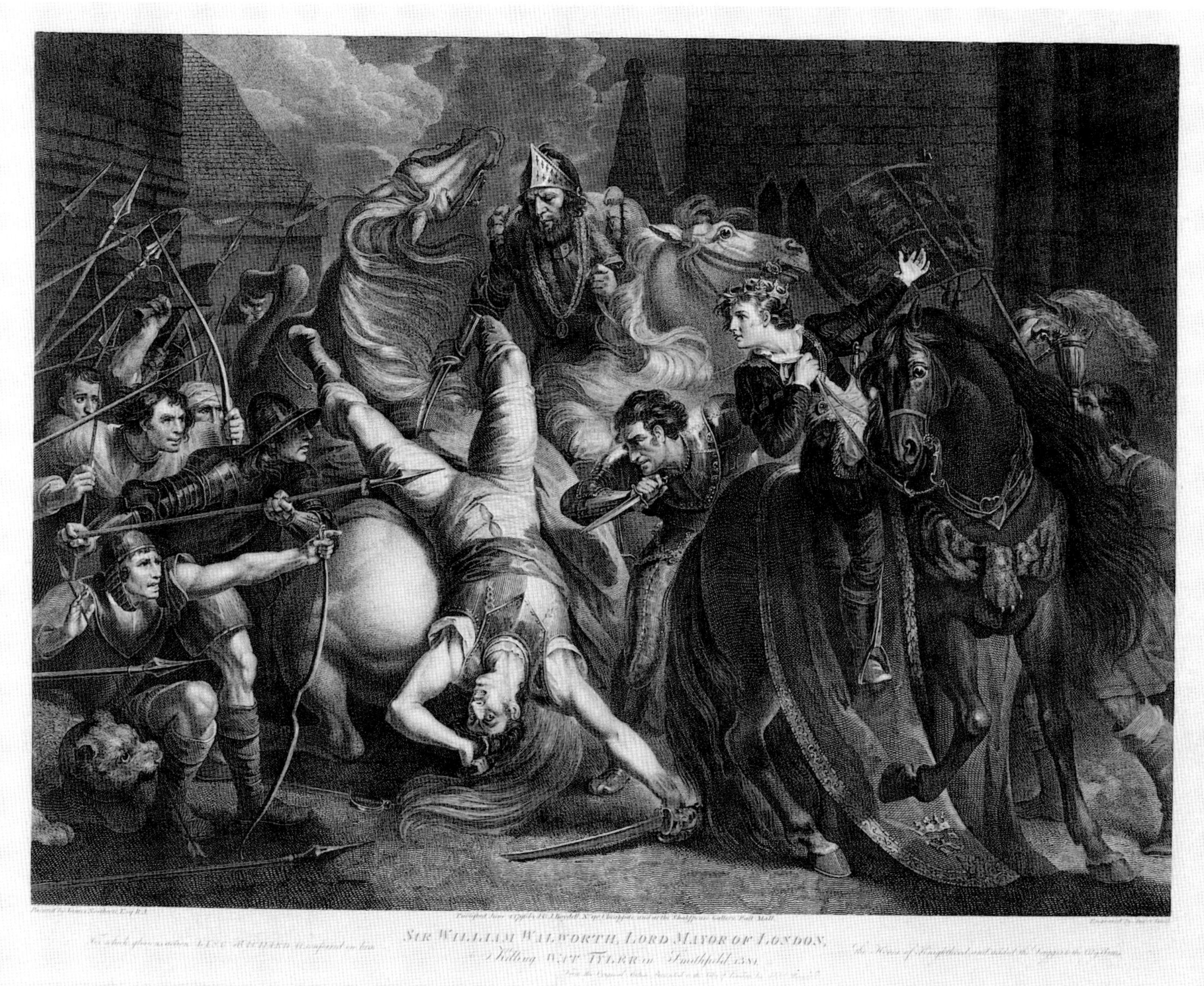

Fuseli maintained a relatively successful (and certainly very high-profile) career as a painter of elevated subjects by using the exhibitions strategically, and by ironically adapting the conventions of high art to the conditions of the marketplace. If one artist defies the opposition between 'intellect' and consumerist 'appetite', it is Fuseli. His career was founded on a fusion, or perhaps confusion, of the ideals of the Academic tradition with the populist demands of the day: if the exhibition public was seen as wanting *outré* pictures, Fuseli was so *outré* that most critics could not make up their mind as to whether he was a genius or a madman.

When Fuseli returned from Italy in 1779, he had a few commissions from his brief stopover in Switzerland, and some hope of new work (notably from Sir Robert Smyth, whom he had met in Italy) but no real prospects for sustained patronage and certainly no great public standing. So, much as Northcote would do a few years later, he set out to produce an exhibition picture that would establish his reputation. The opportunity to create such a work emerged in the summer of 1780, when he saw Reynolds at work on a new picture of the *Death of Dido* (fig. 55). As Fuseli noted in a letter to Sir Robert, he perceived that the President 'himself begins to think he has failed'.[17] With a view to challenging Reynolds's authority as the leading history painter, Fuseli set about executing his own version of precisely the same subject for Smyth (fig. 56); he went on to exhibit this at the Academy in 1781 as a direct affront to the President, whose *Dido* was shown in the same exhibition. Indeed, as newspaper accounts testify, the pictures were hanging on opposite walls of the Great Room.[18] As Fuseli must have hoped and expected, this confrontation provoked considerable critical commentary. As an artist without a secure patronage base whose best outlet at this stage was the exhibition, Fuseli needed to demonstrate his abilities to the public and to distinguish himself from his competitors. The strategy embodied by the *Dido* involved

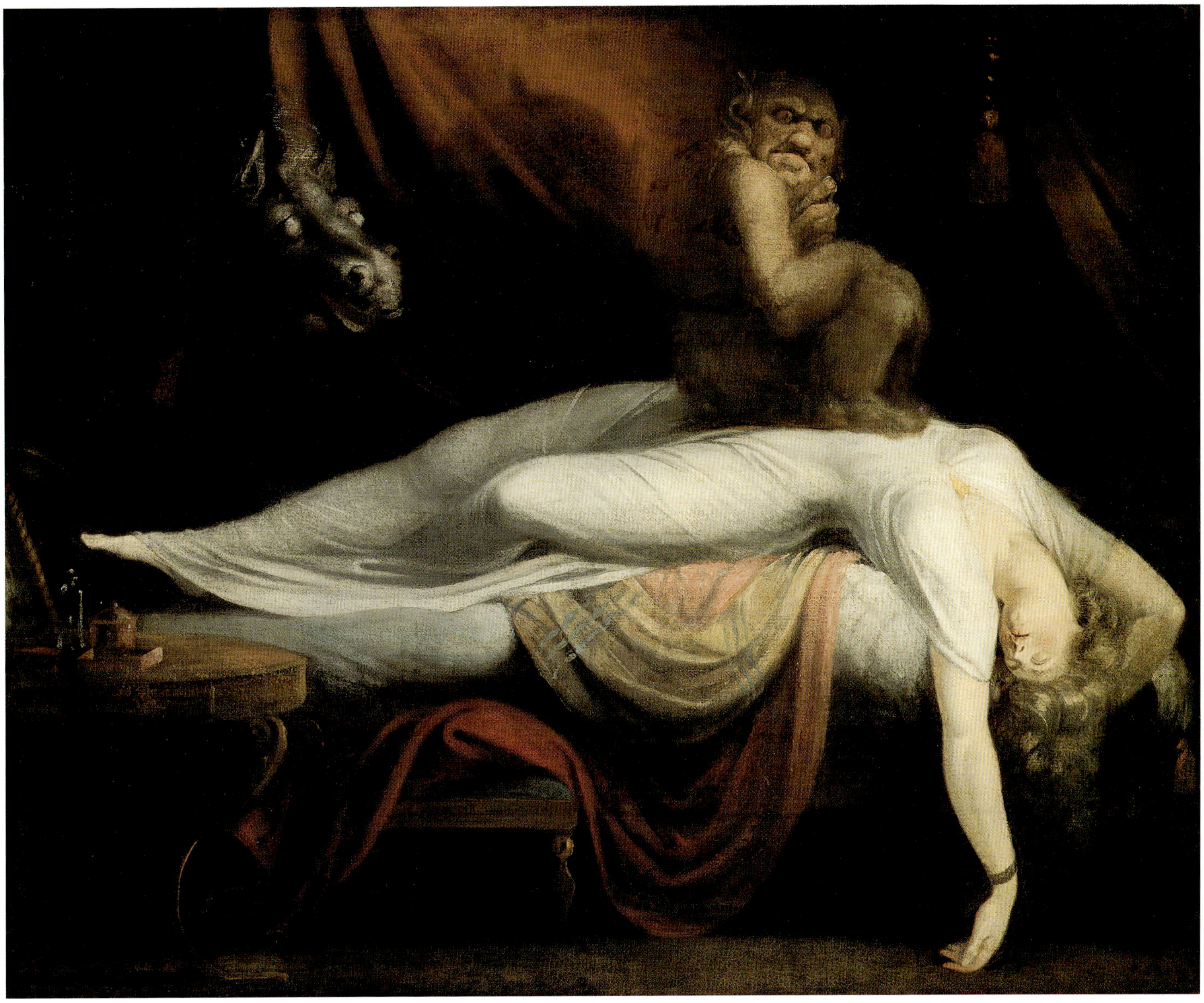

53 (*above*) Henry Fuseli, *The Nightmare*, RA 1782. The Detroit Institute of Arts, Founders Society Purchase with funds from Mr and Mrs Bert L. Smokler and Mr and Mrs Lawrence A. Fleischman.

52 (*facing page*) Anker Smith after James Northcote, *The Murder of Wat Tyler*, engraving of 1796 after lost original exhibited RA 1787. By courtesy of the Trustees of the British Museum, London.

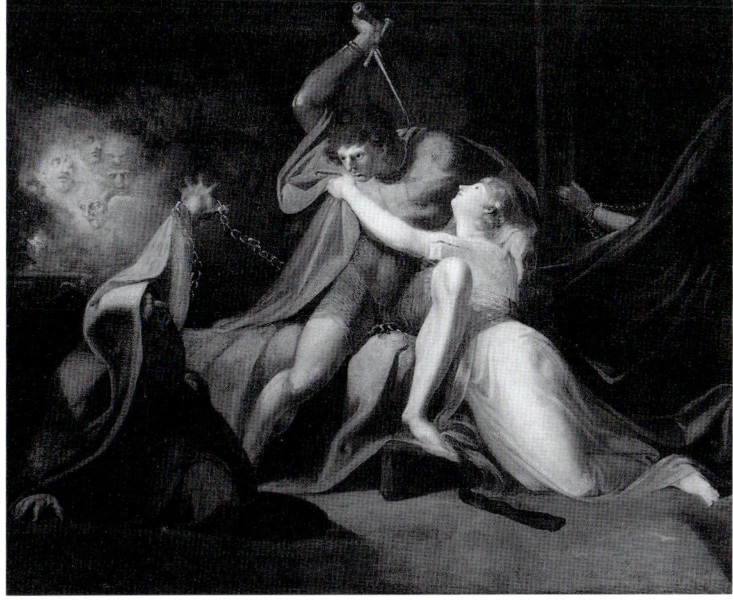

54 (*right*) Henry Fuseli, *Percival Delivering Belisane from the Enchantment of Urma*, RA 1783. Tate, London.

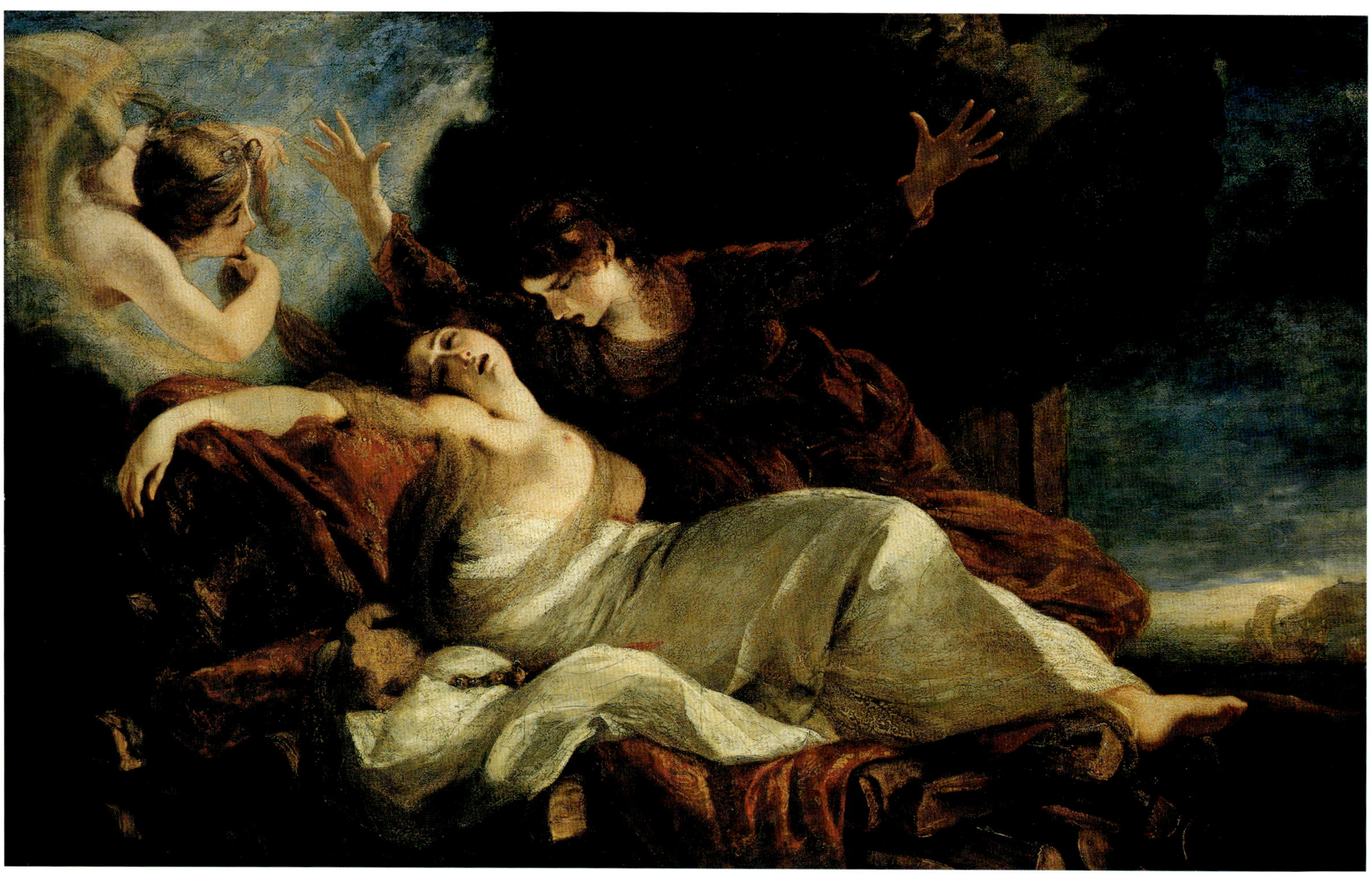

55 Sir Joshua Reynolds, *The Death of Dido*, RA 1781. The Royal Collection © 2001 Her Majesty Queen Elizabeth II.

dramatizing that process of differentiation by means of formal innovations that contrast sharply with the pictorial language deployed by Reynolds. The President's picture is couched in the visual language of seventeenth-century baroque art, evoking an old masterly sense of pictorial texture and depth through a richly manipulated painted surface. His supine Dido is accommodated comfortably within a horizontal canvas. Fuseli's picture looks angular and awkward by comparison. His figures are defined by means of sharp tonal oppositions, entirely unlike the gradual melding of tones that features so prominently in Sir Joshua's work, and he presents a much more complex composition on a vertical format that requires dramatic foreshortening, as awkward as it is technically difficult. The Swiss painter's reward for this effortful performance of showy virtuosity was to be singled out for his 'singularity'. Establishing a theme that was to continue throughout the artist's public career, the critic in the *St James's Chronicle* (28 April–1 May 1781) excused the artist's idiosyncratic awkwardness on the grounds that 'it is often productive of excellent Effects'.

On a later occasion we have firm evidence of Fuseli's deliberate use of the exhibitions to inspire a provocative comparison between himself and another artist, in this case a younger contemporary. In 1793 Thomas Lawrence, already established as a prodigy in portraiture, attempted to claim a reputation as a history painter by exhibiting a large canvas of *Prospero Raising the Storm* (now lost, as Lawrence painted over the image). Like many contemporary depictions of sublime literary themes, this work owed a great deal to Fuseli; indeed it appears that Lawrence had gone so far as to incorporate figures copied from two pictures by the older master. Fuseli – who must have got wind of what Lawrence was up to – responded by exhibiting these very same designs, a sketch from *Macbeth* and a Spenserian subject, in a deliberate attempt to force the comparison. Within a matter of days after the exhibition opened, claims for the priority of either Fuseli or Lawrence began appearing in the press: thus where the *London Packet* (29 April–1 May) maintained that Fuseli's *Macbeth* 'appears to have been made the groundwork of a very large work, *also from Shakespeare*' (i.e., Lawrence's *Prospero*), on 2 May the *Diary* reported that, 'We were assured yesterday from undoubted authority that Mr Lawrence painted his Prospero before Fuseli threw his sketch of Macbeth'. The reporter for the *Oracle* (30 April), meanwhile, wryly asserted that as 'the figures are original to neither the *one* or the *other*', there should really be no dispute.

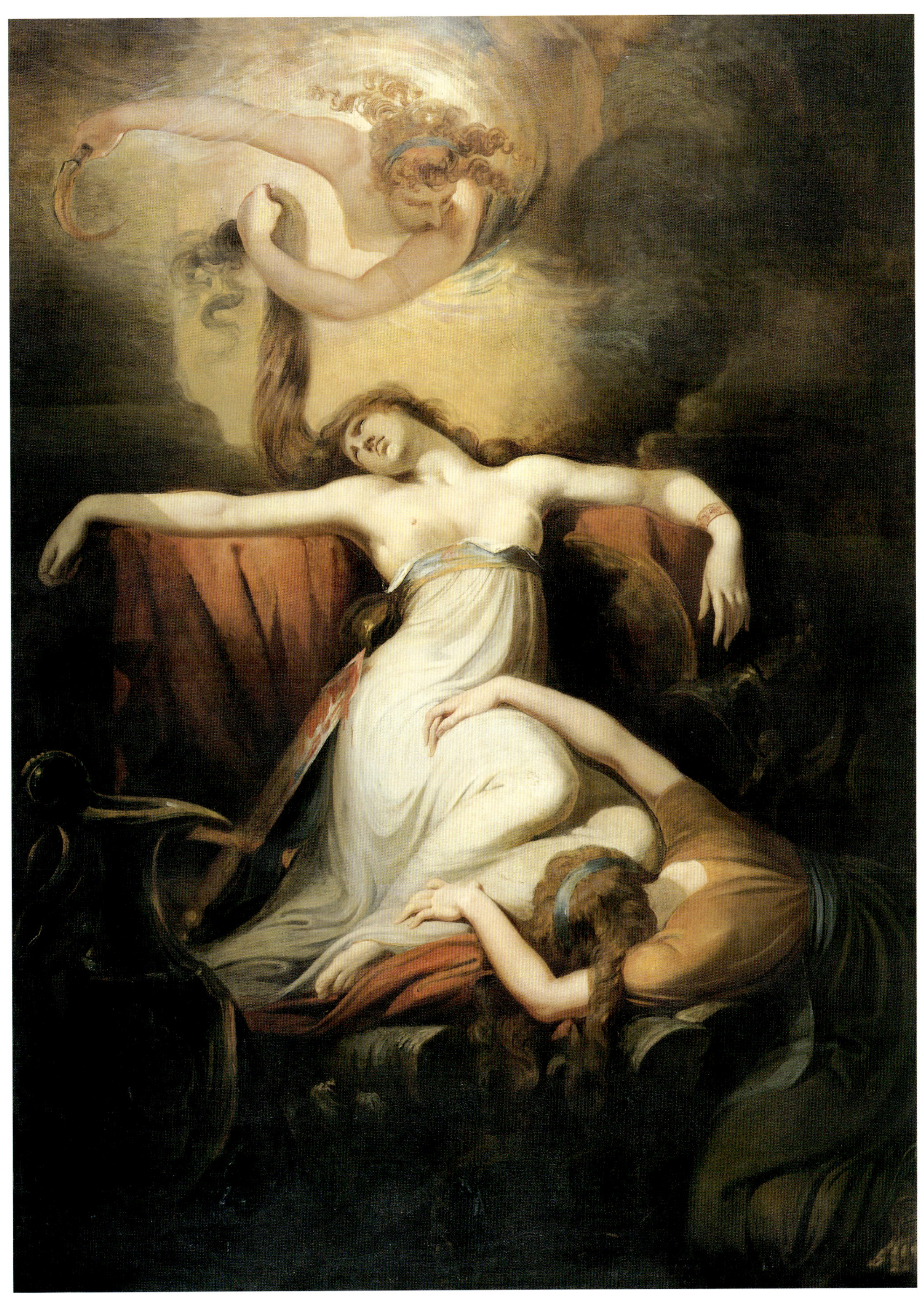

56 Henry Fuseli, *The Death of Dido*, RA 1781. Yale Center for British Art, Paul Mellon Collection.

Aside from these instances of the literally manipulative use of the Great Room, Fuseli needs to be understood as an artist who exploited the very uncertainties about artistic value that haunted Reynolds's *Discourses*. Starting with his aggressive challenge to Sir Joshua's *Dido* in 1781, the author of the *Nightmare* was emphatically identified as an artist defined by his extreme originality. Couched in the emerging vocabulary of 'genius' and the sublime, the characterizations of Fuseli could praise him as an artist of excellence *because* his work was so bombastic. A single comment dating from shortly after his death sums up this line of argument, while recalling the response to his early *Dido*: 'the very *merit* of his style of design consists in it being never by any accident true; for if it had been, it would have rendered all the other merits, of fancy, imagination, &c. that he occasionally displayed, null and void' (*New Monthly Magazine*, 1 July 1825). Very often, Fuseli's perceived originality or 'singularity' prompted reviewers to invoke metaphors of madness, sickness, death or intoxication. Because the artist's mannerisms seemed to put him beyond the realm of the normal, his art could be understood, perhaps, only by being described as originating in physiological abnormality – whether figuratively or even literally ascribed to the artist (there were widespread rumours that he took opium or ate raw pork as a means to inspiration). His typical, trademark distortion of the human form was often seen as a kind of caricature, and, as the *Examiner*'s Robert Hunt explained when he made this point (4 June 1809), 'I do not mean caricature in a qualified but literal sense, where the human passions are pourtrayed [*sic*] from the ravings of a mad-house, and the human form dislocated by the rack'. At other times Fuseli's ostentatious display of scholarship in his choice of subjects and his elaborate treatment of the human figure led to charges that he knew more than was good for his sanity: as early as 1780 we find the accusation that 'he runs some Risk of the old Observation being applied to *him*, that was made on an eminent Man 1700 Years ago, "*Too much learning hath made him mad*"' (*Public Advertiser*, 2 May 1780). Later in the same decade, however, Fuseli would be praised for the exclusivity of his erudition. According to the *Daily Universal Register* for 10 May 1786,

> Fuseli's works are not intelligible to the capacity of the million, they require scientific knowledge to feel their beauties, and resemble fine authors in an obsolete or dead language, which are understood only by the educated, and what is more unfortunate, will never bear a translation.

Yet this remoteness functioned in a very particular way, and certainly not to exclude the general exhibition audience. Indeed the central irony of Fuseli's work, both its bizarre content and unusual formal characteristics, is that while it makes great play with obscurity and exclusiveness, it does so precisely in order to enhance its popular and commercial allure. His representations of ghosts and witches, fairies and horror, have an obvious 'Gothic' quality that still resonates today. Related only very loosely to the sublime described by Burke and other theorists, Fuseli's work has far more in common with the popular literature of his era – that is to say, with the Gothic or romance novels so avidly read by his contemporaries. For certain art critics of the time, this link was patently obvious; the 'gigantic extravagance' of his imagery, according to a review in *La Belle Assemblée* (May 1811), affected the viewer like the 'heroes and dwarfs in the old romances'. The Gothic was a form of literature that used obscurity as a central device, claiming remote origins (with books and short stories supposedly based on ancient, forgotten manuscripts), dealing with shadowy imagery of dungeons and phantasms and, with its irrational plots, cipher-like characters and strange settings, being indistinct in the very texture of its writing. It was all that obscurity which made the Gothic marketable, to a new socially fluid, urban audience (imagined as consisting of impressionable young women) hungry for sensationalism. Fuseli's imagery can be interpreted as acting in an analogous way in the context of the art exhibitions.

With this in mind, we could look again at the *Nightmare*, a work that has always invited a range of interpretations. It has variously been related to folkloric tradition, witchcraft literature, theories of sleep paralysis, and the artist's personal life. Yet rather than opting for one reading or another, we might far more usefully conclude that from the outset the picture's primary purpose has been to generate a potentially endless multitude of such speculations, and in so doing to maximize its own value as visual entertainment. So instead of regarding this as an expression of nascent 'Romanticism', as has more than once been claimed, we should appreciate the *Nightmare* as one realization of a strategy worked out in direct relation to the exhibition public. Another example of much the same approach can be found in *Percival Delivering Belisane*; though this appears to depict some old chivalric legend or romance, as Fuseli admitted it is in fact a subject of his own invention.[19] Here his hero seems to be engaged in a highly important action, but its precise meanings cannot be determined, and were never intended to be. By deliberately shrouding his pictorial stories in an impenetrable veil of obscurity, Fuseli buckles the conventions of high art: for beneath all the gesturing and visual drama of his imagery, there is ultimately a narrative vacuum. On the surface his works may have looked like morally uplifting history paintings – but their main purpose was to create as great a sensation as possible, under the legitimizing banner of the sublime.

Whereas Northcote used 'sublime' sensationalism to make a splash at the exhibition, Fuseli – who made it his business to be exceptional – built his entire career out of making a splash. Both cases dramatize the role of exhibition culture in compromising the conventions of high art. Of a rather different order is Thomas Procter, who for his contemporaries was *the* exemplar of the idealist artist, and, in his tragically short life, the suffocation of idealism in the modern age. Procter's name is now forgotten, but from the mid-1780s until the late 1820s he was enormously admired. A painter and sculptor who received a series of prestigious awards from the Society of Arts and the Royal Academy, as well as enthusiastic commendations in press and in private, Procter died in 1794 at the age of forty-one, after which sad event his reputation rose even higher. Eulogistic accounts of his life were given by Edward Dayes in 1805, Sir Thomas Bernard in 1807 and by J. T. Smith in 1828 in *Nollekens and his Times*. Academic spokesmen, beginning with Benjamin West in his Presidential Discourse of 1794, were no less lavish in their praise; the Professor of Painting John Opie grouped Procter with William Hogarth, Richard Wilson and James Barry as one of the 'injured, but immortal' geniuses of the eighteenth century, while in 1827 his models were displayed as exemplary works by Richard Westmacott, during his Academy lectures on sculpture.[20] Procter's reputation is all the more remarkable inasmuch as all his most famous exhibition pieces were sculptures, and models as opposed to finished works. Late eighteenth-century reviewers hardly ever wrote at length about sculpture in any form, partly because it was put on display downstairs in the Life Academy; as Alison Yarrington demonstrates in Chapter 12 of this volume, sculptors found it particularly difficult to make any impression whatsoever at Somerset House. This makes the fame achieved by Procter all the more worthy of note.

It was with a terracotta model of Ixion, exhibited in 1785 (fig. 57), that Procter initially established his critical reputation. The *Morning Herald* (28 April) said it 'deserve[d] to be distinguished' from every other sculpture in the show, while the *Artist's Repository* declared that 'it would not disgrace the best of our sculptors'.[21] One newspaper even claimed (erroneously) that the king was so impressed with Procter that he had arranged for the artist to be sent immediately to Rome, and that the Academy was to buy the work. The following year Procter exhibited what seems to have been a much larger model, of the *Death of Diomedes*, which again received many favourable notices:

> The death of Diomedes, by Mr Proctor, is evidently a work of great genius, bold, energetic, and sublime; and is a full confirmation of the high opinion which the Public conceived of him last year, from his model of Ixion.[22]

Despite this praise, Procter apparently destroyed his *Diomedes* after failing to find a purchaser. Certainly, he did not exhibit another sculpture until 1792, when he showed the model of *Perithous, the Son of Ixion, Destroyed by Cerberus* (fig. 58). His return to the medium was widely and warmly welcomed in the press, and at least one critic pronounced the work a triumph, well deserving of its unusual placement in the Library, a floor above the room dedicated to the display of sculpture:

> Mr Procter's model is very properly exhibited in the centre of the Academy . . . such a model, perhaps no man in this country, or any one, could have executed. The anatomy is in every point accurate, the lines in a most eminent degree beautiful, and the grouping in a style that sets modern art at defiance. It has the spirit, vigoar [*sic*] and chastity of Grecian art.[23]

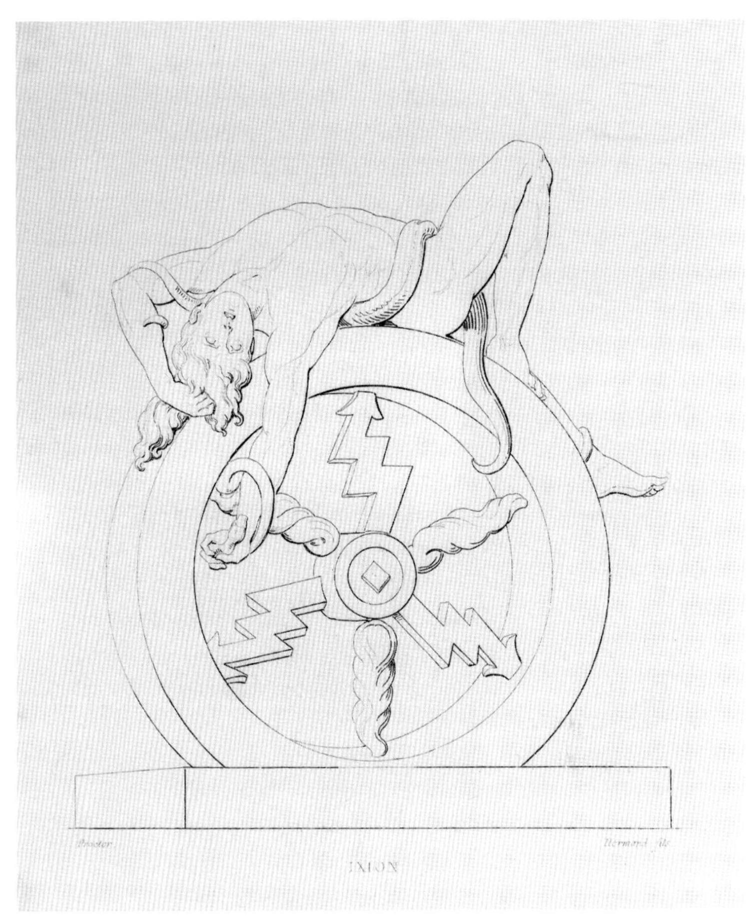

57 C. Normand after Thomas Procter, *Ixion*, engraving after lost terracotta model exhibited RA 1785; from G. Hamilton, *The English School* (1831–2). By permission of The British Library.

58 After Thomas Procter, *Perithous, the Son of Ixion, Destroyed by Cerberus*, engraving after lost terracotta model exhibited RA 1792; from G. Hamilton, *The English School* (1831–2). By permission of The British Library.

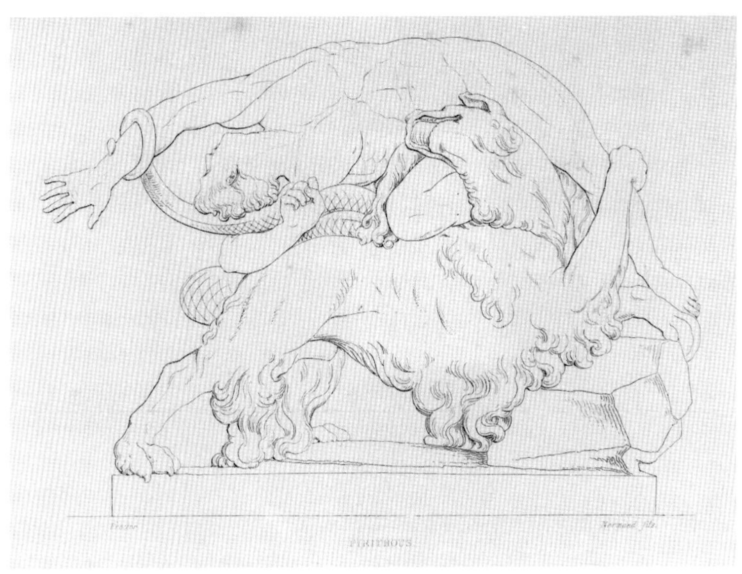

Procter's critical status had certainly been raised high enough for him to be awarded the Academy's Rome Prize in December 1793, with a very significant majority of votes. But the following July he died suddenly before he was able to travel abroad. The circumstances of this event were immediately romanticized, and less than five months later West was proclaiming Procter as one of the best of the moderns, 'whose recent death is a misfortune to the British School, for ever to be lamented'.[24] Procter had rapidly been installed as a lost hero of British art, a position he was to hold for more than three decades.

As far as these early critics and commentators were concerned, Procter's sculptures – now sadly known only from some later outline engravings – represented a rare expression of a pure, ideal art. They dealt with the idealized male nude (the epitome of the Academic ideal), depicted classical narratives, and presented themes of sublime, heroic suffering entirely removed from the frivolity and superficial glamour that appeared to characterize so much contemporary art seen at the exhibitions. The fact that they did not sell, that they remained as models rather than being worked up in marble, and that Procter only just managed to scrape together a living from art, only served to extend his reputation. The fullest and most sophisticated reading of Procter from the period, Sir Thomas Bernard's article in the *Director* for 7 March 1807, brings all these themes into sharp focus. Bernard notes that Procter had a distinct predilection for depicting moments of extreme suffering that were challenging for most viewers, and for rhetorical purposes he offers an apology. If Procter's works were 'all in their nature *pathetic* and *terrible*', this was not because the artist lacked 'a taste for physical or moral beauty'. Rather, it was because Procter was young, ambitious and high-minded. Bernard admits the appeal of the 'softer and more delightful sensations', but is explicit about their social location – in the womanly realm of the home; he implies that Procter's energy was incompatible with privacy and private pleasures. The sculptor's immoderate artistic statements are placed in confrontation with a market Bernard characterizes as supportive only of products which pandered to narcissistic desires and trivial decoration:

> Habituated to the sublime and intellectual branches of the art, he possessed neither disposition nor talent for portrait painting; he could not sketch for the publisher, nor pencil for the manufacturer.[25]

Here and elsewhere Procter is cast in the noble role that Reynolds had prescribed for artists in his ninth *Discourse*. According to this romantic reading, the sculptor's life assumed the dimensions of a tragedy, culminating in poverty and premature death caused by his refusal to bend to the dictates of the marketplace; his sad fate supplied a sentimentally touching example of the failure of high art in Britain as a whole. Yet when seen from a more critical perspective, Procter's achievement appears deeply marked by the spectacular aspects of exhibition culture. Here was an artist without any formal training as a sculptor, and so lacking both the practical skills necessary for professional practice, as well as ready access to the networks of patronage that maintained the trade. Instead his reputation depended entirely on works created only for the exhibition space, and for an audience with an appetite for the novel and sensational. On the admittedly slight evidence of the later engravings, we can read Procter's models as typically sublime conceptions of the human body, recalling the world of torture and sadism of the Gothic novel as much as the classical tradition. Conventional wisdom tells us that idealized nudes were almost completely absent from the Academy exhibitions in this period. When they did appear, on the very odd occasion, this sensationalist aspect often came to the fore. Significantly, when Thomas Banks, a sculptor of the same generation as Northcote and Fuseli, wanted to re-establish himself as a sculptor in London after an unsuccessful sojourn in Russia, he created an *Achilles* (now lost) for exhibition in 1784 that similarly presented a heroically conceived male figure contorted with (in this case emotional) agony.[26] If we look forward to John Francis Rigaud's *Samson Breaking his Bonds* exhibited in 1804 (or a version thereof; fig. 60), Samuel Morse's *Dying Hercules* (RA 1813; fig. 59) or some of William Etty's early exhibits,

59 Samuel Morse, *Dying Hercules*, RA 1813. Yale University Art Gallery.

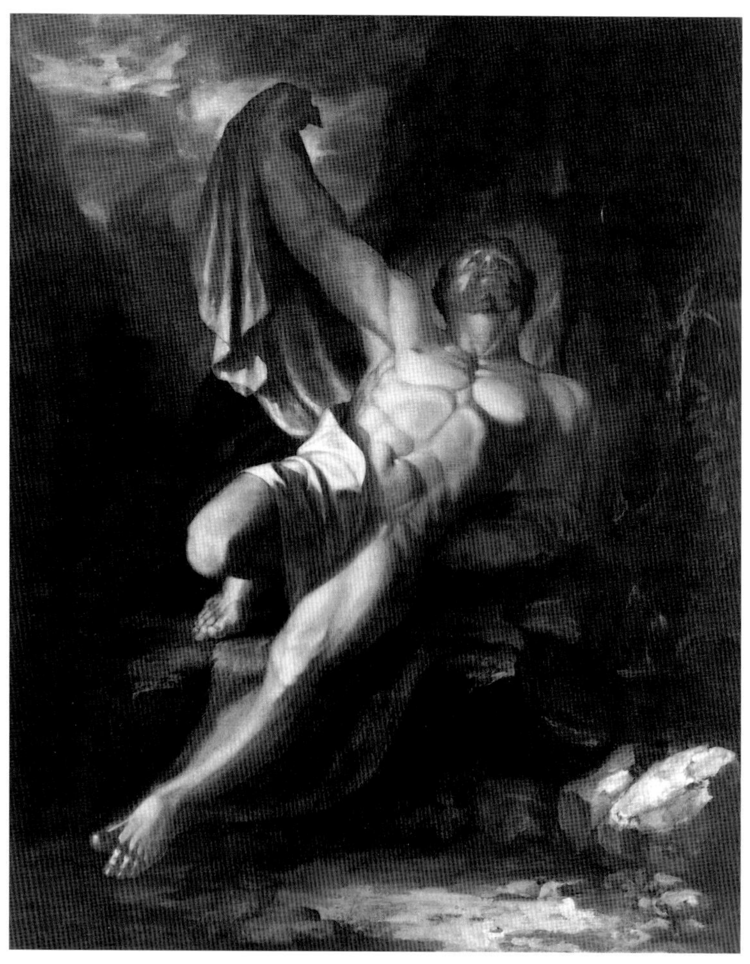

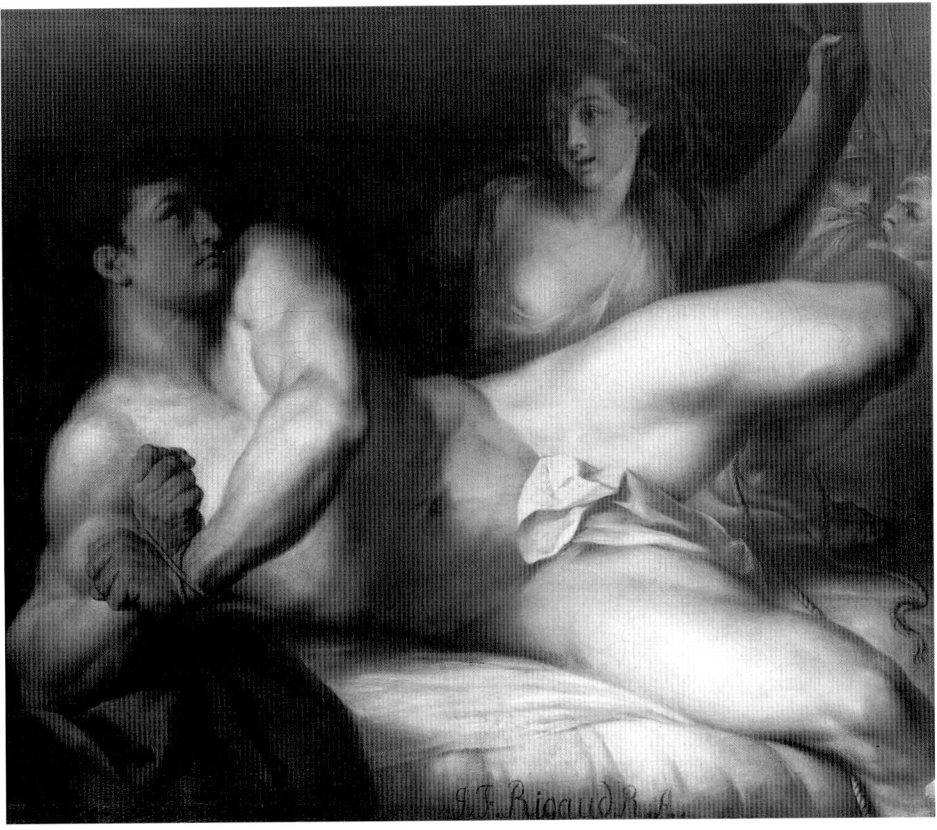

60 John Francis Rigaud, *Samson Breaking his Bonds*, Diploma Picture, 1784–5. Either this work or an autograph replica was exhibited RA 1806. Royal Academy of Arts, London.

we discover a recurring preoccupation with pain, extreme emotion, contortion and stress. The ideal nudes that appeared at the Somerset House exhibitions are among the clearest examples of the 'sharp unnatural Angles' that Skiddy had warned about in the early 1780s. As a genre, the heroic nude was so rarely supported materially, and so overwhelmed in the exhibitions, that when examples were produced for show, the need for artistic showiness in itself tended to become overbearing.

By the early nineteenth century both Northcote and Fuseli increasingly appeared to be relics from a former age – an age that had held out heroic ambitions for high art which were never fulfilled. Art critics had long lamented the paucity of high art in modern Britain, but as the new century progressed the complaints grew louder and more articulate, developing into outright attacks on the Academy, including its exhibiting facilities. So for Robert Hunt in the *Examiner* (7 May 1815), the Great Room was simply not the right place for ideal art:

> It ought to be recollected, too, that the Academy rooms are not on several accounts the best calculated for the display of grand work, and that several of our admired Artists choose to prepare their performances for other places.

One of the artists whom Hunt had in mind must have been the venerable Benjamin West, who in 1814 had organized an independent showing for his enormous canvas of *Christ Rejected*, which attracted visitors in their thousands. Yet such isolated successes failed to stem the growing tide of uniform pessimism about the future of high art. As early as September 1805, a commentator in the *Gentleman's Magazine* had indicated the variety of reasons he believed were forcing artists to give up 'the higher walks of the profession':[27] the rampant nationalism which put pressure on artists to represent only modern-day heroes, the lack of Church or state support, and the decline of the market in prints (marked by the recent collapse of Boydell's Shakespeare Gallery and other entrepreneurial schemes). In the same year Joseph Farington reported Fuseli's despairing thoughts on the situation:

> Fuseli has little hope of *Poetical* Painting finding encouragement in England. The people are not prepared for it. Portrait with them is everything. – Their taste & feelings all goes [*sic*] to *realities*, – The Ideal does not operate on their minds. – *Historical painting*, viz: matter of fact, they may encourage.[28]

Yet as Fuseli's own career shows, 'The Ideal' was not simply absent from the Somerset House exhibitions, and was certainly not ignored by the critics or the public. But it was transformed, made to serve the highest ideals of art and the lowest tastes of the public simultaneously, as well as being loaded with artistic ambition to a disruptive, excessive degree. Paradoxically, it may be in the field of ideal narrative art – a genre that was outmoded, out of place, and under-supported from the very outset of the Academy's occupation of Somerset House – that the impact on art of the new exhibition culture can be most vividly seen.

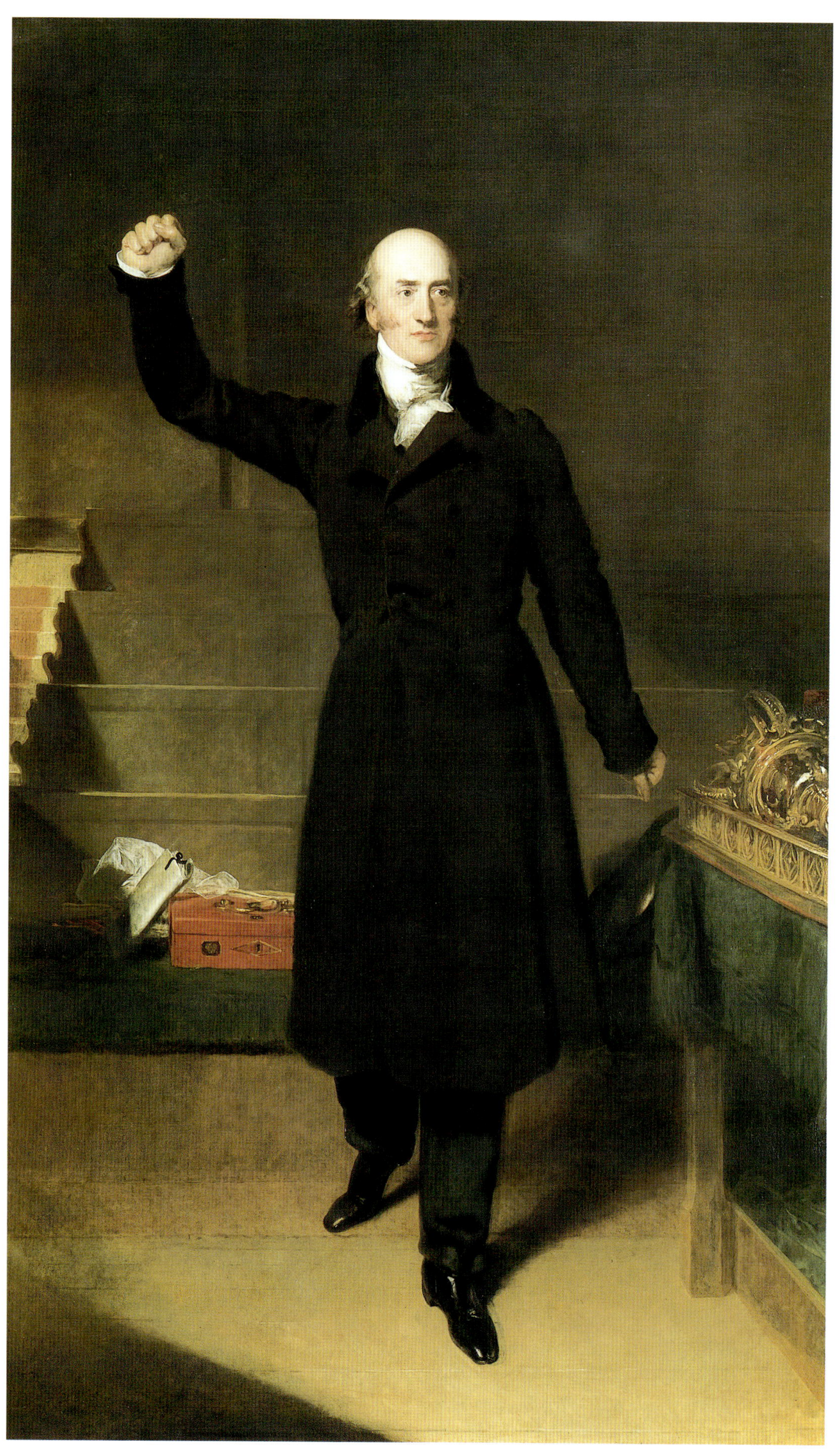

61 Thomas Lawrence, *George Canning*, RA 1826. By courtesy of the National Portrait Gallery, London.

7

'Portrait! Portrait!! Portrait!!!

MARCIA POINTON

'Portrait! Portrait!! Portrait!!!! intrudes on every side; while history, poetry, fiction, fade before the overwhelming invader'.

Annals of the Fine Arts, I (1817), 52

PORTRAITURE WAS THE ROYAL ACADEMY'S source of sustenance and its pervasive poison. Blamed for the failure of history painting and viewed as a sign of the degeneracy of taste, the ever-increasing abundance of portraits on the walls of the Great Room was cause for deep anxiety.[1] 'So long as portrait painting is patronized as "the only true historie", so long must historic painting be dead as an art, for artists must paint to live, and it is too much to expect any one to die a martyr to his love of any peculiar branch', declared John Martin when asked about the effects of the Somerset House exhibitions on young artists. Martin was giving evidence on 24 June 1836 before the Select Committee appointed by the House of Commons to 'inquire into the best means of extending a knowledge of the Arts, and of the Principles of Design among the People',[2] a question that had preoccupied critics and reviewers for two generations (fig. 62). This chapter explores the troubled history of the contribution of portraits to the Academy's exhibitions. Even if the insistence on a causal relationship between the prevalence of portraits and the perceived failure of history painting cannot be taken at face value, we still need to know not merely why the Academy welcomed the 'overwhelming invader', but also what desires and purposes its presence fuelled and fulfilled.

The Royal Academy's Instrument of Foundation required that its members be 'men of fair moral characters, of high reputation in their several professions',[3] but made no stipulation concerning the art that they should produce. The notion of the higher aims of art that informed Martin's dialogue with the Committee had been a familiar part of cultural debate in England long before the Academy's foundation; it grew from the combined effects of an aristocracy avidly collecting Italian old master paintings, the desire of artists to establish a national school of historical painting, and the efforts of theorists familiar with the writings of G. B. Alberti, Roger de Piles, Charles Le Brun and others to promote the cause of grand-style narrative painting. But anti-Catholicism – the Gordon riots broke out just as the Royal Academy exhibition of 1780 was closing – ensured that public patronage for large-scale religious art would never be readily available. Moreover, party political strife, a significant feature of eighteenth-century English life, may – it has been argued – have fatally undermined the development of a unified model of high taste by dividing patrons and preventing the concentration of influence in a few hands.[4] Jonathan Richardson had demonstrated that a taste for art was not evidence of popery, and that gentlemen in general, rather than the nobility exclusively, could acquire such a taste. But Richardson earned his living as a portrait painter, as did Joshua Reynolds, whose Discourses to students of the Royal Academy insisted on the pre-eminence of historical art.

Britain was a commercial society: portrait painters could be hired by aristocrats and merchants alike, and images of these men and their families mingled promiscuously on the walls of the Academy. Johann Zoffany and Francis Wheatley presented genre portraits and conversation pieces which narrated professional and domestic lives with unprecedented conviction and clarity. And

ON ARTS AND PRINCIPLES OF DESIGN. 199

RETURNS of the Number of WORKS of ART EXHIBITED at the ROYAL ACADEMY in each of the last Ten Years (1824 to 1833), distinguishing for each year the Number of Historical Works, Landscapes, Portraits, Busts and Architectural Drawings respectively contributed by Members of the Royal Academy, from the Historical Works, Landscapes, Portraits, Busts and Architectural Drawings, contributed by other Artists.

	MEMBERS.	STUDENTS.	OTHERS.	TOTAL.
In 1824:				
Viz.—Historical and Poetical Works -	22	42	45	109
Landscapes, Views, Animals, &c. -	30	23	166	219
Portraits - - - - - -	70	156	291	517
Sculpture, Statues, Relievos, Gems	7	23	29	59
Busts - - - - - - -	5	24	5	34
Architecture - - - - -	12	27	60	99
	146	295	596	1,037
In 1825:				
Viz.—Historical and Poetical Works -	32	38	66	136
Landscapes, Views, Animals, &c. -	18	19	305	342
Portraits - - - - - -	74	158	181	413
Sculpture, Statues, Relievos, Gems	4	22	26	52
Busts - - - - - -	8	31	21	60
Architecture - - - - -	8	13	48	69
	144	281	647	1,072
In 1826:				
Viz.—Historical and Poetical Works -	30	39	53	122
Landscapes, Views, Animals, &c. -	35	24	218	277
Portraits - - - - - -	58	157	269	484
Sculpture, Statues, Relievos, Gems	7	30	37	74
Busts - - - - - -	9	33	9	51
Architecture - - - - -	8	25	64	97
	147	308	650	1,105
In 1827:				
Viz.—Historical and Poetical Works -	34	38	40	112
Landscapes, Views, Animals, &c. -	52	29	231	312
Portraits - - - - - -	78	136	262	476
Sculpture, Statues, Relievos, Gems	7	26	26	59
Busts - - - - - -	2	26	6	34
Architecture - - - - -	14	29	91	134
	187	284	656	1,127
In 1828:				
Viz.—Historical and Poetical Works -	31	46	52	129
Landscapes, Views, Animals, &c. -	36	24	261	321
Portraits - - - - - -	70	143	309	522
Sculpture, Statues, Relievos, Gems	4	27	36	67
Busts - - - - - -	8	26	15	49
Architecture - - - - -	12	27	87	126
	161	293	760	1,214
In 1829:				
Viz.—Historical and Poetical Works -	33	41	110	184
Landscapes, Views, Animals, &c. -	31	35	180	246
Portraits - - - - - -	75	199	299	573
Sculpture, Statues, Relievos, Gems	7	18	28	53
Busts - - - - - -	4	38	24	66
Architecture - - - - -	11	26	64	101
	161	357	705	1,223
In 1830:				
Viz.—Historical and Poetical Works -	45	62	60	167
Landscapes, Views, Animals, &c. -	40	27	252	319
Portraits - - - - - -	73	150	310	533
Sculpture, Statues, Relievos, Gems	6	33	31	70
Busts - - - - - -	6	40	21	67
Architecture - - - - -	5	33	84	122
	175	345	758	1,278

0.28. B B 4

200 APPENDIX TO REPORT FROM SELECT COMMITTEE, &c.

NUMBER of Works exhibited—*continued.*

	MEMBERS.	STUDENTS.	OTHERS.	TOTAL.
In 1831:				
Viz.—Historical and Poetical Works -	47	34	72	153
Landscapes, Views, Animals, &c. -	37	33	220	290
Portraits - - - - - -	47	163	301	511
Sculpture, Statues, Relievos, Gems	3	32	36	71
Busts - - - - - - -	5	46	21	72
Architecture - - - - -	8	31	98	137
	147	339	748	1,234
In 1832:				
Viz.—Historical and Poetical Works -	39	43	63	145
Landscapes, Views, Animals, &c, -	45	27	224	296
Portraits - - - - - -	69	139	325	533
Sculpture, Statues, Relievos, Gems	10	30	36	76
Busts - - - - - -	3	40	27	70
Architecture - - - - -	12	23	74	109
	178	302	749	1,229
In 1833:				
Viz.—Historical and Poetical Works -	36	51	54	141
Landscapes, Views, Animals, &c. -	49	27	233	309
Portraits - - - - - -	71	185	275	531
Sculpture, Statues, Relievos, Gems	6	38	40	84
Busts - - - - - -	4	44	27	75
Architecture - - - - -	5	27	54	86
—	171	372	683	1,226

Note.—In the early years of the Institution, the Members were not limited in their Contributions to the Annual Exhibitions; but as the Artists of the Country became more numerous, the Members restricted the number of their own Works, and opened additional Rooms for the general accommodation. Of the Portraits, it may be observed, that between two hundred and three hundred, annually, are Miniatures.

RETURNS of the Number of PROFESSORS in the ROYAL ACADEMY; of the Number of Lectures required by the Rules of the Academy to be Annually delivered by each Professor; and of the Number of Lectures which have been Annually delivered by each Professor during the last Ten Years (1824 to 1833).

There are five Professors in the Royal Academy; *viz.* those of Anatomy, Perspective, Architecture, Sculpture and Painting; each of whom is to deliver Six Lectures annually. The Number of Lectures delivered in the Academy, during the last Ten Years, is as follows:—

	1824.	1825.	1826.	1827.	1828.	1829.	1830.	1831.	1832.	1833.	
Anatomy - - -	6	6	6	6	6	6	6	6	6	6	189 Lectures.
Perspective - -	6	4	4	6	–	–	–	–	–	–	
Architecture - -	(a)	–	–	–	–	–	–	6	6	6	
Sculpture - - -	6	(b) 1	(c) 3	3	5	6	6	6	6	6	
Painting - - -	6	(d)	4	6	6	6	6	6	(e)	3	

(a) Professor prevented by a defect in his sight; in the last three years the Secretary read for him.
(b) Professor ill.
(c) Professor died.
(d) Professor died.
(e) Professor resigned.

By Order,

Henry Howard,
Sec. R. A.

INDEX.

62 'Returns of the Number of WORKS OF ART EXHIBITED at the ROYAL ACADEMY in each of the last ten years (1824 to 1833)' from the Report of the Select Committee . . . , *Minutes of Evidence*, London: House of Commons, IX, part ii, appendix (1836). Manchester Central Library.

with the possible exception of Benjamin West, every president of the Academy from Reynolds to Martin Archer Shee (who vigorously defended his colleagues against accusations levelled by the chairman of the 1835–6 Select Committee that they were a 'clique of portrait painters')[5] primarily gained his living through portraiture.[6] The obvious reason was that client demand for portraits exceeded that for any other genre, and artists (as Martin averred) needed (and still do need) an income. Furthermore, the fact that portraits were usually commissioned meant that these paintings had already been paid for by the time they were exhibited, and patrons expected that they would be shown.[7] The exhibition was in this regard less a saleroom than an advertising suite. The Academy itself relied heavily on the income from entry fees to fulfil its own financial obligations, and portraits drew the visitors.

At the 1835–6 Inquiry, it was stated that foreigners were astonished by the quantities of portraits in the annual exhibitions and that, while this could be seen as a reflection of 'the great want of the extension of knowledge of the arts among the people', it was also a measure of the 'great wealth of the country'. There was, claimed one witness, 'no class of art that brings more money to the doors'.[8] Since the Royal Academy needed money, portraits were a necessary evil. They were also a self-perpetuating evil because their exhibition fostered that very interrogative sociability that generated them in the first place and of which they were the measure. Parallel to the spectacular increase in

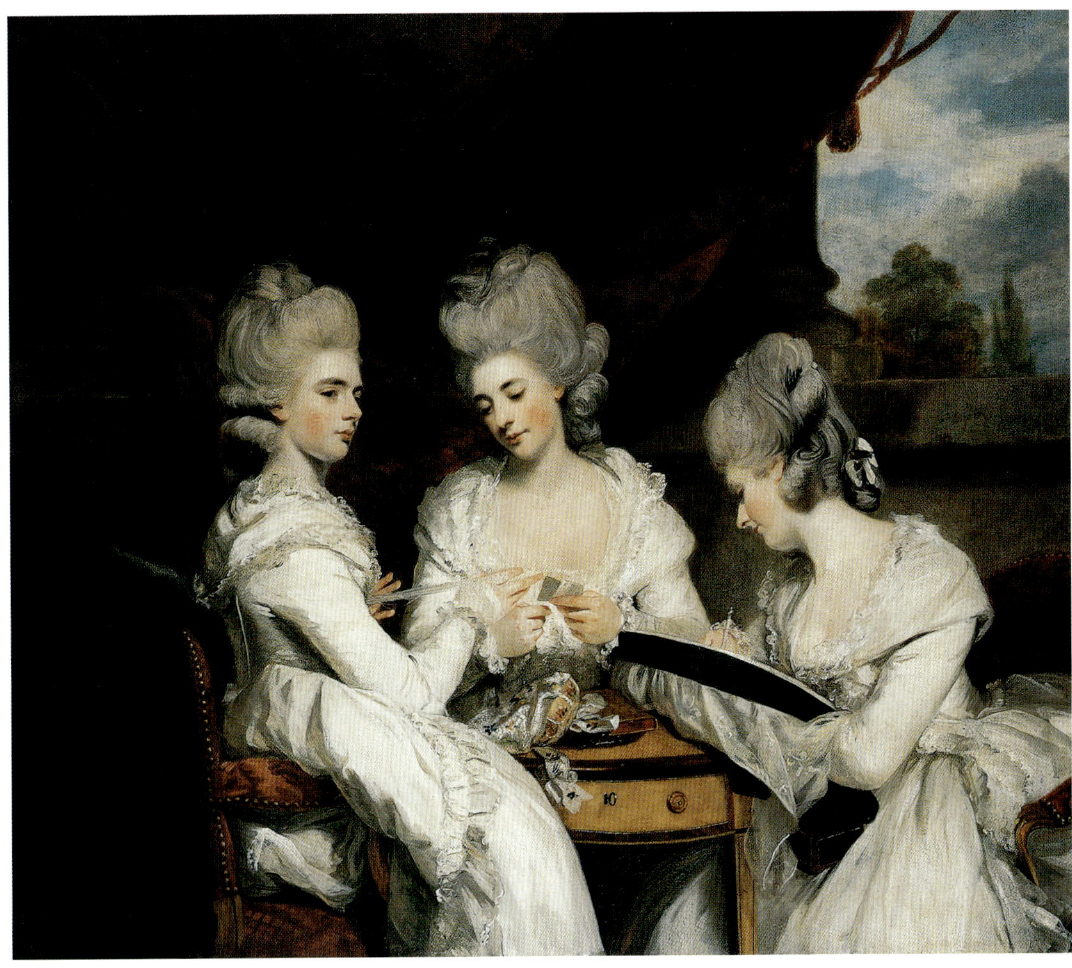

63 Sir Joshua Reynolds, *The Ladies Waldegrave*, RA 1780. National Gallery of Scotland, Edinburgh.

portraits exhibited in the late eighteenth and early nineteenth centuries was the development of an effective national network of newspapers and magazines; with the help of the press, Royal Academy portraits encouraged and responded to an interest in personalities that also linked regional and metropolitan centres through institutions like the theatre and learned societies. By the time the portrait of the child musical prodigy, William Crotch, reached the Academy in 1786, educated men and women throughout England would already have heard of his wonderful performances in Norwich. The portrait lent zest to the cult of such personalities while simultaneously satisfying a craving to match anecdote with facial appearance. Nor was it a small matter that the local artist, in this case the thirty-three-year-old William Beechey, could thereby make the transition from regional to metropolitan practice. Portraits permitted the convivial activity of identification, recognition, self-recognition, emulation and self-projection. And this engagement resulted in a technology of portrait production, supported by a commercial press, designed to ensure that audiences would be held in thrall. Rather like the representational strategies of *Hello!* magazine in our own times, the portrait painter of the late eighteenth century, in the words of writer and critic George Cumberland, 'having discovered that the highest coloured pictures are those which attract publick notice most . . . alters his style, or at least paints in that manner for the Exhibition', resulting in the 'profusion of rosy cheeks, cherry lips, and black eye-brows, which thrust themselves on our notice the moment we enter a modern exhibition room'.[9]

Until the end of the eighteenth century, the majority of portraits were recorded in the official exhibition catalogue in simple class terms (portrait of a nobleman . . . clergyman . . . lady, etc.). Virtually the only individuals given specific identities were members of the royal family – and in the case of George III and Queen Charlotte their unprecedented regal fertility ensured a continuous stream of portraits as their thirteen surviving children grew into adulthood. But visitors were able to exploit this relative anonymity to establish their own credentials in the beau monde, taking their cue from the king who, we are told, delighted in identifying portrait subjects without reference to the manuscript list which was provided for the royal visit.[10] Thus, anyone of distinction would have known that the three splendid young women in Reynolds's portrait of 1780 (fig. 63) were Horace Walpole's nieces, the Ladies Waldegrave. At the turn of the century a trend, perhaps influenced by libertarian tendencies and greater freedom in social relations, led to a change: in the

1805 catalogue more than half of the portrait entries give names of sitters. Simultaneously the professions (medical and legal men in particular) occupied more space on the walls, acquiring greater public visibility.

Visitors to the exhibitions in the period 1780 to 1840 would have viewed images of public and private figures interactively, matching existing knowledge and hearsay to what they saw on view, speculating about personal histories, and sharing anecdotes. They were also able to display themselves among the paintings, sculptures and miniatures, and to enjoy being recognized as well as recognizing others. Ramberg's image of the 1787 exhibition (see fig. 35) depicts visitors eyeing each other – and the President and his guest, the Prince of Wales – as much as looking at paintings. The combination of the beau monde and its imagery attracted a crowd that was numerous and sometimes unruly: in 1806 a writer complained that the exhibition was 'rapidly becoming a mere saloon for a morning lounge to see the likeness of a friend, instead of an academy of painting and a School of Science'.[11] Even the crowds that pushed their way into the exhibition, caricatured by Rowlandson and others (see figs 39 and 44), and visible behind the burly figure of the porter (John Withers?) in John Russell's portrait (frontispiece), did not deter people from coming. The 1808 exhibition, it was announced, 'continues to attract all those with whom the love of the arts, of fashion, or of a lounge, is a motive powerful enough to vanquish the horrors of heat',[12] and by 1826 things had improved so little that the exhibition's 'medley crowd' was described as 'less civilised than at any other place of entertainment, except the minor theatres or galleries elsewhere'.[13] A fan might help to combat the heat but even that could be a site for portraiture (see fig. 38), an ambulant device advertising one's loyalist disposition as well as one of London's most fashionable events.

Portraits (and to a lesser degree other genres) at the Academy were such a major event that an informal system of previewing emerged. What Reynolds and Gainsborough were engaged in was often reported, or at least speculated upon, prior to the show's opening, but there was also much secrecy around the precise identity and appearance of the works to be exhibited. By the early 1820s, professional critics were writing frankly of their attempts to tour the studios in advance of the private view, and even to try to prise out of the Academicians responsible for hanging, or the Royal Academy porters, news of what would be on show.[14] Nor did the passion for portraits fade with the closing of the exhibition at the beginning of June. Many of the most popular portraits were engraved, ensuring their afterlife once the original paintings had left Somerset House to be viewed by a more select, if still numerous, audience on the walls of their owners' dwellings. Valentine Green, for instance, engraved Reynolds's *The Ladies Waldegrave* in 1791, while Charles Heath enjoyed a long-term collaboration with Thomas Lawrence. The engraved portraits exhibited at Somerset House fostered a sense of continuity from one exhibition to another, reinforcing the public identities of certain individuals and endowing particular portraits with iconic status. Take the case of the Duke of Wellington, who towards the end of his life was overwhelmed with the attentions of portrait painters, sitting to Lawrence several times between 1814 and 1817, and again in 1820 and 1824.[15] In 1818 Lawrence's portrait of Wellington mounted on his famous horse Copenhagen, surveying the battlefield of Waterloo, was exhibited to great acclaim, eliciting the comment that 'the sentiment of the picture is so raised above the customary style of Portraiture that we doubt whether we ought to place it in the class of Poetry'.[16] The exhibition in 1830 of William Bromley's engraving after this famous composition (see fig. 199), at a time when Wellington was first minister and at the forefront of parliamentary legislation, was an act of national piety as well as a celebration of portraiture as an art of recognition.

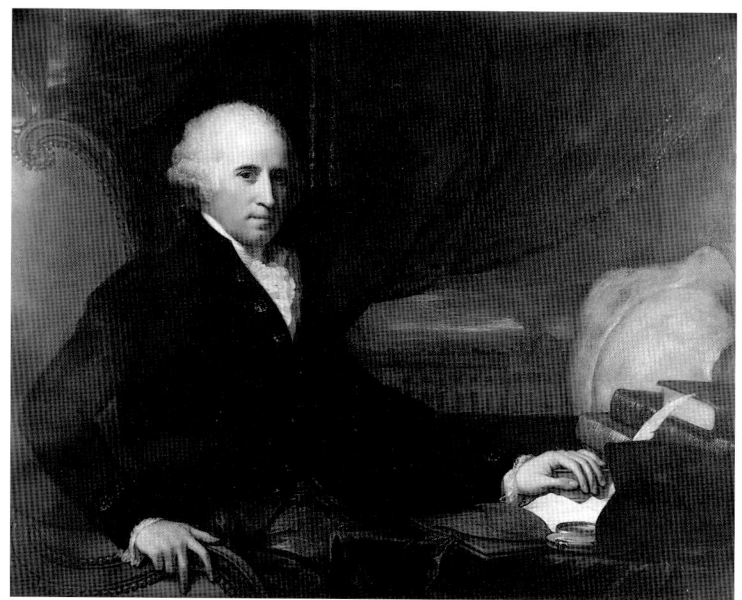

64 Benjamin West, *Self-portrait*, 1792. Royal Academy of Arts, London.

Academicians frequently painted themselves and each other, exhibiting the resulting images in the annual shows. Virtually every exhibition at Somerset House contained a cluster of such portraits. This practice not only further loaded the emphasis on portraits as opposed to other genres, but also intensified the self-referentiality and internalization that were criticized by the Select Committee. One of the most splendid self-portraits (though in this case an unexhibited example) was that painted by Benjamin West on the occasion of his election as President (1792), and now owned by the Royal Academy (fig. 64). Interestingly, West did not represent himself here in the act of painting, but instead showed himself seated at a desk, surrounded by books (including a history of Greece and a history of England) and writing equipment, the fine lace at his wrists and his elegant long-fingered hands suggesting a thinker rather than a practitioner. The background contains a clearly recognizable view of Somerset House, echoing the similar feature that

Reynolds had included in his portrait of its architect, William Chambers (1780). In the intermediate space is a cast of the Belvedere Torso, presumably the example used in the Academy's school (the original belongs to the Vatican). As Allen Staley has remarked,[17] West's portrait appears to make an explicit claim to his right to assume Reynolds's position and, more generally, to his ability to carry out all the obligations of an intellectual and artistic leader to ensure that his adopted country would attain levels of accomplishment to vie with those of antiquity. But whereas Reynolds gave both his own self-portrait and that of Chambers to the Royal Academy, West (perhaps in response not only to his own sense of self-worth but also to an increasingly commercialized environment in the Academy) did not donate his portrait, presumably expecting it to be purchased by the Academy, and it remained in his possession until his death. Surely West's renowned self-esteem was a symptom of his position as an immigrant, and also of the Royal Academy's ambitions as an institution; the history of the portrait is, however, also a sign of the ambiguities that surrounded the relationship of portraiture to ideas of worth, whether financial or artistic.

Royal Academicians were compromised: despite rhetorical declarations of commitment to a hierarchy that placed history painting at its summit, their best artists were portraitists, and both audiences and the budget required that portraits outnumbered other genres. The rage for exhibitions was a rage for portraits; the Academy, for all its royal charter, its annual dinner and its clubbishness, was competing in a market that became, in the period under review, ever more crowded and volatile. London was, from the last quarter of the eighteenth century, full of portraitists, most of whom would never show their wares at Somerset House; among the multiplicity of commodities on offer were likenesses in media ranging from embroidered silk and hair to wax and even butter,[18] alongside services like frame-making, copying and restoration. Mary Linwood's permanent exhibition of embroidered copies was recalled in 1841 as one of 'the lions of London' (fig. 65).[19] Wax modelling was practised by sought-after artists like Samuel Percy and Catherine Andras, who rose to eminence as modeller to Queen Charlotte (see fig. 144);[20] but at the other end of the cultural spectrum there was Salmon's waxwork exhibition, which lasted from the late seventeenth century until Dickens's time, where paying customers could entertain themselves with 'portraits' of subjects ranging from the current royal family back to King Arthur.[21] Against this tide of lesser shows the Academy had to work hard to maintain its dominant position in the public eye, and prominent portraitists who chose to exhibit elsewhere, for all the lamentation over the prevalence of their genre, often aroused indignation. For instance George Romney, who preferred the Incorporated Society of Artists to the Academy, was accused of failing in his duty, whether through 'monstrous affectation, absurd perverseness, or erroneous timidity'.[22]

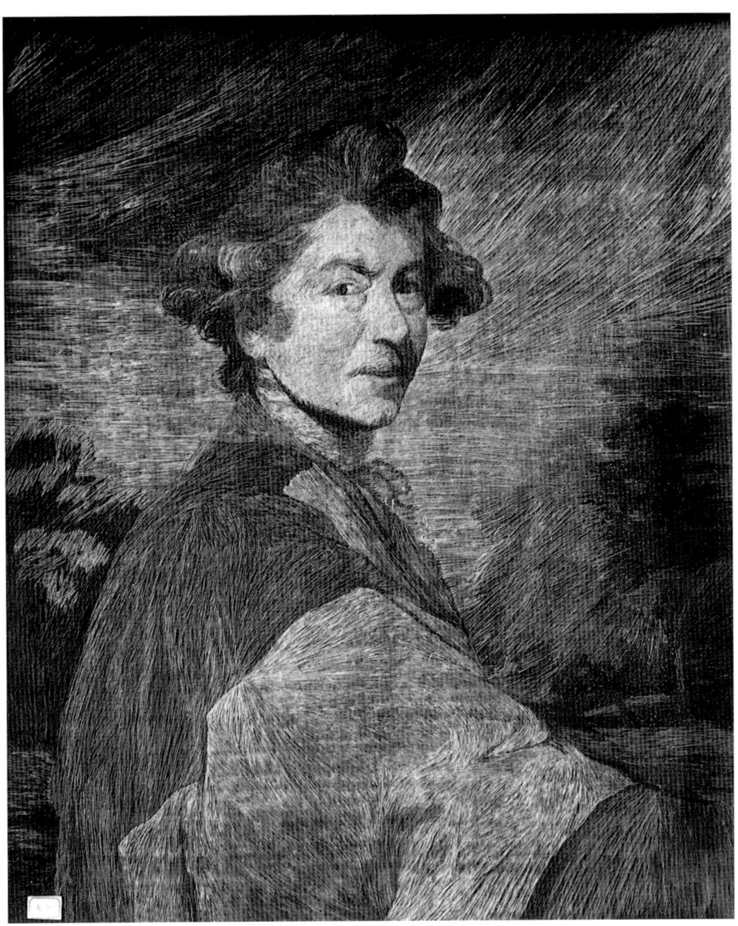

65 Mary Linwood after Sir Joshua Reynolds, *Self-portrait of Reynolds*, date unknown, embroidery. The Bowes Museum, Barnard Castle, Co. Durham.

The dilemma of an Academy that officially viewed portraiture as inferior but which needed it to maintain its position as the premier exhibition venue is well illustrated by the case of John Singleton Copley's *Death of Chatham* (fig. 66), which incorporated no fewer than fifty-five portraits of the members of the House of Lords. Begun around 1779 and completed in spring 1781, its 'appearance at the RA was anticipated with interest and curiosity'.[23] But Copley, wishing to maximize his earnings, instead hired out James Christie's auction room in Pall Mall as the venue for an independent exhibition. Sir William Chambers was so stung when he heard of this plan that he compelled Christie to renege. Quite undeterred, Copley succeeded in securing the alternative space of the Spring Gardens Rooms, regularly used by the Society of Artists, to show his enormous picture. Here the work that Chambers scornfully described as a 'raree show' attracted more than 20,000 paying visitors bringing (it was claimed) profits of around £5,000 for the artist, while the receipts of the Somerset House exhibition fell by a third.[24]

In characterizing a group portrait of noble politicians at a dramatic historical moment as nothing more than a 'raree show', Chambers sought to denigrate Copley's exhibition by associating it with the fairground entertainments of the lower orders.[25] Loss of prospective revenue may have provoked the architect's

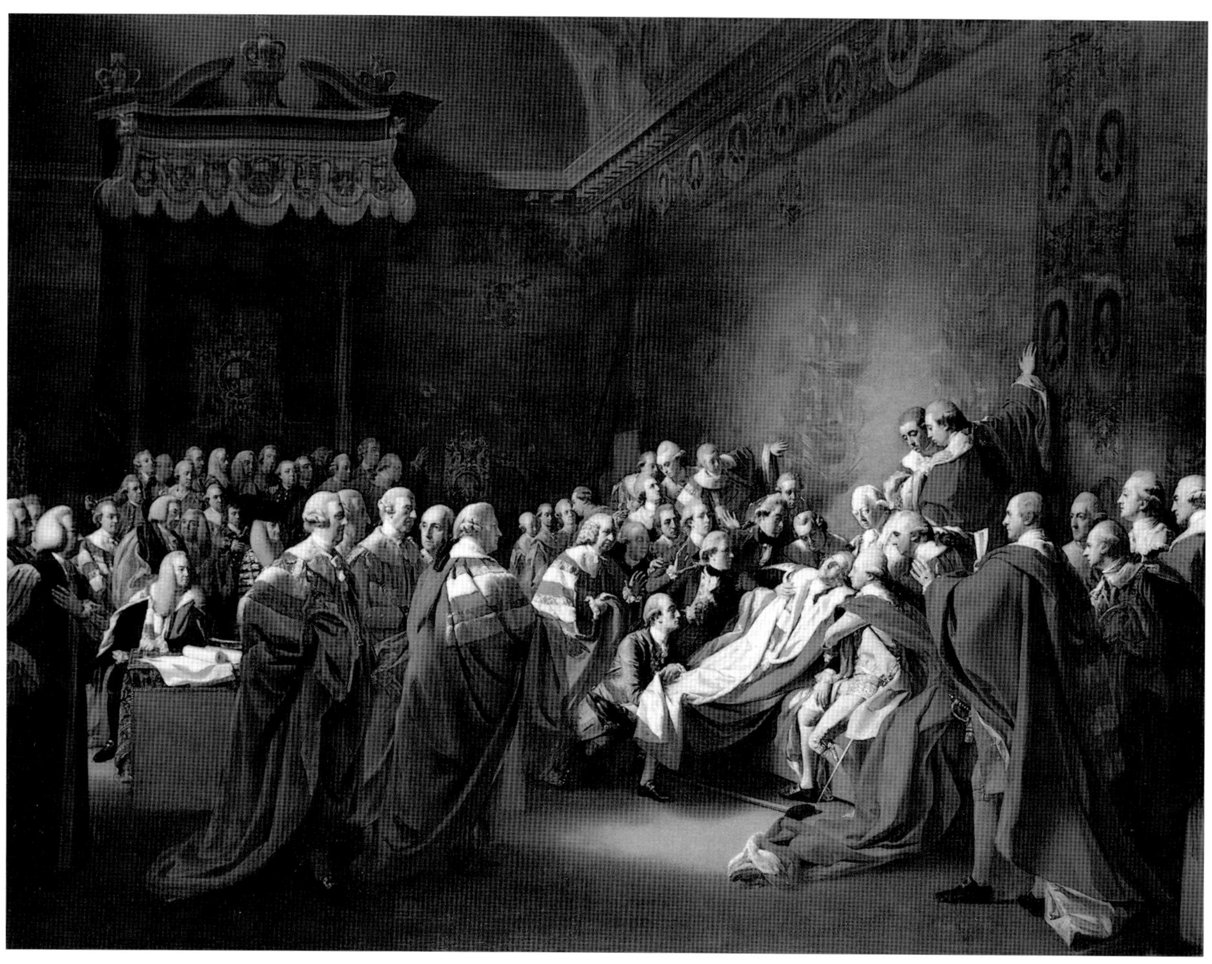

66 John Singleton Copley, *The Death [or Collapse] of the Earl of Chatham in the House of Lords, 7 July 1778*, 1779–81. Tate, London.

anger, but the issue of how to police portrait exhibitions, and the tainting effects of Academicians adopting the strategies of showmen, were of equally pressing concern. In a world where portrait images migrated from the Great Room walls on to ceramic jugs, Bilston enamelware patch boxes, paste plaques, inn signs, wallpaper (the housekeeper's room at Burton Constable, Yorkshire, is papered with a Duke of Wellington wallpaper) and a host of other surfaces, securing the most favoured portrait productions for the walls of the Academy was of more than theoretical concern. Portraits by the best artists could, moreover, be viewed at any time of the year in public and semi-public locations, as well as in private houses, throughout the metropolis: in Westminster Abbey which was filling up with effigies of national heroes, in the premises of the livery companies, in the Royal College of Surgeons,[26] the Society of Antiquaries and, by 1832, also at the National Gallery of Practical Science (fig. 67).[27] Many of the new periodicals, like the *Monthly Mirror*, featured portraits as frontispieces.[28] Wherever they were located, portraits aroused intense interest; as James Northcote tells us, when the French ambassador, Count d'Adhémar, returned to Paris, his London house was opened to the public and the nobility flocked to see

67 Thomas Kearnan, *The Long Room, Gallery of Practical Science, Adelaide Street, Strand*, *c.*1830, etching. The Bodleian Library, University of Oxford, John Johnson Collection.

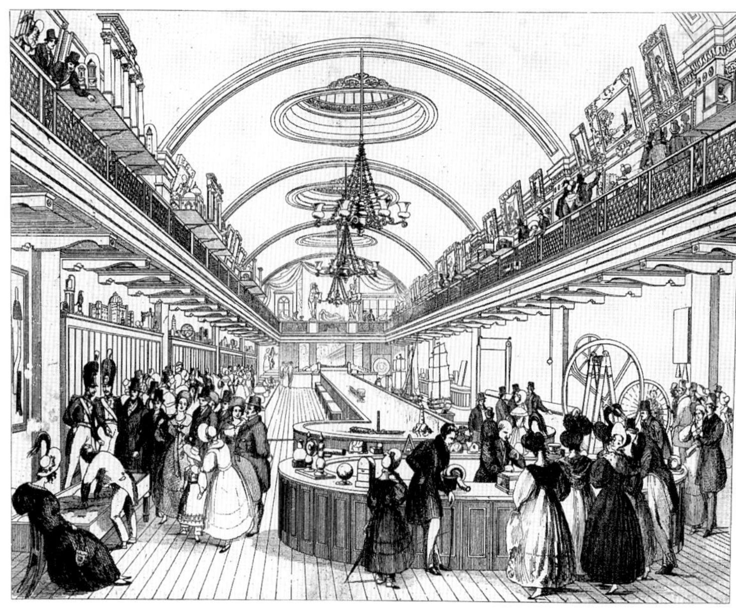

his portraits of Louis XVI and Marie-Antoinette by Vigée-Lebrun.[29] Moreover, Copley's success soon inspired a host of imitators, including Mather Brown, another American-born artist who specialized in semi-fictitious portrait groups based on topical subjects, such as *Lord Cornwallis Receiving the Sons of Tipoo Sahib* (London, Oriental Club). In 1792 Brown, in partnership with the engraver and printseller Daniel Orme, exhibited *Raleigh Destroying the Spanish Fleet* at the European Museum, a gallery in St James's Square founded by yet another American, John Wilson.[30] The extra-Academy exhibition remained popular well into the nineteenth century; when Charles Eastlake completed *Napoleon on Board the Bellerophon* in 1815, he displayed it first in Plymouth and then not at Somerset House but in a large room near the White Bear, Piccadilly.[31]

Published collections of engraved portraits, such as *Iconographia Reynoldsiana: Portraits of the Most Distinguished Characters in the Reign of George III from the Pictures of Sir Joshua Reynolds* (1814)[32] brought the products of the Academician's portrait art into the home. Indeed, the nobility and gentry were specifically invited in prospectuses for such publications to purchase engraved portraits 'to enliven country mansions at low cost'.[33] Viewers were further alerted to the significance of portraiture as a national art and educated in its history by articles like Richard Westall's series 'Opinions on Portraits' published in the *Somerset House Gazette* in 1824. The British Institution's display of 183 portraits of eminent historical characters, accompanied by a catalogue containing biographical accounts, drew huge crowds when it opened in May 1820, and to no one's great surprise. For as the critic Henry Crabbe Robinson remarked, as both 'works of art' and 'memorials' of eminent persons, these portraits were well 'calculated to raise a passion for biography' – despite the doubtful veracity of some of the identifications.[34]

The national 'passion' remarked by Crabbe Robinson, and the widespread belief that viewing portraits was potentially inspirational, contributed to the close identification of portraits with patriotism. Given that the Royal Academy was a public institution, supported by the Crown, it naturally followed that many of the portraits shown at Somerset House elicited comments that were highly nationalistic in nature. This may have been true especially in the case of Sir Joshua Reynolds, because of his dominant position in the art world and his prominence in London society. By and large, contemporary critics trusted Sir Joshua to endow the national art with dignity and distinction; although disputatious comments on his work might focus on the propriety of allegorical portraiture, on composition, attitude or on likeness, such criticisms were minor in comparison to the overwhelming endorsement of Reynolds's genius. Nor did his influence diminish after his death in 1792. Quite the contrary: posthumous exhibitions of his work (notably at the British Institution in 1813), as well as the publication of engraved collections, helped keep Reynolds in the public eye as a benchmark for national excellence.

Efforts to promote Sir Joshua as a modern 'great master' helped fuel what Crabbe Robinson ridiculed as 'John Bullism' – referring to the claims made by John Flaxman and others that British artists were superior to their rivals on the Continent.[35] Britain's growing reputation in the eyes of Europe depended on her military prowess, her liberties and her laws, the Prince of Wales informed his fellow guests at the Royal Academy dinner in 1811. But, he declared, 'the time was fast approaching, if it had not yet arrived, when her superiority in the Arts would be equally acknowledged'. The prince then congratulated the Academy and the country 'on the general excellence and splendour of an Exhibition "distinguished (he said) by Portraits that would not have shamed the pencil of Vandyke"'.[36] The success of portraiture in demonstrating Britain's high level of cultural achievement extended also to miniatures, that genre which 'is to other classes of art what flowers are to the vegetable world', and which by 1816 was regarded as 'nearly equalling [the] French'.[37] Robert Hunt, art critic for the *Examiner*, displayed both patriotism and eloquence in arguing that British supremacy in portraiture made her art of truly European significance. For living proof of this cosmopolitanism one had to look no further than Lawrence: 'we believe it is universally admitted', Hunt claimed in 1827, 'that Sir Thomas Lawrence is the first portrait-painter in Europe', adding that he 'only wants more solidity and depth of effect to render his pictures almost perfect' and thus to equal those of Reynolds, Rubens and Rembrandt. Readers could, it was pointed out, compare Lawrence with the last two painters named, examples of whose work were currently on display at the British Institution.[38]

For the general public, interest in portrait painters was often overshadowed by curiosity about the subjects of their exhibited works. Many critics, too, felt as free to comment on the qualities of the sitters as on the quality of the pictures in which they appeared.[39] Thanks to a well-received portrait shown at Somerset House, a relative nonentity could enjoy a brief moment in the limelight, before reverting to a well-deserved obscurity – a pattern that also embraced a host of minor portraitists. Horace Walpole drew an apt (if hardly original) analogy between the transitory nature of human reputation and the quick turnover of portraits and painters. Within a generation, he observed, the proud possession of the drawing-room would be relegated to the parlour, then to the stairs, then to the country or to the housekeeper's room, before finally being consigned for disintegration to a broker's shop at Seven Dials.[40] Pictures of great men might be expected to avoid this fate, however, for they were a national asset. 'Were not Lord Grenville destined to live in the pages of the Historian', asserted the *Examiner* in 1812, William Owen's portrait of him (fig. 68) 'would carry his harsh but vigorously intellectual countenance down to posterity'.[41] But even the portrait pantheon posed dangers for the dilettante who might 'chuse to spend his day in looking at pictures of wise and great men rather than in conversation with them'.[42] 'Great men' did not, however, necessarily commission those who were, or are today, regarded as great artists. Reynolds, for all his celebrity, did not please George III and his family, who preferred to employ Gainsborough, Zoffany, and later John Hoppner. Those portrait painters who were most highly regarded, most prolific, and most influential in terms of image-making were not always those whose reputations have endured. John Jackson (fig. 69), George Harlow, George Dawe and Henry Pickersgill were enormously esteemed in the first two decades of the nineteenth century; the same is true of Mrs Carpenter, Henry Howard and Francis Grant in the 1830s,[43] along with miniaturists like George Clint and W. C. Ross. When Thomas Phillips died in 1845 he had exhibited continuously for fifty-two years; had it not been for this now little-regarded artist we would have far fewer portraits of the country's leading literary, scientific and legal figures of the first half of the nineteenth century (fig. 70).[44] But perhaps the most dramatic example of fame eclipsed is William Owen, who, extensively lauded in his lifetime, merited no more than a brief paragraph in the 1996 Macmillan *Dictionary of Art*.[45]

68 William Owen, *Lord Grenville*, RA 1812. The Governing Body, Christ Church Oxford.

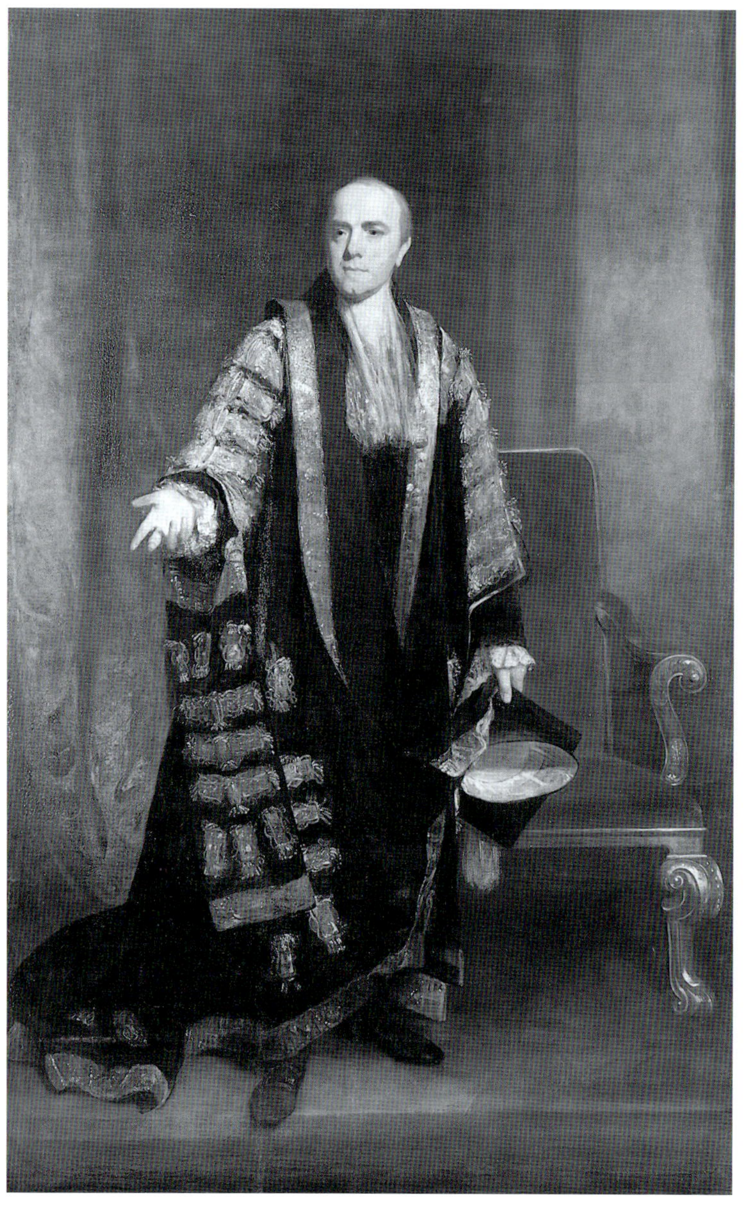

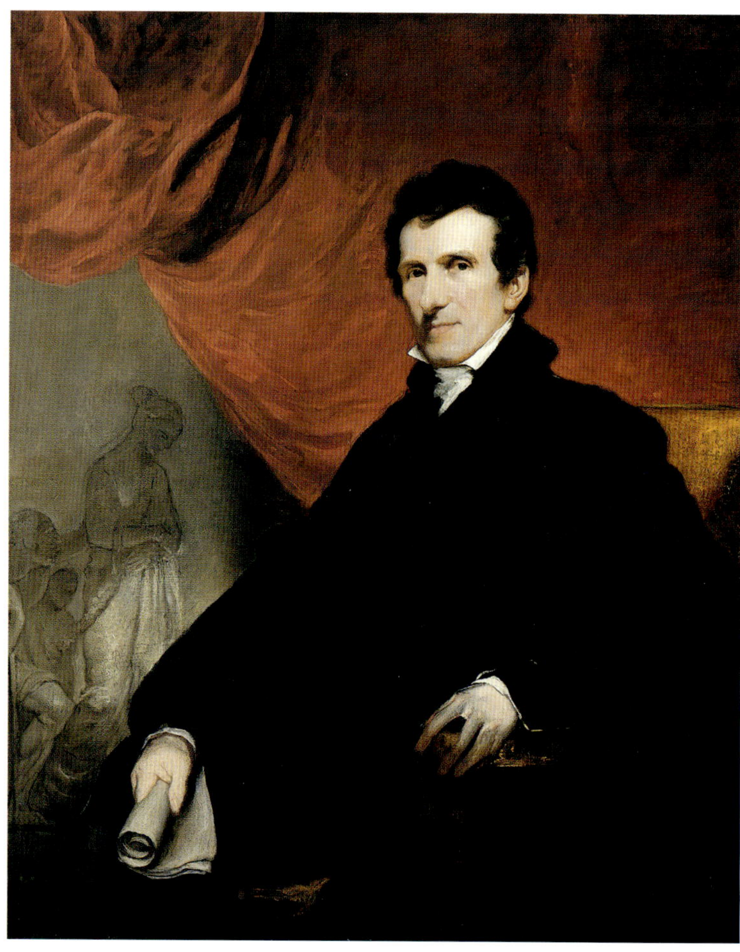

69 John Jackson, *Antonio Canova*, RA (?)1810. Yale Center for British Art, Paul Mellon Collection.

If portrait subjects were to enjoy the fullest exposure to the promiscuous gaze of public and critics alike, their images had to be placed where they could readily be seen by the crowds of visitors to Somerset House. Decisions about hanging were crucial, in other words; yet neither the prominence of the painter nor the fame of his or her subject guaranteed favourable placement. At times there were tensions between the perceived importance of an artist and that attached to a sitter, as vividly registered in the frequent controversies about the Hanging Committee and its decisions. Thus a relatively minor artist like J. P. Davis[46] might reasonably anticipate an advantageous position for his picture of the celebrated beauty, Lady Wellesley, who had recently married – and, when it was not accorded, might either complain himself or persuade his friends to do so. A sympathetic critic (probably Robert Hunt) drew upon a common set of assumptions about the fundamental inseparability of portrait

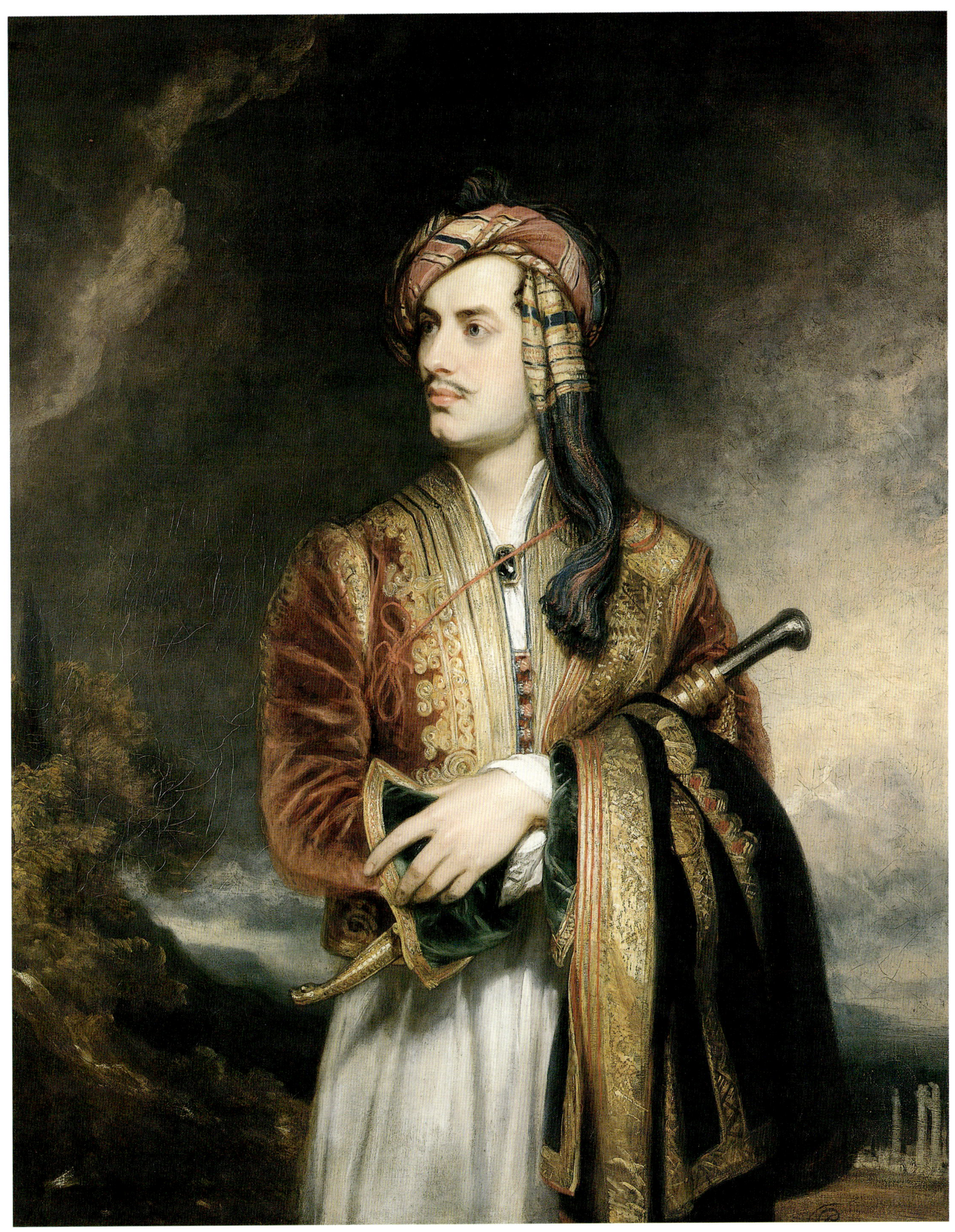

70 Thomas Phillips, *Lord Byron in Albanian Costume*, RA 1814. UK Government Art Collection.

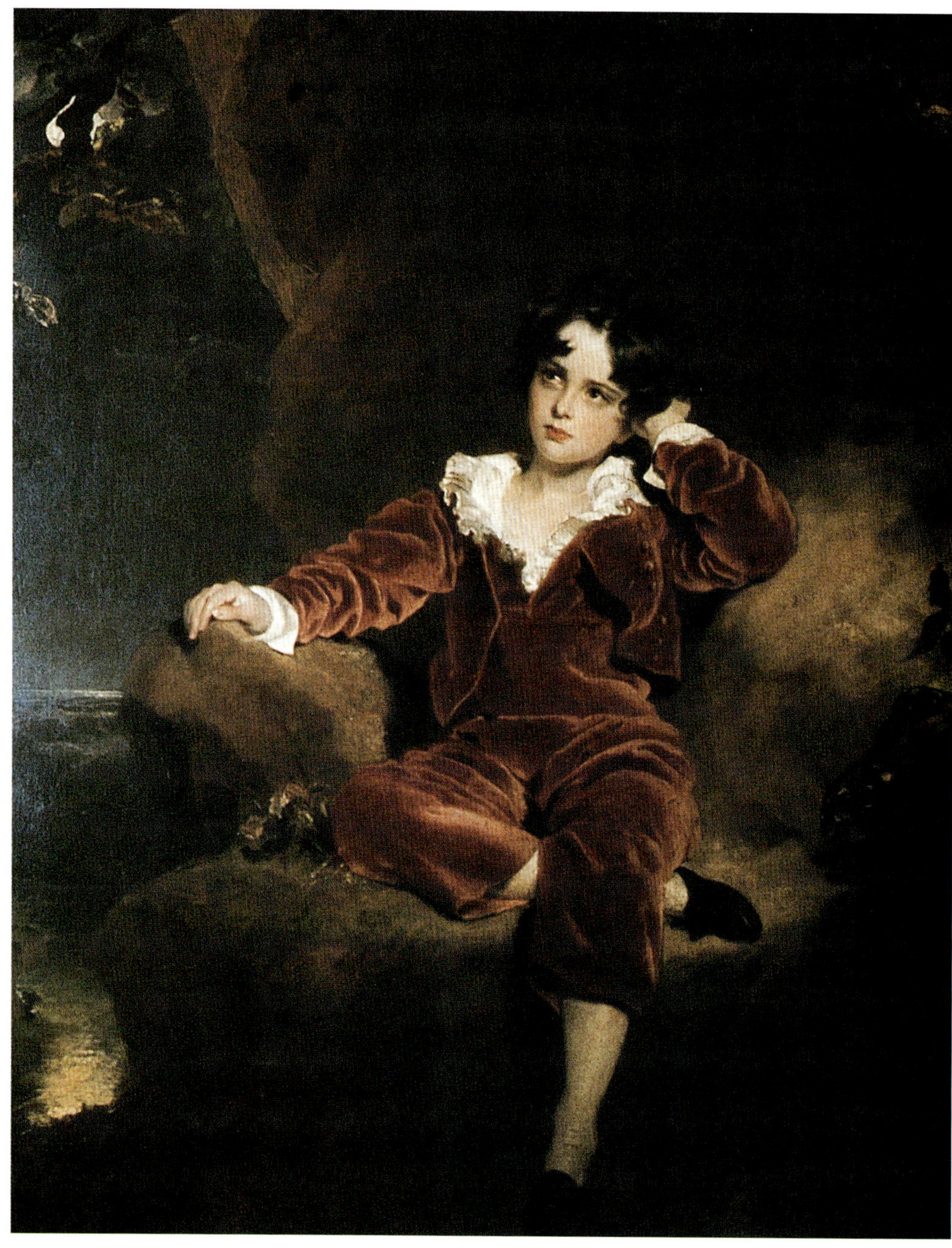

71 Thomas Lawrence, *Master Lambton*, RA 1825. Private collection.

and sitter when he objected to the way in which Davis's *Lady Wellesley* had been

> thrust . . . into a room miserably lighted, and with that light so glaring on the picture, that there are but two or three parts of the room from which it can be seen. . . . Now putting the merit of the work entirely out of the question, has not the public the right to see the portrait of a lady who has so much excited the public curiosity by the reputation of her beauty, and the high rank to which she has so lately been elevated?[47]

Presumably not, would have been the Academy's answer to this question: little-known portraitists who were not Academicians could expect few favours from those responsible for arranging the display. But while the high reputation of certain artistic luminaries might confidently be expected to secure an advantageous position for their works, this did not always prove to be the case. Thus, when in 1825 Lawrence's *Master Lambton* (fig. 71) was hung not in the Great Room but in a smaller chamber (and even then not on the line), and his portrait of Mrs Peel above a doorway, the Hanging Committee was reproved in the press.[48] Further problems were created by the insistence of artists that their images of influential clients be shown in large and flashy frames; it was in vain that the RA Council in 1833 protested about the overpoweringly magnificent surrounds containing Wilkie's full-lengths of King William IV (fig. 72) and H. R. H. The Duke of Sussex.[49]

This was far from being the only occasion when pictures of exceptionally important people demanded and received special treatment. Since such patrons tended to expect their likenesses to appear in advantageous positions, adverse treatment by the Hanging Committee could leave artists in a deeply embarrassing situation. No wonder that emotions ran so high on this issue. It was not simply arrogance that prompted Gainsborough's insistence in 1783 that his small portraits of the royal family (fig. 73) be shown below the line, where he felt they could be properly seen;[50] his threat never to 'send another picture to the Exhibition', unless his instructions were obeyed, features as only one of the many recorded disputes between painters and the Somerset House 'hangmen'.[51] Perhaps the most crucial of their decisions involved the most esteemed position in the Great Room: above the line directly over the mantelpiece on the east wall.[52] It was from here, for example, that Lawrence's portrait of George Canning (fig. 61) dominated the exhibition in 1826.[53] But the issue of hanging extended beyond the positioning of individual works to what was perceived as the problem of a genre driven by the contingencies of location. Words like 'glitter' and 'glare' were habitually employed by early nineteenth-century critics trying to come to terms with the crowded walls. Portraits that were intended for 'the small dark rooms in which pictures in England are hung', and which therefore 'call[ed] for brilliancy and whiteness',[54] seemed strident when encountered *en masse*. The fashion for sharply contrasting light effects and for areas of intense white that had been condemned in Copley's *Sitwell Family* (RA 1786; private coll.) as meretricious glare evolved into a bravura painterly panache in the exhibition pieces of Hoppner, Lawrence and Raeburn, upsetting the visual economy of the Great Room. In the words of one critic, 'The public eye is diverted by the glare of the half-lengths and whole-lengths, from the modest pictures clad in sober hues which peep out amongst them'.[55] But colouristic immodesty was a necessity, if a work was not to risk being overlooked.

72 David Wilkie, *William IV*, RA 1833. Courtesy of the Board of Trustees of the Victoria & Albert Museum, Apsley House, London.

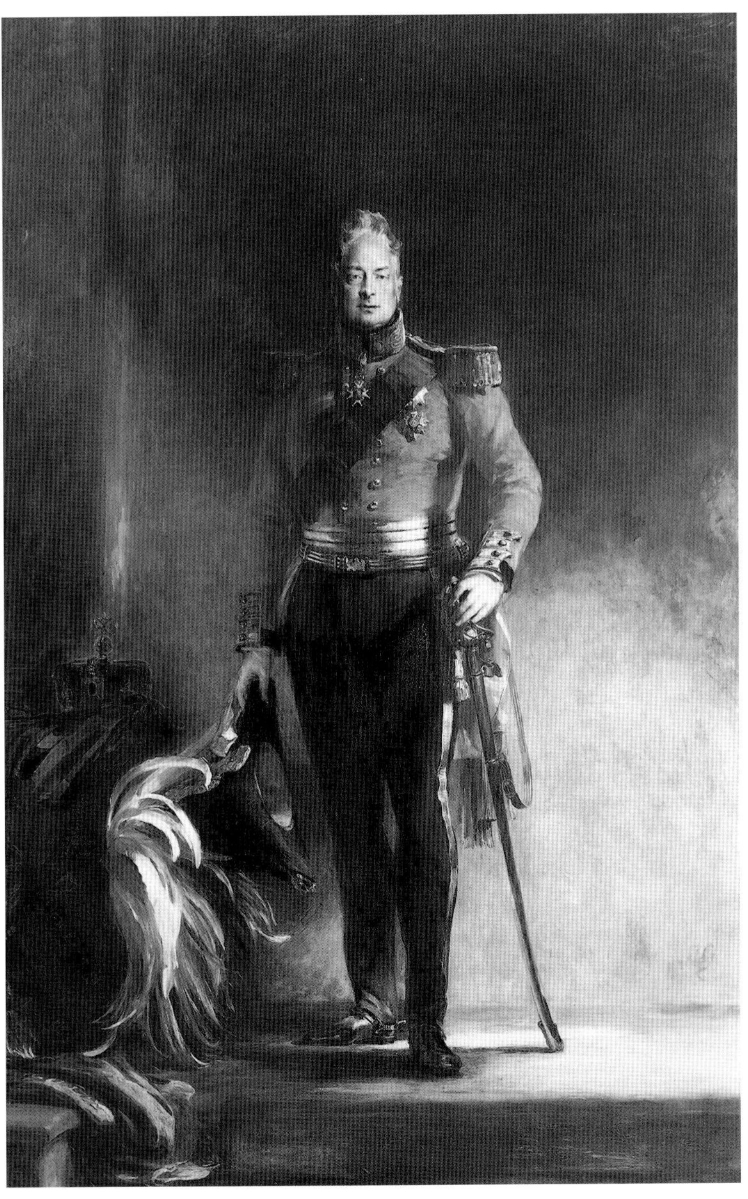

Artists who persisted with delicate tonalities, or who worked in media like pastel that could not be adjusted on varnishing day to the glare around them, sought strategies to counter the effects of the exhibition environment. As early as 1783, for instance, Gainsborough discovered that a group of bust-length portraits hung together as one ensemble could present a more striking effect than if they were presented singly.[56] Doubtless a similar motive underlay the highly popular John Downman's policy of frequently showing his small pastel portraits in groups of six or nine. But there is no doubt that, rightly or wrongly, the Hanging Committee was seen as very powerful and often corrupt and, even when it fulfilled its obligations honourably, the results for many artists could only be disappointing. For, as one critic astutely observed, 'there are many exquisite pictures in the exhibition, but it is curious to observe what little advantage they derive from it'.[57]

In a world prior to visual animation, paint on canvas, especially when proffered in the heightened and animated environment of the RA exhibitions, provoked strong feelings of empathy and generated a critical discourse that was pleasurable precisely because of its deliberate blurring of boundaries between actuality and simulation. Moments of recognition could be genuinely poignant: among Gainsborough's fifteen portraits of the royal family in 1783 was that of four-year-old Prince Octavius, who had died on 3 May, a week after the exhibition opened (fig. 74).[58] Nowadays such a portrait might well be withdrawn in the interests of protecting family privacy, but not so then: indeed, when the queen and the princesses were reduced to tears at the sight (presumably the king and the princes exhibited manly restraint), their display of feelings offered public confirmation of laudable royal sensibilities. While attempts were made to judge the merits of portraits as 'art', distinguishing

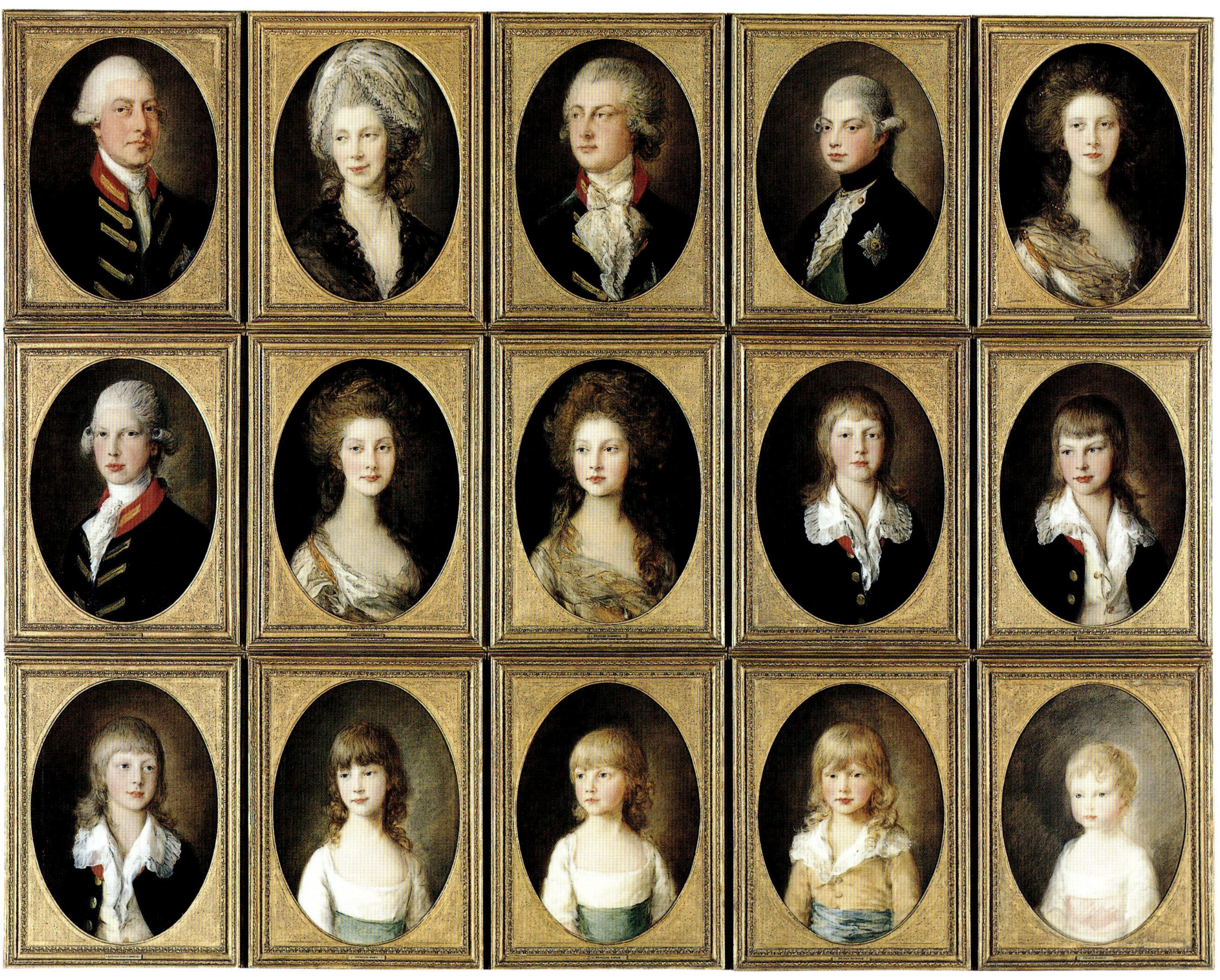

73 Thomas Gainsborough, *The Royal Family*, RA 1783. The Royal Collection © 2001 Her Majesty Queen Elizabeth II.

anything with historical or poetic pretensions over and above simple likenesses,[59] the excitement of viewing could generally be measured in proportion to the degree of recognition involved. Thus in 1810 Lawrence's portraits of political figures gave rise to a parody of the emotional impact that the subjects themselves might, in the flesh, have produced, an impact which underscored the differences of gender, reinforcing ideas of femininity as a soothing antidote to masculine action:

> To mention Mr Lawrence's tasteful and vigorous portraits is to speak of excellence. He has been busy this year among the peculators, parliamentary traffickers, and Golgothites, and the immaculate Melville, merciful Castlereagh, and disinterested Canning, shine on his canvass. – On first looking at them, the complacency with which the sight of the other paintings had filled my mind, was instantly converted into the most uneasy emotions. The pictures appeared, like Draco's laws, to be marked with blood. I thought of my fellow subjects plundered, imprisoned, tortured, death-struck with slow consuming fevers, slain, cities terrified, battered, filled with blood, fired, and the fair and populous face of nature impiously converted into deserts and charnel houses. To relieve my feelings I turned to the amiable objects in No. 8 Portrait of a Lady and her Attendant, W. Owen, RA . . .[60]

When Gainsborough died in 1788, his obituarist in the *London Chronicle* dwelt upon the extraordinary talent that had enabled the artist to give 'not merely the map of the face, but the character, the soul of the original', through an act of imprecision. In a passage perhaps unsurpassed not only in the Gainsborough criticism but also in the analysis of portrait resemblance we learn that the artist 'gives the feature and the shadow, so that it is sometimes not easy to say which is which; for the scumbling about the feature looks like the feature itself; so that he shows the face in more points of view than one, and by that means it strikes every one who has once seen the original with being a resemblance'.[61] The same article also draws a distinction between Gainsborough's portraits of men and women, the latter 'being frequently designed from women that were painted [giving] a general appearance to all his females of painted women'.[62] The implication here is that once a manner is adopted in portrait execution it informs all portraits regardless of the model. Underlying this account of Gainsborough's art is an oscillation between the mechanism through which passing appearances are transformed into a visual vocabulary that guarantees recognition and the sense of portraiture as an art in which ornamentation and design configure a fashionable topical dialect independent of the sitter. And it is the latter which is understood as determined by, as well as defining of, gender.

Likeness is thus a relative matter, embedded in questions of spectatorship, social familiarity and fashion, as well as gender. It is extremely unlikely that everyone viewing portraits at Somerset House in the 1780s would have seen the sitters in the flesh, though this is what Gainsborough's obituarist implies; the point is that there was an assumption, a discursive framework for viewing, predicated upon such expectations of familiarity. Likeness was more about matching an *idea* than replicating an original, and ideas about people, then as now, were shaped by cultural experiences as well as individual disposition. Audiences and critics, holding ideas about subjects, thought it legitimate to comment on likeness whether or not they had seen the sitter. It was upon these grounds that a debate took place in 1786 over the verisimilitude of Reynolds's portrait of the eighty-year-old Lord Chief Justice Mansfield, who, when consulted on the matter, claimed never to have looked in a mirror for a whole generation.[63] Moreover, portraits often masqueraded as subject paintings and, equally, fancy pictures were known (but not officially recognized) to contain portraits. The blurring of genres that was a characteristic of some of Reynolds's portraits – whether representing women as classical personages or child subjects in fancy dress – was acknowledged by Northcote when he told Hazlitt: 'Portrait often runs into history, and history into portrait, without our knowing it'.[64] By 1840 the inventions of Nièpce and Daguerre were familiar to a wide audience;[65] within a couple of decades these would lend to portraiture an entirely novel set of possibilities regarding questions of likeness, facture and gender that formed the armature for analysing the genre in the late nineteenth century.

I would like to stay with the terms 'likeness', 'facture' and 'gender' and to add a further term, 'modernity', suggesting that it was this constellation, unique to the genre, that guaranteed portrait painting's pre-eminence at the RA in the period under review. It was not only for economic reasons that portraits exerted such a powerful public allure. They constituted an important arena within which to construe notions of a modern social identity, whether by comparing similarities or contrasting differences. For the aristocracy a common language was required, even if such a language accommodated certain variations (as with, for example, the choices in drapery/dress, powdering/natural hair that divided Reynolds and Gainsborough). Against this common standard the differences implied by images of racial others (fig. 75), or of middling men who had risen to fame for one pre-eminent achievement or another (fig. 76), could be measured. Likeness is by this measure less a question of aesthetics than of politics. The preoccupation with likeness also, however, manifests a concern with the growing gulf between image and referent, between a portrait representation and its subject, that had already been felt in Reynolds's day. Early nineteenth-century readers were invited to look back to the era of Hudson, Highmore and Hogarth, and to observe that 'our modern Raffaeles will make your picture independent of

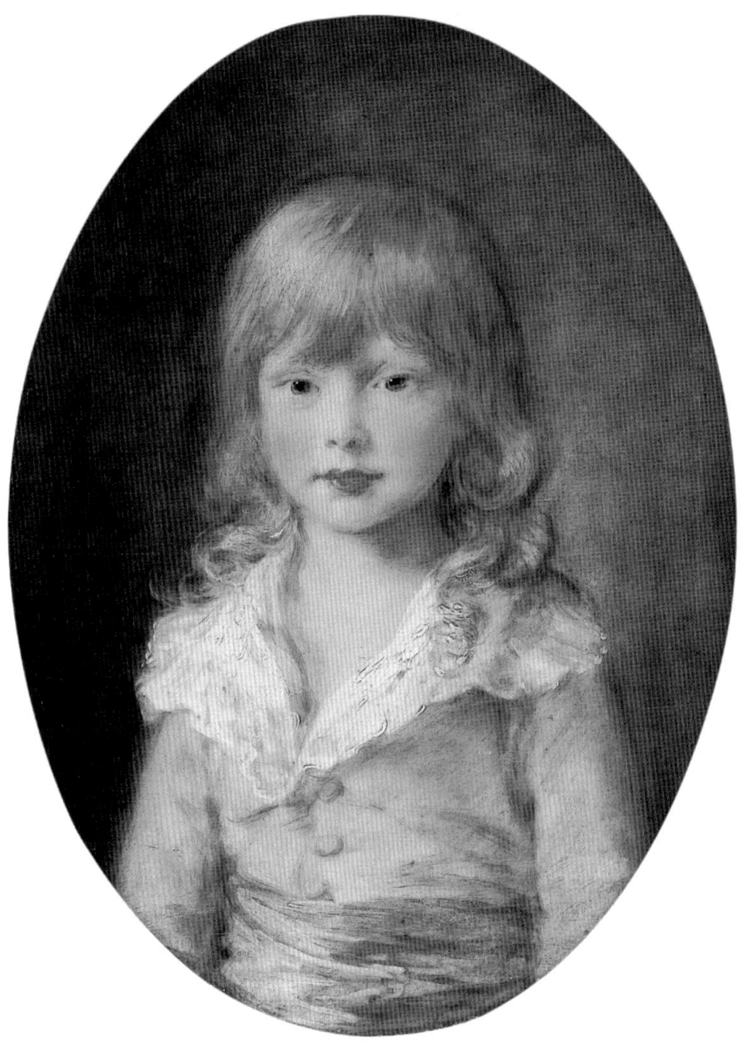

74 Thomas Gainsborough, *Prince Octavius*, RA 1783. The Royal Collection © 2001 Her Majesty Queen Elizabeth II.

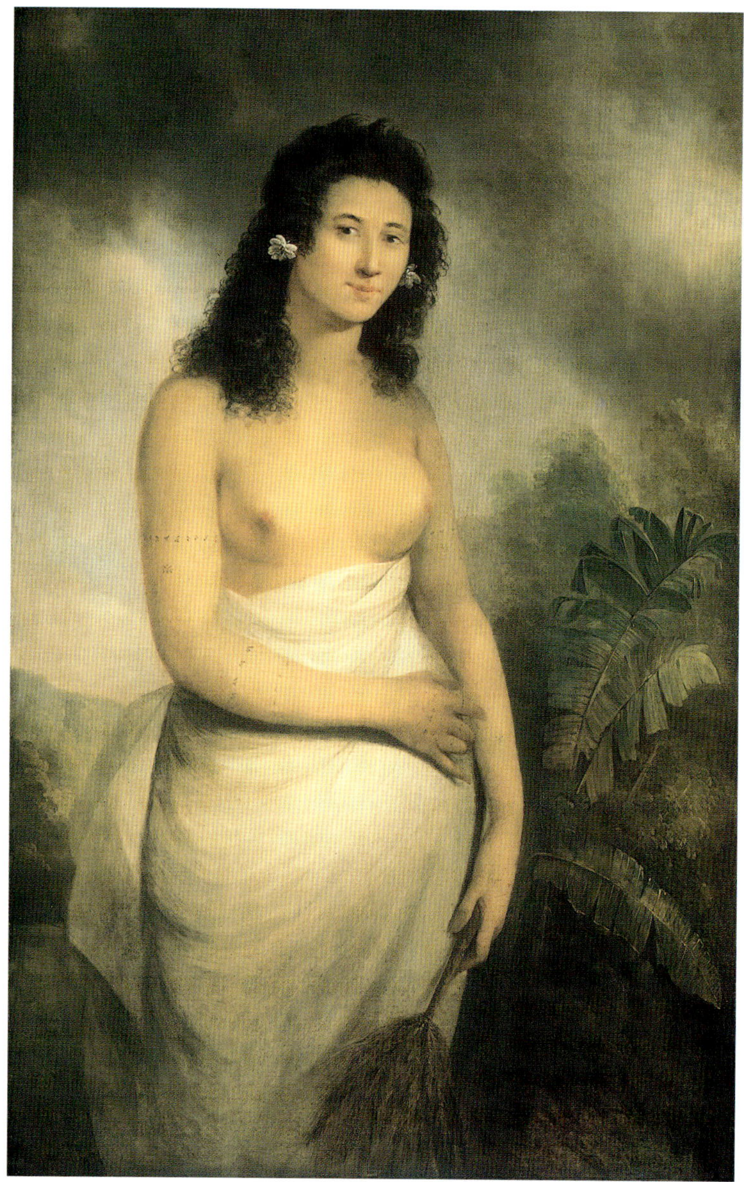

75 John Webber, *Poedua, Daughter of Oree, Chief of Ulaietea, of the Society Islands*, RA 1785. National Maritime Museum, Greenwich.

yourself', unlike the old-style portraits 'all stiff and awkward' but bearing 'an inveterate likeness to the original'.[66]

By now the art of portraiture had come to be recognized as what we would call a matter of interpretation. The diversification of portrait imagery (portraits constituted around 45 per cent of all exhibits between 1788 and 1829) inflected a fractured world in which appearances were delusory and identities transitory; this was a world where people could present contradictory faces. Thus Charles James Fox, whom it was not easy for anyone to paint without giving him a likeness, could be represented in extremely close resemblance to the original but not in pleasing resemblance, as the fierce man of public office rather than the good-humoured acquaintance.[67] On the other hand, David Wilkie, an artist of quintessentially Scottish vernacular, was portrayed by his friend Andrew Geddes not, as might have been anticipated, at work in his studio or in his native environment, but posing at leisure clad in an exotic oriental silk dressing gown (fig. 77). The individual itemization of luxury goods that had been a feature of Zoffany's conversation pieces gives way by the early nineteenth century to an all-enveloping fetishization of surface detail in which texture and substance is dwelt upon for its own sake. Reviewers responded with enthusiasm to this glorification of an explicitly contemporary material world, speaking of the ebony lustre on a pair of shoes almost in preference to the owner of the feet thus fashionably clad. Beechey was praised in his 1809 portrait of Mr and Miss Cockerell not for the faces of his sitters or their expressions but for the 'elegant modern costume and polished personal deportment' depicted.[68] Martin Archer Shee epitomized this trend: 'shewy' and 'fashionably modern', his portraits seemed unnatural and transparent, with everyday objects – flesh, wool or wood – seeming 'alike to be made of glass' (like the vitrines in the new shopping arcades). Paintings that were not then, as they are today, cus-

76 Carl Frederik von Breda, *Matthew Boulton*, RA 1793. Birmingham Museums & Art Gallery.

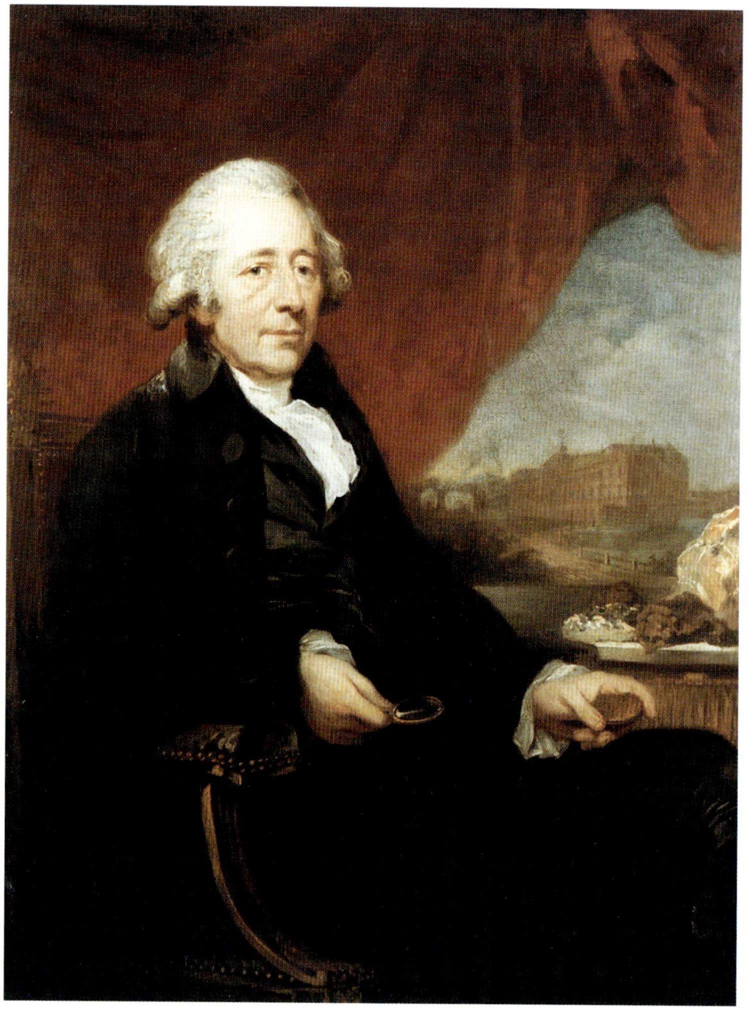

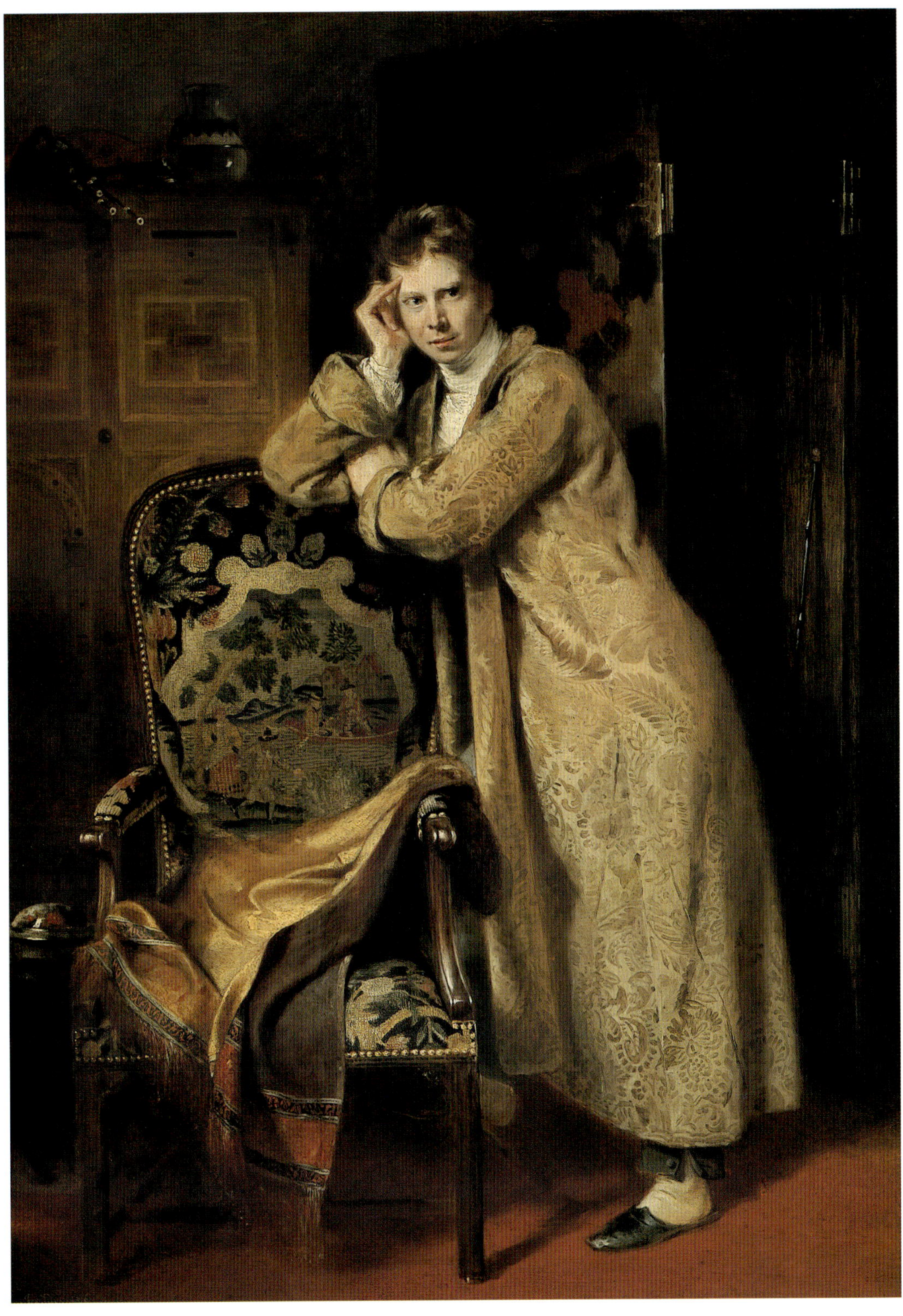

77 Andrew Geddes, *David Wilkie*, RA 1816. Scottish National Portrait Gallery, Edinburgh.

tomarily covered with glass, suggested to critics a quality of fragility, impermanence or effeminacy; instead of flesh-and-blood individuals, these works depicted 'pretty, sentimental, love-sick girls, with uplifted eyes, sitting on [Shee's] favourite lumps of sugar candy'.[69]

The art of caricature, offering subversive alternative personae for celebrities, both contributed to and profited from the proliferation of portraits and the destabilizing of identity that accompanied that proliferation. The canvases from which these caricatures often derived might, like a camera obscura or like Cornelius Varley's graphic telescope, show a persuasively 'exact' resemblance. But this, it was argued, was never sufficient – for this would tell you little of the work as art nor to what class or grouping a person belonged. What attracts the attention of critics

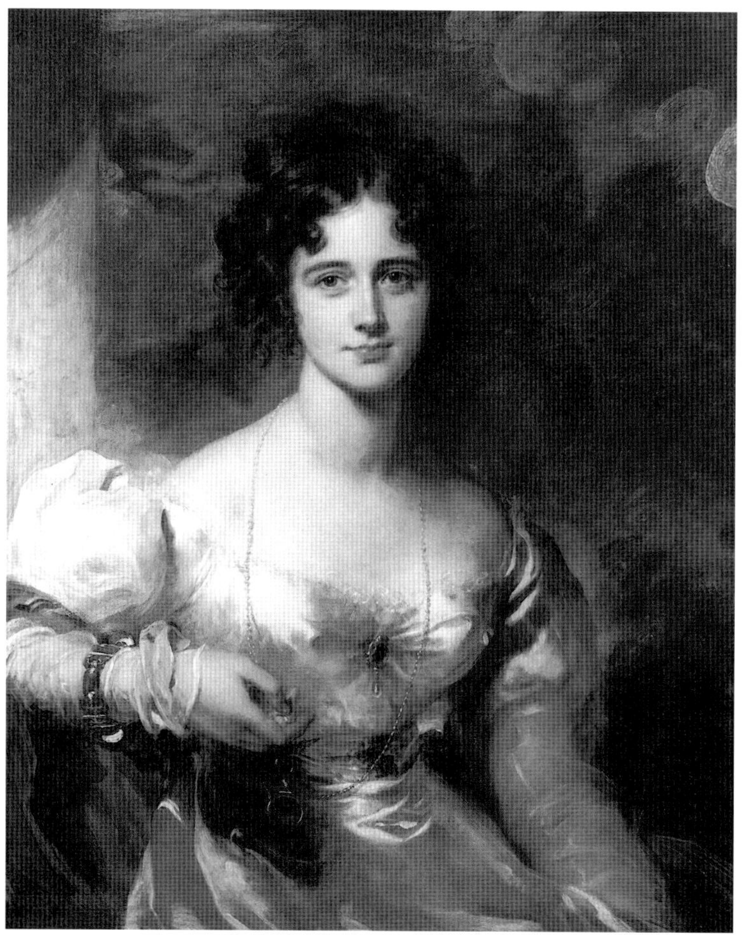

78 Sir Thomas Lawrence, *Miss Croker*, RA 1827. Albright-Knox Art Gallery, Buffalo, N.Y., Seymour H. Knox Fund through special gifts to the fund by Mrs. Marjorie Knox Campbell, Mrs. Dorothy Knox Rogers and Mr. Seymour H. Knox, Jr. 1945.

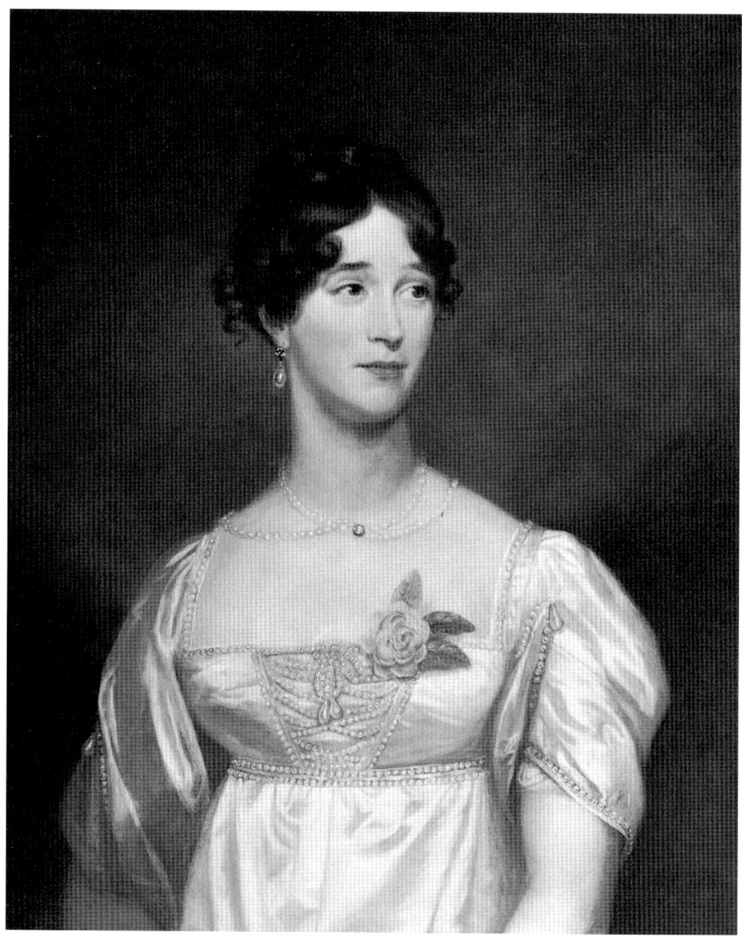

79 James Northcote, *Lady Elizabeth Whitbread*, RA 1810, Lord Howick, Howick Grange.

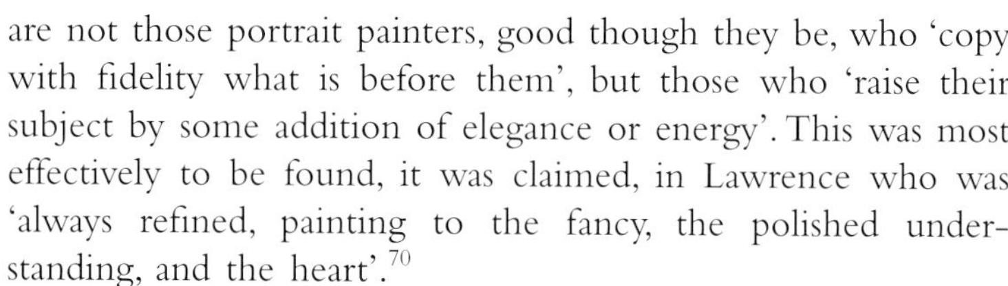

are not those portrait painters, good though they be, who 'copy with fidelity what is before them', but those who 'raise their subject by some addition of elegance or energy'. This was most effectively to be found, it was claimed, in Lawrence who was 'always refined, painting to the fancy, the polished understanding, and the heart'.[70]

Thus as a new generation of professional critics struggled for a vocabulary – and the value-added of portraiture in the early nineteenth century is designated variously as elegance, energy, fancy, poetry, refinement – likeness became increasingly problematic as a yardstick of success. After all, any artist could produce a resemblance and waxworks and silhouettes were there to prove it. So the identities of public figures in a world no longer governed by court protocol or sumptuary legislation were mapped on canvases valued for the kind of bravura of execution that could be marvelled at in a public exhibition. If likeness, *tout court*, is at issue it should be immaterial whether the subject is male or female. But, as we have observed already with Gainsborough, execution may draw attention to detail – to dress, complexion, accessories and to questions of style and fashion as contemporary visual vocabularies. Lawrence was thus praised for his female portraits and when, in 1827, he exhibited his painting of a famous beauty, Miss Croker (fig. 78), the work attracted an audience of men who stood 'before it in half-circle admiring its loveliness';[71] we may infer from this anecdote that the beauty of the subject combined with Lawrence's fluidity of handling and his brilliance of colour in ways likely to inflame spectators' desires. Through this process the identity of a sitter is crystallized in the moment of public recognition. It is for this reason that an unnamed contemporary is supposed to have said: 'Phillips shall paint my wife and Lawrence my mistress'.[72] Beechey, on the other hand, while recognized as endowed with special gifts in the rendering of female subjects, was sufficiently restrained to enjoy the sobriquet 'the Ladies' Apelles'.[73]

Artists like Hoppner, Wilkie, Beechey, Shee, Lawrence and Raeburn reinvented the painterly economy of the portrait while establishing their credentials on the walls of Somerset House. Their work stood for the modern in an exhibition where it was possible still unashamedly to quote Van Dyck (as does Northcote with *Lady Elizabeth Whitbread* of 1810, fig. 79), and where new-made men like

Thomas Telford (fig. 80) were displayed in canvases that competed in grandeur with the most ambitious imagery of the newly crowned king (fig. 81).[74] Certainly Reynolds had painted professional men from the law, the Church and the armed services as well as friends from the literary world; but the social realm in which Reynolds's pupil James Northcote moved was distinctively more demotic. The sitters whose likenesses he exhibited at the Royal Academy between 1803 and 1823 spanned the nation, and included landed gentry like Ralph Leycester; Charles Abbot, Baron Colchester and Speaker of the House of Commons; Edward Jenner, famed for his discovery of vaccination; Samuel Taylor Coleridge; the radical writer William Godwin; King George III; the great engineer Isambard Kingdom Brunel; and the boy actor Master Betty. Unlike history painting which invoked noble collective endeavour, portraiture by the early nineteenth century demonstrably generated a discourse of fragmented individualism. The annual display of portraits licensed critics to fixate upon detail in the interests of invoking a person whose individual biography might be defended on grounds of patriotism. But through the very act of communication in an exhibition environment where artistic visibility was predicated upon overstatement, the image displayed highlighted the momentary, the fashionable and the modern at the expense of a wider allegiance to a class, a nation or a history. The professional success of large numbers of portrait artists of the 1820s–40s was assured. But among the visitors to Somerset House were those who came for reasons of nostalgia, or for reassurance of a world unchanging. For them it was disconcerting to encounter an environment 'in which the merciless splendour of the painter's pallet put nature out of countenance, and in which the unmeaning grimace of fashion and folly was the only variety in the wide dazzling waste of colour'.[75]

80 Samuel Lane, *Thomas Telford*, RA 1822. Courtesy of the Institution of Civil Engineers, London.

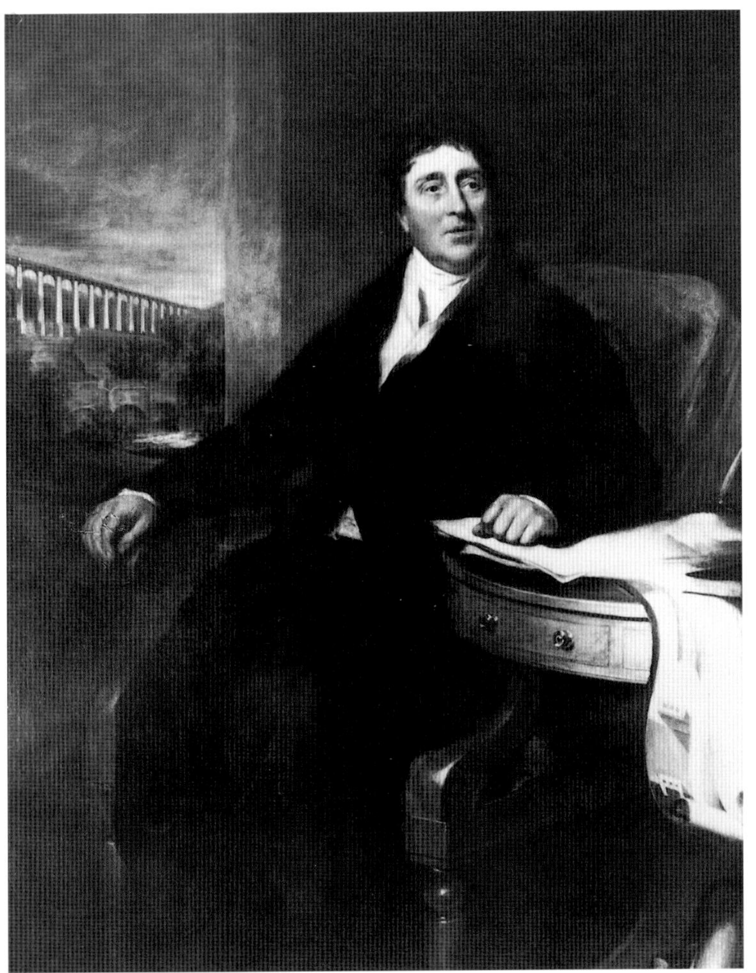

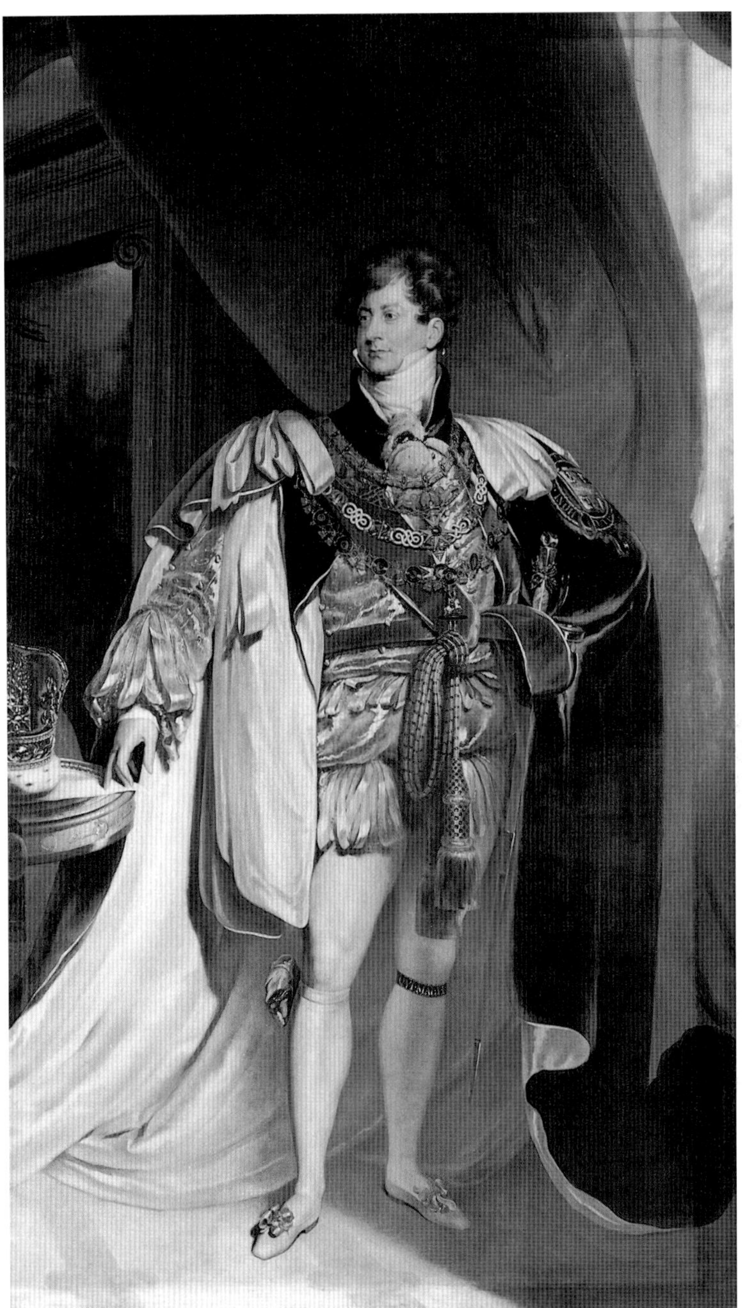

81 Thomas Lawrence, *George IV in his Coronation Robes*, RA (?)1822. The Royal Collection © 2001 Her Majesty Queen Elizabeth II.

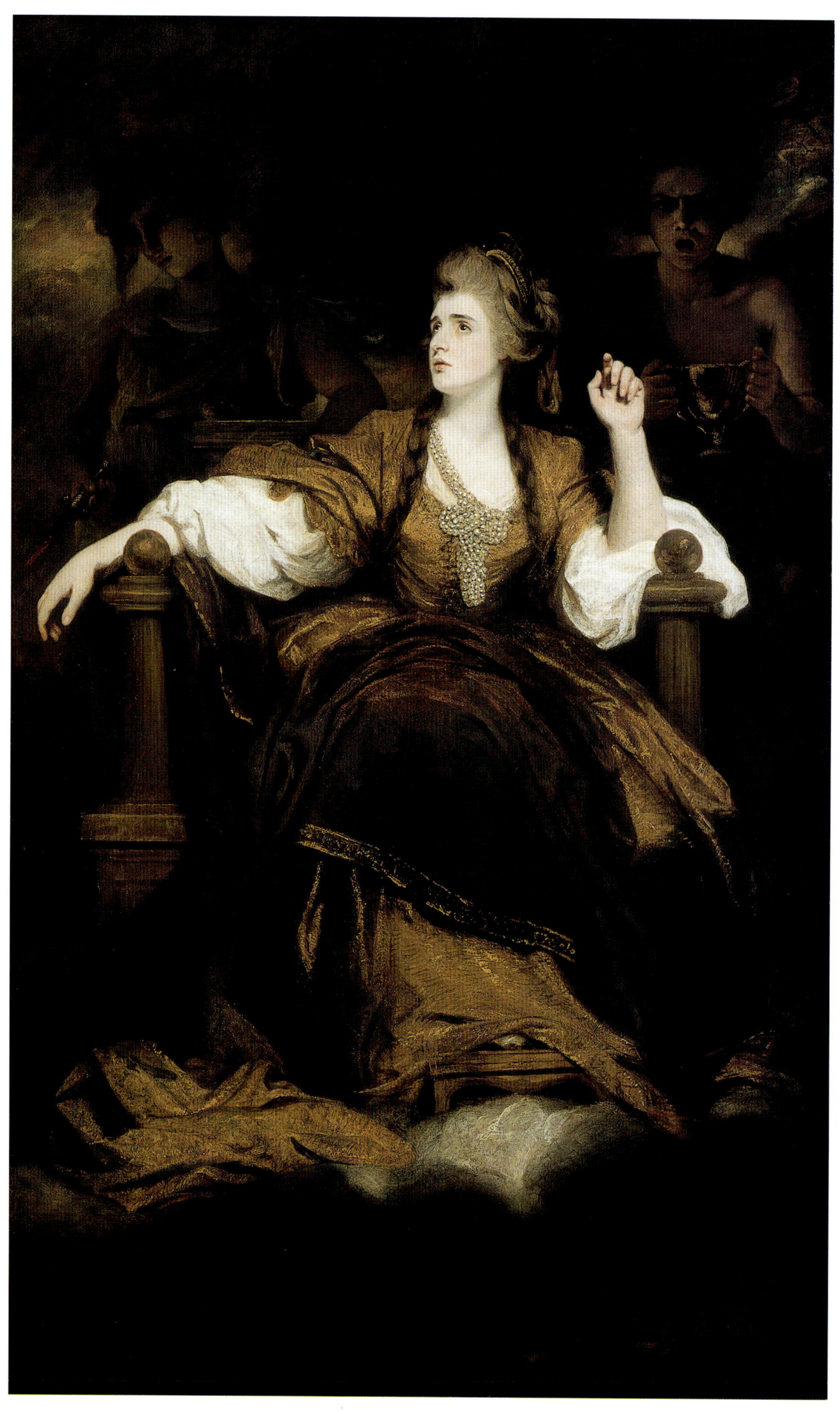

82 Sir Joshua Reynolds, *Mrs Siddons as the Tragic Muse*, RA 1784. Courtesy of the Huntington Library, Art Collections and Botanical Gardens, San Marino, California.

8

The Spectacle of the Muse: Exhibiting the Actress at the Royal Academy

GILL PERRY

IN THE WINTER OF 1782/83 the actress Sarah Siddons marked her return to the Drury Lane Theatre by appearing eighty times in seven different parts. She opened in one of her most famous roles, as Isabella, the heroine of Garrick's eponymous tragedy,[1] which played regularly to full houses. The following season she took the stage fifty times in twelve different parts, while in 1784–85 she clocked up no fewer than seventy-one performances in seventeen roles (eight of them new). Although it was then normal policy for popular theatres to produce a wide repertory each season, a seemingly insatiable public demand for Siddons's performances provoked this unusually heavy workload, encouraged by the guarantee of substantial commercial success. During the same decade portraits of Siddons featured frequently at the Royal Academy, further contributing to her extraordinary visibility. Thus as the actress's winter seasons at Drury Lane were drawing to a close, her audiences shifted their attention to Somerset House, where the object of their adulation appeared in painted form. When the annual exhibition opened in the spring of 1784, Sir Joshua Reynolds's full-length of *Mrs Siddons as the Tragic Muse* (fig. 82) generated both popular frenzy and excitement among the critics, who almost universally applauded Siddons as a tragic actress and the status of the artist's work. The following year in a revival of Garrick's popular patriotic play *The Jubilee*, Siddons was wheeled on to stage as 'the Tragic Muse', in the pose given her by Reynolds – the point being both to exploit the picture's fame and to give an added dimension of nobility to her performance in the drama. But if here art supported theatre, the theatre also supported art by lending its pulling power to the annual exhibitions. The two forms of spectacle enjoyed a symbiotic relationship, both fuelling and fuelled by the culture of celebrity.

This give-and-take, which functioned partly as a form of mutually beneficial advertising, was encouraged by the physical proximity of London's main centres of dramatic and visual art. Somerset House in the Strand was an easy walk from Drury Lane or Covent Garden, and but a short carriage ride from the King's Theatre in the Haymarket. The Royal Academy, like the theatres, was a key venue in the social diary of the educated and genteel Londoners (of both sexes), as it was for foreign visitors to the capital, all participating in what John Brewer has called 'the flamboyantly hedonistic life of fashionable society'.[2]

In this context the theatrical portrait possessed a special appeal, which contemporary painters were quick to exploit. Numerous leading Academicians exhibited examples of the genre, including, apart from Reynolds, Thomas Gainsborough, Johann Zoffany, William Beechey and Thomas Lawrence. At the RA, portrayals of actors or actresses in their stage roles provided the viewing public with a 'memory' of performances previously witnessed in the theatre, while contributing to another form of spectacle – that on offer at the exhibitions themselves. The popularity of this form of portraiture also attests to the lively cultural exchange between the worlds of the dramatic and visual arts during the second half of the eighteenth century. Not only were Reynolds and Gainsborough, for example, both keen devotees of the London stage, but they numbered such influential theatrical figures as Garrick and Richard Brinsley Sheridan among their closest friends. Sir Joshua befriended – and painted – several successful actresses apart from Sarah Siddons, including Mary Robinson and Frances Abington, whose portraits he also showed at the Academy.

During the late eighteenth century professionals in both fields were engaged in comparable battles for respectable social status;

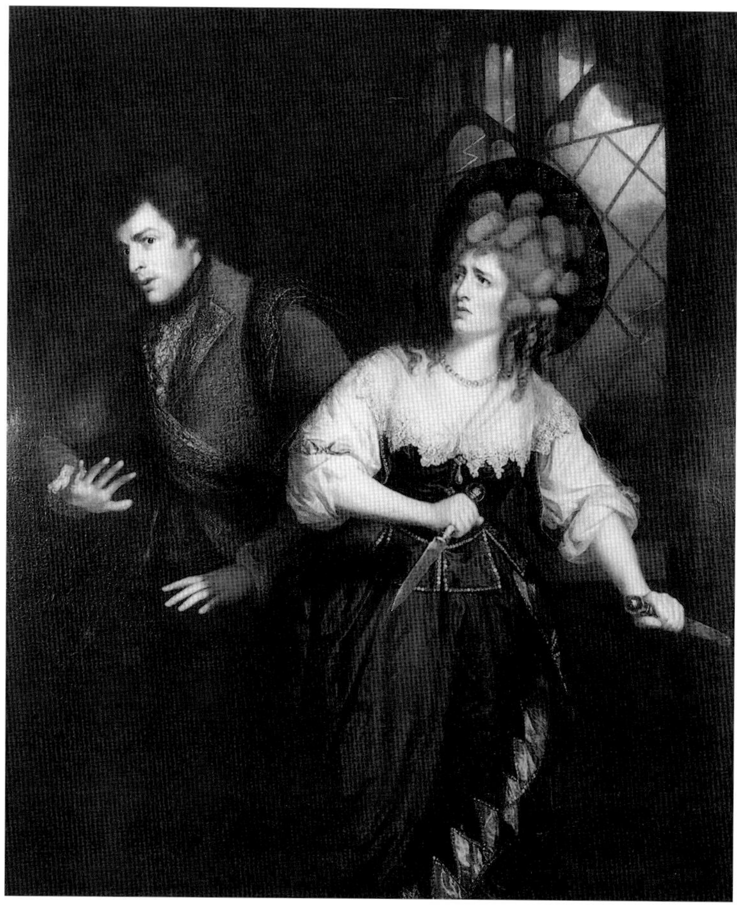

83 Thomas Beach, *Sarah Siddons as Lady Macbeth and John Philip Kemble as Macbeth*, RA 1786. The Garrick Club, London.

these struggles took place under the constant scrutiny of an ever-expanding phalanx of critics writing for newspapers and magazines, who generally supported efforts by artists, actors and their respective institutions to raise public perceptions of their work. Journalistic reviewers of the theatre and the fine arts – doubtless the same writers often covered both fields – shared an overlapping vocabulary, as a reflection of the basic assumption that the two disciplines involved visual display for public consumption. This close and multi-layered relationship is crystallized in the portraits of theatrical performers which regularly attracted so much attention at the annual exhibitions. Here I shall be discussing the reception of several prominent examples from the 1780s and 1790s, in particular with a view to understanding how the spectacle of the exhibition helped to mediate the meanings of these pictures to a contemporary audience. Issues of gender, class, patronage and professional status are all at stake here.

Though the Academy and the patent theatres had been established by royal charter, none operated under the direct patronage of the Crown,[3] and they all depended on their paying customers to keep them in business. But in both arenas the pressure to attract as large an audience as possible occasionally ran into conflict with the creative aspirations of an ambitious few to promote the most serious and elevated forms of art. At least as eloquently as any other artefact, the actress portrait encapsulated this tension between the aesthetic and the commercial. Some of the same anxieties were generated by images of (male) actors – though not to the extent provoked by the spectacle of the actress. The presentation of her painted image within the setting of a royal academy prompted a range of disturbing questions about the nature and function of its exhibition space. Were the Academicians selling out to commercial demands and the pressures of fashion? How could the prominence of so many actress portraits avoid contaminating a temple of high art with the questionable morality of the theatre and a dangerous feminine sexuality? Wouldn't such pictures compromise the Academy's dignity, which was never that secure at the best of times? Although rarely formulated in so overt a fashion, such questions proved hard for reviewers to ignore. They were aware, for instance, of sexuality as an issue, with respect not only to images of actresses, but also to feminine portraiture in general. In April 1786 at least three London papers carried the same (anonymous) paragraph:

> The R.A. opens on Monday next, when all those whose portraits are to be exhibited will hasten to enjoy the triumphs of self-love and vanity. This annual display of paintings, however, is a tax on the public, beyond the mere shillings demanded at the door. Every girl who has her face hung up, and has probably paid the artist only in amorous coin, immediately raises her price on her chance customers. Instances have been known, when the fair frail one, who would have been content to sell her beauty for a few guineas, has declared her resolution to take nothing less than a Bank note, after her apotheosis at Somerset Place.[4]

Not just vanity, but lust, greed and pride – at least four of the seven deadly sins are on offer here, brought into play by the pictures of 'fair' women on view at the Academy. Here the shilling demanded at the door is presented in uneasy conjunction with the 'amorous coin' of the artist's model, and the wages of sin of the prostitute – a social category inextricable from that of the actress. Images of the latter were inescapably present at the exhibition of 1786, where the *Morning Chronicle* (5 May) took the profusion of theatrical scenes as evidence of a 'dramatic furor' that had 'seized' contemporary painters.[5] The most widely discussed products of this 'furor' were three large-scale portraits: Thomas Beach's *Sarah Siddons as Lady Macbeth and John Philip Kemble as Macbeth* (fig. 83), Hoppner's *Mrs Jordan as the Comic Muse* (fig. 84; see below), and Mather Brown's *Joseph Holman and Anne Brunton as Romeo and Juliet*.

One important reason why works like these attracted so much critical attention is that they were seen as raising portraiture to the level of history painting, thus helping at least partially to provide the exhibitions with what they perennially lacked:

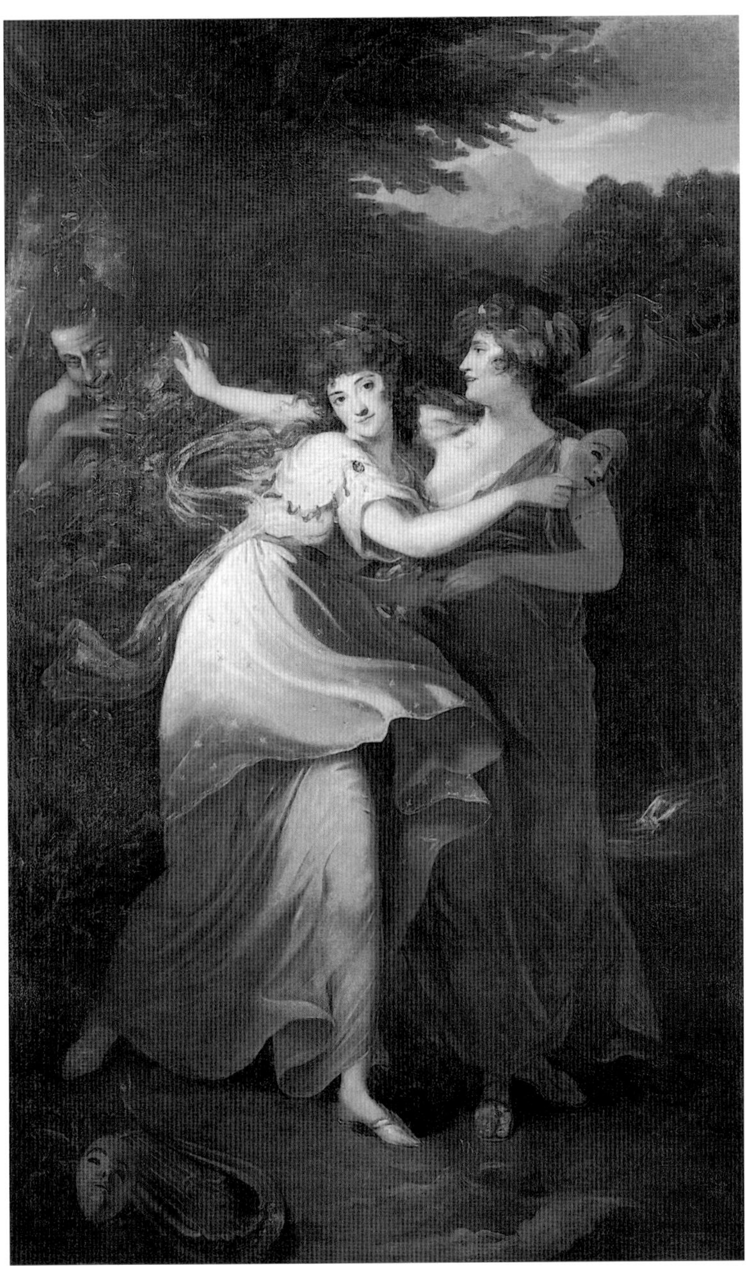

84 John Hoppner, *Mrs Jordan as the Comic Muse*, RA 1786. The Royal Collection © 2001 Her Majesty Queen Elizabeth II.

serious 'works of imagination'.[6] But this was a role which portraits of actresses, no matter how dramatically conceived, were in certain respects profoundly ill qualified to play, on account of their morally problematic (sexual and fashionable) subject matter. No wonder, then, that contemporary reviewers often found it difficult to decide what to say about these works – whether to class them under the headings of vanity and commerce with the worst tendencies of portraiture, or to emphasize those intellectual and imaginative aspects which linked them to historical art.

* * *

1782 and the representation of 'our celebrated women'

On 23 March 1782 the *Public Advertiser* carried an announcement that the forthcoming Royal Academy exhibition would feature no fewer than six full-length portraits by Thomas Gainsborough – of the Prince of Wales, Colonels Tarleton and St Leger, the Duke of Dorset, the dancer Giovanna Baccelli, and Mrs Robinson the actress, known as 'Perdita' after the character in Shakespeare's *The Winter's Tale* (fig. 85). But shortly before the show opened the *Dorset* and the *Robinson* were unexpectedly withdrawn. While we cannot be entirely certain of Gainsborough's motives, it is possible that he was anxious not to stimulate prurient gossip by exhibiting two of his sitters in provocative juxtaposition to two others: for in 1781 Mary Robinson had

85 Thomas Gainsborough, *Mrs Robinson: Perdita*, intended for RA 1782, but withdrawn prior to opening. Reproduced by permission of the Trustees of the Wallace Collection, London.

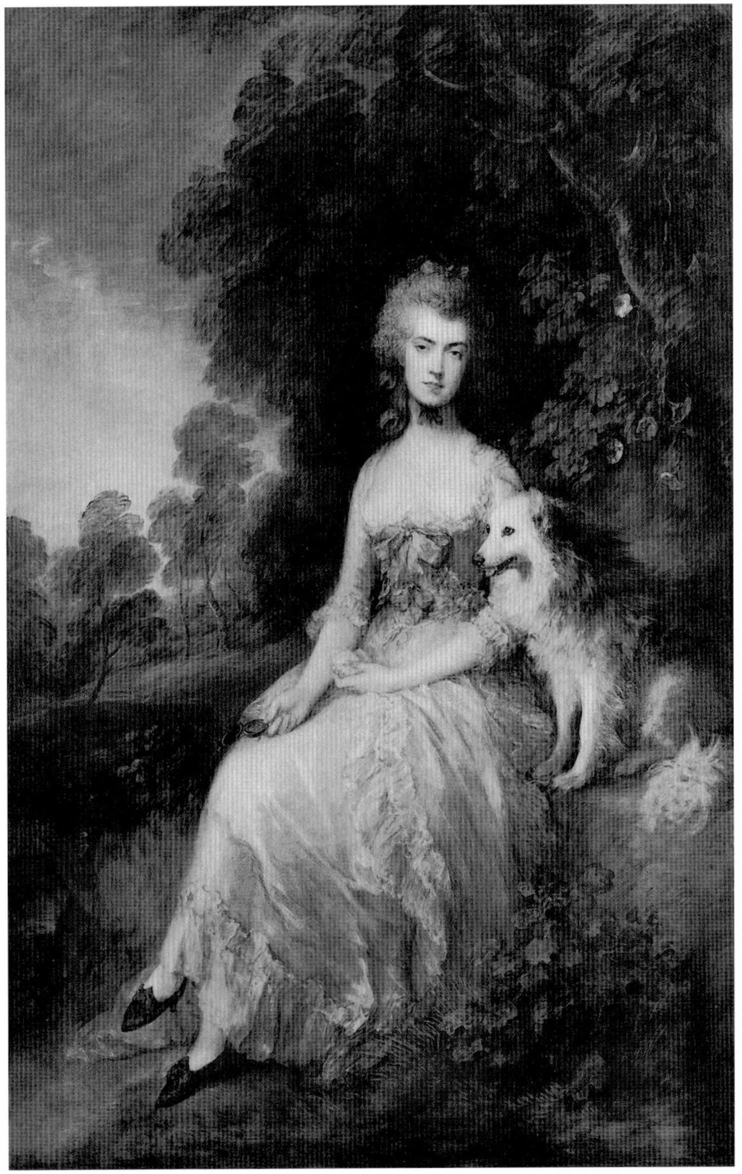

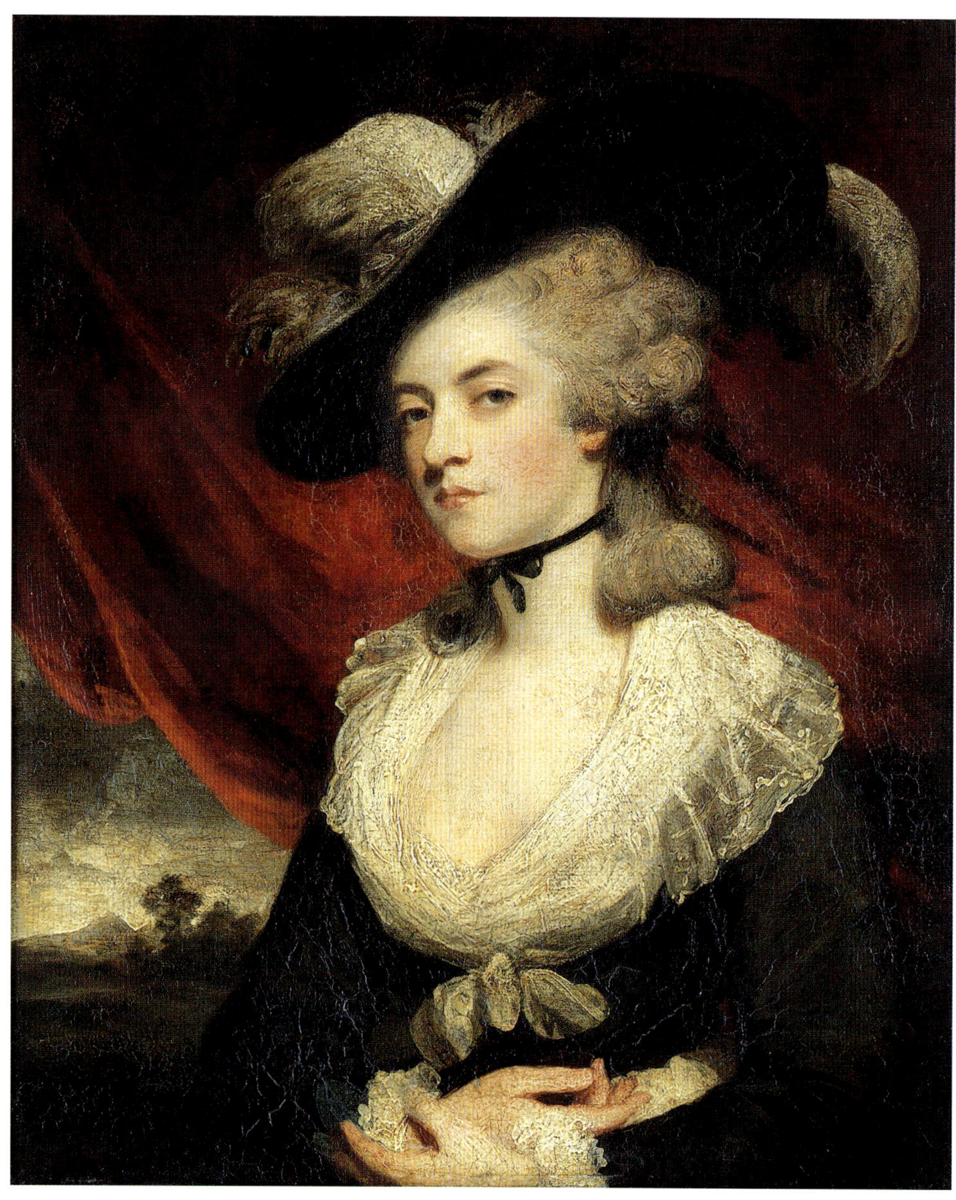

86 Sir Joshua Reynolds, *Mrs Robinson*, RA 1782. The Rothschild Collection, Waddesdon Manor (The National Trust).

engaged in a short-lived but notorious affair with the Prince of Wales, whereas Baccelli had been living with John Frederick Sackville, 3rd Duke of Dorset, since 1779. Although portraits of royal or noble sitters were frequently juxtaposed with those of well-known actresses, on this occasion the artist and/or his male patrons (each having commissioned the image of his respective mistress) may have judged the practice ill-advised.[7] It is easy to imagine how two Gainsboroughs of a 'great' man and his lover, when put on display in the same exhibition, would have invited viewers to consider the social and sexual relations involved; though if the newspaper report was correct, and such had been the artist's original plan, this suggests that neither the prince nor the duke was entirely loath to advertise his possession of such a celebrated 'beauty'.

A more specific reason for Gainsborough's withdrawal of his *Mrs Robinson* is suggested by a gossipy article which appeared in the *Public Advertiser* two weeks before the opening of the 1782 show. Here it was claimed that once her royal liaison had come to an end, the actress had blackmailed the king into giving her £5,000 as 'hushmoney', in return for not publishing the letters sent her by the prince.[8] The same article also introduced Gainsborough's name into this sordid context, by comparing his painting with recent portraits of Robinson by George Romney and Reynolds – the last of which did appear at the Academy shortly afterwards (fig. 86). Of the three works, Sir Joshua's was declared the 'best', and Gainsborough's dismissed as an inadequate likeness. Given that the latter prided himself on his ability to capture a close resemblance, this criticism may have come as the final straw, prompting him to remove a promised exhibit already tainted with so many scurrilous rumours. One wonders if concerns about the RA's own reputation made at least one or two of its members breathe a sigh of relief.

Robinson may have been disappointed, however – not only because she'd been deprived of an opportunity to publicize her talent, but also because portraits exhibited at the Royal Academy lent an undeniable air of dignity to sitters of (then) questionable respectability. This arose from the setting itself and the company: on the walls of Somerset House, likenesses of actresses appeared alongside those of women of wealth and/or title, and were often virtually indistinguishable from them. But this did not stop anxieties about the sexual and social status of female performers from influencing exhibiting strategies, or from shaping the critical discussion of their portraits. This is what the *Gazetteer and New Daily Advertiser* of 30 April had to say about Reynolds's *Mrs Robinson* – listed in the catalogue simply as *Portrait of a Lady* (no. 22):

> Through the hands of eminent painters we have our *celebrated* women handed down to posterity, as well as through the pens of historians, we have our *celebrated* men; with what difference of example, the *virtuous* part of the public will decide. The above is a portrait of Mrs Robinson, well known under the name of 'The Perdita', dressed in a black riding habit, hat and feather, and of whom we may say with the poet 'who would not think that being innocent?'

This gendered perception suggests that because painters deal in appearances, they can produce adequate records of famous women; but since men are renowned for their character and deeds, they require the treatment in depth of the historical text. Though both men and women can be useful as examples, the difference implied between them here is easy to grasp: for 'the virtuous' will see that exemplary males are meant to inspire emulation, while 'celebrated women' are not. Other reviews of Reynolds's picture made a similar use of moralizing innuendo. On 30 May 1782, for instance, the *Public Advertiser* singled out the 'short' three-quarter size, commenting drily: 'An unconverted Magdalen should never be painted below the waist'.

The costume worn by Mrs Robinson elicited remarks from several contemporary reviewers, who noticed that Reynolds had, in a sense, depicted the actress 'in character' – that is to say, in the character of a particularly celebrated old master painting. Her pose, plumed hat and dark bodice all recalled Rubens's *Chapeau de paille* (now London, National Gallery), which Reynolds had admired on his recent trip to Antwerp. If this reference complimented Sir Joshua's visual wit and erudition, at the same time it alluded to the role-playing for which Robinson had become notorious in both her professional and personal life. Famous on stage for her extravagant costumes, she often rode in her carriage around the West End of London as 'the belle of Hyde Park', dressed in equally exotic clothes. Though Reynolds had devised a self-consciously 'art-historical' way of mediating Robinson's theatrical and social performances, even the most complimentary reviewers found it hard not to refer to her seductive sexuality. The *St James's Chronicle* of 27 April called this 'the most flattering likeness that has yet appeared of the celebrated Mrs Robinson', before the critic went on to express his surprise that 'we have not been told of some astonishing Effects which her charms produced in the Artist employed'. For how, we are meant to infer, could the painter have resisted so beguiling a creature? Evidently the seductive power exerted by the actress when on stage could be transferred, at least in the imagination, to her role both as the artist's model and as the subject of a publicly exhibited painting. Hence some of the moral anxieties that clustered around portraits of 'our celebrated women'. In viewing such works, aesthetic appreciation might be tainted with desire.

Giovanna Baccelli was another sitter whose ambiguous social status affected assessments of her portrait (fig. 88). Gainsborough's painting shows the dancer executing a specific movement from the ballet *Les Amans surpris*, a performance for which she had won popular acclaim in 1781–82. In late eighteenth-century England, the status of dancer or ballerina was at least as problematic as that of actress. High art portraits of dancers were rare, and the profession was all too easily identified in the press with 'the higher order of impures'.[9] To a large part this was because the ballet demanded a display of active bodily exertion which ran counter to contemporary ideals of modest femininity and encouraged a voyeuristic discourse of sexual innuendo. Reviews of Baccelli's dance performances, like those of actresses on stage, were generally gossipy and replete with irony, filled with many more comments on physical appearance and dress than on the quality of her work.[10] From 1779 onwards, when Baccelli set up home with the Duke of Dorset, she became the focus of intense press and public interest which the display of Gainsborough's portrait can only have fuelled. On this occasion – as was so often the case for exhibited images of female performers – the critics spent a great deal of time arguing whether the painter had achieved an accurate likeness; and though most had doubtless seen Baccelli in person, they were unable to reach any consensus.[11]

When the subject of an exhibited portrait was an actress, dancer or courtesan, the 'likeness' debate often took on an overtly sexualized dimension. On 2 May 1782, for instance, the *Public Advertiser* spoke of Gainsborough's *Baccelli* as 'a good moral likeness'; by contrast, his small oval of *Grace Dalrymple* (fig. 87) was 'not a good moral likeness; – the Eyes are too characteristic of her Vocation'. Dalrymple was a well-known *demi-mondaine*, popularly nicknamed 'Dally the Tall', notorious for both her beauty and her numerous highly publicized affairs. What worried the writer for the *Public Advertiser*, paradoxically, was that Gainsborough's picture was *too* close to its subject, inasmuch as it was seen to betray her lack of moral character. The critic found her expression simply too alluring, as evidence of a threatening feminine sexuality that had no right to be seen in respectable society. To be deemed acceptable for public exhibition, portraits of women of dubious repute had to undergo a form of masquerade: such sitters had to be given 'polite' masks, even if

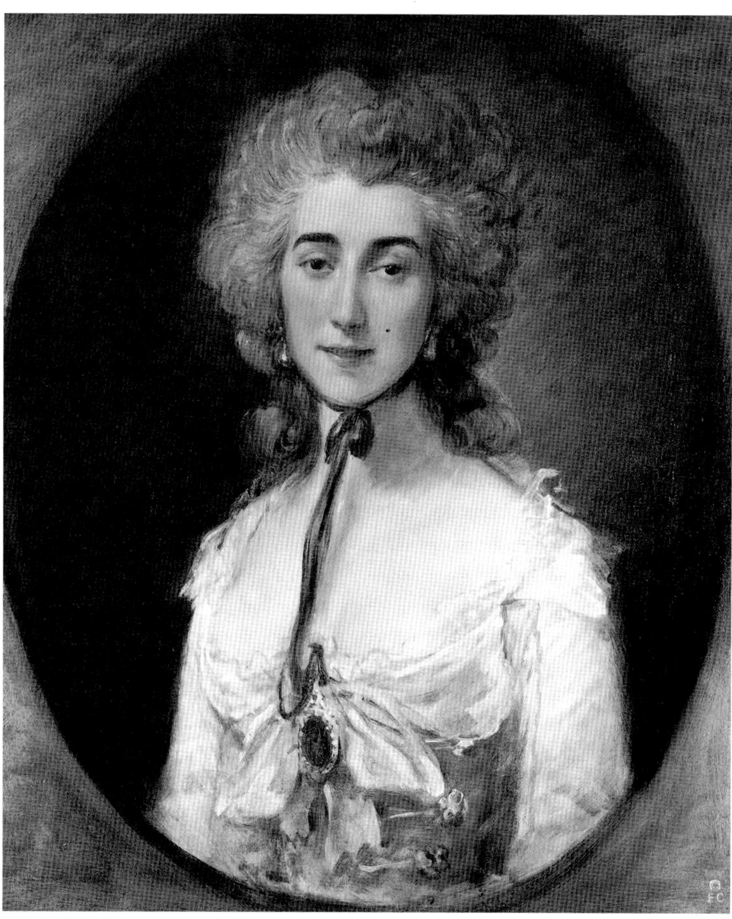

87 Thomas Gainsborough, *Grace Dalrymple*, RA 1782. The Frick Collection, New York.

these made it hard to tell them apart from 'proper' members of their sex.

The issue of 'likeness' presented further problems in relation to images of female performers and theatrical portraits in general. If an individual was to be painted in her or his stage role, how accurate a representation of the dramatic disguise should the artist provide? Critical responses suggest there was little agreement about the desirability of 'naturalness' in pictures of this sort, apparently because what could be called 'natural' for an actress might be judged both artificial and immodest by contemporary standards of feminine beauty. This dilemma prompted a rather ambivalent assessment of Gainsborough's picture by the critic for the *Gazetteer* (1 May), who explained that in order to represent 'an Italian opera Dancer, the artist was not only obliged to embellish, but if he would be thought to copy the original to *lay on his colouring thickly*; in this he has succeeded for the face of this admirable dancer is evidently paint-painted'.

The portrait shows Baccelli rouged and powdered, the exaggerated whiteness of her skin appearing in sharp contrast with her dark (Italian) features. But if this was a concession to the truth of her disguise, stage paint, like the activity of acting itself, inescapably also symbolized deception and falsity, the opposite of a natural 'likeness'. In contemporary culture this form of masquerade was regarded as characteristically *feminine* behaviour. Women – actresses being the most obvious examples – used make-up, or so it was often claimed, to give themselves the look of modesty and innocence; but in so doing they simultaneously exhibited their capacity to dissemble and deceive. When exposed in the public domain, the image of a 'paint-painted' dancer, who was also mistress to no less a personage than a duke, may have helped bring such anxieties to the fore. In 1786, as W. T. Whitley has observed,

> It was asserted that French visitors to our exhibitions were shocked at the indelicacy of placing, close to the portraits of women of rank and virtue, the presentments of these notorious persons, triumphant, as it were, in vice. 'In Paris' remarked one writer, 'such portraits would on no account be admitted; the name of the King is a sufficient check upon them to keep a just decorum in *his* Academy, and it is no small reflection upon our Academicians here to have as little regard for the dignity of their master as they seemingly have for their own'.[12]

If the presence of such portraits threatened the dignity of this *royal* institution, for the women thus depicted the process worked in reverse, by making hierarchical distinctions harder to discern. In this respect Gainsborough's *Giovanna Baccelli* is rather unusual in the degree to which it signals the subject's involvement with the stage – though the setting, in 'nature', would seem to conjure up the more prestigious context of a rural estate. Mary Robinson, too, was only one of many female sitters, often of the highest social class, whom Reynolds dignified with the trappings of old master art; he also adopted the conventions of allegory for noble ladies and actresses alike.

One factor that enabled such artistic conduct was the fluidity of the actress's social identity. Though traditionally associated with prostitutes (Nell Gwynn might be cited as a historical example), towards the end of the eighteenth century the more successful female members of the acting profession were beginning to claim, and to be granted, a status much more akin to that of the respectable members of their audience.[13] In many of their dramatic roles actresses could assume the demeanour of 'ladies', while off-stage they increasingly found themselves treated as such, even by aristocratic women like the Duchess of Devonshire. Sexual liaisons between actresses and noblemen were becoming more and more public; and if this sort of familiarity bred contempt – in the form of scurrilous press reports, caricatures and the like – it nevertheless provided the women in question with an entrée into the very highest social circles. Here the most spectacular example was that of Dorothy Jordan, who moved in with the Duke of Clarence (later William IV) in 1791, and bore him ten children during the next twenty years, when he left her in favour of a partner deemed more appropriate for a future king. One result of such liaisons was that many portraits

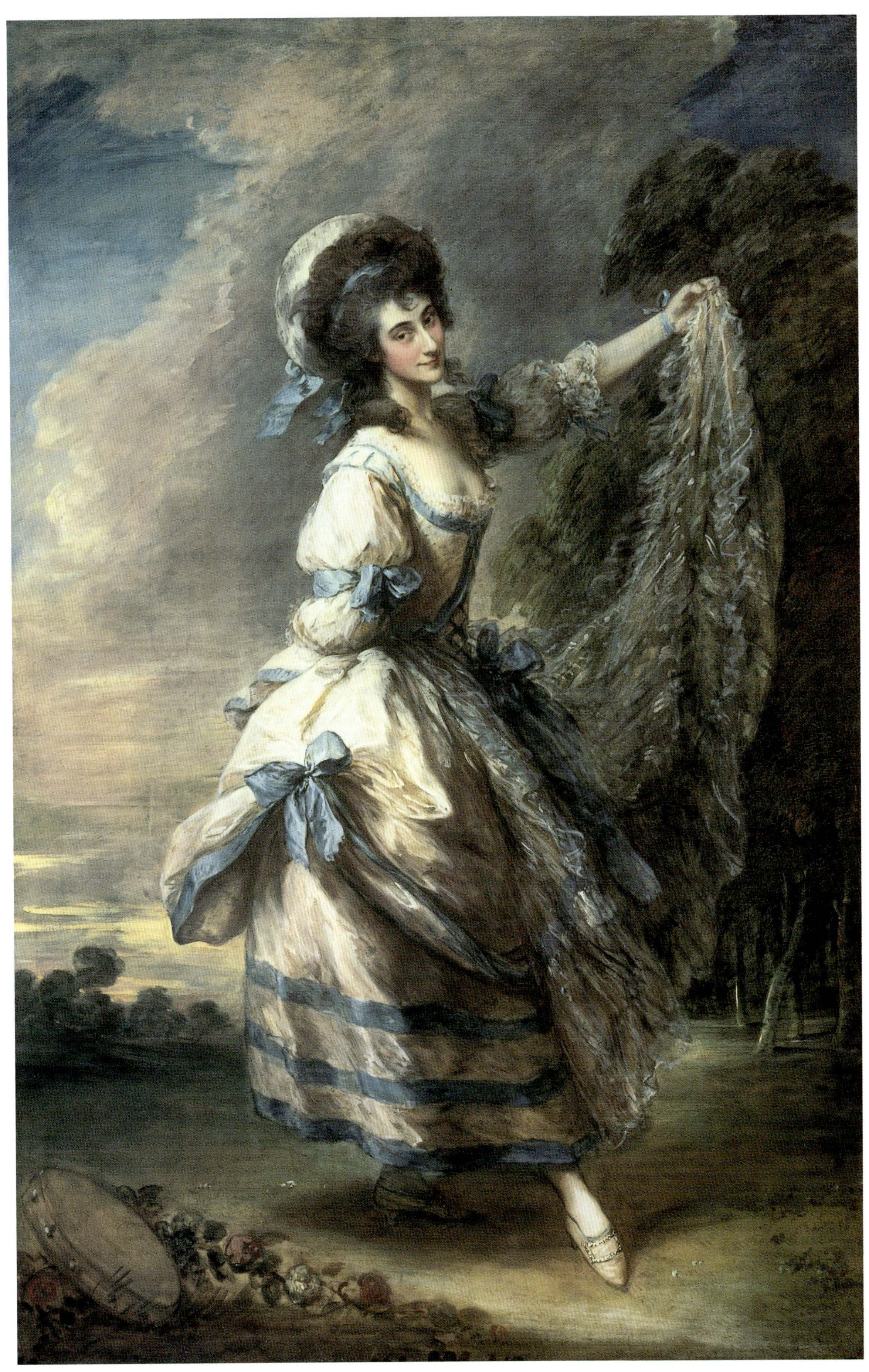

88 Thomas Gainsborough, *Giovanna Baccelli*, RA 1782. Tate, London.

of women performers were commissioned by, or done for the approval of, their noble lovers.[14]

The crossing of class boundaries involved in these relationships found its rough equivalent at the annual exhibitions. Here the setting enabled a form of *déclassement* through the unsystematic display of so many portraits, while encouraging a somewhat confused (and often veiled) critical discourse on feminine sexuality which at times acquired an added piquancy due to the nature of the institution. For this was, after all, the *Royal* Academy. At its private views, dinners, award ceremonies and the like, the monarch and his family – the Prince of Wales most prominently of all – enjoyed a high degree of visibility which was widely publicized in the press. Their physical presence, however, was problematized by the regular display of portraits of various royal mistresses, including Robinson and Jordan. Somerset House provided a social and aesthetic space in which such alliances were both legitimized and worried about.

Exhibiting 'divine excess': the spectacle of Sarah Siddons

Of all the actresses whose portraits appeared at the Somerset House exhibitions in the last two decades of the eighteenth century, none enjoyed a higher profile, or a higher reputation for personal respectability, than did Sarah Siddons. During this period over twenty pictures of her were shown at the Royal Academy, beginning in 1780 with William Hamilton's *Mrs Siddons as Euphrasia in 'The Grecian Daughter'* (fig. 90); three years later crowds reputedly thronged the same artist's studio to see his portrait of the actress as Isabella, which according to newspaper reports was finished too late to make the opening of the RA show (fig. 89). This insatiable curiosity about paintings of Siddons was fuelled by the full houses that watched her at Drury Lane, and by a flurry of newspaper reports about the effects of her performances on her audiences, which included some of the country's most eminent personages. In 1783, if contemporary accounts are to be believed, George III and Queen Charlotte saw five Siddons performances in a single month, and were reduced to tears on each occasion. On 24 April the *Morning Herald* mischievously predicted that in the forthcoming RA show:

> Mrs Siddons will be so numerously exhibited in her tragic characters, that the very daggers she is to be in the act of drawing, will be sufficient to hang every second picture in the academy upon, in case the President should think it expedient to convert them into *pegs*!

While complimenting Siddons's talent for Shakespearian tragedy, the mock-heroic notion of using Lady Macbeth's daggers as picture hooks suggests an underlying fear that the Royal Academy might itself be overwhelmed by a surfeit of images of melancholy and pain, and by the powerful emotional responses

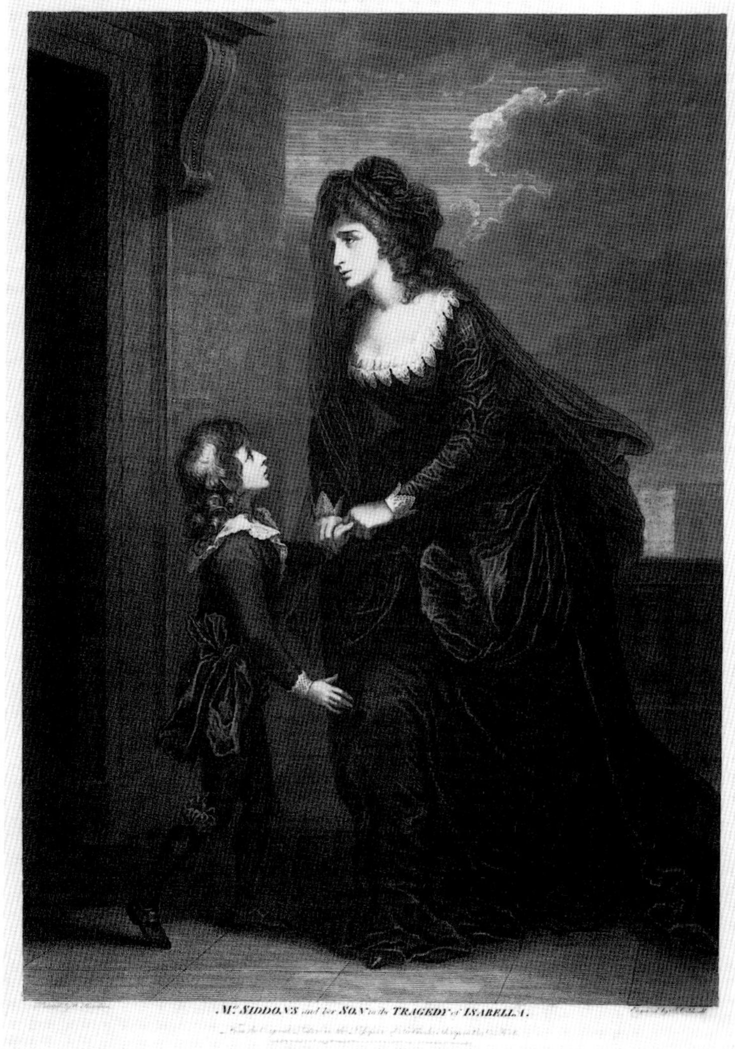

89 James Caldwall after William Hamilton, *Sarah Siddons as Isabella*, mezzotint of 1785 after lost painting of 1783. Courtesy of the Huntington Library, Art Collections and Botanical Gardens, San Marino, California.

these tended to evoke. According to the actress's biographers, the king and queen were far from being the only spectators to be reduced to tears or gasps, as they were thrilled by her 'divine excess'.[15] In September 1798 the stage journal the *Monthly Mirror* included a burlesque piece based on the reaction of a Dublin audience to one of Siddons's early performances as Isabella:

> Several fainted, even before the curtain drew up; but when she came to the scene of parting with her wedding ring, oh, what a sight was there! . . . One hundred and nine ladies fainted, forty-six went into fits, ninety-five had strong hysterics. The world will scarce credit the assertion, when they are told that fourteen children, five old women, a one-handed sailor, and six common council men actually drowned in the inundation of tears that flowed from the galleries, lattices and boxes, to increase the briny pond in the pit.[16]

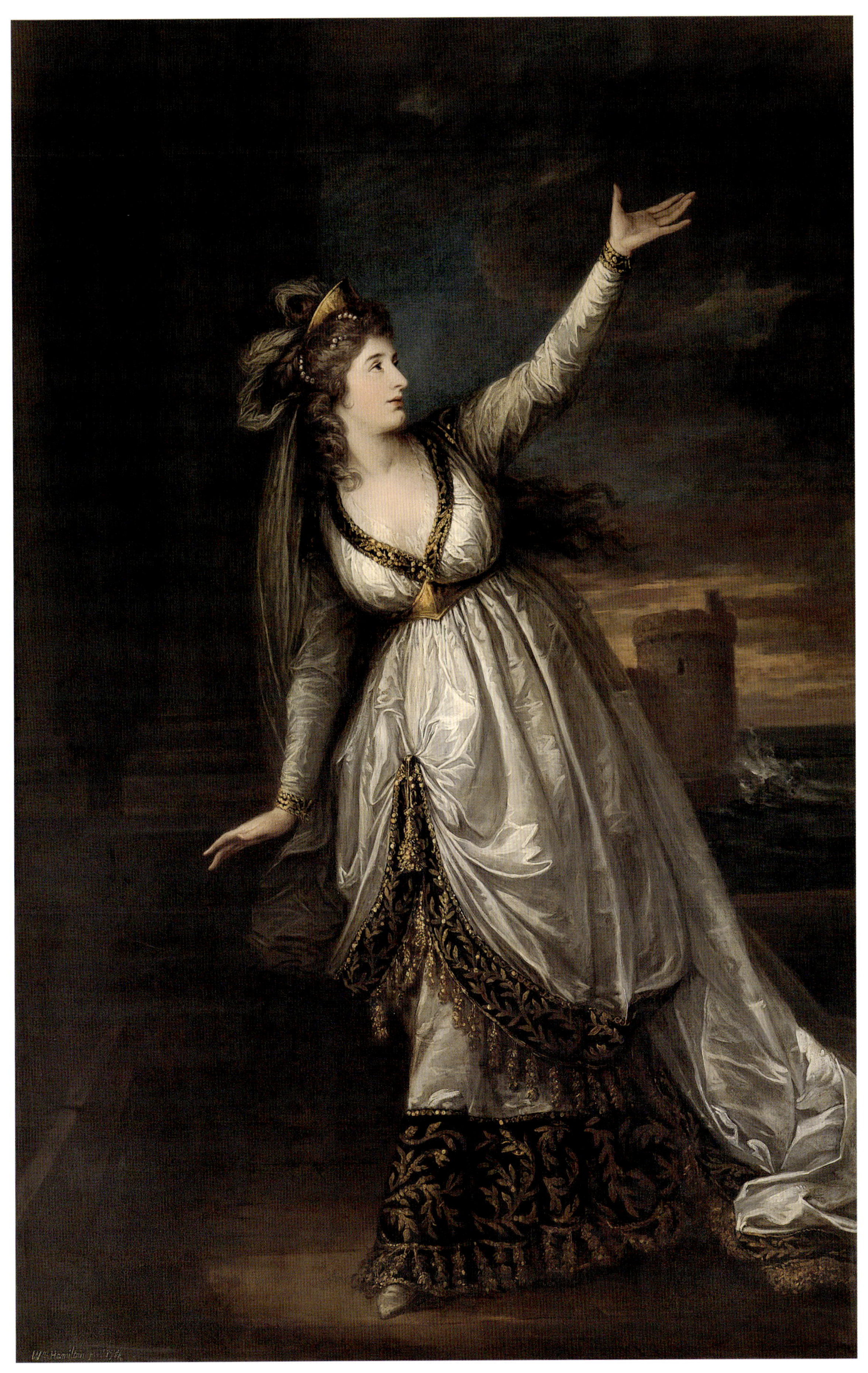

90 William Hamilton, *Mrs Siddons as Euphrasia in 'The Grecian Daughter'*, RA 1780. Town Hall, Stratford-upon-Avon.

As a female performer vividly expressing her feelings on stage, Siddons enabled a public outpouring of emotions by both sexes. What they admired, perhaps above all, was her tremendously versatile range of facial expressions and her ability to convey several types of passion at once.[17] Her appeal may have been especially strong for the growing numbers of women in the audience, who found themselves moved when Siddons played out 'feminine' tragedies of maternal grief or lost love[18] – though, as common participants in this feminized culture of sensibility, many men proved themselves equally adept at crying and weeping when confronted by the same spectacle of anguish.

Painted portraits of Siddons in sentimental tragic roles must have held an additional charge for those exhibition viewers (both female and male) who had already indulged their emotions when they had seen her in person on the stage. But feminized emotional reactions to theatrical performances were not directly translatable into aesthetic responses to pictures on display at the Royal Academy. Crying and hyperventilating did not form part of the conventional repertoire for the cultivated consumption of art, nor is there any known documentary evidence to suggest that such behaviour took place within the confines of Somerset House. When mediated through the conventions of high art, any actor's forms of expression had to be subtly recoded. What this meant in Siddons's case, since she specialized in tragedy, was that portraitists were able to represent her in accordance with the rules governing the most serious and dignified form of pictorial art – history painting in the grand style. Thus Hamilton's *Siddons as Euphrasia* cast Siddons in an idealized upward-gazing pose, as influenced by Charles Le Brun's 'expressive heads'[19] as by her evocative passions on stage. A similar, spiritually enraptured look recurs in Reynolds's *Mrs Siddons as the Tragic Muse* (fig. 1), which could justly be described as even more 'divine' in its excess than the spectacle of the actress weeping on stage. On this occasion, as has often been observed, Sir Joshua pulled out all the stops to create a *tour de force* of visual grandeur and classical erudition. The dark old-masterly colouring; the appropriation of the pose of the prophet Isaiah from Michelangelo's Sistine Chapel ceiling; the introduction of framing figures personifying the Aristotelian notions of terror and pity[20] – these were only some of the features which led contemporary critics to proclaim *Mrs Siddons as the Tragic Muse* a truly 'historical portrait'.[21] Reynolds had successfully endowed a celebrity likeness with the trappings of high mythological art, in a potent combination which carried metaphorical possibilities beyond Siddons's symbolic and theatrical role-playing as the personification of tragedy. Following the opening of the 1784 show, press reviews waxed lyrical about the work's 'dignity', 'sublimity' and 'excellence', using language borrowed from the critical discourse on history painting. In this image of the actress then, Reynolds had produced one of his most bravura pieces, a portrait which could be claimed as evidence of the elevated aspirations of the British School.

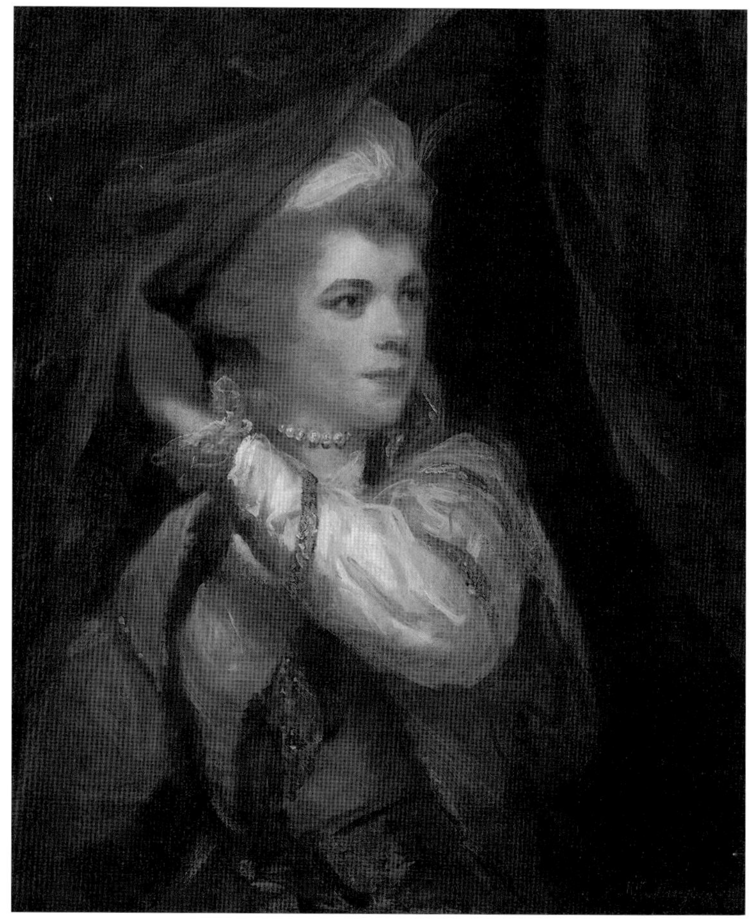

91 Sir Joshua Reynolds, *Mrs Abington as Roxalana*, RA 1784. Private collection.

It was not simply the painter's deployment of art-historical allusions which offered the spectacle of Siddons the possibility of 'sublime' status. The model of respectable femininity which she was seen to embody was crucial in enabling these symbolic possibilities. According to contemporary biographers, she led an exemplary domestic life as a faithful wife and mother, qualities that helped inscribe her name 'in the highest rank of theatrical merit'.[22] Her apparently respectable private morality allowed her dramatic powers to overshadow the less honourable associations of her very public profession. Thus with Siddons we have the exceptional case of an actress whose sexuality functioned as a trope for both the moral and professional status of the theatre, and the authority of British art, contributing in a fruitful manner to the exchange of discourse between the two disciplines. It is hardly surprising that the reviewer of the *Public Advertiser* felt that with the *Tragic Muse*, Reynolds had surpassed all his previous artistic 'Performances'.

Aided by a good hanging position on the line in the Great Room (see the far right of Angus's engraving after Dodd in fig. 34), *Mrs Siddons as the Tragic Muse* was the star of the show, overshadowing the other actress portrait that Reynolds exhibited in

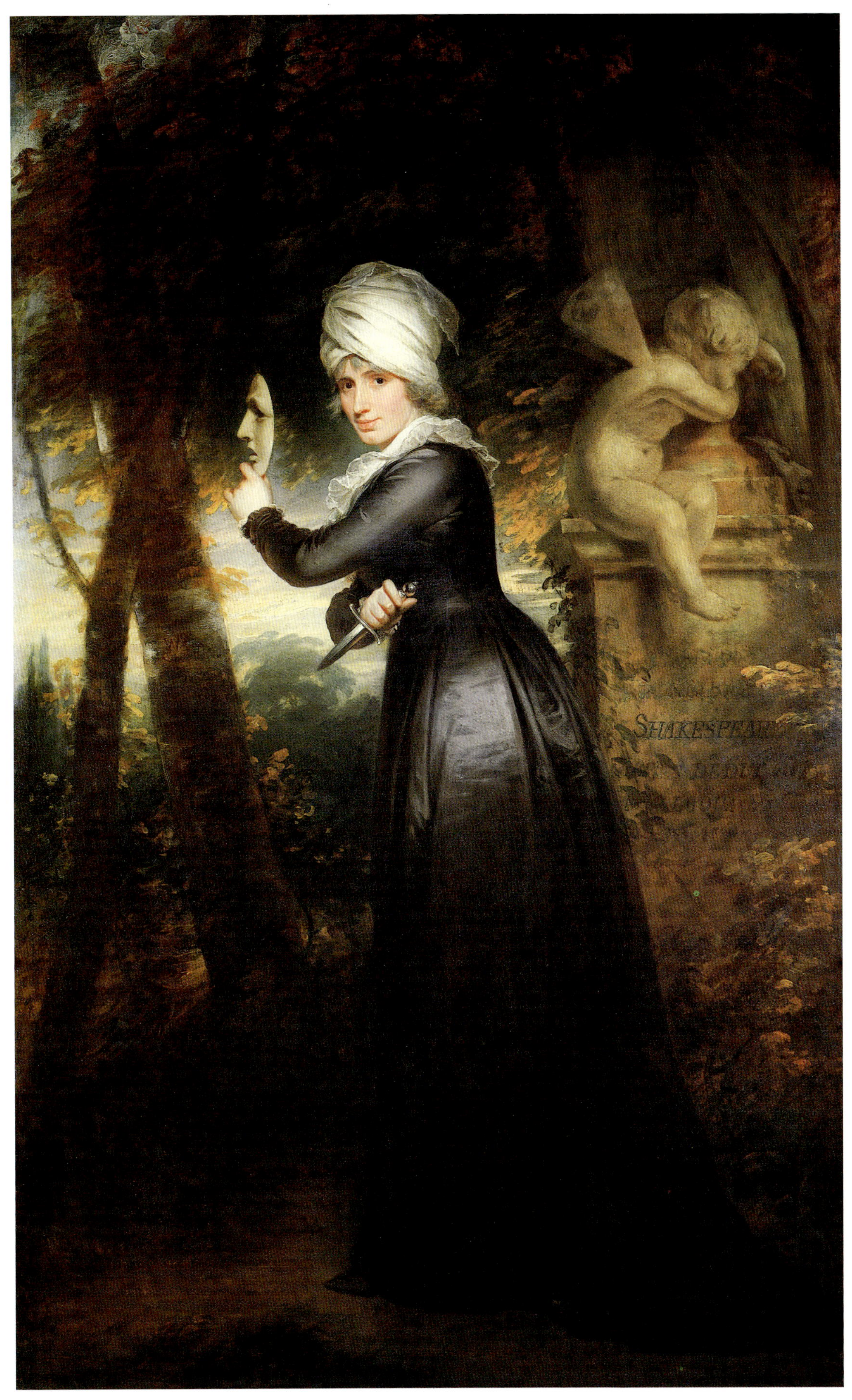

92 Sir William Beechey, *Sarah Siddons with the Emblems of Tragedy*, RA 1794. By courtesy of the National Portrait Gallery, London.

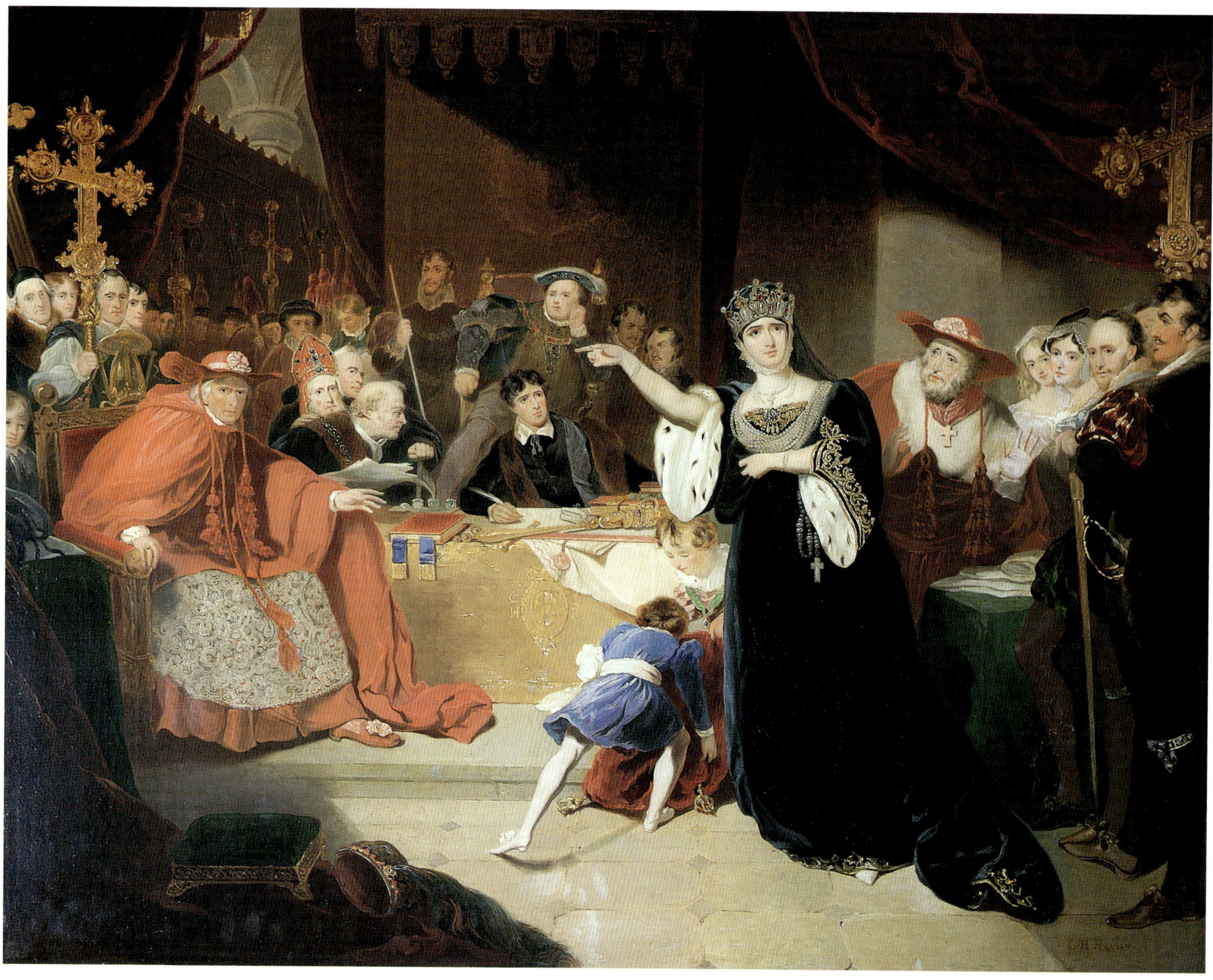

93 George Henry Harlow, *The Court for the Trial of Queen Katherine*, reduced autograph replica of painting exhibited RA 1817 (Sudeley Castle Trustees). From the RSC Collection with permission of the Governors of the Royal Shakespeare Company, Stratford-upon-Avon.

1784, *Mrs Abington as Roxalana* (fig. 91). Sir Joshua's grandiose production proved a hard act to follow, and it was ten years before a comparable full-length of the actress in generalized tragic mode appeared at the Academy. This was William Beechey's *Sarah Siddons with the Emblems of Tragedy* (RA 1794; fig. 92), which sets its subject in a woody grove, and shows her holding a bloody dagger and a tragic mask. The plinth behind her is engraved with the word SHAKESPEARE, which in this context probably refers to her celebrated Lady Macbeth. But the inevitable comparisons with the late Sir Joshua's canonical image made Beechey's effort a critical failure, which seemed to offer neither a good likeness of Siddons nor a convincing representation of Melpomene.[23]

Despite the popularity of Reynolds's *Tragic Muse*, he seems to have had some difficulty selling the picture. Correspondence between the artist and his engraver Valentine Green in 1783 indicates that the work was probably originally commissioned by Sheridan, then the manager of Drury Lane, as a particularly ambitious form of advertisement for his theatre and its greatest female star. But after its exhibition the painting returned to Reynolds's studio, where – reportedly priced at 1,000 guineas – it languished for six years, until a buyer finally appeared in the person of a French former minister to Louis XVI.[24] In fact many of Sir Joshua's portraits of actresses – including the Rubensian image of Mrs Robinson discussed above – remained in his personal collection. This may partly reflect the artist's personal attachment to the pictures and their sitters (about which there was much speculative gossip); but it also suggests that while such paintings may have been extremely good at generating publicity, their value as marketable commodities was far from secure.

Whatever its economic value, the social value of an exhibited actress portrait was never in doubt, at least from the sitter's point of view. Rather than simply echoing her appearances on stage, the dignified poses which Siddons was given by Reynolds and other painters were also seen as confirmation of her 'aristocratic' demeanour. As Robyn Asleson has noted, 'Keenly aware of her ambivalent and anomalous position, Siddons was careful to imbue her every gesture and glance – whether on or off stage – with a gravity appropriate to the high seriousness of the tragic mode'.[25] Even after her official retirement from the stage in 1812, portraits of Siddons in tragic and regal roles continued to appear (albeit less frequently) at the Academy. What later became one of the most famous of all of her images was actually exhibited five years after the actress had retired: this was George Henry Harlow's *Court for the Trial of Queen Katherine* (fig. 93), showing Siddons in the trial scene from Shakespeare's *Henry VII*. So popular did this painting become that it was used as the model for subsequent stagings of the play, and some seventy years later, Ellen Terry famously based her interpretation of Queen Katherine's role on Siddons's appearance in Harlow's image, thus helping to consolidate a visual history of 'Siddonian' poses.

Comedy, femininity and pantomime

Exhibited portraits of comic actresses raised a different set of critical issues, in which the performer's seductive power – on stage and on canvas – often came to the fore. On 29 April 1784 the critic of the *London Chronicle* had the following words of praise for Reynolds's *Mrs Abington as Roxalana*:

> Who that looks on the portrait of Mrs Abington, does not immediately trace the Muse of Comedy! The witching smile, the fascinating air, the roguish eye, the seductive blandishments of Thalia, are all most critically pictured in her accomplished representative.

Although this passage has clearly been composed in response to the painted image, the actress is described as if she were on stage, seducing her (male) audience with her 'roguish' charms. But if the exhibition provided a forum where the actress could extend her flirtatious blandishments to the contemporary audience for art, by doing so she might endanger the cultivated image which the Royal Academy assiduously sought to promote. Unlike the tragic actress, the alluring femininity of her comic counterpart, whose performances often involved bawdy or flirtatious elements, was not easily translated into an acceptable form of high art. In 1786 Reynolds would ruminate on the parallels between comedy and the lower, more naturalistic forms of art, comparing 'Comedy, or Farce' with 'the inferior style of Painting' which sought to imitate nature rather than improve upon it. In contrast, he draws an analogy between tragedy and the grand manner, which selects and reorganizes from nature and pre-existing art.[26] But the commercial and popular success of comedy, and of its best-known actors and actresses, helped to generate its own affirmative critical discourse, which sought to reframe Reynolds's antithesis between 'natural' and higher truth. Speaking of the actress Dorothy Jordan, the anonymous author of an *Essay on Comic Genius* (1786) argued forcefully for the important moral lessons that comedy could offer; in his view, 'A writer or an actor who constitutes a successful picture of the lower virtues and contemporary vices, is . . . more valuable to the interests of society', than 'a luxuriant Poet' or 'a sublime Actor'.[27] By locating the socially improving power of comedy in its ability to represent ordinary life – in its 'naturalness', in other words – this great admirer of Jordan's talent sought to salvage her professional reputation, and in so doing to combat the innuendoes of moral impropriety that dogged her both on and off the stage.

The theoretical opposition between the relative statuses of tragedy and comedy was implicated in the critical response to several large-scale theatrical portraits in the RA show of 1786: one reviewer coupled Thomas Beach's *Sarah Siddons as Lady Macbeth and John Philip Kemble as Macbeth* with Mather Brown's *Joseph Holman and Anne Brunton as Romeo and Juliet* as supporting the 'dignity of tragedy', while he suggested that Hoppner's *Mrs Jordan as the Comic Muse* belonged merely in 'the comic department'.[28] Of these three works the Hoppner seems to have aroused the most widespread critical concern.[29] Listed in the catalogue as *Mrs Jordan in the Character of the Comic Muse, Supported by Euphrosyne who Represses the Advance of a Satyr*, this full-length image prompted the obvious comparisons with Reynolds's *Siddons* of two years earlier. The younger artist's implicit challenge to Sir Joshua's authority must have conjured up the oft-discussed rivalry between their respective sitters; Jordan's portraits appeared almost as frequently as Siddons's at the Academy shows of the 1780s and 1790s. The long title of Hoppner's composition suggests that Euphrosyne may here be shown protecting Jordan (Thalia) from the lecherous voyeurism of the male theatre-goer (the satyr).[30] But the allegorical components, while offering the image a superficial dignity, also serve to confuse the possible layers of sexual innuendo. Jordan's figure is both prettified and desirable, beguilingly revealing an ankle and gazing at her spectator, but also apparently repulsing the satyr. Her sexuality could easily be interpreted as both seductive and refusing, an ambiguity reinforced by her dance-like contorted pose. Critics were troubled by this twisted and alluring body, focusing on the odd 'display' of her limbs and what the *Morning Herald* of 10 May rather inexplicably described as her 'dwarfish' stature. While Siddons's 'sublime' pose and expression in Reynolds's *Tragic Muse* had enabled associations

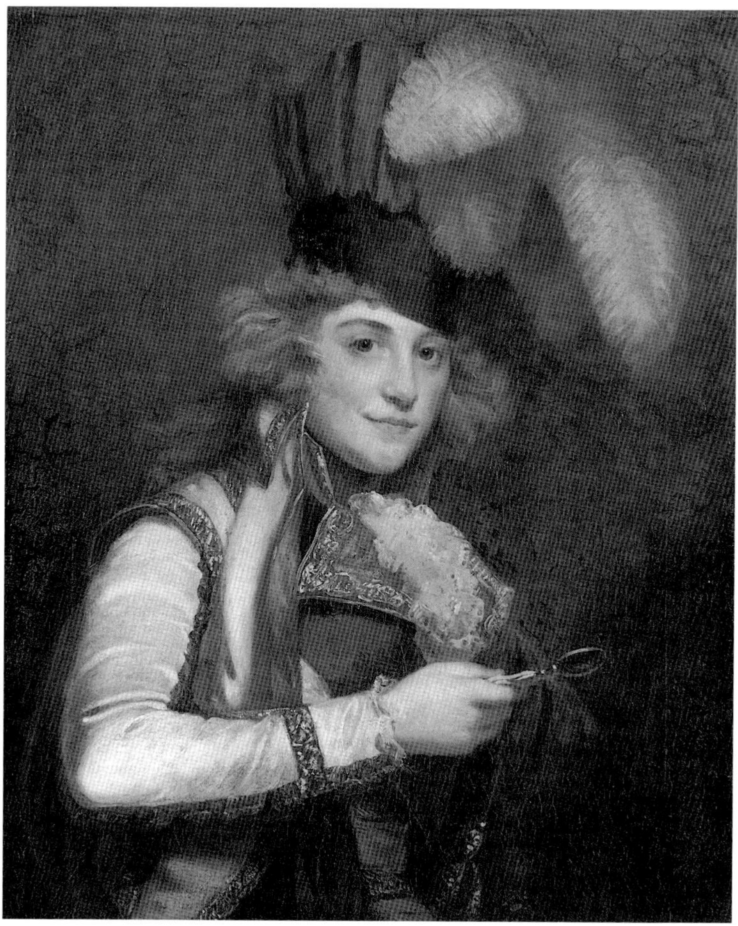

94 John Hoppner, *Mrs Jordan as Hippolita in 'She Would and She Would Not'*, RA 1791. By courtesy of the National Portrait Gallery, London.

with elevated classical allegory, Hoppner's Jordan seemed to be rooted in the cruder and more 'naturalistic' theatre of comedy.

In the previous discussion of Gainsborough's *Baccelli*, it was argued that the task of painting a dancer, as opposed to an actress, primarily involved representing the spectacle of the female body in movement, without the redeeming trappings of tragedy or allegory. But we should not underestimate the important meanings conveyed by the representation of bodily motion in theatrical portraiture, or how this might be sexually coded in images of actresses. In the critical discourse on the physicality of male and female stage players that emerged during the second half of the eighteenth century,[31] attempts were made to separate (in theory at least) a more refined theatre from the 'barbarism' of dancing and pantomimes, with their connotations of bawdiness and threatening feminine sexuality. In 1786 an anonymous contributor to a pamphlet entitled *The Green Room Mirror* declared that

> The rapid progress from barbarism to refinement has strongly recommended, as an ornament to a civilized nation, *Theatrical Amusements*, which from their general support, has [*sic*] annihilated that frivolity of the Drama, so conspicuously predominant in the ruder ages: the *Tragic Muse* nearly obliterated the derogating impression of *Dancing, Ballad-singing*, and *Pantomimes*.[32]

Because comedy was regarded as close to pantomime, which by the late eighteenth century had come to be associated with an unseemly emphasis on the body and spectacular attention-seeking effects, the status of the comic actress proved especially worrying. And when her image went on display at the Royal Academy exhibitions it entered a space that certain critics viewed as already tainted with the 'frivolity' of 'the ruder ages': in 1818 the *Annals of the Fine Arts* accused Academicians of producing 'pictures hurried up like new pantomimes at the theatre, and with no other object than that of the theatre, of producing a temporary effect'.[33]

Hoppner's *Mrs Jordan as the Comic Muse* epitomizes the conflicting interests that emerged when theatrical performances by women were translated into the medium of high art. In his attempt to play down the frivolous associations of pantomime and the notoriously seductive appeal of the comic actress, Hoppner employed confusing signifiers; he used allegory to dignify comedy, albeit an allegory of sexual pursuit and repulsion. Other (non-allegorical) portraits of Jordan which appeared at the RA during the 1780s and 1790s were less confusing in their coding and therefore seem to have attracted relatively little critical attention. Among these were several paintings showing the actress in her famous cross-dressing roles (or 'breeches parts'), including Hoppner's *Mrs Jordan as Hippolita in 'She Would and She Would Not'*, (RA 1791; fig. 94).[34] When attired as a man on stage, Jordan's physical attributes – particularly her legs and ankles – were provocatively visible, thus enhancing her sexual appeal. When mediated through Hoppner's portraits, however, the element of sexual ambiguity was restrained in favour of a more thoroughly feminized effect playing on the continuities between the obvious delicacy of the actress's features and the ornamental richness of her clothing. But in the light-heartedness of such images there also lies a tension between Jordan's masculine disguise and her supposedly 'natural' femininity – a tension which generated the work's erotic charge, its ability to provoke desire in the spectator.

After Reynolds's death in 1792 the allegorical actress portrait seems to have fallen gradually out of fashion. Many paintings of leading stage performers continued to grace the walls of Somerset House, but as time went on they tended more and more to show these individuals as they actually appeared in the theatre. While painters like Lawrence and Harlow continued to exhibit large-scale portraits of actors or actresses 'in character',[35] there was a growing demand for images that were smaller, more intimate and more detailed – for what might be called 'theatrical conversation pieces', usually of comic subjects, which painters like George Clint, Henry Singleton and Samuel de Wilde supplied in considerable numbers. Many of their works were never exhibited at the Royal Academy, and when they were, they attracted far less critical attention than the more ambitious products of the previous and current generations.

The class of pictures discussed in this chapter conferred considerable benefits on the Somerset House exhibitions. Portraits of actresses in famous roles helped draw the London theatre audiences into a space devoted to the visual arts, generated a great deal of critical attention, and lent a certain seductive glamour to the shows as a whole. If their presence left the Academy open to charges that it was degenerating into nothing more than a fashionable commercial spectacle, then this may have seemed a relatively small price to pay. From the standpoint of the actress whose image made it on to the walls of the Great Room, there were certain obvious rewards. A portrait that succeeded in capturing public attention could be an invaluable advertisement, particularly if the work was subsequently engraved and distributed to an even larger audience. Meanwhile the exhibited painting, hung alongside likenesses of her social superiors, could enhance the performer's status and buttress her claim to professional dignity. Yet paradoxically, her regular appearance at the Academy, and the criticisms which this frequently provoked, could reinforce the power relationships that alienated the actress from social respectability. In both painted and written forms of portraiture, she was often represented as a sexualized spectacle of femininity acting out a role. Whether her painted portrait represented the theatre of tragedy or comedy, the actress was always at risk of being merely the star of the pantomime.

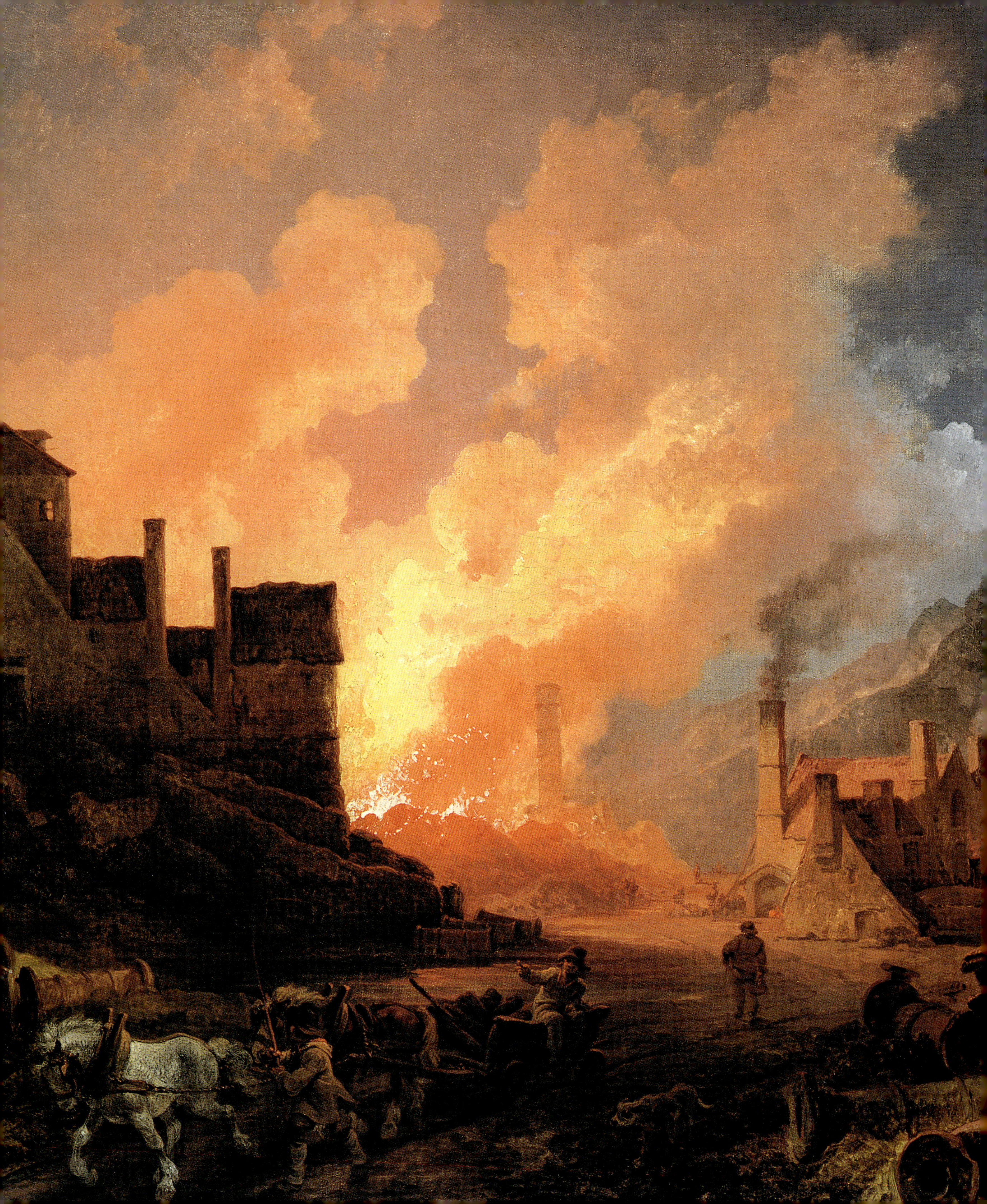

9

Landscape-O-Rama: The Exhibition Landscape at Somerset House and the Rise of Popular Landscape Entertainments

ANN BERMINGHAM

REMARKING ON THE SIZE OF SOME of the entries in the Academy's exhibition at Somerset House in 1818, the reviewer for the *Literary Gazette* speculated: 'Whether it be owing to the dismantling of our navy that has made canvas cheap, we cannot say, but there is no want of prodigious expanse in a number of subjects'.[1] Among the 1,039 paintings exhibited, portraits predominated and history painting was little in evidence. 'Variety', the reviewer noted, resided in landscape, where one could find 'some poetical and fancy productions of considerable merit'.[2] Augustus Wall Callcott's *Mouth of the Tyne* (present whereabouts unknown) and J. M. W. Turner's *View of Dort* (New Haven, Yale Center for British Art) came in for particular praise, Callcott's for its vivid realism and Turner's for its light-filled colour.[3]

A number of aspects touched on by this reviewer – size, naturalistic as well as imaginative realizations and luminous colouristic effects – bear closer examination when thinking about the aesthetics of the nineteenth-century exhibition landscape. The scale of the Somerset House exhibitions and their popularity encouraged artists to inflate the size of their works and to introduce eye-catching effects into their landscapes. Far from exhibiting a modest naturalism, exhibition landscapes of the early nineteenth century often produced breathtaking visual displays. In their calculated manipulation of scale, perspective and atmosphere these works approached the look of those popular 'o-rama' landscape entertainments: the panorama and the diorama.[4] Both of these enormous and illusionistic commercial attractions provided their viewers with a powerful visceral sense that they were in the presence of a real landscape. It is the intersection of the visual experience of these popular landscape spectacles and the aesthetics of the exhibition landscape of the early nineteenth century that interests me here. My argument is that the visual qualities borrowed from the panorama and the diorama enabled the exhibition landscape to compete in the Great Room of Somerset House, and created for it a new audience. In addition, I shall claim that the fertile cross-pollination between the exhibition landscape and the popular landscape entertainments of the period needs to be understood in the context of metropolitan modernity. Thus, the success of the exhibition landscape cannot be viewed as a simple compensation for the loss of rural nature, but must be seen as a positive response to urbanism.

As much as a panorama or diorama, the Academy's annual exhibition was its own kind of visual spectacle. A reviewer for the *Champion* vividly evoked the experience of looking at art in the Great Room:

> Let us fancy to ourselves an Exhibition Room whose large walls shall burst out upon the subdued eye, covered top to bottom, with florid pictures in glittering frames . . . the whole mass worked up, in desperate competition among its individual parts, to the tone of a nosegay of artificial flowers.[5]

The effect of paintings stacked floor to ceiling on the walls of the Great Room was visually overwhelming.[6] Since the founding of the Academy the size of the annual exhibition had steadily grown, from 500 to 600 items in the 1770s and 1780s, to between 800 and 900 in the 1790s. After the turn of the century, the totals crept upward from 1,100 in 1800 to 1,214 in 1828. While the

De Loutherbourg, *A View of Coalbrook Dale by Night*. Detail of fig. 101.

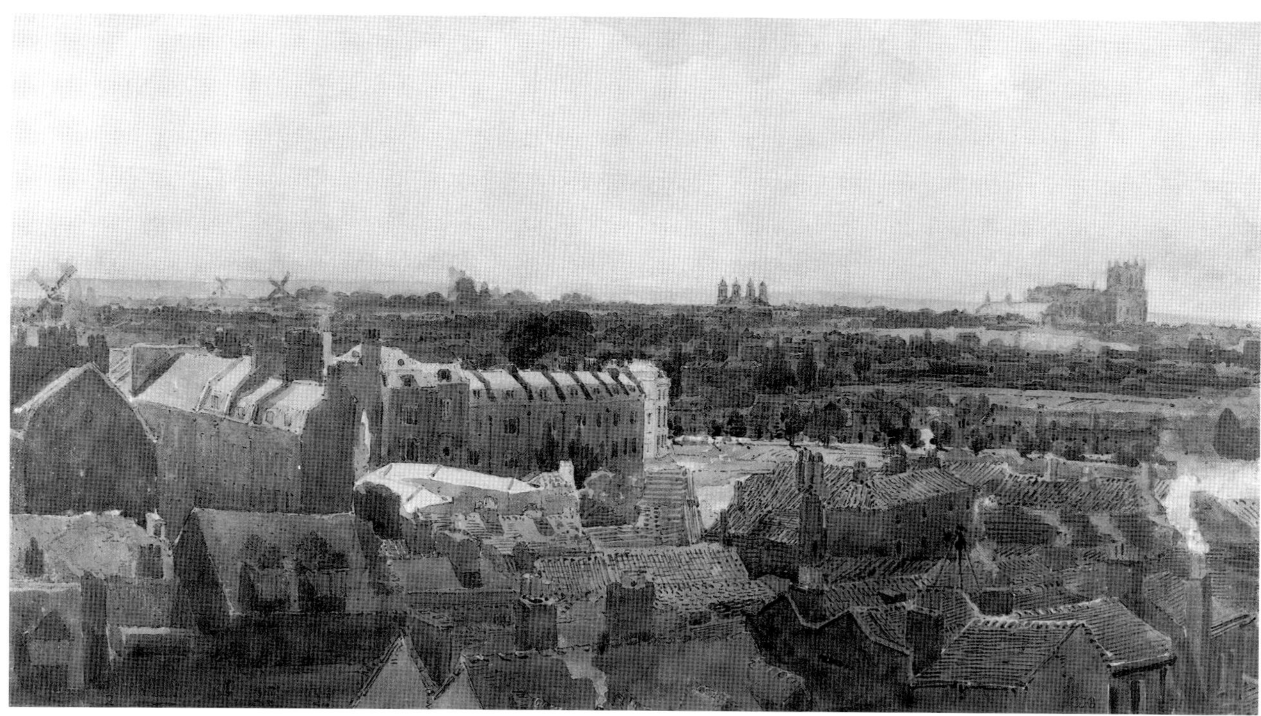

95 Thomas Girtin, *Westminister and Lambeth*, study for the *Eidometropolis*, 1800–01, pen and watercolour. By courtesy of the Trustees of the British Museum.

actual number of paintings that could be hung in the Great Room fluctuated between around 210 and 230 (a considerable reduction from the 1780s and 1790s, when there had sometimes been more than 260), depending on the size of the entries, the tendency in the early nineteenth century for artists to inflate the size of their works and to heighten their colour intensified the room's overpowering effect.[7] To compete for attention a landscape needed to stand out from the Great Room's cacophony of styles, sizes, colours and effects. The sheer visual noise of the room, to say nothing of the noise and crush of the hundreds of spectators who daily visited it, called for fortissimo, bravura performances like Callcott's *Mouth of the Tyne*, with its illusionistic depictions of water and sky, or Turner's *Dort* with its bold, broad expanse of luminous golden light.

In such a setting size was an advantage. However, large paintings were not particularly welcomed. Joseph Farington reported in 1802 that the portrait painter John Hoppner complained that 'exhibiting colossal sized portraits of woemen [*sic*] has done harm as it makes common sized portraits appear trifling'.[8] Portraits were not the only large-scale works; history paintings, especially the contributions of the Academy's President, Benjamin West, had grown, too, reaching mural size as in the case of West's *Death on a Pale Horse* (RA 1817; Philadelphia, Pennsylvania Academy of the Fine Arts). In order to hold their own, landscapes, particularly in the hands of Turner and James Ward, were challenging history painting in their size and in the sublimity of their subjects. Ward's *Gordale Scar* (RA 1815; London, Tate Britain), measuring 13 feet 8 inches wide by 10 feet 9 inches high, was intended to refute Sir George Beaumont's pronouncement that because of its immensity the Scar was unpaintable.[9] At Somerset House in 1815 the picture received mixed reviews. The *New Monthly Magazine* admired its sublime effects but also called them 'mechanical', while the *Sporting Magazine* thought *Gordale Scar* 'coarse, dark' and 'ostrogothic'.[10]

In addition to drawing attention to one's work, size could help guarantee that a painting got hung on or close to the coveted line (see Chapter 2 in this volume). The rule was that all large pictures had to be placed above this moulding with the bottoms of their frames resting on it so as to preserve its continuity. Pictures above the line were tilted forward so that they got good light and could be seen to advantage from below, whereas the works beneath were fated to be viewed through the hats, coats, trousers and skirts of the spectators.

While size was a way to command attention and to secure a good place, it also offered the spectator a temporary refuge from the room's visual confusion. Large paintings provide the viewer with an opportunity to become lost in the portrayal and to gaze at the depicted scene without an awareness of either the frame or what lies outside it. It is this aspect of the large exhibition landscape – the way it invites the viewer to forget the circumstances in which it is being viewed – that relates it most closely to the panorama and diorama and it is these landscape entertainments and their popular appeal that I wish first of all to consider.

* * *

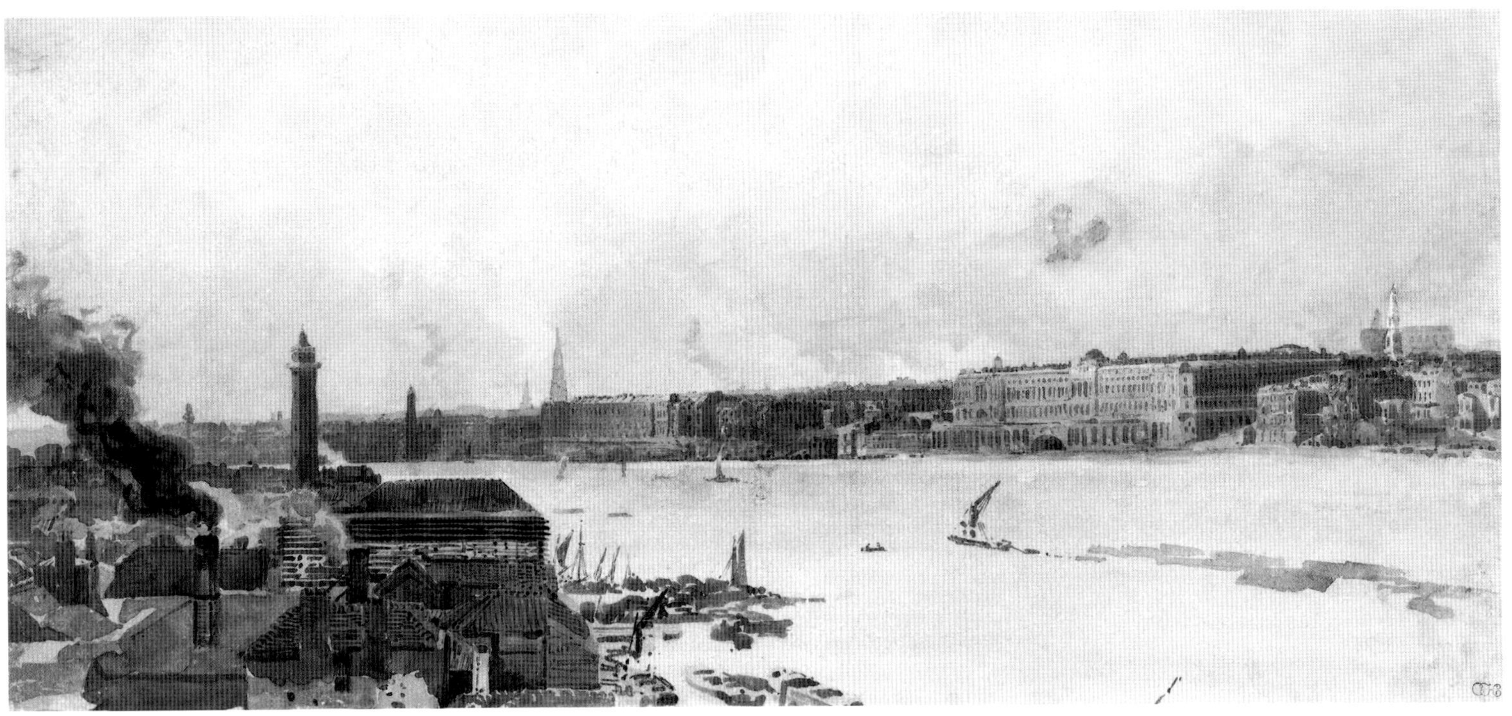

96 Thomas Girtin, *The Thames from Westminister to Somerset House*, study for the *Eidometropolis*, 1800–01, pen and watercolour. By courtesy of the Trustees of the British Museum.

Upon viewing Robert Barker's panorama of London, Sir Joshua Reynolds reportedly took the inventor by the hand and said, 'the present exhibition proves it is capable of producing effects, and representing nature in a manner far superior to the limited scale of pictures in general'.[11] It was precisely the notion that the manipulation of size, scale and perspective could produce a better way of realizing painted landscape scenery that inspired Barker to advertise his invention as a 'New Improvement in Painting', and as 'la nature à coup d'oeil'. In advertising Barker's view of London in 1791, *The Times* coined the term 'panorama' from the Greek words for 'all' and 'view'.[12] Panoramas called for special buildings or 'rotundas' which were drum-like structures attached to traditional porticoed entries. Far from being a passing novelty, the panorama flourished. Barker's Leicester Square rotunda prospered under his hands and later those of his son, Henry Aston Barker, who managed it until 1823 when he sold it to John Burford and his son Robert, who kept it going until his death in 1861. Soon after Barker set up business in Leicester Square, two other rotundas sprang up, in the Strand and Regent's Park. In August 1802 Thomas Girtin opened his *Eidometropolis* at Wigley's Great Room in Spring Gardens; it continued to receive paying customers until March 1803, several months after the artist's death the previous November. A panoramic prospect of London taken from the roof of the British Plate Glass manufactory on the south end of Blackfriars Bridge (figs 95 and 96), the *Eidometropolis* was not a great success – presumably because its vantage point did not permit the depiction of popular London sights in sufficient detail, and because it essentially repeated a view made by Barker a few years before. Undaunted by this failure, Girtin was preparing a panorama of Paris at the time of his death.

Although a British invention, the panorama did not remain an exclusively British experience. The American engineer Robert Fulton was granted a licence to open a panorama in Paris in 1799; Fulton then immediately sold the licence to James Thayer, who erected two rotundas – one in the gardens of the Hôtel de Montmorency-Luxembourg and the second on the Boulevard Montmartre. In the summer of 1799 Thayer opened a panorama of a *View of Paris from the Tuileries* painted by Pierre Prévost. This was followed by Prévost's panoramas of Lyon (1801), Amsterdam (1804), Rome and Naples (1805), as well as panoramas of military subjects such as *The Evacuation of Toulon by the English in 1793* (1800) and *The Fleet at Boulogne Preparing to Invade England* (1806). In 1799 and 1800 Barker exhibited his panorama of London in Hamburg and then Leipzig, where Goethe found its effects 'remarkable' and 'enchanting'.[13] By 1802 the panorama had become, as Constable said, 'all the rage', and by the end of the first decade of the nineteenth century it was an international sensation, with rotundas established in Berlin, Basle, Vienna, Amsterdam and New York, and panorama paintings circulating through most major European capitals.[14]

As the example of Girtin reminds us, panorama painting was not necessarily looked down upon as an unworthy occupation for serious artists. In addition to Girtin, William Daniell, Edward Dayes, Joshua Cristall, William Mulready, Ramsay Richard Reinagle, David Roberts, Clarkson Stanfield and the American

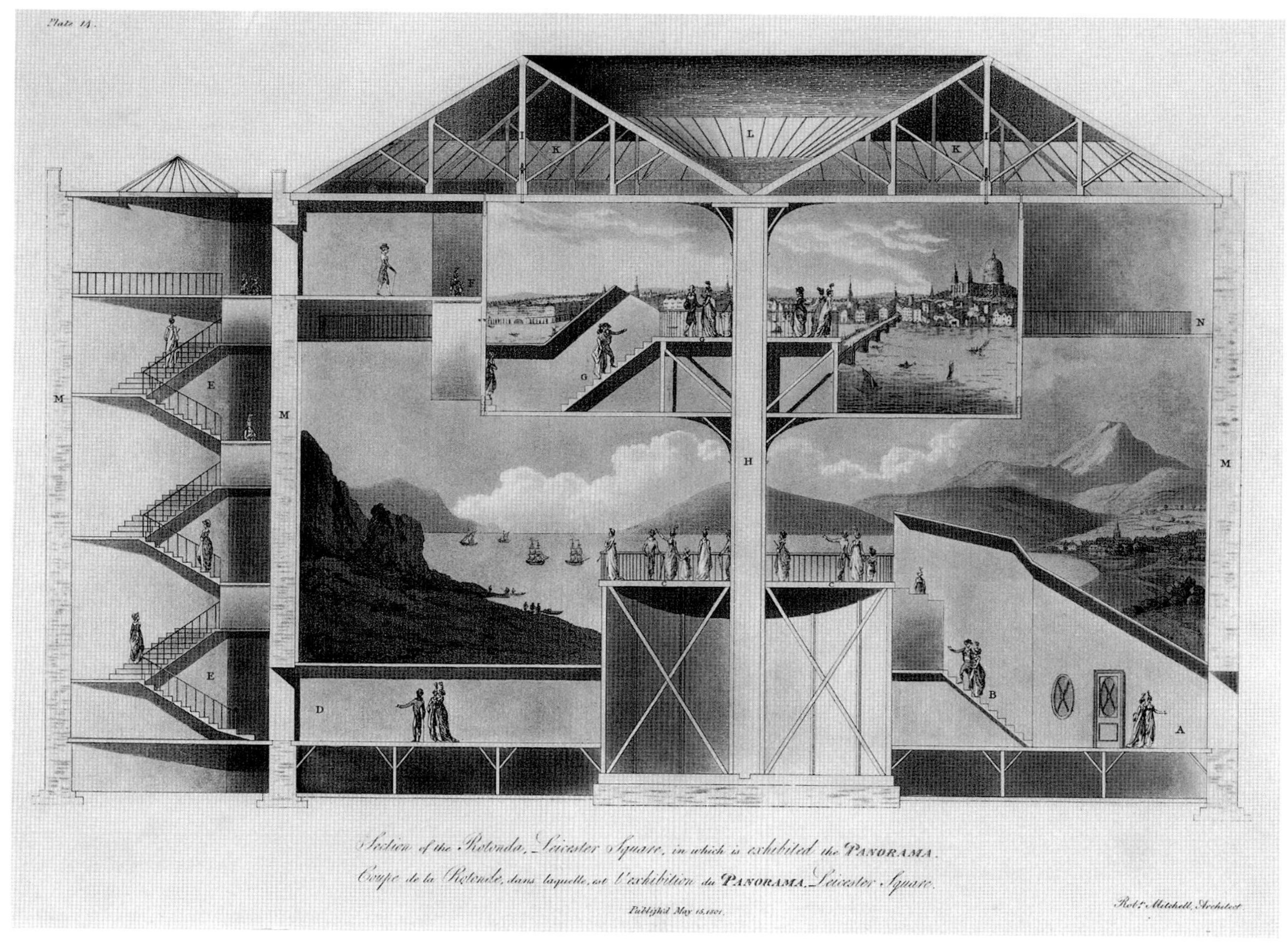

97 Robert Mitchell, 'Section of the Rotonda, Leicester Square, in which is exhibited two panorama's on two different floors', coloured aquatint from his *Plans and Views in Perspective, with Descriptions of Buildings Erected in England and Scotland* (1801). By courtesy of the Trustees of the British Museum.

John Vanderlyn all produced panorama paintings. Reinagle regularly painted for the Panorama Strand and was part owner of that establishment; Roberts and Stanfield executed not only moving panorama paintings, but also dioramas at Drury Lane.

Panoramas were landscape paintings in the round, enveloping their viewers in a 360 degree illusion of a city or the countryside viewed as if from a high vantage-point. After paying the entrance fee (a shilling in London), visitors entered the panorama through a dark tunnel and mounted a round platform in the centre of a round room (fig. 97). The room was illuminated from above by a skylight set into the centre of an umbrella-shaped dome, the curvature of which masked the top edge of the canvas and created a gradual transition from the illusionistic painting on the wall to a ceiling painted to look like the sky. The lower portion of the canvas was disguised by the creation of a false terrain containing three-dimensional objects that aimed to make the transition from the foreground to the illusion on the wall entirely imperceptible. The observation platform of Barker's panorama of the *Grand Fleet at Spithead in 1791*, for instance, was constructed to look like the poop deck of a frigate, and proved so effective at creating the illusion that one was on board ship that Queen Charlotte, for one, felt seasick.

As this suggests, the panorama's 'new improvement in painting' consisted first and foremost of its powerful illusionism. The suppression of the frame and of anything that might distract from the sensation of a three-dimensional view allowed spectators to experience the illusion as a real landscape. Writing to his brother in Philadelphia, the artist Charles Robert Leslie reported that Barker's panoramas of 1812, the *Siege of Flushing* and the *Bay of Messina*, were so convincing that 'I actually put on my hat imagining myself to be in the open air . . . such is the astonishing effect that can be produced by a strict adherence to Nature'.[15] The somatic reactions of Queen Charlotte and Leslie to the panorama also recall the sensations one was expected to feel in the presence of the sublime, which stretched the limits of human endurance. The panorama in this sense domesticated what had in the eighteenth century been an experience of real landscape scenery, and mechanically reproduced it as a popular commercial attraction.

Virtual reality combined with topographical accuracy were

the hallmarks of the panorama. While the first gave spectators the visceral thrill they desired, the second allowed the painters and promoters of panoramas to declare them to be 'educational'. As early as Barker's panorama of London, visitors could purchase for sixpence an anamorphic diagram of the view which identified its important features. Recalling Burford's panorama in Leicester Square, which was famed for its views of foreign cities, John Ruskin later exclaimed that, 'it was an educational institution of the highest and purest value, and ought to have been supported by the government as one of the most beneficial school instruments in London'.[16] The panorama's educational benefits derived from its topographically exact treatment of subjects of national, historical and cultural interest. Battles of the French and Napoleonic wars, views of major European capitals and exotic cities, as well as landscapes of historical or religious interest such as Rome or Jerusalem – all these were common subjects for panoramas.

As a form of topography a panorama painting began with preliminary drawings, made on the spot, of the view to be reproduced. Alone among the great panorama entrepreneurs, Henry Aston Barker made his own drawings; most others hired trained professional artists like Reinagle, while Robert Burford used drawings supplied by army officers stationed in different parts of Europe and the Empire in order to construct his panoramas of military battles and views of foreign cities.[17] No matter who was responsible for the initial studies, accuracy was a common point of pride. In the case of a battle scene, survivors and veterans would be consulted as to the truth of the depiction; meanwhile, for urban panoramas numerous detailed distant and close-up views of major monuments would be made, so that the exactness of their representations could be assured. All of these preparatory drawings would then be massively enlarged, transformed into polygonal views, painted on sections of canvas and arranged cylindrically with the joints between each panel softened so that the illusion looked seamless.[18]

Given its origin in topography it is not surprising that the panorama's artists and subjects should have derived, in part, from the military. Before the 1820s the conventions used in mapping to delineate different terrains were not regularized or accurately descriptive.[19] Their shortcomings made topographical elevations of tremendous importance, since they enabled one to see what the mapped landscape would look like when encountered on foot. Those best trained in making such elevations were military men (like those hired by Burford), who also had the advantage of being located in those places the public, especially during the war years, was especially curious about: battlefields, continental cities, and the far-flung reaches of the growing Empire. Hence the ties between panorama painting and the militarism and imperialism of the early nineteenth century were both understandable and close.

Topography linked the panorama to picturesque tourism and to estate portraiture. With the institution of the picturesque tours of the Reverend William Gilpin and others at the end of the eighteenth century, the experience of an unfamiliar place was made a wholly visual one. Popular sites such as the English Lakes or Tintern Abbey were to be visually consumed and rated on a scale of picturesqueness, while tourists were encouraged to imagine that they could know a place simply through the contemplation of its visual features. The possibility of making travel into a complete visual simulation, so that one did not even have the bother of packing, makes the panorama the logical end point of the picturesque approach to viewing landscape. Another connection with the picturesque sensibility, and in particular with its supposed 'improving' effects on the mind, was the panorama's presentation of the view as an 'educational' experience. It also had ideological as well as formal ties to the topographical genre of estate portraiture: the panorama's elevated viewpoint and its powerful sense of place recall views of country seats where the estate grounds are shown extending beyond the house

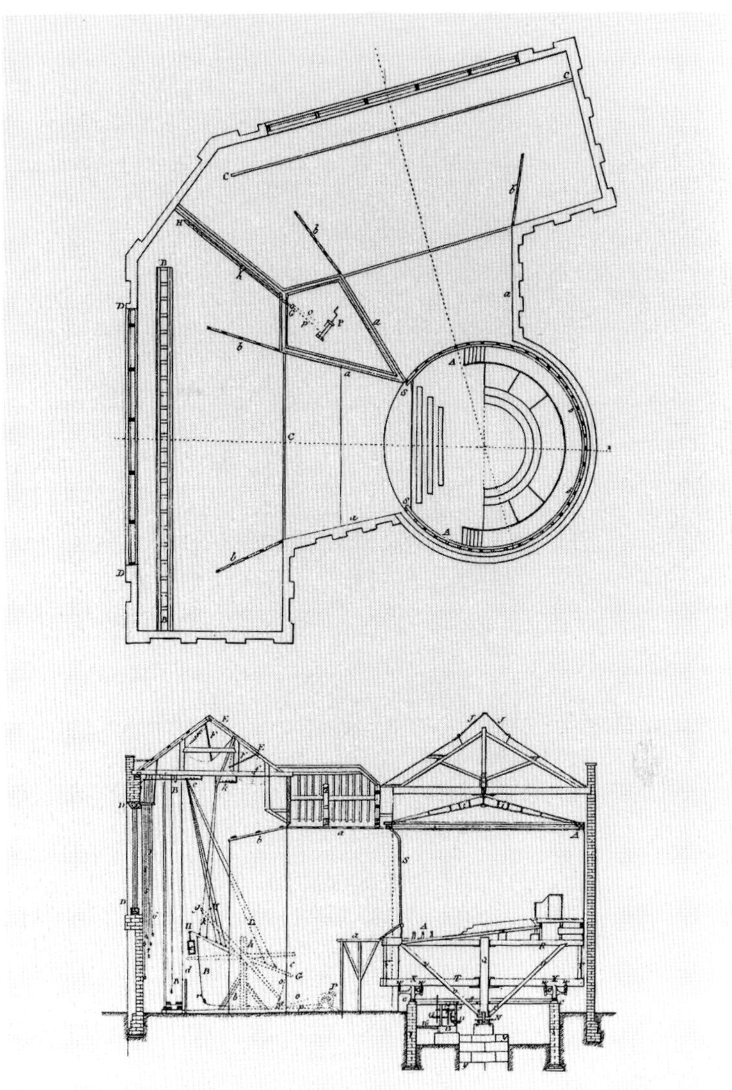

98 A. Pugin and J. Morgan, 'Plan and Section for Arrowsmith's Diorama Building, London', engraving from *J. D. Dinglers Polytechnisches Journal*, 17 (1825).

and merging into the surrounding landscape. Such extensive prospects and commanding viewpoints have been associated with a way of seeing that is of a piece with land ownership.[20] With the arrival of the panorama, however, the visual domination of the landscape associated with the privileged and proprietary viewpoint of the landowner became a mass visual experience.

If the panorama was a spectacle of special events and places, the diorama was a spectacle of special effects. Its inventor – better known for the daguerreotype – was Louis Jacques Mandé Daguerre (1787–1851), who opened the first diorama in Paris in 1822. The entertainment was so successful that a year later he built a second such establishment in Regent's Park. Unlike the circular format of the panorama, the diorama was painted on a flat screen (fig. 98). To create the proper illusionistic effect, diorama buildings were constructed so that viewers entered the auditorium in near darkness, and when the curtain went up they sat looking at the 70 × 45 foot transparency from 40 feet away. In front of the transparency was a false terrain and behind it was a screen or a number of screens on which various elements of the scene were painted. The total illusion as well as the individual painted screens could be illuminated from above and behind, depending on what special effects were desired. Blinds of coloured silk and cotton were used to colour and vary the light. When one scene was finished the whole auditorium rotated 45 degrees and another scene magically materialized. The illusion of depth, projection and three-dimensionality created by the lighting was so strong that viewers often threw objects at the screens to convince themselves that the things they saw were not real and were simply painted on a flat surface.[21]

Unlike the panorama, which presented a continuous view, the diorama offered a continuous narrative, adding to the illusion the dimension of time. Each diorama scene underwent a series of visual transformations which unfolded over the course of about fifteen minutes. For instance, Daguerre's *Effect of Snow Seen through a Ruined Gothic Colonnade* (1826) opened with the building and its surroundings shrouded in thick fog which by degrees burned off, revealing an extensive snow-covered, sun-filled valley (fig. 99).[22] While the panorama drew on the popular interest in views of cities and the scenes of famous Napoleonic battles, the early diorama capitalized on the popular taste for the sublime and the Gothic. From the start Daguerre paired his dioramas so that one scene would be an exterior sublime landscape, and the other a Gothic interior. In 1822, for instance, he paired a view of the Sarnen Valley in Switzerland with an interior view of a side chapel in Canterbury cathedral.

99 Louis Jacques Mandé Daguerre, *Diorama: Effect of Snow Seen through a Ruined Gothic Colonnade*, 1826. Collection Gérard Lévy, Paris.

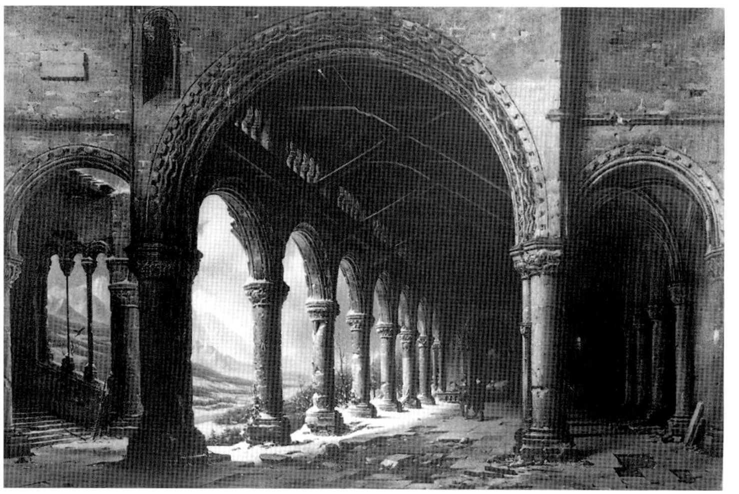

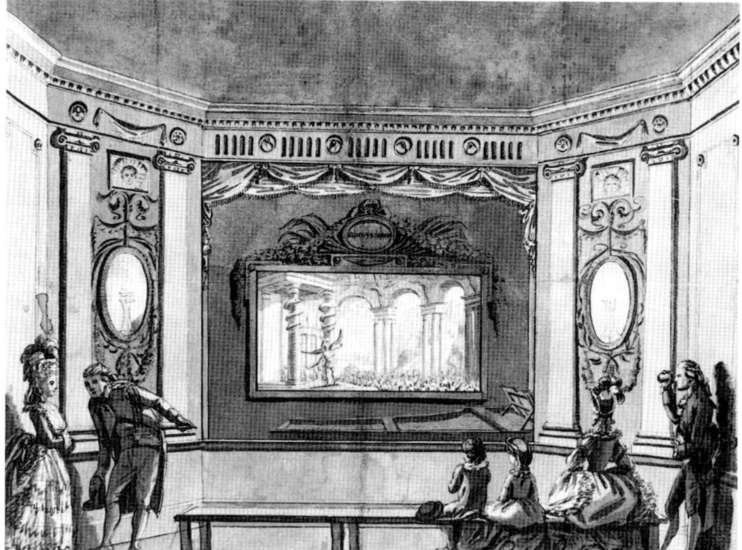

100 Edward Francis Burney, *The Eidophusikon*, *c.*1782, watercolour. By courtesy of the Trustees of the British Museum.

In the diorama, it was not enough to have the sensation of being present at the scene; one had to be emotionally gripped as well. The diorama's simulation of sublime special effects such as fires, storms, sunsets and sunrises thrilled and unsettled its audiences. The self-possession of the panorama viewer, who was free to move about the viewing platform and take in the landscape as she or he wished, must be contrasted with the experience of the diorama viewer who, seated in a darkened room, was the passive spectator of the illusion's dramatic effects.[23] In this way the diorama looks backs to its origins in the theatre – not only in its reliance on the technology of transparencies, which had for two centuries been standard equipment for the staging of illusionistic effects, but also in its creation of a visual narrative through changing light effects.

In its technology and its narrative approach to landscape, the diorama also looks back to Philippe Jacques de Loutherbourg's *Eidophusikon*, first exhibited at his London house in 1781 (fig. 100). Before building his *Eidophusikon*, the artist had worked for the actor-manager David Garrick revolutionizing scene design and lighting at Drury Lane. One of de Loutherbourg's innovations in the theatre was the dramatic use of coloured trans-

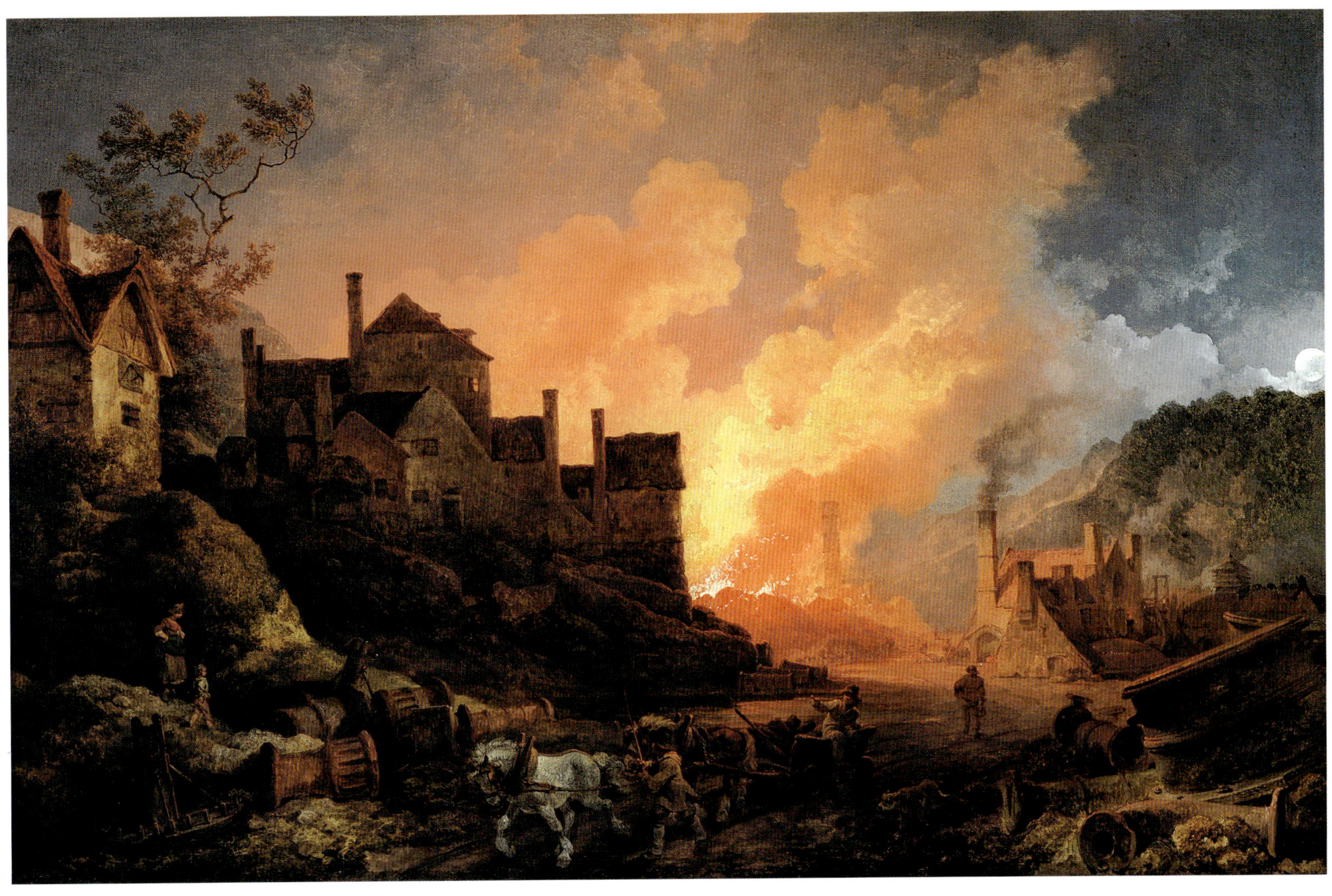

101 Philippe Jacques de Loutherbourg, *A View of Coalbrook Dale by Night*, RA 1801. Science Museum, London.

parencies in order to simulate various light and weather effects.[24] Following on the heels of his wildly successful pantomime at Drury Lane, the *Wonders of Derbyshire* (1779), which showed eleven different localities in the Peak District at various times of day, the *Eidophusikon, or Representation of Nature* presented five landscape views seen at changing times of the day and under varying light and weather conditions.[25] Following its début in 1781, de Loutherbourg exhibited his invention in 1782, 1786 and 1793; in the nineteenth century, exhibitions of it were mounted by others.[26] A description of one of the views 'Aurora; or, the Effects of the Dawn, with a View of London from Greenwich Park' gives some idea of what viewers experienced:

> The houses and trees were cardboard cutouts and placed in exact perspective. The foreground, which resembled a heath, was constructed of cork to appear like moss or lichens. When the curtain went up the whole was bathed in the indeterminate sort of light that precedes dawn, and then a faint light appeared along the horizon. The scene took on a hazy, grayish tint, then a saffron yellow tone gilded the clouds gliding past in the misty dawn. Colour and light gradually increased in intensity until the sun came up, illuminating first the tips of the trees and hills, the towers and domes, and finally the entire landscape, revealing a sparkling summer morning in all its brilliance to the amazed spectators.[27]

The effects achieved by de Loutherbourg were so extraordinary that they enchanted many painters, most notably Thomas Gainsborough, who returned to see the show many times and who built for himself a small peep-box fitted with glass transparencies of landscape scenes.[28]

Critics of de Loutherbourg's exhibition landscapes inevitably alluded to their reliance on effects derived from the theatre. Remarking of *A View of Colebrook Dale by Night* (RA 1801; fig. 101), an anonymous reviewer observed that

> The mechanical dexterity of this Artist has been always justly admired. . . . But this excellence has been so much his aim, that he has neglected excellencies of a higher kind. Hence he seldom looks at the modest beauties of nature, or thinks them perhaps beneath his Attention. There is too much of a gaudy

glare in all his Works, though indeed they may all be considered as strong proofs of genius but genius not regulated by sound taste. In the Picture before us, the Artist has attempted too much. He has given a vivid representation of the artificial light resulting from the foundry, but not contented with what should have been the great object, he has attempted also to shew *Moonlight* and the *Break of Day*: The general aspect of this Picture is like the *nocturnal Transparencies* which excite so much vulgar admiration in our *Print Shops*.[29]

The reviewer glosses the relationship between de Loutherbourg's light effects and conventions derived from the theatre – that is, the use of two contrasting lights, one warm and the other cool. These could also be found in the small-scale transparencies sold by printmakers for domestic decoration and entertainment, showing cottages ablaze or gypsy camp fires set against the silvery moon. Joseph Wright of Derby also often employed this double light system, mainly in his nocturnal landscapes.

While the panorama depended for its illusionistic effects on a vast horizontal format and a manipulation of linear and aerial perspective, the diorama, like the *Eidophusikon* before it, depended on the careful orchestration of colour and light. Given its hyperrealism and its attention to special optical effects, it seems only fitting that its creator should have been the inventor of the daguerreotype. And, given this, it seems almost uncanny that Daguerre's assistant, who arranged for the opening of the diorama in London, was the younger brother of John Arrowsmith, the London art dealer. A few years later the elder Arrowsmith would bring to Paris a different triumph in optical realism, John Constable's *Hay Wain* (London, National Gallery) – or, as it was then known, in diorama fashion, *Landscape: Noon*.[30]

By pointing out the personal links between Gainsborough and the *Eidophusikon* and Constable and the diorama, I wish to underscore the way in which these artists shared with the landscape entertainments an abiding interest in and sensitivity to the visual effects of size, colour and light as well as the emotional and narrative possibilities of the depiction of natural phenomena. Such painters may well have been inspired by these popular spectacles to pursue their own formal innovations, innovations that echoed or coincided at certain points with the panorama's and diorama's 'new improvements' in landscape. The work of artists like Gainsborough and Constable and the advent of popular landscape spectacles are indicative of a visual culture that had come to value and expect unusual and dramatic optical effects in its painted representations of landscape.

More specifically, it seems to me highly likely that Gainsborough directly incorporated lessons learned from the *Eidophusikon* into his later landscapes such as *Mountain Valley with Sheep* (RA 1783; Edinburgh, National Gallery of Scotland) and his numerous variations on the 'cottage door' theme. The large-scale format, delicate light and lush colourism of these paintings are new elements in his style, and play a large part in his works' visual impact and emotional sentiment. It was during this phase of his career, when he was experimenting with transparencies and with unusual effects of colour and light, that Gainsborough became especially concerned with the conditions under which his paintings would be seen. His constant battles with the Hanging Committee of the Royal Academy centred on the effect his works would have when hung in the Great Room at Somerset House. He preferred to show them in his own gallery in Schomberg House, where the light could be strictly controlled in order to make his imagery appear to maximum advantage. In addition to Gainsborough's preoccupation with colour and light at this time, a further inspiration from the *Eidophusikon* is suggested by his practice of fashioning miniature landscapes out of cork and mirrors for the purposes of landscape sketching. Such three-dimensional models suggest something like the false terrain employed by de Loutherbourg and the later panoramists and dioramists.

John Constable's connections with the popular landscape entertainments of his day are more indirect. We know from his letters that he admired the panorama and diorama as intriguing illusions, but that he did not consider them to be art. Nevertheless, Constable's own increasingly large horizontal landscapes of the 1820s and 1830s, with their theatrical manipulations of light, suggest a sensibility alert to the panorama's power of size and to the diorama's dramatic narratives of changing weather and times of day. Yet the increase in size brought Constable's ambitions as a colourist into conflict with his need to rely on those broad areas of tone that his large landscapes required if they were to cohere as unified compositions. In his cloud studies as well as his analysis of the work of Claude and Rubens, the painter struggled to infuse his large landscapes with dramatic patterns of light and dark, or what he called the 'chiaroscuro of nature'. The result was a sacrifice of the colouristic naturalism that had distinguished his earlier works. Constable's panoramic landscapes of the later 1820s and 1830s such as the *Beach at Brighton, the Chain*

102 Thomas Girtin, *Kirkstall Abbey*, 1800, watercolour over pencil. By courtesy of the Trustees of the British Museum.

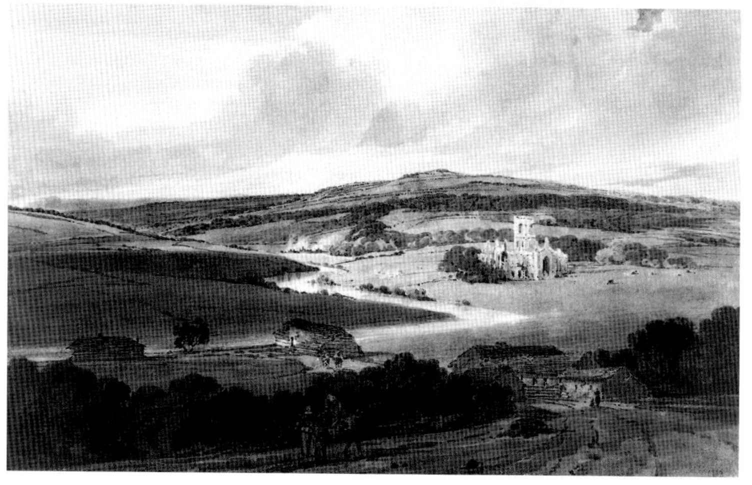

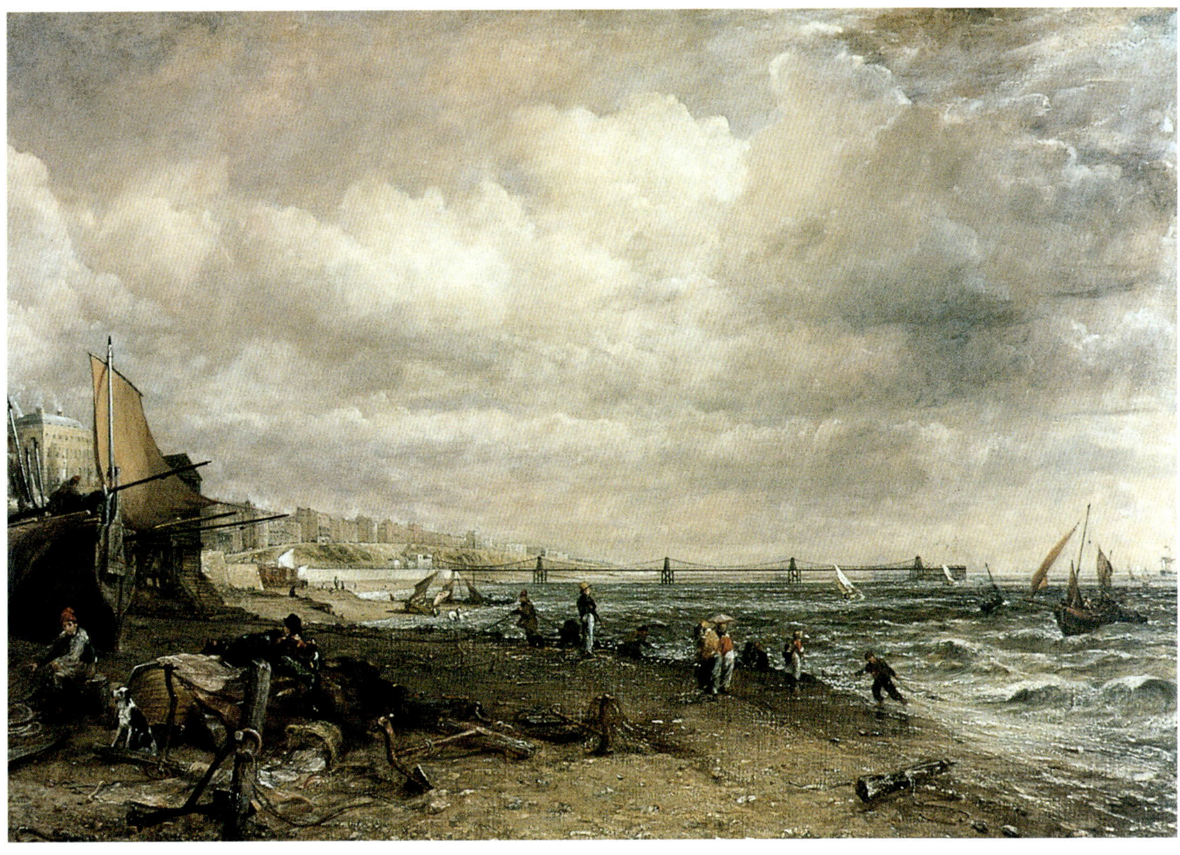

103 John Constable, *The Beach at Brighton, the Chain Pier in the Distance*, RA 1827. Tate, London.

Pier in the Distance (RA 1827; fig. 103) and the *Opening of Waterloo Bridge* (RA 1832; see fig. 122) take on the silvered tone of landscapes seen in a smoked mirror.

The emergence and popularity of panoramas and dioramas coincide with two distinct phases in the history of early nineteenth-century British landscape painting. First of all, the panorama emerges at the moment when topography was once again in the ascendant under a renewed concern for naturalistic depiction of local English scenery. Girtin's and Turner's transformation of topography brought to the genre a breadth of handling derived from the classical landscape tradition, enabling visual fact to be wedded to a simple and harmonious structural form. Whereas other painters may have sought to create visual drama by working on a large scale, the 'sublimity' of these two young artists' topographical views came not from the size of the support but from the internal scale. Views like Girtin's *Kirkstall Abbey* (1800; fig. 102), while small in size, created the sense of a sweeping scale, an effect that was magnified by the broadness of the handling. Watercolour was the preferred medium because its transparency allowed the carefully delineated outlines of forms to show, while its luminosity enabled artists to treat atmospheric conditions in a naturalistic way. It is significant that Barker's first panorama, a view of Edinburgh (1789) was painted in the topographers' preferred medium of watercolour. Girtin's own *Eidometropolis*, which was renowned for its atmospheric effects and for 'representing objects of [*sic*] the hues which they appear in nature', was sketched first in watercolour before being translated into oil, a common practice among panoramists.[31]

The heightened realism of panorama painting took the realism of the topographical watercolour a step further. Echoing the sublime topography of Girtin and Turner, the producers of panoramas employed a large internal scale, and this, when combined with the spectacle's large size and its 360 degree format, evoked vast expanses of space – a sense of sublimity that owed at least as much to this manipulation of forms within the scene as it did to the painting's actual size. In addition, the panorama's attention to the effects of light and atmosphere, particularly as it affected the illusion of spatial distance, can be related to similar concerns in the topographical watercolour. The atmospheric effects achieved by Girtin and Turner depended on gradated veils of transparent watercolour wash that defined the arc of the sky and softened the outlines of distant objects. Comparable techniques were used in the panorama, to create the illusion of vast distances and to obscure the seam between the top of the painting and the ceiling of the room. For example in John Knox's panorama of the *View of Loch Lomond and Ben Lomond* (1810), clouds of mist rise from the lake and blend with the cloud-filled sky (figs 104 and 105). As in the topographical watercolour, the vantage-point in the panorama is elevated and the sky dominates the composition. Yet perhaps the most

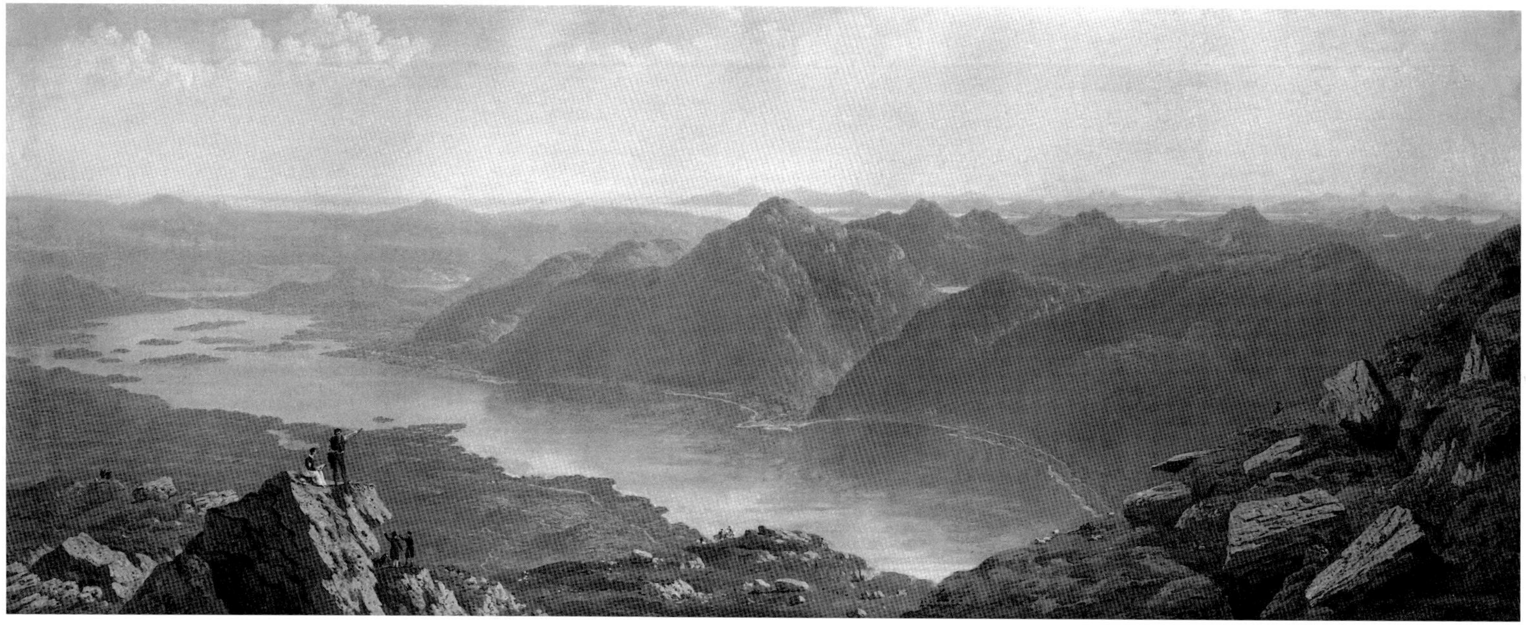

significant link is the way in which both forms cultivate a factual, almost artless look, an appearance of recording the actual features of the view directly rather than according to the conventional formulas of studio productions. It is only when we become aware of the clever use of the winding river in *Kirkstall Abbey* to direct the eye into the distance that we see it as a compositional device as well as a feature of the landscape.

The panorama demonstrated that nearly all the naturalistic effects found in the topographical watercolour could be transferred into a large-format oil painting. This was an important lesson, for it provided artists with a means to convert a naturalistic topographical view into an exhibition landscape in a way that did not depend on classical precedents and formulas. Some distinctions, however, had to be made when it came to the treatment of light. The time of day most often represented in the panorama was noon, which complemented the central skylight illumination of the room. To represent dawn or twilight would mean that in one portion of the panorama the sun would have to be represented as shining directly in the viewers' faces, silhouetting that portion of the landscape before them. To avoid this, the light depicted in the panorama tended to be even rather than dramatic, and shadows were kept to a minimum. Landscape painters could not follow this recipe exactly without losing the sense of distance; nevertheless, in works like Girtin's *Kirkstall Abbey* or Constable's *Dedham Vale: Morning* (RA 1811; fig. 106) the shadows are limited to the foreground where they suggest the presence of passing clouds, while the rest of the landscape is illuminated with an even light that picks out the most distant features of the view.

More than Girtin or Constable, it was Turner who, in his large exhibition landscapes from around 1810 until the 1830s made the most of what had by now become the conventions of panorama painting. As Professor of Perspective at the Academy since 1807, Turner was not only a master of its mathematical complexities but was adept in using perspective as an expressive tool. In his extraordinary picture of *Rome, from the Vatican* (RA 1820; fig. 107) the panoramic view of the city in the centre of the composition is flanked on the right by a deep perspectival view of the loggia; a similar view to the left is abruptly cut off by the edge of the canvas. This vast painting, measuring 11 feet wide and nearly 6 feet high, marked the three-hundredth anniversary of Raphael's death; in the foreground Turner included a figure of the artist together with his mistress, surrounded by many of the Renaissance master's best-known works. While the scene's highly saturated golden colour attracted a certain amount of press criticism, its oblique perspective and atmospheric effects elicited general praise. *Rome, from the Vatican* creates the illusion of seeing the hot, steaming city below from within the cool shelter of the loggia; standing before it the observer feels surrounded by the view, a sensation directly akin to that of the panorama.

Paintings like this, which celebrated real or imagined scenes from the past, were termed 'historical landscapes' – that is to say, they were landscapes that incorporated relatively small-scale figures representing historical, mythological or biblical narratives. Deriving from seventeenth-century examples such as Nicolas Poussin's *Deluge*, this genre had come to Britain largely thanks to the agency of Richard Wilson, whose *Destruction of the Children of Niobe* (1759–60; New Haven, Yale Center for British Art) had initiated a competition between history painting and landscape that continued well into the nineteenth century. Historical landscapes competed with history paintings proper not only by encroaching on their traditional subject matter, but also by treating such themes on a substantial scale, and in both respects by aspiring to the highest levels of intellectual dignity and cultural prestige. Also referred to as 'poetical landscapes', such

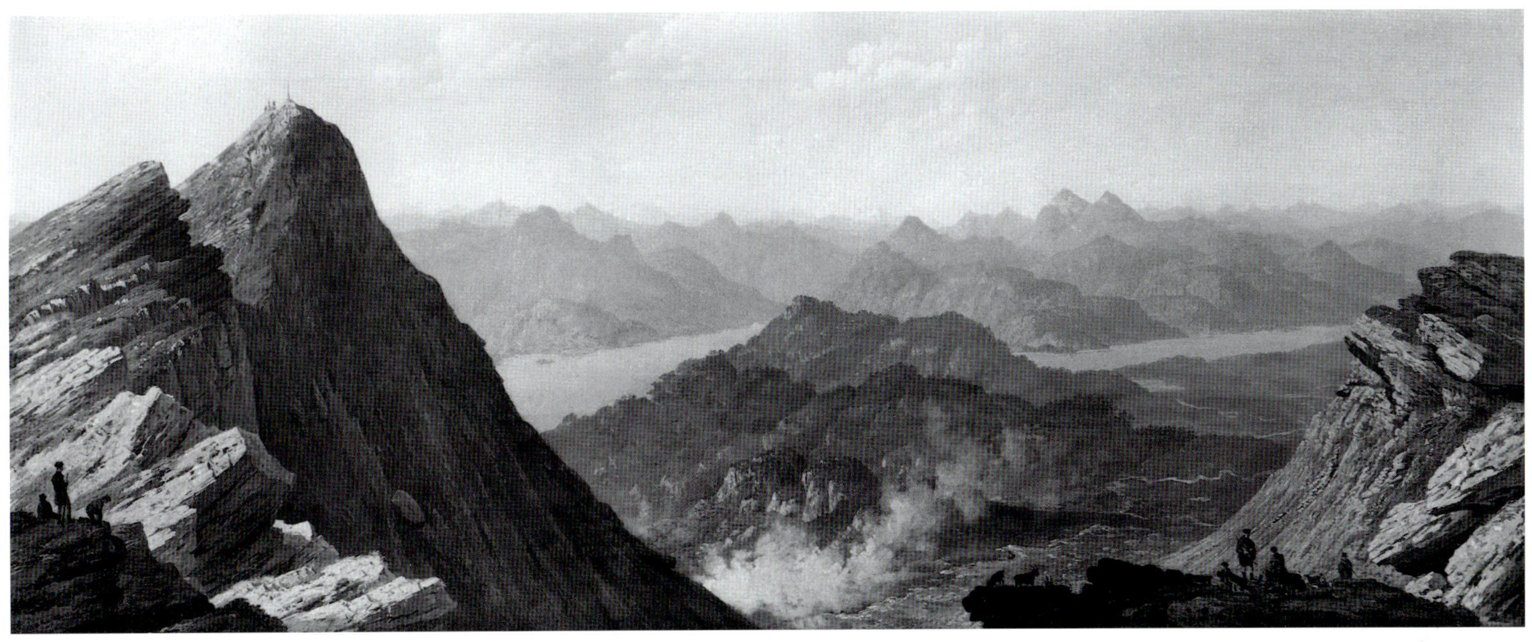

105 John Knox, *South-western view of Ben Lomond*, 1810. Glasgow Museums: Art Gallery & Museum, Kelvingrove.

104 (*facing page*) John Knox, *South-western view of Loch Lomond*, 1810. Glasgow Museums: Art Gallery & Museum, Kelvingrove. This and figure 105 are either studies for or reduced replicas of Knox's panorama of *Loch Lomond and Ben Lomond*.

106 John Constable, *Dedham Vale: Morning*, RA 1811. Elton Hall Collection.

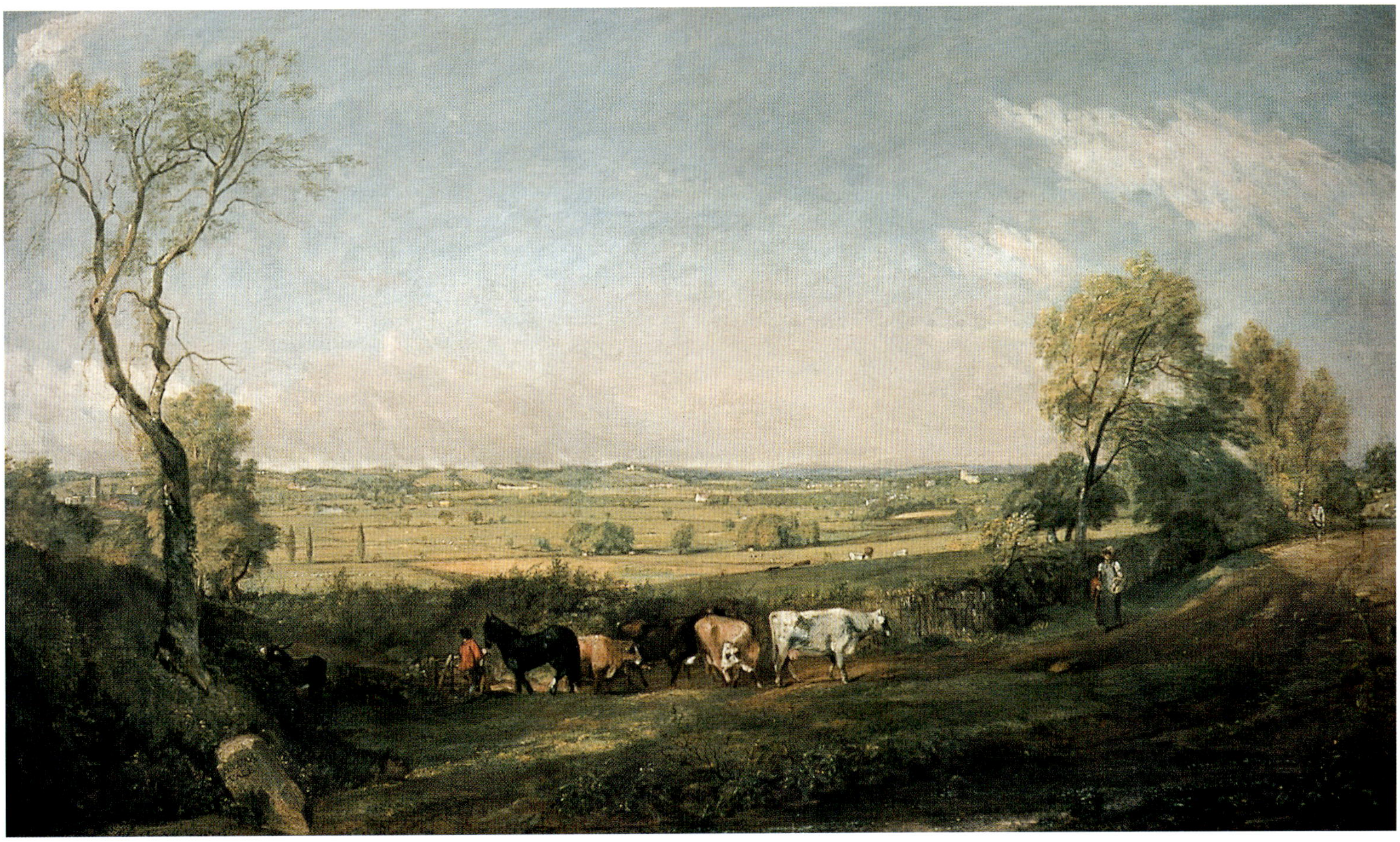

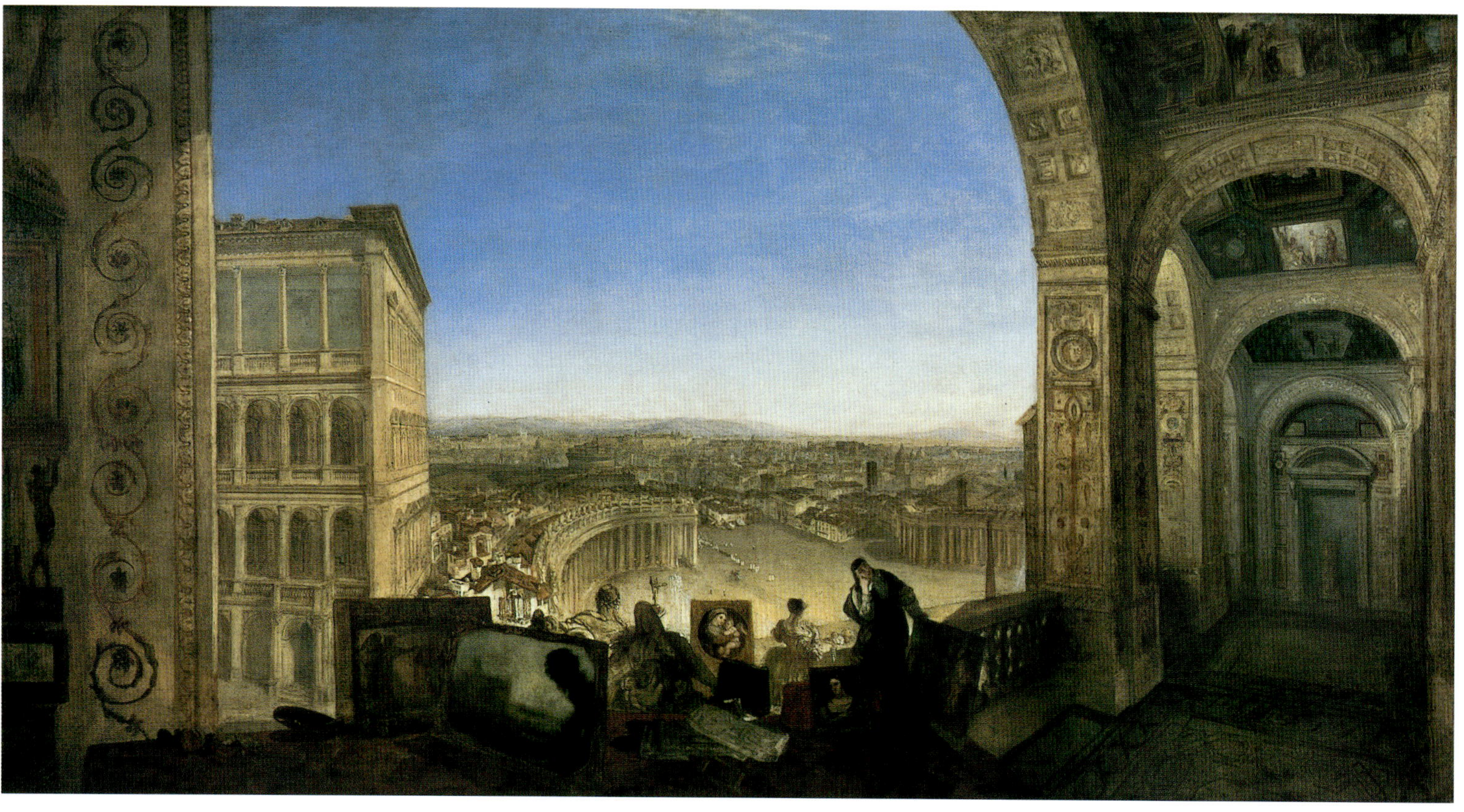

107 J. M. W. Turner, *Rome, from the Vatican. Raffaelle, accompanied by La Fornarina, preparing his Pictures for the Decoration of the Loggia*, RA 1820. Tate, London.

works often took the form of the panorama or borrowed its effects.

Aside from compositions by Turner like *Rome, from the Vatican*, the panorama's dramatic manipulations of perspective can also be found in the historical landscapes of John Martin and Francis Danby. Their biblical and apocalyptic visions of cosmic destruction were anticipated by Turner in such works as his *Fifth Plague of Egypt* (RA 1800; Minneapolis Institute of Art) and are no doubt related to the rise of millenarianism.[32] Paintings like Martin's *Joshua Commanding the Sun to Stand Still upon Gibeon* (RA 1816; London, Grand Lodge of the Masonic Order) treat landscape objects as architectural forms and apply the rules of linear perspective so that rocks, cliffs, clouds and ocean waves are organized along orthogonals to create the illusion of deep receding spaces. Among these vertiginous caverns tiny human figures scramble for their lives. Such perspectival tricks and manipulations of scale were perfected by Francis Danby, and in paintings like *An Attempt to Illustrate the Opening of the Sixth Seal* (RA 1828; fig. 112) they were combined with melodramatic displays of spectacular light effects and intense colour. The *Sixth Seal* was a huge success. Visitors to the Academy in 1828 crowded around the work, which the *London Weekly Review* called 'the most striking picture in the present Exhibition', and which the *Athenaeum, Literary and Critical Journal* praised as 'sublimely imagined and powerfully executed'.[33]

The colourism and lighting in Danby's works approximate the luminous effects created earlier by de Loutherbourg and Daguerre; indeed one year before his triumph at the Academy, Danby had designed a diorama of the Deluge which he never built. As this suggests, while the panorama anticipated the birth of the sublime topographical watercolour, the diorama coincided with the heyday of the poetical or historical landscape.

While the panorama demanded even lighting from above, the diorama's *raison d'être* was its spectacular instances of illumination. Like the *Eidophusikon* before it, the diorama's illusionistic magic depended on back- or front-lit scenes (figs 108 and 109). With back lighting, landscape objects would be silhouetted darkly against a glowing sunset, fire or moonlit sky, whereas when lit from the front they would be crisply illuminated against a light-filled variegated sky. The back-lit view closed off the distance and made the foreground objects appear to project outwards; the front-lit view opened up the distance and created the impression of recession behind the picture plane. We find Turner employing both of these conventions, and in his two views of *Mortlake Terrace* (RA 1826 and 1827; figs 111 and 110) he demonstrated – in almost textbook fashion – the different effects that lighting could have on a single landscape scene. In the first he shows the seat of William Moffatt illuminated from the front on an early summer's morn, and a year later, in a view

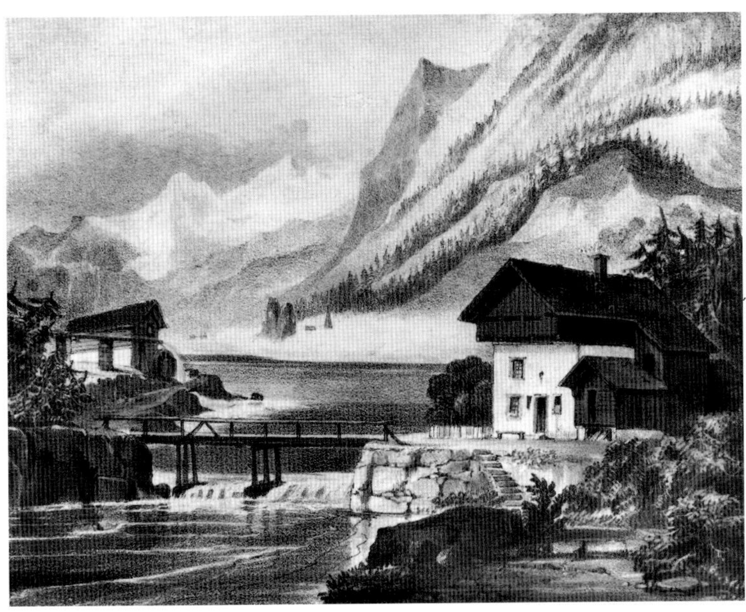

108 After Louis Jacques Mandé Daguerre, *Alpine Scene: Morning*, *c.*1836, coloured lithograph. Gernsheim Collection, Harry Ranson Humanities Research Center, The University of Texas at Austin.

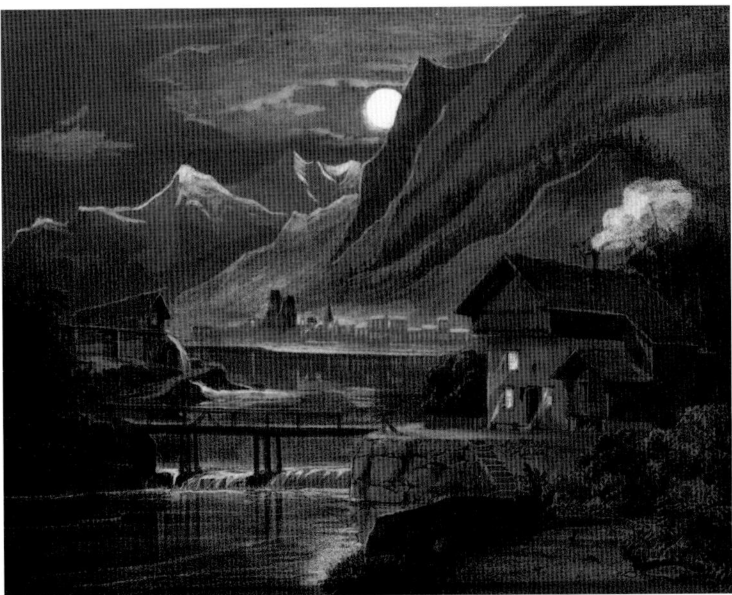

109 After Louis Jacques Mandé Daguerre, *Alpine Scene: Night*, *c.*1836, coloured lithograph. Gernsheim Collection, Harry Ranson Humanities Research Center, The University of Texas at Austin.

taken from the same spot, but turned 180 degrees, he depicted the terrace illuminated by the setting sun.

In his historical canvases such as the *Decline of the Carthaginian Empire* (RA 1817; fig. 114) or *Ulysses Deriding Polyphemus* (RA 1829; fig. 115) Turner most often employed back lighting, and it was with back lighting that he indulged in his most spectacular colouristic effects. Derived from the seaport compositions of Claude Lorraine, the *Decline of the Carthaginian Empire* depicts a receding architectural perspective against a brilliant golden sky. The format is panorama-like in its extreme horizontality, with the canvas measuring nearly 8 feet wide by $5\frac{1}{2}$ feet high. The luminosity of the light and the high saturation of the colour in Turner's painting surpass anything found in Claude; moreover, there is more incident in the foreground of Turner's work than one finds in any of the seventeenth-century master's harbour scenes. Like the false terrains of the panorama or the

110 J. M. W. Turner, *Mortlake Terrace, the Seat of William Moffatt, Esq., Summer's Evening*, RA 1827. Andrew W. Mellon Collection, National Gallery of Art, Washington, D.C.

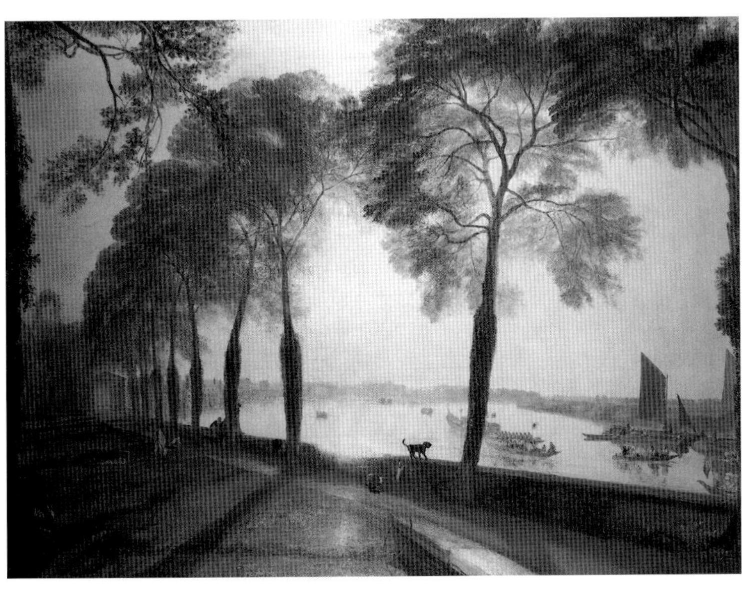

111 J. M. W. Turner, *Seat of William Moffatt, Esq., at Mortlake. Early (Summer's) Morning*, RA 1826. The Frick Collection, New York.

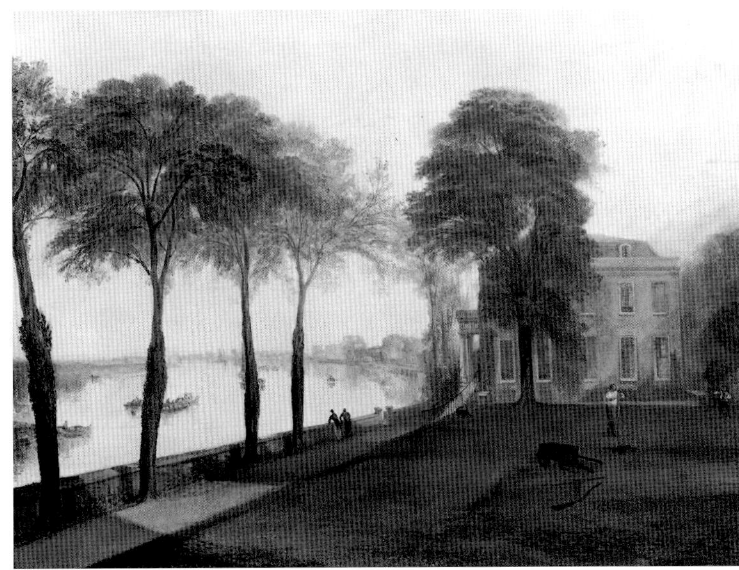

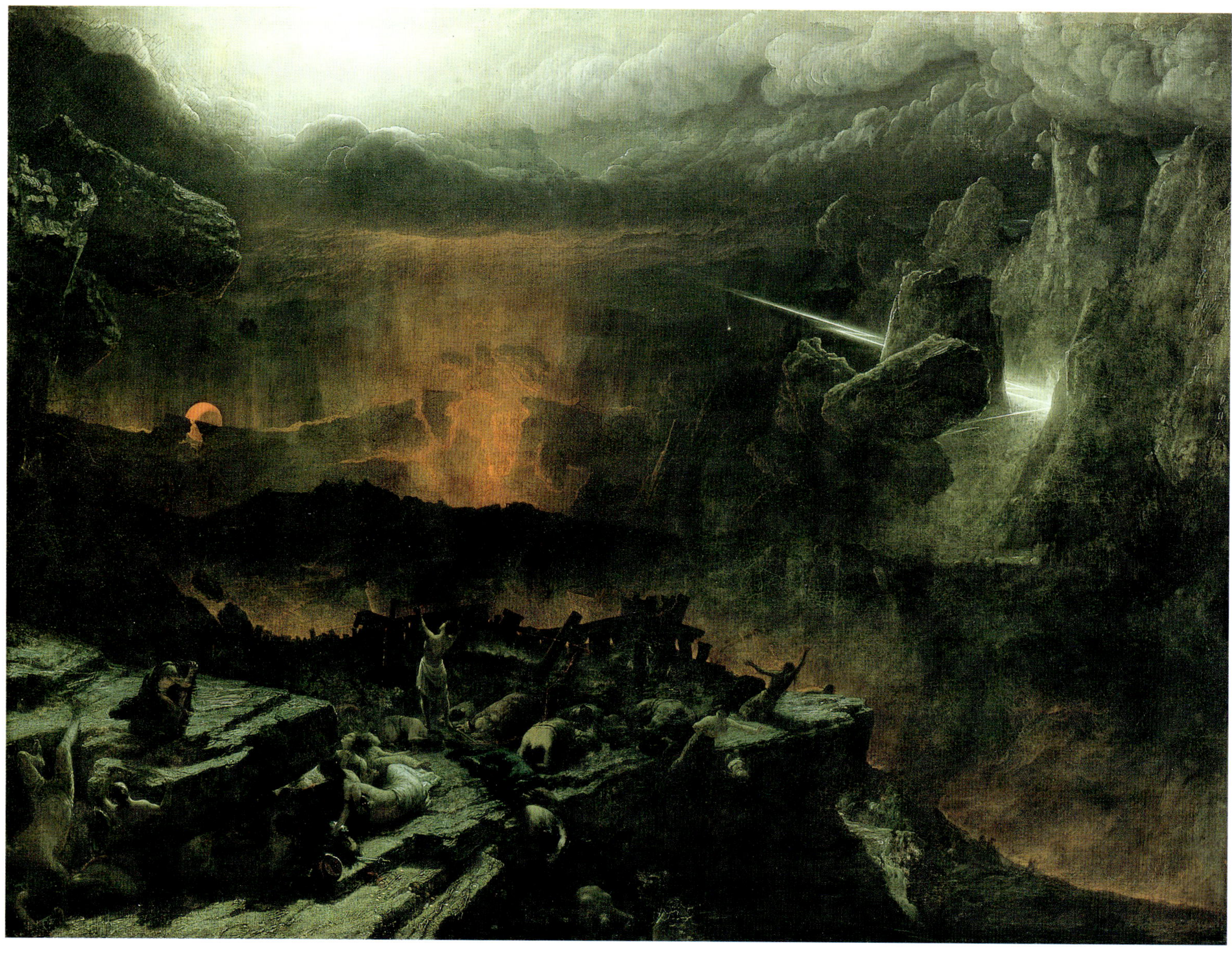

112 Francis Danby, *An Attempt to Illustrate the Opening of the Sixth Seal*, RA 1828. By courtesy of the National Gallery of Ireland, Dublin.

diorama, the clutter in the foreground of Turner's painting appears to project towards the viewer, and by setting the scale these objects create an illusion of deep space that is abruptly closed off by the blaze of the setting sun.

The illumination of the *Ulysses* is even more extraordinary. The heat of its glowing reds, oranges and yellows contrasted with patches of intense blue sky and sea pushes the painting beyond the realm of naturalism. Not surprisingly, perhaps, the painting's colouristic excesses came in for harsh criticism from the press. The *Morning Herald* called it 'colouring run mad', while the *Literary Gazette* accused Turner of trying to put out the eyes of his critics just as Ulysses had put out the eye of the Cyclops. But the *Athenaeum* defended the painting, on the grounds of its 'poetical feeling' and the 'ease and boldness' with which it was achieved, reminding its readers that the subject was 'not drawn from common reality'.[34] Since Ruskin, we have been used to thinking of Turner's colour as inspired by natural phenomena – the sun, the marbles and lagoons of Venice, the clear, blue Alpine air, etc. – yet the sheer theatricality of Turner's use of colour suggests effects borrowed from the stage as much as, if not more than, from life.

The advantages of transferring effects found in the popular landscape entertainments to the walls of Somerset House are obvious enough. Size and intense colour gave landscape paintings a visibility that enabled them to compete with portraits and history paintings. This was important, for landscape demanded a different mode of visual attention on the part of its viewers, one that was not easily maintained in the crush of the exhibition room. Unlike landscapes, portraits often work on the principle of the single gestalt. They represent figures in the foreground and their format is usually vertical. Their simple compositions silhouette the dramatic poses of their subjects, and their bright

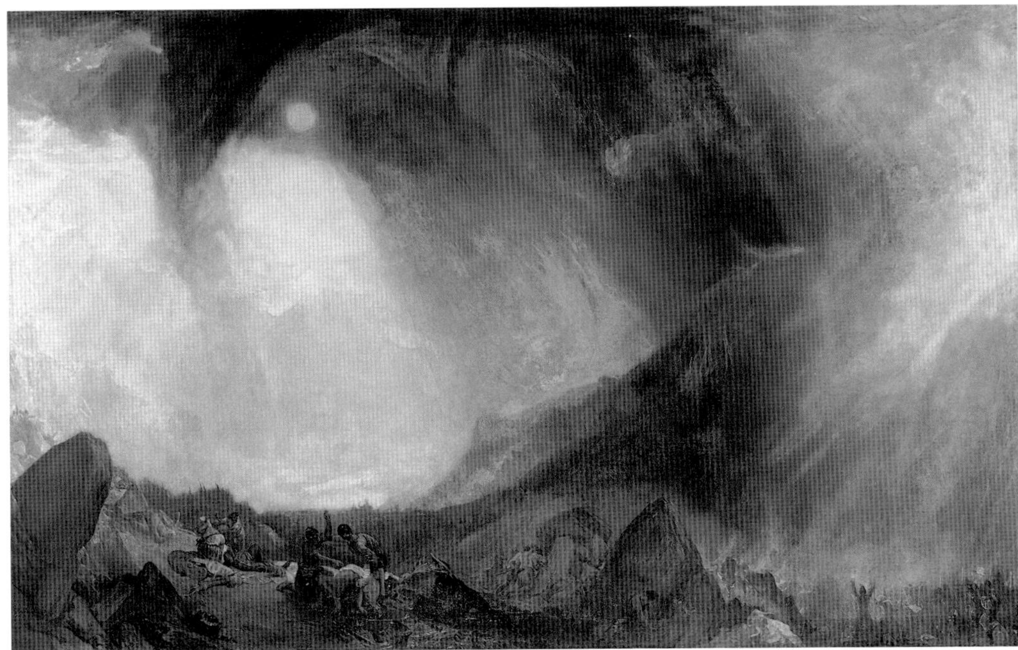

113 J. M. W. Turner, *Snow Storm: Hannibal and his Army Crossing the Alps*, RA 1812. Tate, London.

tonality and strong colour notes – all elements orchestrated with particular effectiveness by Sir Thomas Lawrence – heighten their visual éclat. History paintings tend to draw the viewer's attention to the centre of the composition. While more complex than portraits, their compositions usually cohere around a central figure or action. Hung on the line and angled forward, they could be taken in at a glance. By contrast, landscapes tend to be horizontal in format, inviting the eye to trace a pedestrian itinerary though the landscape from left to right and from foreground to background. Landscape demands a leisurely kind of viewing, since its composition is made up of different spatial zones and it includes a variety of objects and effects. The larger the landscape and the more diverse the number of its naturalistic incidents and details, the more visual attention it demands.

By adapting the panorama's and diorama's size and perspectival effects, landscape painters could resolve some of the problems the exhibition room posed for their genre. The correlation between the spatial effects of these entertainments and the vast scale, ruptures of space and plunging perspectives that one finds in the more sublime historical paintings of Turner, Martin and Danby suggests an attempt on the part of these artists to create compositions that replicated the visceral thrills of the panorama and diorama. Rather than the leisurely pastoral walk through Arcadia indulged in by Constable and others, these artists sought to destabilize their viewers' perceptions and plunge them into a vast spatial abyss. We know for instance that Turner insisted that his *Hannibal Crossing the Alps* (RA 1812; fig. 113) be hung below the line so that its vortex-like composition could be experienced at eye level.[35] When viewed from this angle its centrifugal spatial composition is more immediately felt, and one gets the sensation of being drawn into its chaotic whirlpool. Such compositions commanded the visual attention of the spectators through manipulations of space that were clearly sensationalistic, and which had not been seen before in landscape painting.

Such spectacular colour and theatrical light effects were also new to landscape painting. Colour is always a problem in large landscapes. If treated too literally and assertively the local colour of natural objects can fragment the composition. Sir George Beaumont's proverbial 'brown tree' was more than just a throwback to an older tonal style of landscape painting, it was also an acknowledgement of the need to harmonize and downplay the local colours of a landscape so that the composition maintains the proper visual impact.[36] Many landscapists such as those of the Norwich School created landscapes of enormous breadth and realism through the careful calibration of colour to tone. Nevertheless, such modest and subtle essays in naturalistic perception were, as Constable discovered, doomed to obscurity when hung in the Academy.

Remarking on the high colouring of many of the entries, the *Mirror of Fashion* observed, 'the mischief of those glaring exhibits is, that it forces the artist to have recourse to glitter.'[37] The result was that the colour key of the exhibition as a whole was raised to a high note. In 1807 the *Monthly Retrospect of the Fine Arts* reported,

> It has lately become a fashionable opinion among painters, that all pictures which are to be exhibited must be coloured above nature, to prevent their being either overborne by the works of others, or overlooked by visitors in so large a room. This has *sometimes* led them into a meretricious colouring, in which, attempting to be splendidly attractive, they have become offensively gaudy.[38]

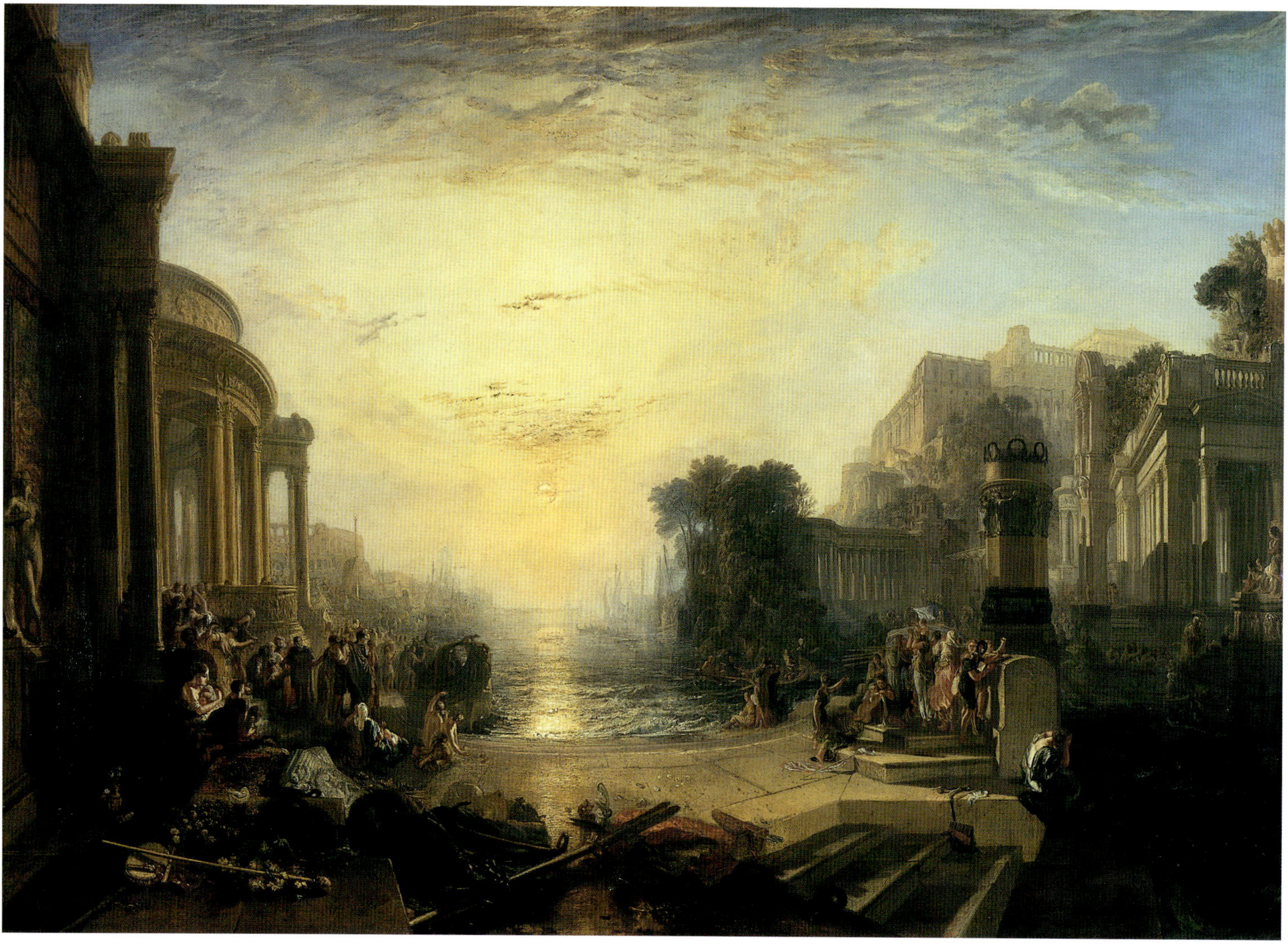

114 J. M. W. Turner, *Decline of the Carthaginian Empire – Rome being determined on the overthrow of her Hated Rival, demanded from her such Terms as might either force her into War, or ruin her by Compliance: the Enervated Carthaginians, in their Anxiety for Peace, consented to give up their Arms and their Children*, RA 1817. Tate, London.

The *Champion's* critic went further, calling the exhibition room a 'gaudy display'. He went on:

> It will not require two seconds reflection to be convinced that such an Exhibition-room must be the destruction itself to the young artist, of promising powers but of diffident temper. Has he toiled with anxious heart, but patient hand, for months and months, in his secluded study to catch the soft simplicity and sober effect of nature. . . . Its faithful tints are lost in the universal [gl]are, as the genuine lustre of a pearl would be lost if thrown admidst a heap of painted glass beads; – its truth be thought weakness by the mob who are in search of effects that nature never presents.[39]

Turner's revolution was to transcend the tension between tone and the local colour of objects in landscape, and to turn instead to the use of a dominant single colour. Landscapes like the *Ulysses* are powerful near-monochromatic statements, modulated not with light and dark but with harmonizing and complementary tints. The transparency of its colouring, its monochromatic intensity, its pure saturation, and its high key all find their counterparts in the diaphonous colouristic effects of the diorama. Due to the brilliance of his colour, Turner's exhibition landscapes could, and did, more than hold their own in the Great Room.

The conclusion to be drawn from this, in particular from the example of Turner and his successes at the Academy, is that the conditions of the Great Room cut against English naturalism in landscape painting. One could even go further and say that by 1820 the Great Room had made naturalism in the exhibition landscape painting a thing of the past. Forced to inflate the size of their works, and to heighten their visual impact by dramatic manipulations of perspective, colouring and subject matter, ambitious landscape painters abandoned the style that had previously been the hallmark of the English School. The inability of Con-

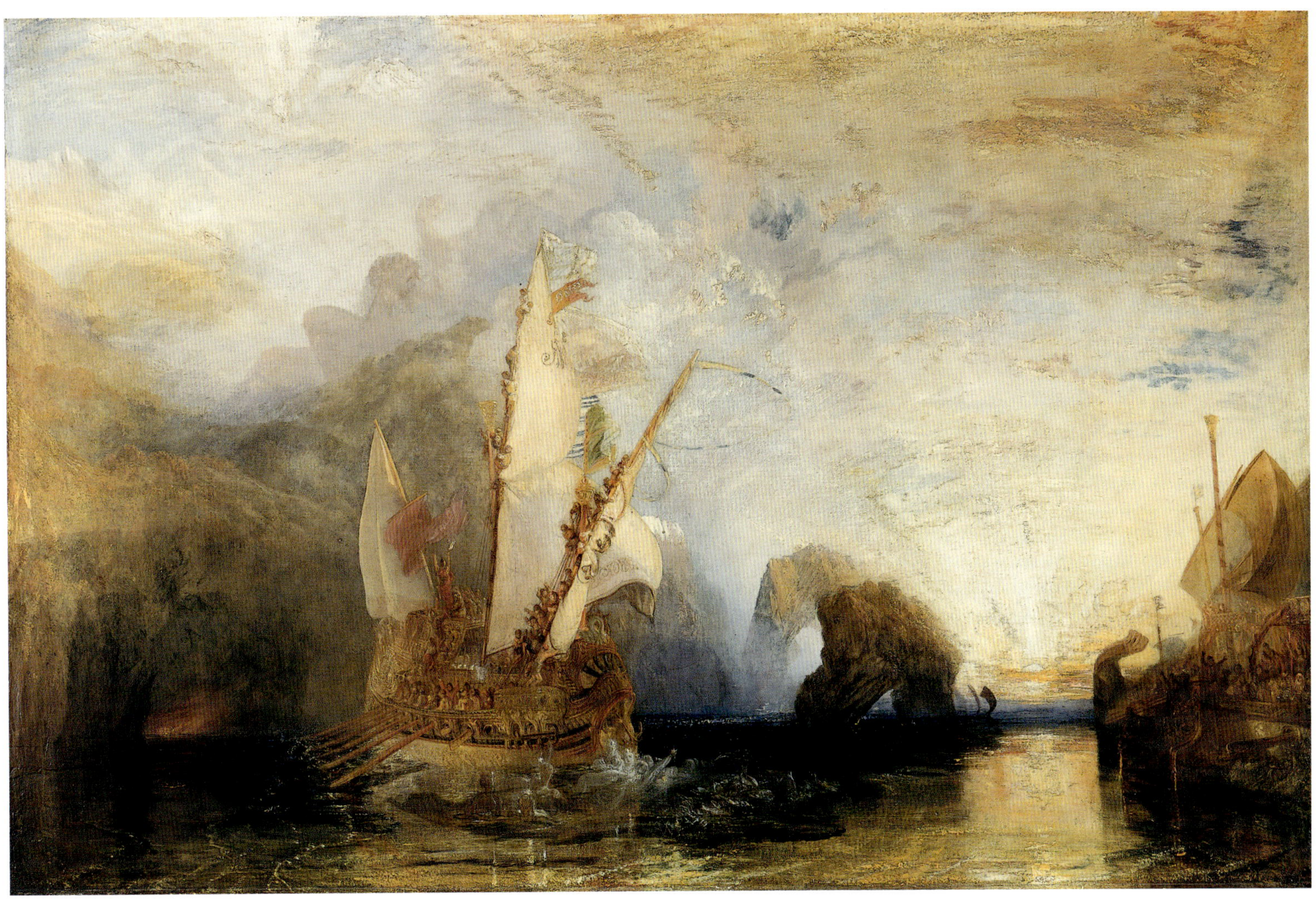

115 J. M. W. Turner, *Ulysses Deriding Polyphemus – Homer's Odyssey*, RA 1829. National Gallery, London.

stable to adjust his naturalistic style of the teens to the demands of the exhibition room of the twenties is only one example of the Great Room's casualties.

Yet as much as it hastened the death of naturalism, the Academy exhibition produced a new kind of landscape, one calculated to command the attention of the ever-growing crowds by satisfying their longing for escapism and transcendence. Like the panorama and diorama, or the *Eidophusikon* before them, the exhibition landscape of the early nineteenth century seduced its viewers by creating illusions in which they could lose themselves. For the length of the time it took to gaze at these spectacles, the social experience of viewing could be recast as a private, intense, individual one. In the presence of these awe-inspiring scenes of nature *in extremis*, the sensation of the crowd, the noise and the heat of the room could be temporarily forgotten and replaced by other more sublime sensations. This should not be seen as an unhappy privatization of the viewing experience, for it was an experience whose pleasure depended wholly upon the viewer knowing that it was only an illusion. Its very escapism acknowledged the presence of the urban crowd. Rather than a rejection of reality, the exhibition landscape must be seen as an acknowledgement of reality: not the reality of its subject – for indeed nature was hardly real at all for the born-and-bred Londoners who crowded into the Great Room – but the reality of its viewing situation. Borrowing its technologies of vision from the popular landscape entertainments of its day, the exhibition landscape transformed nature into urban theatre. It was this new, mass experience of landscape that the Great Room produced and that we find embodied in the exhibition landscapes of the 1820s and 1830s. Appropriately enough it was the cockney Turner, and not the countryman Constable, who remade landscape painting into a genre capable of speaking to the urban crowd. Turner did this by dramatizing the conditions of their spectatorship as a spectacle of nature. It was a transformation in tune with the popular landscape entertainments of the day and with their audiences' desire for visual experiences that produced sensations of domination and dislocation. At Somerset House visitors could enjoy an experience of landscape that no longer recalled rural nature but rather the nature of the new, urban metropolis.

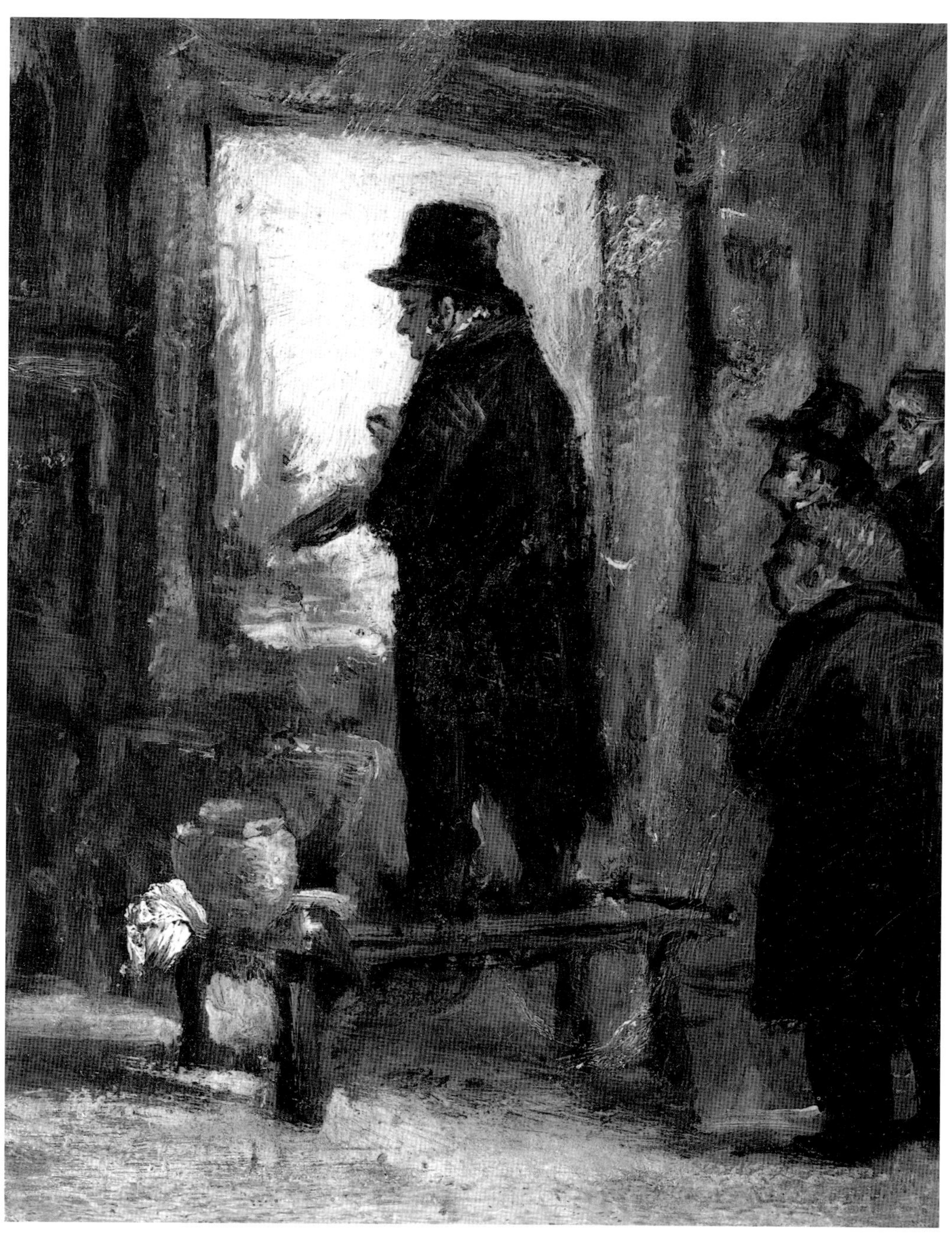

116 Charles West Cope, *J. M. W. Turner Painting in Somerset House*, oil on card, *c.*1828. This is the only known image of Turner painting in Somerset House, though apparently not on Varnishing Day. According to Cope's son, this little sketch shows Turner demonstrating his skills while acting as 'Visitor' in the Royal Academy Schools, 'with some of the porters or sweepers looking on'.

10

Turner Fires a Gun

MICHAEL ROSENTHAL

IN 1809 THE COUNCIL OF THE ROYAL ACADEMY resolved that

> Three days or more according to the convenience of the arrangement . . . shall be allowed to all Members of the Royal Academy for the purposes of varnishing or painting on their Pictures, in the places which have been allotted to them, previous to the day appointed for the annual dinner in the Exhibition Room.[1]

Consequently, prior to the opening of each annual exhibition, members could spend what frequently amounted to five days working on their entries *in situ*, mindful of the company their pictures were keeping on the crowded exhibition walls. George Dunlop Leslie wrote how these were 'nearly the only occasions on which the Academicians and Associates meet together in almost perfect freedom and equality', and fondly remembered the 'fun and friendly chaff'.[2] More than any of his colleagues, perhaps, J. M. W. Turner hugely enjoyed and exploited varnishing days, revelling in the sociability, and in the opportunity to paint in a public forum. In 1811, notes John Gage, 'he worked away on all four of these days', while four years later the *Sun* reported of *Dido Building Carthage, or the Rise of the Carthaginian Empire* (fig. 117) that, when 'we *first* saw this Picture, the yellow predominated to an excessive degree, and though the Artist has *since* glazed it down in the water, it still prevails far too much in the sky' (my emphases).[3] Evidently members of the press were privy to the final preparations, and were even prepared to go so far as to comment critically on progress made during the varnishing days.

By the 1830s Turner had developed his varnishing day ritual into an early form of performance art (cf. fig. 116). The painter Edward Villiers Rippingille recalled that

> He came, they said, with the carpenters at six in the morning, and worked standing all day. He always had an old, tall beaver hat, worn rather off his forehead. . . . His way of work was quite unlike that of the other artists. . . . His colours were mostly in powder, and he mixed them with turpentine, sometimes with size and water, and perhaps even with stale beer . . .[4]

The most spectacular instance of this practice occurred not at Somerset House but at the rival British Institution, where in 1835 Turner exhibited the *Burning of the Houses of Lords and Commons* (fig. 118); 'the picture when sent in', recounted Rippingille (again), 'was a mere dab of several colours and "without form and void" like chaos before the creation', before the master, as if he were 'a magician, performing his incantations in public', teased the subject into form.[5] Leslie later recalled how Turner had on occasion submitted to the Academy 'pictures . . . with only a delicate effect, almost in monochrome, laid on the canvas', which 'had probably been painted for some time, as they were quite dry and hard; all the bright colour was loaded on afterwards, the picture gradually growing stronger in colour and effect during the three varnishing days'.[6] On occasions such as these, the artist would have been sending in canvases that were essentially lay-ins, what we now refer to as his 'colour beginnings'. But given the fact that Turner had to submit titles and quotations (when appropriate) for the exhibition catalogue – though this went to press just prior to the opening of each show, after all the works had been given their final positions – from the outset he must have had some knowledge of the pictorial superstructures he would build on to these chromatic foundations. This ability to see into the future made him seem all the more like a magician, whose arcane skills and knowledge of mysteries underpinned the seemingly miraculous illusions that he achieved.

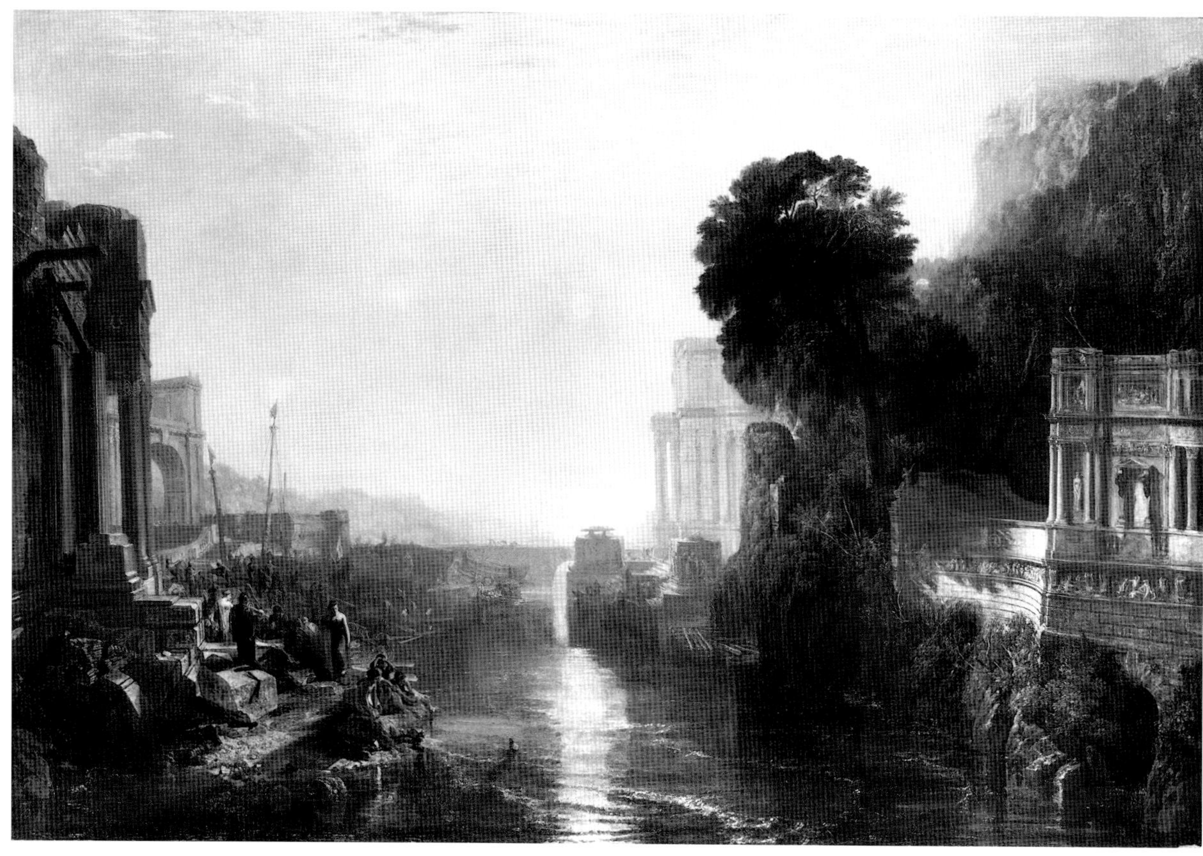

117 J. M. W. Turner, *Dido Building Carthage, or the Rise of the Carthaginian Empire*, RA 1815. National Gallery, London.

Beyond providing Turner with a public setting in which to display his mastery, varnishing days also gave him a chance to mingle with his fellow artists. Richard and Samuel Redgrave describe how, in these special circumstances,

> Much of precept, much of practice, and much of common experience were interchanged. The younger members gained much from the elder ones, and many useful hints and suggestions from one another. Who does not recollect the valuable remarks of David Wilkie, William Etty, C. R. Leslie, John Constable, and William Mulready, and, above all, Turner? Though from him . . . [advice] was conveyed in dark hints and ambiguous phrases.[7]

Edwin Landseer, for one, admired Turner's capacity 'to detect errors' and suggest improvements 'after the pictures [had been] placed', calling him, 'without exception . . . the best teacher I ever met with'.[8] It was the young Landseer who was said to have provided reciprocal assistance in 1827 by cutting out the shape of a dog from a piece of paper, colouring it black, and sticking it on to the parapet in *Mortlake Terrace, the Seat of William Moffat, Esq. Summer's Evening* (see fig. 110); Turner acknowledged that the addition enhanced the sense of depth which he had been trying to achieve, and proceeded to adjust 'the little dog perfectly', before varnishing 'the paper and . . . painting it'.[9]

But we should also bear in mind the Redgraves' acknowledgement that 'Turner . . . was quite aware of the greatness of his own powers, and jealous of their proper recognition', for at times a strong element of competitiveness could enter into the proceedings.[10] Speaking of the paintings that the artist had bequeathed to the nation, G. D. Leslie felt obliged to remind his readers that

> No idea can be formed from these pictures in the National Collection of the intensely brilliant effect that they possessed when first exhibited. Turner went about from one to another of them on the varnishing days, piling on, mostly with the knife, all the brightest pigments he could lay his hands on . . . until they literally blazed with light and colour. . . . Artists used to dread having their pictures hung next to him, saying that it was as bad as being hung beside an open window. They caught your eye the instant you entered the room.[11]

While there were many artists who tried to ensure that their works stood out from the hundreds of canvases which crammed the exhibition walls, Turner's purposes went beyond the simple goal of bringing his own landscapes into prominence: except at the very beginning of his career, his reputation would in itself have ensured that his paintings attracted plenty of attention. Often he aimed to distinguish himself from his fellow exhibitors

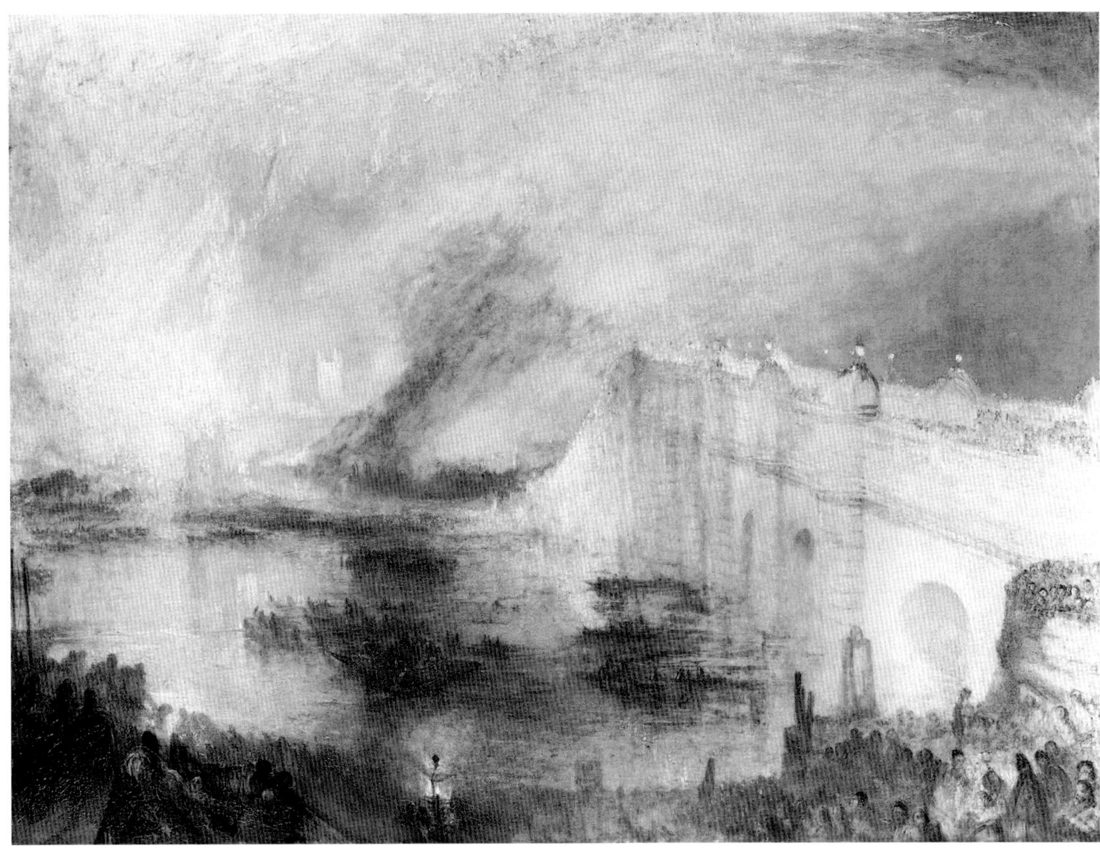

118 J. M. W. Turner, *The Burning of the Houses of Lords and Commons, 16 October 1834*, exhibited British Institution 1835. Philadelphia Museum of Art: The John Howard McFadden Collection.

in quite particular ways. Thus in 1833, when Clarkson Stanfield submitted a *Venice from the Dogana* (fig. 119) on a relatively large canvas (51 × 65½ in), Turner responded with his *Bridge of Sighs, Ducal Palace and Custom-House, Venice: Canaletti Painting* (fig. 120); not only was this far smaller (20 × 32½ in), but it first appeared at Somerset House as a 'colour beginning', for Turner reportedly painted the entire composition during the course of the varnishing days.[12] The *Morning Chronicle* of 6 June 1833 recorded that he had chosen his theme only after hearing that 'Mr. Stanfield was employed on a similar subject – not in the way of rivalry of course, for he is the last to admit to anything of the kind, but generously, we will suppose, to give him a lesson in atmosphere and poetry'.[13]

Exhibition reviewers understood this as a contest, one they judged Turner to have won. For the *Spectator*, the opportunity to play the two works off against each other revealed that Stanfield, in comparison to Turner, was 'what a mere talent is to genius'. *Arnold's Magazine* saw a larger triumph: 'viewed from whatever distance, Turner's work displayed a brilliancy, breadth, and power, killing every other work in the exhibition'. And as far as the critic for the *Athenaeum* was concerned, though Turner 'imagines he has painted in the Canaletti style: the style is his, and worth Canaletti's ten times over'[14] – so there was competition with an Italian old master, as well as with a contemporary Englishman. To complicate matters still further, Turner's old friend George Jones had a view of *Ghent* (untraced) hanging next to the *Bridge of Sighs*. This was highly coloured, so Turner upped the key of his sky to outdo it, but Jones had not spent all his ammunition. Later he recalled what had happened next: 'I introduced a great deal more white into my sky, which made his look much too blue. The ensuing day, he saw what I had done, laughed heartily, and said I might enjoy the victory'.[15] This rivalry seems to have been an entirely cordial affair, but not so that between Turner and Stanfield, who, as a younger follower, had to be put in his place.[16]

Where Stanfield's *Venice* lacked for nothing in the way of picturesque figures or topographical precision, Turner took certain obvious liberties with the cityscape, and introduced an anomalous historical element, in the person of the eighteenth-century artist, Canaletto, who appears at the lower left, painting on a canvas already enclosed within a bright gilt frame. Turner, whose hints to those he meant to help could be oblique, *may* have been making a point to Stanfield along the lines of Henry Fuseli's well-known censure of 'the last branch of uninteresting subjects, that kind of landscape which is entirely occupied with the tame delineation of a given spot'.[17] That is, he may have been implying that landscape art should aspire to something higher than mere topographical documentation. In this context

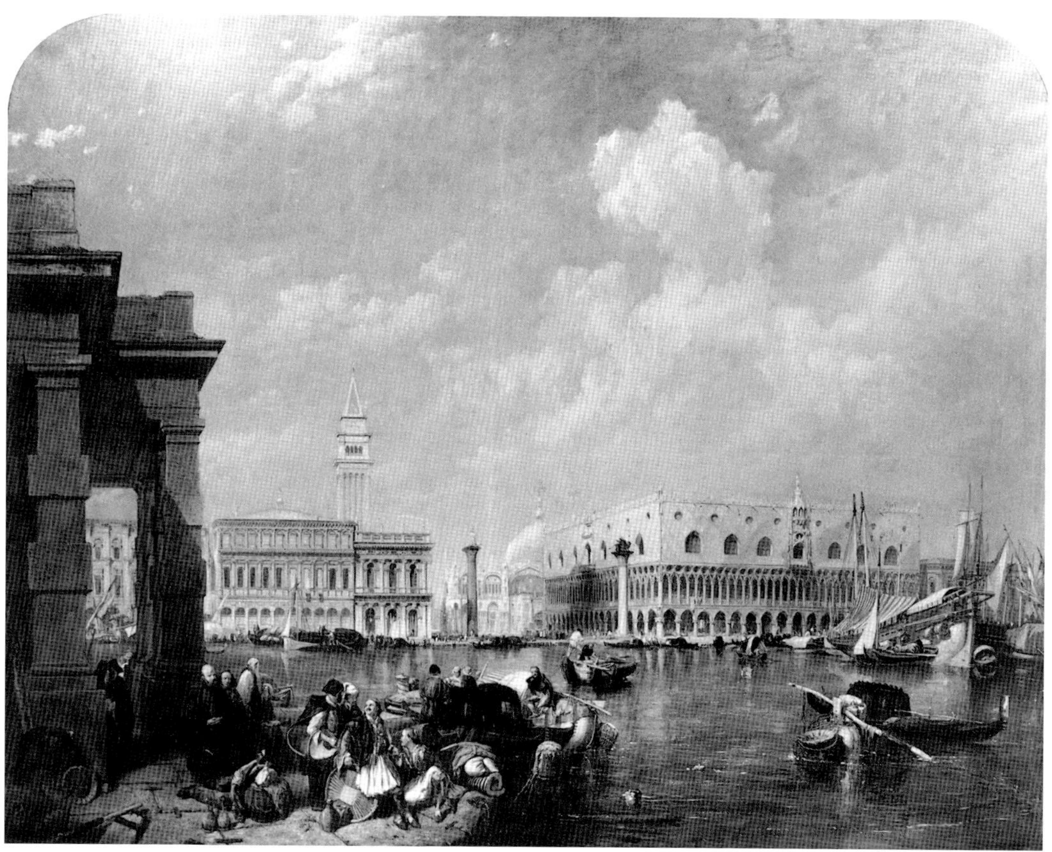

119 Clarkson Stanfield, *Venice from the Dogana*, RA 1833. Bowood House, The Trustees of the Bowood Collection.

we should note that Canaletto is shown working with his back to the scene, as if to demonstrate the need not simply to copy the visual, but to distil its features through intellectual reflection; precisely what Turner himself had done, in conjuring up his illusion. The curious portrayal of Canaletto painting his composition on a framed canvas, just as Turner himself had done with his own *Bridge of Sighs*, may have been meant as a further lesson to Stanfield, that performance – not size – is the be-all and end-all.

Turner did not discriminate when it came to rivals. The previous year had seen an incident involving his exact contemporary, John Constable, which is best recounted in the words of the latter's first biographer, the American painter Charles Robert Leslie:

> In 1832 when Constable exhibited his *Opening of Waterloo Bridge* it was placed in the school of painting – one of the small rooms at Somerset House. A sea-piece by Turner, was next to it – a grey picture, beautiful and true, but with no positive colour in any part of it. Constable's *Waterloo* seemed as if painted with liquid gold and silver, and Turner came several times into the room as he was heightening with vermilion and lake the decorations of the city barges. Turner stood behind him, looking from the *Waterloo* to his own picture, and at last brought his palette from the great room where he was touching another picture. And putting a round daub of red lead, somewhat bigger than a shilling on his grey sea, went away without saying a word. The intensity of the red lead, made more vivid by the coolness of his picture, caused even the vermilion and lake of Constable to look weak. 'He has been here', said Constable, 'and fired a gun'. . . . The great man did not come into the room for a day and a half; and then, in the last moments that were allowed for varnishing, he glazed the scarlet seal he had put on his picture, and shaped it into a buoy.[18]

To add insult to injury, the sea-piece in question, *Helvoetsluys* (fig. 121) was far smaller than *The Opening of Waterloo Bridge* (which measured well over three by six feet) (fig. 122), as if to show that largeness of scale was not the only means of attracting attention on the walls of Somerset House.

Turner shrewdly calculated his move. In a gesture addressed to his fellow artists – and to Constable in particular – he first threw down the red blob as a gauntlet of his competitive (and critical) intentions – and then returned to his canvas at the last possible minute, to transform a marker of painterly aggression into something as simple as a mere buoy, an indicator of the right path to follow. For the exhibition audience, the buoy would have been just that, a natural component of the scene; but to those who had enjoyed the privilege of witnessing the final

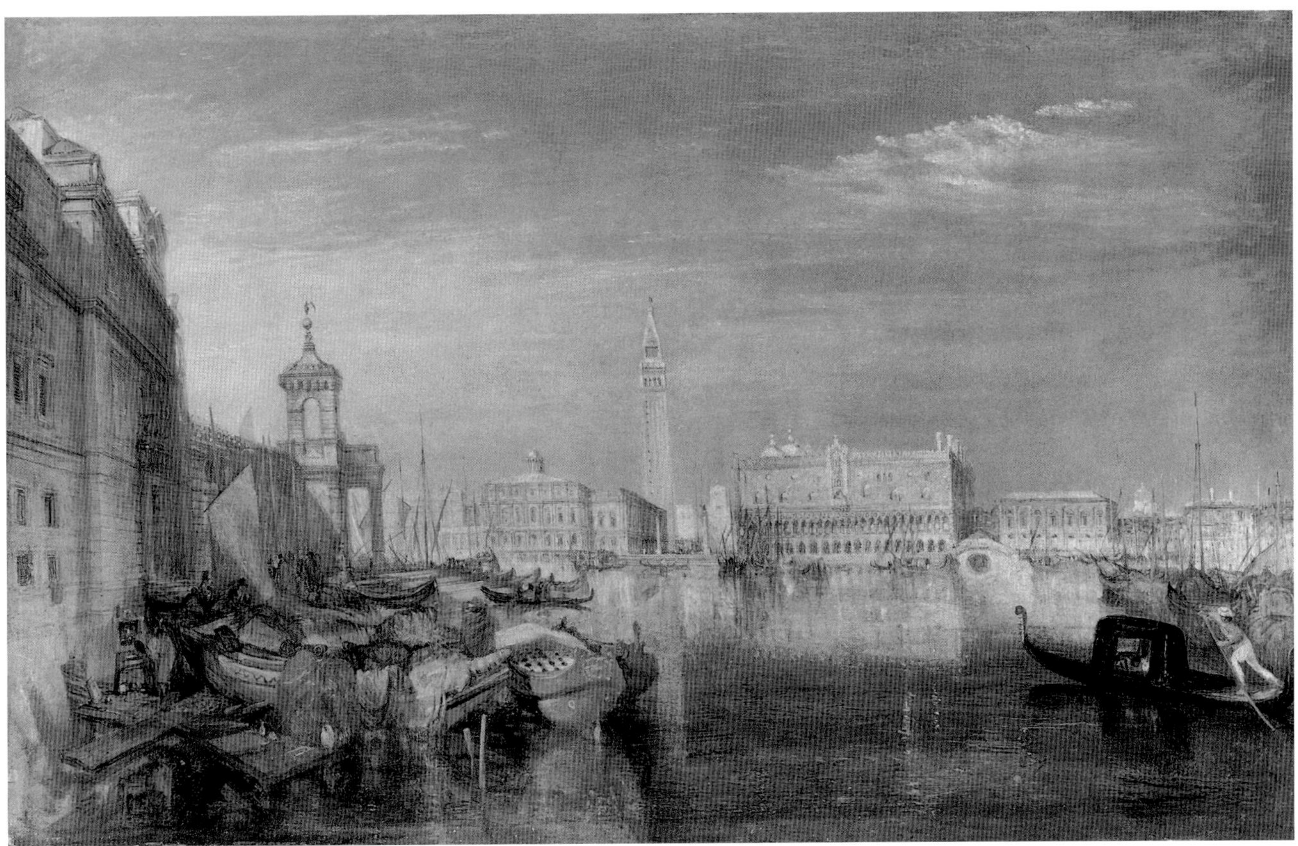

120 J. M. W. Turner, *Bridge of Sighs, Ducal Palace and Custom-House, Venice: Canaletti Painting*, RA 1833. Tate, London.

phase of the picture's genesis, Turner had supplied much richer food for thought. Constable's 'fired a gun' phrase points up the combative nature of the encounter, acknowledging the impact of the red against the greys and greens as akin to a visual explosion, so startling as to make his own ambitious composition fade into insignificance. Perhaps he felt that his painting had been terminally wounded – that he had met his own 'Waterloo'. For Turner, this may have been sweet revenge. In 1831, Constable, then a member of the Hanging Committee, had replaced a Turner with his own *Salisbury Cathedral from the Meadows* (fig. 123), apparently after the arrangement of the exhibition had been virtually fixed.[19] That the victim of this sleight-of-hand was more than a little displeased is made clear from David Roberts's account of a soirée given soon afterwards by General Phipps, a prominent amateur of the arts (the account has been transcribed, with its often idiosyncratic spellings, from Roberts's manuscript):

> It was at one of these partys that an extraordinary scene took place, at least it was to me. Constable, Turner & Munro of Novar were of the party, Constable a conceated egotistic person, whatever Leslie may have written to the contrary, was loud in describing to all the severe duties he had undergone in the hanging the Exhibition [*sic*]. According to his own acount nothing could exceed his disinterestedness or his anxiety to discharge that Sacred Duty. Most unfortunately for him a Picture of Turners had been displaced after the arraingment of the room in which it was placed. (I am writing now of Somerset House). Turner opened upon him like a ferret; it was evident to all present Turner detested him; all present were puzzled what to do or say to stop this. Constable wriggled, twisted & made it appear or wished to make it appear that in his removal of the Picture he was only studying the best light or the best arraingment for Turner. The latter coming back invariably to the charge, yess, but why put your own there? – I must say Constable looked to me and I believe to every one else, like a detected criminal, and I must add Turner slew him without remorse.[20]

Exhibiting was extremely competitive, and members of the Committee of Arrangement had to be seen to be scrupulously impartial. It is debatable, though, whether Turner went so far as to 'detest' Constable, for, though never close, the two appear to have enjoyed cordial relations, as well as some mutual understanding. And their jousting at the Academy in 1832 fell entirely within the norms of conventional exhibition behaviour, even if Constable felt hard done by as a result.

Other problems with *The Opening of Waterloo Bridge ('Whitehall Stairs, June 18th 1817')* were of the artist's own making. To start with he had taken a risk by straying out of his usual thematic arena, and into one dominated by other

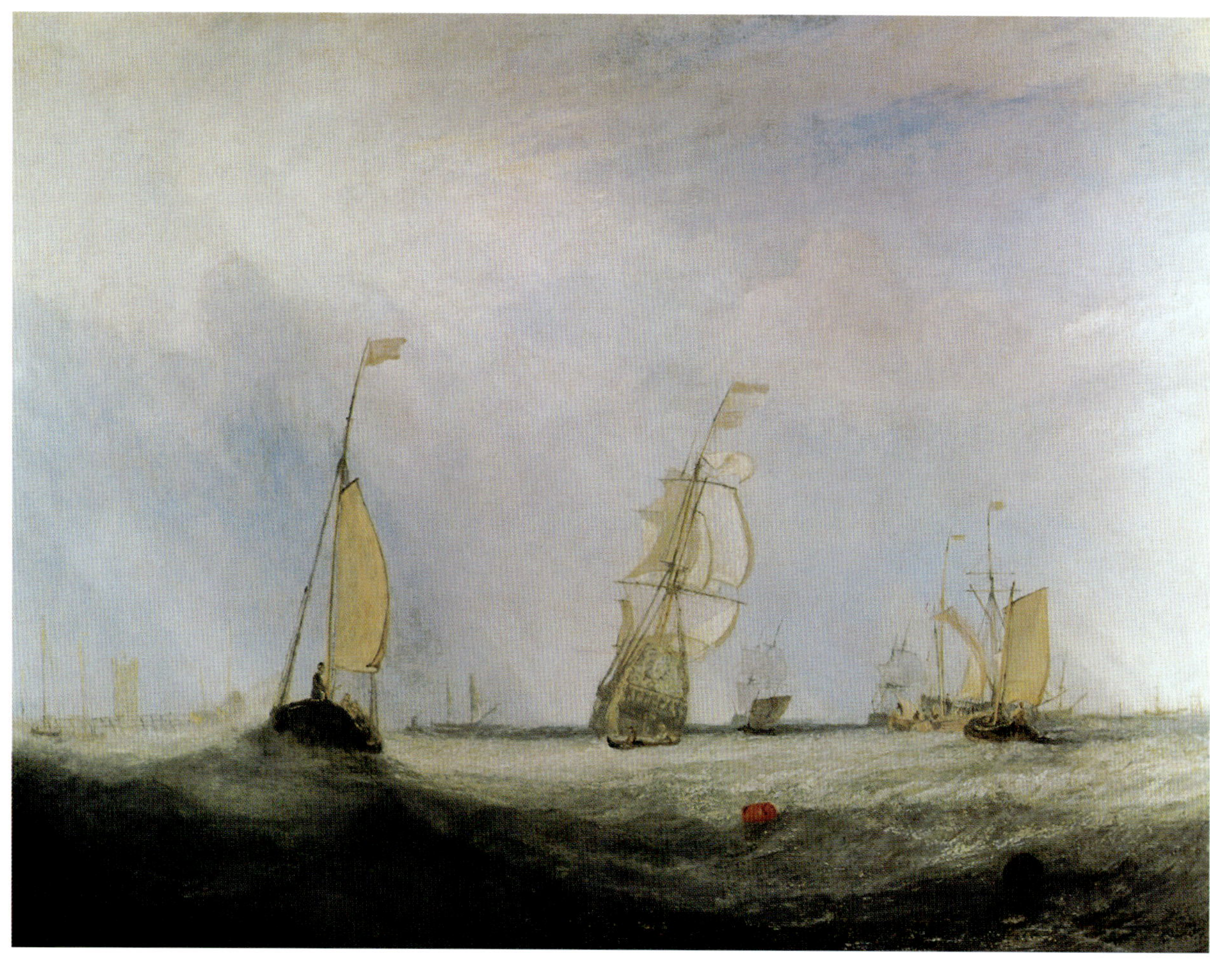

121 J. M. W. Turner, *Helvoetsluys*, RA 1832. Private collection.

well-established specialists; Constable had not previously exhibited a major metropolitan subject, nor would he ever do so again. After many years of trying, by around 1820 he had painstakingly built up a reputation as a painter of rustic landscapes, and once having established this identity in the public eye, he seems to have been of two minds as to the best career strategy to pursue. There were obvious advantages in continuing to plough the same furrow, thus meeting the expectations of the exhibition audience and confirming a name for excellence in a particular line; but there was also the temptation of trying to create a larger patronage base by branching out into something new. Constable's inability to decide between these two options probably goes a long way towards explaining why he worked on his *Waterloo Bridge* for well over a decade, signalling his intentions on several occasions to show it at Somerset House, only to change his mind at the last moment. Indeed delay was a factor right from the outset, since after witnessing the opening of the bridge Constable waited three years before deciding to record the event in paint. He then came close to completing the composition at several points during the first half of the 1820s, only to lapse into dissatisfaction and discouragement. Twice – in 1826 and then again in 1829 – he temporarily abandoned the project, before gathering his energies for a final push in the winter of 1832 – though by now with few hopes that his picture would be a success.

In late February Constable told his engraver David Lucas that he was 'dashing away at the great London – and why not? I may as well produce this abortion as another – for who cares about landscape?'[21] Eleven years previously, in a more sanguine state of mind, he had referred to his paintings as his beloved 'children', whom he felt reluctant 'to expose . . . to the taunts of the Ignorant'[22] at the annual exhibitions. His much more brutal description of *Waterloo Bridge* is entirely typical. Such remarks are part and parcel of the profound anxiety and alienation that persistently characterize Constable's correspondence of the 1830s, in the wake of his wife's death and a succession of professional and private disappointments. But his moods could swing from depression to optimism, even when referring to a painting that had proven such a source of frustration for so many years. Affectionately referring to his *Waterloo Bridge* as 'The Lord Mayor's Show', Constable told Lucas how he believed it

> rather too good a 'joke' to be received into *our* Church. Nothing can I fear make him either 'apostolic', or 'canonical',

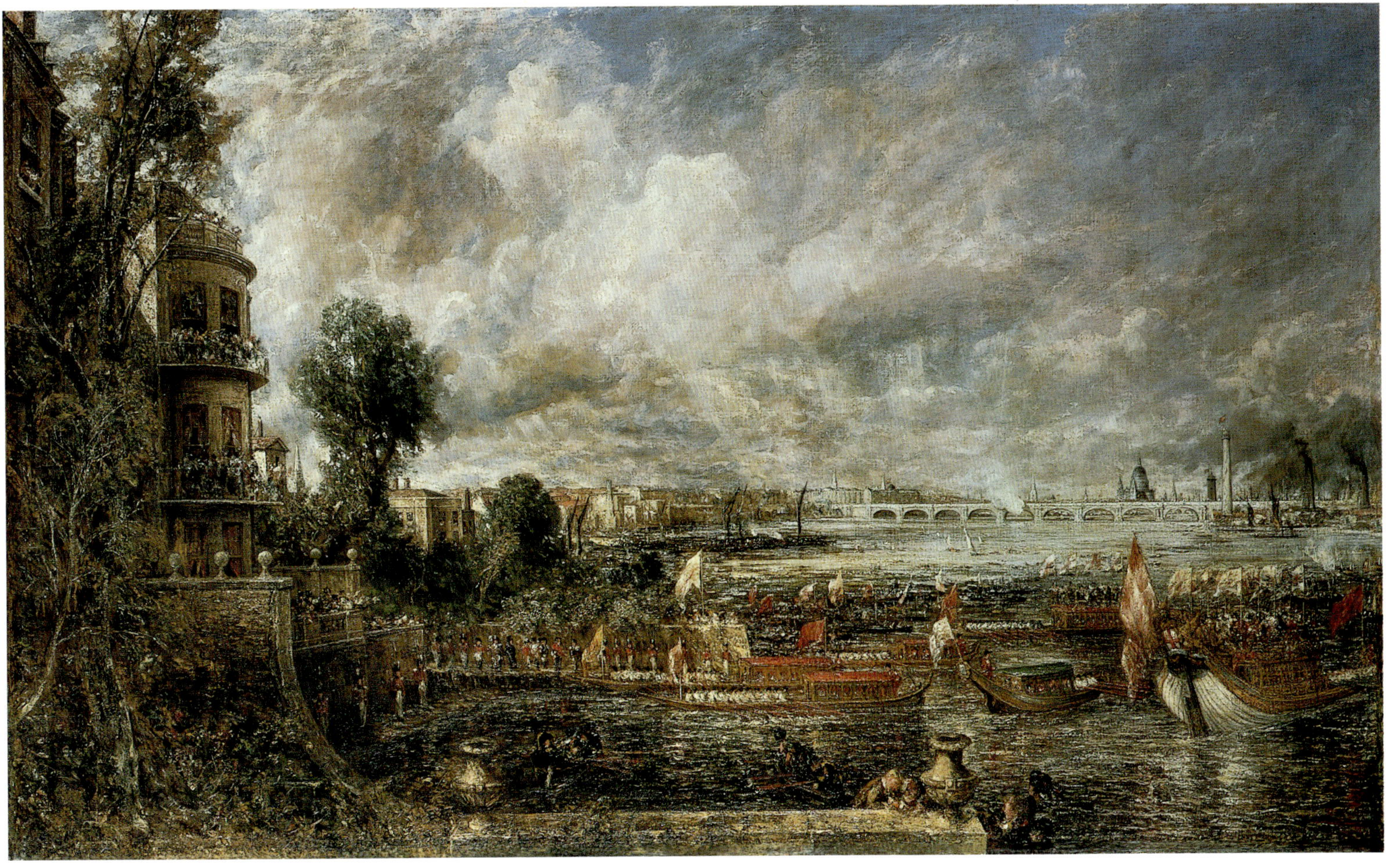

122 John Constable, *The Opening of Waterloo Bridge ('Whitehall Stairs, June 18th 1817')*, RA 1832. Tate, London.

> so uncongenial is any part of this hideous 'Gomorah'.
> J.C.
> And yet, after all the Waterloo is a famous composition, and ought to give much pleasure to all. But it is the devil – and I am 'sore perplexed'.[23]

Although cryptic to the point of obscurity, what the painter seems to be saying here is that his picture may be too good for Somerset House (which is at the same time the Royal Academy: '*our* Church' and a site of fashionable excess: a 'hideous "Gomorah"'), but that he still harbours hopes for the work's success. The 'Lord Mayor's Show' nickname (which R. B. Beckett thought referred to 'the decorated barges on the river')[24] suggests that the composition, rather than commemorating an event of almost fifteen years before, was now serving itself as a vehicle for display, communicating shifting colours and succeeding illusions in a way analogous to the appearance of the civic ritual itself. This factor will need to be borne in mind when we come to inspect the paint surface.

His picture's state of finish was giving Constable considerable anxiety in the days just prior to the opening of the show. On 24 April, in a letter to C. R. Leslie, he reported on an encounter in the Academy with the artist Thomas Stothard, who had first given him his opinion of David Wilkie's much-heralded large history painting, *John Knox Preaching before the Lords of the Congregation* (London, Tate Britain):

> As a set off, he says 'Wilkie's picture is not agreeable Sir – brown and heavy' – and of myself he gives a rather worse account, 'Very unfinished Sir – much to do – figures not made out Sir' – and this being I fear the general opinion they have put it where it can only be seen to the greatest disadvantage, in the traffic between the doors and the doors in the new room – the light of the worst kind for my unfortunate 'manner' & also coming across mine, had you seen it, I am sure you would not have let me send it out of my house in so sad a condition – there I deserve my punishment. Besides that, to add to all the horrors of our annual show, it is also retributive, & I have my deserts for I played the devil with others.[25]

Constable had, of course, 'played the devil with others' by switching his and Turner's landscapes the previous year, and now had little choice but to accept the 'punishment' he 'deserved'. Yet even with the episode of the 'gun' still to follow, things may not have been as bad as he imagined. Certainly Leslie

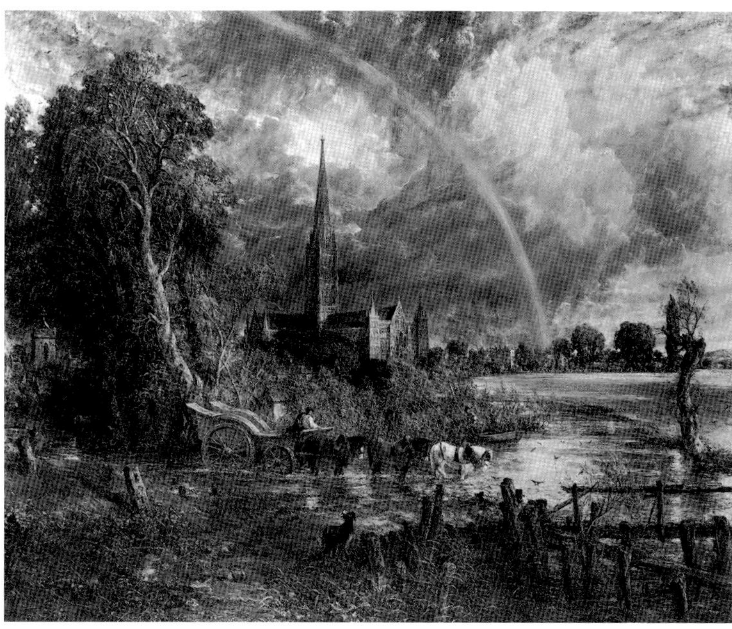

123 John Constable, *Salisbury Cathedral from the Meadows*, RA 1831. National Gallery, London.

– who along with Turner watched Constable at work during varnishing days – failed to mention the bad hanging of *Waterloo Bridge*, and no one in the press thought it worthy of comment either.[26]

Nor, as we shall see, did reviewers take much notice of the subject matter of Constable's large exhibition-piece, which features the Prince Regent setting out from Whitehall Stairs *en route* to the ceremonial opening of the newly built bridge, seen in the distance. If the specifics of this narrative seem rather marginal to the effect of the canvas as a whole, this is in part because its dynamic surface textures draw so much attention to themselves. The paint has been heavily worked with the palette knife to obtain pictorial cohesion through colour and texture, as rich scumbles of white create their own harmonies, while the reds of the barges find a muted response in the roof-tops to the left: this chromatic balance is of a comparable order to that which Sir Joshua Reynolds had commended in Titian's *Bacchus and Ariadne* (London, National Gallery).[27] In more obvious terms the composition reprised another Venetian tradition of more recent origin: while nodding generically to earlier Thames paintings by such British artists as Samuel Scott, the principal reference is to Antonio Canaletto's *The Thames from the Terrace of Somerset House, Westminster Bridge in the Distance* (*c.*1746–50, Royal Collection), the design of which Constable has effectively reversed, now with Somerset House in the background. Evidently Turner was not the only landscape artist of the 1830s who wished his achievements to be measured against Canaletto's. Hence a mid-eighteenth-century painting that had celebrated the contentious modernity of the newly built Westminster Bridge came to serve as the model for a cityscape where the traditional interests of the establishment, as personified by the Prince Regent, seem to cohere harmoniously with those of the City of London.[28] Although ostensibly picturing an event of 1817, the scene includes, on the right-hand side, the shot tower built in 1826, as if to hint at British martial qualities. This cavalier attitude towards chronology, together with the impressive painterly sweep of the impressive canvas as a whole, speaks of ambitions beyond the merely documentary or topographical. It is fitting, then, that Constable referred to the painting as his 'Thames', or, simply, as 'London'.

He also called it 'my Harlequin jacket' in recognition of its exceptionally (for him) showy colouring of silvers, blues and reds.[29] The shot that Turner fired was expressly designed to counteract this: not just by stealing some of Constable's pictorial thunder, but also by making his *Waterloo Bridge* look vulgar in its gaudiness, and undermining its moral probity by tarring his rival's overloaded palette with the brush of continental decadence.[30] No nineteenth-century artist was more aware of colour and its potential significance than J. M. W. Turner; no one knew better than he how the deployment of colour could elevate landscape art to the level of a universal poetry, or debase painting to a mere servant of the senses. He may have spotted *Waterloo Bridge* as an exercise in colourism that had originated in sixteenth-century Venice, and his gunshot intentionally blew away these aspirations.

In an important sense, then, what Turner did to Constable in 1832 was fundamentally analogous to the lesson he taught Clarkson Stanfield a year later. On both occasions, he offered his rivals a pointed reminder of the civic function of the fine arts, of the modern painter's responsibility to promote a cause higher than the merely factual or the gratuitously ornate; suggesting, too, that the walls of the Royal Academy exhibition, as befits the ethos of the institution, constituted by far the best arena for such arguments to be made. As the *Monthly British Magazine* reminded its readers in 1830, the 'object an artist or painter should always have in view, is to interest and excite the imagination, instruct the understanding, and delight the heart of the spectator'.[31] This ambition was something that Turner wished to communicate to his fellow artists, and to the Academy public at large.

He also did this by exhibiting works dealing with the history of art. Thus besides representing Canaletto at work in the *Bridge of Sighs*, in 1833 he also showed *Van Goyen Looking Out for a Subject* (fig. 124), a sea-piece in the Dutch manner that features the famous seventeenth-century master standing in his own vessel (the inscription on the stern reads VAN G), as he searches nature for new sources of inspiration. This portrayal, which conforms to what was believed to have been Van Goyen's actual practice, reminds us of Turner's own well-known determination to experience rather than simply observe his landscape subjects, as he had done for *Staffa, Fingal's Cave* in 1832 (New Haven, Yale Center for British Art).[32] But aside from situating his work within an old and illustrious tradition of naturalistic landscape art, with the *Van Goyen* he also put forward a case for going

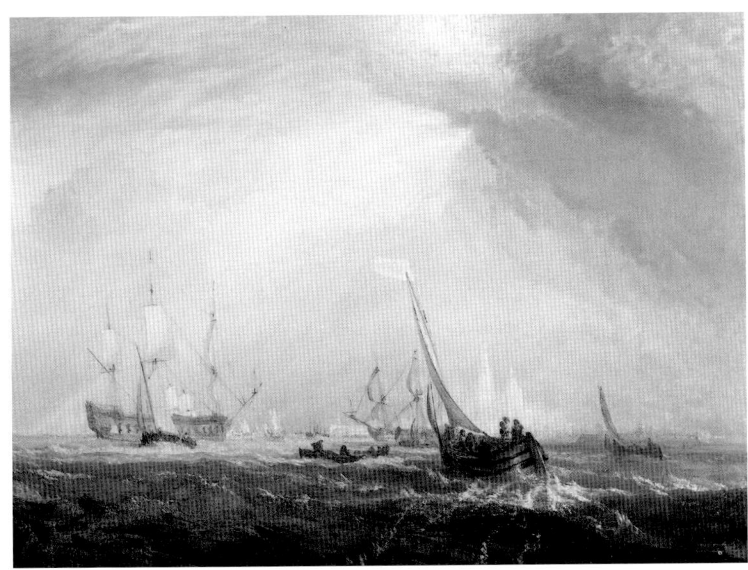

124 J. M. W. Turner, *Van Goyen Looking Out for a Subject*, RA 1833. The Frick Collection, New York.

beyond the merely observable, and into the realm of the historical imagination. This elevating approach was entirely consistent with academic theories of art, and with the procedures that Turner had followed ever since his student days, when Reynolds's *Discourses* had taught him to assimilate the art of the past before refining and improving it through direct observation of nature. While it was right for a modern artist to try and emulate the old masters, he could also show how they might be surpassed.

Thus by the early 1830s, Turner had begun to use the exhibitions as a pedagogic platform, a place for the display of images increasingly preoccupied with the theme of art itself. Perhaps the most overtly didactic of his pictures from this period is the small *Watteau Study by Fresnoy's Rules* (fig. 125), which went on show in the School of Painting at the Academy in 1831. Its catalogue entry included the following couplet from William Mason's translation of Charles du Fresnoy's *De arte graphica*:

> White, when it shines with unstained lustre *clear*,
> May bear an object back, or bring it near[33]

As these lines suggest, Turner's canvas offered a demonstration of the pictorial effects achievable through the use of white, while also suggesting that past theory and practice sanctioned the bright tonalities of his own work. A few contemporary commentators picked up the point: a review in the *Library of the Fine Arts*, for instance, admired 'his lights merging in depths, his depths thrown deeper by his lights'.[34] But one reason why Turner had felt it necessary to become so didactic must stem from the critical incomprehension that had begun to greet his work during the later 1820s, and had peaked in 1830 with the vitriolic reception of the Rembrandtesque *Jessica* (fig. 126) and *Pilate washing his Hands* (London, Tate Britain).[35] The *Morning Chronicle* (3 May) wrote of *Jessica* that it looked 'like a lady getting out of a large mustard-pot', which insult so

125 J. M. W. Turner, *Watteau Study by Fresnoy's Rules*, RA 1831. Tate, London.

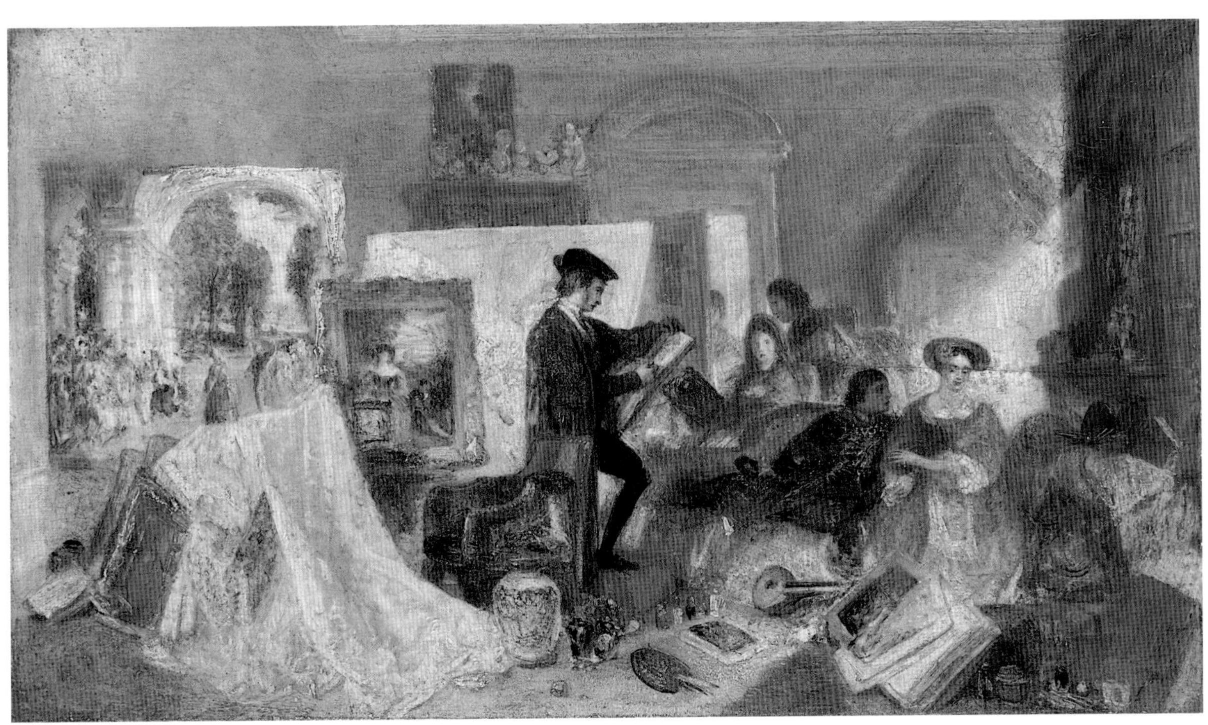

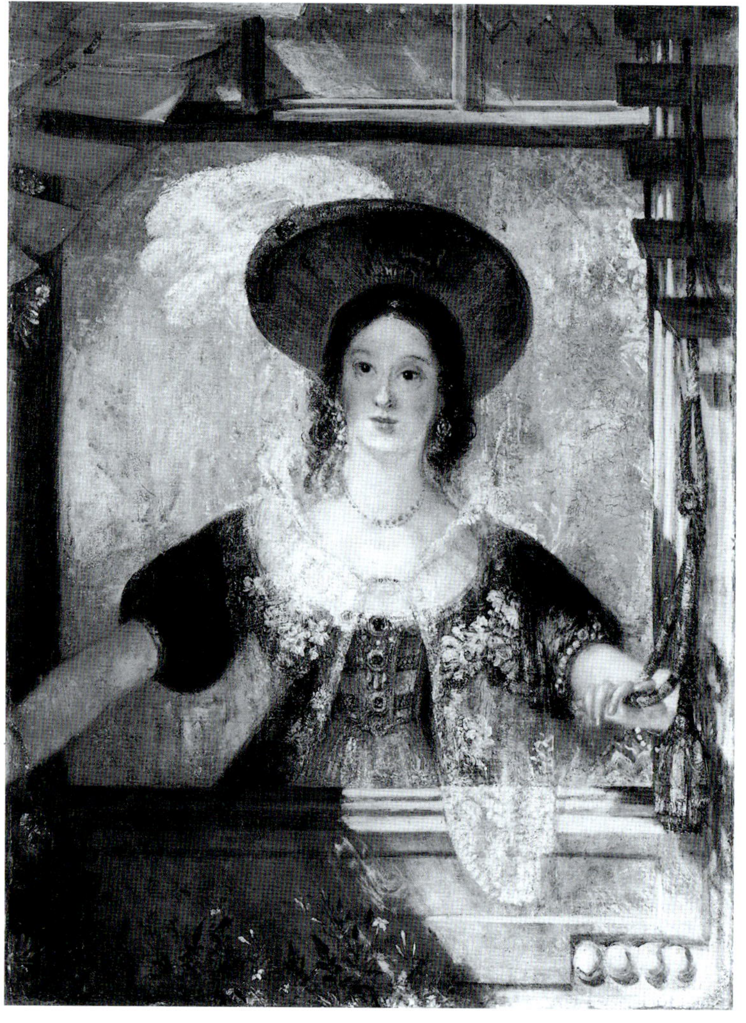

126 J. M. W. Turner, *Jessica*, RA 1830. Tate, London.

delighted the *Literary Gazette* (29 May) that it found 'the temptation to piracy to be irresistible'.

During the same years Constable's critical fortunes underwent a similarly precipitous decline. At the Royal Academy in 1827 he had prompted some uneasiness with the *Beach at Brighton, the Chain Pier in the Distance* (see fig. 103), and by 1829 the attacks on what was perceived to be his mannered way of painting had grown in both volume and ferocity.[36] *The Times*'s review of *Salisbury Cathedral from the Meadows* was characteristically scornful:

> A very vigorous and masterly landscape, which someone has spoiled since it was painted, by putting in such clouds as no human being ever saw, and by spotting the foreground all over with whitewash. It is quite impossible that this offence can have been committed with the consent of the artist. (6 May 1831)

Another critic wrote of 'a confusion of colours, a smudginess of effect . . . that is painful to look upon' – and, of Turner's exhibits, could only sigh, 'What is to be said of this artist?'[37]

The following year, when *Waterloo Bridge* and *Helvoetsluys*, important works by two of England's senior landscape specialists, hung adjacent to one another, no contemporary commentary even came close to recognizing Turner's silent act of pictorial subversion (an act which was, arguably, also an indication of respect). *The Opening of Waterloo Bridge* was a serious and complex landscape, an ambitious exercise in colouring set within a highly regarded artistic tradition. This Turner recognized when he put down his red marker, out-colouring Constable with the force of his chromatic contrast; in part to revenge an injustice committed at the exhibition of 1831, but also to acknowledge what his rival's picture was about. Yet if the critical response is anything to go by, nothing whatsoever of this was noticed at the time. Only the *Athenaeum* reviewed *Waterloo Bridge* and *Helvoetsluys* together. It disliked Constable's colour but made no mention of Turner's.[38] Elsewhere other connections were made, based not on physical proximity but on theme. Thus the *New Monthly Magazine and Literary Journal* mentioned landscapes 'by Callcott, Stanfield, Constable, and Jones', wrongly claiming that, 'The three last-named exhibit pictures of the opening of London Bridge'.[39] This was an understandable mistake, perhaps, given that the inauguration of the span at Waterloo had long

127 George Jones, *The Opening of London Bridge*, RA 1832. The Trustees of Sir John Soane's Museum.

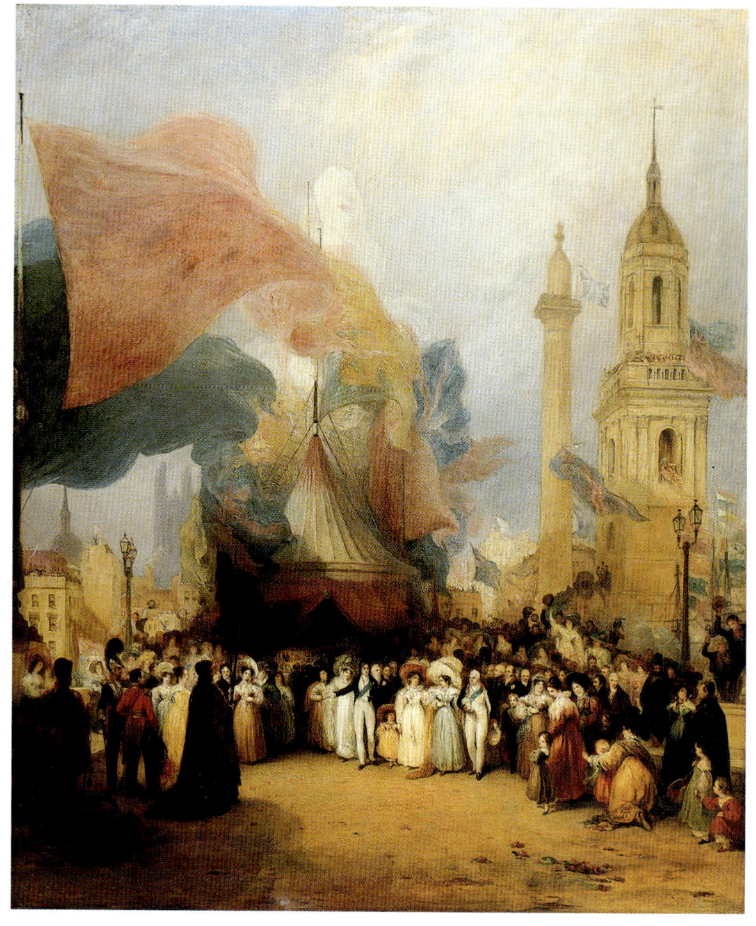

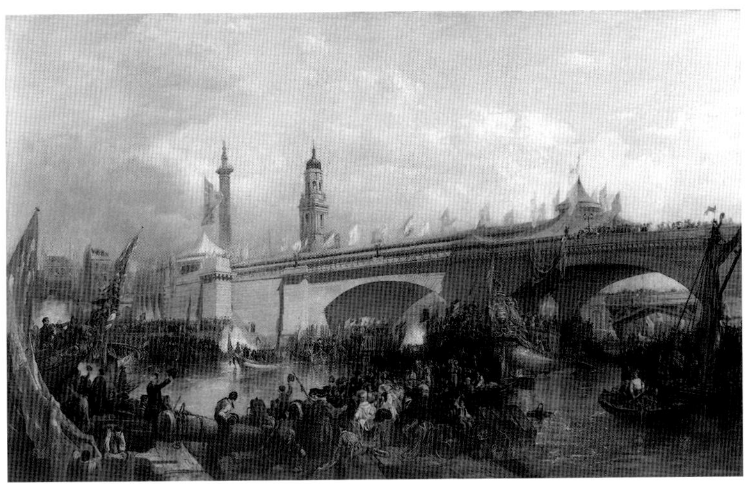

128 Clarkson Stanfield, *The Opening of London Bridge*, RA 1832. The Royal Collection © 2001 Her Majesty Queen Elizabeth II.

since been eclipsed by other events much fresher in the public memory – including the construction of London Bridge further east along the Thames, the opening of which, on 1 August 1831, Jones and Stanfield had portrayed.

If the *New Monthly*'s critic failed to consult his catalogue, other commentators seem to have paid no attention to the pictures. *The Times* thought *Waterloo Bridge* 'so similar in its general design to the other two, that, but for the assurance of the catalogue (which cannot be wrong), we should have thought it belonged to the same subject'.[40] In fact there were vast differences between the three compositions. Jones (fig. 127) pictured the throng on the new London Bridge. Stanfield (fig. 128) took his view through the crowds on the river bank and picked out the ceremonial barges, the banners, and other events of the opening (in a rare moment of critical insight, the *London Literary Gazette* noticed 'also that which might "point a moral" in the dilapidated remains of the old bridge, seen through the arches of its proud successor'.)[41] Elsewhere, the *Spectator* alluded to a general displeasure amongst the Academicians that Stanfield, who was not one of their number, had been commissioned to produce his view by William IV.[42] But of any more analytical or profound critical writing there is virtually none. It is certainly possible that the odd individual viewer may have been more perceptive, although given the sheer numbers of paintings and people to be found within Somerset House, even this likelihood seems fairly remote. An exhibition critique of 1820 had put the problem in a nutshell:

> Many, very many fine pictures there are on these walls: pictures which, in their several ways, have never been surpassed, and but seldom equalled, in any place or at any time. But to examine them critically is impossible; for what with the glare above, and the crowd below; and the heat, both above and below; one cannot be sure of a single idea in such a place, and little or nothing can be carried away from it but dust and the head-ache.[43]

This may be an exaggeration, but given the fact that professional art critics found it almost impossible to say anything worthwhile – 'Painting is a Mystery' confessed 'Ignoramus' in *Blackwood's Edinburgh Magazine* in 1831 – it is hard to imagine most if any lay viewers gaining anything but the most superficial impression from the bewildering multitude of works on show.[44] Varnishing days were an entirely different matter, however. It was then, and perhaps only then, that the exhibiting artists could establish a mutually enriching relationship with their 'public' – a 'public' limited, of course, to their colleagues and a small number of *cognoscenti*. Under these intimate circumstances, before the anonymous throngs of paying customers took over Somerset House, painters could indulge in a meaningful give-and-take with one another, in the illusion that their achievements mattered, that their ambitions were understood. One imagines that the sense of community on varnishing days must have been particularly palpable for two veteran landscape artists, both now in their late fifties, who for different reasons were beginning to feel that the world had passed them by. Faced with incomprehension on the part of most critics, and with indifference from the great majority of viewers (most now a good deal younger than themselves), Constable and Turner could at least take pleasure from their mutual understanding, from playing games that made sense at least to one another, though perhaps to them alone. In the seclusion of the Academy, Turner fired his gun, and Constable heard it loud and clear. But did anybody else? In the spring and summer of 1832, with the highly divisive campaign for parliamentary reform about to reach its peak, English society at large had more important things on its mind – issues of greater urgency than a couple of ageing painters trying to teach each other a lesson or two on the walls of Somerset House.

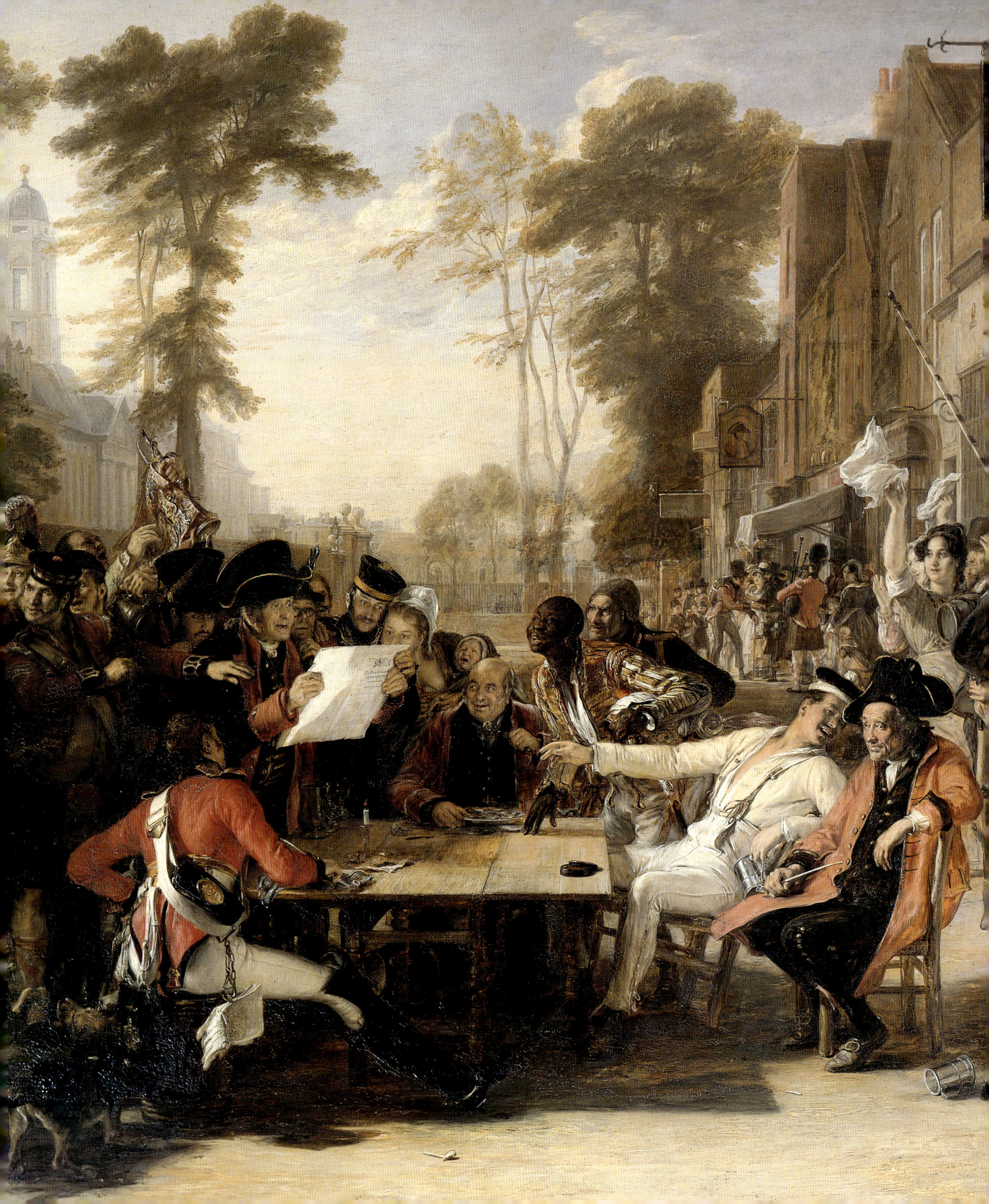

II

Crowds and Connoisseurs: Looking at Genre Painting at Somerset House

David H. Solkin

> The Crowd was so great on Tuesday, by People pressing into the Exhibition-Room in the Strand, that a deal of Mischief was done; one of the Porters, who was empowered by the Society to see Decorum observed, was knocked down, and otherwise greatly abused.
>
> *St James's Chronicle*, 14–16 May 1761

The history of regular public art exhibitions in London began in the early 1760s with scenes of turbulent confusion. Not only were there too many people, but there were too many viewers of the wrong sort; writing on behalf of the artistic community, Samuel Johnson complained to the Society of Arts, which had hosted the initial display (in 1760), that the event had been 'incommoded by the intrusion of great Numbers whose stations and education made them no proper judges of Statuary and Painting, and who were made idle and tumultuous by the opportunity of a shew'.[1] Though the speedy imposition of a shilling admission charge soon succeeded in keeping the poor out, overcrowding remained a perennial problem, even after the annual exhibitions, now under the aegis of the Royal Academy, moved further east along the Strand to Somerset House. Newspapers periodically aired complaints about the oppressive heat, the foul odours and the unwelcome jostling that greeted visitors to the Great Room; and while public decorum may have only rarely been disturbed, the spectre of disorder was never far away.[2]

As far as the exhibiting artists were concerned, the near-constant crush of potential patrons may have been excellent in principle, but its benefits in practice were extremely mixed. The painters who stood to gain the most and lose the least from this situation were presumably those whose canvases hung above 'the line', where they were guaranteed more or less unimpeded visibility. No matter how many people were standing on the floor, there was nothing to stop them from gazing at the full-length portraits, large history paintings and panoramic landscapes which dominated the upper levels of the Great Room, leaning out on the armature that bridged the space between the line and the coving. But often the smaller pictures hanging closer to the floor must have been virtually invisible to the vast majority of spectators, simply because there were so many other bodies standing in the way. These works could be seen, though only from quite close up, and by very small numbers of people at once. Thus the line, positioned eight feet above the floor, roughly demarcated a boundary between two regimes of spectatorship: a public form of viewing directed at the paintings above, and a private, occluded gaze at those underneath.

Above the line, the most effective exhibition pieces tended to be those which represented dramatic actions or famous personages, and which did so in broad visual terms designed to create a clear impression from a considerable distance; not surprisingly the biggest canvases and the grandest manners often fared the

Wilkie, *Chelsea Pensioners* . . . . Detail of fig. 142.

best, and took up most of the space in contemporary press reviews. But if the smaller works underneath garnered far less critical attention, they were much better equipped to stimulate the acquisitive desires of those ordinary exhibition-goers – doubtless the vast majority – who were prepared to contemplate spending limited sums on modest examples of modern art. The goods on show below the line principally consisted of bust- or half-length portraits, miniatures, picturesque views, seascapes and humble narratives of everyday life, together with the occasional still life or sporting scene; and because most of these pictures were designed to appeal to 'middling' buyers of relatively unadventurous tastes, the artists in question had little reason to try and create strikingly singular exhibition-pieces, capable of challenging the visual and discursive supremacy of the larger paintings higher up.

This commercial logic dovetailed neatly with the Academy's own practical and ideological needs. For if far more aesthetic excitement was generated above the line than below, one important consequence was that the pictures commanding the greatest amount of attention were also those that could be most easily seen by the greatest number of viewers – hence facilitating the circulation of the visiting throngs. Moreover, the same unequal visual economy was entirely in keeping with the Royal Academy's commitment to the cause of public, grand-style art, and with its corresponding ambivalence towards the inferior and commodified forms of painting available in the open marketplace. Yet there was always a danger that this order of priorities might be overturned by the viewing public, whose general preference for works far removed from grandeur was widely, if regretfully, acknowledged. As early as 1772 Sir Joshua Reynolds had expressed his apprehension that the practice of holding regular displays would tempt artists to abandon the elevated path of classical idealism in favour of depicting the particular appearances of common nature; for the 'lowest style', he conceded, was bound to be 'the most popular, as it falls within the compass of ignorance itself; and the Vulgar will always be pleased with what is natural, in the confined and misunderstood sense of the word'.[3] In actuality the real problem lay not with 'the Vulgar' *per se* – since the poor were effectively excluded from the annual shows – but with the respectable middle classes, who made up the bulk of the exhibition audience. Though such viewers may have been just about persuaded to accept the superior prestige of history painting, with its heroic themes and ideal forms, there was widespread acknowledgement that most took far greater pleasure from works that dealt in specific truths, and with subjects closer to their own experience – not just portraits and landscapes, as well as depictions of significant contemporary events, but also scenes of 'common' or 'familiar' life, rich in detailed visual incident.

Genre painting, as this branch of art would later come to be called, belonged to a tradition originating in the seventeenth-century Netherlands, where its most celebrated practitioners had included Adriaen Brouwer, Adriaen van Ostade, and David Teniers the Younger. In Reynolds's rather condescending words, these were painters who had 'applied themselves . . . to low and vulgar characters, and who express[ed] with precision the various shades of passion, as they are exhibited by vulgar minds'; he put William Hogarth into the same humble category.[4] It was probably on account of their reputation for vulgarity that these artists inspired few imitators in late eighteenth-century England. Although every Somerset House exhibition featured a significant minority of genre scenes, between 1780 and 1805 these tended to owe much less to Hogarth and his Netherlandish predecessors than to the sentimental domestic dramas of Jean-Baptiste Greuze, or Thomas Gainsborough's elegant pastorals. If this allegiance was determined on the one hand by the moral imperatives of a self-consciously polite social order, on the other it was partly shaped by the viewing conditions in the Great Room, where small paintings rendered in precise detail were more than likely to get lost. In addition to 'cleaning up' the Dutch tradition of lowlife imagery, Greuze and Gainsborough had adopted a more generalized visual idiom, and one which worked on a larger scale better suited to the spaces of the public exhibition.

The lessons learned from their (and especially Greuze's) example were most consistently demonstrated by William Redmore Bigg, whose works appeared in every Royal Academy show between 1780 and 1827. Since a high proportion of his exhibits were designated as for sale, and many of them were subsequently issued as prints, there were exceptionally strong commercial reasons for Bigg to design his compositions in such a way as to try and leave a lasting impression upon the minds of any potential buyers in the exhibition audience. At an early point in his career he came to appreciate the value of producing genre scenes large enough (typically 40 × 50 in.) to merit placement right below the line, just above the heads of the visitors.[5] Within his favoured horizontal format Bigg strove as best he could for maximum legibility, typically by giving a dominant compositional role to a relatively small number of figures; these he arranged to tell simple visual stories of his own invention, featuring an obvious moral element, and fleshed out with sufficient details to retain the viewer's attention beyond his or her initial glance. In each case further guidance for the viewer was provided by a title designed to signal the main thrust of the plot, and to provoke interest in its dramatic content. This combination of tactics also had the advantage of inviting more or less extended exegeses from newspaper critics, whose responses modelled those that Bigg sought to elicit from members of the public at large. In 1795 his picture of the *Truants Discovered* (fig. 129) provoked one reviewer to summarize its principal attractions, and to note why Bigg had become a perennial favourite at the Royal Academy shows:

> There is generally a considerable share of merit in the productions of this Artist, and we notice them with peculiar pleasure, because it seems to be always his aim to inculcate some moral principle, or to impress some amiable affection

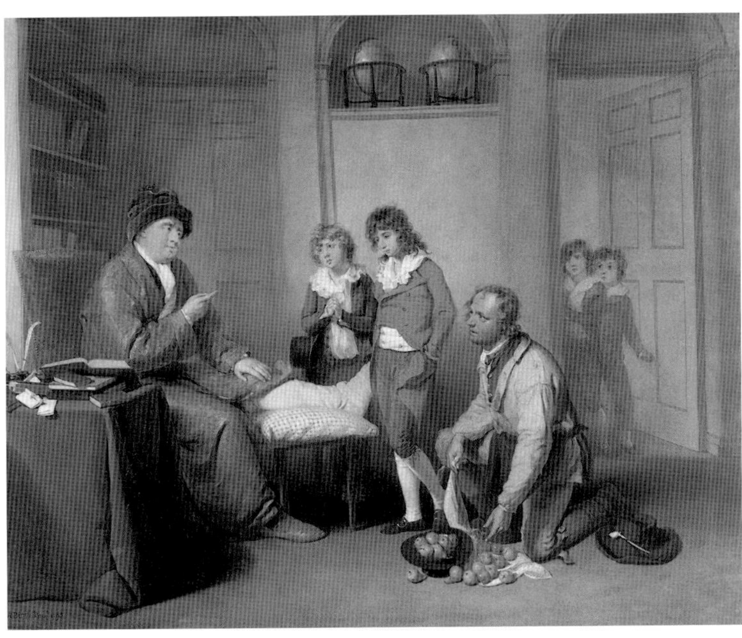

129 William Redmore Bigg, *The Truants Discovered*, RA 1795. Private collection.

> upon the heart. The story here is well told. There is a good expression of benevolence in the face of the School-master, and a due appearance of contrition in the Boys. This subject will make a good engraving.[6]

Other contemporary exhibition-pieces by Bigg elicited similarly appreciative commentaries of somewhat greater length, cataloguing the feelings displayed by the various characters in his little dramas. By the 1790s, this kind of self-conscious exercise in the culture of sensibility had become a standard feature of English literary and art criticism; but even if the journalistic reviewers were working to their own discursive agenda, their reactions cannot have been fundamentally different from those of many other members of the exhibition audience. Like many comparable scenes by the almost equally popular George Morland (e.g., *The Benevolent Sportsman*, RA 1792; fig. 130), Bigg's pictures evidently aimed to provoke a response in two stages: an immediate apprehension of the anecdotal action as a whole, followed by a closer reading of the expressions shown by the various participants. The whole process might last only a minute or two – though presumably this was enough time to leave some imprint on the viewer's memory, and to do so without impeding the slow circulation of the Great Room crowd. For a commercial painter like Bigg, who required a constant stream of buyers for his paintings and the prints made after them, there were obvious advantages in a pictorial formula that so readily invited the spectator's engagement, but which did not detain him (or her) for terribly long. The approach was one from which the artist rarely deviated throughout a long and productive career.

But Bigg's appeal was far from universal. While the popularity of his work was hardly ever in doubt, it was generally assumed that most of his admirers came from the less discriminating strata of the exhibition public. One early nineteenth-century critic condescendingly described these as people 'who, without indulging a fastidious taste, examine the works of Art by the criterion of a general knowledge of Nature'.[7] This commonsensical approach shaped their preference for genre scenes representing a 'nature' that may have been tidied up, selected and moralized, yet which to them provided a convincing (and appealing) simulacrum of contemporary English life. Viewers with more 'fastidious tastes', however, rejected the sentimental banalities of Bigg and other artists in favour of an altogether different form of genre painting, one that both the Academy and most of its middle-class audience regarded as irredeemably 'low'.

During the late eighteenth and early nineteenth centuries, the London art market witnessed a dramatic rise in the prices paid for small scenes of peasant life by David Teniers and other seventeenth-century Dutch and Flemish masters.[8] Fuelling this boom was an elite of extremely wealthy connoisseurs and collectors – led by no less a figure than the Prince of Wales – who were clearly not bothered in the slightest by the supposed 'vulgarity' of the imagery they so admired. A fine painting was in their eyes an object of private pleasure, beautifully crafted and made for the pleasurable appreciation of gentlemen of taste; what (in theory) distinguished their tastes from those of their social inferiors was precisely the connoisseurs' ability to treat matters of form as distinctly separate from those of content – although 'low' subjects, too, were clearly not lacking in allure. The fact that the Netherlandish genre painters had specialized in the depiction of boors and drunkards only underscored their ability

130 George Morland, *The Benevolent Sportsman*, RA 1792. Fitzwilliam Museum, Cambridge.

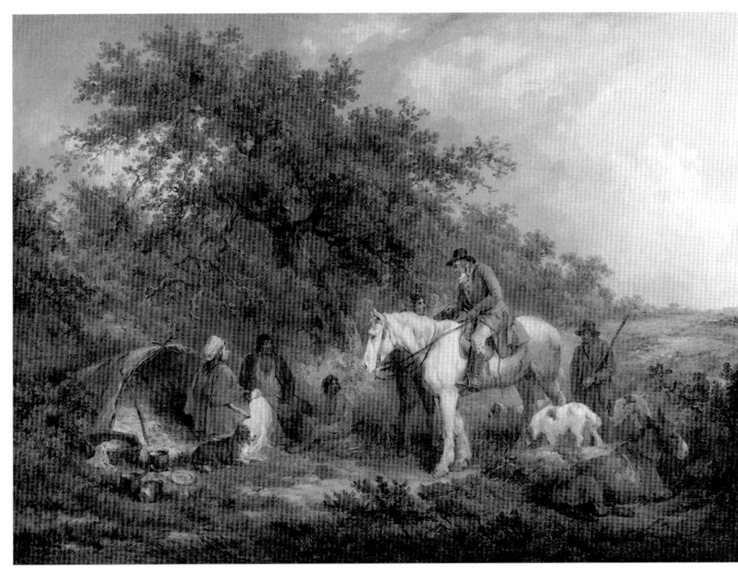

to redeem such low themes through exquisite handling, colour and chiaroscuro – or at least so it was often argued by the turn of the nineteenth century. In one of the most succinct statements of this point of view, the writer and collector Richard Payne Knight praised seventeenth-century Dutch and Flemish artists for having produced 'the finest pictures of the greatest masters of the art, considered abstractly as the art of painting – that is, the art of employing colours to imitate visible objects, with the greatest possible degree of skill, judgment, taste, and effect'.[9] Such encomiums implied a double rejection – not only of what was perceived to be the vulgar (i.e., bourgeois) preoccupation with subject matter, but also of the Academy's commitment to an elevating art that addressed the mind; instead the connoisseurs insisted on the primacy of the exquisitely cultivated eye, and on close and long looking as the best (and only) basis for exercising a properly informed aesthetic judgement. While the operations of this superior gaze may have been at home in the privacy of the gentleman's cabinet, however, they ran into trouble in the crowded spaces of Somerset House. Out in public, aside from being out of place, the connoisseur's pretensions proved vulnerable to satiric attack, his concentration on the minutiae of painting technique exposed as myopic ignorance, or as indicative of an acquisitive temperament governed by irrational and lascivious desires.[10]

Given such hostile attitudes, as well as the antagonism of an artistic profession anxious to secure a reputation for intellectual dignity, it is hardly surprising that the claims of connoisseurship were overshadowed for so long by the countervailing authority of academic art theory. Change would come eventually, but not until the first decade of the nineteenth century. Three events that occurred in 1806 marked a key moment in this process: the first exhibition hosted by the British Institution, which supplied an alternative space for the display of modern and old master art under connoisseurial direction; the opening to the public of the Marquis of Stafford's collection, which was especially rich in its holdings of Netherlandish genre; and last but certainly not least, the ecstatic reception accorded a curious little picture called the *Village Politicians* (fig. 131) at that year's Royal Academy show.

Painted by a twenty-one-year-old Scotsman named David Wilkie, who had arrived in London only the previous year, the *Village Politicians* marked the first public appearance of a prodigy hitherto unknown outside an extremely narrow circle of art world insiders. The canvas itself was modest in size, less than thirty inches wide, and its brownish tonalities were anything but eye-catching; yet notwithstanding its unprepossessing appearance and its author's virtual anonymity, this work generated a degree of interest entirely disproportionate to its scale, its comically low subject matter and its position below the line. The engraver Abraham Raimbach later recalled what had happened:

> When the exhibition at Somerset House opened in May, 1806, and the *Village Politicians* was seen by the public, Wilkie's reputation was at once established; the effect was electrical, and it might be compared without exaggeration to that produced by Byron's *Childe Harold*. It was well placed, though not centrically, in the great room, and was from the first day constantly surrounded by a group of gratified spectators. Though not very forcible in its effect, its simplicity of arrangement, the novelty of its style, and beauty of its execution, excited an interest quite unexampled within the walls of the Royal Academy.[11]

'There was a daily crush to see [the painting]', confirmed Wilkie's biographer, Allan Cunningham; 'crowd succeeded crowd of gazers and wonderers from morning till night'.[12] What, it seems fair to ask, drew and kept them there?

If Raimbach's recollection is to be believed, people clustered around Wilkie's first exhibition-piece mainly to admire its formal and technical qualities – and the engraver may very well have been right to suggest that this was something which Somerset House had never witnessed before. Surely the connoisseurs' interest in matters of style and execution had been brought into play on previous occasions, and focused on other pictures; but in 1806, arguably for the very first time, such viewing practices became a significant part of the exhibition experience for very large numbers of visitors. In effect, the *Village Politicians* appears to have acted the part of a Trojan Horse, as the vehicle for introducing a set of aesthetic values – and a mode of spectatorship – into an alien, hitherto hostile setting.

Whether or not this effect was aimed for from the outset, the indisputable fact remains that a small number of leading connoisseurs of Dutch art stage-managed Wilkie's astonishing London début. At some point during the early part of April 1806, the amateur landscape artist Sir George Beaumont and his friend Lord Mulgrave – who were both to play leading roles in the British Institution – visited the young Scotsman in his studio, and straight away placed orders for pictures (the *Blind Fiddler* in the former's case, *Rent Day* in the latter's). On 12 April Joseph Farington wrote in his diary that Beaumont had called, 'quite enthusiastick about a young man of the name of Wilkie. . . . He has painted several pictures in which He has exhibited the low Scotch character in familiar scenes, in a manner . . . almost equal to Teniers in execution and superior to him in variety of character'.[13] Deeply impressed by the *Village Politicians*, Sir George and Mulgrave 'spread the fame of the picture round the bright circles to which they belonged'.[14] One member of their coterie of collectors was the merchant John Julius Angerstein; and according to Alan Cunningham it was he who openly declared at that year's Royal Academy dinner, held just prior to the opening of the show, that Wilkie's picture 'had all the spirit of Teniers and the humour of Hogarth . . . [he] pointed it out to the company as the star of the collection'.[15] Within three days Angerstein's comments had been picked up by the press, some sections of which evidently required a bit of prompting to pay tribute to a painting which they would normally have disregarded. Thus the *Morning Herald* of 6 May was quick to make

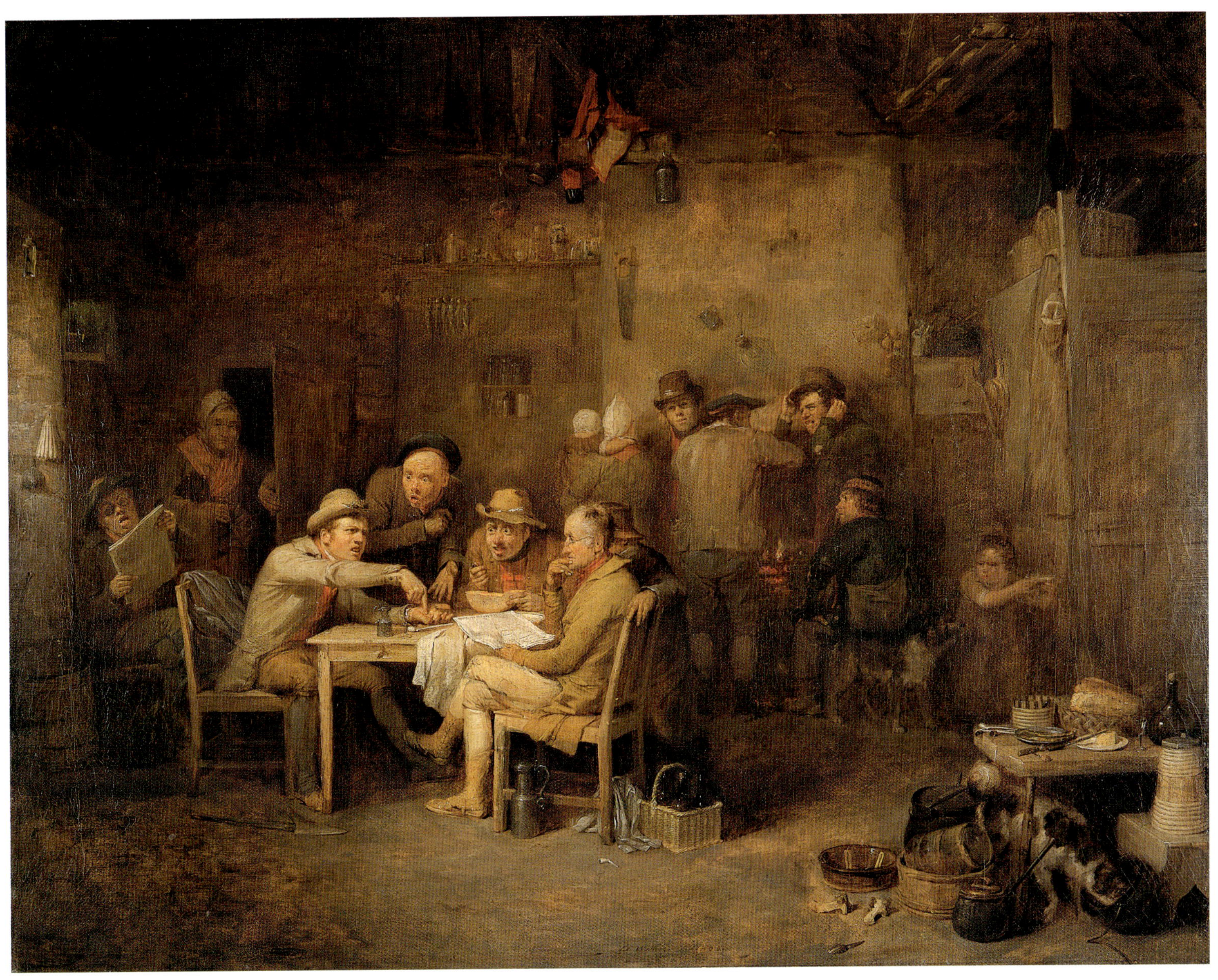

131 David Wilkie, *The Village Politicians*, RA 1806. The Earl of Mansfield.

amends for its initial lapse in proper discrimination: 'We yesterday noticed the principal Pictures. One we accidentally overlooked. It is the 'Village Politicians,' the production of a young Scotsman, not more than 18 years of age. It has all the truth of Teniers, with all the humour of Hogarth'.[16] Though not everyone accepted the comparison with Hogarth, virtually every commentator acknowledged Wilkie's closeness to Teniers – and more to the point, perhaps, they showered the picture with praise for this very reason. Notwithstanding the Flemish artist's well-known predilection for vulgar subject matter – and notwithstanding, too, the low and comic character of the *Village Politicians* itself – a juvenile exercise in the manner of Teniers was hailed as one of the greatest achievements of the modern British School. The connoisseurs – and Wilkie – had triumphed.

But a survey of the contemporary critical response to the *Village Politicians* suggests that the victory belonged to another constituency as well. For even as the reports carried by newspapers and magazines took the connoisseurs' frame of reference as their point of departure, certain critics immediately began modifying it slightly to suit the different interests of their broadly middle-class readership. Thus where Wilkie's champions among the great *cognoscenti* stressed his dependence on Teniers, a number of journalistic reviewers chose instead to present both artists as equals, allied in pursuit of natural truth. According to the *Monthly Magazine*, 'Mr Wilkie may be said to have looked at nature with the same spirit and eye that Teniers would have looked at it, and he has delineated the ale-house politicians of Scotland with the same fidelity that Teniers has represented the Dutch and Flemish boors'.[17] Similarly, the *Village Politicians* prompted a writer of a review that appeared simultaneously in the *Public Ledger* and the *Star* to

> congratulate the admirers of the art on the several examples (this eminently conspicuous among others) which have been set within these two or three years, mostly by young men, indicative of a returning taste for Nature and Truth, in preference to that which has no other sanction but the pedantic *dictum* of those whose chief claim to applause is that of most tenaciously following each other in a beaten track, which time has rendered familiar to the meanest capacity.[18]

Though we cannot be certain which other young artists this reviewer had in mind – he may have been referring to John Varley's pupils, the precocious landscapists William Mulready, John Linnell and William Henry Hunt – I think we can gauge with some clarity what he and other early admirers of the *Village Politicians* meant by its 'Nature and Truth'.

The kernel of the answer lies in Sir George Beaumont's comment to Farington, when he cited Wilkie's 'variety of character' as that which marked him out as superior to Teniers. Beaumont was referring to the remarkable precision with which Wilkie had managed to differentiate the several actors in his comic drama, and this opinion soon echoed throughout the press. 'The characters are admirably defined and *varied*',[19] the critic for the *Sun* was happy to report; while the *Public Ledger* praised 'the characteristic expression of the *different* faces introduced'.[20] Meanwhile the *Morning Post* applauded the picture as 'evinc[ing] an intimate knowledge of vulgar nature, and a facility in expressing the *various* passions by which she is actuated, that are unrivalled in the present day' (my emphasis throughout).[21] As this final phrase suggests, the critics who praised Wilkie's variety were also hinting at the shortcomings of his rivals and immediate predecessors, whose works now seemed to offer an unsatisfactorily general characterization of lowlife types. Viewers grown accustomed to the standards of naturalism set by W. R. Bigg, Francis Wheatley or George Morland must have been astounded by the uncanny particularity of each of the figures in the *Village Politicians*, and by the way in which not just faces but bodies were so crisply distinguished one from the other. Rather than sharing in the single character of brutish inebriation – and it is worth noting that some are drinking whisky and others beer – these would-be 'politicians' manifest a range of identifiable passions, from the most thoughtful and self-absorbed to expressions of surprise, and even anger. The most thorough analysis of the different players and their roles appeared in the fashionable monthly magazine *La Belle Assemblée*, and it is worth quoting at some length:

> This picture evidently represents a scene of the politicians of lower life, collected in a public house after the labours of the day, disputing upon some points of politics, which may be supposed, at that moment, to have interested every class of society, and to have found its way into the shop of the mechanic, and the cottage of the husbandman. The idea is original. The principal figure which appears in this groupe [*sic*], is a young carpenter, who, from the shrewd winking of his eyes, the expression of his mouth, the extended arm, and the acute angle of the wrist, and the end of the fore-finger on the table, happily conveys a self-approbation of the sagacity and superiority of *his* mind over those of his hearers; while the man before him, who is evidently a blacksmith, seems to hold his sentiments cheap notwithstanding all his self-consequence and dictatorial parade. These two figures are admirably characteristic of the conceit which a little knowledge produces upon vulgar minds; they evince great observation of rustic nature, and the influence of the little heats of parties and politics upon such as would naturally be supposed beyond the sphere of their operation. The expression of the face of the man, reading the paper, indicates with much felicity his composed and settled acquiescence in the conclusions of his own mind, – his undaunted adherence to his own opinions, amidst the din of his battling associates. He is easy and quiet, and *thinks for himself*, whilst another man, in the opposite part of this picture, is scratching his head, seemingly sensible of his not having the eloquence of the 'haranguing carpenter,' but tolerably confident in his own mind, that he is the best informed in the room. – The accompaniments to these figures are happy and appropriate, and every way expressive of the inside of a house that retails whiskey.[22]

Though this passage is from the tradition of critical writing that had produced the laudatory description of W. R. Bigg's *Truants Discovered*, there are profound differences between these texts, and the images which inspired them. Whereas Bigg's approach involved the deployment of an easily legible storyline implying a sequence of events starting before and concluding after the moment depicted, in the *Village Politicians* this form of narrative gave way to a carefully orchestrated set of social interactions, which combined to describe a situation, rather than a plot. It took time for the spectator to figure out exactly what was going on: the title may have helped to indicate the overall scenario, but the role played by each participant could be deduced only from a microscopic scrutiny of facial and bodily signs. Viewers had to look long and closely at the plethora of details that Wilkie had provided, and this could be done only by a very small number of spectators at a time; no wonder, then, that crowds gathered and generated more crowds, as people struggled to see what all the fuss was about. Once they'd finally managed to position themselves in front of the picture, it invited them to indulge in two distinct forms of connoisseurial viewing: an aesthetic connoisseurship of formal qualities and painterly skill, perhaps to begin with, but also a social connoisseurship of the minds and bodies of the 'low'.

If the first sort of knowledge was limited to the experience of an elite of wealth and taste, the second just as clearly was not.

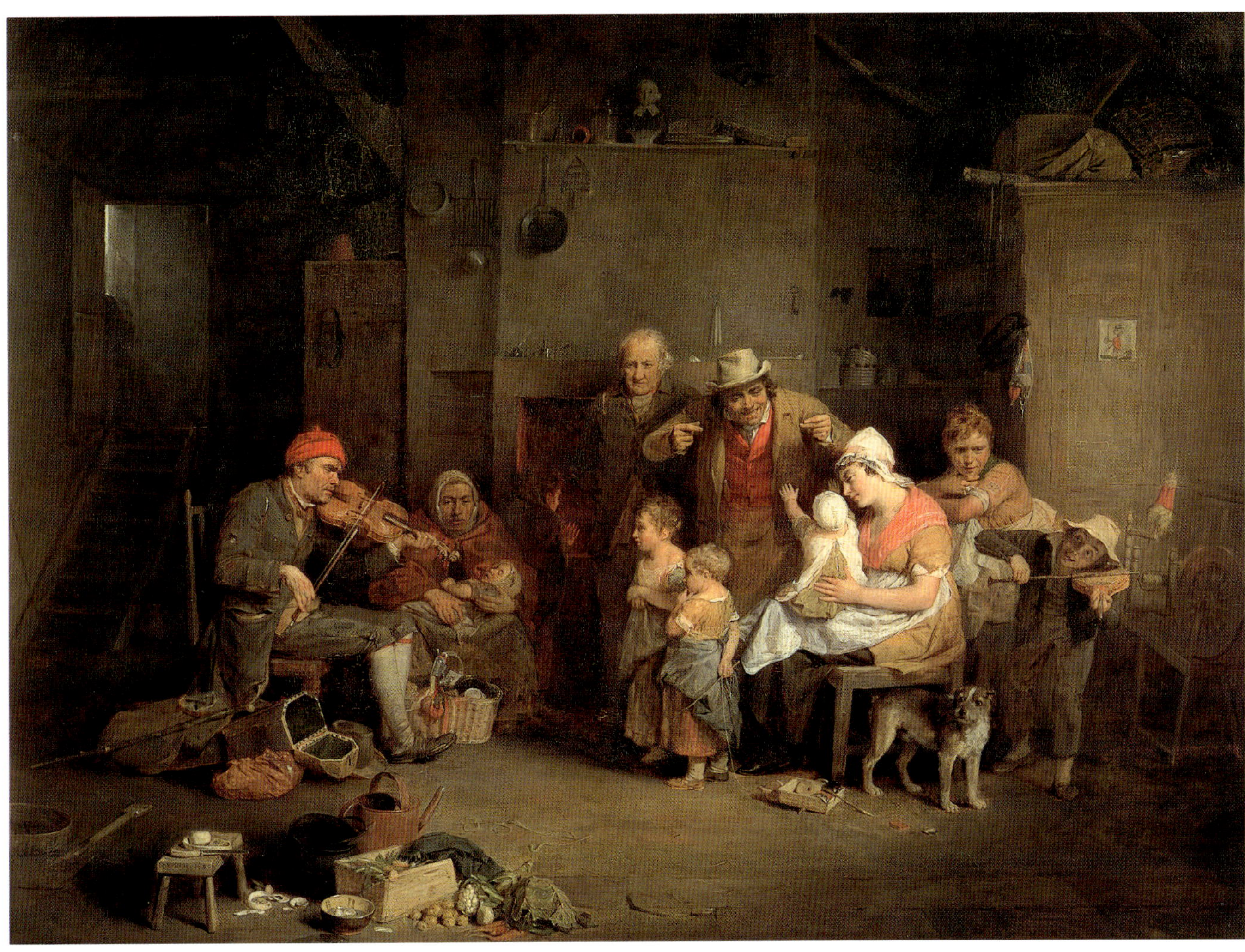

132 David Wilkie, *The Blind Fiddler*, RA 1807. Tate, London.

On the contrary: by this point in British history the ability to identify human character on the basis of external evidence had come to be understood as a crucial marker of bourgeois identity. As Jon Klancher has observed, in the early nineteenth century 'being "middle-class" will finally mean being in a position to "read" social signs correctly. . . . [by] reading society as a symbolically instructive text, the middle-class reader edges away from any class identity of his own, standing outside the order of social classes to the extent that he can textualize it'.[23] To a degree perceived to be unmatched by any other contemporary artist, Wilkie instantiated this ability to 'read' society, and to 'know' the passions which motivated the lower orders; thus the *Village Politicians* presented the average exhibition-goer with a complex 'social text' to be considered directly in relation to the human 'nature' that the painting ostensibly described with such truth.

One important by-product of Wilkie's new formula for genre painting was to alter the dynamics of viewing in the Great Room – and one wonders whether everyone was pleased with the results. The cramming of so much significant detail on to so small a canvas surface encouraged visitors to spend a disproportionate amount of time in front of a work that fell far short of fulfilling the elevated civic aims of Somerset House's architect, and of the Royal Academy itself; indeed there is evidence that certain Academicians were less than overjoyed by Wilkie's initial triumph.[24] Moreover, the enormous interest excited by the *Village Politicians* must have caused certain practical problems: at a social event where overcrowding was a perennial and growing concern, the appearance of a new type of picture capable of creating crowds on its very own cannot have been an entirely welcome development. Questions, too, would eventually arise as to whether such paintings could be properly appreciated in an environment pre-eminently unsuited to the kind of viewing that they ideally required.

For the time being, however, Wilkie was content to build on the success of the *Village Politicians* by producing even more elaborate versions of the same basic formula. His next exhibition-piece, the *Blind Fiddler* of 1807 (fig. 132), featured slightly fewer figures, but a far more varied cast of characters and activities: men, women and children spanning three generations, mothers and fathers, husbands and wives, children ranging in age from

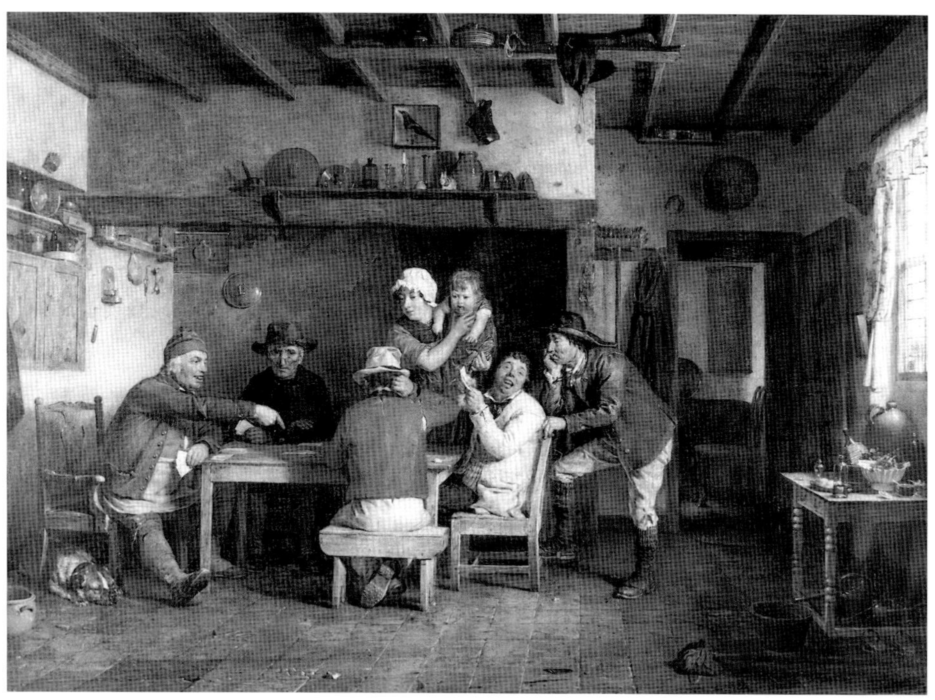

133 David Wilkie, *The Card Players*, RA 1808. The Lord Denham.

infancy to youth, the respectable and the destitute poor, performers and audience, with expressions varying from the roguish and the delighted to the solicitous and the sad; and on top of these a veritable cornucopia of minutely detailed accessories rich in decipherable meanings – one could go on and on. This was a temptation that contemporary reviewers found extremely hard to resist; now several newspapers strove to outdo one another in regaling their readers with prolonged readings of the minutiae of Wilkie's new work,[25] which was widely judged to have surpassed the merit of its predecessor. According to Allan Cunningham, the *Blind Fiddler* was deliberately hung beside a picture of 'overpowering brightness'; but 'The human nature which [Wilkie] had stamped on the whole scene triumphed over all; the pictures of the academicians, in the same room, with all their scientific colouring and glow, failed to attract. The visitors crowded to the *Blind Fiddler*, and *Jupiter presenting to Diana her Bow and Arrows* [by John Francis Rigaud], *Flora unveiled by the Zephyrs* [by Richard Westall], nay, even the *Sun rising through Vapour*, or *The Blacksmith's Forge* [both these latter works by Turner] . . . were disregarded in comparison'.[26] Though Cunningham may have been guilty of some degree of exaggeration, reports published at the time of the exhibition confirm that Wilkie's picture was regarded as 'deserv[ing] the first notice', as the one undeniable '*chef d'oeuvre*' on display.[27] Once again, the strategy for securing public attention that had been launched with the *Village Politicians* had worked to perfection, and at the expense of those more elevated but less discursive images that bore the Academy's highest aspirations.

The next year, however, Wilkie seems to have disappointed many members of his audience. Having come to expect him to depict a striking diversity of characters and incidents, his admirers found much less worth reading in the *Card Players* (fig. 133), and the critics were not slow to suggest that its author had lost his way. 'This picture', wrote a reporter in the *News*, 'is yet more highly finished than "The Village Politicians," or, "The Blind Fidler," [*sic*] indeed so much so, as to bear inspection with a glass of considerable magnifying power, but it has gained nothing by it'.[28] The Teniers-like *Card Players* may have been a fine painting for the few tasteful admirers of old master art (Wilkie's patron was HRH The Duke of Gloucester), but it offered far too little to the many *aficionados* of 'vulgar' human nature who formed the bulk of the exhibition audience. The magnifying glass – long established as a satiric trope of myopic connoisseurship – here revealed only an empty sign.

Wilkie partially made up for this lapse the following year, with *Rent Day* (fig. 134) and the *Cut Finger* (fig. 135). Largely the product of work carried out in 1807, *Rent Day* adheres quite closely to the basic format of the *Blind Fiddler*, which was commissioned at the same time. In both pictures the main action takes place on the left-hand side, where we are asked to begin our investigation; then traversing horizontally across the composition, our eyes register the varied actions and responses of the assembled figures, as we gradually build up our understanding of the group as a whole. *Rent Day* takes the differentiation of character to an extreme degree, to the point where it threatens to become a distraction. As one modern scholar has justly observed, the right half of Wilkie's image constitutes 'almost a catalogue or encyclopaedia of the odd things faces can do, coughing, arguing, gnawing the end of a stick, grimacing with effort, swallowing food'.[29] The results were not to everyone's taste. At least one critic objected – presumably certain viewers did as well – to the grossness of some of the behaviour depicted, which was

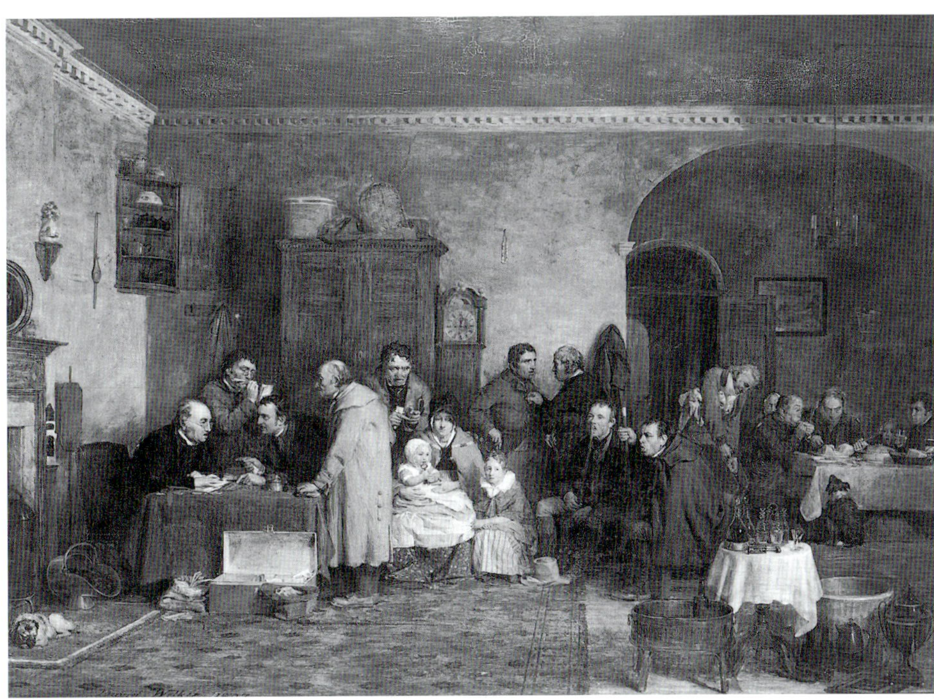

134 David Wilkie, *Rent Day*, RA 1809. Private collection.

135 (*below*) David Wilkie, *The Cut Finger*, RA 1809. Private collection.

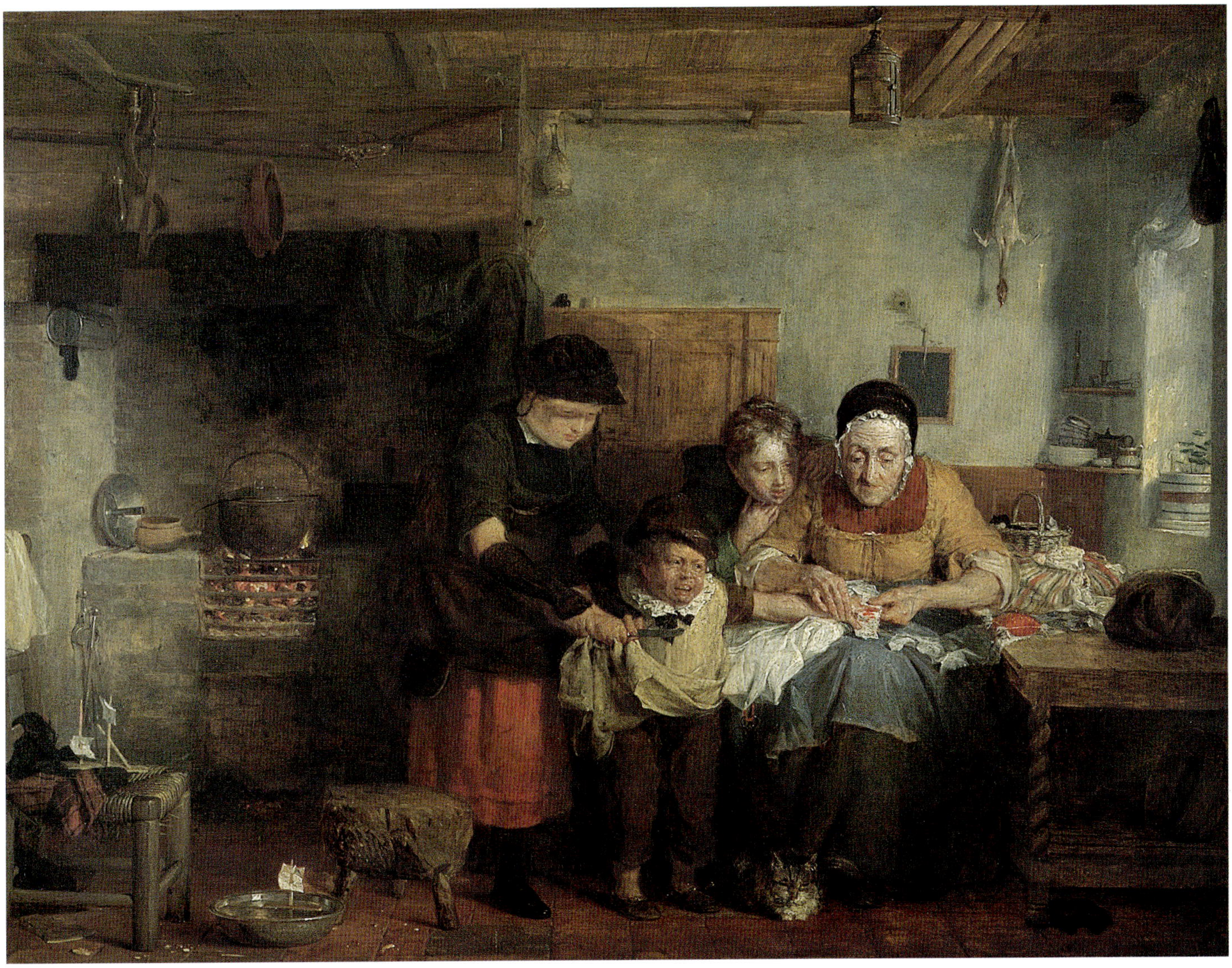

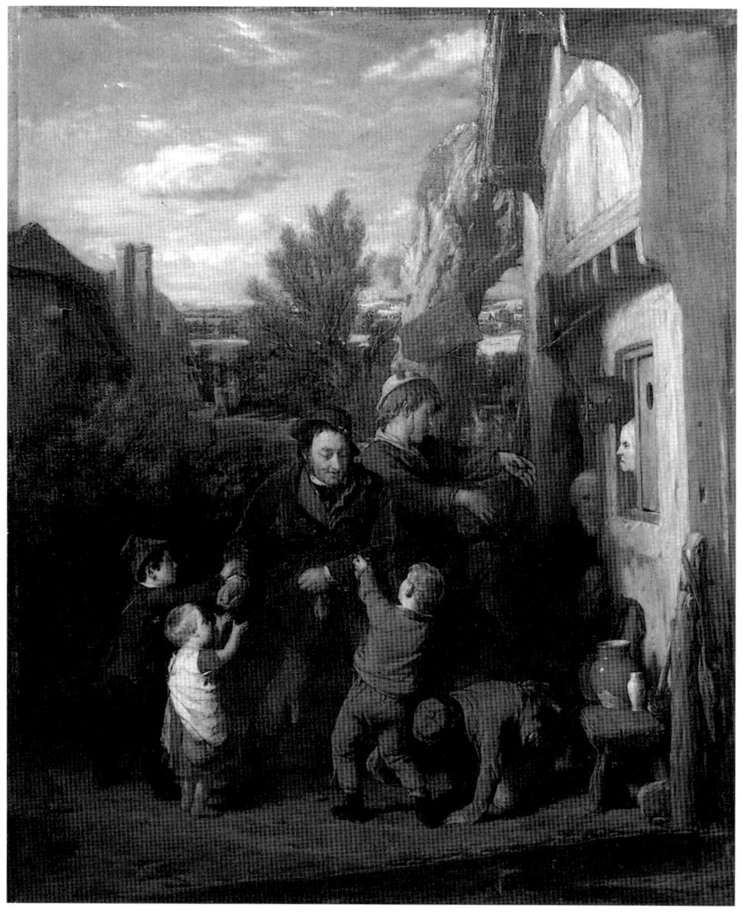

136 William Mulready, *Returning from the Ale-House*, RA 1809; background repainted 1817; re-exhibited as *Fair Time*, RA 1840. Courtesy of the Board of Trustees of the Victoria & Albert Museum.

taken as an affront to middle-class sensitivities;[30] sometimes 'vulgar' conduct did not bear being looked at too closely. As with the *Card Players* at the previous RA, if for quite different reasons, *Rent Day* may have better suited the connoisseurs (including Wilkie's patron Lord Mulgrave) than the exhibition public at large.

This was not the case with the *Cut Finger*, however, where Wilkie turned away from 'situation' in favour of telling a story. Here there are just four figures, whose expressions and positions are closely focused on a unifying action which implies both a previous incident (the cut) and a resolution to follow (the cure) – just like the narrative structure of a conventional history painting, or of works by the previous generation of British genre specialists. Certainly, the *Cut Finger* presents a wealth of details to be read; but these remain clearly subordinate to the overall theme, which (with the help of the title) we grasp more or less at first glance. While Wilkie's change in strategy may have been prompted in part by financial considerations (scenes with more figures cost more to produce, but his patrons were reluctant to adjust their payments accordingly), by now, with his celebrity fully established, he may no longer have felt it necessary to fill his imagery with quite so much attention-grabbing incident. Inevitably, this greater economy of means reduced the amount of viewing time demanded by his composition. And in the overpopulated confines of Somerset House, this may have had a highly desirable effect.

By 1809 Wilkie had inspired several young artists to follow his example, and they tended to adopt one or other of the pictorial strategies represented by his contributions to that year's

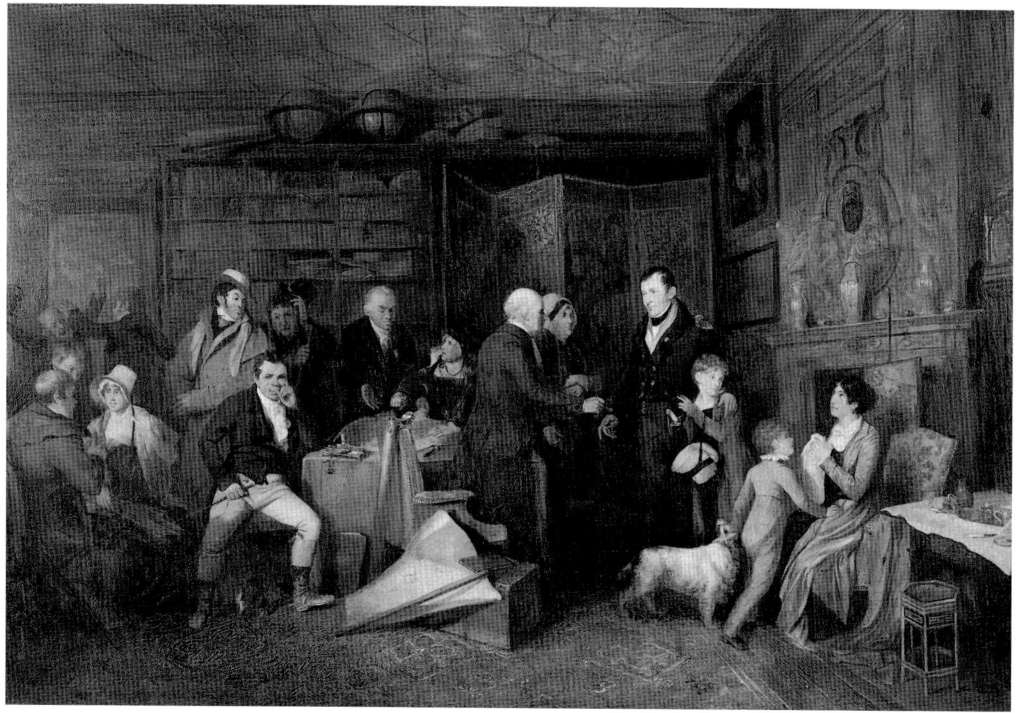

137 Edward Bird, *The Reading of the Will Concluded*, RA 1811. Bristol City Art Gallery.

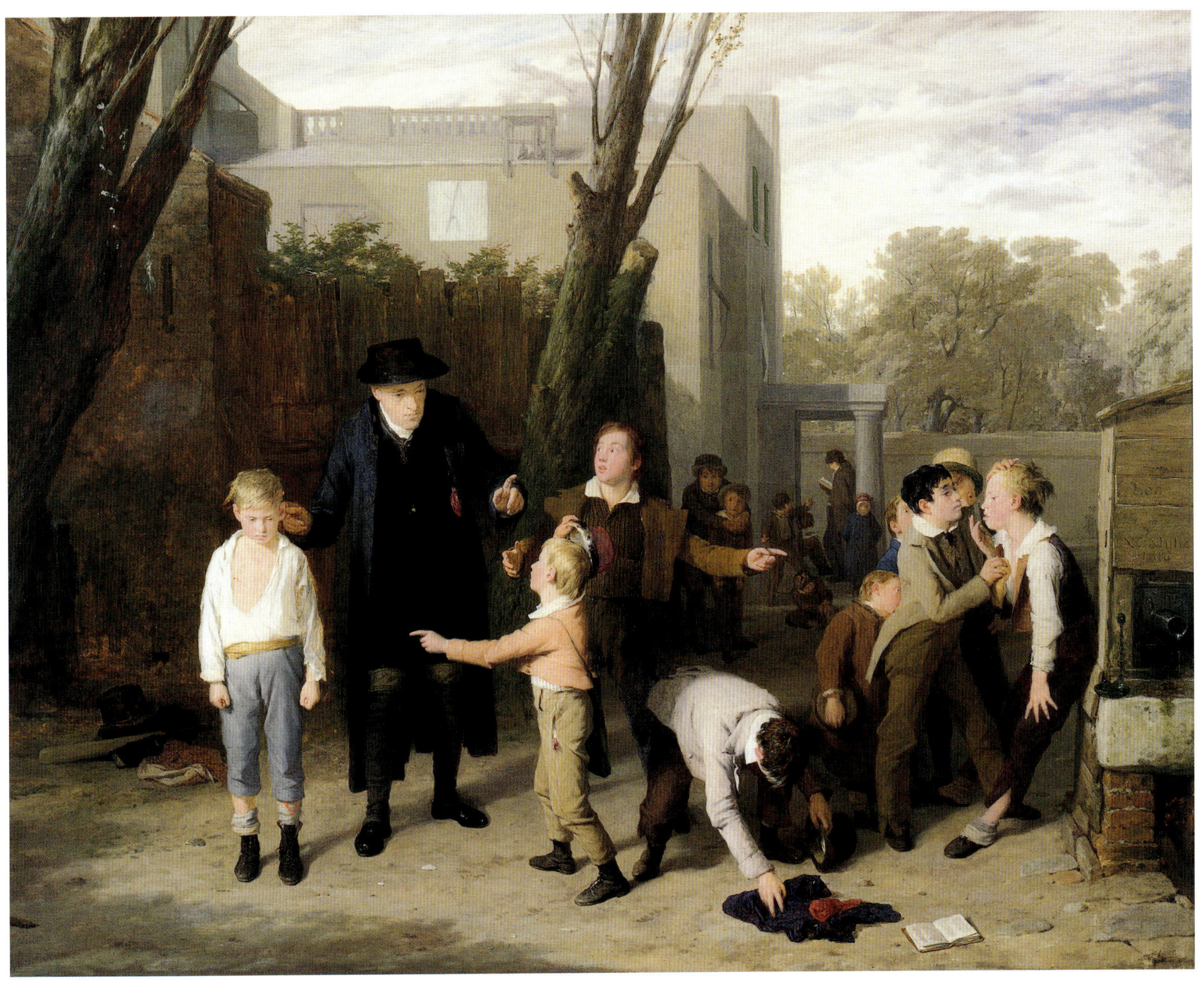

138 William Mulready, *The Fight Interrupted*, RA 1816. Courtesy of the Board of Trustees of the Victoria & Albert Museum.

exhibition. The Bristol artist Edward Bird took the path signposted by *Rent Day*, the *Blind Fiddler* and the *Village Politicians* with *Good News* (unlocated), showing a motley assortment of English villagers listening to a cobbler reading out a press report of patriotic importance. At the same display visitors could also admire William Mulready's *Returning from the Ale-House* (fig. 136), which, like the *Cut Finger*, focuses on a single action. In the years to come both Bird and Mulready would develop their respective approaches to produce exhibition favourites: Bird in 1811 with the *Reading of the Will Concluded* (fig. 137), another complex study in group psychology, and Mulready in 1816 with the *Fight Interrupted* (fig. 138), a schoolyard drama hailed as *the* 'point of attraction in the great room'.[31]

Wilkie, meanwhile, seems temporarily to have had serious doubts about the wisdom of exhibiting at the Academy, feeling perhaps that the kind of buyers he wished to attract and the viewing practices he sought to encourage were ill served in the chaotic setting of Somerset House. In 1810 he absented himself altogether – to bitter complaints from certain quarters – and two years later he organized his own retrospective in fashionable premises at 87 Pall Mall, an event clearly intended to enhance his standing with the elite. Though the wealthy collectors of old-master art remained his most consistent source of patronage, between 1813 and 1823 Wilkie also continued to solicit the favour of his middle-class admirers, with annual contributions to the Academy shows. His strategy here was to try and play both

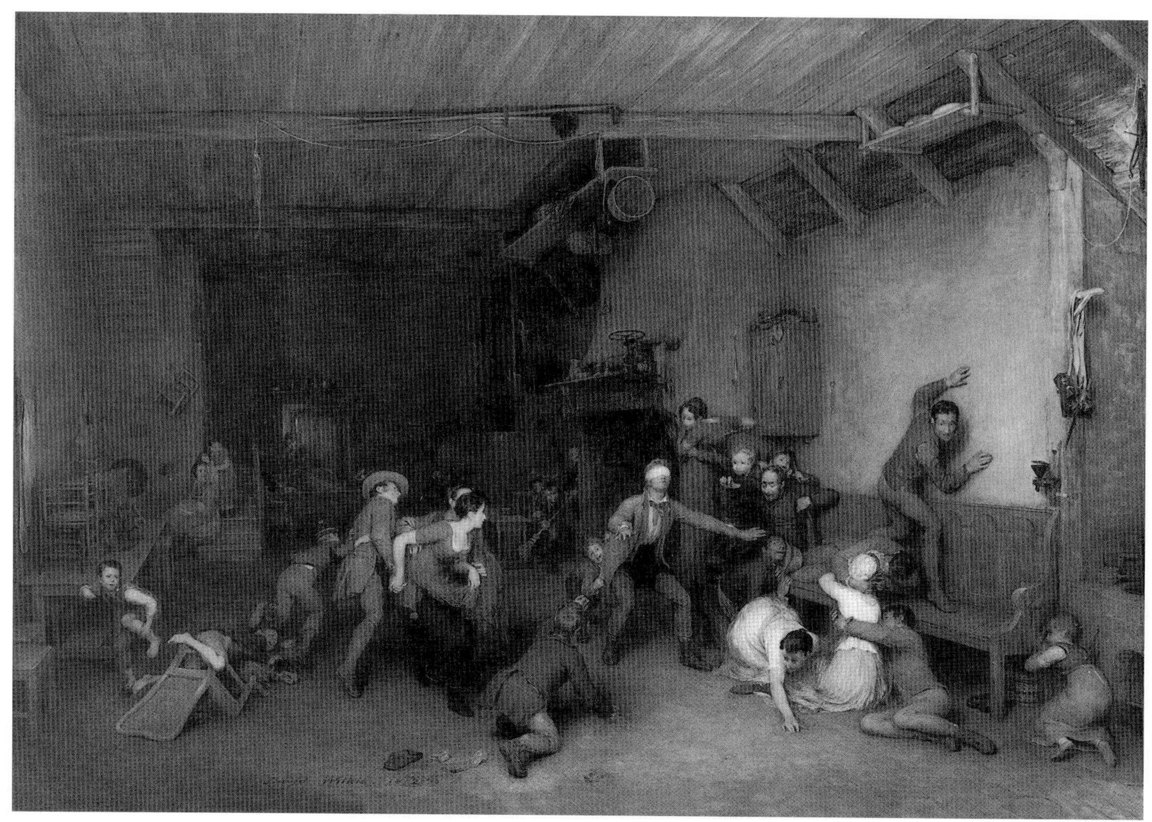

139 David Wilkie, *Blind Man's Buff*, RA 1813. The Royal Collection © 2001 Her Majesty Queen Elizabeth II.

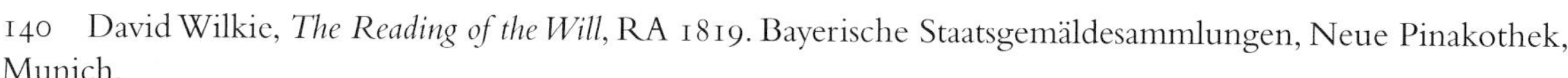

140 David Wilkie, *The Reading of the Will*, RA 1819. Bayerische Staatsgemäldesammlungen, Neue Pinakothek, Munich.

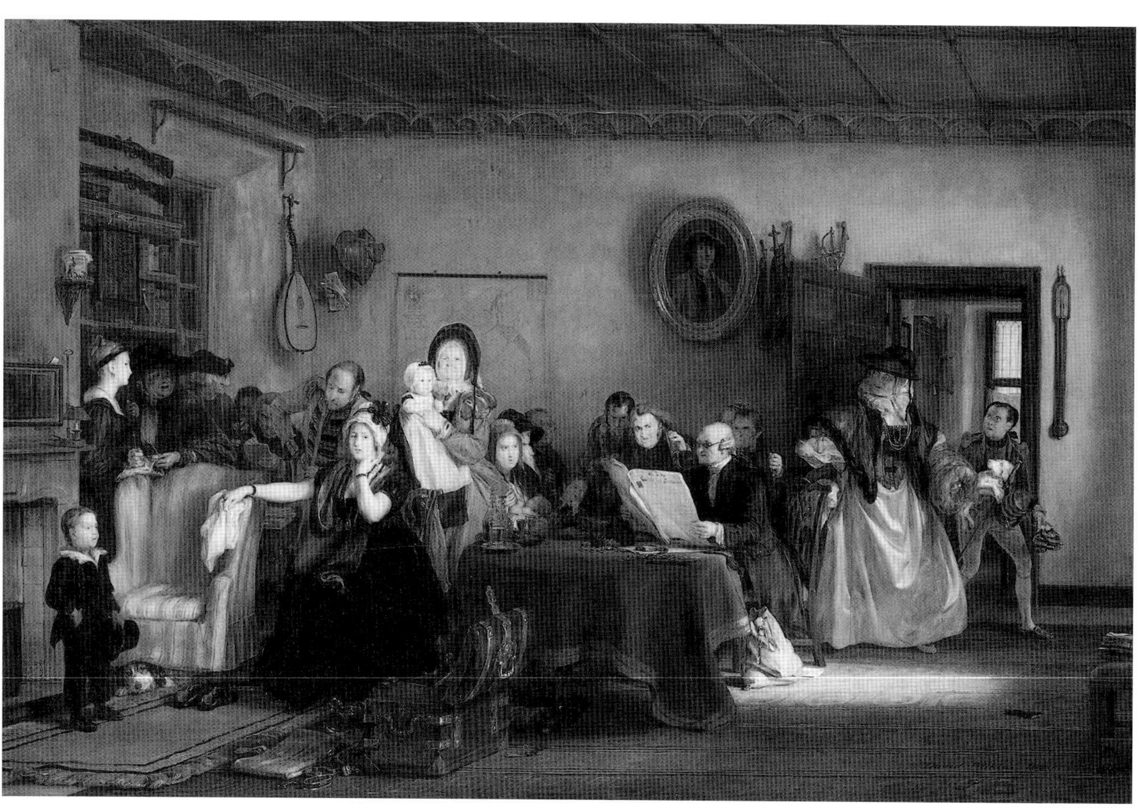

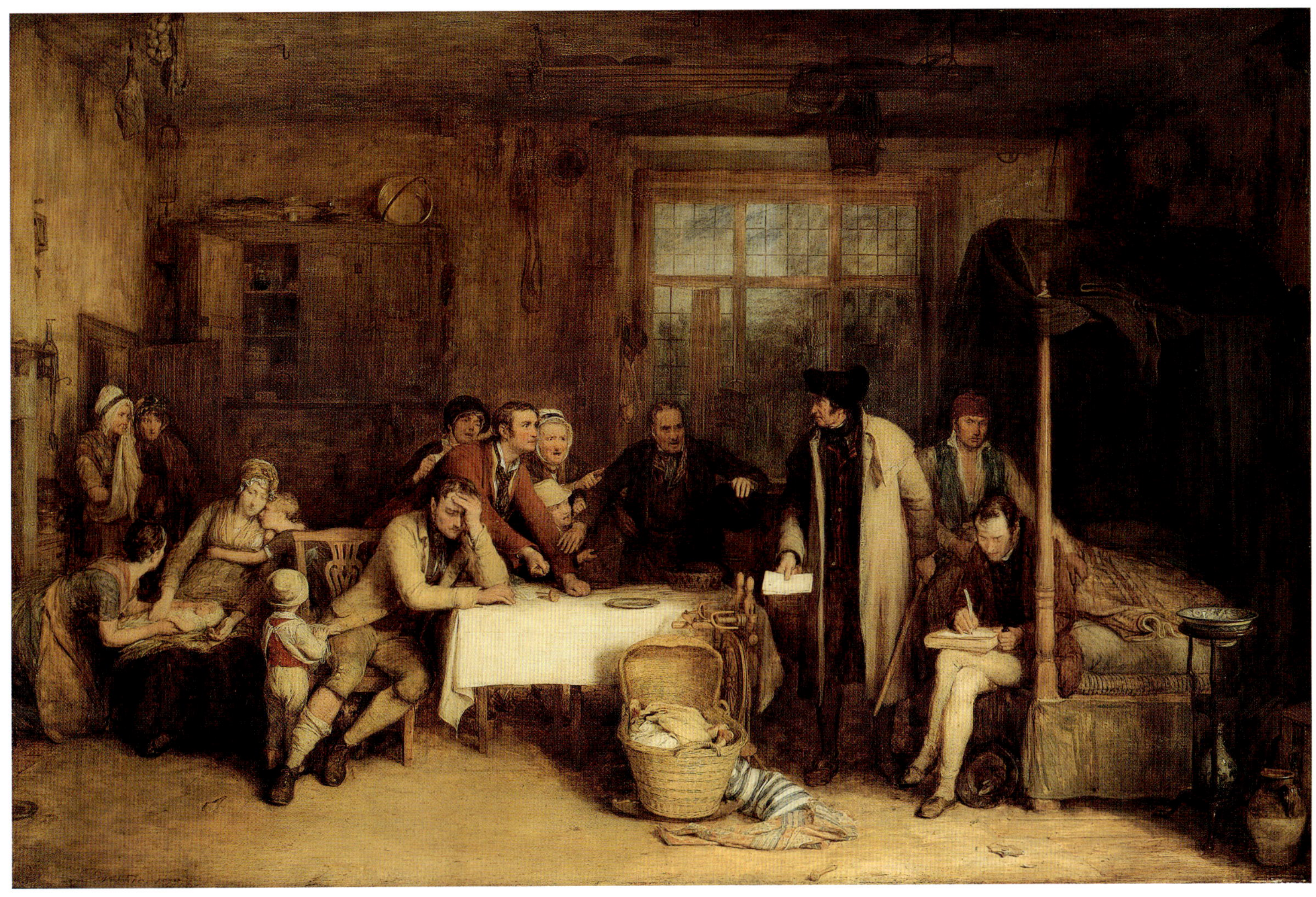

141 David Wilkie, *Distraining for Rent*, RA 1815. National Gallery of Scotland, Edinburgh.

sides off against the middle: to give the connoisseurs virtuoso performances overtly in the style of the Dutch old masters (for instance, the Ostade-like *Blind Man's Buff* (fig. 139) and its companion the *Penny Wedding*, shown in 1813 and 1819 respectively; both painted for the Prince Regent); and to meet the demands of the general public for touching moral and sentimental narratives, with works like *Distraining for Rent* (RA 1815; fig. 141) and the *Reading of the Will* (RA 1819; fig. 140).

Although on the whole Wilkie managed this balancing act with considerable aplomb, occasionally fears were expressed that his popularity did little honour to the true value of his work. Thus after seeing the crush of people around the *Reading of the Will* (commissioned, as it happens, by the King of Bavaria), the critic Thomas Wainewright wrote that, 'it offends me to the soul, to see a parcel of chuckleheaded Papas, doting Mamas, and chalk-and-charcoal faced Misses . . . crowding and squeezing, and riding upon one another's backs, to get sight – not of the faces of the folks reading the Will, but of the brass clasps of the strong box wherein was deposited the Will'.[32] This condescending sneer could boast a distinguished heritage, traceable at least as far back as Reynolds's attacks on the materialistic tastes of the bourgeois audience for art; and by the 1820s, with between 70,000 and 90,000-plus visitors attending each year's Royal Academy exhibition, certain commentators began to complain that the modern art experience was degenerating into a showy entertainment for the delectation of the ignorant.

It was in this context that Wilkie enjoyed what has generally been regarded as the crowning moment of his career, with his *Chelsea Pensioners Receiving the London Gazette Extraordinary of Thursday June 22d, 1815, Announcing the Battle of Waterloo!!!* (fig. 142). In the RA catalogue for 1822 the declamatory title is followed by an exceptionally long description, amounting almost to a set of instructions for reading the picture as the record of a long line of great English military victories:

> The picture represents an assemblage of pensioners and soldiers in front of the Duke of York public-house, Royal Hospital-row, Chelsea. The light-horseman on the left has just

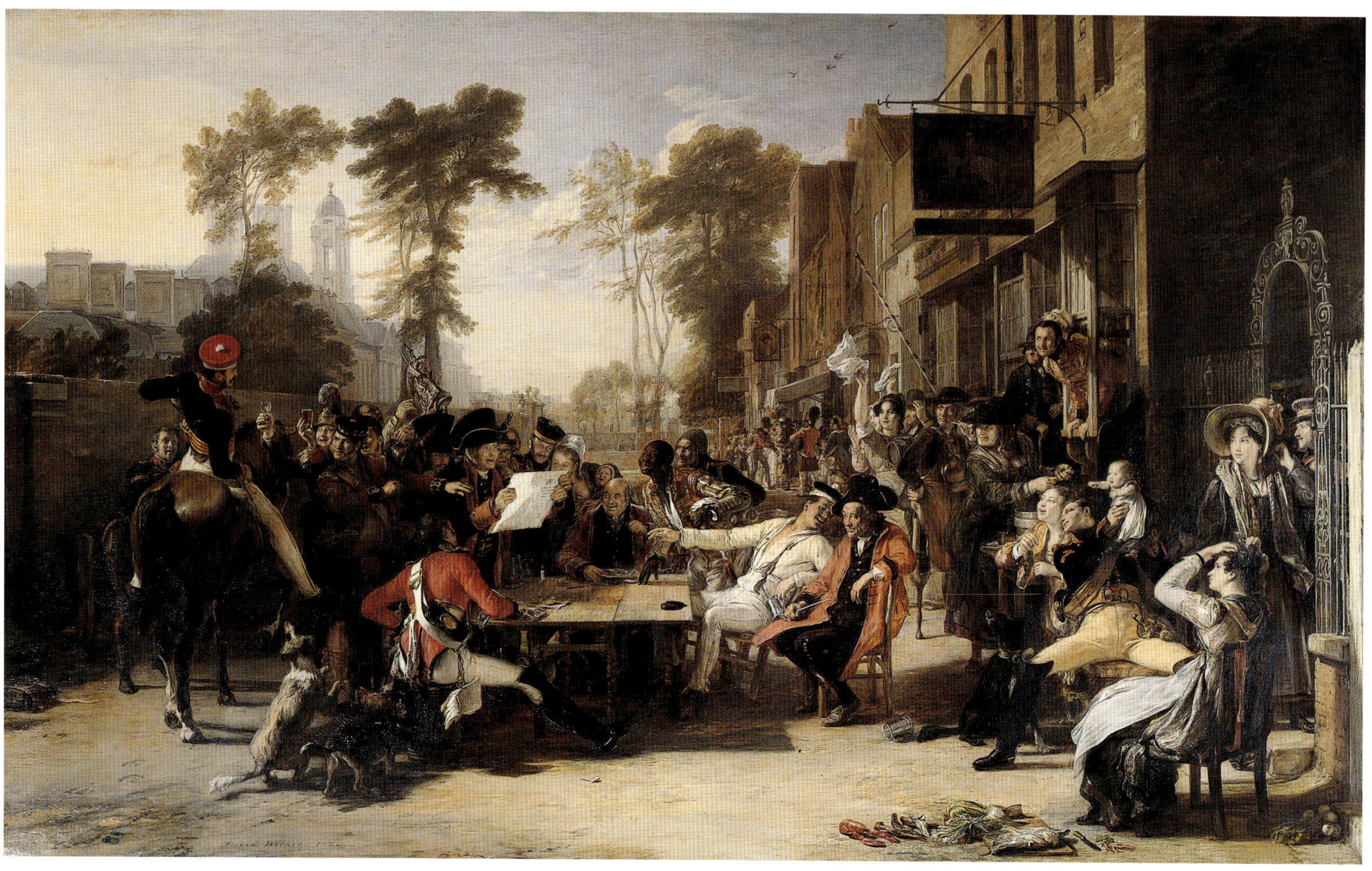

142 David Wilkie, *Chelsea Pensioners receiving the London Gazette Extraordinary of Thursday June 22d, 1815, Announcing the Battle of Waterloo!!!*, RA 1822. Courtesy of the Board of Trustees of the Victoria & Albert Museum, Apsley House, London.

arrived with the Gazette, and is relating further particulars to his comrades, among whom is a Glengarry Highlander, who served with General Graham at Barossa.

The Gazette is in the hands of an old pensioner, a survivor of the Seven Years War, who was at the taking of Quebec with General Wolfe, and is now reading aloud to his companions the details of the Victory of Waterloo. Opposite to him is a black, one of the band of the 1st regiment of Foot Guards, who was in France during the Revolution; was present at the death of Louis XVI, and was afterwards servant to General Moreau, in his campaigns in Germany during the revolutionary war.

Next to the black, in a foraging dress, is an Irish light-horseman, explaining the news to an old pensioner who was with General Elliot during the bombardment of 21 months and 21 days, at the memorable siege of Gibraltar; and behind the black's head, is that of a soldier who served with the old Marquis of Granby.

Farther to the right is a corporal of the Oxford Blues, who was at the Battle of Vittoria; and at his feet is a black dog, known to the officers and men by the name of 'Old Duke', who followed that regiment all over the Peninsula.[33]

This description mentions only a minority of the actors in Wilkie's celebrated composition; a host of contemporary newspaper accounts surveyed its contents at far greater length. But more clearly than any of these other reports, the text in the catalogue – which viewers presumably held in their hands as they stood in front of the painting itself – indicates how the *Chelsea Pensioners* was looked at, and why that process must have taken so long. On a canvas just over five feet wide, we encounter approximately fifty figures, as well as a host of significant architectural features and other accessories, all delineated with an astonishing degree of precision. There are uniforms aplenty, but no two are precisely identical; and amongst the plethora of minutiae one can even make out the heading of 'The London Gazette Extraordinary' on the newspaper that has captured the attention of the assembled multitude.

The picture's original viewers, too, were positioned as the readers of a record of a great historic event; but whereas it is possible for many people to hear one news report simultaneously, there was so much to be examined in the *Chelsea Pensioners* that it ended up by virtually disappearing behind the seething crowds of curious spectators. One reviewer lamented that 'The occupation of stations by the hour in front of favourite pieces, is hardly fair in an Exhibition crowded by visitors; and especially when ladies get their poke-bonnets within the frames, the pictures are endangered and all vista shut out'.[34] Soon the organizers felt forced to intervene: 'Wilkie's picture is so much admired', the *European Magazine* reported shortly after the opening, 'that it is difficult to approach it; and the Academy has been compelled to put a bar before it, to prevent its admirers from touching it'.[35] Significantly, there was a recent precedent for this action: a year earlier the British Institution had placed a barrier in front of John Martin's *Belshazzar's Feast* (private collection), a biblical blockbuster which most serious judges regarded as a piece of meretricious showmanship; the reminiscence could hardly have pleased Wilkie or his patron, the Duke of Wellington. One wonders exactly how they felt about the extraordinary popularity of the *Chelsea Pensioners*. Within the painted scene, in the words of one reviewer, 'taste and chastity' reigned; here the artist had 'pick[ed] and cull[ed] . . . agreeable, not disgusting objects . . . [which were] alike pleasing to the most delicate Miss, the most fastidious Gentleman, and humble boor'.[36] In the space in front of the picture, however, an unseemly chaos ruled: people stood, refusing to move on, they jostled one another and the canvas, while social distinctions suffered together with the dignity of art itself. No wonder that the *Literary Gazette* made the tongue-in-cheek suggestion that 'on future occasions the pictures of Wilkie may be hung near the ground, [so] there will then be a chance of seeing them; and let the first rank kneel, the second stoop, and the third will only have to cast their eyes down'.[37] Just seven years after the Battle of Waterloo, this image would have conjured up memories of the serried front lines of Wellington's infantry, the soldiers positioning themselves one behind the other on three different levels, in order to maximize the impact of their guns.[38] By implication the Great Room had itself become a battlefield, a chaotic struggle for visibility in need of discipline and rule. But since 'rank' meant not only 'row' but 'class', a second joke may also have been intended here, bringing to mind a ludicrous scenario wherein the topmost levels of the social hierarchy (the people of 'the first rank') would switch places with the lowest, in pursuit of the best vantage-point from which to look at Wilkie's work; the only way of restoring hierarchical order, it seems, was to start by turning the world upside down. Notwithstanding the flippancy of this recommendation, it pointed to a real problem which had been brewing in Somerset House ever since the appearance of the *Village Politicians*.

This problem came down to one of distinction, or rather the lack thereof, between the different strata of the exhibition public. The appearance in public of a new form of modern genre painting that successfully elicited intensive scrutiny from a large and heterogeneous art audience created a situation that was fraught with potential for unhappiness. From the standpoint of the connoisseurs – and perhaps from the artist's, too – Wilkie's works required a privileged form of spectatorship that could properly be exercised only in private, and by a select few, away from the throngs of crass 'Papas' and 'Mamas' who admired pictures for utterly the wrong reasons, and who did not know how to stand back so that their superiors could see. An elite could not behave as such when submerged within the crowd. Nor was the situation much better for most ordinary middle-class exhibition-goers. Not only was it enormously difficult for them even to approach the works they most wanted to see, but the closer they got the harder it became to escape from other people like themselves. As a result, instead of enjoying a pleasurable opportunity to 'textualize' the low Other, they became forcibly entangled in the physical, irrational and disorderly aspects of their own class identity – in characteristics that they urgently wished to displace on to the vulgar subjects of genre painting itself. While Wilkie's art may have been designed to encourage the most refined form of aesthetic appreciation, within the increasingly crowded confines of the public exhibition it had come to engender precisely the opposite, a collective reaction uncomfortably reminiscent of the disorderly rituals of carnival. No wonder that the Academy sought to remedy this situation by placing a barrier between its visitors and the *Chelsea Pensioners*. And no wonder, too, that the 'success' of this picture was not something that Wilkie, or indeed any other Academician of his generation, would ever try to repeat.

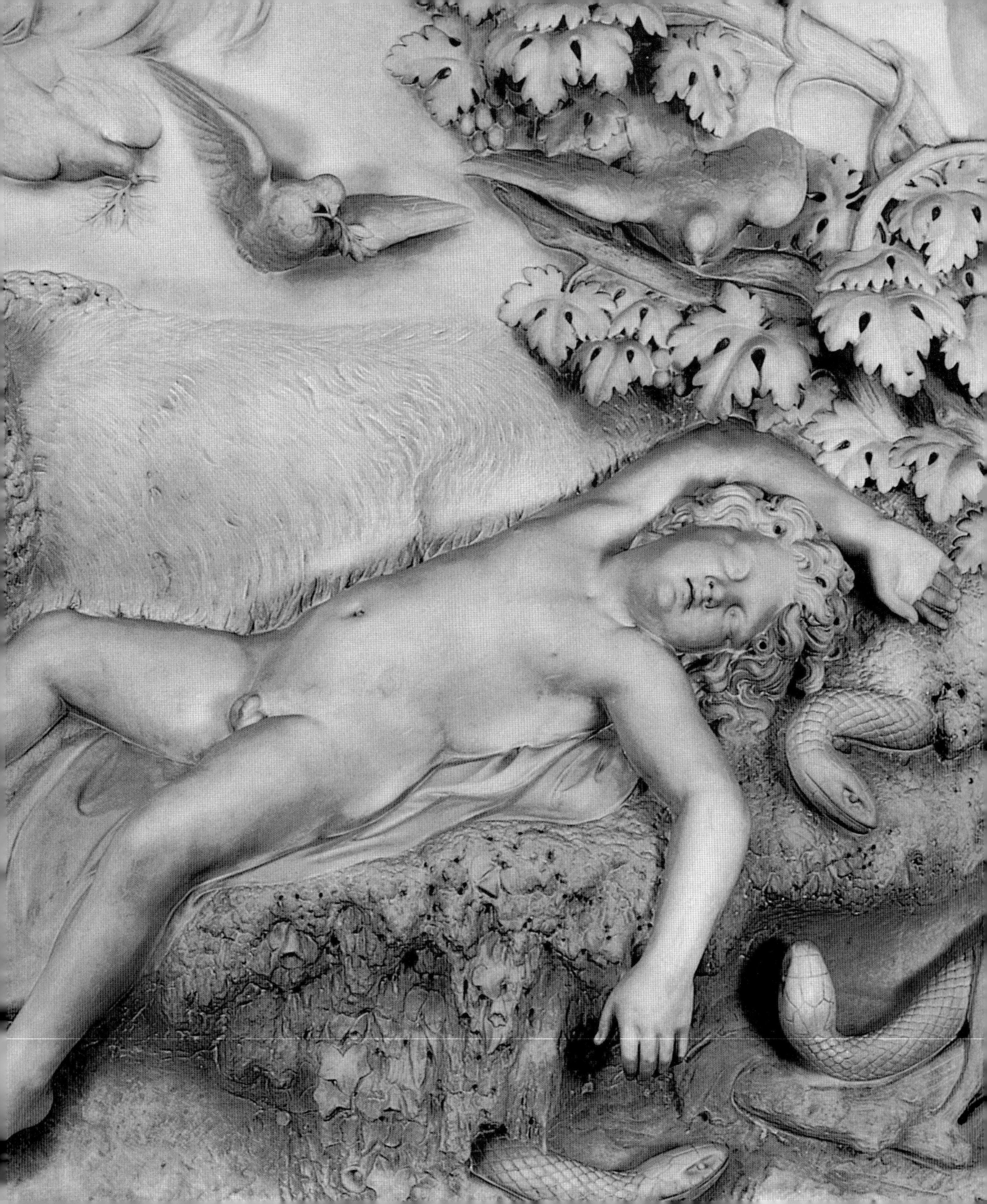

12

Art in the Dark: Viewing and Exhibiting Sculpture at Somerset House

ALISON YARRINGTON

> We have not visited the Sculpture; and it is not likely, that we shall see much of it in the dungeon to which it is doomed at Somerset House.
>
> *Literary Gazette, and Journal of the Belles Lettres,* no. 492 (30 April 1825), 283

ALAS, POOR SCULPTURE! Relegated to the nether regions of the Royal Academy exhibitions, sculpture suffered greatly by comparison with the sister art of painting, whose virtual monopoly of the Great Room also ensured that it received the lion's share of critical attention. Those who did venture into the 'dungeon' at Somerset House often found much to admire in the 'high' and 'distinguished' standard of the sculpture on display, and much to lament about the 'untoward darkness' that impeded its wider appreciation.[1] Such treatment seemed especially iniquitous in the decade following the end of the Napoleonic wars, when contemporary sculptors came to be acknowledged as constituting a praiseworthy national school distinguished above all by its naturalness and simplicity, as opposed to foreign deception and artifice. During this period the Royal Academy exhibitions also regularly featured major works of 'poetic' sculpture that elicited enthusiastic reviews in newspapers and magazines – though judging simply by the amount of coverage given to the different media, the public's engagement with sculpture might appear to have been almost moribund, little more than a footnote to the main text of painting. Yet even if it played second fiddle at Somerset House, sculpture had other important resources at its disposal that made it a cultural force to be reckoned with. Although painting may have been more popular (at least at the annual exhibitions), the more functional, commemorative qualities of sculpture ensured its national prestige. From 1795 until Waterloo and its immediate aftermath, moreover, it received more state funding than any other art, bringing it into sharp focus in the public arena.[2] Additionally, partly due to the acquisition of ancient sculpture for national collections, and in particular the purchase of the Elgin Marbles, a flourishing debate took place about the sculptural canon, particularly during the second decade of the nineteenth century. These various developments ensured that sculpture's place in English society at large remained very much a live issue towards the end of the Hanoverian period, while its problematic treatment at the fashionable playground of Somerset House provoked intense and anxious scrutiny.

The changing place of sculpture at the Academy exhibitions mirrors its paradoxical status as one of the most significant and insignificant of media. In the early years of the institution it was displayed in the annual exhibitions primarily in the company of architectural drawings, emerging for the first time as a separate entity as late as 1811. At its first exhibition in 1769, there had been only six sculptures among the 136 works exhibited, with a 'medallion of the King' by John Bacon placed first in the catalogue.[3] Among the exhibitors were the three founding sculptor-members of the Academy – Joseph Wilton, Agostino Carlini and William Tyler – who all showed works on a small scale, mainly busts and

Westmacott, *The Dream of Horace.* Detail of fig. 160.

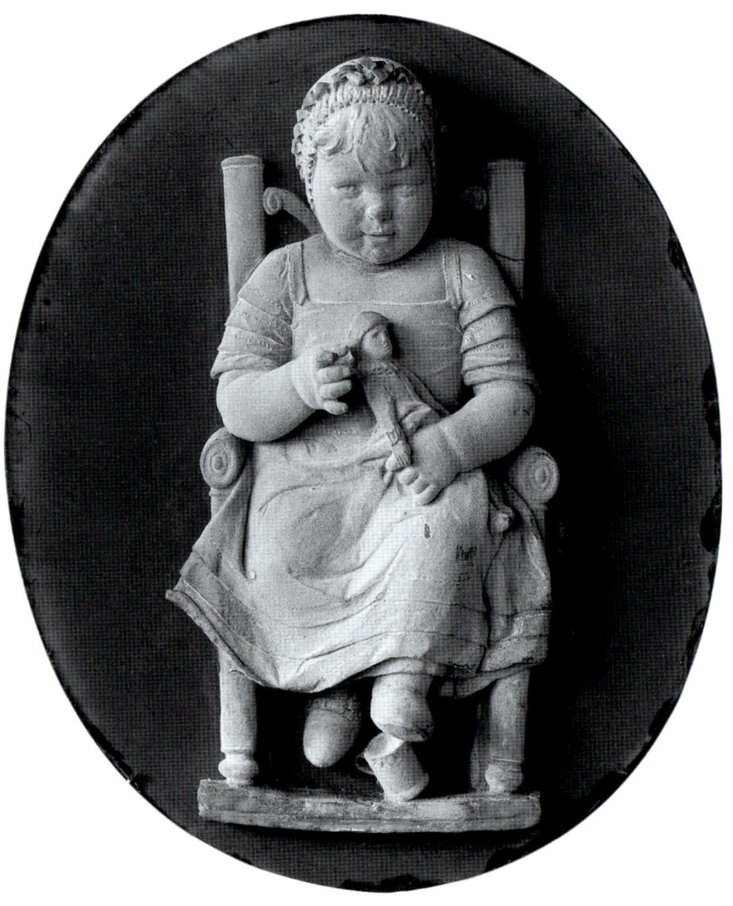

143 John Flaxman, *Figure of a Child* (possibly his sister Mary Ann), RA 1772, wax. Courtesy of the Board of Trustees of the Victoria & Albert Museum.

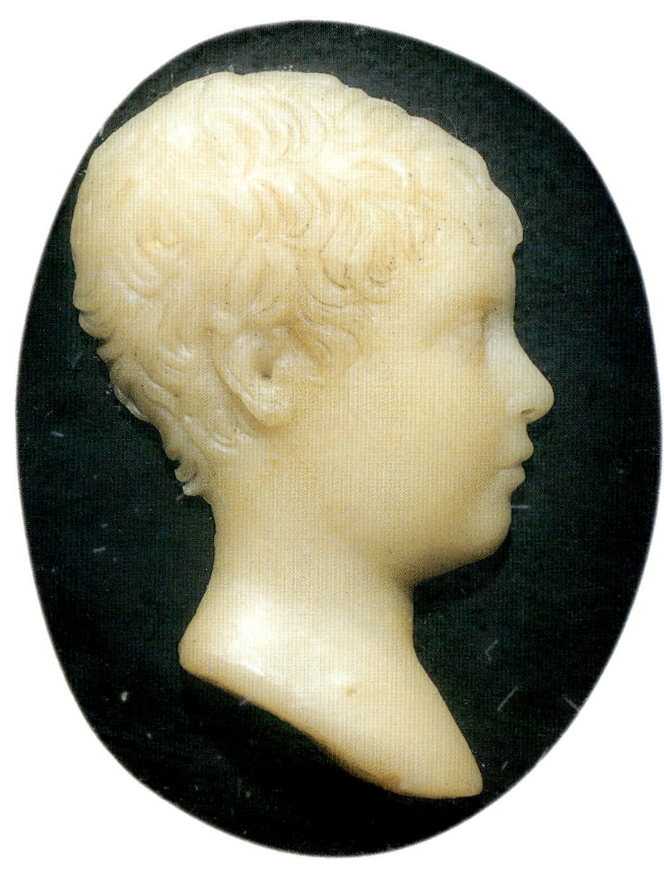

144 Catherine Andras, *Princess Charlotte*, 1801, RA 1802, wax. Courtesy of the Board of Trustees of the Victoria & Albert Museum.

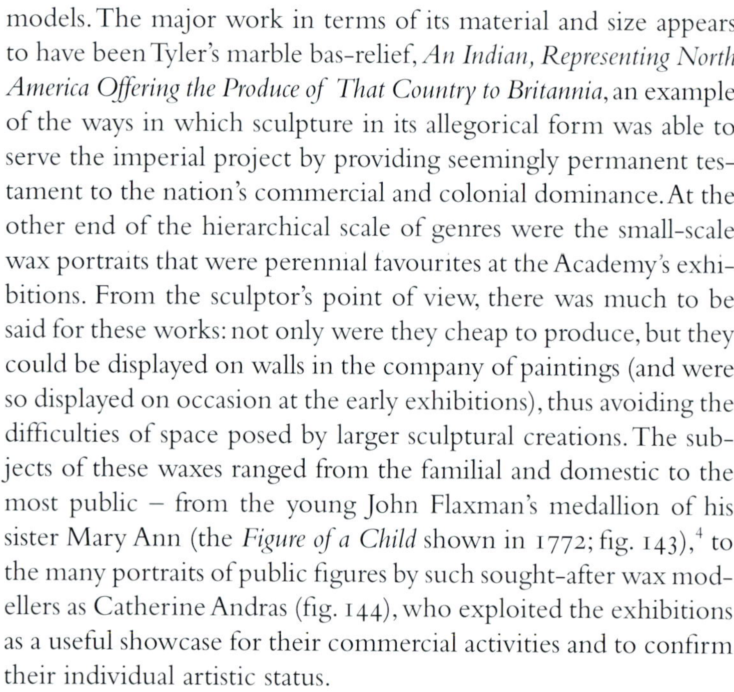

models. The major work in terms of its material and size appears to have been Tyler's marble bas-relief, *An Indian, Representing North America Offering the Produce of That Country to Britannia*, an example of the ways in which sculpture in its allegorical form was able to serve the imperial project by providing seemingly permanent testament to the nation's commercial and colonial dominance. At the other end of the hierarchical scale of genres were the small-scale wax portraits that were perennial favourites at the Academy's exhibitions. From the sculptor's point of view, there was much to be said for these works: not only were they cheap to produce, but they could be displayed on walls in the company of paintings (and were so displayed on occasion at the early exhibitions), thus avoiding the difficulties of space posed by larger sculptural creations. The subjects of these waxes ranged from the familial and domestic to the most public – from the young John Flaxman's medallion of his sister Mary Ann (the *Figure of a Child* shown in 1772; fig. 143),[4] to the many portraits of public figures by such sought-after wax modellers as Catherine Andras (fig. 144), who exploited the exhibitions as a useful showcase for their commercial activities and to confirm their individual artistic status.

In the more generous exhibition space of Somerset House the mixing in of sculpture with works in other media gradually diminished and eventually ceased, with generally beneficial results for its status and identity within a developing national school. During the early years on the Strand site sculpture did feature in the Great Room, but only in a very minor key, with small waxes, medallions and intaglios placed around the fireplace (see fig. 165). It is worth noting that coloured waxes were deemed ineligible for inclusion,[5] presumably because of their connections with the debased sculptural forms – life-size, clothed wax figures – abhorred by Reynolds and Joseph Nollekens as mere copies after nature, that were displayed in popular and highly commercial venues. However, it was not commerce itself that disqualified such works, but modes of display and representation. Sculptors specializing in small wax medallions and busts who exhibited at the Royal Academy, such as James Tassie and Alexander Mackenzie, certainly ran commercial enterprises but their works could nevertheless be accommodated within the decorous mode of portraiture. It was the 'other' vulgarizing exhibitions staged by sculptors such as Mrs Salmon, Patience Wright and Madame Tussaud that were considered to be beyond the pale of art.

Apart from restrictions arising from the classification of sculpture as art or popular entertainment there were other very practical problems that precluded larger, more ambitious, works from being displayed in the heart of the exhibition in the Great Room. These arose from the physical limitations and internal geography of Somerset House; it was simply too difficult and dangerous to carry large, heavy objects up (and down) the Chambers staircase and to place them on an upper floor not designed to support their concentrated weight. Academicians would be aware of instances elsewhere in the capital of the structural damage that could result from the interior location of large-scale sculptures. Francis Chantrey, for instance, by the end of the second decade of the nineteenth century a stalwart of the Royal Academy, could cite personal instances of having to deal with such matters. In 1827 Harriet Lady Coutts had to pay Chantrey to employ carpenters to strengthen the stair of her house at 1 Stratton Street, Piccadilly, so that his marble statue of her late husband could be placed in the dining room.[6] A few years later in 1832 the sculptor was obliged to repair structural damage to Westminster Abbey when, during its installation in St Paul's Chapel, the weight of his statue of James Watt caused the arch of the vault beneath the chapel's threshold to give way.[7] To cater for such potentially catastrophic events at Somerset House on a regular basis and on a far greater scale was simply not practical.

Another possible reason for the absence of sculpture from the perennially overcrowded Great Room is the simple fact that painters dominated the Royal Academy at every level of its activities and on a proportional basis would necessarily be allocated the greatest share of the exhibition space.[8] It could be argued that such dominance in this elite cultural arena was potentially damaging to sculpture's national prestige; its secondary role to the more glamorous art of painting apparently confirmed by its exclusion from the primary exhibition galleries. Had the Academicians wanted to proclaim sculpture's importance it would surely have been possible to include some busts and small-scale models for major works in the upper rooms, but there is no evidence that this was ever petitioned for by the sculptors themselves. Indeed, it is arguable that sculptors may have preferred their work to be viewed separately from their sister art rather than being overshadowed by it amidst the gaudy display of the Great Room, however prestigious the location.

Whatever the reasons, the fact remains that at Somerset House sculpture in its various elite forms was displayed in the dark confines of the Life (or Model) Academy on the ground floor, which most exhibition-goers visited last on their grand tour (if at all) and immediately after encountering the sometimes dubious miscellanea found in the 'Artist's Purgatory' of the Antique Academy.[9] As was the case with the paintings upstairs, the vast majority of the exhibited sculptures were portraits (usually busts); but examples of major public sculptures as well as allegorical and ideal subjects – often termed 'poetic' – were also on display. Poetic sculptures were increasingly seen as far more significant indicators of the current status of the art – evidence that, again as with painting, spoke of the emergence of a national school with its own particular brand of Englishness.[10] Whilst the demand for portraiture and church monuments continued to be the economic mainstay of sculptors' studios in Britain, the production of prestigious and expensive 'gallery' pieces, usually based on subjects from the classical past,[11] was vital if practitioners were to compete on the international stage, where the spotlight was centred firmly upon Italy's thriving sculpture market. In England the single most crucial exhibition venue for sculpture was the Royal Academy in that it bestowed, if only by inference, its stamp of approval upon selected works. Sculpture's emergence – quite literally – from the shadows of insularity demanded clever footwork and executive bravura in order to attract attention, but first and foremost it required access to a large audience – a requirement that the Academy was best equipped to fulfil. As *Blackwood's Edinburgh Magazine* pointed out in 1823, the Somerset House exhibition provided competition and publicity; opportunities for purchase, criticism and the comparison of styles; and, or at least so it was hoped, 'an assurance of a fair trial of merits'. But most importantly it had 'the immediate power of attracting the public eye'.[12]

The location of sculptures at Somerset House worked against these notions of 'fair trial' and 'immediate power' of attraction. Initially housed together where they remained until 1811, architectural drawings and sculpture were disadvantaged until this date by their mean and gloomy accommodation, a sign to the undiscerning visitor of their apparent common institutional subservience to painting. The setting inevitably hindered efforts to gain public attention no matter how virtuoso the performance of any individual work; sculpture danced in the wings while painting gave the performance on stage. Another frustration arising from sculpture's physical location was that most reviewers, until the mid-1810s at least, tended to write their commentaries in the sequence in which the exhibition was visited. With the Great Room dominating this artistic pilgrimage and the Life Academy coming last, sometimes there was simply not enough space remaining to review sculpture; and even though relatively few works were on view in any given show, the column space devoted to individual works, particularly prior to 1811, was usually quite meagre.[13] On occasion, however, the juxtaposition of architecture with sculpture could work to mutual advantage, particularly when architectural projects made provision for a high sculptural content as part of designs for grandiose public schemes. Among the most talked about of these were the various monuments envisioned in the period from 1799 to 1803 to commemorate British and allied victories in the war with France. For example the Duke of Clarence's proposed pillar of naval celebration received extensive publicity in 1799, inspiring the production of several utopian (and impractical) grandiose designs that attracted considerable interest at Somerset House (e.g., fig. 145). Later, after the victories of 1814 and 1815, there were several proposals for monuments and palaces for the Duke of Wellington where sculpture formed an important part of the symbolic decoration. In such cases sculptors and architects could demonstrate that they possessed the talents to create works of

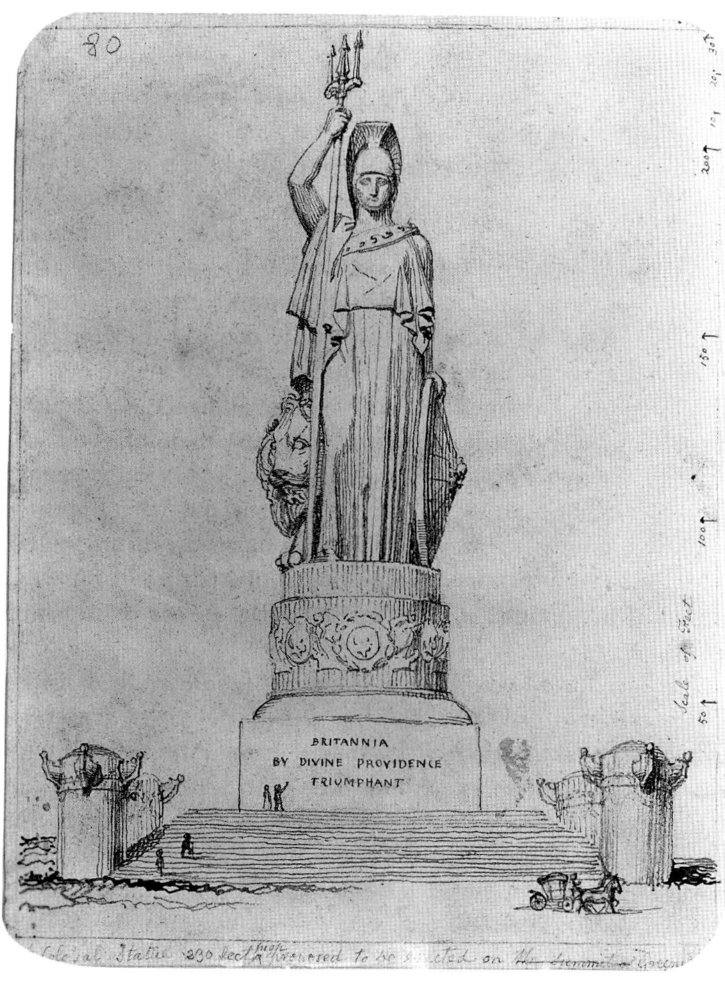

145 John Flaxman, *A Sketch for a Colossal Statue of Britannia Triumphant, Proposed to be Erected upon Greenwich Hill*, 1799, RA 1801, pencil, pen and ink. Courtesy of the Board of Trustees of the Victoria & Albert Museum.

great ambition, sometimes tending to one composite goal, even if the possibility of these ever being executed was decidedly remote.

Despite these occasional moments of symbiosis, British sculptors and architects must have breathed a collective sigh of relief in 1811, when their respective productions were finally allocated spaces of their own; at the RA this event marked a significant elevation of the prestige of sculpture, even if it remained very much in the numerical minority and in its established position at the tail end of the exhibition trail. The pressures for such a rise in status had been building for some time. A year earlier, in the spring of 1810, John Flaxman had been appointed the Academy's first Professor of Sculpture.[14] As he acknowledged in his inaugural lecture, this comparatively late development in the institution's history had come about largely as a result of the 'increasing taste of the country' for the art, and more specifically because of sculpture's popularity as a means of celebrating 'British heroes and patriots'.[15] At the exhibition that followed Flaxman's promotion and at the moment when sculpture at last appeared to be receiving equal recognition within the institution, J. C. F. Rossi was the sole sculptor represented on the Committee of Arrangement. Flaxman's contributions to what was effectively his inaugural exhibition were from commemorative monuments that were characteristic of his particular brand of restrained simplicity: the monument to Josiah Webbe (fig. 146),[16] an important East Indian commission, along with his bas-relief *Instruct the Ignorant* (fig. 147) – works that prompted Robert Hunt, one of the most perceptive and enthusiastic reviewers of sculpture, to claim in the *Examiner* that they 'might be contemplated with pleasure by Peidias [i.e., Phidias] himself'.[17] But although there were other examples of commemorative and poetic subjects, notably by Richard Westmacott, the majority of works on display were inevitably busts.[18] These attracted most of the somewhat scant critical attention then given to sculpture in the reviews, with Flaxman and Nollekens being singled out for praise.[19]

Flaxman's professorship was confirmed at the time when discussions were taking place at the Academy concerning the improvement of its exhibition rooms. These centred upon the lighting of the Great Room and the creation of more exhibition space in the upper storey, not the problematic viewing space of the Life Academy. With the conversion of the Secretary's room into 'an additional Exhibition Room' next to the Great Room, for the first time architectural drawing and sculpture each gained its own exhibition forum. This move had been proposed jointly to the Council by an architect and a sculptor, John Soane and Nollekens, suggesting that they represented the views of their two professions in seeing it as mutually advantageous. Approval of this significant change came too late in the year to have much if any effect on the selection of objects for the 1811 exhibition, and only five more works of sculpture than the previous year were included.[20] The dominance of portrait sculpture remained intact; indeed the removal of the drawings from the walls would allow for further shelving for the display of more busts and small models in the future. None the less, for the first time in its history, sculpture could be seen as a separate – if minority – category within the Royal Academy, a development that heralded its gathering strength. The *Examiner*'s Robert Hunt felt sufficiently emboldened by this and other exhibitions held in London to claim that both sculpture and painting were 'rising from the state of torpor to which for many years past they were reduced'.[21]

By 1813 the 'new and better arrangement' of pieces in the sculpture section was noted, but the press reports give no specific indication as to why this was the case.[22] One discernible change was the unprecedented pre-eminence given to so-called poetic subjects. If the visitor to that year's sculpture section followed the sequence given in the catalogue the first work that he or she would encounter to introduce the display was a life-size mythological subject, rather than a representative of the more popular categories of bust and church monument. William Theed's seated figure of Mercury (now lost) 'as large as life'[23]

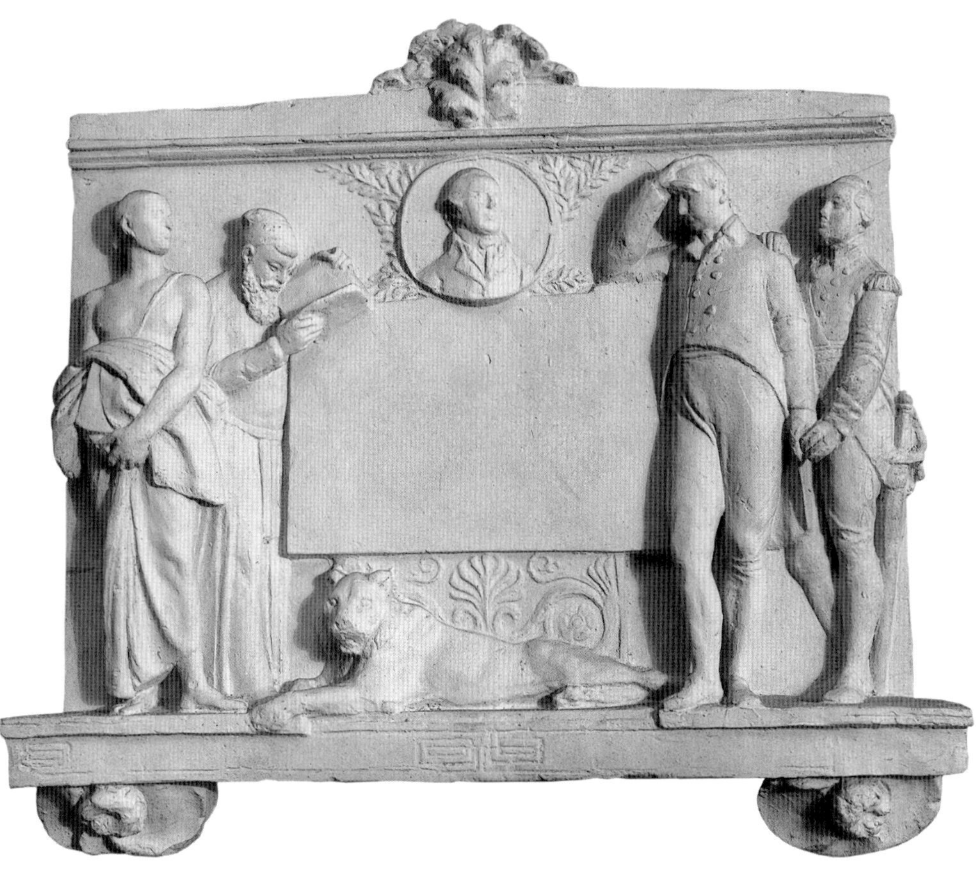

146 John Flaxman, model for a monument to the late Josiah Webbe, Esq., RA 1810, plaster. College Art Collections, University College, London.

147 John Flaxman, *Instruct the Ignorant*, monument to Abraham Balme, RA 1810, marble. Cathedral Church of St Peter, Bradford.

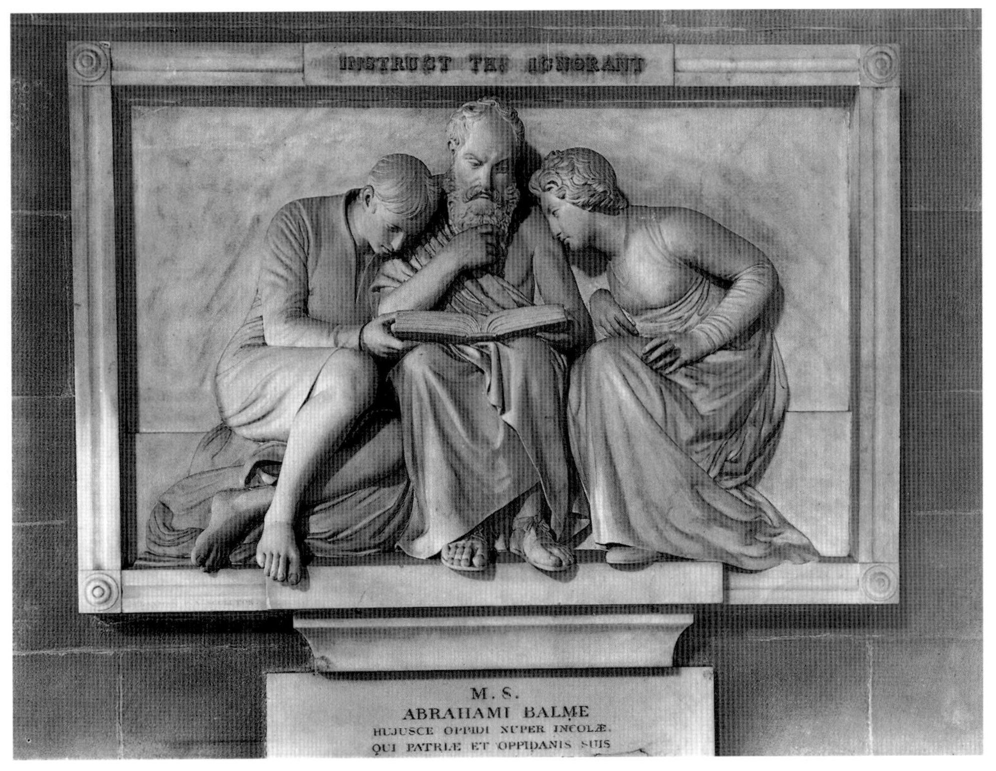

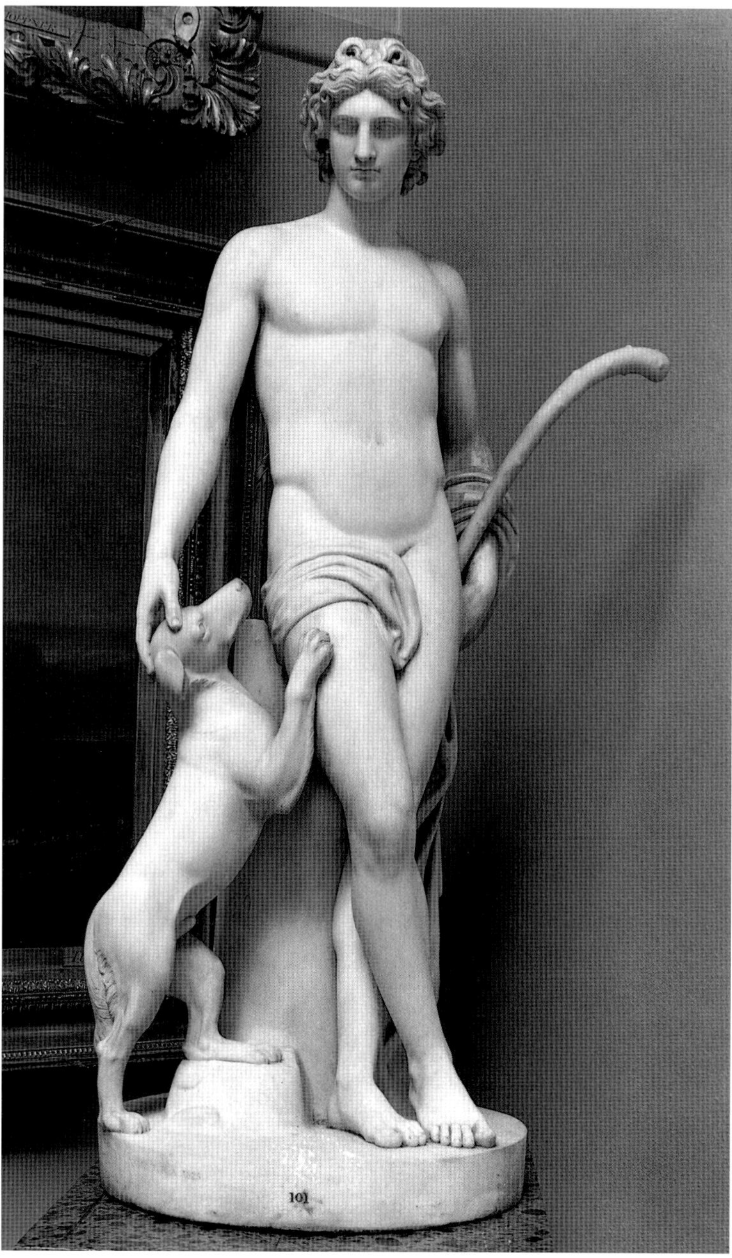

148 John Flaxman, *Pastoral Apollo*, RA 1824, marble. Petworth House, The Egremont Collection (The National Trust).

signalled the serious ambition of sculpture at the Royal Academy, as much as each year the use of quotation on the title page of the exhibition catalogue formed an epigraph to the entire theatre of display. This elevated tone was to continue, notably in the following year when Flaxman's model for the Petworth *Apollo* (fig. 148) took on this role, in effect welcoming viewers to the room and presiding over its contents. In 1813, amidst the usual plethora of portrait busts,[24] seven works stood out in this most elevated category, of subjects from classical mythology, the final number of the catalogue being Humphrey Hopper's *Bacchante*.[25] If we take the catalogue order as reflecting the actual arrangement of sculpture (and there is little other documentary evidence of this, or any as to the actual appearance of the room), visitors encountered busts on the shelves around the room interspersed with the occasional small model, church monuments and their offshoots in small groups featuring both private and public commissions. This latter category included both Westmacott's relief of the *Progress of Navigation* (fig. 149) for the government memorial to Admiral Collingwood, destined for St Paul's Cathedral, and his marble high relief of a young woman about to cut some corn that formed part of a church monument to a Leicestershire gentleman.[26] To one commentator, the sculpture placed in the Life Academy gave 'proofs of rapid progress', and raised the expectation that 'Britannia will have one day to boast of as much glory as Athens and Rome'.[27] Indeed the comparatively large number of major poetic sculptures within a space devoted entirely to that art must have encouraged the idea that nationally sculpture's fortunes were in the ascendant.

Hunt was, unusually among critics at this date, prepared to give generous space to sculpture in his reviews for the *Examiner*. It is through his commentary that we may gain insight into the ways in which sculpture was encountered within the Royal Academy exhibition, though he wrote from a particular reformist stance opposed to the excesses of a fashionable elite. In his commentary on the 1816 exhibition he argues that, as part of the round of fashionable entertainment of the polite classes, viewing sculpture has less to do with educated understanding than with the pursuit of false pleasures:

> To the many, placid, unobtrusive, unornamented Statuary, has no more charms than plain bread and meat to the vitiated palate of the gourmond [*sic*] or epicure, or than the entertainment of mind to mere lovers of the bottle and of cards, or nature-dressed fields and open day-light of heaven to the daily driver up and down Bond-street, and the incessant visitor to candle-light assemblies. After looking therefore, at dazzling masses of colour, it is impossible they can endure the grey and grave aspect of sculpture.[28]

Such viewers were, in Hunt's eyes, like children, 'best pleased with what is gaudy'; unable to resist the temptation of too many rich treats, they were incapable of appreciating sculpture's positive contribution as a wholesome last course to a balanced and healthy visual diet. The critic proposed to overcome consumer resistance simply by reversing the order in which the exhibition was viewed, so that visitors confronted sculpture 'before their eyes [were] debauched by that gay wanton of fancy – colour!' Hunt himself had already tried to encourage something like this idea in his reviews of the previous year; here instead of saving sculpture for the end of his discussion, in the position corresponding to its appearance at the end of the exhibition, he gave it a more central role, after his consideration of poetical and historical paintings but before landscape and portraiture. Clearly what Hunt had in mind was to rescue contemporary sculpture from its marginal position in British art-critical discourse, and to restore it to the elevated place he felt it justly deserved, placing

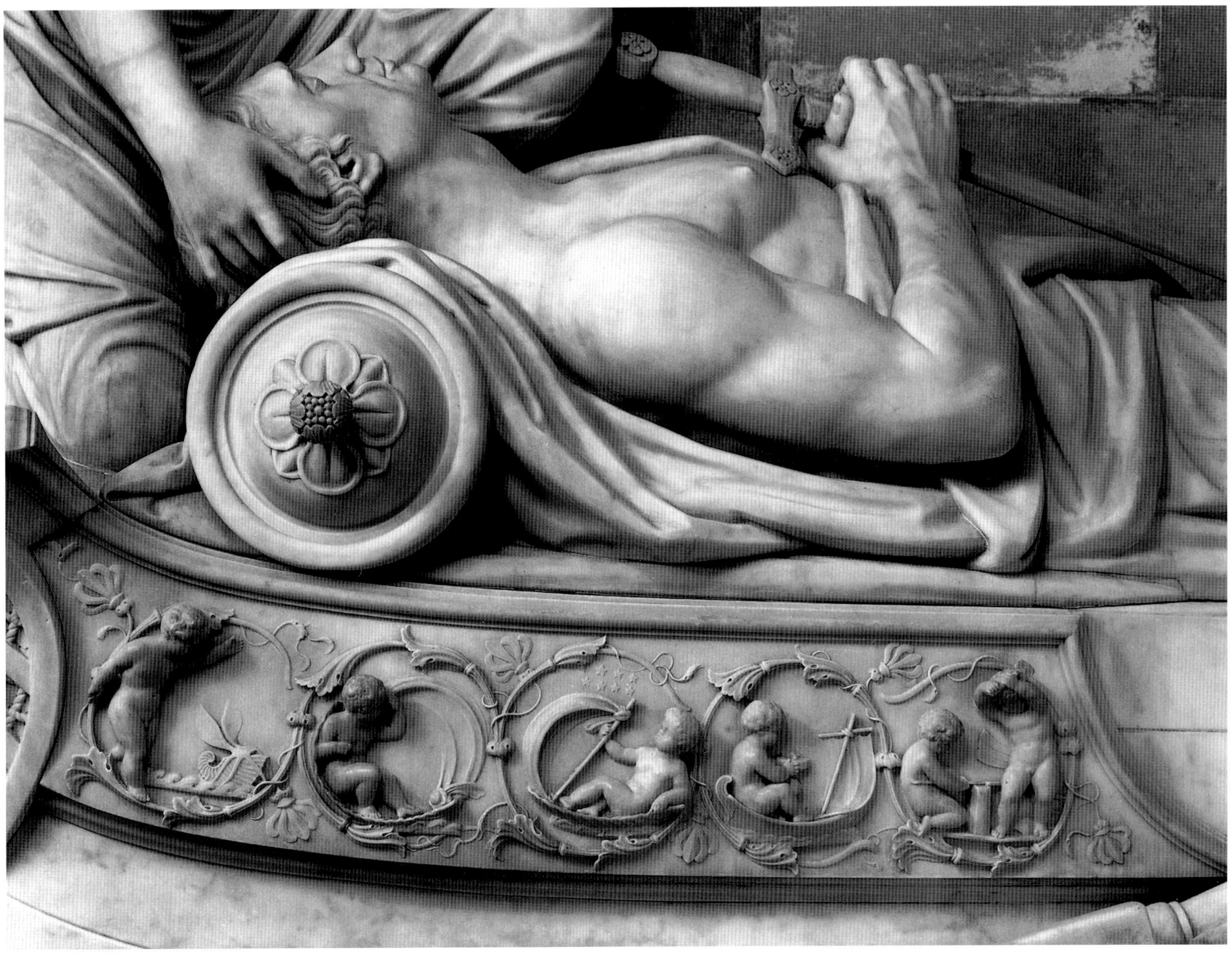

149 Richard Westmacott, *The Progress of Navigation*, relief on the monument to Lord Collingwood, RA 1813, marble. St Paul's Cathedral, London. The relief was displayed on its own, and the monument completed four years later.

it centre stage rather than as a postscript or 'afterpiece' to painting.[29] However, he had to contend with the fact that at the Royal Academy exhibition, unlike in St Paul's or in the private collections such as those being amassed by Thomas Hope, Richard Payne Knight, the 6th Duke of Devonshire and the Earl of Egremont, sculpture was viewed at a disadvantage, at the last point on an exhausting tour by members of a public who were widely acknowledged to be little versed in the finer points of the art.

Within the 'National Temple of the Chromatic Muse'[30] sculpture could easily appear dreary to the disenchanted eye. In 1816 a French visitor (not necessarily an impartial observer) to the exhibition dismissed the sculptures, 'in a little room on the ground floor', as 'few in number, and for the most part utterly mediocre in execution',[31] suggesting that whatever ground sculpture may have made nationally it was still undistinguished internationally. For some, however, sculpture's position at the end of the exhibition was an advantage:

> On a sultry day, the coolness of this room is as refreshing as a glass of ice-cream: – it is like a bath at the end of a journey, on a dusty road. After we have been dazzled by the glare and contrast of colours, and wearied by the pressure of the throng of gazers in the upper rooms, we are instantly relieved on entering the appartment appropriated to Sculpture, by its comparative solitude, and by the chaste simplicity of the works which are there assembled . . . we feel as if, after having run a long career of pleasure and dissipation, we had towards the close of life, withdrawn from the gay illusions of society.[32]

How would the visitor encounter the sculptures arranged in

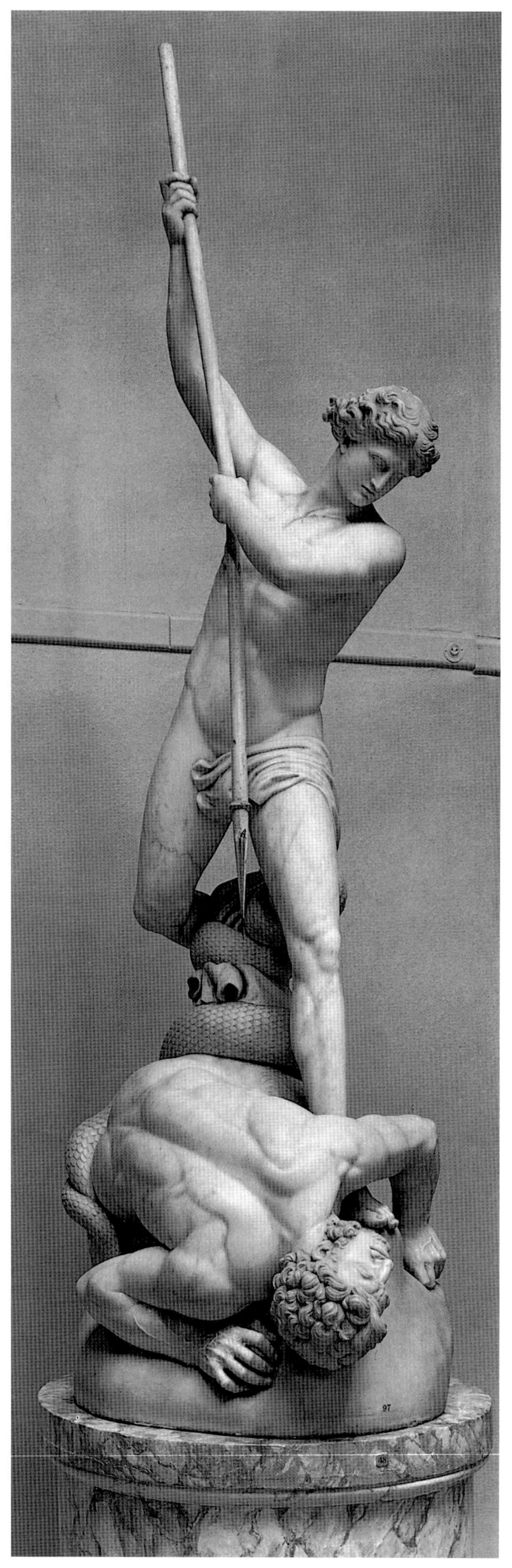

this limited space? There was a seat for the exhibition-weary, 'a little shaded niche which is so accommodatingly placed between the windows' from which the sculpture could be viewed in comfort.[33] The works were crowded together, and this in itself could make viewing difficult, with 'interference of statues with groups, and of busts ill seen'.[34] The Committee of Arrangement appears to have tried to place works to their best advantage,[35] but those on a large scale, such as Flaxman's *Satan Overcome by St. Michael* (fig. 150) designed for the lofty sculpture gallery at Petworth and forming the centrepiece of the 1822 exhibition, were almost impossible to view. As one commentator lamented, 'It is hardly possible, in this confined room, to judge of, much less do justice to, this towering group, or to the elevated grandeur of the conception'.[36] Despite the need to consider each work individually it was almost impossible to do so. At the 1825 exhibition, for instance, the *London Magazine* found something almost comic in the incongruous juxtaposition of Richard Freebairn's *Psyche* with Samuel Manning's model for a monument to John Wesley – and yet 'something grand withal, for the eye, and the mind's eye, seem to take in two systems of mythology at a single glance'.[37]

Portrait busts were the dominant genre in the sculpture section. Most, together with small-scale models, were placed on shelves running along the walls – as Ebeneezer Rhodes commented, 'on the shelf' was 'an emphatic expression, denoting beyond the reach of the eye';[38] and certainly individual works could easily be overlooked. Sculptors, like painters, had to try and make their works catch the eye, either by having the support of a member of the Committee, as with Nollekens's support for Chantrey at the 1811 exhibition when he placed the sculptor's bust of Horne Tooke (fig. 151) in a prominent position; or by ensuring that the quality made it shine out – hence Peter Turnerelli's disappointment in 1820, when the Council would not allow him to replace one of his plaster busts with the belatedly finished marble version.[39] Why such an arrangement was preferred over the use of pedestals is not difficult to grasp: for not only did this allow the Committee to maximize the number of sculptures in the exhibition, it also ensured the safety of pieces that were often both costly and vulnerable. Moreover it left more space free in the centre of the room for the display of larger sculpted productions.[40] Yet even if the validity of these functional considerations was generally conceded, the utilization of a shelf densely packed with works was felt to downgrade their status, and to impede proper viewing: 'Busts intended for a nich [*sic*], or pedestal, to stand alone, and, in the dignity of their worth and the estimation of their character, shed a lustre on surrounding objects, are here huddled together, placed on shelves as in a

150 John Flaxman, *Satan Overcome by St Michael*, 1826, marble. Petworth House, The Egremont Collection (The National Trust). The plaster model now in the College Art Collection, University College, London was exhibited at the RA in 1822.

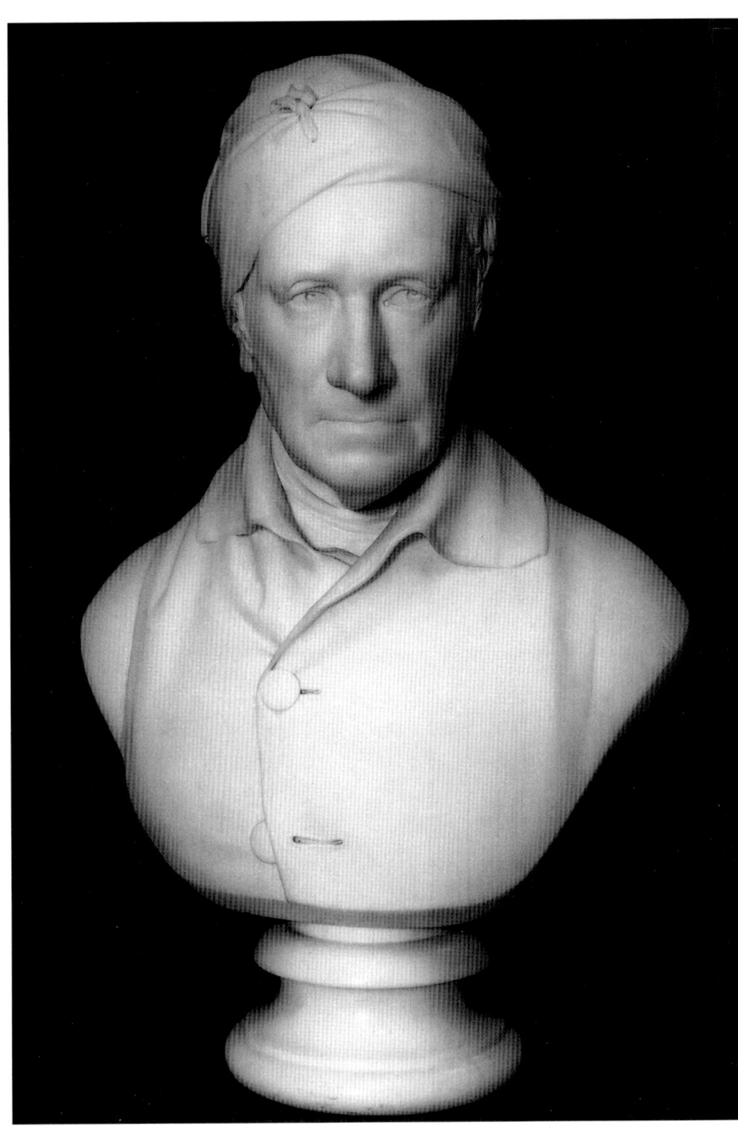

151 Francis Chantrey, *John Horne Tooke*, 1818, marble. Fitzwilliam Museum, Cambridge. The damaged plaster model (Ashmolean Museum, Oxford) was exhibited at the RA in 1811.

figure-maker's shop. [. . .] It is not with the sculpted portrait as with the painted', complained one reviewer in 1822.[41] 'Were it not for their names where would be their distinction?' critics often wondered, especially when the busts of 'illustrious persons' were presented in this way.[42] Rapport with the object – the imaginative interplay of viewer and viewed – suffered greatly in such restrictive and crowded circumstances; but what were the ideal circumstances of viewing sculpture against which the annual exhibitions could be judged? And if portrait busts laboured under these difficulties, what of poetic sculpture, the highest form of the art?

By the early nineteenth century a consensus had been reached that for best effect poetic works should be displayed in a purpose-built environment, one which would allow the properly attuned viewer to become fully absorbed in an act of aesthetic contemplation. Such activity was essentially private, knowing and, above all, discriminating. When viewing such pieces it was essential that the gaze should operate with concentrated intensity, without having to contend with the distractions of other works, or with the frustrations of inadequate lighting. By contrast with the conditions on offer at Somerset House, we might cite the success achieved by Thomas Hope's Flaxman Room at Duchess Street (fig. 152), or the environment created at Woburn Abbey for Canova's *Three Graces*. The Woburn Temple of the Graces attracted a great deal of critical interest, some of which was focused on the Somerset House exhibition of 1818, where related sculptures and Wyatt's drawing of the architectural ensemble were on public view.[43] Canova's group itself was less easily accessible, even for visitors to Woburn itself – unless, of course, they were personal acquaintances of the Bedford family.[44]

The Reverend Thomas Frognall Dibdin, an English visitor to Paris in the summer of 1818, had an encounter with a sculpture by Canova in a private collection, which emphasized the significance of setting for the process of viewing. The collection of the Marquis de Sommariva in the rue du Bas Rempart – 'among the most distinguished, and the most celebrated in Paris . . . eminent for sculpture'[45] – provided the setting in which to gaze

152 After Thomas Hope, 'The Flaxman Room, Duchess Street', engraving from *Household Furniture and Interior Design executed from designs by Thomas Hope* (1807).

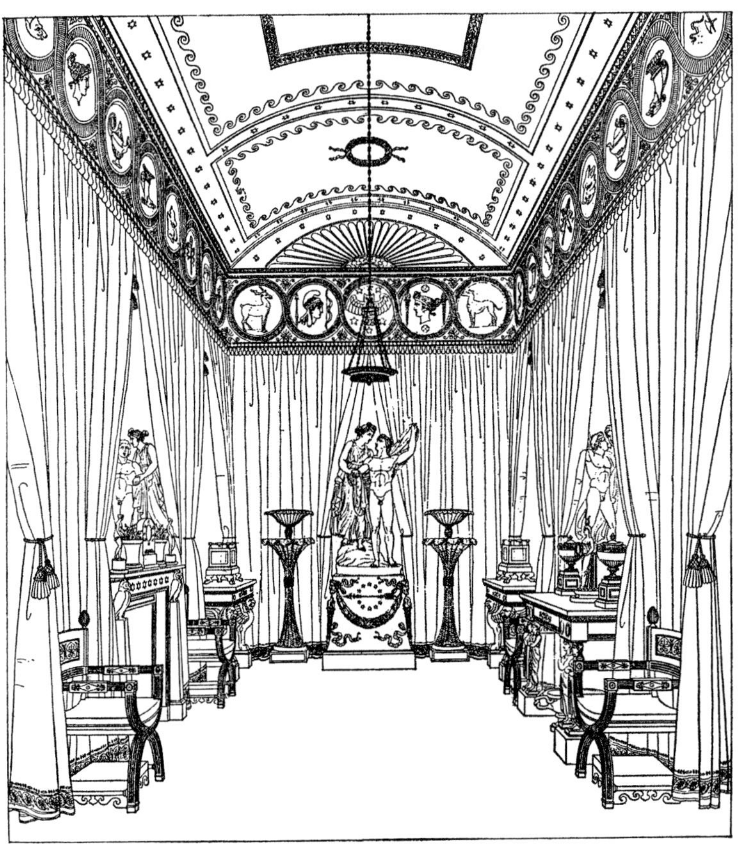

upon Canova's *Magdalene*. This was an event shrouded in pleasurable mystery for Dibdin: 'you observe a door, or aperture, half-covered with silken drapery of a greyish brown tint. There was something mysterious in the appearance, and equally so in the approach'. Most essentially this was a lone pilgrimage – 'not a creature besides myself was in the rooms' – and for five minutes he was 'lost in surprise and admiration'. His consumption of the nuanced marble surface was enhanced by its context: 'The windows are hid by white curtains; and the interior is hung all over with the same grey silk drapery [as covers the entrance]. A glass, placed behind the figure, affords you a view of the back while you are contemplating the front'. Dibdin in this 'ingenious', but probably 'too artificial', environment spent a 'full three-quarters of an hour' looking. While doubtless intending to impress his readers with his concentrated study of Canova's work, the reverend author at the same time conjured up an ideal set of viewing conditions, allowing for long and close, uninterrupted scrutiny of the desired sculptural object.[46] The situation at Somerset House could hardly have been more different.

What the Royal Academy exhibitions highlighted for many knowledgeable contemporary observers was a tension between what was understood to be an essentially closed and cultured, epicurean experience – an elite response involving the use of highly developed imaginative faculties – and a public domain where the aesthetic lay open to misinterpretation by the undiscerning majority. This issue was to raise more overt concerns later in the century, especially in the context of the various international exhibitions that were staged in Europe from 1851 onwards, and in particular in relation to the sculpted nude. But the huge open spaces of these later shows allowed sculptures to be isolated within structures that seemed to provide some protection for the object from uneducated viewing, and in turn protected the public from too close a study of the naked body. This was the case with John Gibson who at the 1862 International Exhibition in London, ordered that his *Tinted Venus* was to be placed with other works by himself and Harriet Hosmer in a temple-like exhibition stand designed by Owen Jones, thus preventing the public from having access to the works except at a considerable distance.[47] Smaller, vulnerable works could also be separated from the public by being placed in exhibition cases, such as the exquisite purpose-built case by Paul Hankar containing Charles van der Stappen's mixed media sculpture *Mysterious Sphinx* at the 1897 Tervueren Congo exhibition.

There was simply not room in the Somerset House Model Academy to allow such protective barriers to be raised, and with the works exhibited firmly under the heading 'Sculpture' there could be little opportunity for misinterpretation. There was certainly no opportunity for any committee arranging the sculptures to create the sort of sympathetic surroundings offered by certain private galleries. For sculpture in public collections, the niceties of display could be discussed and determined over a far longer period of time, as took place most famously in the case of the Elgin Marbles. On the page opposite Hunt's review of the 1816 Royal Academy exhibition, the *Examiner* carried a lengthy article on the debate then raging about how these ancient masterpieces should best be presented:[48] opinions differed as to the optimum height for their display, the best form of lighting, and on the need to place the larger pieces such as the Ilyssus and the Theseus on pedestals with castors for more effective study. And what sort of environment would set off the works to maximum advantage? According to the *Examiner*, 'The room should . . . be lined with green baize, the best colour to give value to the colour of the marble; and every pedestal should be covered with the same stuff'.[49] Although green baize was used at Somerset House as the backdrop to the paintings in the Great Room, there is no evidence that decorative embellishments of this or any other sort were ever used in the Life Academy. Much later, at the Royal Academy exhibition of 1894, baize was employed, to wrap the base of Bertram Mackennal's *Circe* – not for the purpose of enhancing the sculpture's appearance, but to protect the viewer from being corrupted by the orgy represented on the encircling relief. Contamination could sometimes be a two-way street.[50]

The arrival of the Elgin Marbles, together with the prominent role played by the artistic community in the subsequent parliamentary deliberations on their purchase, gave an enormous boost to the confidence of British sculptors, and encouraged an emerging move towards truth to nature within the ideal – a trend identified above all with the works of Baily, Chantrey, Flaxman and Westmacott. It was at the Royal Academy exhibition of 1817 that this 'school' seemed to come of age and it is no coincidence that the significance of the Elgin Marbles was highlighted on the title page of that year's catalogue with its quotation from the Select Committee report.

In that year the sculpture section at Somerset House contained seventy-one works and was noteworthy in featuring several major poetic works, including those by the Italian Antonio Canova, widely acknowledged as the greatest sculptor of the age. It was Canova's participation that made the 1817 exhibition so special for his British colleagues who had already fêted him in person during his earlier visit to England,[51] several of whom he assisted by proposing them for membership of the Accademia di San Luca in Rome. In such august company the achievements of British sculptors in the realm of poetic sculpture had an especially important part to play. Richard Westmacott, the Academician who had arguably the closest professional links with Canova, was brought in to supervise single-handedly the arrangement of the sculptures, as no sculptor was included in the Committee of Arrangement.[52]

In Britain poetic sculptures, other than the rare commissioned gallery piece, usually took the form of single figures ultimately intended for church monuments, but initially exhibited independently, under titles – such as *Resignation*[53] or *Family Affection* – clearly designed to enhance their sentimental character. In 1817 the poetic tone of the display was set by such a piece, Flaxman's *Maternal Love* (fig. 153). This was listed as the first item

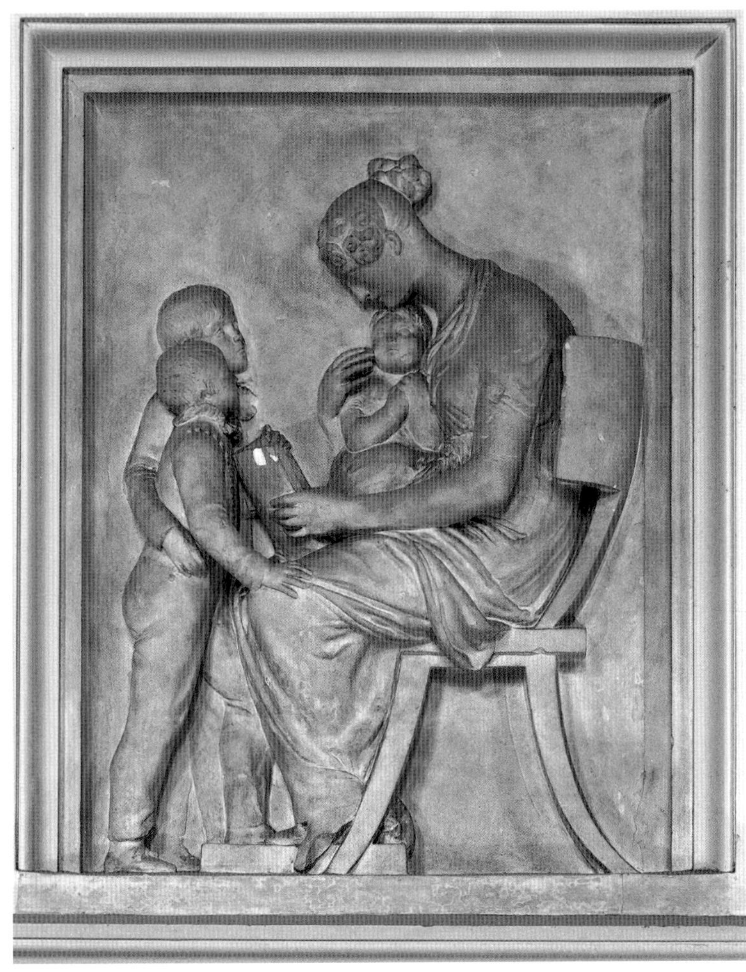

153 John Flaxman, *Maternal Love*, RA 1817, plaster. College Art Collections, University College, London.

in the sculpture section of the catalogue before Canova's *Terpsichore* and *Hebe* (fig. 154) A large group of busts and models followed on from these, presumably ranged along the ubiquitous shelves; other poetic works included Kendrick's *Prometheus Chain'd* and a statue of Flora (executed for the Earl of Darnley) by the rising star of English sculpture, Edward Hodges Baily.

As in the previous year, the Academy exhibition of 1817 featured a prominent array of sculptures dealing with the highly popular themes of war, victory and heroism. Here a number of Chantrey's studio assistants came to the fore, with David Dunbar attracting considerable interest with his interpretation of Robert Burns's *The Soldier's Return*: 'She sunk within my arms, and cried,/Art thou my ain dear Willie?'; another of Chantrey's assistants, Joseph Theakston, exhibited sketches for monuments to Major General Gillespie, General Hay, Major Generals Packenham and Gibbs and Generals Gore and Skerrett. Further models for national monuments to commemorate the victorious war dead had been put on display by Baily: *Fame Encouraging Genius, by Directing his Attention to Britannia, who is Raising a Trophy to the Memory of her Deceased Heroes*, and *Fame Embracing a Victory Supporting the Dying Hero*. Not surprisingly, there was also a bust of the Duke of Wellington, modelled by Humphrey Hopper. Also in keeping with the theme of war and its aftermath, Canova exhibited his bust of Peace.

Canova's presence at this exhibition encouraged comparisons between the acknowledged leader of international neoclassicism and the nascent English School. Given the nationalistic fervour of the period, most critics championed their fellow Britons. The work that attracted the most enthusiastic praise, from reviewers and visitors alike, was Chantrey's *Sleeping Children* (fig. 155), the

154 Antonio Canova, *Hebe*, 1808–14, RA 1817, marble. Devonshire Collection, Chatsworth.

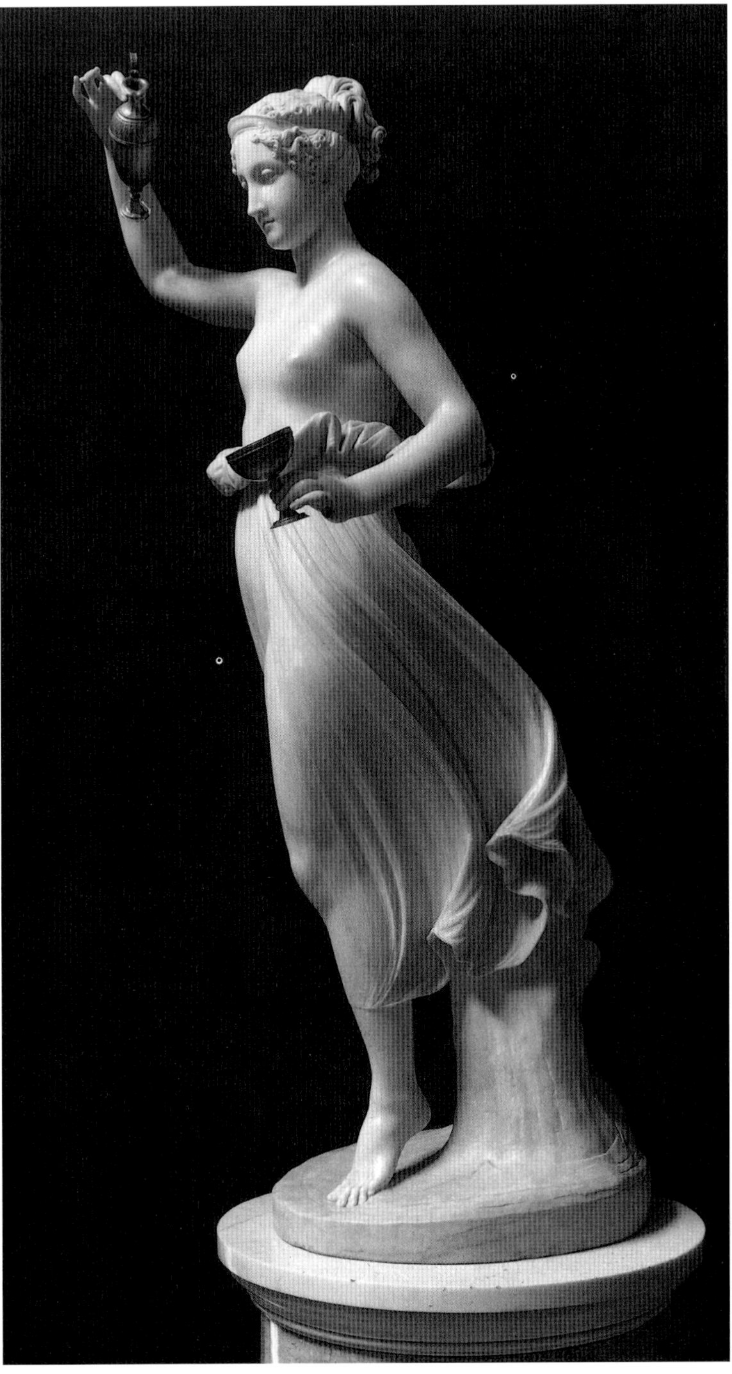

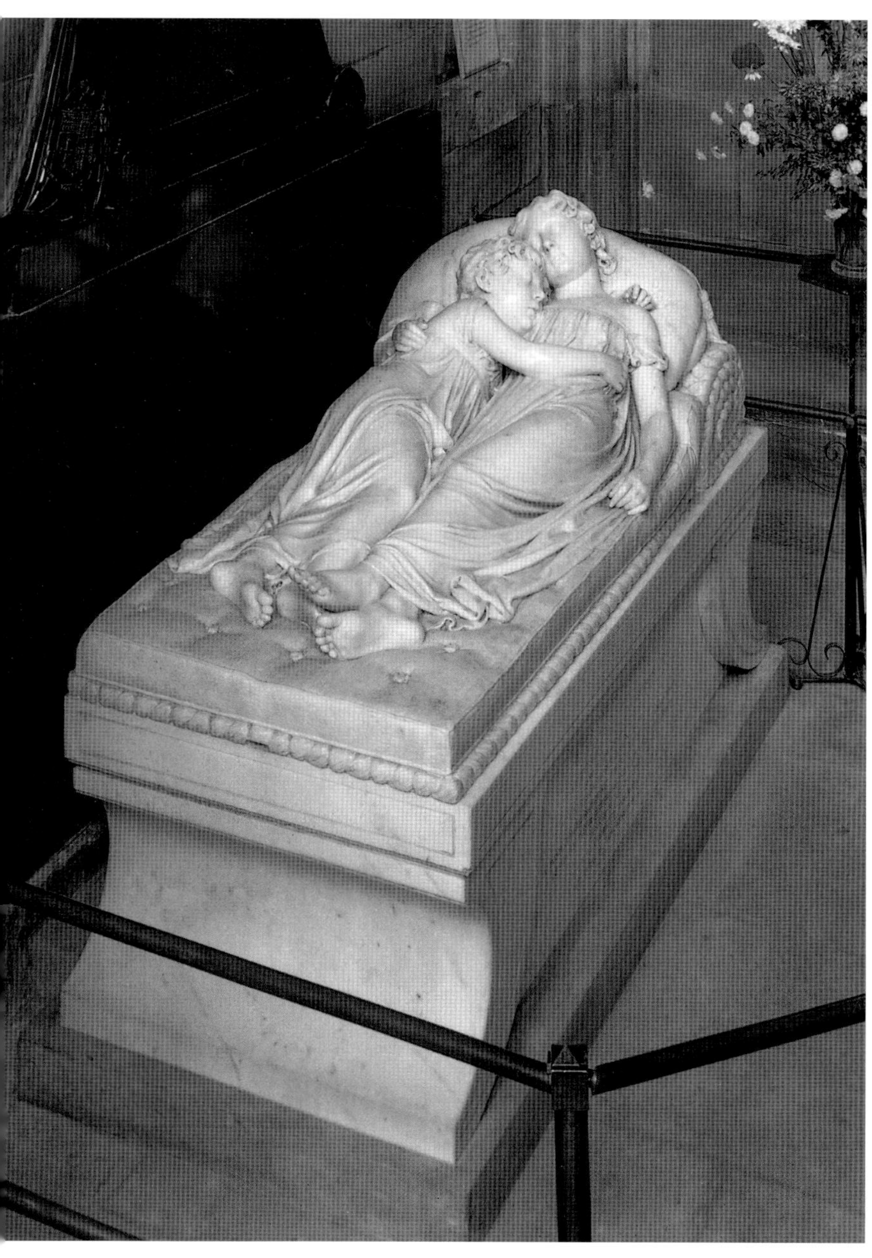

155 Francis Chantrey, *The Sleeping Children*, monument to Ellen Jane and Marianne Robinson, RA 1817, marble. Lichfield Cathedral, Staffordshire.

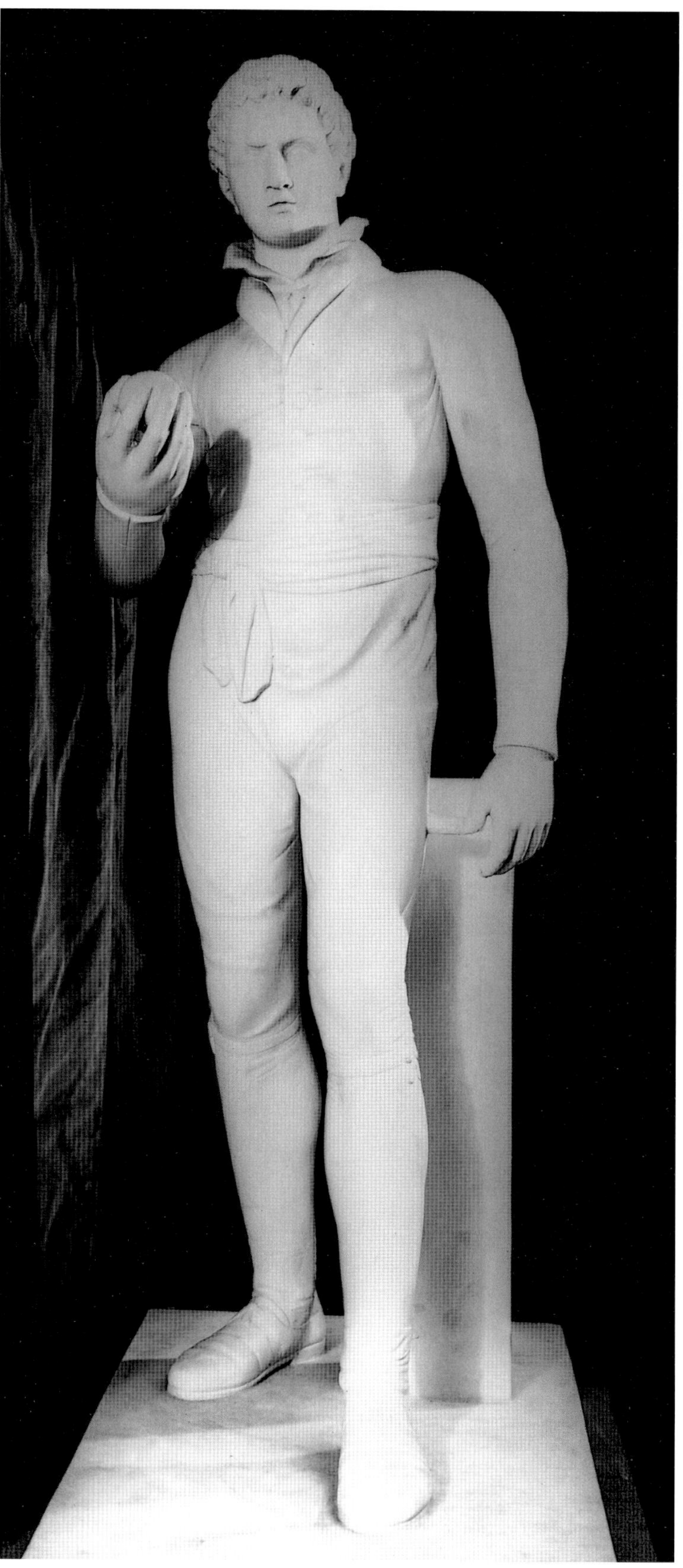

156 Henry Rossi, *Bowler*, 1825, marble. Duke of Bedford, Woburn Abbey, Bedfordshire. Rossi exhibited a model of a bowler at the RA in 1819, presumably a preliminary design for the *Model of a Statue of a Bowler to be Carved in Marble* shown in 1824.

marble monument to the Robinson children made for Lichfield Cathedral. Universally praised as the epitome of a home-grown and untainted response to nature, the *Sleeping Children* struck contemporary observers as offering an eloquent contrast to the highly acclaimed but more artificial style of Canova's works in the same exhibition.[54] In Chantrey's piece the poetic was lauded as enshrined in its most natural form, allowing the free flow of sensibility through a totally cohesive modern subject. Its effect on the exhibition audience was little short of electric, and from this point onwards Chantrey would almost cease to exhibit works based on literary sources or classical mythology; instead he followed the path begun with his *Sleeping Children*, by seeking

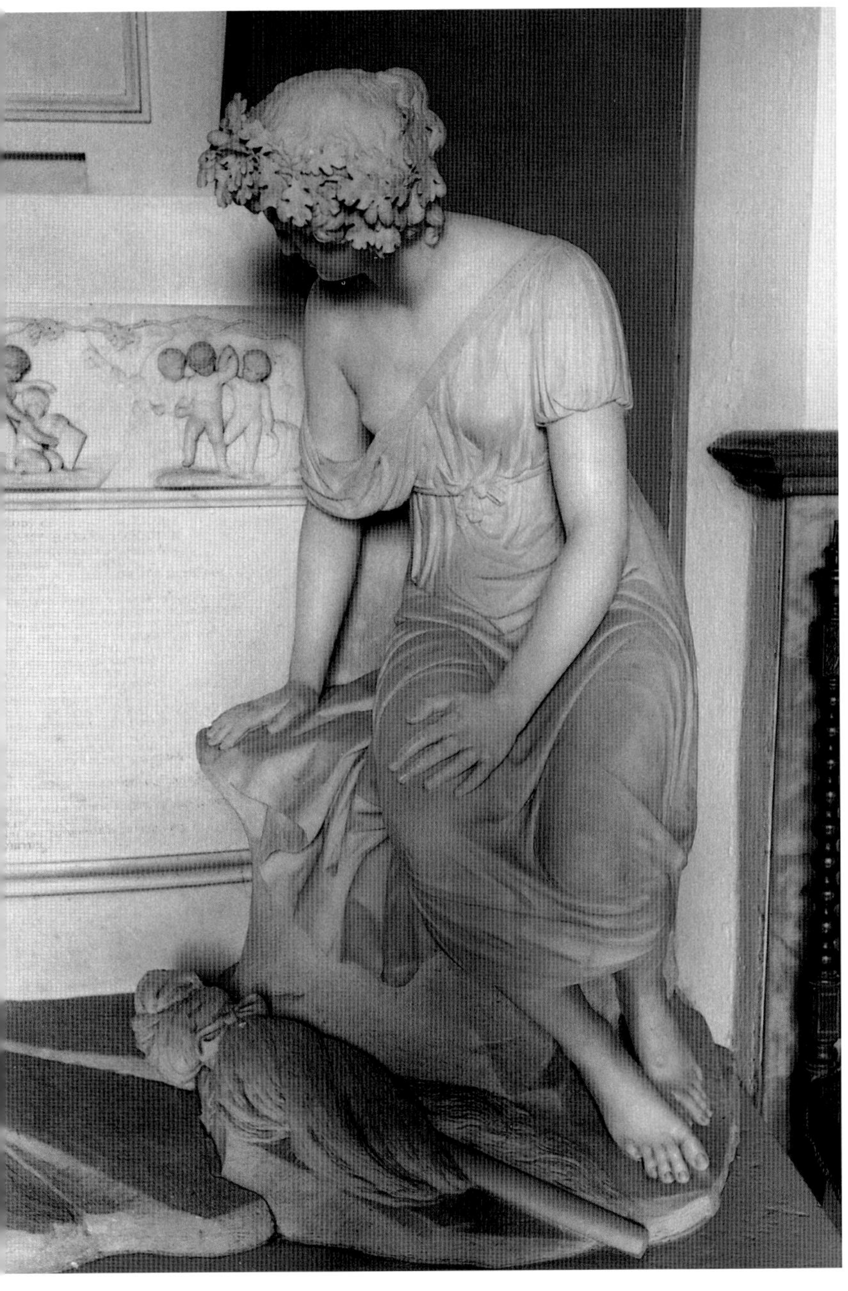

157 Richard Westmacott, *Peasant Girl*, figure from the monument to Lord and Lady Penrhyn, RA 1819, marble. St Tegai's, Llandegai, Gwynedd.

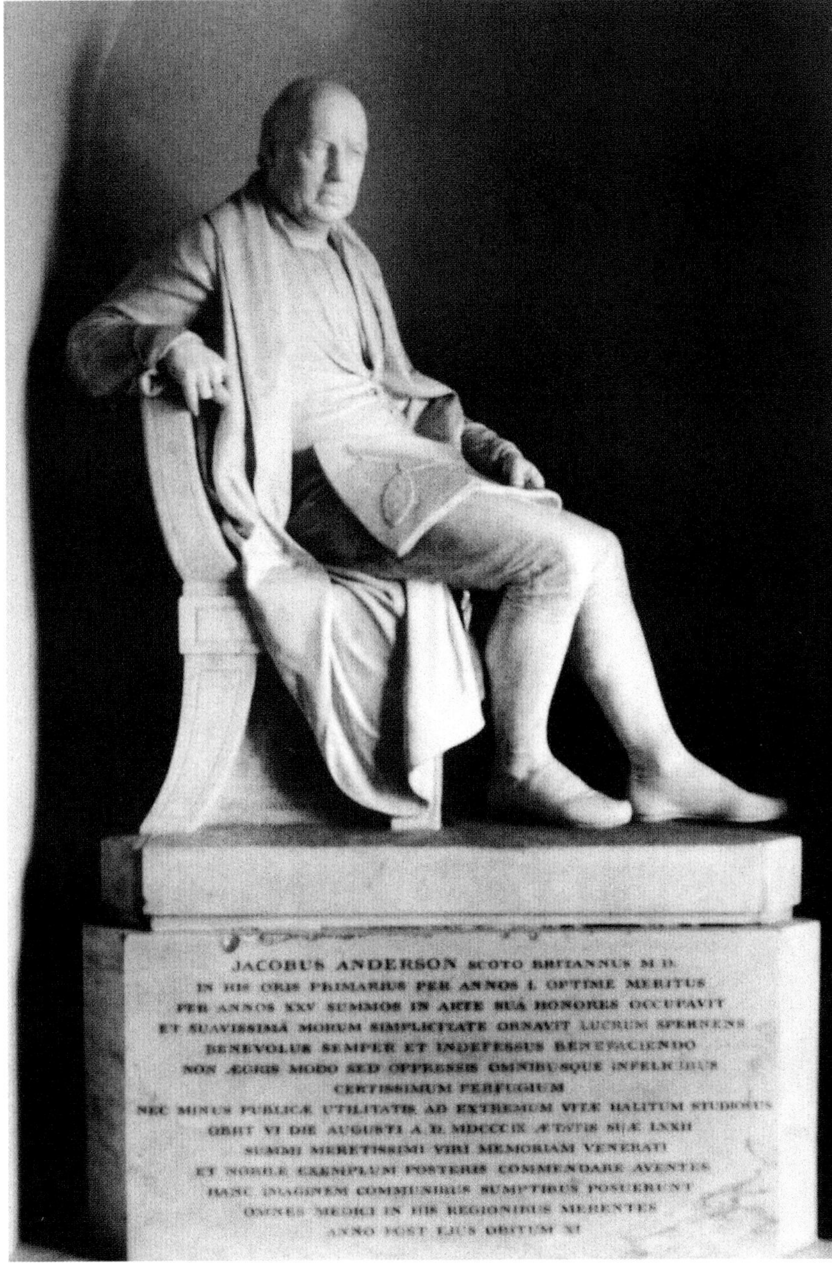

158 Francis Chantrey, monument to Dr James Anderson, RA 1819, marble. St George's Cathedral, Madras.

to incorporate the poetic and ideal in themes of a more literal nature. It was left to Baily, Behnes, Flaxman, Gott, Gibson and Westmacott to carry forward the ideal and poetic in more traditional mode.

If the 1817 exhibition stands out as a moment when the English School was seen in full flower, that of 1819 is of particular interest on account of both the continuing quality of the poetic works on show, and the unprecedented number of sculptors included on the Committee of Arrangement – a situation which prompted some rather snide remarks about the inability of sculptors to hang pictures.[55] Flaxman, Chantrey and Rossi were all members, though it was the last who seems alone to have been responsible for setting out the sculptures in the Life Academy.[56] Here the strengths of the modern English School could be seen to particular advantage in the first five items listed in the catalogue. All executed on an impressive scale, these were a seated figure of a peasant girl taken from Westmacott's monument to Lord and Lady Penrhyn (fig. 157);[57] Baily's *Hercules throwing Lychas into the Sea*, made for Joseph Neeld (untraced); Chantrey's seated figure of Dr Anderson (fig. 158); and Henry Rossi's plaster models, the *Cricketer* and *Bowler* (fig. 156), his attempts to represent modern athletes in a mode that would rival

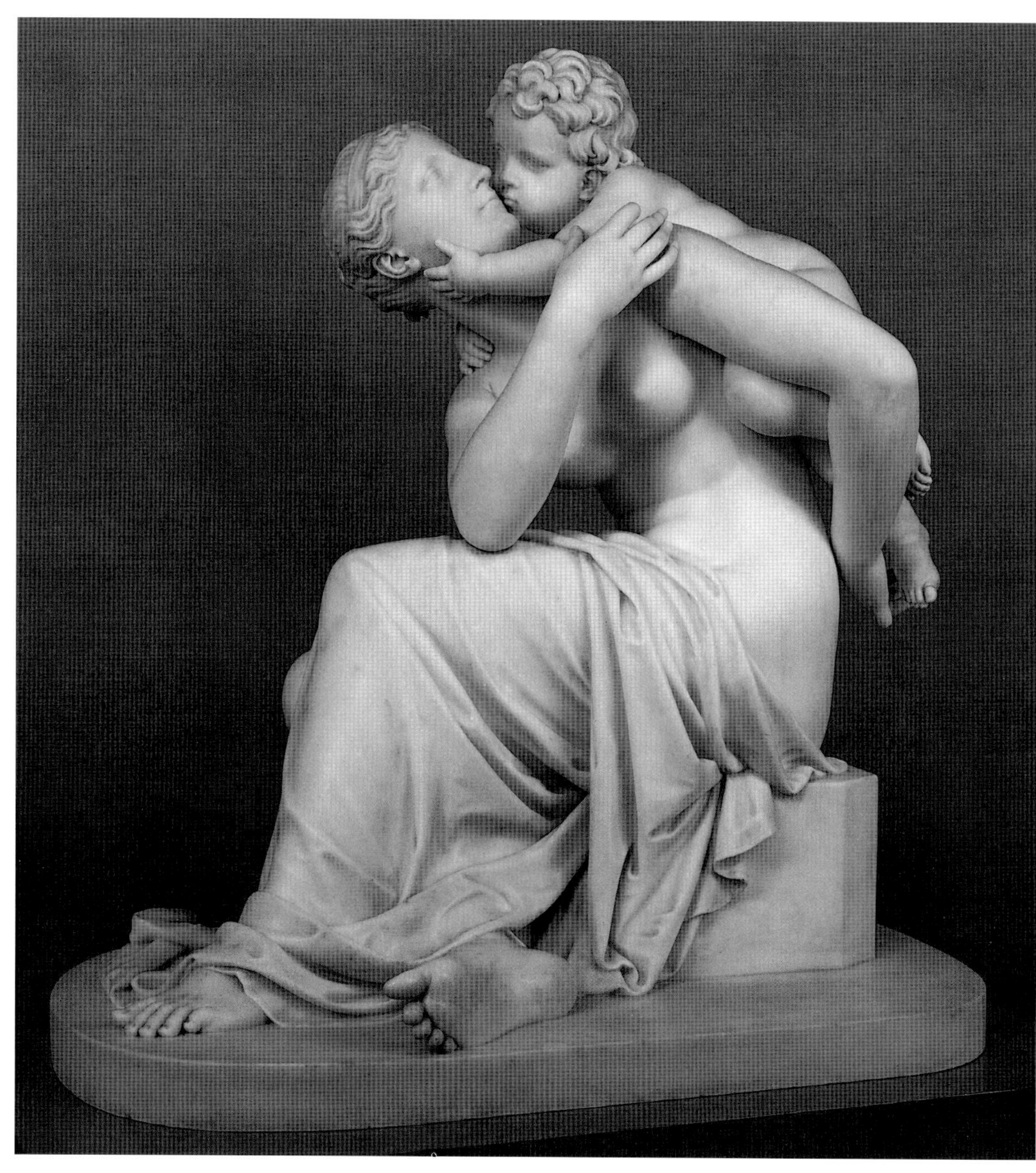

159 Edward Hodges Baily, *Affection*, RA 1823, marble. Courtesy of the Board of Trustees of the Victoria & Albert Museum.

the ancients. In subsequent years examples of ambitious poetic sculpture in whatever form – by Baily, Freebairn, Chantrey, Flaxman and others – continued to have a major impact at the annual exhibitions. Thus in 1823, when the Academy featured Canova's *Danzatrice* (various versions, none identifiable with RA exhibit) in posthumous tribute to its author, its presence appeared to confirm how far British sculpture had improved on his example, in the short space of just six years. Indeed by now certain critics were prepared to say that the British sculpture was 'preferable even to the best foreign modern sculptor, the late Canova'.[58] Baily's *Affection* (fig. 159) – 'the soul of loveliness' displaying 'the higher captivations of the heart'[59] – and Westmacott's rendering of *The Dream of Horace* (fig. 160), 'this fabled and poetical incident' – provided the best evidence for the triumph of a distinctive national school: were they to be placed 'in the British Museum surrounded by the Antique itself . . . they would not appear as in strange company'.[60]

In demonstrating their continuing strengths through works of 'high' art, sculptors were aided by demand from aristocratic purchasers who in the 1820s were busy developing private sculpture galleries, notably the Dukes of Devonshire and Bedford as well as the Earl of Egremont. By now the institutional situation had improved, too, with Flaxman's appointment as professor in 1810 marking the moment when the Academy belatedly acknowledged sculpture as an art of truly public significance. Its status – much promoted by Hunt in the pages of the *Examiner* – may have benefited still further from its subsequent isolation in the context of the exhibition. The enhanced position that sculpture secured in the second decade of the nineteenth century at publicly available and elitist sites can be seen to have fostered a native ambition to compose large-scale sculptural groups to rival those of Italian or other European sculptors. However, this was not simply a turn to some historically specific past, but an original synthesis of what was in essence a form of romantic

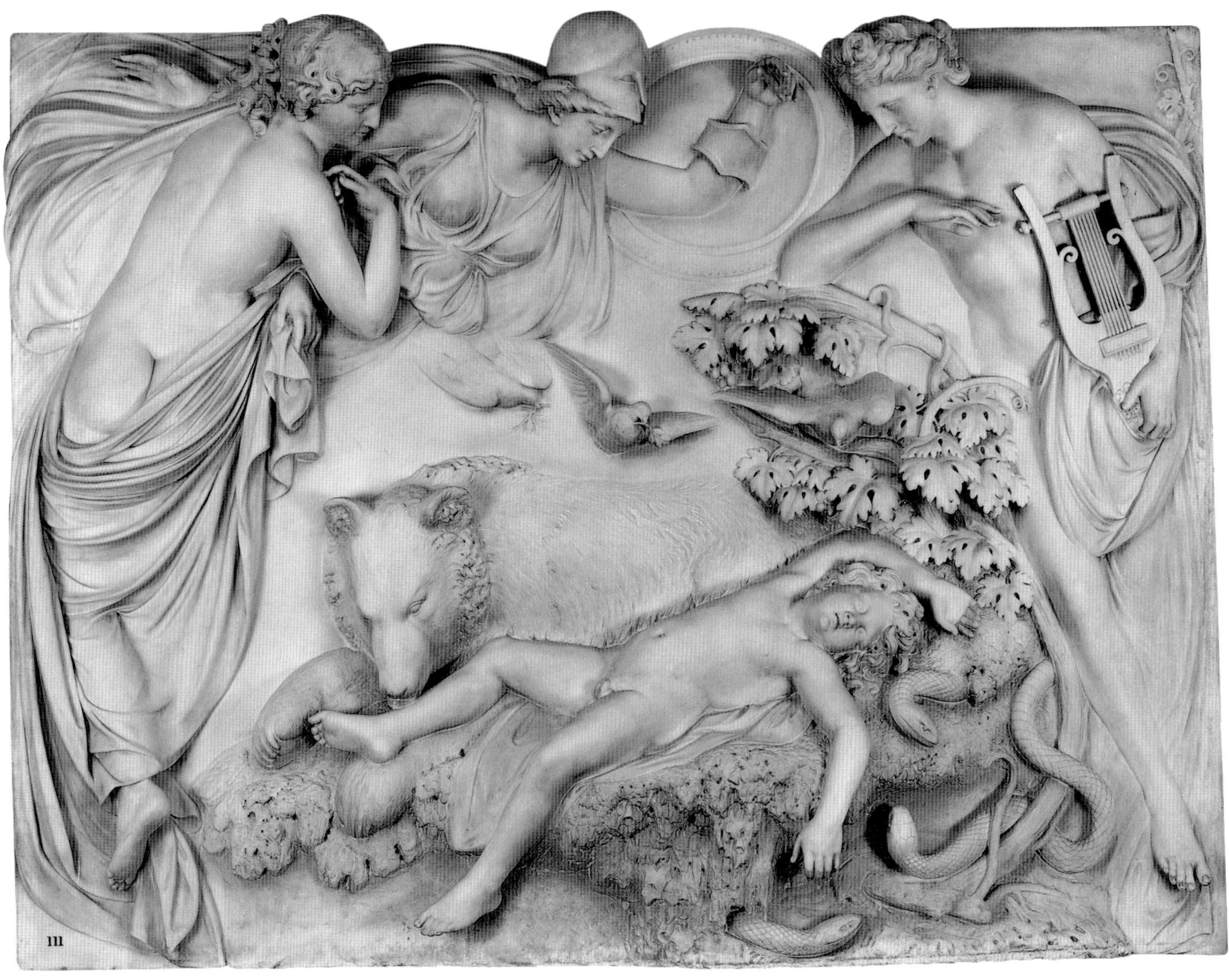

160 Richard Westmacott, *The Dream of Horace*, RA 1823, marble. Petworth House, The Egremont Collection (The National Trust).

Hellenism. It was actually *au courant*, a contemporary and even prescient poetic appropriation of classical themes. What sculptors presented at the Academy was a regular parade of ambitious, poetic works that adhered to the tenets of the Reynoldsian grand style – and did so far more effectively, it might justly be argued, than contemporary efforts in the equivalent field of history painting, which attracted less public interest and patronage alike. Although at the annual exhibitions painting physically ruled the roost, despite being confined to the 'dungeon' on the ground floor, sculpture continued to flourish and to gain recognition as one of the defining triumphs of the modern English School. Rather like the contemporary Romantic poetry of Keats, much vaunted in the columns of the *Examiner*, poetic sculpture grew in prominence because at the same time that it attracted the emotive gaze of the rapt observer, it could also be regarded as chaste and even remote from common experience. This paradox proved fruitful in a variety of ways. Even in the twilight zone of the Academy exhibition what might have appeared as an after-thought could actually promote a sense of mystery and wonder equivalent to poetic inspiration – the poetry of sculpture. In Somerset House sculpture may have lain dimly in the dark, but there were still ways in which its qualities could be brought into the light.

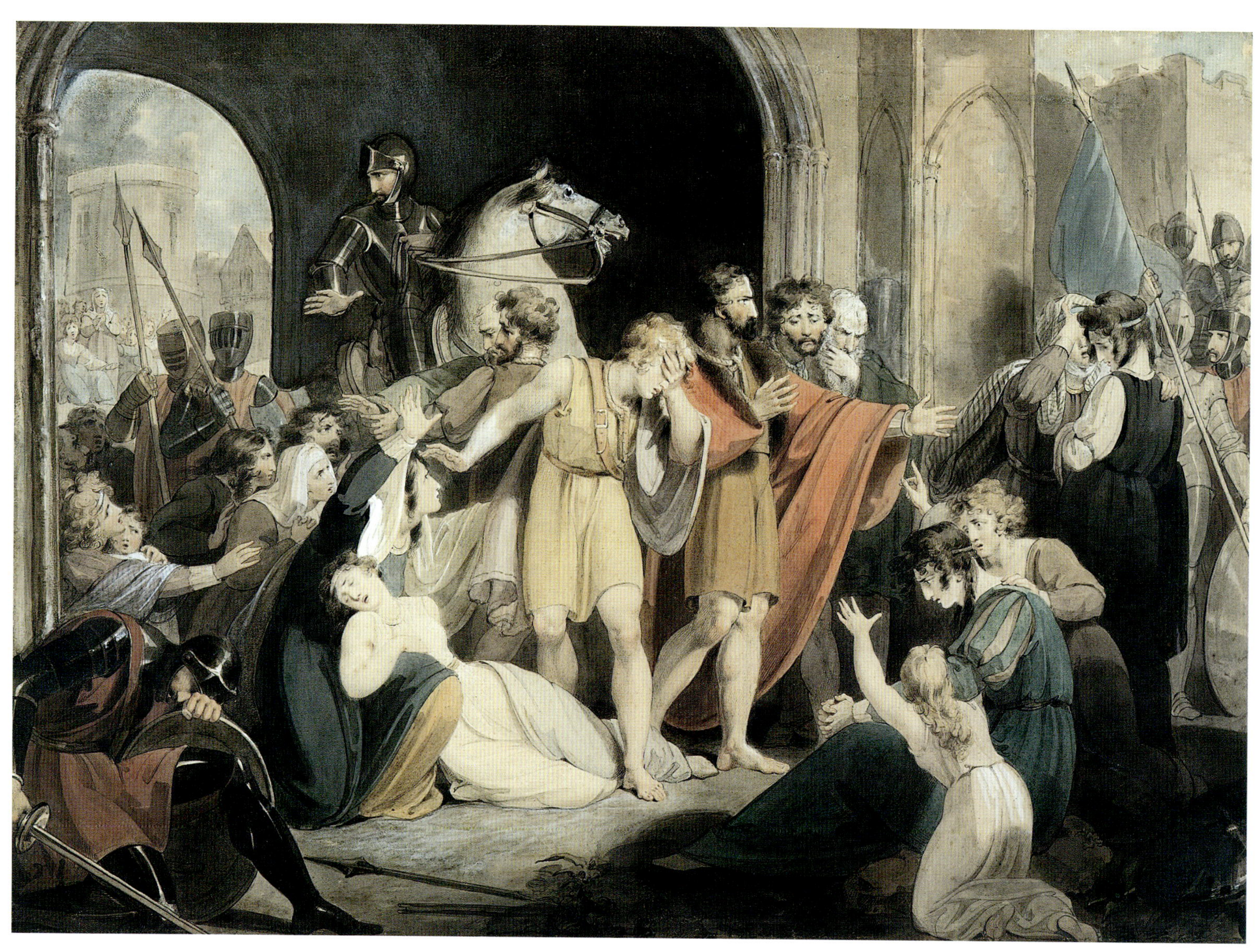

161 Richard Westall, *The Brave Burghers of Calais*, RA 1791, watercolour and pen and ink. Musée des Beaux-Arts et de la Dentelle, Calais.

13

Watercolourists and Watercolours at the Royal Academy, 1780–1836

GREG SMITH

THOUGH THE TITLE OF THIS CHAPTER may sound simple and straightforward, it is, in fact, fraught with problems of definition. Specifically, the term 'watercolourist' is generally understood today to cover those fine artists who specialize in using the watercolour medium on paper, but this meaning did not develop until well into the nineteenth century. It is certainly true that a group of specialist practitioners emerged around the turn of the century, and a faction termed themselves 'painters in water colours' in distinction to draughtsmen, but they constituted a small proportion of the artists who exhibited works at the Academy which employed the watercolour medium. What then of the subject specialist who painted both in oils and watercolours, or the miniaturist who used watercolours, but painted on ivory? What, too, of the amateur who employed a few monochrome washes, or of the architect who used the medium, or employed others, to realize visions of his designs? Then there is the problem of what constitutes a 'watercolour', again a term which did not emerge until after the period under consideration. The simplest and most neutral definition – all works which employ the medium – has the advantage of clarity, but is unwieldy, covering perhaps as much as half of all the exhibits.[1] The obvious alternative contemporary definition, of watercolour as a category of high art associated with a narrow tradition of innovative specialists, implicitly operates a range of exclusions which simply do not accord with the historical evidence. Constricting the field in this way makes for attractive exhibitions and publications, but only at the expense of a broader understanding of watercolour as a highly diverse and changing set of cultural practices.

My response to these problems is twofold. Firstly, I have adopted the broadest possible definition of watercolour commensurate with certain pragmatic decisions relating to the book's organization. This means, for instance, that I do not look at architectural drawings, which are dealt with elsewhere in this volume, but I do cover miniatures, which are often considered as a separate issue altogether.[2] Since my aim throughout is to invoke something of the richness and variety of watercolour practices as they entered the public domain, I will also touch upon areas such as portrait drawings, the work of amateurs, and less ambitious works related to publishing projects. Secondly, my response to the problematic identity of the watercolourist is to confront the issue directly by looking at the role the Academy played in the emergence of a new independent profession. This development, I suggest, represents a key episode in the fragmentation of the artistic domain, as an enlarged art market supported a growing specialization of practices. I am particularly concerned with a small group of watercolourists – as distinct from a large number of practices – because the RA's treatment of them and their work was in turn symptomatic of forces which were transforming the Academy's position within the artistic domain.

The wealth of available material suggests numerous ways of organizing my coverage, and it begs the question of the advisability of seeking to discuss the whole period of the Academy's stay at Somerset House. Since there has been no systematic attempt to treat the subject, and the archive contains significant details which have not been considered, I have adopted a structure which seeks to answer three very specific questions, both to provide a basic introduction to the subject and to gather together material from which an analysis of broader shifts in the artistic domain might be developed. My starting point is to ask in turn: what was the position of practitioners at the Academy, and how did it change? Where were their works shown? What forms did they take, and how were they were presented? The first section considers the position of the watercolourist in relation to the institutional politics of the Academy, and focuses on the way in which factional struggles contributed to the emergence of an independent profession. The second describes how these contentions were played out in the rooms at Somerset House and how the display spaces mapped out a media hierarchy. I hope to show how and why it was that one faction of artists who employed watercolours became the first professional sub-group who not only bridled at the limitations of the Academy, but seceded in an attempt to elevate their status elsewhere. And, finally, consideration is given to the range of exhibited works which employed watercolours, and to the ways in which their different functions determined, or were reflected in, their display – a further aim being to offer some initial thoughts on the broader question of what effects exhibitions may have had on the appearance of the works shown.

The struggle for recognition and status: watercolourists, miniaturists and the Academy

Beginning with the earliest commentators on the profession, it was widely accepted that it was the Academy's antipathy to watercolourists which provoked an honourable section of the artistic community to secede and form a series of independent institutions, starting in 1804 with the Society of Painters in Water Colours (SPWC).[3] Supporters of the watercolourists pointed, in particular, to a law passed in 1772 by the RA's General Assembly, which stated, 'That Persons who only exhibit Drawings cannot be admitted as Candidates for Associates';[4] this, they argued, was both a symptom of the prejudice and a source of deep offence. However, there is no evidence that the law initially caused any sense of resentment. It is not just that in the 1770s there was no group whose members identified themselves as specialist practitioners, but it is difficult to think of many eighteenth-century professional artists, certainly amongst those who are recognized today as major watercolourists, who did not also paint and exhibit at least some works in oils.[5] At the same time, the law did not define what was a 'Drawing', and more specifically it did not proscribe practitioners on the basis of their use of a particular support or medium. The definition of 'painting' could thus extend to pastels, even though their execution on paper means they are classified as drawings today; miniatures, too, tended to be classified as paintings despite their use of watercolour.[6] Moreover, although there was a general consensus that the use of a few washes to tint a predominant line constituted a drawing, larger, more highly worked watercolours, often incorporating the use of gouache and functioning as a framed object for domestic decoration, could still be defined as paintings. I am not arguing that the Academy did not prosecute a media hierarchy, but that a law forbidding membership to those 'who only exhibit Drawings' reflected its broader professionalizing project, which, as in the case of engravers, sought to promote the interests of the artist – defined as the disinterested man called to an intellectually ennobling practice – over the artisan or mechanic. Thus, although the reasons for the introduction of the law were never stated, it was presumably the initial association of the watercolour medium with frankly artisanal practices such as colouring maps and prints, and the production of simple stained drawings for copying in the less prestigious areas of reproductive prints and book illustration, rather than an attack on watercolourists *per se*, which motivated the Academy's proscription of draughtsmen.

The fact that an uncontroversial measure aimed at one artisanal aspect of watercolour practice came to be interpreted as discriminating against more ambitious practitioners arose from a complex range of factors. One of the most important was the emergence of a new type of 'painting in water colours' which was widely seen as a major advance, both on the stained or tinted drawing, and on the opaque gouache. The term was first used at the beginning of the 1790s in relation to Richard Westall's historical scenes. Works such as the *Brave Burghers of Calais* (RA 1791; fig. 161) were praised widely for surpassing 'any thing of the kind we have ever seen any where', and by 1795 Westall could be hailed as the 'Founder of a particular School'.[7] Such watercolours, it was often claimed, marked a major advance because they had 'a solidity not exceeded by an oil picture', and displayed a new 'depth, and force'.[8] The theme was developed further in relation to the landscapes of Thomas Girtin and J. M. W. Turner, which from the mid-1790s attracted sometimes extravagant praise. In the case of the latter, critics were even prepared to extend favourable comparisons with oils to the great masters of the past. The *London Packet*, for instance, claimed that an 'effect' such as the sunset in *Caernarvon Castle* (RA 1799; fig. 162) 'is given with the precision and brilliancy not surpassed by the best works of Claude de Lorrain', while other Turner watercolours elicited comparisons with Rembrandt's paintings.[9] The display of *Caernarvon* in close proximity to Girtin's equally ambitious *Beddgellert* (fig. 163) resulted in unprecedented critical attention for landscape watercolours and linked the artists' names as twin pioneers of a prestigious new art.

The reformulation of 'painting in water colours' as a 'modern art' which employed transparent colours to produce works which could vie with oils may have been expected to have improved the practitioners' status at the Academy, but initially it merely highlighted their inferior position. Thus, the period during which spectacular changes in watercolour practice took place was also marked by a hardening of the definition of painting within the Academy; effectively, it now became synonymous with the use of oils on canvas, with the law of 1772 now being used to exclude the growing number of artists who specialized in using watercolours. This did not affect Turner or Westall who, early in their careers, broadened their practice to encompass oil painting and quickly achieved academic honours. Girtin, however, was more typical of a younger generation who saw

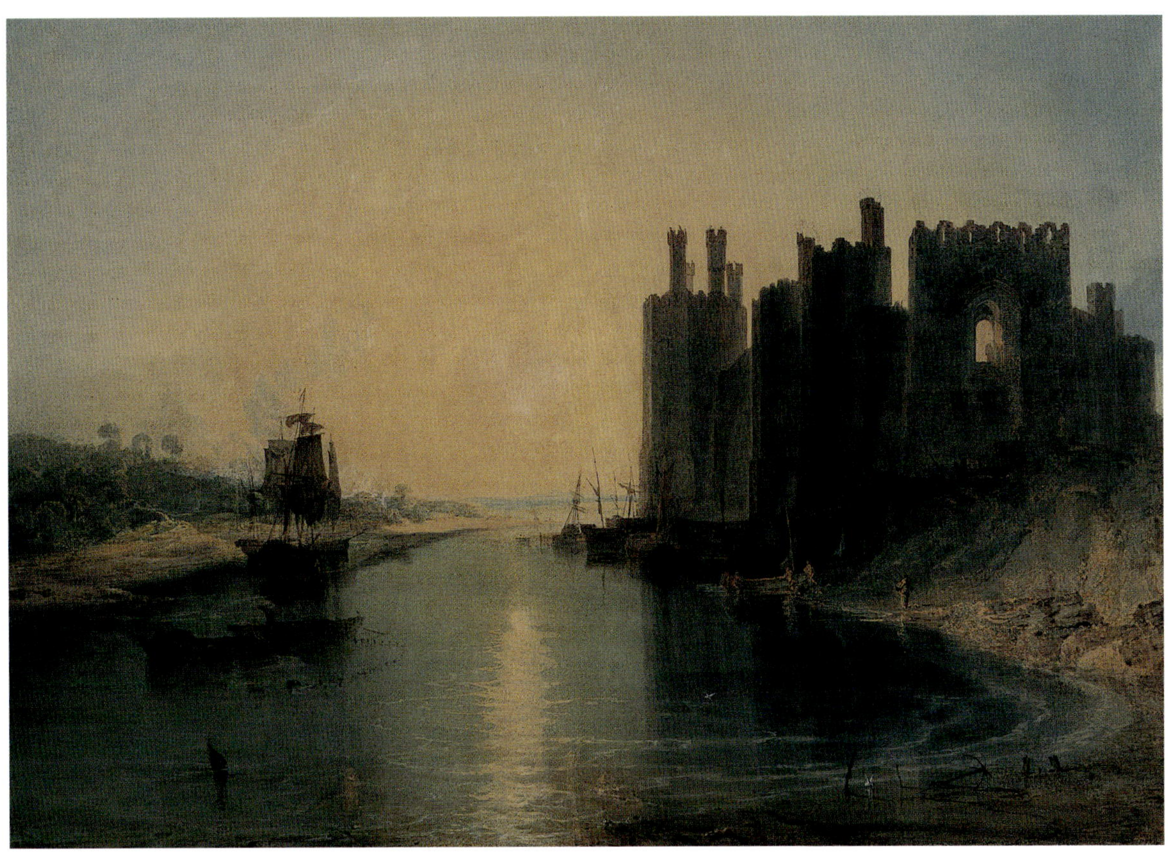

162 J. M. W. Turner, *Caernarvon Castle*, RA 1799, pencil and watercolour. Private collection.

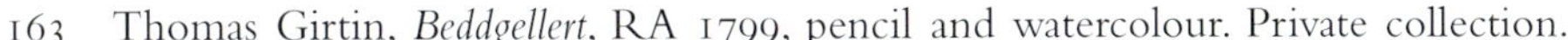

163 Thomas Girtin, *Beddgellert*, RA 1799, pencil and watercolour. Private collection.

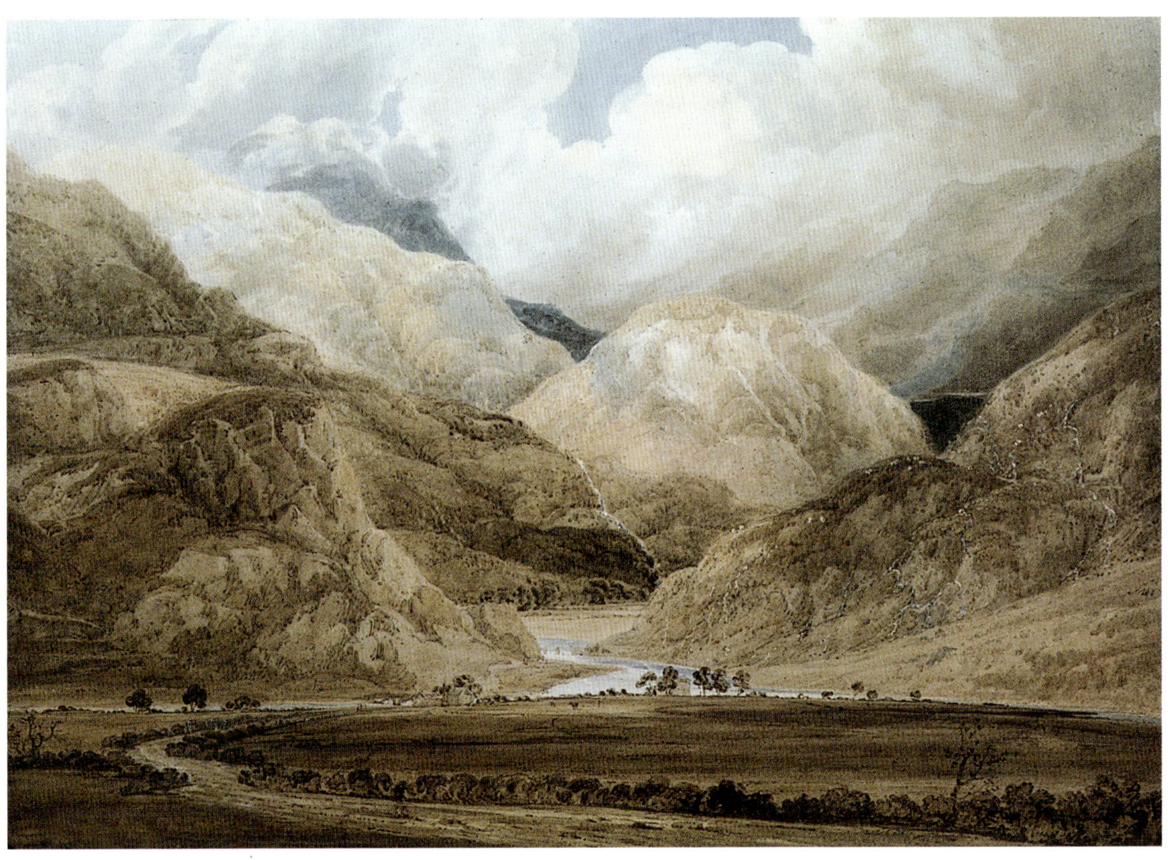

economic advantages in confining themselves to the production of watercolours; these benefits included the requirement of a smaller financial outlay by the artist, a wider range of patrons, and the security to be derived from supplementing their income from teaching. Watercolourists were free to exhibit one-off paintings in order to qualify, but such expedients were a humiliating reminder of their subordinate position. For Girtin the results were particularly mortifying: after having shown the required oil in 1801 (the untraced *Bolton Bridge*) he then failed to attract a single vote in the subsequent election. The hardening of attitudes against watercolourists and the increasing factionalism which was the corollary of the specialization of practices is perhaps even better illustrated by Francis Towne's unsuccessful efforts to be elected an Associate Academician. In all he put his name forward no fewer than ten times, and by 1803 was becoming desperate. In a letter to a friend, the Academician Ozias Humphrey, Towne made it clear that he felt that his role as a 'provincial Drawing Master', together with his use of watercolours, had frustrated his academic ambitions. He was keen to stress that 'I never in my life Exhibited a Drawing', and that 'at fourteen years of age I began to paint in oil'; adding that from early in his career he had 'painted . . . views from drawings after nature, and some of these were of a large size'. My 'profession is that of a landscape painter', Towne protested, but to no avail.[10] This was not an artist who was seeking to be defined as a painter on the basis of exhibiting the occasional oil, but an established exhibitor who believed himself unfairly stigmatized by his use of the watercolour medium.

I suggest that there are three main reasons why the Academy toughened its stand against watercolourists at the very moment when so much was being written in celebration of the spectacular 'progress' of their art. Firstly, the emergence of the specialist watercolourist was just one facet of a rapidly growing artistic community which, given that the number of Academicians and Associates remained fixed, reacted with growing frustration to the RA's exclusivity. Secondly, there is evidence that the commercial success of a new generation of watercolourists was seen as a threat to oil painters. This was of particular concern to the prominent collector and amateur Sir George Beaumont, who claimed that the 'progress of landscape' was being impeded by 'the great encouragement given to tinted drawings almost to the exclusion of oil painting'.[11] According to Beaumont, the medium was clearly 'inferior' to oil, 'but as it is more easily acquired and the artists can afford to work for a lower price, all the rising and promising young men give themselves up to it'.[12] The commercial and critical success initially enjoyed by the SPWC only increased concern amongst a faction of the Academy that oil painting 'wd. be neglected' as a result.[13] Thirdly, such comments provide evidence of the increasingly aggressive way in which the media hierarchy was being challenged, and of the resulting antagonism between the polarized groups. The watercolourist and drawing master William Marshall Craig was especially outspoken, using his lectures at the Royal Institution in 1806 to argue 'the superiority of water over Coloured painting'.[14] The 'practice of painting in water-colours', he concluded provocatively, 'will . . . make good its unrivalled pretensions, and become, finally, the current process of the painter's art'.[15] An anonymous writer in *Le Beau Monde* was more reasoned in his criticism, but he squarely laid the blame for the secession of watercolourists on 'defects of the code of laws' which, he argued, are characterized by 'ambiguity and apparent contradiction'. In particular, he continued, the institution must settle 'what is meant by the Academical distinction between Painting and Drawing'; he went on to attack the idea that oil 'must preserve its natural ascendancy' when artists such as Henry Edridge, and earlier Thomas Girtin, 'had with materials presumed to be inferior . . . produced superior works of art'. Works like Edridge's portrait of the Bishop of Durham (RA 1809; fig. 164), which were 'wrought up to high perfection', showed how the Academy was engaged in the 'silly substitution . . . of mode of attainment, for attain-

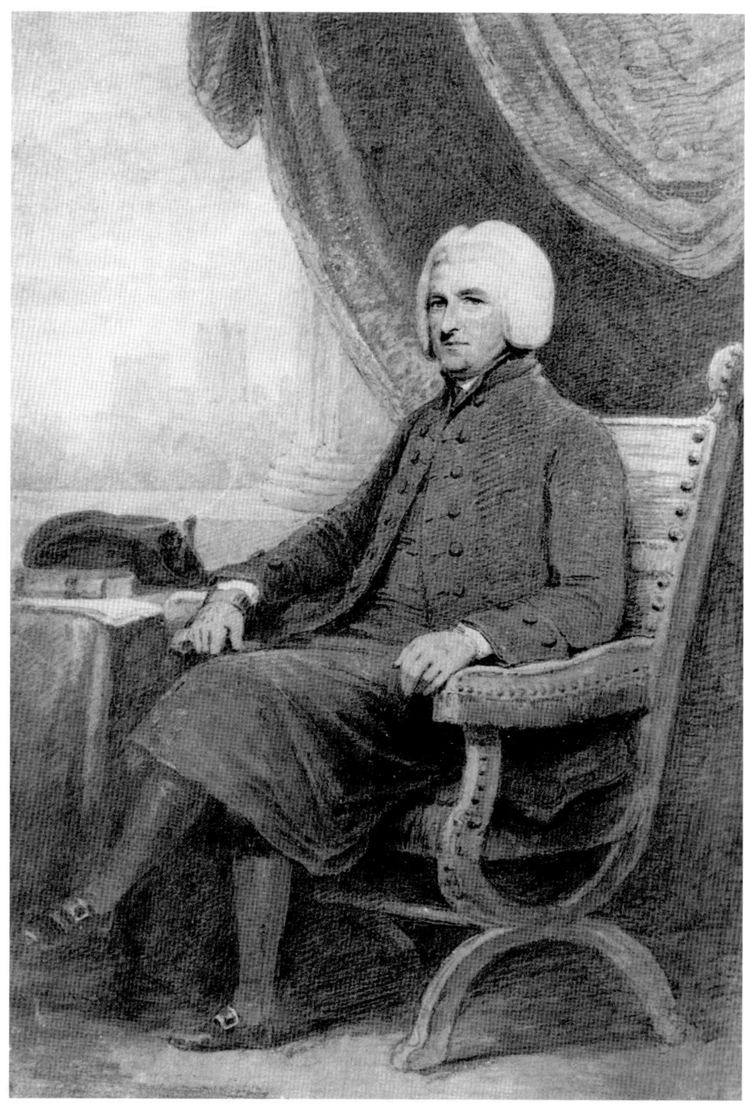

164 Henry Edridge, *The Bishop of Durham*, RA 1809, pencil and watercolour. Private collection.

ment itself'.[16] While Joseph Farington was sympathetic to Edridge's ambitions, John Hoppner's response was typical of the factional view. Make an allowance for Edridge, he argued, and 'Glover, Heaphy etc. (and) a Herd of Water Colour painters wd. have a right to offer themselves'.[17]

One of the most notable points about Farington's support for Edridge – and this was a view maintained ironically by Craig, too – was the notion that practitioners in watercolours might be defined as painters as long as they were miniaturists.[18] Such was the confusion over definitions that both the apologist for academical distinction and the watercolourists' most outspoken supporter overlooked the fact that the status of the miniaturist at the Academy had seen a rapid decline. Ozias Humphrey had been the last to have been made an Academician, in 1791, and in the 1808 exhibition none of the 140 miniatures listed were by a member of the RA. Humphrey himself talked of the 'disgrace' attendant on being a miniaturist, and according to Walter Henry Watts, writing in 1806, the Academy had dramatically shifted its attitude from its earliest years; they had not then found it 'derogatory' to 'the character of the institution to admit miniature painters to a share in its honours', he complained.[19] Moreover, the miniatures were no longer hung prominently around the fireplace in the Great Room, as shown in Ramberg's view of the 1787 show (fig. 165); since 1793 they had been moved downstairs. For the Academician Martin Archer Shee this was just, since miniaturists were at the very bottom of the artistic ladder. He argued that because of 'the prompt means of subsistence which miniature-painting affords to every manufacturer of a face, it will always be the refuge of imbecility: a receptacle for the poor and disappointed in art'.[20] The situation faced by miniaturists was particularly difficult, for not only were they badly treated at the Academy, but the Society of Painters in Water Colours made a point of excluding portraits from their exhibitions. It is not surprising, therefore, that a group of miniaturists and portrait specialists, together with other watercolourists excluded from the SPWC, formed a second society in 1807.[21] Membership was open to any professional artist 'in those departments for which water colours and chalks are employed', including 'Portraits', and the body considered calling itself the New Society of Painters in Miniature and Water-Colours, before settling on the Associated Artists in Water-Colours.[22] The enterprise was not a success, however; it collapsed in debt in 1812, after the leading miniaturists had already withdrawn, forced to accept that their future lay as a marginal group within the Academy.

In contrast, the more restrictive policy of the SPWC was to prove highly successful: although the impact of their exhibitions may have attracted envious glances amongst some Academicians, it prompted others to rethink their attitude towards watercolourists. Farington recorded the favourable reaction of a number of members to their earliest exhibitions; Thomas Lawrence was said to have been 'in raptures' over the 1808 show.[23] Two years later the President Benjamin West privately expressed the opinion that 'the law which prevents Artists who make drawings such as those by Westall & Heaphy from becoming Members of the Academy' was wrong. 'The law', he continued, 'was made against inferior works done on paper, but the works now produced are of a quality not then known'.[24] Members may have been concerned by suggestions in the press that the secession of so many watercolourists had resulted in a decline in the exhibitions, and, despite the opposition of men like Hoppner to the 'herd of Water Colour painters', the law that discriminated against those 'who only exhibit Drawings' was

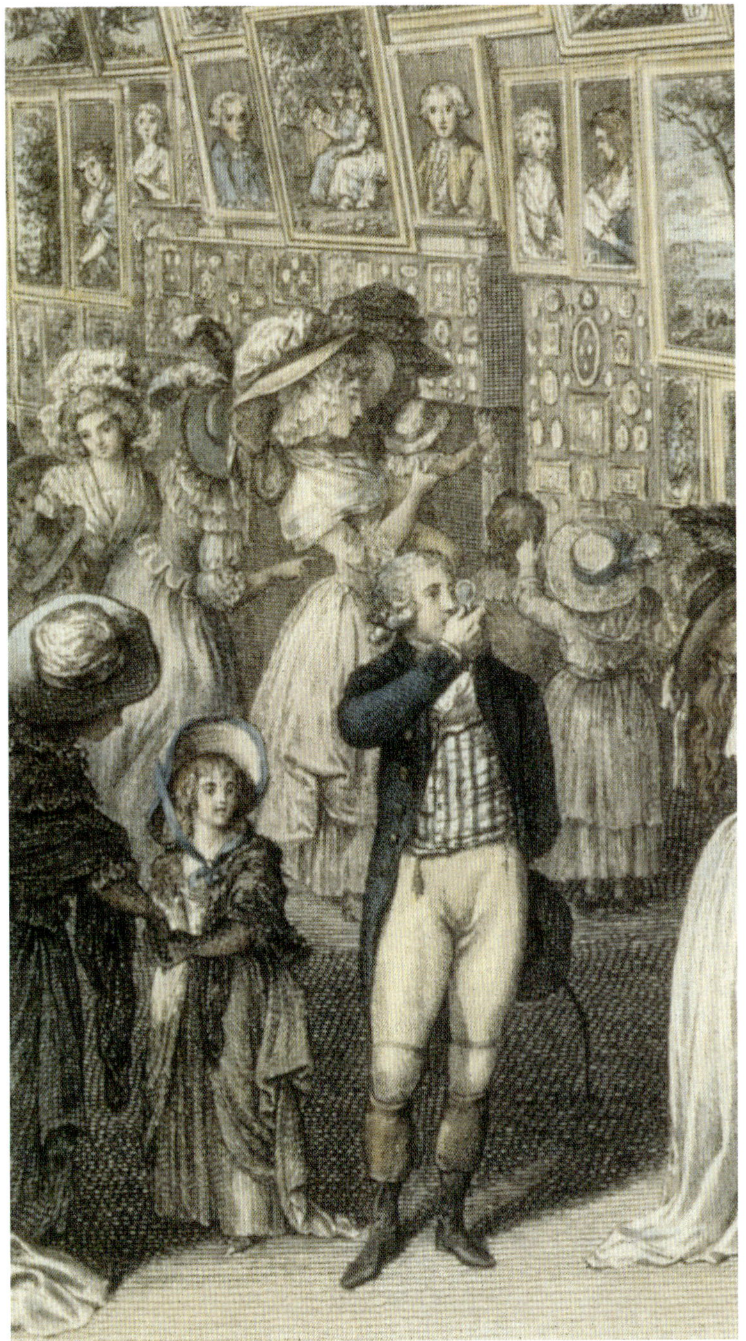

165 Pietro Martini after Johann Heinrich Ramberg, *The Exhibition of the Royal Academy 1787* (detail of fig. 36), engraving. By courtesy of the Trustees of the British Museum.

revoked as being 'repugnant to the honour & interests of the Royal Academy'.[25] In practice, however, this did not placate the feelings of the watercolourists; no specialist watercolourist was elected a member in the remainder of the Somerset House period, and there was little prospect of change if, as another regulation required, candidates for Associate status first had to resign their membership of other institutions. The policy change of 1810, therefore, removed one of the symptoms of the media hierarchy without radically changing the watercolourists' position.

Banished to the 'Lower Rooms': the media hierarchy and the politics of display

Watercolourists and their supporters may have protested about the Academy's constitution, but the negative effect of the media hierarchy manifested itself with the greatest force at the practical level as a result of decisions made annually by the members of the Hanging Committee. This was particularly the case following the Academy's move to more spacious and luxurious apartments at Somerset House in 1780, which, though it reflected well on the institution, simultaneously highlighted its hierarchical bias. Hitherto oil paintings, miniatures, watercolours and sculpture had been mixed in the same room, and though there is no visual or textual evidence to suggest how drawings fared in the Academy's first home in Pall Mall, the absence of specific complaints about their placement suggests that there was a rough and ready equality. In the new building, however, the initial division of the exhibition space into three – the Great Room and the Ante-room upstairs, and the 'Exhibition-Room of Sculpture and Drawings' on the ground floor – gave a visible form to the media hierarchy; the position of the lower room, it was implied, was commensurate with an inferior branch of the arts. This was certainly the view of John Downman, who wrote to the Academy to state 'that if his Drawings were not placed in the Great Room they should not be exhibited'; two years later he again protested about the fact that his works had been denominated 'Drawings' and therefore consigned to the lower floor.[26] Thomas Hearne employed another tactic in 1788 which, according to the *St James's Chronicle*, showed up the arbitrary and unfair behaviour of the Academy. Hearne, the paper declared, had submitted a view of *Tintern Abbey* (untraced) which, although 'highly finished' and 'varnished, instead of being covered with Glass', was 'only a tinted Drawing'. Presumably, the critic continued, 'the Academick Council . . . mistook it for a Painting in Oil; and therefore, instead of ordering it below, placed it in the Great Room'.[27] The slight to the status of watercolourists was not improved by the opening up of the rooms on the first floor after 1792. This allowed for the inclusion of many more works, but the location, size and, in the case of the Antique Academy, the utilitarian function of the room contrasted poorly with the grand public space above.

Complaints about the placement of watercolours at Somerset House went much further than objections to the illiberal policy towards non-members; the disposition of their works also impaired their chances of finding buyers, and of attracting either critical attention or the interest of potential patrons. One of the watercolourists' main grievances related to the practice of showing oils and watercolours together; this, it was claimed, was detrimental to the latter which were said to suffer from comparison with large and brightly coloured canvases. The inclusion of a watercolour in one of the crowded top-floor galleries, a privilege granted only occasionally even to Academicians, was likely to be a hollow victory. As one writer noted in 1788, a drawing by Sandby 'suffers in its force from being oppressed by the strength of Hercules' – a reference to Sir Joshua Reynolds's monumental painting nearby[28] – and Farington noted that the decision of a significant group of 'Artists who only exhibit drawings' to found their own exhibition society in 1804 was partly taken 'on acct. of paintings being hung among drawings, which destroys the effect'.[29] The issue was even more pressing for those whose watercolours were shown downstairs, where, according to one of the founders of the SPWC, William Henry Pyne, they were often 'mixed with pictures in oil, in crayons, and with works discreditable to the art, and arranged with no regard to the tout-ensemble'.[30] The insensitive way in which oils, and inferior examples in particular, were allowed to dominate even the lower rooms was seen by the Society's supporters in the press as proof that an Academy of Arts was in fact an oligarchy of painters.[31]

The watercolourists' disenchantment with the Academy was compounded by the fact that the room set aside for glazed drawings and sculpture in 1780 was entirely unsuited to their display. One writer called it a 'miserable . . . place . . . unworthy a Royal institution' in which 'every man who exhibits . . . is injured', while the *St James's Chronicle* suggested that the poor quality of works shown there was probably due to the fact that 'Artists will not be so imprudent as to lend good Drawings to be disadvantageously viewed in such a Place'.[32] Indeed, the *Chronicle* undertook a campaign against what it saw as the Academy's 'narrow and illiberal Policy' in general, and its treatment of drawings in particular. The 'dark Rooms on the Ground Floor', the critic mocked, had been contrived by Sir William Chambers 'after some Chinese Example . . . to conceal, not to exhibit, the Works of the Artists', adding that 'Small Drawings require a good deal of Light'.[33] The extension of the exhibition into the first-floor rooms improved the situation. This allowed for the separation of drawings and sculpture, and in 1795 the Council Room was set aside for the most important watercolours and drawings. It was here, in the years up to 1809, that the majority of the watercolours of Turner, Thomas Girtin, Richard Westall and John Sell Cotman were displayed. None the less, the space still suffered from a major problem, since, as the *Literary Panorama* noted, works 'which are seen by side lights from several windows, have but too often a vicious glare dazzling upon them, whereby their true effect is injured'; moreover, as another writer noted, the reflection of light on the glazed watercolours made them resemble 'so many pier glasses' (i.e., mirrors).[34] This was also a problem for miniatures after they lost their prestigious position in the Great Room, as was the fact that 'spectators necessarily intercept the light, and prevent it from falling on those pictures which are hung below the level of the rest'.[35] It is debatable whether works in watercolours were placed at a greater disadvantage than the majority of oils at the Academy, but the artists themselves felt that the exhibitions did not allow their talents either collectively or individually to 'be fairly evinced . . . nor could the public justly appreciate the merits of such a separate department of art'.[36]

The decision to revoke the law denying membership to those who exhibited only drawings might have been expected to have led to improvements in the display of watercolours, but attempts at amelioration were blocked by a hostile faction of the Academy. This had made its views felt in 1810, when it was decided to appropriate the Council Room for the display of the members' diploma pictures, leading to the dispersal of the watercolours around the lower rooms. Farington was particularly upset by the policy and pointed out that the most prominent academician/watercolourist, Richard Westall, had as a result withheld 'two drawings made for Mr. Chamberlain, which alone wd. have raised the credit of the Academy in this department of the art above all external competition'.[37] A year later, however, the Academy changed its practice yet again, possibly in order to compete with the SPWC. It opened up a new gallery next to the Great Room and this was used primarily for the display of watercolours; as a result these works gained a new prominence on the upper floor, and just as importantly, better lighting conditions. At the same time, the Academy also addressed another of the watercolourists' grievances; namely, that the exhibition offered artists little chance of securing sales. They thus employed an 'Agent . . . to answer Enquiries respecting those Works which are to be disposed of'.[38] As one newspaper critic noted, this was a major departure for an organization which had 'hitherto abstained from' such a policy 'from an apprehension that it might injure the dignity of the Institution'.[39] The shift in attitude produced an improvement in the display, and may well have encouraged Turner to show a substantial group of his watercolours at the Royal Academy for the first time since 1806.

A year later the situation changed once again. The Academy then resolved, Farington noted, that 'under the present circumstances' (he does not say what these were) 'pictures in Oil only shd. be exhibited in the new room'.[40] At least one critic protested at the expulsion of 'Water-colour Paintings' from a 'properly lighted' room, complaining that they were once more 'thrust into the lower rooms . . . with the inferior oil paintings . . . under all the disadvantages of side lights and dark corners'.[41] Perhaps the demise of the SPWC in its original form in 1812 meant that the Academy no longer felt threatened; in any case, further changes took place in the following year. The experiment with an agent to help with sales was discreetly dropped, the diploma pictures were hung in the Council Room, and the watercolours were once again moved to the first floor. Thereafter, there were sporadic complaints about what one critic termed a veritable 'lumber-room, into which things of all shapes and descriptions are thrown, and huddled together', while another complained that the 'general arrangement' of this 'purgatory . . . makes one year so closely resemble another, that we can hardly persuade ourselves we are not looking at the last exhibition'.[42] Nothing came of such protests, however, and even the watercolours of those Academicians such as Turner and Constable who practised in both media were shown in the lower rooms. In fact, there was little opposition from the watercolourists themselves, who more and more came to recognize that their future, like that of a growing number of other specialized professional groups, lay outside the Academy.[43] The exhibitions continued to contain numerous watercolours, but in the last two decades of the Academy's stay at Somerset House the most important practitioners concentrated their efforts elsewhere, and the shows shifted from being a showcase for the best works to providing an opportunity for young artists to establish their reputation.

Private art and public display: the function of watercolours and their presentation at exhibitions

The ways in which watercolours are presented nowadays rarely correspond to their original appearance, and shifts in taste, the impact of the art market, and modern conservation requirements means that it needs a leap of imagination either to picture their overall effect at the Academy or to assess the initial visual impact of individual works. The loss of material evidence is unfortunate because it obscures the works' original function, making it easy to forget that the majority of watercolours were produced for private consumption or in relation to sometimes complex chains of production which imposed their own limitations and requirements; public display was rarely their primary purpose. The specific danger of ignoring the issue of function is, I suggest, that it can encourage the simplistic view that there is a causal relationship between the advent of exhibitions and stylistic developments which are interpreted as being predicated on the need to make a strong visual impact.[44] A brief discussion of the function and the original appearance of the range of exhibited works which employed watercolours may encourage a subtler approach to the question, as well as correcting the distortions in our appreciation which are the inevitable outcome of modern conventions of display.

More is known about the way in which miniatures were originally presented at the Academy than perhaps any other category of work which employed watercolours. Frames and settings were always regarded as integral to the image, and a large number of miniatures survive unchanged, particularly because their

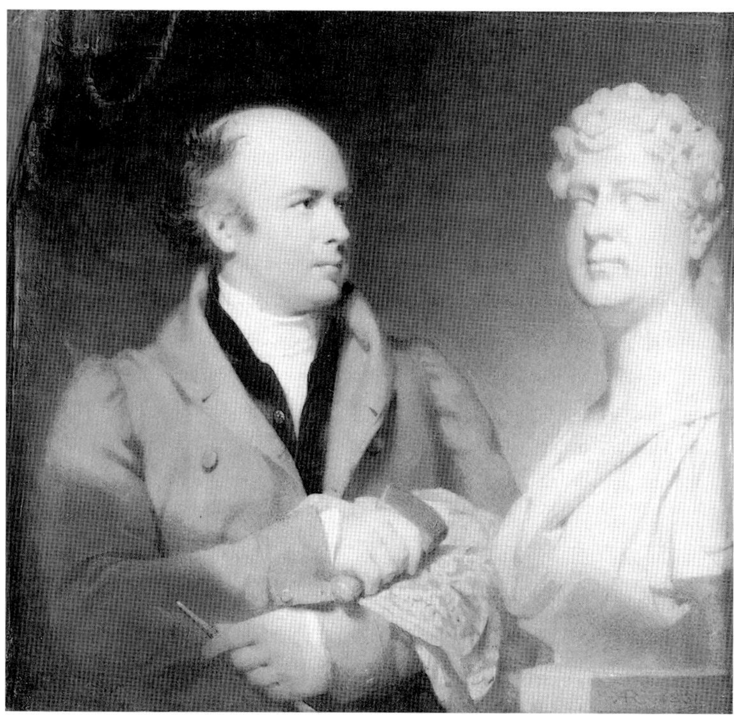

166 Andrew Robertson, *Sir Francis Chantrey*, RA 1831, watercolour on ivory. The Royal Collection © 2001 Her Majesty Queen Elizabeth II.

condition has suffered less than framed works on paper. We also have more information about their display from the Academy's laws which not only stipulated that all pictures must have a 'gilt frame', but also prescribed its maximum size; this rose from no 'more than one Inch of Framing' in 1791 to 'two inches and a half in width and one in depth' by 1818.[45] The Ramberg view of the Great Room in 1787 provides visual evidence, illustrating a number of features which remained constant throughout the period (see fig. 165). These range from the way in which the Hanging Committee followed the principle of showing all of the miniatures together, to the manner in which artists often grouped together their smallest oval works and displayed them mounted on a back board; the view also illustrates the presence of a smaller number of larger pieces, many of them in ornate frames. The image is especially significant in that it highlights the degree to which exhibitions disrupt the function of miniatures, transforming, albeit for a short period, an object which was created for silent and private perusal and for handling – and one with a strong association with jewellery – into part of a public spectacle. This should make us wary of attributing solely to the influence of exhibitions changes which occurred during the period, such as the increase in the average size of miniatures, the introduction of more ornate frames, and the growing adoption of a rectangular format – associated with the display of miniatures as cabinet pictures. Miniatures had to fulfil a series of specific functions and although ambitious compositions such as Andrew Robertson's portrait of Sir Francis Chantrey (RA 1831; fig. 166) might be shown as a way of promoting the artist's reputation, the market dictated production. 'Small miniatures', Robertson ruefully noted, are 'what one must live by'.[46]

Two other categories of portraits featured prominently at the Academy: the pastel and the portrait drawing. The presentation of the former is unproblematic since the frame was again an integral part of the piece; the fragile surface means that pastels have to be framed and glazed, and they presumably qualified as 'paintings' at the Academy on those grounds. The frames followed the common pattern of the period which saw a shift from simple mouldings to broader, more complex forms, and, if they were not close-framed, a gold mat was increasingly substituted for a black border. Portrait drawings were also often framed for domestic display, but their informality and lack of finish signified a different commodity.[47] The use of paper, rather than ivory, allowed for larger works and the introduction of full-length poses which followed oil paintings, whilst the more detailed treatment of the face and hands – with the background left in various degrees of incompletion – balanced this infor-

167 Henry Edridge, *Lord Paget*, RA 1808, pencil and watercolour. By courtesy of the National Portrait Gallery, London.

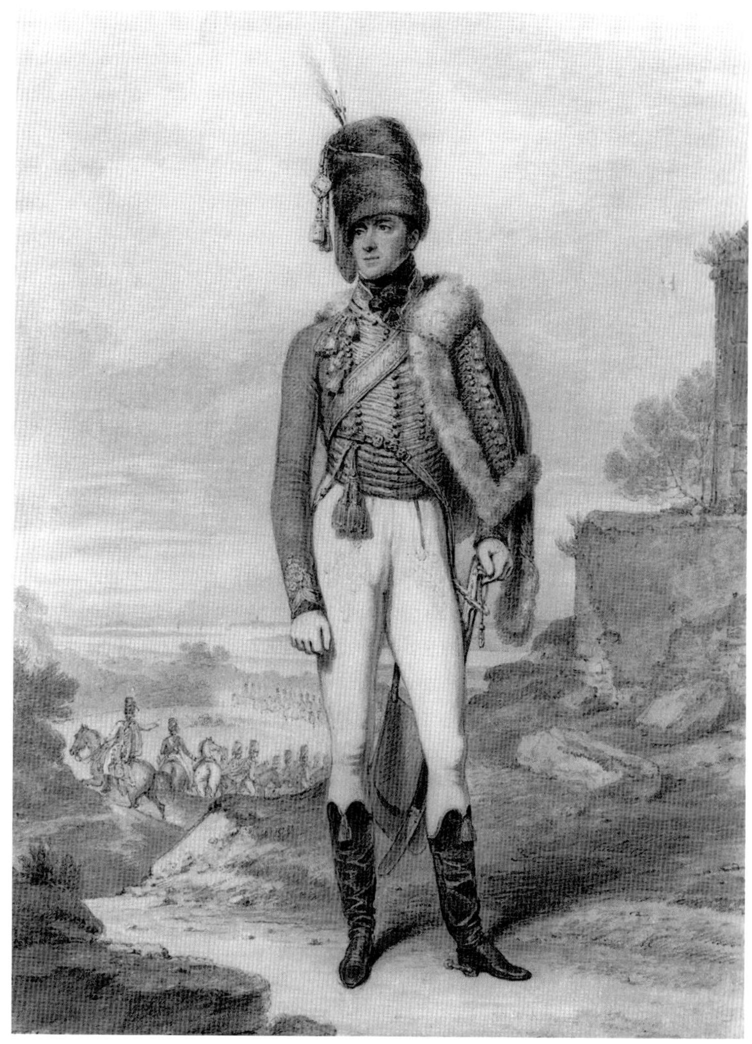

mality with the finish of the miniature. Examples such as Henry Edridge's *Lord Paget* (RA 1808; fig. 167) could, of course, be kept in the portfolio or in albums for private perusal in the library, but more commonly they were shown within smaller domestic spaces, as befitting a type of image that usually provided an intimate visual record of a loved one.[48] Many portrait drawings were conceived as framed objects designed to fit into specific private settings; the circumstances of public display were essentially alien to them. And as with any commissioned work, portraits could appear in the exhibition only with their owner's prior consent. Though an artist might select his or her Academy submissions with a view to achieving the maximum impact at Somerset House, the desires of patrons had to be taken into account first of all.

But the circumstances were rather different when an exhibit had been made on a speculative basis, since its notional function then remained to be determined by its purchaser. The indeterminate status of such drawings was enhanced by the fact that the frame and glass were rarely included in the asking price, so that works for sale were usually designed to fit frames which the artist kept aside for the exhibition.[49] Unfortunately, it is not possible to say precisely what proportion of the large number of landscapes, flower pieces, history and genre subjects shown every year came into this category because, although artists could mark their works for sale in the catalogue, they did not always do so. However, marked copies of the 1812 exhibition catalogue suggest that the proportion for sale remained relatively low – perhaps 10 per cent; this and other evidence tends to confirm Robertson's claim that in general 'few' sales 'come from the Exhibition', and that 'business comes more from connection, or from pictures seen in private'.[50] Certainly, none of the major landscapes by Turner and Girtin was marked for sale. Outstanding pieces such as *Caernarvon Castle* and *Beddgellert* were exhibited as public demonstrations of the artists' success in securing the support of prestigious patrons, and as magnets for future commissions.

The impact made by these two artists has encouraged the common misconception that 'painting in water colours' did not begin until the 1790s with the production of their large-scale watercolours designed to be framed for domestic display. It certainly suited the interests of one faction of practitioners to cultivate this idea, but in fact artists had employed bodycolour to produce large works which were closely framed in the manner of oil paintings throughout the eighteenth century. Bodycolour, also known as gouache, involved the addition of chinese white, which rendered the watercolour opaque. Inventories record how such 'paintings' were glazed and formed an important part of the decoration of smaller domestic spaces within large houses and the main rooms of humbler homes; moreover, although it was not their main purpose, such works could also hold their own with oils in exhibitions. It is often forgotten that Paul Sandby exhibited numerous gouaches such as *Morning* (RA (?)1795; fig. 168), and that these were always close-framed in distinction to his

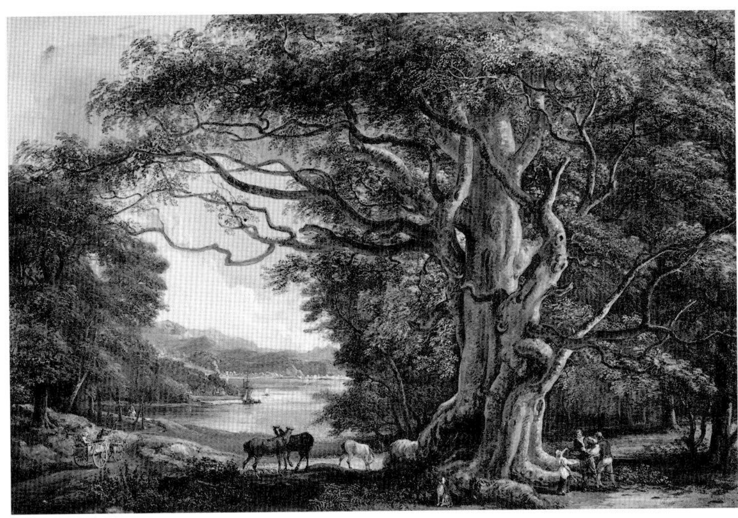

168 Paul Sandby, *Morning*, RA (?)1795, bodycolour. Courtesy of the Board of Trustees of the Victoria & Albert Museum.

'stained drawings'; John Laporte and George Barret, Senior were others who showed such works at the Academy. The bright and often garish colours of these 'paintings' are disturbing to modern tastes, and this may have been one factor in their declining popularity towards the end of the century, when a new generation of artists developed the potential of transparent watercolours to produce a similarly striking and large commodity which could satisfy changing standards of naturalism.

Gouaches suffer from their own conservation problems, but as they are less liable to fading they have tended to survive more often in their original frames than 'pure' watercolours. The taste for cream mounts and simple frames, compounded by the need to protect the image from the damaging effects of light, means that a framed watercolour is more likely to have been altered than any other category of work. Only a few of the larger works by Turner or Girtin, for instance, remain attached to their original stretchers and retain their frames, and, as in the case of the former's *Chryses* (RA 1811), these objects are usually in private collections. Unfortunately, the loss of material evidence is not counterbalanced by any images of watercolours at the Academy's exhibitions; however, the view of the 1807 exhibition of the Society of Painters in Water Colours from the *Microcosm of London* (1808; fig. 169), and a drawing by George Scharf of the gallery of the New Society of Painters in Water Colours in 1834 (London, Victoria & Albert Museum), give us some idea of the increasing complexity and size of frames, and of the way artists/collectors followed the fashions set by painters.[51] Evidence that a similar shift took place within the domestic environment comes from two views of major collections of Turner's watercolours: the depiction of the interior of Walter Fawkes's London home (*c.*1819, private collection), and the later record of the appearance of Benjamin Windus's library (1835, fig. 170). These images offer a timely reminder that the watercolour frame was first and foremost a piece of domestic furniture, and not simply

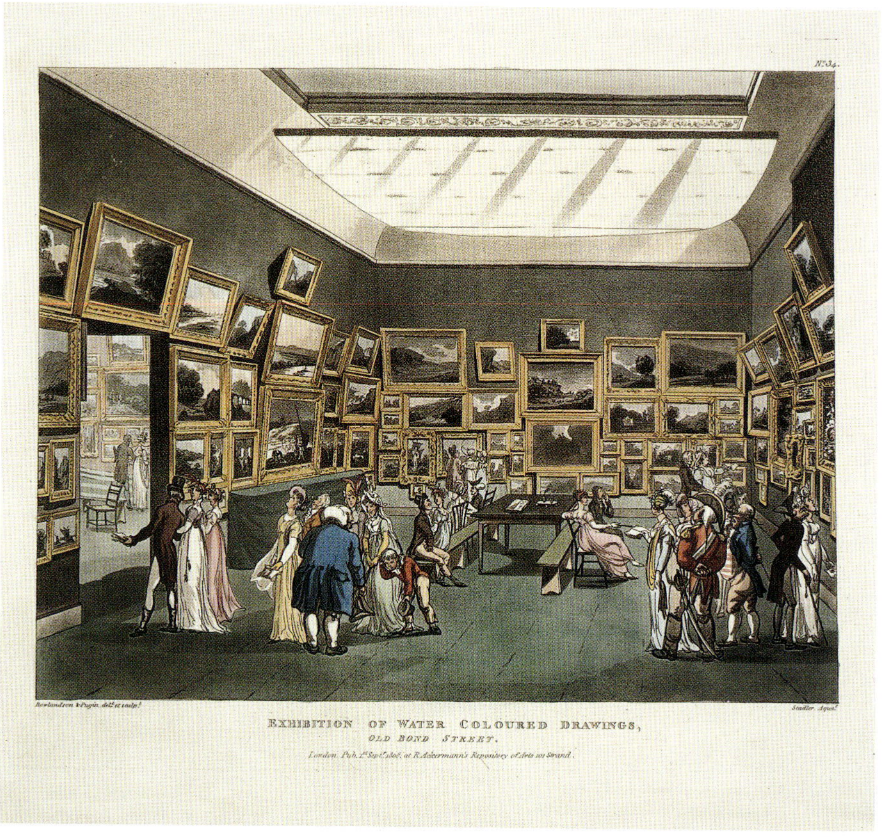

169 Joseph Stadler after Thomas Rowlandson and Augustus Pugin, *Exhibition of Water Coloured Drawings, Old Bond Street*, hand-coloured aquatint from *The Microcosm of London* (1808). By permission of The British Library.

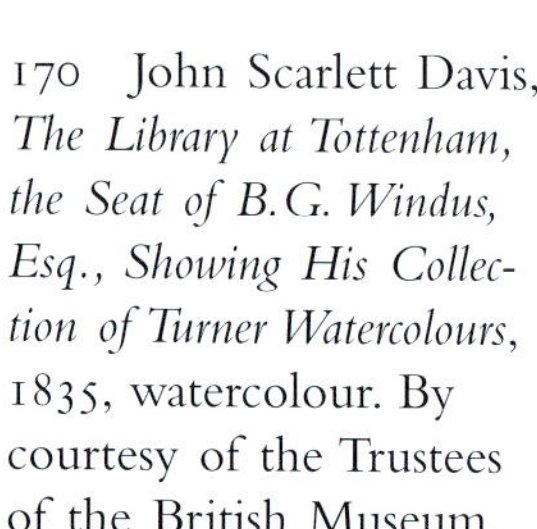

170 John Scarlett Davis, *The Library at Tottenham, the Seat of B.G. Windus, Esq., Showing His Collection of Turner Watercolours*, 1835, watercolour. By courtesy of the Trustees of the British Museum.

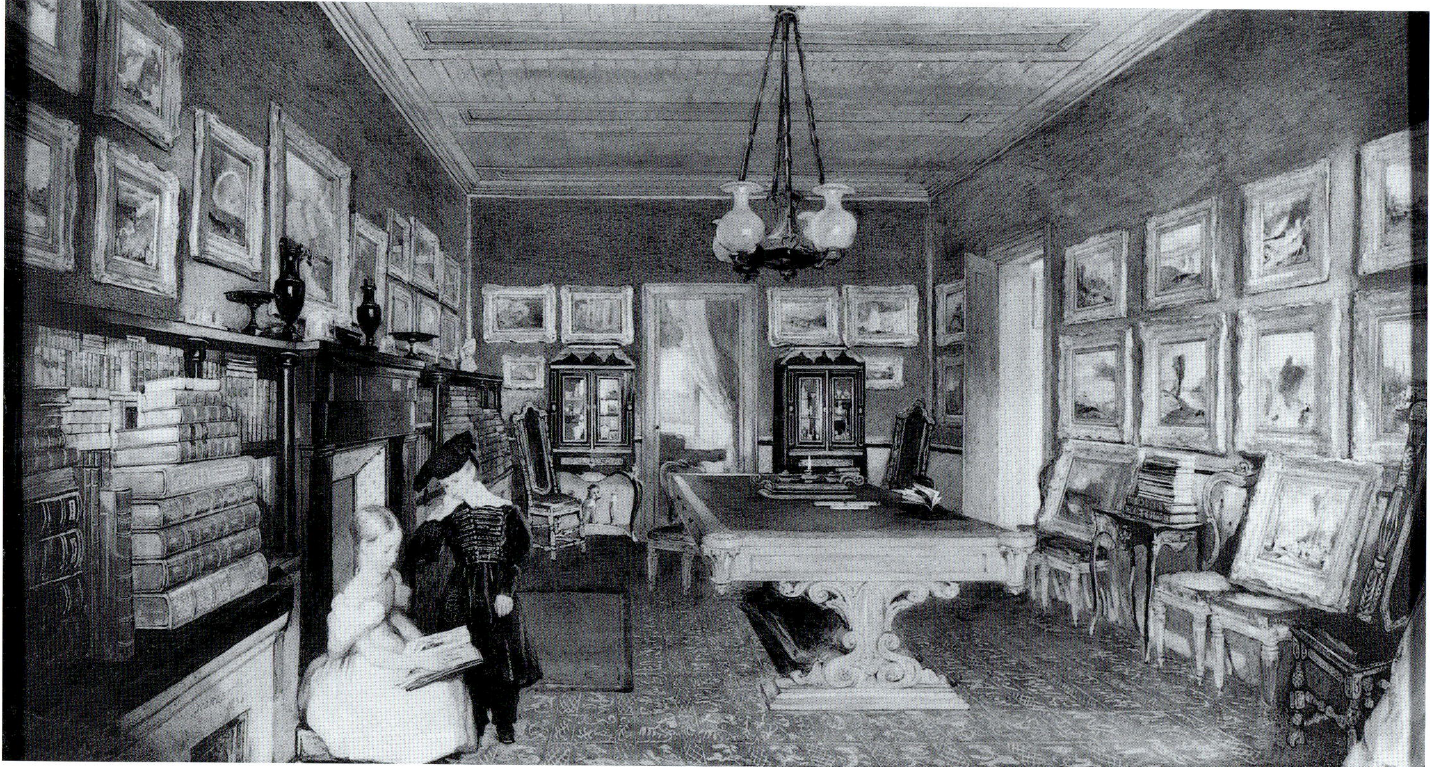

a means to attract attention in the competitive space of the public exhibition.

The majority of watercolours, however, were designed for close perusal and handling, and for this reason were kept in portfolios and albums in the library; consequently, they were usually mounted on a secondary support which was often decorated

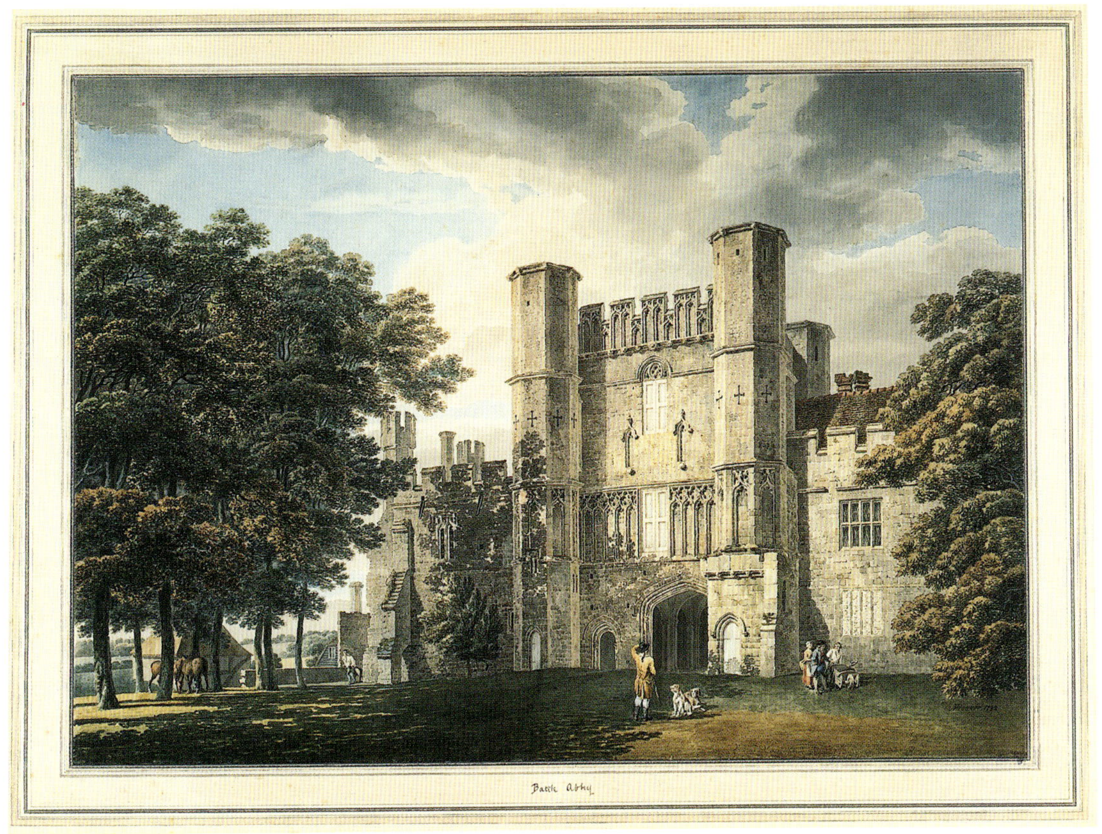

171 Michael Angelo Rooker, *The Gatehouse of Battle Abbey*, RA 1792, pencil and watercolour, with an original mount. Royal Academy of Arts, London.

with a decorative border. Unfortunately, these, too, have been subject to radical changes, and in a reversal of the fate of the framed work, the substitution of a new broad mount has allowed collectors and museums to present works designed for handling as framed objects. The widespread loss of original mounts also means that it is impossible to say what proportion of works shown at the Academy were designed for the portfolio. The conventional wisdom is that the practice became less common around the turn of the century, but the detailed research which might confirm this has not been carried out. What can be said, however, is that an older generation of artists such as Paul Sandby, Edward Dayes, Michael Angelo Rooker and Thomas Hearne continued to produce and exhibit watercolours mounted in this way, and that this reflected their primary function. Rooker's view of the gatehouse of Battle Abbey (RA 1792; fig. 171), mounted with its title added to the border, is a good example of a work which, despite its size and degree of finish, was never framed and was purchased specifically for the portfolio. Such mounts were not just designed to offer physical protection to the works they contained, or to highlight them visually; in addition, they represent the appropriation of a well-established convention associated with the collection of old master drawings. Moreover, the development of the framed 'painting in water colours' did not mean that smaller and less finished drawings ceased to appear at the Academy, though they may have looked lightweight by comparison; many patrons continued to commission and purchase drawings for reasons unconnected with display.

My contention that larger works designed for domestic display, either in gouache or watercolour, formed a small fraction of the total number of exhibits, applies with equal truth to one of the most substantial categories of watercolour featured in the exhibitions: works designed to be reproduced. These were submitted throughout the period in order to advertise the publication of prints, and we might expect that the practice encouraged the production of more imposing works, especially as their production costs were low compared with those of their reproduction. However, the wide range of types of prints which were aimed at different sectors of the market meant that there was neither a common prototype nor a single way of presenting the works in the exhibitions. Book illustrations encompassing small-scale figurative subjects, topographical views and scientific specimens, and prints for framing including smaller stipples, more prestigious engravings, as well as larger, often hand-coloured aquatints, each had their own specific requirements which determined the form and the presentation of the prototype. Edward Dayes's *Queen Square, London* (RA 1787; fig. 172) is typical of many works, including those of Paul Sandby, which were exhibited with a broad wash mount prior to being published as aquatints in the same format. Aquatint was especially valued for

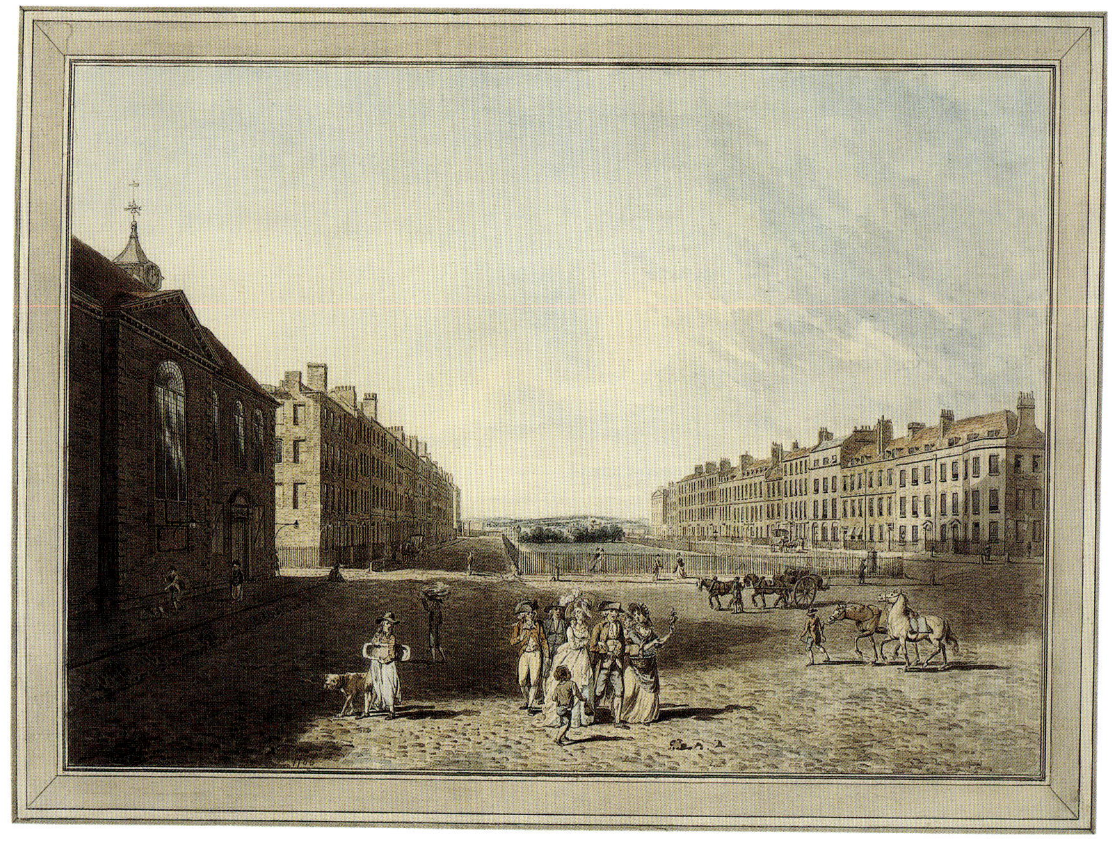

172 Edward Dayes, *Queen Square, London*, RA 1787, watercolour, with an original mount. Yale Center for British Art, Paul Mellon Collection.

its capacity to reproduce watercolour washes and the stained drawing in particular, but by printing in colours, and with the addition of hand-colouring, the watercolourist Richard Westall, for example, was able to publish elaborate reproductions after his own highly finished watercolours which were designed to be close-framed like their prototypes. It must be admitted, however, that Westall's enterprise was unusual, and that more commonly artists were constrained by the limitations of the media used in the reproductive process. The contractual relationship between artist and publisher compelled the former to find a balance between making a strong impact in the exhibition space and producing a commodity that would work well as the model for a print.

Last but not least, we need to mention one category of artists who uniquely enjoyed complete control over their own productions: amateurs. Unfortunately, although in any given exhibition works by amateurs constituted as much as 10 per cent of the total shown – and most of these must have been watercolours of some sort – only a handful of exhibits can be securely identified. The fact that these pictures were produced for pleasure, and were given or exchanged rather than sold, underlines their exceptionally private nature; however, they were not confined to simple washed drawings designed for the portfolio. In addition to oil paintings, amateurs showed miniatures, portrait drawings and more finished watercolours, as well as works that, unusually for the exhibition, were listed as 'sketches', and this variety would have been reflected in the presentation of their work. The sizeable presence of the work of amateurs in the exhibitions is particularly significant for the way in which it points up a crucial contrast with that of the professionals: they alone were exempt from economic constraints and were able to pursue their art for its own sake. The exhibition may have been the key location in which artists staked a claim to personal reputation, and where they collectively negotiated professional status and identity, but the process also identified the limits imposed by the market. Arguing for their position within the Academy was one thing, but squaring those ambitions with the realities of commerce was another. Works which employed watercolours performed many different functions, but the exhibition both smoothed over those differences and highlighted one feature that was common to the work of all professional artists: their works were commodities. Exploring the function of the works via a detailed reconstruction of their original presentation can not only help us to see the way that watercolours were originally displayed, but can also shed important light on the professional project itself and the difficulties it faced.

14

Exhibiting Architecture: Strategies of Representation in English Architectural Exhibition Drawings, 1760–1836

NICHOLAS SAVAGE

ON FRIDAY, 3 MAY 1776 the *Morning Post, and Daily Advertiser* carried a remarkable column-length introduction to a review by 'Philo-Architectus' of 'the architectural Designs now exhibiting at the Royal Academy in Pall Mall'.[1] Although ostensibly addressing the issue of how a visitor should judge an architectural design shown in the exhibition – namely that it was 'not by the excellence of the *drawing*, but by that *design*'s being, or supposed to be carried into execution, that the full and true effect ought to be estimated' – the reviewer's real purpose, as his title 'The Architects' Mirror' suggests, was to draw attention to the disadvantages with which exhibiting architects had to contend as compared with painters and sculptors. Philo-Architectus's perceptive view of these, which is clearly that of an architect as opposed to a connoisseur or potential client, may be summarized as follows. Firstly, since 'the chief difficulty in forming a right judgement of an architectural design' lay in the fact 'that there is no exact standard in nature to regulate our judgement by', it was not surprising that architecture, although 'a noble art', received no ready understanding in the exhibition, especially amongst an audience in which 'almost every person thinks himself qualified to judge of a painting, because he supposes himself sufficiently acquainted with the works of creation'. Secondly, although it could not 'be denied but that the most elegant and well designed structure may be executed from the rudest draughts', and 'that an architect may be very eminent in his profession and yet (strange as it may sound) not capable of making a *drawing* worthy of a school-boy's notice', it was none the less the case that 'the best architectural designs should be expressed somewhat gracefully, and especially when exhibited to public view, otherwise they cannot among paintings be introduced with propriety' and 'the most ingenious architect by not paying a little attention to his *drawing*, may lose the merit of his *design* how excellent soever it may be'. Thirdly, whereas 'when the painter and sculptor have finished their pieces of art, their work is done, and the reward due to their merit may consequently (and oftentimes does) immediately follow, not so the architect', whose designs can be judged only on the basis of the buildings they propose and not on the beauty of their drawings which in any case 'will probably be buried in oblivion' for want of a client with sufficient taste, time and money to carry them out. And finally, there was the problem that a design that has not been executed might appear for that reason alone to be of less account than one that has. Although an architectural design may exist only on paper, what mattered was that 'it might be executed', or, in other words, that its significance as a design lay in its potential to be realized irrespective of any actual translation into bricks and mortar.

I open this chapter with Philo-Architectus's 'Mirror' because it shows how, almost from the start, certain underlying problems concerning the nature and purpose of architectural drawings were brought to the surface in the exhibition and were to affect both their reception and their evolution as an autonomous genre over the next half-century. Philo-Architectus's repeated insistence upon the importance of the distinction between a *design* and the *drawing* in which it is represented depends on the notion, stemming ultimately from Plato, that the former exists independently of the latter, not as a particular realization in built or graphic form, but as a prior idea or concept in the architect's

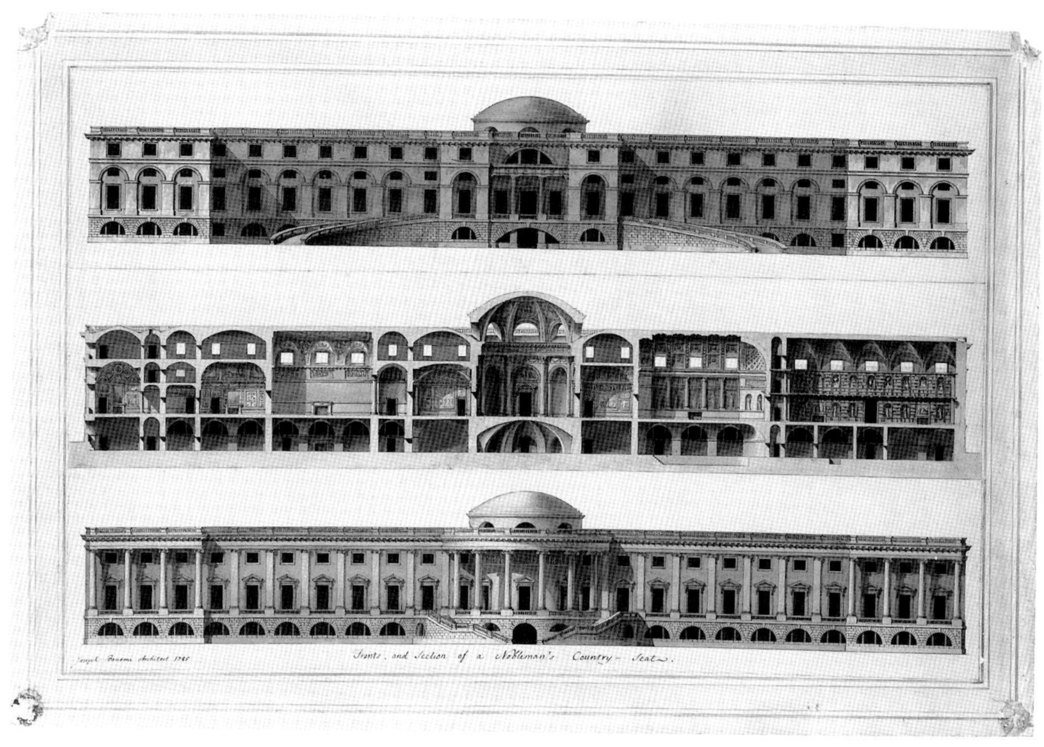

173 Joseph Bonomi, *Fronts and Section of a Nobleman's Country Seat*, RA 1785, watercolour. British Architectural Library, Royal Institute of British Architects, London.

imagination. Unlike the painter or sculptor, whose art is to be judged according to what it expresses in paint or models in clay, the architect's design remains in a sense locked in his or her head, the drawings or other means by which it is communicated being either 'tools' to enable its execution or 'reports' on its imagined effect upon the eye. In the context of the exhibition this alienation becomes all the more intense because, on the one hand the functional nature of 'tools' (working drawings and, one suspects, three-dimensional architectural models as well) tended to disqualify precisely those representations which suggested a direct relationship to the reality of a building and the process of its construction; while on the other, the approximate nature of imaginative 'reports' on the effect of an architect's design (be they in his own hand or in that of an accomplice) always ran the risk of appearing false precisely to the degree that they pretended to the autonomy of art. Caught in this double-bind of having to be both factual (i.e., faithful emissaries of the architect's ideas) and expressive of the effects of their execution in built form, drawings of designs prepared for exhibition purposes were forced to develop new strategies of architectural representation that diverged from those which had evolved in books and prints or were the natural product of architectural practice. My aim here is to suggest some of the ways in which these strategies are evident in aspects of the form and content of exhibited architectural drawings during the period.

Although these aspects are raised in more or less the order in which they appear, it is not my purpose to propose a history of architectural exhibition drawings as a genre for the simple reason that too few have survived for a meaningful narrative to be proposed. And even if this were not the case, it is important to guard against the idea that architectural drawings must parallel in some way the stylistic development of other, contemporaneous art forms. Like photography – another deeply 'compromised' form of visual expression – the architectural exhibition drawing has its own history which, although yet to be written, is quite distinct from that of other drawn and painted media, in spite of its appropriation of the latter's methods and motifs. Concentrating instead on the unique contradiction at the heart of its enterprise will also make it clearer how the exhibition of architectural designs at the Academy during this period followed no simple line of progression but evolved a growing multiplicity of different means of representation which functioned in parallel rather than succession.

One of the simplest strategies of the architectural exhibition drawing – what might be termed its opening gambit – is easily overlooked, namely that of forming a matching or contrasting group of works by the same architect. Although an exhibitor had of course no control over the placing of his submissions, the need to achieve a symmetrical hang meant that drawings that formed a natural group were always likely to be viewed favourably by the Hanging Committee, especially in the early years when pressure on space had not yet become a major issue. In architecture, however, the most natural grouping is between plans, elevations and sections of the same design, which in visual terms will balance on the wall only with another design represented in the same way. Such pattern-making tends to

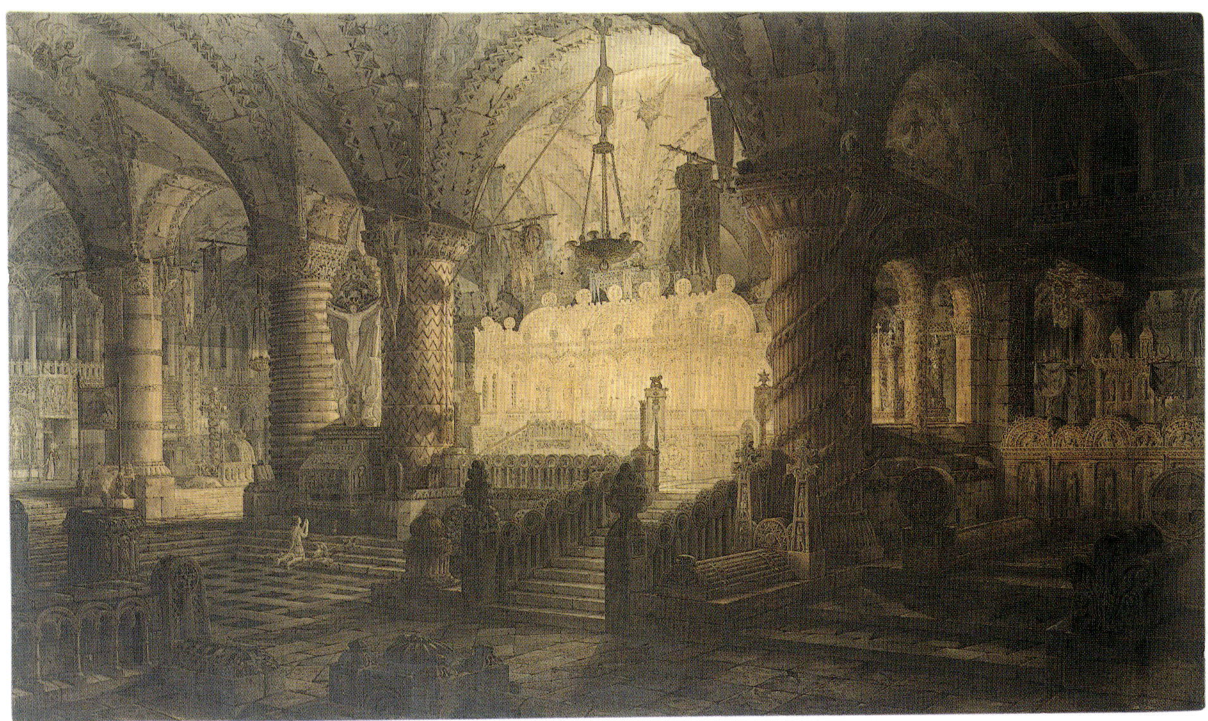

174 J. M. Gandy, *The Tomb of Merlin*, RA 1815, watercolour. British Architectural Library, Royal Institute of British Architects, London.

emphasize the abstract, mechanical quality of orthographic and planimetric *drawings* at the expense of their legibility as *designs*, especially when displayed in a miscellany of other works on paper, as architecture invariably was at the Academy until 1793. The evidence of the catalogues suggests in fact that after the first decade of exhibitions the traditional series of plan, elevation and two sections to show a single design – such as, for instance, Edward Stevens used to exhibit his design of *A Town Mansion for a Person of Distinction* in 1766 – was to be seen only rarely in the exhibition. The matter-of-fact office-drawn plan, elevation or section, rendered in pen and ink with grey and pink washes used as conventional codes to indicate exterior surfaces and sections of solid parts, could convey the authority of the architect effectively enough in the workplace and on site. But once removed from its role as part of the architect's explanation of a proposed design to a client or series of instructions to the builder, and placed instead in a public exhibition of works of art, this kind of representation ran the risk of appearing to lack the element of 'grace' that Philo-Architectus felt was necessary in such a context.

Thus although architecture had made only a slight showing in public art exhibitions in Britain by the time the Academy first opened its doors at New Somerset House in 1780, from the start its representation was never restricted to the straightforward 'Office of Works' drawing. When a young William Newton, for instance, exhibited *A Piece of Architecture in Perspective* at the first of London's art exhibitions in 1760, he probably hoped that its pictorial quality would help to redress the more utilitarian manner in which he represented his accompanying *Design for an Academy*.[2] In spite of the obvious drawback of this strategy – there was no guarantee that the juxtapositions upon which it depended would be detectable in the hang – contrasts between different modes of representation and variety in their selection of subjects remained an important factor in architects' submissions to the exhibition. It can be seen at work in Joseph Bonomi's pairing in 1785 of two interior views of the Pantheon in Rome alongside an ambitious design for a vast country mansion – *Fronts and Section of a Nobleman's Country Seat* (RA 1785; fig. 173) – and in his combination the following year of two exterior views and a further interior perspective of the same ancient Roman building alongside a spectacular watercolour of the fitting out of a proposed library for Lansdowne House (*Design of a Library for a Nobleman in Town* (RA 1786); Bowood, The Trustees of the Bowood Collection).

The attempt to set up connections and contrasts between drawings exhibited by the same architect was taken to its furthest extreme by Joseph Michael Gandy, whose numerous exhibits at the Academy from 1800 to 1838 repeatedly drew attention to the ironic incongruity between what a modern architect was asked to design and what his imagination was capable of producing by bracketing together, for instance: *Pandemonium* (RA 1805; private coll.) with the *New Phoenix Fire Office at Charing Cross*; a *Design of an Entrance to a Public Bath Built at Lancaster* (RA 1806) with a recreation of the *Odeum or Music-school* described by Pausanias; the *Tomb of Merlin* (RA 1815; fig. 174) with a *Ball Room*; *A Geometrical Elevation of Part of the*

Fronts of an Idea for an Imperial Palace . . . Estimated to be Built in Ten Years at £300,000 per Annum (RA 1824) with *A Sketch of the Alterations and Additions Now Erecting for General Sir Robert Bolton near Chipping Norton*; *An Idea of the Staircase Leading to the Gates of Heaven* (RA 1832) with *Design for the Entrance Hall at Ince, a Seat of H. Blundell Esq.*; and so on. Gandy is usually portrayed as a somewhat tragic figure, a failed architect dependent upon Sir John Soane's employment and protection to make ends meet. This picture should, I think, be modified by the recognition of a sense of humour at play in the above juxtapositions. No one without his tongue somewhat in his cheek could have exhibited a painting entitled *The Fugitives* (RA 1822) in the same year as a *Perspective Sectional Plan, Elevation and Section, of . . . Part of the Arrangements of Lancaster Prison. . . .* Perhaps taking his cue from J. M. W. Turner's quotation of his 'Fallacies of Hope' poem, Gandy also pursued the idea of exhibiting a sequence of related drawings over successive years. Thus, for five consecutive years between 1824 and 1828, he linked a series of perspectives of his British imperial palace project by means of cross-reference and quotation in the catalogue, and right at the end of his long exhibiting career, attempted to expound a narrative concerning the mythic origin and progress of architecture by exhibiting a sequence of three related watercolours in 1836, 1837 and 1838.[3] The spatial difficulty of comparing the same artist's works in the exhibition, if this was already not encouraged by the hang, is here compounded by that of having to rely on the visitor's memory of previous years, so it understandably remained a more or less unique experiment. Reliance on sequence, even more than juxtaposition, stemmed from the conditions under which books and portfolios worked rather than from the needs and limitations of a public exhibition space.

One could view all this variety and contrast within individual architects' exhibits simply as evidence that, being naturally keen to make the most of the visual resources and design opportunities available to them, they revelled in the freedom afforded by ambiguity and vagueness as to what constituted the best means of exhibiting their art. This freedom was illusory, however, because what they were really up against was the intractable exigency of having to condense the essential qualities, intricacies and beauties of a building on to generally a single sheet of paper. Whether out of natural limitations as a practising architect or because of his particular abilities as a draughtsman, it fell to John Yenn, an otherwise undistinguished pupil and follower of Sir William Chambers, to be the first regular architectural exhibitor to grasp the implications in graphic terms of this fundamental requirement of the *exhibition* as opposed to the *project* drawing. Employing a stock repertoire of visual effects to enliven orthographic elevations, such as rain-streaked ashlar surfaces, repoussoir trees, smoking urns and chimney-pots and stormy skies (tricks that had been learned in Chambers's office and would have been recognizable in many of the drawings of his fellow pupils, among whom Edward Stevens, Thomas Hardwick, James Gandon and Thomas Whetten were regular exhibitors at the Academy in the 1770s), Yenn took the lead in establishing a strategy whereby the representation of part of a building – usually its principal façade but sometimes a longitudinal section – stood for its totality. Exhibiting virtually every year at the Academy from 1771 to 1782 and again sporadically in the 1790s, from 1773 onwards Yenn took the plunge of abandoning ground plans altogether, and indeed thereafter never showed more than one drawing per design in the exhibition.[4]

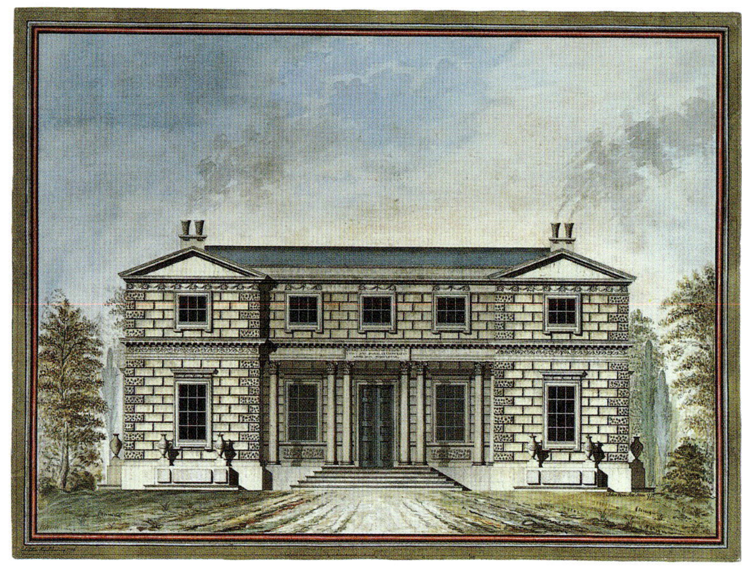

175 John Yenn, *A Casine for a Gentleman's Park*, RA 1776, watercolour. Royal Academy of Arts, London.

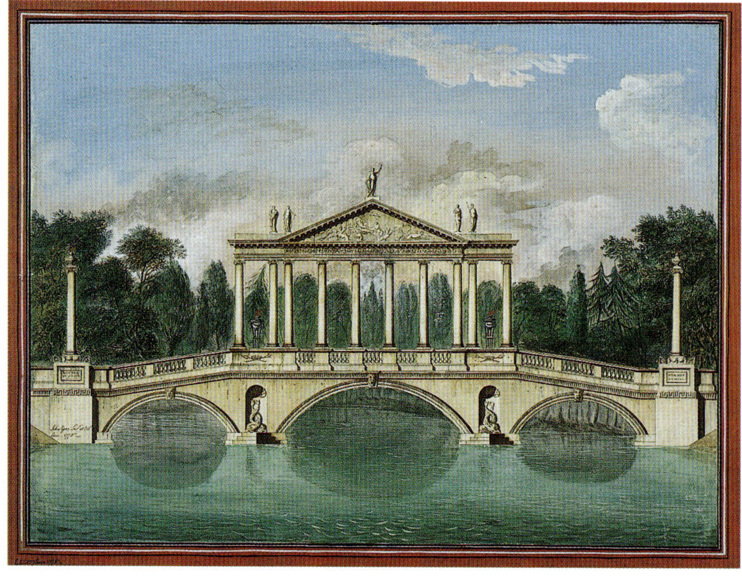

176 John Yenn, *A Design for a Bridge, in the Manner of the Palladian Bridge . . . at Wilton*, RA 1775, watercolour and bodycolour. Royal Academy of Arts, London.

In keeping with the critical principles outlined in the introduction to his review, Philo-Architectus had commented only on the merits and demerits of Yenn's designs in 1776 for *A*

Casine for a Gentleman's Park (RA 1776; fig. 175) and *A Villa* and not at all on their manner of presentation.[5] Yenn's typical rendering in these drawings of orthographic elevations set in flat planes of stylized 'trees, ground, and sky' was perhaps less in danger this year of being criticized by Philo-Architectus for being 'too apt to captivate the eye and mislead the judgement', since he abandoned the use of gouache which had been a feature of his exhibits in 1775 (fig. 176).[6] Paradoxically, in Philo-Architectus's opinion such visual props in an orthographic drawing were more likely to distract the eye and 'mislead the judgement' than if the design was shown in perspective. Thus he praised Chambers's *Plan and Elevation of a Mausoleum* (RA 1776; figs 177 and 178) in particular, observing 'that the whole being in perspective produces the most pleasing effect'.[7]

According to Philo-Architectus, out of the eighteen architectural drawings in the 1776 exhibition only one other, John Dotchen's *Villa Designed for a Gentleman in Middlesex*, was similarly shown in perspective. (This incidentally provides valuable corroboration of the statistical evidence derivable from catalogue descriptions, unreliable as these can be in specific instances, about the rarity of perspectives in the architectural section of the exhibition at this date.) Interestingly, in the case of Dotchen's villa design, Philo-Architectus finds the way that it is 'perspectively exhibited' valuable because this reveals, not so much its beautiful 'effect', but rather a 'little blemish' which 'could not have been seen if the design had not been in *perspective*'. The usefulness of perspective to architects and the public in general lay as much in its ability to expose the faults, as in its capacity to express the beauties, of a proposed design. Philo-Architectus puts his finger here on a key advantage of architectural perspective in the exhibition context, namely its capacity to synthesize visual information which, when shown orthographically, has to be dispersed between several different drawings and/or forms of representation.

Chambers's resuscitation in 1776 of an advanced Franco-Italian perspective drawing, dating from his heady years in Rome a quarter of a century earlier, was probably not intended to be a statement about the merits of this particular form of presentation. That Philo-Architectus interpreted it as such was, however, quite revolutionary in 1776 because it ran counter to the neo-Palladian, Office of Works tradition of architectural draughtsmanship that had predominated in England since the early eighteenth century. Stemming ultimately from Alberti's rejection of perspective on the grounds that it distorted the intellectually prefigured 'lineaments' upon which a design was founded, this tradition had established strong roots in English architectural engraving since the publication of *Vitruvius Britannicus* (3 vols, 1715–25), Colen Campbell's nationalistic celebration of the rise and progress of 'regular' (i.e., classical) architecture in Britain. What Philo-Architectus is registering here then is a quite new expectation that an architectural drawing should provide the means of judging how a design might appear in relation to an observer in a particular place once it has been carried

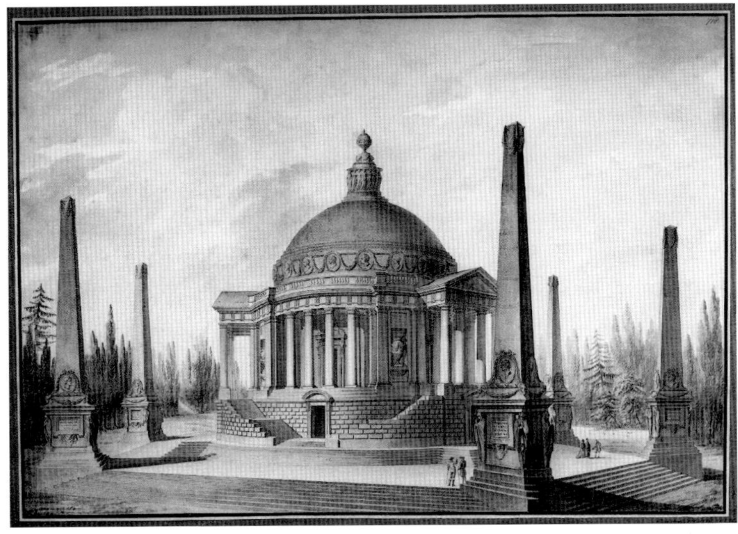

177 William Chambers, *Elevation of a Mausoleum*, RA 1776, watercolour. The Trustees of Sir John Soane's Museum.

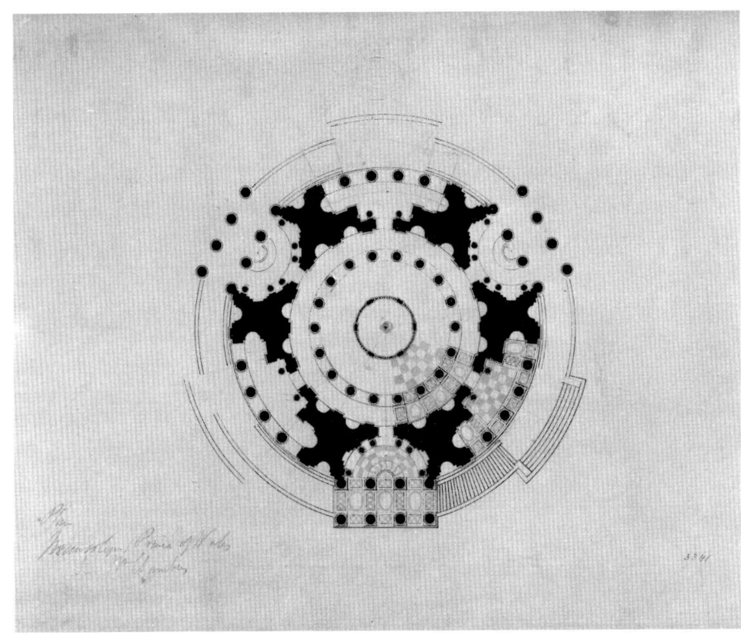

178 William Chambers, *Plan . . . of a Mausoleum*, RA 1776, watercolour. Courtesy of the Board of Trustees of the Victoria & Albert Museum.

into effect, rather than simply marking out and defining the organization and dimensions of its constituent elements in relation to itself (what Alberti had called its 'concinnitas') independently of any single, and therefore necessarily partial and distorted, viewpoint. The notion, a by-product of an emerging taste for 'picturesque' scenery (already evident in the popularity of William Gilpin's tours, which began to circulate in manuscript in the 1770s), that buildings could generate feelings and associations in common with specific types of landscape, is already at work in the ambiguity of Philo-Architectus's use of the word 'effect'.[8] Another influence, more directly relating to architecture, stemmed from Piranesi via Clérisseau to Robert Adam, who had written in 1773 of a concept of 'movement', in which 'the rising and falling, advancing and receding, with the convexity and concavity, and other forms of the great parts' of a composition had 'the same effect in architecture, that hill and dale, fore-ground and distance, swelling and sinking have in landscape: That is, they serve to produce an agreeable and diversified contour, that groups and contrasts like a picture, and creates a variety of light and shade, which gives great spirit, beauty and effect to the composition'.[9] Although Philo-Architectus might have been able to distinguish in his own mind between the effect of a building and the effect of its picture, such a distinction must have been generally lost upon an audience predisposed to the idea that the former might be quite properly understood in terms of the latter, and who had anyway come to the exhibition expecting to see finished works of art, not mere representations of them.

In spite of Philo-Architectus's advanced opinions, to judge from the catalogue descriptions architects seem to have remained generally conservative about adopting perspective in exhibition drawings throughout the 1770s and much of the 1780s. In 1780 for instance, even though the number of architects exhibiting rose steeply to thirty-two (compared with a mere fourteen the previous year), not one chose to describe what he exhibited as a 'view' or perspective of his design. It is possible that some of the drawings listed in the catalogue as 'designs' or even 'elevations' were in fact perspectives, but the fact that architects did not describe their designs more precisely in terms of any particular manner of the presentation suggests that, as far as these exhibitors were concerned, what still mattered most was that the visitor should be able to distinguish between an artist's topographical *view* of a building and an architect's drawing of its *design*. The need to maintain this distinction in the catalogue descriptions was paramount for as long as architectural designs were shown indiscriminately with topographical drawings and watercolours in the Life (or Model) Academy on the ground floor (or 'Exhibition Room of Sculpture and Drawings' as it was called until 1793 when the majority of non-architectural drawings began to be located in the Antique Academy). One might suppose perhaps that the necessity of holding their own alongside topographical views and watercolour landscapes in the exhibition would have quite quickly pushed architectural drawings towards an adoption of the same visual language. However, in so far as this influence may have operated, its opposite was equally at work, since the greater the requirement that architectural designs be visually distinguishable from topography in the same exhibition room, the more likely it was that they would stick with the geometrically drawn elevations in preference to perspectives. Although the evidence of the catalogues is difficult to interpret, if one takes the descriptions of exhibited architectural designs at face value, a pattern emerges, in which the number of plans and sections, though never common, gradually diminishes, and an equally gradual underlying trend towards a greater number of perspectives emerges in the 1780s. This strengthened noticeably from 1793, when architectural designs started to predominate for the first time in the Life Academy, and again, from 1811, when architecture was transferred *en bloc* up into the Library.[10]

Another important reason for the slowness with which perspectives were adopted by exhibiting architects – and why they never entirely superseded other modes of representing architecture in the exhibition – lies in the fact that what they show of a building is always dependent upon the choice of a specific viewpoint (unlike orthographic projections which show all points equally parallel to the picture plane). Unfortunately it is impossible to choose a viewpoint that can claim to reveal the true effect of a design without also being suspected of hiding other parts. In perspective there is, by definition, always an area hidden from sight, which becomes greater the lower or nearer the artist's viewpoint. Because of its size the closer one is to a building, the more *partial* one's view of it becomes, and the further away the more distracted one is by what the surrounding and intervening space contains. One solution – admittedly rare in either drawn or printed media – was to block out this space entirely, so that the building floated anchorless in a void. Soane experimented with this idea in a two-point 'perspective view of the entrance front' of Chillington Hall, Staffordshire, published in 1788.[11] For the exhibition however such drastic measures seem to have been generally out of the question, although it is possible that the Royal Institute of British Architects' austere, beautifully drawn central-point monochrome perspective of the east front of the Grange, Hampshire, by William Wilkins was the drawing exhibited at the Academy in 1809 or 1820.[12] The opposite approach to the problem of the partial nature of what perspective reveals was simply to walk round the building and show it from a previously hidden side – a typical example of this additive solution is Bonomi's pair of views of Rosneath, Dumbartonshire, exhibited at the Academy in 1806 (fig. 179).[13] Such doubling-up however is a denial of perspective's real source of expressiveness, which lies precisely in its capacity to persuade us to imagine what it fails to show; hence the effect of a pair of views of the same building from opposite sides is rather to cancel each other out, unless the artist at the same time quite drastically alters the angle and scope of viewing point.

Bonomi's use of complementary perspectives in the exhibition is a sign of loss of faith in the truth-telling function of this mode of representation, being in effect an attempt to reclaim for it the reliability associated with geometrically drawn elevations of the different sides of a building. The same uncertainty may be seen in the way a number of his exhibited perspectives of designs for country houses – such as those of Longford Hall, Shropshire (RA 1797; private collection) and Laverstoke Park (RA 1799; fig. 180) – reveal somewhat stark, ruler-drawn and harshly shadowed buildings that fail to occupy the rudimentary landscapes in which they are placed.[14] Such a 'failing' may seem rather odd in an architect whose early career had been built

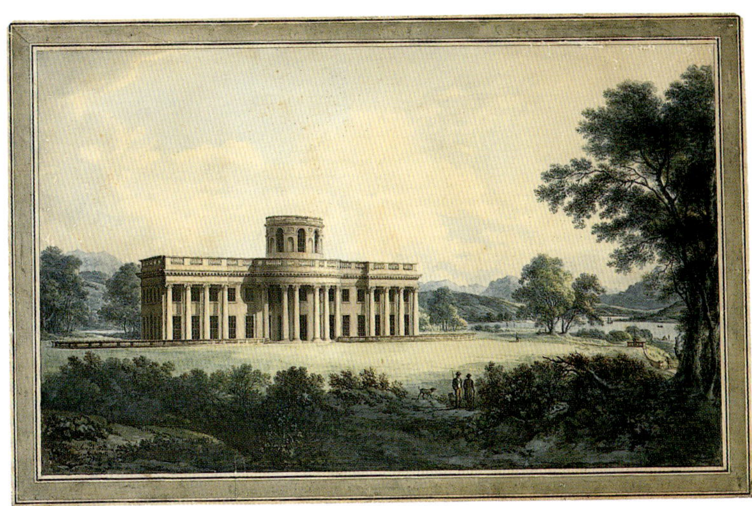

179 Joseph Bonomi, *South-east View of the House now Building at Roseneath, Dumbartonshire* . . . , RA 1806, watercolour. British Architectural Library, Royal Institute of British Architects, London.

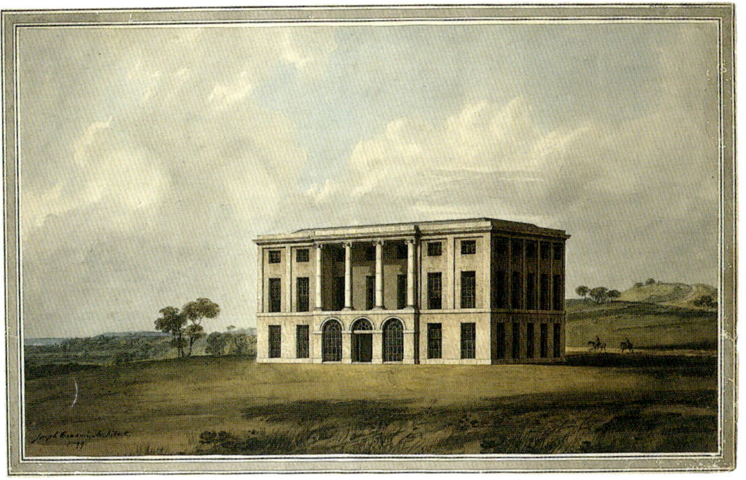

180 Joseph Bonomi, *Design for Laverstoke Park, Hampshire, for Henry Portal*, RA 1799, watercolour. British Architectural Library, Royal Institute of British Architects, London.

upon exceptional gifts as a draughtsman and who had done so much in the late 1770s and early to mid-1780s (both during and after his employment by Robert Adam), to develop perspective for the sensitive portrayal of the interplay of interior and exterior architectural space and light within the same drawing. What we are looking at here is not so much a falling off of powers in one individual, but evidence of a modification of strategy in which the art of *designing* a building is seen to reassert itself over the mere portrayal of it.

Such a reassertion of the primacy of design over drawing (expressed in this case as that of geometry over nature) became more necessary rather than less as the alienation of the architect from any direct means of representing his art in the exhibition reached its logical outcome in the employment of other hands to produce part or all of the requisite drawings. In one way the employment of a specialist draughtsman to produce exhibition drawings – as for instance James Wyatt seems to have done from early on in his career – was simply an extension of an existing division of labour between an 'office principal' and his draughtsmen which was already customary in large architectural practices by the last quarter of the eighteenth century. The difference of course was that in the context of an exhibition there was a danger that the public might suspect that the draughtsman of a design was its author; hence Wyatt's concern that his senior office assistant, John Dixon, should not appear before the public as an architect-exhibitor in his own right, and the effectiveness of Farington's lobbying against Thomas Malton's candidacy for election to the Academy in 1795 on the grounds that he was 'only a draughtsman of buildings, but no architect'.[15] Such determination to maintain a public perception of the architectural drawing as the product of an architect's mind rather than the artist's pencil is nowhere more poignantly epitomized than in the suppression of acknowledgement of the hand responsible for its production. The fact that Wyatt exhibited his second design for Fonthill (RA 1798; fig. 181) without J. M. W. Turner's name appearing either in the watercolour itself or the catalogue entry, is evidence not simply of a powerful convention at work (which, incidentally, has remained more or less effective in the architectural section of the Summer Exhibition up to the present day), but also of the defensive stance that architects had to adopt when they found themselves exhibiting by proxy.

Wyatt was in the end unable to prevent Dixon from exhibiting at the Academy, and his employment of Turner as an architectural draughtsman was not repeated.[16] A very much more fertile meeting of minds proved possible between the maverick John Soane and Joseph Gandy, the most brilliant and inventive architectural draughtsman of his generation. It is clear from the

181 James Wyatt, *Projected Design for Fonthill Abbey, Wiltshire*, RA 1798; watercolour by J. M. W. Turner. Yale Center for British Art, Paul Mellon Collection.

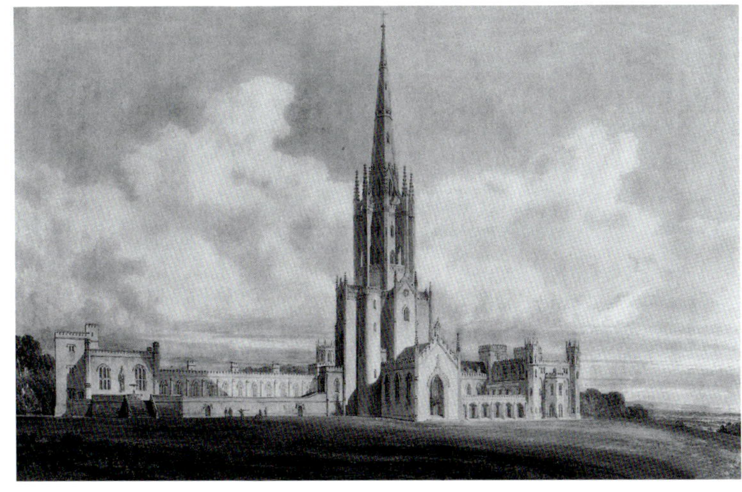

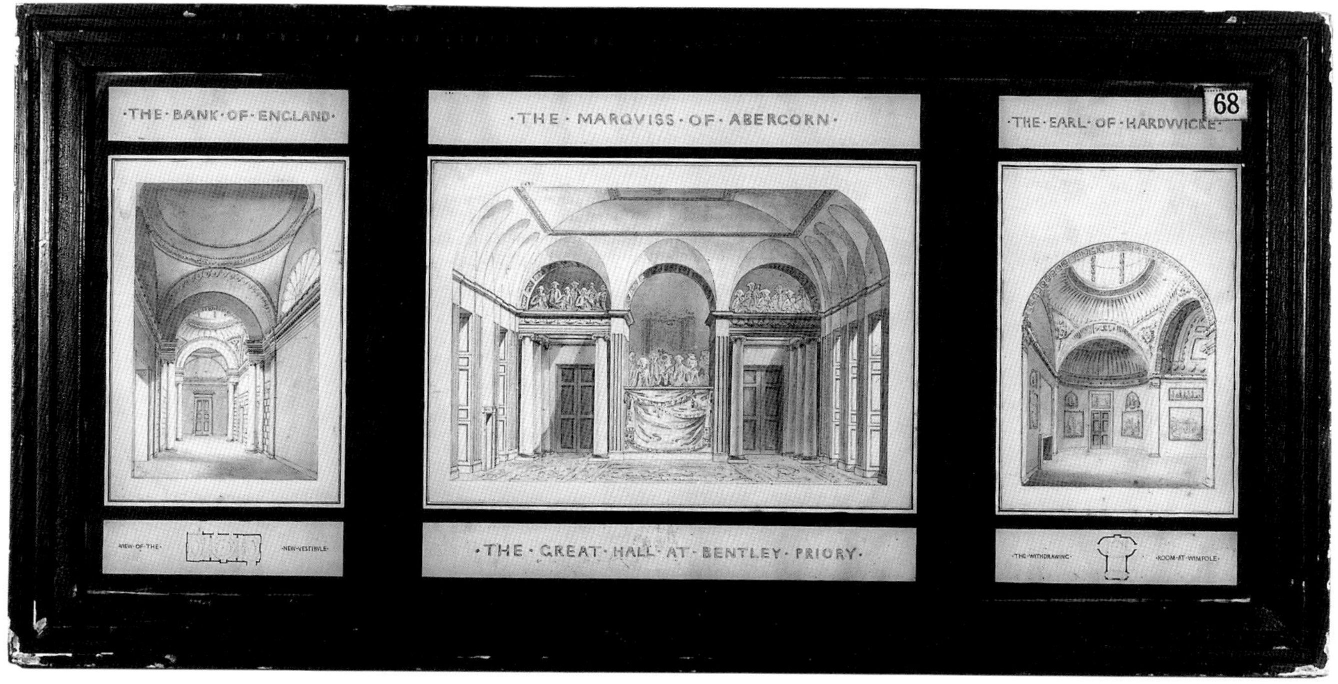

182 John Soane, *Vestibule, at the Bank of England; the Great Hall, Bentley Priory; and the Withdrawing Room at Wimpole*, RA 1792, watercolour by Thomas Chawner (a pupil). The Trustees of Sir John Soane's Museum.

history of their relations that the long series of architectural exhibition watercolours that Gandy produced for Soane were the product of a deep collaboration between the two men, rather than of the former being given a free hand or of the latter dictating precisely what he required. Soane's contribution to this partnership is generally assumed to be strictly that of choosing and supplying the designs he wished Gandy or other draughtsmen in his office to prepare for showing at the Academy. This assumption, however, has obscured the fact that Soane was responsible for at least two important strategic innovations in the representation of architecture in the exhibition.

The first of these – the introduction of textual explanations and glosses both in the labelling of exhibited drawings and in their catalogue descriptions – is more significant than it may seem, since it evinces Soane's lack of confidence in the capacity of architectural representation alone to convey his message to the public. Although Soane was obviously trying in this way to convey more – and different – things about his work in the exhibition, the fact that he felt the need to exhibit his work over and over again in virtually every year of his long career from 1772 to 1836, is indicative not of mere commitment to the Academy but of an almost obsessional need. However, rather than view this as a peculiarity in Soane's make-up (a restless desire for public approbation, for instance), it is more fruitful to see how it trapped him in the coils of the contradictory nature of architectural representation itself. Similarly, Soane's second major innovation – the use of composite depictions of the same or related designs in a single drawing – should, I think, not simply be seen as a personal quirk (or a trick to cram more of his work into the exhibition) but recognized as a response to the impossibility of 'showing it' (i.e., architecture) 'as it is' (or might be) by means of any one image or mode of representation.

In what was probably the earliest composite drawing he exhibited – containing interior views of the vestibule of the Bank of England, the great hall at Bentley Priory, Middlesex, and the drawing-room at Wimpole Hall, Cambridgeshire (RA 1792; fig. 182) – Soane used a triptych format simply to bring out the common formal and spatial characteristics of his designs, adding thumbnail ground plans in the caption area. The same format, arranged vertically, was used for *The Bank Stock Office, Constructed without Timber* (RA 1794; Soane Museum), but this time showing two views of the same interior (seen from positions at a 90 degree angle from one another) with, in the centre, a detailed plan of the vaulting. But these are tentative beginnings compared with *The Elevation, Plan, Longitudinal Perspective Section and Other Parts of a Design for a National Monument, to Perpetuate the Glorious Achievements of British Valour by Land and Sea* (RA 1818; fig. 183), which, like its accompanying *Perspective Representation of the Exterior* (Soane Museum), was probably drawn by Gandy. Ostensibly Soane and Gandy's purpose here is simply to attract the eye, but in creating a kind of *trompe l'oeil* of contrasts in scale and modes of depiction, they also throw into relief the contingent nature of each image. They used the composite cartouche device again, more decoratively, to reveal the intricate spaces of Soane's house in Lincoln's Inn Fields (RA 1822; Soane Museum), the National Debt Redemption Office (RA 1823; Soane Museum), and to compare built and unbuilt versions of

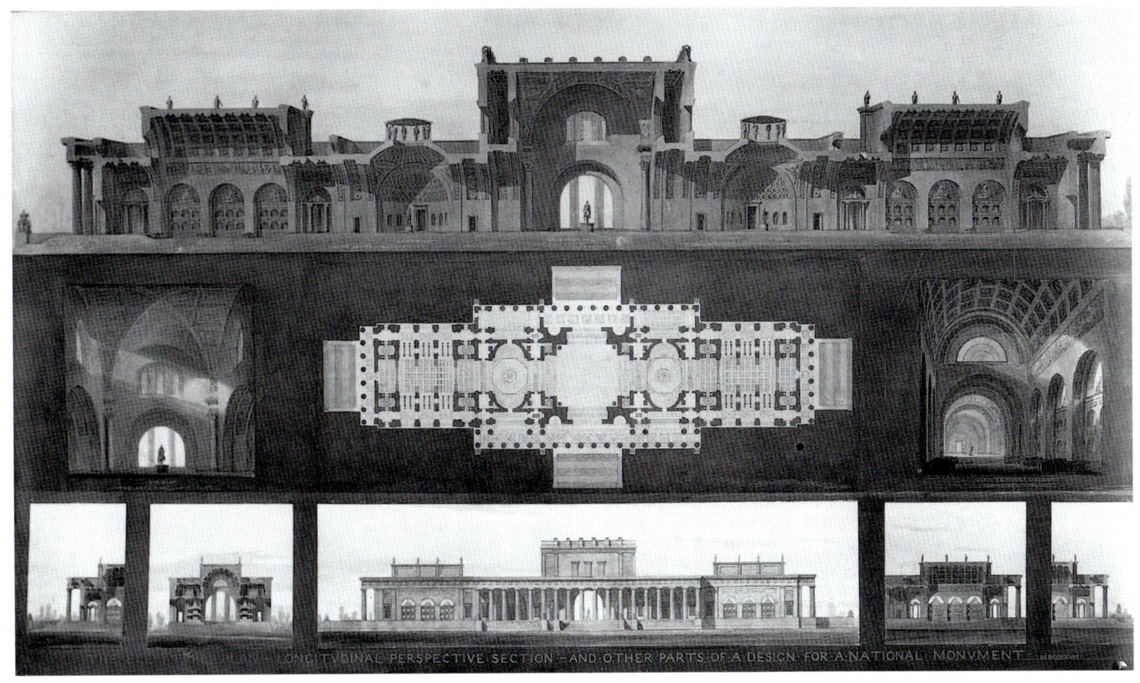

183 John Soane, *The Elevation, Plan . . . Section and other Parts of a Design for a National Monument . . .*, RA 1818, watercolour probably by J. M. Gandy. The Trustees of Sir John Soane's Museum.

184 John Soane, *An Architectural Study: Subject, the Picture Gallery and Mausoleum of the Late Sir Francis Bourgeois, at Dulwich*, RA 1823, watercolour by J. M. Gandy. The Trustees of Sir John Soane's Museum.

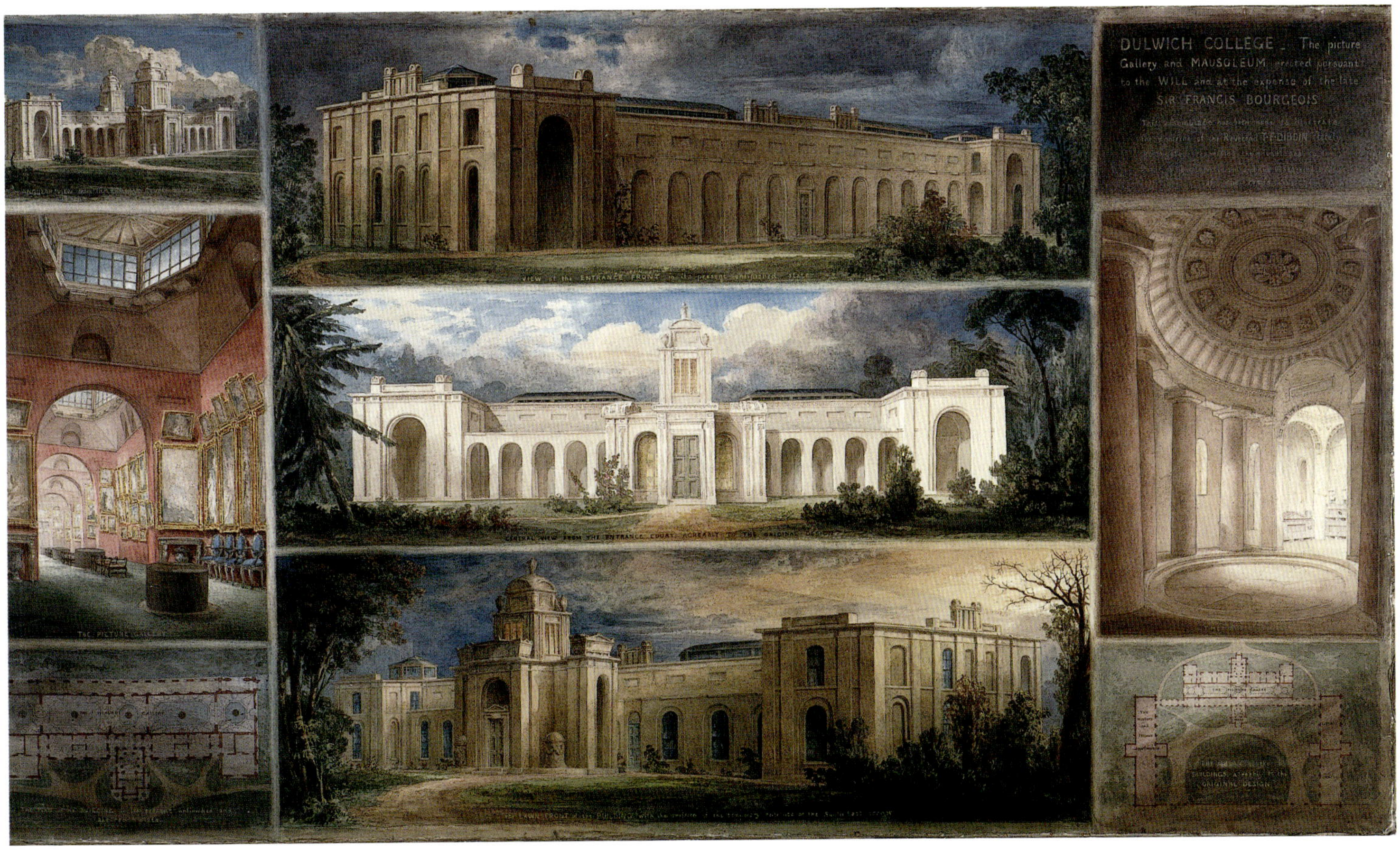

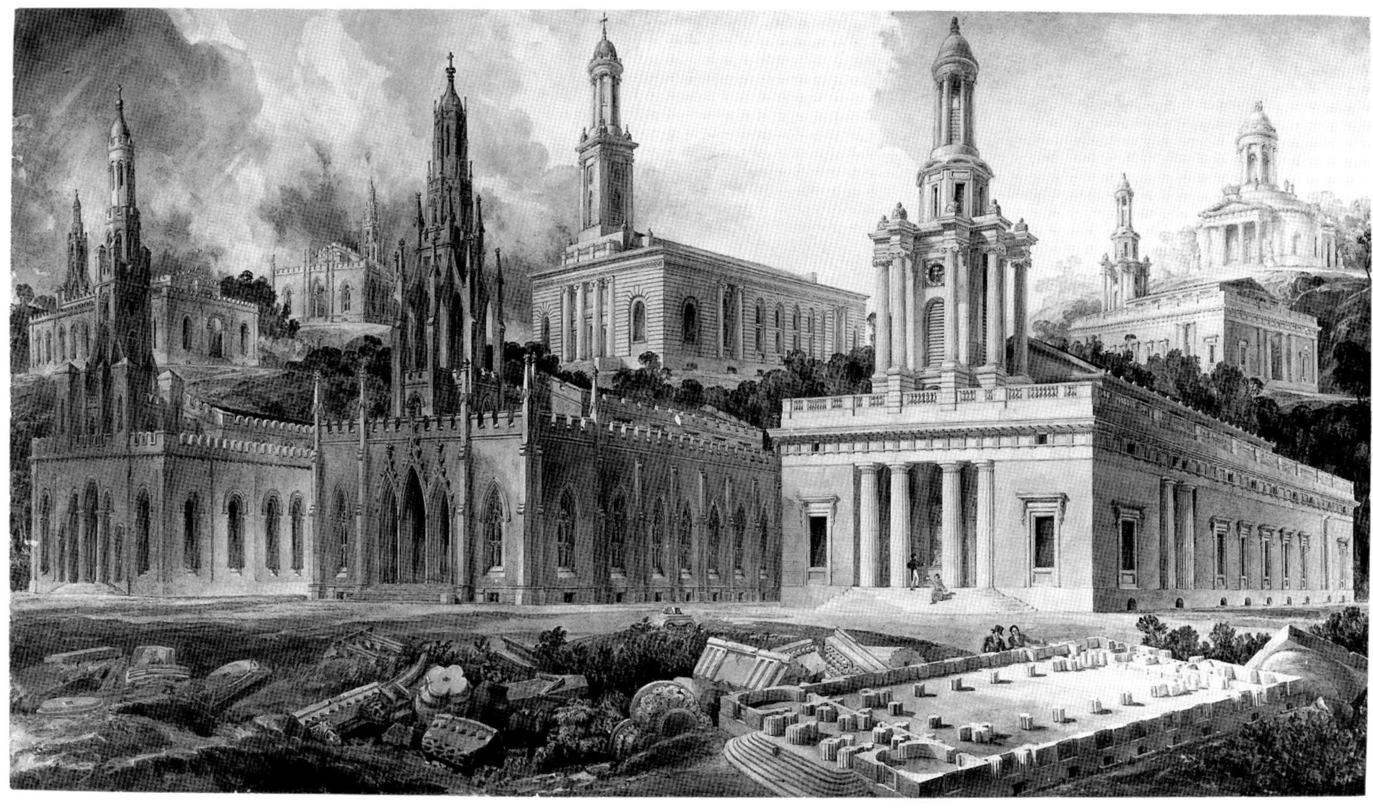

185 John Soane, *A Groupe of Churches, to Illustrate Different Styles of Architecture*, RA 1825, watercolour by J. M. Gandy. The Trustees of Sir John Soane's Museum.

186 John Soane, *A Design for a National Entrance into the Metropolis, Intended to Combine the Classical Simplicity of the Grecian Architecture, the Magnificence of the Roman Architecture, and the Fanciful Intricacy and Playful Effects of the Gothic Architecture*, RA 1826, watercolour by J. M. Gandy. The Trustees of Sir John Soane's Museum.

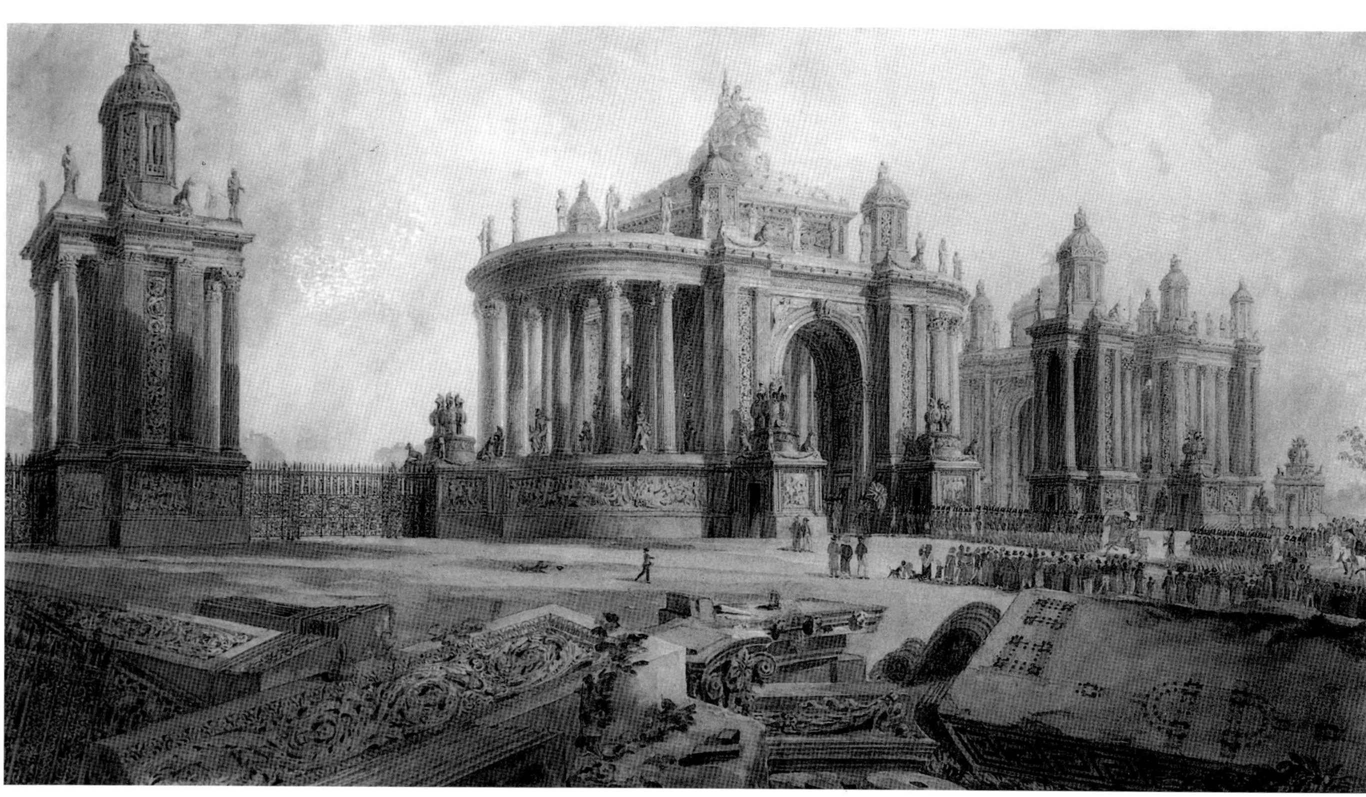

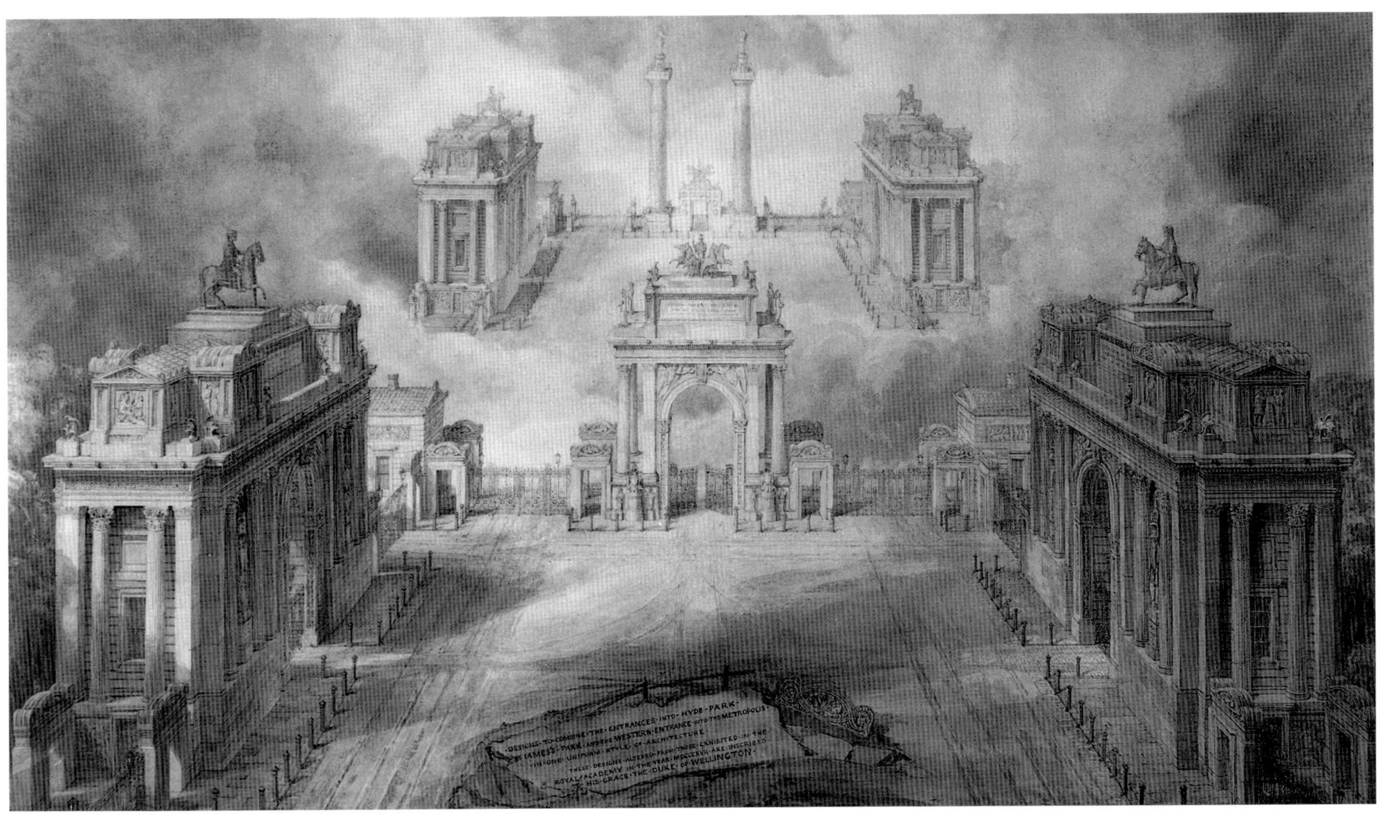

187 John Soane, *Designs to Combine in the Same Uniform Style of Architecture, the Entrances into Hyde Park, St James's Park, and the Western Entrance into the Metropolis . . .*, RA 1829, watercolour by J. M. Gandy. The Trustees of Sir John Soane's Museum.

Dulwich Picture Gallery and Mausoleum (RA 1823; fig. 184). It was a short step from these to the idea of combining different designs by means of vignettes that shaded off into each other to form an architectural capriccio, as for instance in *A Groupe of Churches, to Illustrate Different Styles of Architecture* (RA 1825; fig. 185), or of sneaking additional representations into perspective views, like the miniature ground plan that appears on a fragment of architectural ornament in Gandy's worm's-eye view of *A Design for a National Entrance into the Metropolis . . .* (RA 1826; fig. 186). This effort to unite disparate representations of a design into one image could sometimes lead to bizarre effects, as when Gandy attempted to show Soane's *Designs to Combine in the Same Uniform Style of Architecture the Entrances into Hyde Park, St James's Park*, [etc.] (RA 1829; fig. 187) in a single, central-point perspective, but taken from different heights. The apogee of Soane's development of a composite strategy of representation is reached, appropriately enough, near the end of his exhibiting career, with *Sketch of the First Design for a New State-Paper Office . . . with a Section Shewing part of the Interior, and a Perspective Plan of the Ground Floor* (RA 1833; fig. 188). This extraordinary drawing is probably unique in the history of architectural representation in showing the ground plan, section and view of a building as distinct images combined into a single, unified space. The usual way of achieving this would have been to adopt the Renaissance convention (deriving ultimately from Baldassare Peruzzi's famous project drawing of St Peter's in the Uffizi) of showing a sectional perspective with the cutaway portion of the building in the foreground revealing part of its plan.[17] Instead, by cramming disparate images into the same pictorial space, Soane manages to express not only the difficulties that he had to overcome on such a constrained site but a tension arising out of the contradictory nature of architectural representation itself which would have been quite lacking had he been content to submit to the conventions of a particular mode of architectural drawing.[18]

In effect both of Soane's strategies – the knitting of words with images and of images with images – were borrowed from books, and intended, like Gandy's appropriation of the idiom of the 'apocalyptic sublime' in his own exhibits, to serve a discourse concerning the condition of architecture itself in the modern world. To grasp this aspect of the content of architectural exhibition drawings, which is quite distinct from that of conveying the true effect of executing a design, we must retrace our steps to 1781, when the Academy's Professor of Architecture, Thomas Sandby, scored an unprecedented triumph in the exhibition with two drawings of *A Bridge of Magnificence* over the Thames, linking the river front of New Somerset House with Lambeth on the opposite bank (fig. 189).[19] It is possible to describe Sandby's success in such terms because the critical response it evoked in the press marks it as the first, and even perhaps only, time that an architect's design became one of the principal attractions of

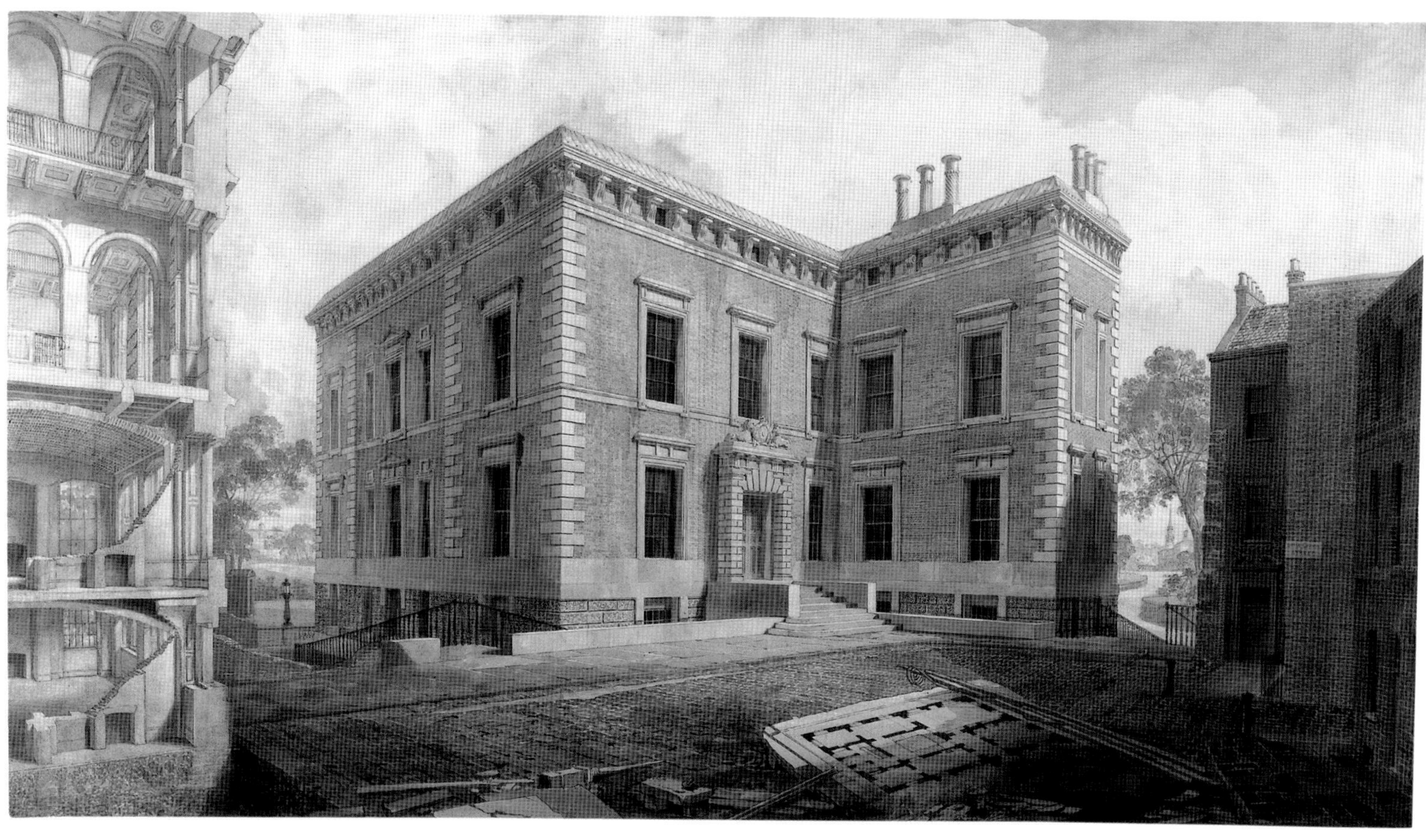

188 John Soane, *Sketch of the First Design for a New State-Paper Office, to be Erected in Duke-Street, Westminster . . .*, RA 1833, watercolour by J. M. Gandy. The Trustees of Sir John Soane's Museum.

the exhibition. According to a typical reviewer, Sandby's drawings gave 'a grand Idea of the Objects to which the young students of the Royal Academy are directed. This Bridge, on Paper', he went on, 'is a most beautiful Object' – does this refer to the drawing or to the design? one wonders – 'and the Execution of the Design in Stone would surpass in Grandeur, Magnificence, and Elegance, every Thing that has been, or even described before our Time'.[20] Described rather tellingly by another reviewer as 'a very magnificent Exhibition of Architecture', what mattered about Sandby's bridge was not its design (which the same reviewer found faulty, in that at high tide 'the Arches would not have space enough, to be correspondent with the superstructure and the rest of the Design') but rather its claim to express the idea of 'magnificence', which Sandby had expounded in his lectures to the Academy students and which he now wished to convey to the mind of the exhibition visitor.[21]

Oddly enough, Sandby's example does not seem to have produced any immediate imitators. The probable reason for this was that until the 1790s the exhibition was more or less dominated by a younger generation of architects – many of them former pupils of Sir William Chambers or, like William Thomas, George Richardson, John Plaw, James Malton, Robert Morison and even Soane in his youth, authors of architectural pattern books who regarded the exhibition as another chance to publicize their wares among potential clients in London. Such men could not risk appearing before the public with impossibly grandiose and expensive schemes, while the older generation of established architects almost without exception stayed away.[22] Chambers, one of the godfathers of the exhibition since its inception in 1760, did not exhibit again after 1777, and of the three other architect founder-members of the Academy, George Dance showed only three architectural designs between 1770 and 1785, thereafter confining himself to portrait drawings (with one exception in 1799); William Tyler, though a practising architect, preferred to show sculpture between 1769 and 1779, appearing in the exhibition as an architect on only seven occasions thereafter between 1780 and 1800; and Thomas Sandby, despite his professorship, had exhibited only as a topographical artist since 1771, and was to crown his success in 1781 by showing his last work at the Academy, a *View of the Gothic Gallery at Strawberry Hill* (RA 1782; Victoria & Albert Museum).[23] Impressive in its detailed rendering of the gothick tracery of the gallery's ceiling and miniature versions of the pictures on the walls (in spite of being unfinished it was exhibited in the Academy's Great Room and received favourable notices in the press), Sandby's topographical view of an interior in which he had played no role as

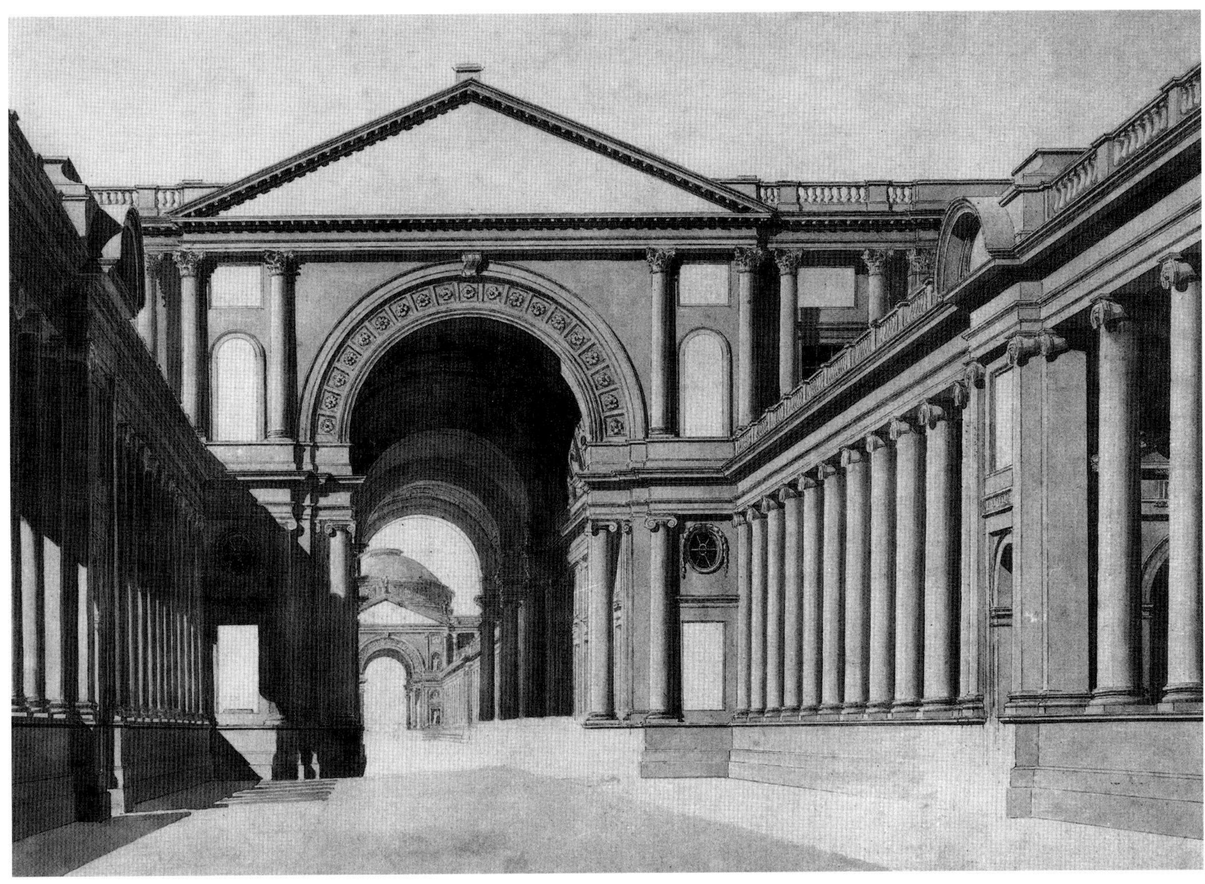

189 Thomas Sandby, *A Bridge of Magnificence: View from the Entrance on the Bridge*, RA 1781, watercolour. British Architectural Library, Royal Institute of British Architects, London.

an architect could not have been in more pointed contrast to his *Bridge of Magnificence* the previous year.

The real significance of Sandby's bridge design lies in the fact that it influenced later generations of students at the Academy who, as Soane recalled in his own lectures thirty years later, had had an opportunity of witnessing the drama of its unrolling every year from about 1776 until Sandby's death in 1798.[24] The example that it set in this pedagogic context made a much more powerful impression than its ephemeral success with the general public in the exhibition arena. As an idealized design for a monumental public building, for which no commission existed or was ever likely to exist, Sandby's bridge prefigured the determination of a subsequent generation of architects – epitomized in particular by Soane – to use the Academy's exhibition as a forum for dramatizing the nobility of architecture when practised as a civic art (rather than as a trade) and the concomitant responsibility of the architect to contribute the products of his toil, skill and knowledge to the public realm.

The duties and responsibilities of the architect to his client and to society at large became a burning issue in the late 1780s and early 1790s, and in the absence (until the founding of the Institute of British Architects in 1834) of any professional body with enough general support to be able to define who was, and who was not, entitled to call himself an architect, the Academy exhibition functioned to some degree as forum for both leaders and aspirants within the profession to express their hopes and fears for the well-being of architecture in the modern world. Although the sharp practices and shoddy workmanship of speculative architects, builders and surveyors bitterly complained of in the following review of the 1788 exhibition could only realistically be addressed by reforms in professional practice, such criticism must have encouraged those entering architecture as a career to try to use the exhibition as a means of dissociating themselves from its target:

> Wyatt and Paine jun. have distinguished themselves in the architectural line. The generality of the other performances are beneath criticism. Could some of our famed architects (whose works remain memorials of their genius) rise from their graves, and view the despicable works of these sons of the *hod* and children of the *chip*, how would they tremble for the reputation of their art. We consider the major part of these Gentlemen as so many locusts, by whose means the nobleman is duped, and the fair tradesman robbed of his property and deprived of the means of supporting his family. A man of true genius and abilities must blush to profess himself of this

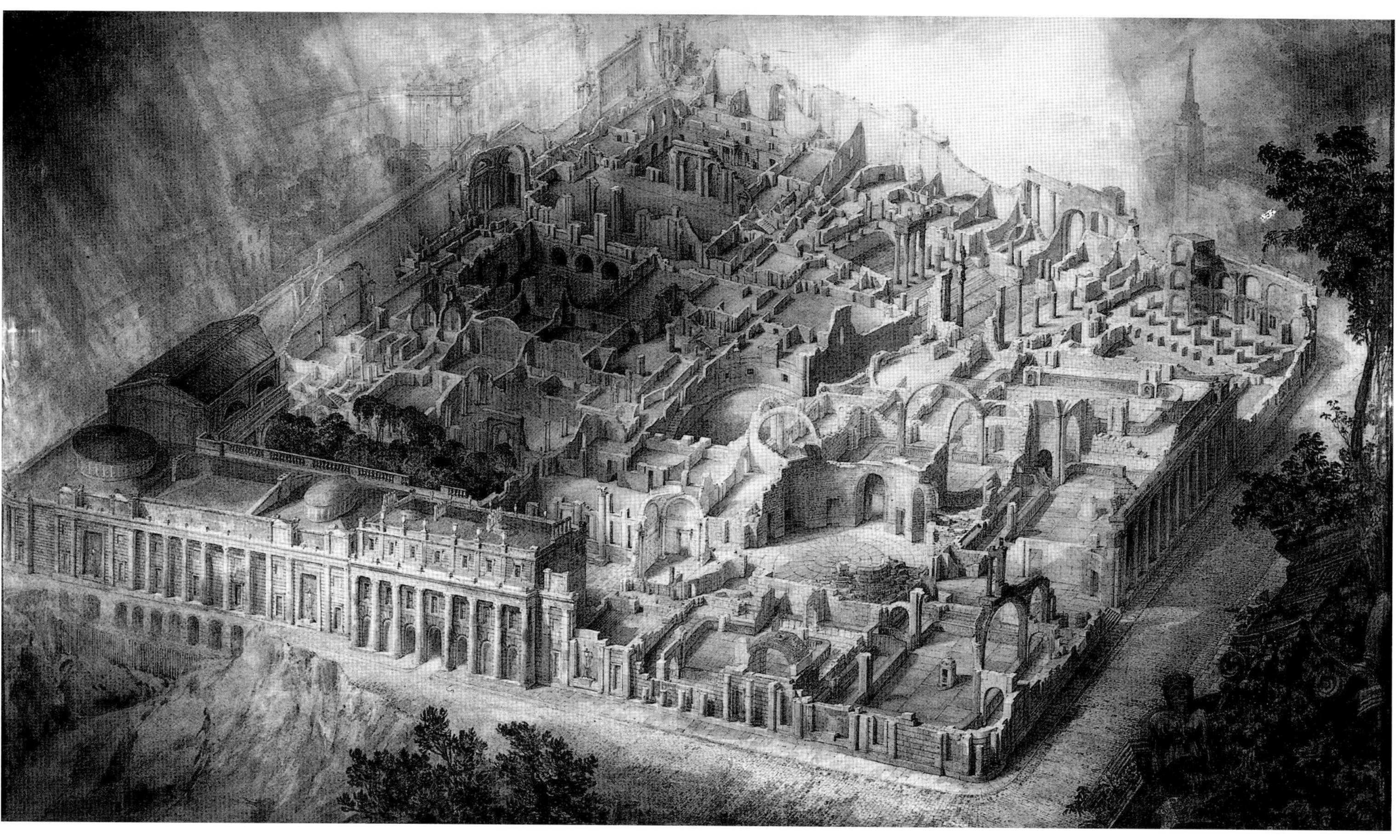

190 John Soane, *A Bird's-Eye View of the Bank of England*, RA 1830, watercolour by J. M. Gandy. The Trustees of Sir John Soane's Museum.

> branch of the arts, when he reflects, that the title of architect and surveyor is bestowed on some of the most contemptible and illiterate beings in the creation.[25]

It may have been this attack that roused Soane to write in September 1788 the classic definition of an architect's responsibilities: 'The business of the architect is to make the designs and estimates, to direct the works and to measure and value the different parts; he is the intermediate agent between the employer, whose honour and interest he is to study, and the mechanic, whose rights he is to defend. His situation implies great trust; he is responsible for the mistakes, negligences, and ignorances of those he employs; and above all, he is to take care that the workman's bills do not exceed his own estimates. If these are the duties of an architect, with what propriety can his situation and that of the builder, or the contractor be united?'[26] Soane's rallying cry went unheeded almost to the end of his life.

In the meantime one way of redressing the ill-repute of the profession was to exhibit works that could be seen as scholarly, intellectual, poetic and monumental in character. These were precisely the attributes of the highest sphere to which the visual arts could traditionally aspire, namely history painting. Credit for the realization that the concerns and subject matter of history painting – defined as the depiction of significant human actions or events – might be appropriated to the needs of representing the true nature, origins and progress of architecture as an art and science, undoubtedly belongs first and foremost to Joseph Gandy. Although the earliest examples in the exhibition of a literary or mythopoeic representation of architecture seem to have been three Homeric subjects shown by Jeffry Wyatt (later Wyatville) in 1798, 1799 and 1800, it is highly likely that the idea upon which these were based dates from the period when Wyatt was working alongside Gandy as a pupil of his uncle, James Wyatt, between 1792 and 1794.[27] The most significant feature of Gandy's peculiar vision of architecture is his exploitation of what might be termed the last remaining strategy for the representation of architecture: that of placing it in the fourth dimension. Unlike all the depictions of architecture so far discussed, which exist in a timeless state, practically all Gandy's imaginary exhibition pieces involve the evocation of a historical, literary or mythological moment concerning the fate of architecture in the past, present or future. Sometimes, as in his famous bird's-eye view of Soane's Bank of England (RA 1830; fig. 190), there is a deliberate ambiguity about where to place what we see in time (it is both a cutaway sectional perspective of the existing structure and a premonition of future ruin). More usually however his imagining of architecture sets the past against the present,

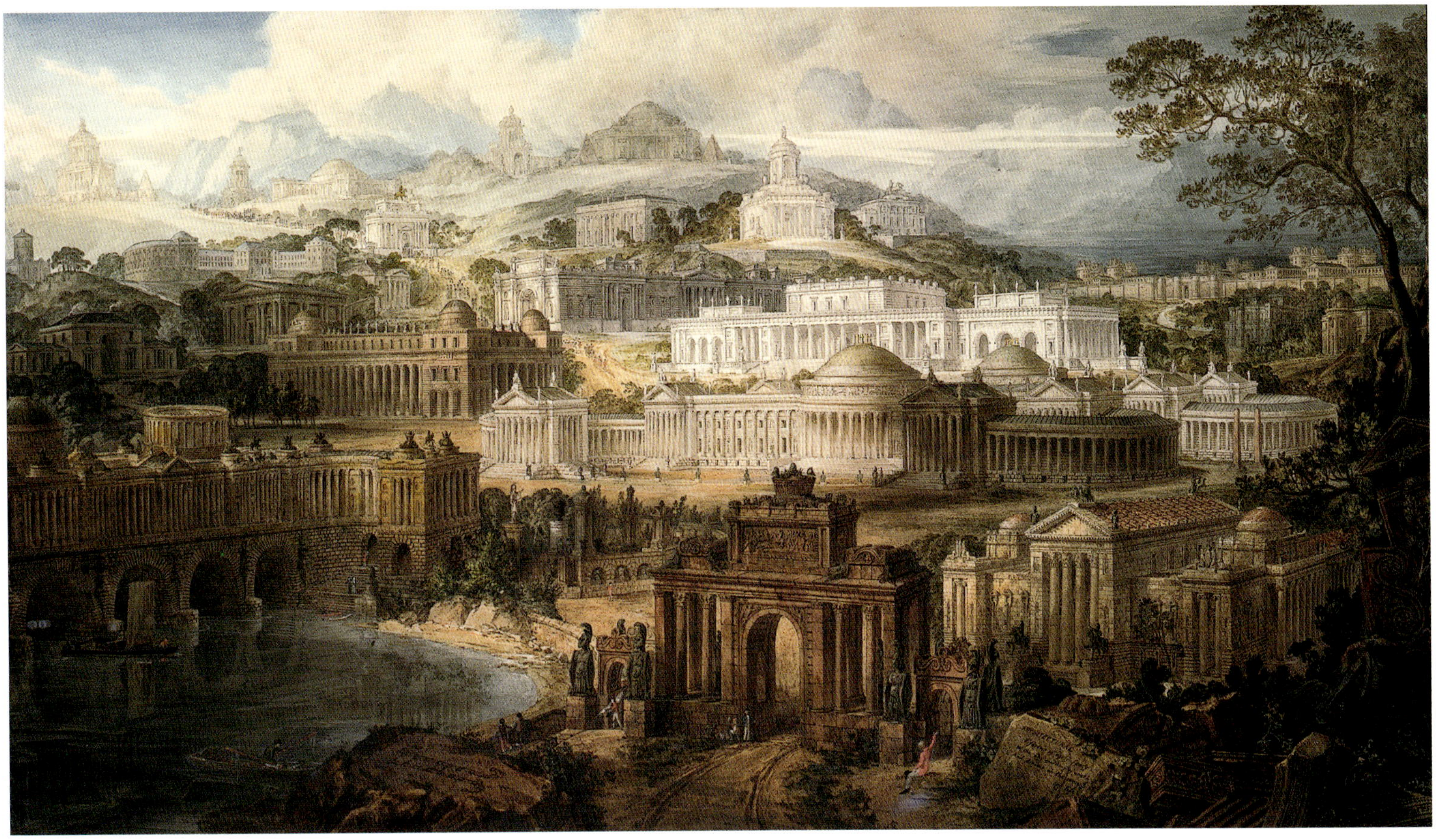

191 John Soane, *Architectural Visions of Early Fancy, in the Gay Morning of Youth; and Dreams in the Evening of Life*, RA 1820, watercolour by J. M. Gandy. The Trustees of Sir John Soane's Museum.

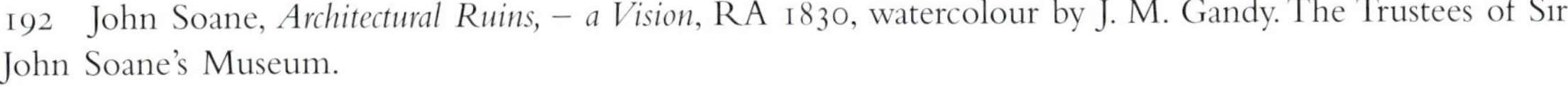

192 John Soane, *Architectural Ruins, – a Vision*, RA 1830, watercolour by J. M. Gandy. The Trustees of Sir John Soane's Museum.

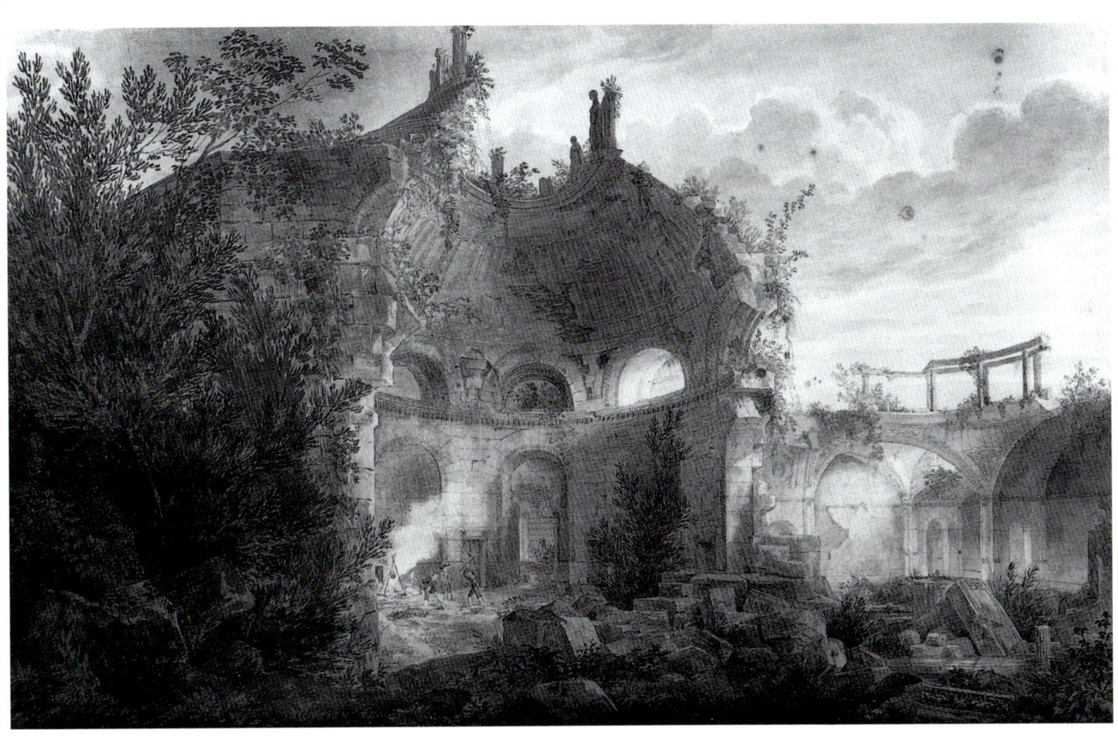

either in chiliastic warnings of impending doom (*Pandemonium, or Part of the High Capital of Satan and his Peers* (RA 1805) and inevitable decay (the Bank of England rotunda in ruins (RA 1832: *Architectural Ruins, – a Vision*; fig. 192)), or laments for beauties no longer of this world (*Tomb of Merlin* (RA 1815; see fig. 174)) and evaporated hopes and lost opportunities (*Architectural Visions of Early Fancy* (RA 1820; fig. 191)).

Gandy's appropriation of history painting can also be seen to have appropriated him, in the sense that it led him literally into painting and exhibiting, with considerable critical success, such works in oil as *Jupiter Pluvius, Lebadea* (RA 1819; private coll.). Soane, his great supporter and the person who understood his extraordinary gifts as an architectural draughtsman best, warned the students in his lectures of the dangers of attempting to tread Gandy's path, reminding them in effect that as soon as architectural drawing becomes an end in itself – or, in other words, a work of art in its own right – it has abandoned its only purpose, which is to represent the creative processes of architecture but not to supplant them. Only in the realm of archaeological re-creations of ancient sites – where the imagination could be seen to be held in check by apparent truth to historical evidence – was it possible to carry forward to some degree Gandy's legacy. Thus the precedent set by what were probably the earliest such scholarly restorations to appear in the exhibition – Robert Smirke's *Temple of Minerva at Sunium*, the *Acropolis of Athens*, and the *Temple of Jupiter Olympus at Agrigentum* (RA 1805; RA 1808 (Royal Academy); RA 1810) – would culminate through the influence of Gandy's example in C. R. Cockerell's great exhibition pieces, *Tribute to the Memory of Sir Christopher Wren* (RA 1838; private coll.) and *The Professor's Dream* (RA 1849; Royal Academy). The hard fact remained as true inside the exhibition as outside it: the architectural drawing was not a work of art. Ultimately this is why the various strategies of representation negotiated by architects in the exhibition of their work reveal not simply their individual abilities as designers but a truth about architecture itself.

15

Printmakers and the Royal Academy Exhibitions, 1780–1836

Sarah Hyde

What has come to be called 'the engravers' battle' is a fairly well-known episode in the history of British art: the newly founded Royal Academy refused to grant full academic status to engravers, sparking a conflict with the profession which remained unresolved for over eighty years.[1] The practical consequences of this schism, however, have often been exaggerated; indeed two of the most respected authorities on British prints have even wrongly claimed that 'engravers were excluded from membership [of the Academy] and prints were not shown' at its exhibitions.[2] In fact prints *were* shown, but in very specific circumstances. Let us first see what these were, before attempting to assess their implications.

Critical opinion has differed widely about the significance of the engravers' conflict with the Academy. In the most recent specialist study of the development of British printmaking, Timothy Clayton has presented the story in personal and individual, rather than social or ideological, terms, declaring that 'Petty personal animosity shaped the future of the artistic establishment'.[3] This is in sharp contrast to the view expressed in the mid-1970s by Raymond Williams, that the exclusion of printmakers from full membership of the late eighteenth-century Royal Academy played a crucial part in strengthening and popularizing the emerging distinction between the modern notions of 'artist' and 'artisan', the latter being demoted to 'skilled manual worker' without 'intellectual', 'imaginative' or 'creative' purposes.[4]

In this context it is worth recalling that the 'memorial' of 28 November 1768 concerning the foundation of the Royal Academy was addressed to George III by a group of 'Painters, Sculptors and Architects of this Metropolis'.[5] Printmakers did not form part of the Academy as it was originally constituted. However, at a meeting in the following March it was decided to confer on six engravers the special categorization of 'Associate':

> A Number of engravers, not exceeding six shall be admitted Associates of the Royal Academy . . . these Associates shall not be admitted into any of the Offices of the Society, nor have any role in their Assemblys . . . each . . . shall have the liberty of exhibiting two Prints, either compositions of his own or Engraving from other Masters, which have not been published, & that these be the only Prints admitted in the Royal Exhibition.[6]

Thus the class of 'Associate' was originally framed solely for the purpose of categorizing printmakers; it was not until the end of 1769 that the Academy decided to introduce a second group of Associates, this time consisting of twenty painters, sculptors or architects. The creation of this new class demoted the earlier group to 'Associate Engravers' (AEs) whose rights were more limited than those given the now more prestigious title of simply 'Associates' (ARAs).[7]

These complicated manoeuvres, and the minutes of the first few years' Assembly meetings, clearly demonstrate the difficulties the Academy had in framing the constraints which were to govern its association with the printmaking profession. The procedures for electing Associates and Associate Engravers were repeatedly altered, but the final regulations, crucial for the future relationship between printmakers and the Academy, stipulated that 'Vacant seats of Academicians' were to be 'filled from Associates only',[8] that is, painters, sculptors and architects. 'Associate Engravers' were a subordinate category, from whose ranks no one could rise to the status of Academician. None the less, the diploma creating both forms of Associate Member contained the words 'and appoint you ——— Gent. to be one of the Associates';[9] in other words, a social as well as an artistic distinction was being conferred on printmakers as well as painters, sculptors and architects, although the deliberations of

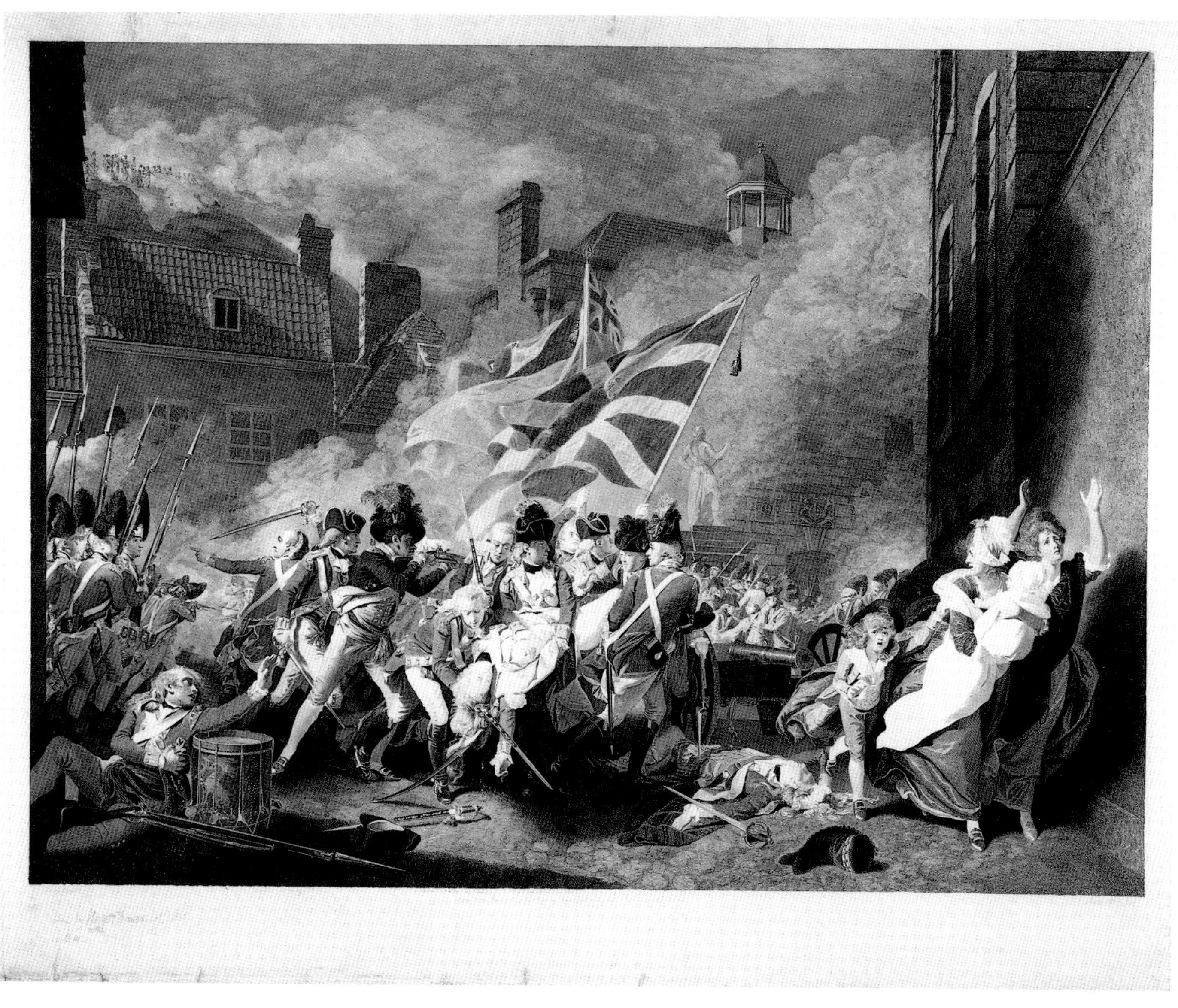

193 James Heath after John Singleton Copley, *The Death of Major Peirson*, RA 1795, etched proof. By courtesy of the Trustees of the British Museum.

the early Academicians show that they were uncertain as to whether or not men who were engravers by profession merited such prestige.

These discussions formed the background to the engravers' situation at the beginning of the Academy's residence at Somerset House. In theory a maximum of twelve prints could have been shown at each annual exhibition: two by each Associate Engraver. But in practice the average number of prints shown each year was between two and three during the first twenty years, rising to around four from the first decade of the nineteenth century. These low numbers were partly due to the difficulties the Academy had in recruiting Associate Engravers; for the first sixteen years after its establishment, and occasionally after that, the Academy was unable to fill all six places. However, given that even when there were six AEs they never all exhibited at once, and on two occasions no prints were shown at all,[10] a more likely explanation seems to be that the Council did not regard itself as in any way obliged to include all prints submitted by Associate Engravers. In 1784 several prints and drawings were accepted to be hung 'if room can be found';[11] the fact that only one print was shown that year suggests that the Council was prepared to use the chronic lack of space in Somerset House as an excuse to show less than the full complement of prints allowed by the regulations.

Space, or rather location, was another contentious issue for engravers. In the first decade or so at Somerset House prints were shown in the 'Exhibition Room of Sculpture and Drawings' (the room on the ground floor which served as the Life Academy), but from 1793 they were moved to the Antique Academy on the first floor. This remained the main place where prints were displayed, with the occasional foray into the Library (the smaller room next to the Antique Academy); even more infrequently the work of favoured engravers such as Francesco Bartolozzi was hung in the Council Room, the largest of the Academy's suite of rooms on the first floor. The poor conditions in which prints were shown seemed to engravers and reviewers alike an injury added to the insult of the special conditions of their Associate status. Anthony Pasquin (the pseudonym of John Williams, himself an engraver) records that prints were sometimes not exhibited in a room at all, but on what appears to have been the first-floor landing. He describes James Heath's etched proof of Copley's *Death of Major Peirson* (fig. 193; misspelled as 'Pierson' on the print) as being hung in 'a dark passage leading from the library to the Antique Academy' where it 'cannot be surveyed for a moment by any curious visitor'; this then leads him to ask 'of what texture the organisation of Engravers are formed, at least in this country, as they appear willing to submit to any insults, which the folly and arrogance of Royal Academicians may impel them to commit'.[12]

Contributing to the growing chorus of complaints from engravers was the fact that from 1793 onwards prints were shown in the same room as large oil paintings, a disadvantage highlighted in 1802 by the opening of the British School, a commercial gallery where prints and drawings were shown in a room separated from paintings. Visibility was also a problem: in the late 1820s and 1830s the *Literary Gazette* compared the poor lighting conditions in the Antique Academy to both purgatory and hell, complaining that it was virtually impossible to make out whether the exhibits were works of art or not,[13] and that 'some of the works exhibited might just as well be hung with their faces to the wall.'[14]

Given these conditions, it is not surprising that the majority of British printmakers boycotted the Academy, refusing to put their names forward for election as Associate Engravers, and thus surrendering the chance of contributing to the annual summer exhibitions. As a result, the prints shown at Somerset House were in no way representative of the wider output of British printmakers at the time. The most celebrated prints of the period – by William Woollett after West, William Wynne Ryland after Angelica Kauffmann, Raimbach and Burnet after Wilkie, W. B. Cooke and E. Finden after Turner, and David Lucas after Constable, to name but a few examples – never appeared at the Academy, for the reason that their producers refused to submit to the indignity of being categorized as an Associate Engraver.

The prints that were exhibited were an ambitious mixture of portrait, historical and landscape subjects, in the main after works by contemporary British painters, most of whom were members of the Academy. Although portraits made up around 45 per cent of exhibited prints, the proportion of historical subjects was also high (around 30 per cent), and the number of landscape prints correspondingly low (around 6 per cent), suggesting that those engravers who did accept Associate Engraver status were willing and able to present themselves in terms of the Academy's acknowledged hierarchy of subject matter. Valentine Green chose to emphasize his work after history paintings by prominent Academicians, including Benjamin West, Henry Singleton and Maria Cosway (e.g., fig. 194); likewise Bartolozzi showed his print after John Singleton Copley's *Death of Chatham* (RA 1792; fig. 195), and James Heath his reproductions of Copley's *Peirson* (RA 1795), Wright of Derby's *Dead Soldier* (RA 1797; fig. 197) and West's *Death of Lord Viscount Nelson* (RA 1811; fig. 196). As is clear from these examples, engravers frequently exhibited military subjects with distinctly nationalistic overtones.

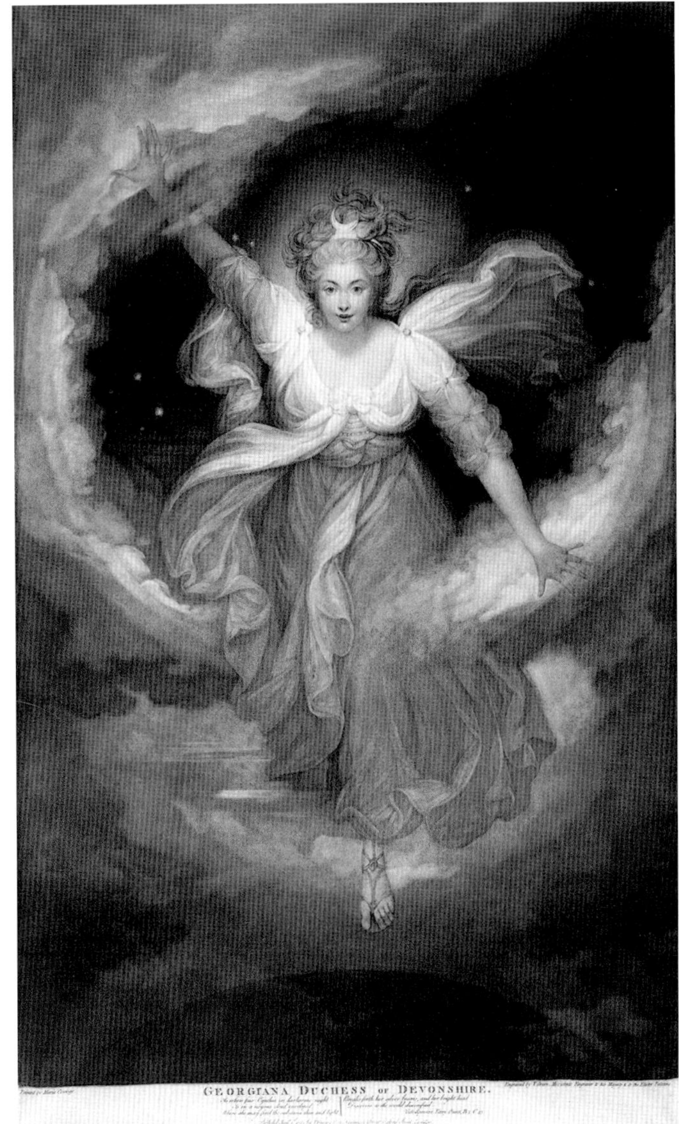

194 Valentine Green after Maria Cosway, *Georgiana, Duchess of Devonshire as Cynthia*, RA 1783, mezzotint. By courtesy of the Trustees of the British Museum.

The vast majority of printmakers chose to show reproductions of contemporary paintings, many of which were themselves exhibited at the Academy, although hardly ever in the same year as the print (a notable exception being James Heath's print and Benjamin West's painting of the *Death of Nelson*, both of which were shown

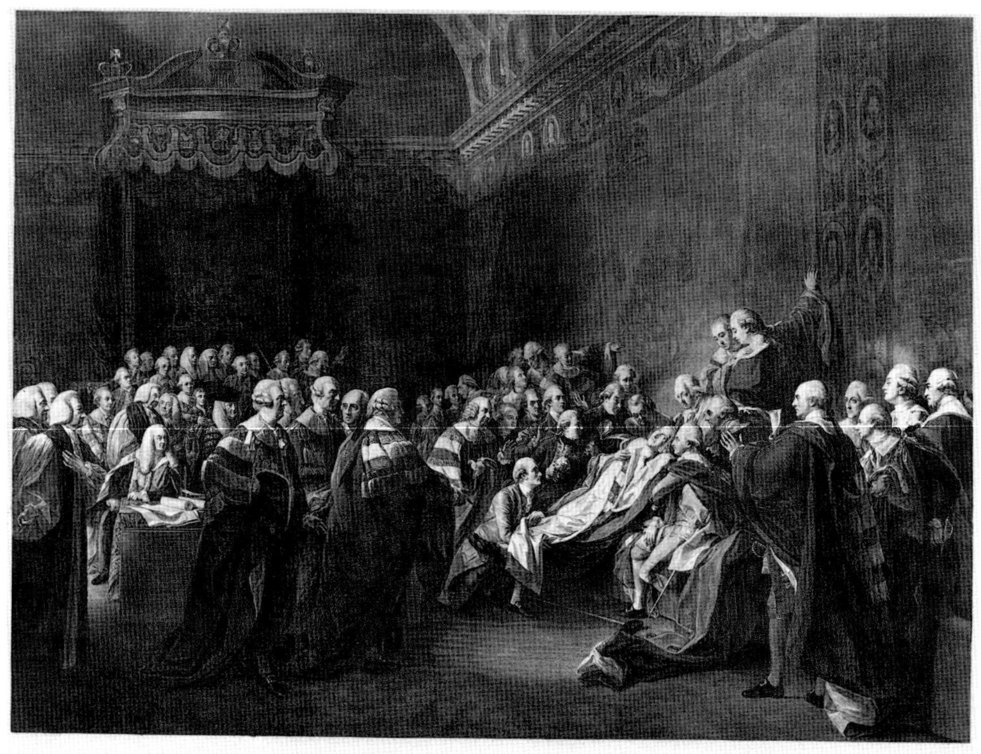

195 Francesco Bartolozzi after John Singleton Copley, *The Death of Chatham*, RA 1792, line engraving and etching, proof, 3rd state. Courtesy of the Board of Trustees of the Victoria & Albert Museum. An etched proof from an earlier state was exhibited in 1792.

196 James Heath after Benjamin West, *The Death of Lord Viscount Nelson*, RA 1811, line engraving. By courtesy of the Trustees of the British Museum.

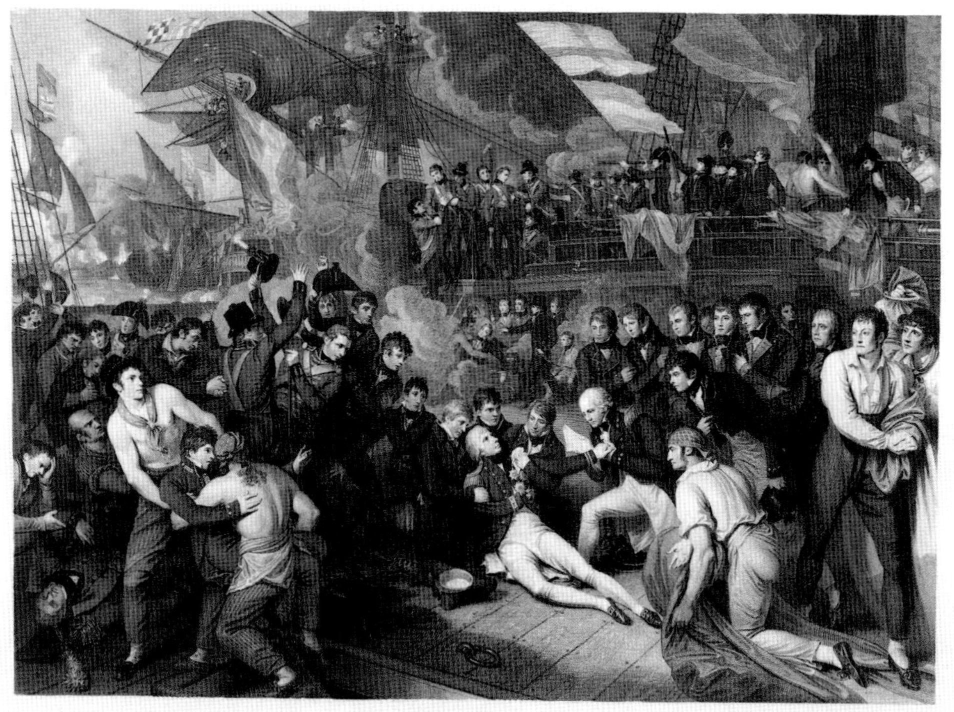

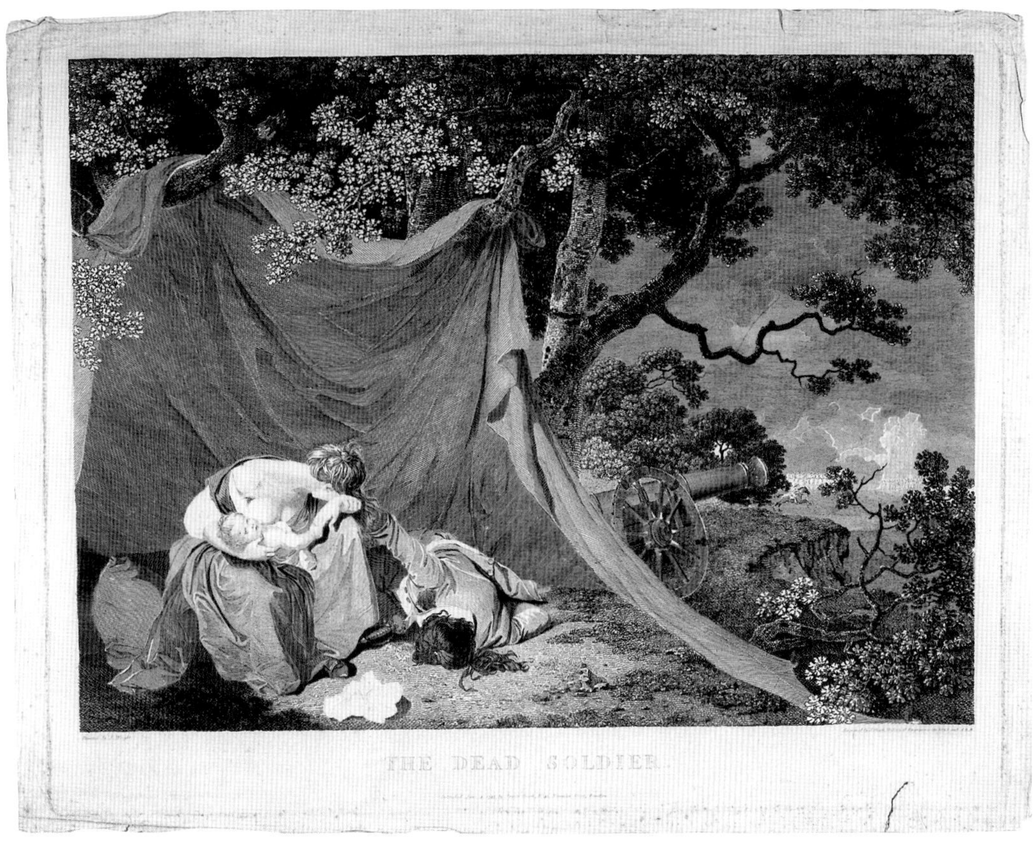

197 James Heath after Joseph Wright of Derby, *The Dead Soldier*, RA 1797, etching and engraving. By courtesy of the Trustees of the British Museum.

198 John Browne after Salvator Rosa, *Apollo (Attended by the Muses) Granting Long Life to the Cumean Sibyl*, RA 1781, line engraving and etching. By courtesy of the Trustees of the British Museum.

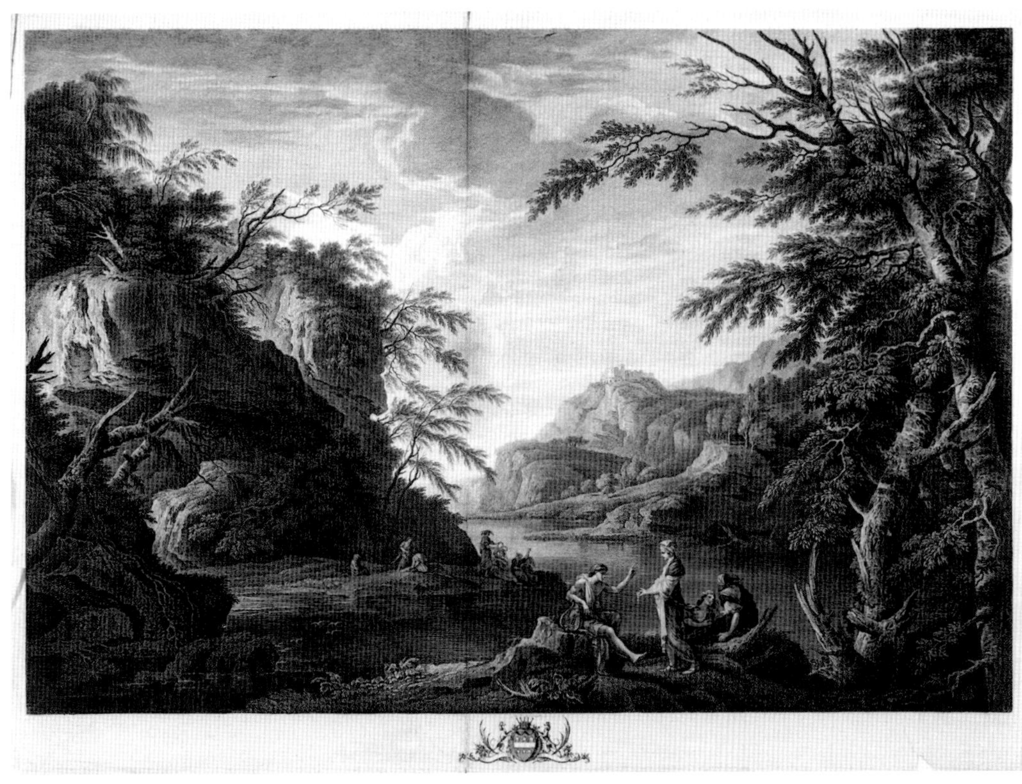

in 1811, although not, of course, in the same room). A much smaller number of respected old masters were also represented. These were mostly seventeenth-century painters such as Poussin, Salvator Rosa (fig. 198) and Murillo, as well as a significant number of Dutch and Flemish artists: Backhuysen, Both, Cuyp, Ostade, Rubens, Snyders, Swanevelt, Terborch and van de Velde. The range of work exhibited, however, diminished noticeably towards the end of the period, becoming ever more dominated by portraits, including a flurry of prints after Lawrence around the time of the painter's death in 1830 (e.g., fig. 199).

Most Associate Engravers chose to exhibit work in what continued to be the most prestigious (and time-consuming) of printmaking techniques, namely the combination of engraving and etching usually referred to as 'stroke' engraving. The less prestigious 'dotting manners' were less in evidence, although the presence of Valentine Green as Associate Engraver for almost forty years (from 1775 to 1813) meant that mezzotint was regularly included. Stipple, on the other hand, despite – or rather because of – its fashionable popularity outside the Academy, was virtually absent except for a handful of works by Francis Haward (fig. 200) and Joseph Collyer (fig. 201) shown in the late 1780s and 1790s. Notably, the only print from Boydell's Shakespeare Gallery to be exhibited was not a stipple but a line engraving: Anker Smith's *Scene from The Tempest* after William Hamilton, shown in 1799 (fig. 202). The prestige of 'stroke' engraving was confirmed by the display of proof impressions by John Browne, Joseph Collyer, James Fittler and Francesco Bartolozzi; the latter exhibited a proof stage of his *Death of Chatham* in 1792 in order to show the immense amount of carefully etched line work which preceded the final bravura touches with the burin.

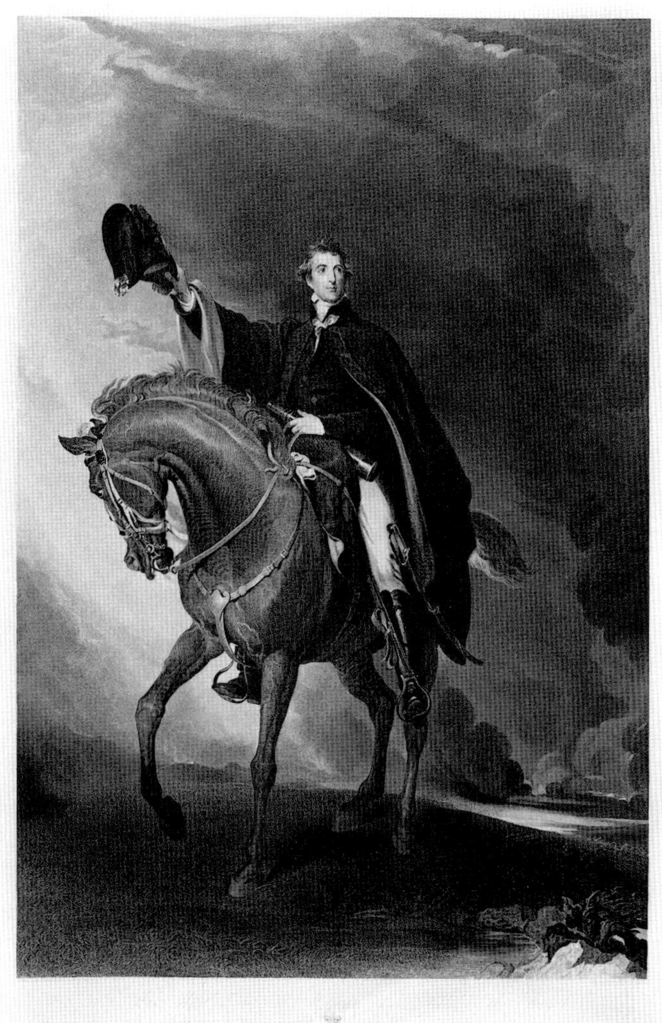

199 William Bromley after Sir Thomas Lawrence, *The Duke of Wellington on Horseback*, RA 1830, line engraving. By courtesy of the Trustees of the British Museum.

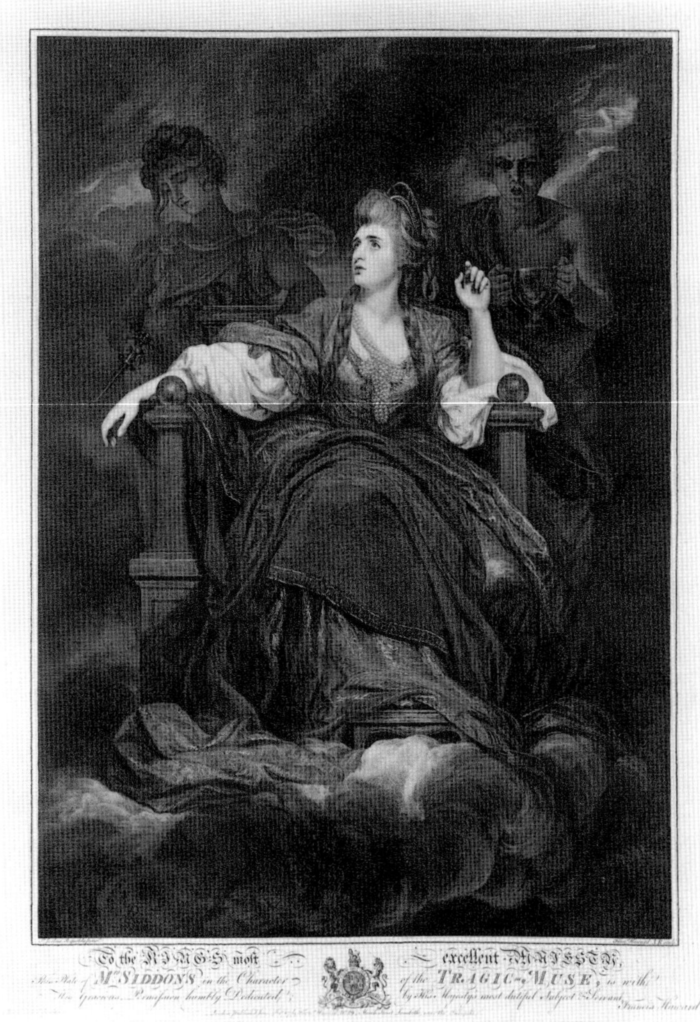

200 Francis Haward after Sir Joshua Reynolds, *Mrs Siddons in the Character of the Tragic Muse*, RA 1787, stipple. Courtesy of the Board of Trustees of the Victoria & Albert Museum.

As interesting as what was shown is what was not. Not surprisingly, the late eighteenth-century flood of comic, satirical and caricature prints never made it on to the Academy's walls. More unexpected is the complete absence of genre scenes: no examples of the huge output of prints after paintings by the likes of George Morland, Francis Wheatley, W. R. Bigg or David Wilkie were ever exhibited. This was in spite of the fact that William Ward, who produced large numbers of genre prints, was elected Associate Engraver in 1814; he exhibited only portrait prints and one historical subject. Furthermore, many of the most recently developed printmaking media failed to make an appearance. The scorn with which Joseph Farington refers to aquatint as 'a low branch of that art'[15] helps to explain the complete absence from the Academy shows of this and other newly developed techniques such as crayon manner and soft-ground etching. No practitioners of the new technique of wood engraving were elected, and the older technique of woodcutting, now largely associated with the cheapest, popular prints, was also excluded. One new technique – lithography – did feature, but not until twenty-five years after its first appearance in England.[16] Although the lack of detail given in the Academy's catalogues makes it impossible to be certain, it also seems that no examples of colour printing ever went on view.[17]

201 Joseph Collyer after John Russell, *Portraits of HRH the Princess of Wales and Princess Charlotte*, RA 1799, stipple. By courtesy of the Trustees of the British Museum.

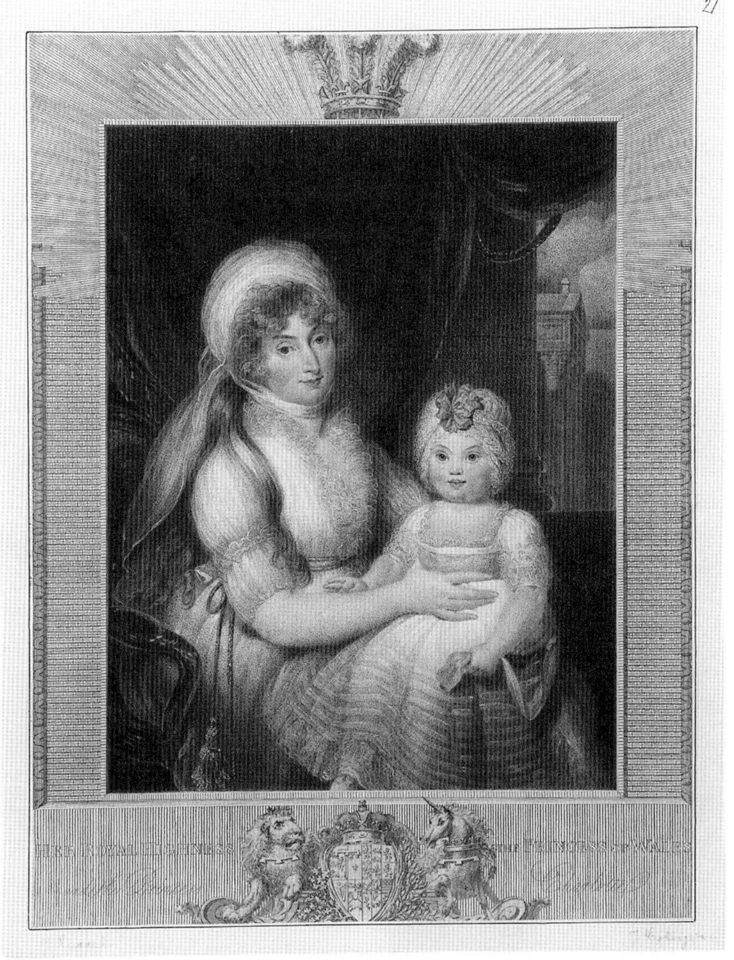

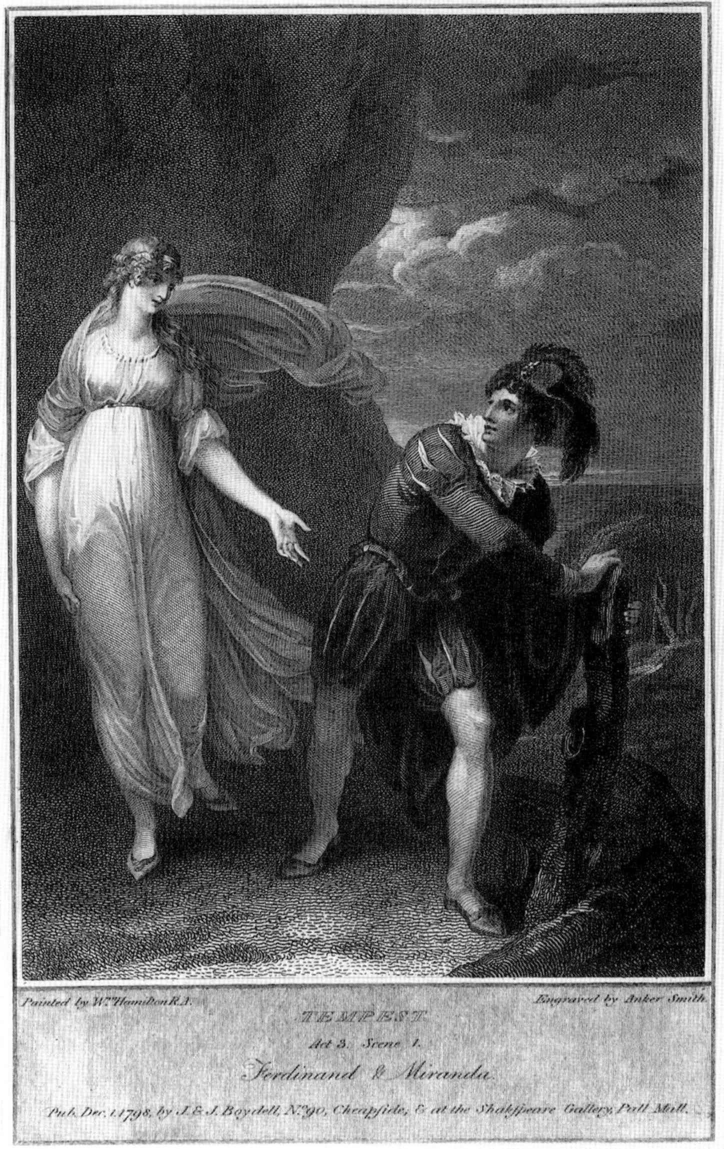

202 Anker Smith after William Hamilton, *Scene from The Tempest*, RA 1799, line engraving. By courtesy of the Trustees of the British Museum.

What is less clear is how these 'exclusions' (if that is the correct term) were effected. Although the Academy Council indirectly controlled what was shown by selecting the Associate Engravers who were allowed to exhibit,[18] there is no evidence that they directly censored the *types* of prints which Associate Engravers showed, although the policy of admitting prints only 'if room can be found' obviated the need to give specific reasons for rejection. It seems likely that engravers also policed their own exhibits, submitting mainly the kinds of prints they knew would be acceptable to the academic hierarchy. While there are known instances of the Council refusing to accept specific prints, this appears always to have been, at least ostensibly, on grounds other

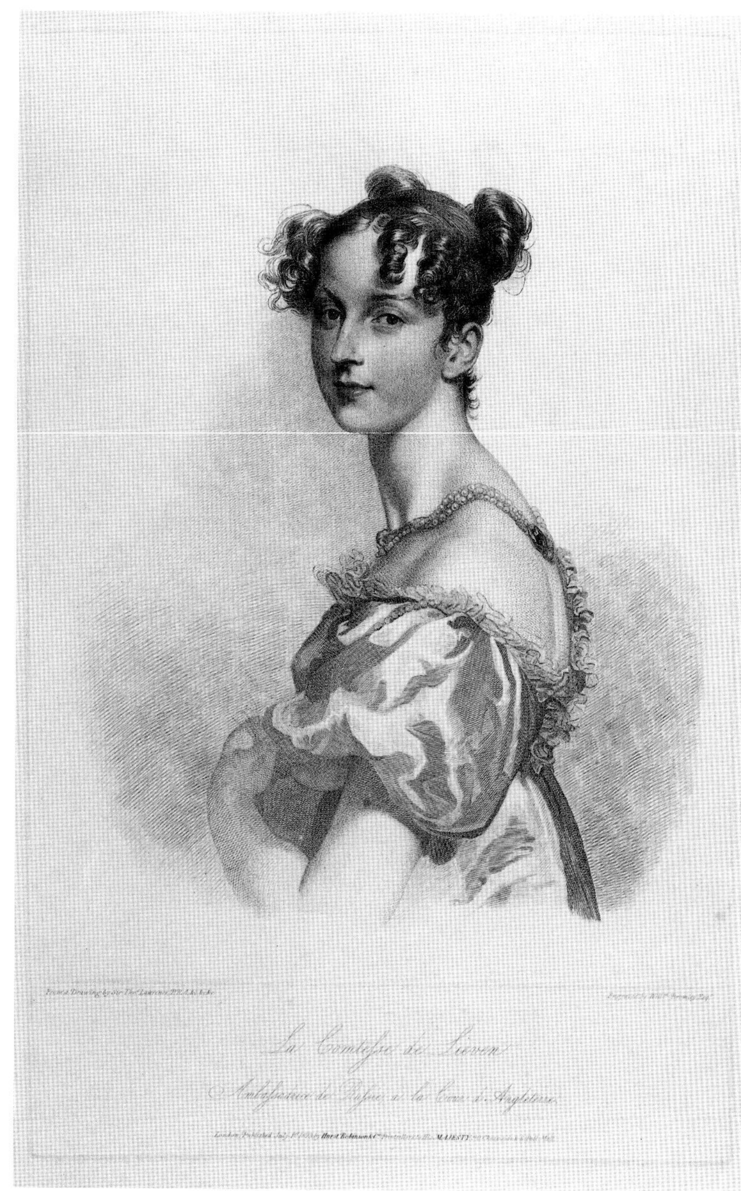

203 William Bromley after Sir Thomas Lawrence, *Countess Lieven*, RA 1823, line engraving and etching. By courtesy of the Trustees of the British Museum.

than the subject matter or medium of the print concerned. Thus the Council repeatedly frustrated engravers' attempts to display more than two works in any one year,[19] and, at least initially, attempted to enforce the ban on exhibiting prints that had already been published. Nevertheless, both these regulations were broken at least as many times as they were enforced.[20]

The question here is whether this pattern of behaviour suggests a consistent policy or a particular ideological stance. Clearly the Academy was unhappy with the possibility that the inclusion of prints in its exhibitions might appear to grant these works a status approaching that of the oil paintings appearing alongside them – and yet the institution was unwilling simply to exclude prints altogether. The root of its determination that prints should not be given the same status as painting seems to have been a broad prejudice against 'mechanic' arts, which were seen as demanding physical or technical skill, but little, if any, intellectual input. Furthermore, many Academicians felt that their displays should not include works of art produced in multiples, since, by their very nature, these could be viewed in many different places at any one time. Implicit here was the belief that novelty and uniqueness were among the main factors that brought spectators thronging annually into Somerset House. This argument was used against the engravers in 1812, when the Academy Council argued that the very existence of the institution depended on it exhibiting new work: 'in a society . . . supported solely by the produce of its Exhibitions, there is a particular necessity for bringing forward *original* Artists, who, alone are capable of supplying sufficient novelty, and interest to excite public attention, without which, the Schools, the charitable Fund, and the Establishment itself must fail'.[21] The problem for engravers was that these same criteria of uniqueness, novelty and originality conflicted with the very nature of contemporary printmaking practice.

In addition to being produced in multiples, eighteenth- and early nineteenth-century British prints were overwhelmingly reproductive: with very few exceptions, they replicated in line, and sometimes tone, the compositions of oil paintings. The fact that contemporary prints were both multiples *and* reproductions caused problems not only within the Academy, but also outside it, in contemporary newspapers. The prints that were exhibited at Somerset House received hardly any critical attention in the press; and when they were discussed, the few column inches devoted to printmakers' work were invariably dominated by complaints about the poor exhibiting conditions in the Antique Academy. For the most part, reviewers agreed that 'in the lower rooms of the Royal Academy there is seldom anything of sufficient importance to call for particular mention'.[22] This was not merely careless neglect: echoing the argument used by Diderot at the Paris Salons, most journalists deemed it unnecessary to pay special attention to objects whose nature as multiples meant that they could already be widely seen.[23] Very rarely did critics pay attention to the nature of printmaking itself. The one exception was Anthony Pasquin who, because he was an engraver, was in a position to write unusually explicit and detailed criticism of printmakers' techniques: he declared, for instance, that 'engravers of this country are too fond of executing with what is termed, a *square* graver, instead of a *lozenge graver*'.[24] Pasquin was, however, well aware that printmakers' technical virtuosity could not be seen to its best advantage in the circumstances of the Academy's exhibitions, advising James Heath against exhibiting proof impressions, because 'the surrounding glare makes what is in itself too faintly expressed appear more so'.[25]

Instead of commenting on the technical aspects of the prints on view, most critics focused on their reproductive nature. Occasionally, a sympathetic reviewer such as Pasquin was ready to defend engravers at the expense of painters: thus he noted of the drapery in the *Death of Major Peirson* that, 'There is an hardness in

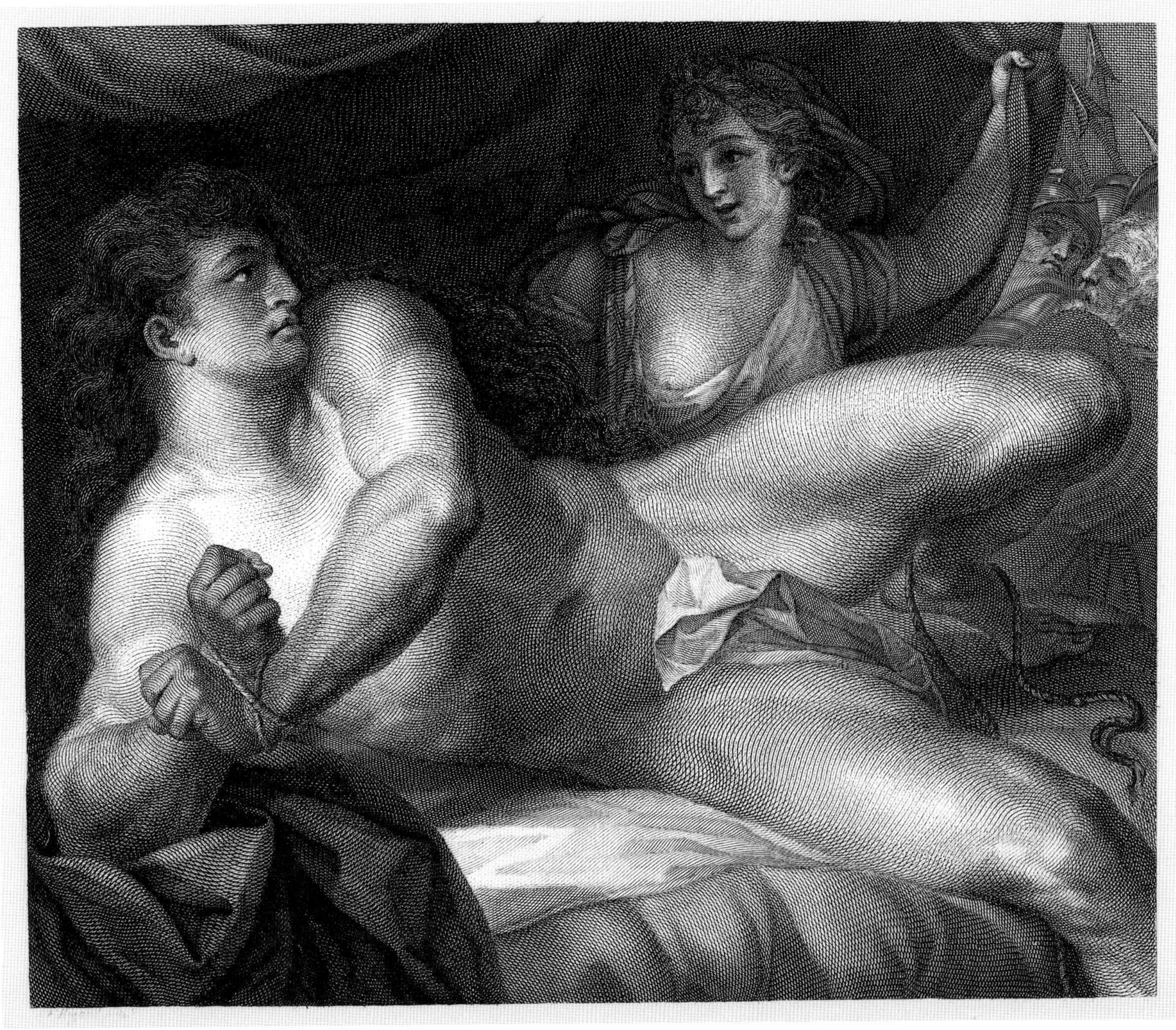

204 Francesco Bartolozzi after John Francis Rigaud, *Samson Breaking his Bands*, RA 1797, etching. By courtesy of the Trustees of the British Museum.

the folds for which the painter, Mr. COPLEY, is more responsible than Mr. HEATH'.[26] For the most part, however, reviewers praised engravers for faithfully copying their original: William Bromley's *Countess Lieven* after Thomas Lawrence (fig. 203) was claimed to have 'all the charms of the original drawing . . . except colour, for it is to the life in its fleshy tones, and the lines everywhere else are what we think any other kind would be less in contact with the truth'.[27] Occasionally, the best prints were even said to exceed the quality of their originals: Bartolozzi (himself a Royal Academician, accepted on the basis of his painting, despite being a practising printmaker) showed an etching after Rigaud's *Samson* (fig. 204; see also fig. 60) which was described as 'a graphic jewel freely copied . . . inasmuch as the transcendent mighty genius who etched it, has infused a fire and correctness on the copper which none but himself could conceive'; Bartolozzi's performance was compared to 'Apollo singing a modern ballad – he sublimes the melody even of a vulgar tune'.[28]

Whether or not the engraver managed to surpass the original painting, the fact that the finished product could be seen as a reproduction presented problems for the Academy, whose regulations, drawn up in 1769, forbade the exhibiting of copies: 'No Picture copied from a Picture or Print, a drawing from a

Drawing, a Medal from a Medal, a Chasing from a Chasing, a Model from a Model or any other species of sculpture, or any copy shall be admitted in the Exhibition.'[29] This detailed list was made necessary because, as we have seen, having agreed to accept as Associate Engravers men whose output consisted solely of reproductive prints, the Academy had made itself unable to exclude copies altogether. This, however, begs the question as to why the Academy did not decide only to allow the exhibition of 'original' prints (prints designed and engraved by the same hand). Likewise, if 'originality' and 'newness' were to be the criteria for successful exhibitions, why did printmakers themselves not respond by moving from reproduction to creating and exhibiting 'original' prints?

The answer, as far as concerns the Academy, was bound up with the fact that most original prints were made by painters, whose training gave them the confidence to invent compositions, but who lacked the lengthy technical training necessary to allow them to carry this out in engraving. Painters thus tended to make prints using etching rather than engraving,[30] but since contemporary critical opinion still largely preferred the high finish of professional engravers' work, and derided the sketchy quality of artists' etchings, most painters made 'original' etchings for private interest, not for public exhibition. Those who, rather than becoming painters, underwent the complex lengthy training (commonly a seven-year apprenticeship) of a professional engraver, rarely produced original compositions of their own invention. The only engraver to argue that printmaking could and should be used to make original art, just like any other technique, was William Blake, who believed that engraving was simply 'drawing on copper, as Painting ought to be drawing on canvas . . . and nothing else'.[31] But on this point, as on so many others, Blake's was an isolated voice.

The failure of engravers to produce original prints should thus be seen in the context of the social status attached to their profession, the lowly nature of which also explains why contemporaries attached more significance to the distinction between prints made by painters and those made by engravers (as opposed to the modern distinction between reproductive and original prints). Many painters, such as Angelica Kauffman,[32] could, and did, make both 'original' and 'reproductive' prints, without labouring the difference between the two. However, the freedom of professional printmakers was considerably more restrained. The very apprenticeship process through which engravers were trained marked and separated them as a group distinct from artist/painters, so that anyone categorized as a professional engraver who had the presumption to try and make a print 'from his own designing' was quickly reminded by his academic 'superiors' of the limitations of his powers.[33] What this suggests for the Royal Academy exhibitions, of course, is that the oddities and inconsistencies of the regulations governing the display of prints can in part be attributed to the fact that it was as much the social and professional status of the producers, as the nature of the products, that the Academy set out to control.

This question of social control lies at the heart of the most important questions concerning the relationship between engravers and the Academy: exactly why the Academy persisted in categorizing engravers as lesser members, why engravers failed to force a change to this policy until 1853, and whether the consequent conditions for exhibiting prints notably affected the wider development of printmaking during the period. When challenged to defend its policies in 1809, the Academy rejected the engravers' demands for better treatment without explanation, citing its inability to alter statutes that had been sanctioned by royal authority.[34] Three years later the Academicians admitted that indeed it *was* in their power to overturn the regulations in question, but claimed they had previously insisted otherwise in order to spare 'the feelings of their Brother Artists'. The real reason, they now revealed, was that the arts were based on

> those intellectual qualities of Invention and Composition, which Painting, Sculpture and Architecture so eminently possess, but of which Engraving is wholly devoid; its greatest praise consisting in translating with as little loss as possible the beauties of these original Arts of Design. With such an important difference in their intellectual pretensions as Artists, it appear'd to the framers of this Society that to admit Engravers into the first class of their Members, would be incompatible with justice and a due regard to the dignity of the Royal Academy.[35]

I would argue, however, that this was not the only, or even the main reason for the engravers' marginalization. After all, as engravers repeatedly pointed out, other techniques with even less pretension to an intellectual basis were given better treatment at Somerset House.[36] What made engraving a special case was its uniquely close relationship with painting, and the fact (which the RA could not bring itself to acknowledge) that painters necessarily depended on engravers to publicize their compositions. It is hardly surprising that the Academicians went to such lengths to deny their intimate association with a 'mechanical' profession which threatened both their social aspirations and their desire to be seen as practitioners of a liberal art. It is certainly true that many painters felt a strong prejudice against any one of their number who had a whiff of the engravers' workshop about him: Joseph Farington and Robert Smirke were reduced to near panic at the thought that the Academy might have been tricked into electing as a painter-Academician a man who was really an engraver.[37]

The engravers' own inconsistencies also contributed to their failure to improve their lot. Their first concerted campaign, led by John Landseer (an Associate Engraver from 1806), involved engravers who were themselves too strongly imbued with academic ideology to dispute it effectively. Also crucial were the difficulties that engravers experienced in establishing a coherent and powerful community of interest.[38] Landseer himself was speaking for only one group of printmakers ('stroke' engravers of history subjects) and he was always ready to criticize other groups, such as those engaged in 'chalk manner' prints, in colour printing, lithography or relief printing. His claim for raising the status of engravers depended first and foremost on the 'translation' argument alluded to in the Academy Council's statement above; Landseer argued for the intellectual content of engraving by claiming its status was analogous to such literary works as Pope's celebrated translations of Homer. This argument divided Landseer from much contemporary printmaking practice, and nowhere more dramatically than in the case of colour printing. Since to him the use of colour suggested that printmakers were trying to produce a facsimile of a painting – a mere copy rather than a translation from one medium to another – Landseer strongly counselled against its use in engraving. He blamed the current fashion for colour prints on publishers who commissioned such works 'with the view of making the copy, in their own vulgar estimation, approach nearer to its original'.[39] Colouring an engraving, he argued, was as absurd as colouring a diamond. Here Landseer once again shows himself to be more in line with Academy thinking than one would expect from an 'opposition' spokesman, as it was surely because most Associate Engravers realized that the Academy itself would also view colour printing in this light that they did not show colour prints at its exhibitions.

The fragmentation of the engravers' profession was due less to Landseer's arguments than to developing relations between printmakers and the growing body of print publishers whose capital accumulation was turning them into a newly powerful group of 'middle men'. The fear which Landseer voiced of the power of such men was another thing that many engravers had in common with the Academy. The desire to distance high art from commercial concerns must have been an important factor in the original decision to restrict engravers to Associate status; yet the fact that this same fear motivated many engravers made it especially hard for them to counter the Academy's arguments. Once again it becomes painfully clear that Landseer was fighting not for the print publishing industry as a whole, but for his particular section of it. He blamed the fragmentation of the profession on the publishers' introduction of new, labour-saving techniques in order to increase profits, which in turn robbed his own, older technique of line engraving of its commercial viability. Landseer hoped that if the Academy would agree to support the engravers' claims this would facilitate the resurgence of the independent line engraver. Effectively, he was asking the Academy to support his efforts to restrict the activities of publishers to selling only, keeping them behind the counter and preventing them from straying out of what he considered to be their 'proper orbit' – that is to say, from dictating decisions which properly belonged to engravers themselves, such as their selection of image and technique. Any engraver choosing to work with such a businessman was, in Landseer's eyes, selling his birthright for a mess of pottage.[40] However, Landseer's denunciation of contemporary print publishers (most notably his comments about the recently deceased John Boydell) can only have confirmed the Academy's belief that, if engravers were admitted to full membership, it would not be long before the commercial interests of publishers would become all too nakedly apparent on the walls of Somerset House.

Although it may now seem obvious that the 'battle of the engravers' with the Royal Academy masked the fact that the opposing sides shared an intense dislike of the developing forces of commerce, the triumph of commercialization seemed anything but inevitable at the time. Landseer, for example, was convinced that the revival of line engraving, visible in the work of engravers reproducing Wilkie's paintings, signalled the possibility of a return to an older pattern of independent line engravers producing prints whose quality would be recompensed by the generosity of an educated audience, in the teeth of the activities of print publishers who at every turn reduced the quality of their products in order to cut costs and maximize profits. Landseer and many Academicians hoped that this process of turning back the clock would be helped by the Academy's exhibitions, which would provide an opportunity to appeal directly to potential patrons, thus cutting out the need to deal with middle men – whether picture dealers or print publishers. As part of its own, largely hopeless, effort to stem the tide of commercialization, the Academy did its best to prevent its exhibitions from being seen simply as a shop window, and particularly as a place for advertising print sales: in 1785 the Council refused to accept two paintings by Angelica Kauffmann which appeared to have been submitted by a publisher rather than the painter herself.[41] But even if the flood of genre prints was kept from the exhibition walls, the vast majority of genre *paintings* shown at the Academy were available as reproductive prints, and publishers rightly assumed that the exhibited oils advertised their prints quite as well as if the prints themselves had been shown. Exhibited prints may have been sparsely reviewed, yet new print publications were advertised and assessed with increasing frequency, so that the public was never in danger of remaining unaware of their existence.

In retrospect, it is clear that the engravers' boycott of the Royal Academy and its exhibitions, and their attempts to gain the right to full academic status, constituted a minor, and largely vain act of resistance to the larger processes of capital accumulation and the development of bourgeois art markets, which both parties hoped the Academy might be able to reverse. It is ironic, then, that it was an attack by members of the middle class, at the close of the Academy's residence on the Strand, which began to pave the way for the final admittance of the engravers into the citadel in the 1850s.[42] The pressure for reform of the Academy, which had come to be seen by bourgeois radicals as a bastion of aristocratic and artistic privilege, was acknowledged by the 1835 Select Committee set up to enquire into its accountability, among other questions. As part of its overall brief, the Committee was to look into the engravers' claims, and although they failed to win their argument immediately, the way was now open for the state to endorse the view of engravers as victims of academic despotism and aristocratic privilege.

Yet by the time engravers were admitted to full academic status in 1853, it was clear that Landseer's ideal, of independent line engravers publishing their own prints to be sold by printsellers reduced to shopkeeper status, could never be realized. Samuel Cousins, the first printmaker finally to be elected to the newly conceded status of Engraver Academician, was not a line engraver, but an expert in the new mixed method of steel engraving whose basis was not line but mezzotint. The major changes in the printmaking profession – in particular the new tendency of publishers such as Ackermann to commission prints after drawings and watercolours, thus cutting out the expense of either commissioning or buying the copyright of a major oil painting – had further increased the Academy's irrelevance to the industry's development. Important though the conflicts between the engravers and the Academy were to the development of cultural production in nineteenth-century Britain, they meant that, whereas the RA's exhibitions had a demonstrable effect on the development of painting in oils and watercolours, they had less impact on the wider development of printmaking. Even from its earliest days, the Academy had never been the only place where prints could be exhibited. Around a hundred printmakers who were unwilling to become candidates for the degraded Associate Engraver status exhibited instead with the Free Society and the Society of Artists between 1760 and 1791, and more did so later at the British School and the British Institution. Even after the demise of the two earlier institutions, the development of projects such as Boydell's Shakespeare Galley and Macklin's Poets' Gallery continued to provide venues in London where reproductive prints were exhibited, the 'Gallery' of the title applying not only to the exhibition room but also, by extension, to the folio or other publication to which it was hoped that visitors would subscribe. Arguably, it had always been in such printed 'galleries' that the intricacies of engraving could be viewed to their best advantage, rather than on the walls of Somerset House.

16

Foreign Exhibitors and the British School at the Royal Academy, 1768–1823

ANNE PUETZ

AT LEAST 250 FOREIGN EXHIBITORS CONTRIBUTED to the Royal Academy exhibitions at Somerset House (for a breakdown see p. 253, Tables 1 and 2). Though a small proportion of the overall number of contributors, their presence raises a number of significant questions about the larger world in which they operated: about patterns of economic and artistic migration during a turbulent era in European history; about the development of the art market, both in Britain and on the Continent; and about the formation of a distinctly British political and cultural identity at a time when the nation fought and emerged triumphant from a prolonged and difficult war with France. It is this last issue that will concern me most of all, as I examine how the presence of the Academy's foreign exhibitors interacted with efforts to define the particular character of *British* art.[1]

In order to make sense of this overall phenomenon, I shall be presenting a series of three case studies, each involving one or two artists who can be taken as representative of a standard type of foreign practitioner: the long-term settler; the political refugee; and the Continental painter or sculptor whose works were sent in from abroad, or were submitted to the Academy by a British patron. As we shall see, it makes sound historical sense to analyse these different types in chronological order. In so doing, moreover, we shall be in a position to assess how the 'foreign' evolved as a signifier, within the discourse of the visual arts in Britain, between the 1770s and the 1820s. At the beginning of this period, a foreign exhibitor's origins and style seem to have mattered little if at all; by the end, however, they had come to matter a great deal.

The creation of a native school of art had been, of course, the Royal Academy's professed *raison d'être* at its foundation in 1768. After decades of debate about the best organizational structure for the systematic education of young artists, the proponents of William Hogarth's notion of an art with solidly local connotations, and taught in an informal and egalitarian way, lost the argument to those who favoured a hierarchical model based on established Continental academic theory and practice. Thus England's Royal Academy took as its model the most prestigious of its European counterparts, the French Académie Royale de Peinture et Sculpture.

The new institution's doctrines, as most authoritatively formulated in Sir Joshua Reynolds's *Discourses*, similarly derived from the mainstream tradition of European art theory. This placed its central emphasis on a broadly Neoplatonic conception of art, in which ideal beauty was to be distilled from observable reality according to a set of objective rules. In Reynolds's formulation, the most dignified art was one that abstracted 'general' from 'particular' nature, and transcended all local (including national) characteristics in favour of expressing a universal ideal of visible beauty and moral truth. In theory at least, British high art was meant to look like – and not different from – high art elsewhere in Europe.

The thirty-four founding members of London's new Academy included no fewer than nine artists of foreign origin, most of whom had received a classical academic training in Italy (see p. 254, Table 3). This large percentage reflected the relative weakness of the native art tradition, and its longstanding dependence on immigrants; throughout the eighteenth century, furthermore, foreigners had played a prominent part in British art education. In a memorable acknowledgement of this dependence, Reynolds would later describe foreign artists as contributing the 'manure' needed to 'accelerate' the growth of the British School.[2] The

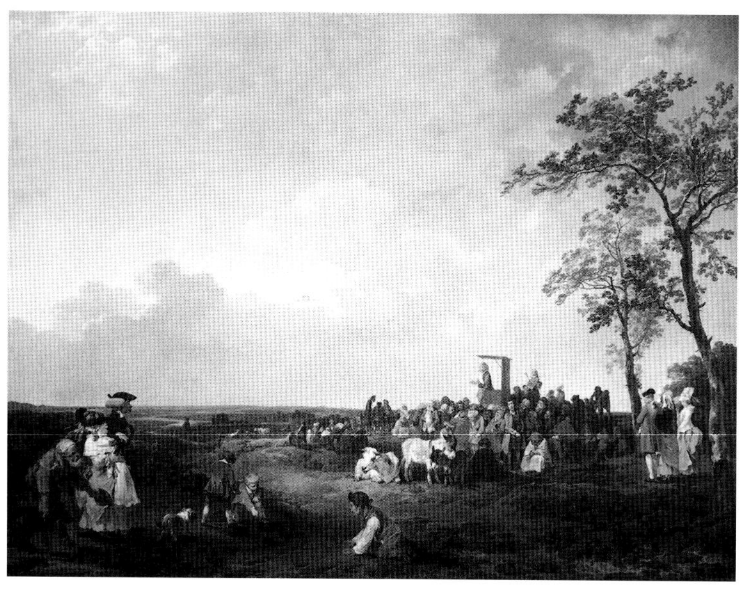

205 Philippe Jacques de Loutherbourg, *A Midsummer Afternoon with a Methodist Preacher*, RA 1777. National Gallery of Canada, Ottawa.

Academy's early statutes facilitated the absorption of useful foreign talent by opening its membership to all suitably qualified artists, irrespective of national origin, as long as they were 'of fair moral characters', not part of any rival exhibiting society, and resident in Great Britain.[3] Access to membership, at least for French artists, was further eased by admitting 'the Academicians of the French Academy of Painting, Sculpture, and Architecture . . . to the drawing Academy and Lectures'.[4] Such openness is indicative of the fact that most of the Academy's British founder members were steeped in a culture of easy cosmopolitanism. Along with Reynolds, its first President, and its Treasurer William Chambers, many had spent extended periods of study abroad, chiefly in Rome or in Paris; there they had not only attended to the art of the past, but had also come into close contact with numerous contemporary French and Italian masters.[5]

For a variety of reasons, therefore, the British system was prepared to accommodate those immigrant artists who came to London in search of patronage and professional advancement. Foreign history painters could count on an especially warm welcome during the Academy's early years, when there was a real sense of urgency underlying its desire to measure up to its continental counterparts. Hence the RA's immediate acceptance of the Turin-born Jean François Rigaud, who within a year of his arrival in 1771, had been elected an Associate member and was displaying work at the institution's first exhibition rooms in Pall Mall.[6] On several subsequent occasions reviewers praised Rigaud for his commitment to the noble cause of historical art; in 1781, for instance, when he showed a sketch for a Deposition altarpiece for the Sardinian ambassador's chapel, it was regretted that the finished painting was not likewise present 'as it [the exhibition] greatly wants the Help of large and good Pictures to enable us to swallow with less Disgust the Quantity of small Trash with which it abounds'.[7] But the realities of the London marketplace forced Rigaud to manufacture a greater range of pictorial commodities, and to adjust his exhibiting strategy accordingly: of the sixty canvases he displayed between 1772 and 1784, only fourteen were histories while the remainder were portraits (e.g., fig. 206). A number of critics sympathetic to the Academy's agenda to produce, and to be *seen* to produce, art in the highest genre, emphasized Rigaud's exhibited history paintings over his more numerous portraits; though until the mid-1780s the latter, too, when noticed, also elicited general approval, above all for their precise draughtsmanship and expressive rendering of likeness. That Rigaud's reputation as a portraitist sharply declined from 1784 onwards may have been due, at least in part, to the contemporaneous appearance at the exhibitions of a new generation of ambitious native-born competitors, headed by John Hoppner, and followed by William Beechey and Thomas Lawrence.[8] Significantly, however – especially in light of what we shall learn below of the different treatment of other Continental artists a few years later – neither Rigaud nor his portraits were criticized for being foreign, but rather on the grounds that any artist whose academic honours derived from the production of history painting should be discouraged from taking up 'lower', if more lucrative, alternatives, especially when this threatened to take patronage away from deserving young British painters. The fact that critics made no issue of Rigaud's nationality presumably owes a great deal to his own ceaseless and anxious efforts at assimilation, beginning with the anglicization of his first names to 'John Francis' at his Academy début in 1772.[9]

In contrast, Philippe Jacques de Loutherbourg, who also arrived in London from Paris in the autumn of 1771, appears to have actively cultivated a colourful, 'foreign', even exotic self-image.[10] The RA catalogue for 1773 describes him as 'Painter to the King of France and Member of his Royal Academy, and of the Academy of Painting at Marseilles' – an impressive string of titles occasionally reiterated by reviewers throughout the 1770s – and he was rapidly established in exhibition reviews as 'this celebrated foreign artist' or 'this very ingenious foreigner'.[11] Such terms speak eloquently of the prestige bestowed on the exhibitions by the participation of an internationally renowned artist, whose public profile was enhanced by his celebrated stage designs (1773–81) for the actor-manager David Garrick and his successor Richard Brinsley Sheridan at Drury Lane. At times an awareness of de Loutherbourg's nationality found expression in discussions of his style of painting, and in particular of his lush colouring, which one critic thought was 'evidently like that of most of his countrymen, adopted from Berney [the French landscape and marine artist Claude-Joseph Vernet]'.[12]

But the same stylistic qualities did not prevent the artist's comic rural scenes of the seventies from being widely admired as masterly and unrivalled expressions of quintessentially '*English*' humour. For works like *A Midsummer Afternoon with a Methodist Preacher* (RA 1777; fig. 205), critics hailed de Loutherbourg not just as the heir to, but as the superior reincarnation of the orig-

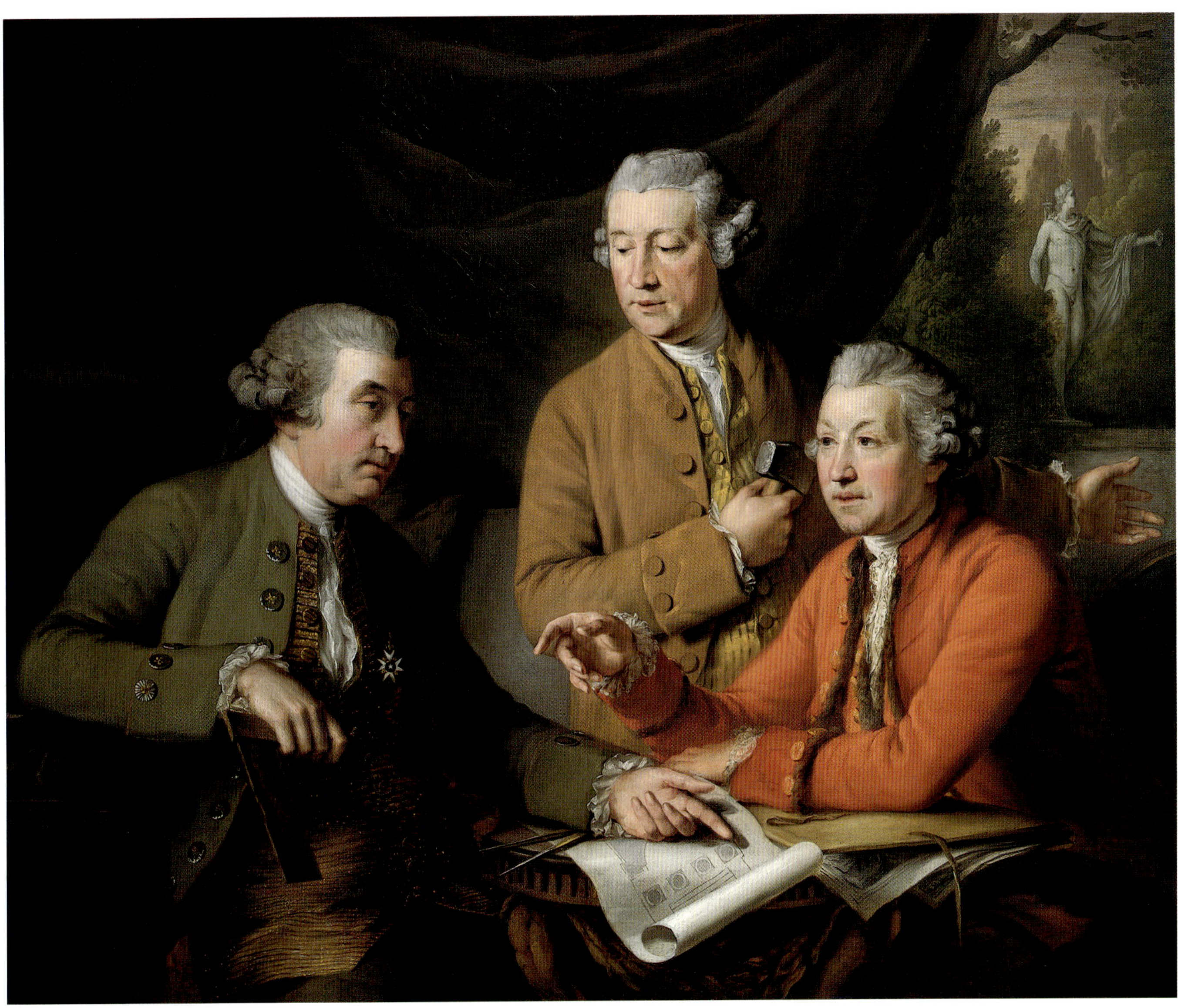

206 John Francis Rigaud, *Sir William Chambers, Joseph Wilton and Sir Joshua Reynolds*, RA 1782. By courtesy of the National Portrait Gallery, London.

inal native genius, William Hogarth.[13] And like Hogarth, though in very different circumstances, the French master proved adept at identifying and filling gaps in the marketplace. During the 1770s he was perceived mainly as a painter of landscapes filled with comic incident – of works that offered no competition to the picturesque views and country house portraits associated with Richard Wilson and George Barret, or to the rustic pastorals that were a speciality of Thomas Gainsborough's. But by 1784, the deaths of Wilson and Barret, together with Gainsborough's boycott of Somerset House, left de Loutherbourg as the uncontested leader in the field of exhibition landscapes – an 'artist unrivalled in his line', as the *Morning Post* put it in 1785.[14]

From 1784 to 1787 de Loutherbourg capitalized on the growing appeal of tourism in Britain, which had begun to complement the patrician 'Grand Tour' by flooding the exhibitions with picturesquely rendered scenes of Derbyshire, the Lake District and Wales. Always prolific, in 1784 and again in 1785 he reached new heights by putting ten works on show; nine of these were hung in the Great Room – the premier exhibition gallery – in 1784, and all ten in the year after. Although the domination of the Great Room by the productions of Academicians to the detriment of non-members would later come under critical attack, during the 1770s and 1780s it was generally regarded as part of an Academician's duty to provide the exhibitions with as many pictures as possible, and preferably in a variety of types. In 1784, de Loutherbourg, alongside Reynolds, was declared 'a chief Supporter of this Year's Exhibition', while in the following year his works were judged outstanding 'amidst the general penury'.[15]

His exploitation of the London public's interest in popular native tourist attractions appears to have paid off handsomely, at least judging by the prominence his British views were given

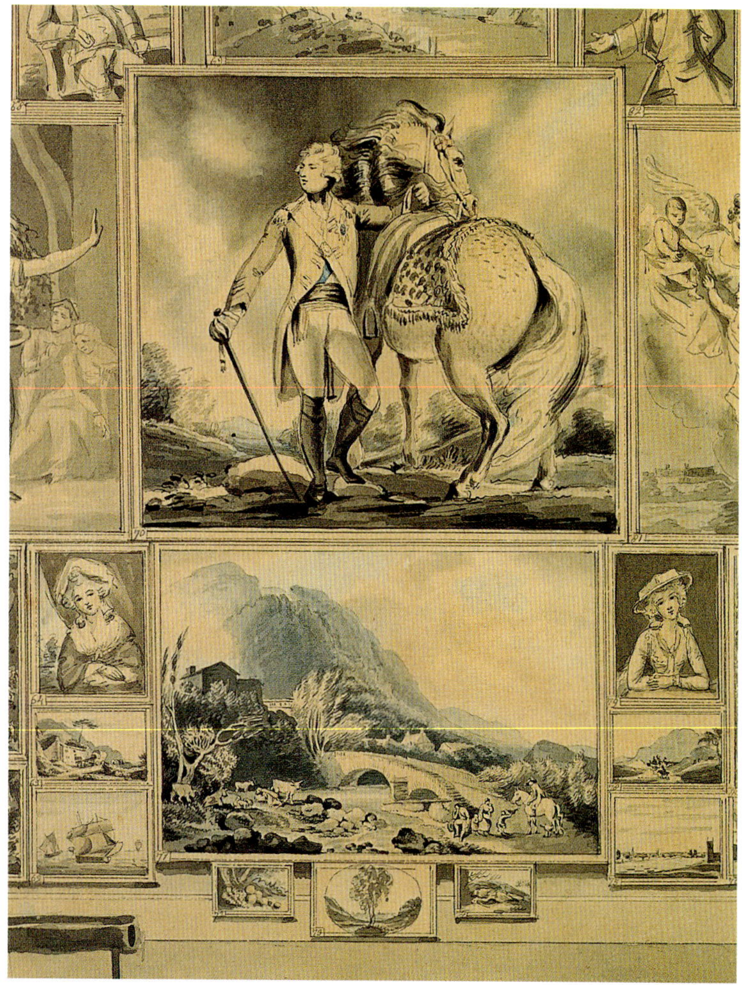

207 Edward Francis Burney, *The Royal Academy Exhibition of 1784: The Great Room, North Wall* (detail of fig. 17, showing de Loutherbourg's *Brother Bridge* hanging below Reynolds's *Prince of Wales*), pen and watercolour. By courtesy of the Trustees of the British Museum.

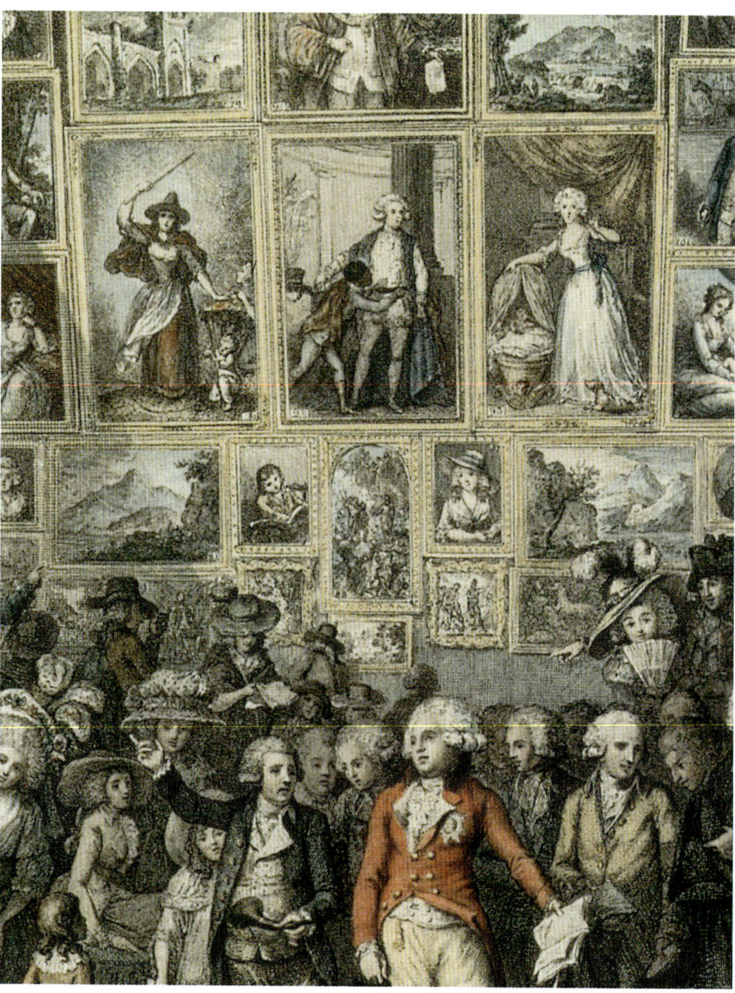

208 Pietro Martini after Johann Heinrich Ramberg, *The Exhibition of the Royal Academy, 1787* (detail of fig. 36, showing de Loutherbourg's *Grasmeer* [*sic*] and *Snowdon* hanging below Reynolds's *Prince of Wales with a Black Servant*), engraving. By courtesy of the Trustees of the British Museum.

within the overall hang of the Great Room. Perhaps the most desirable situation was in the centre of the north wall, which usually featured a full-length royal portrait by a leading Academician, flanked on either side by other full-lengths of important sitters or by large-scale history paintings. In 1784, this space (fig. 207) was dominated by Reynolds's huge portrait of the Prince of Wales (see fig. 22), with de Loutherbourg's highly praised *Brother Bridge, which divides Westmoreland from Cumberland* (unlocated) hanging directly underneath. Three years later a position of comparable importance was given to his views of *Grasmeer [sic] in Westmoreland – an Evening* and *Snowdon from Llan Berris Lake, with the Castle of Dol Badon [Dolbadern]*, which appeared below Sir Joshua's portrait *The Prince of Wales with a Black Servant* (fig. 208; and see fig. 3). It is a significant indication of the Academy's (and its supporters') understanding of British art as stylistically pluralist that this powerful evocation of national identity – juxtaposing an image of the heir to the throne with two pictures of celebrated local scenery – could be achieved by a British painter working in a combination of Flemish and Venetian idioms, and a Frenchman steeped in the manner of his own native school.[16]

De Loutherbourg's exhibits of 1784–87 owed their great popularity not only to his use of a familiar national subject matter, but also to what was customarily called the artist's 'happy stile'.[17] This 'stile' or 'manner' consisted of a repertoire of techniques which ultimately derived from French academic practice, featuring neat and spirited draughtsmanship, a highly finished and varnished paint surface, and contrasting areas of vibrant colours. Such formal qualities combined literally to spotlight de Loutherbourg's exhibits within the crowded display of the Great Room. As an artist who had learned how to negotiate a similarly competitive set-up in the Paris Salons (where he showed prolifically between 1762 and 1771), he was well placed from the outset to outdo his British rivals in the manipulation of the visitor's gaze.

Critics were not just speaking metaphorically when they described the artist's works as among the 'brightest ornaments of the exhibition', and as 'shining forth' among the rest with uncommon 'lustre' or 'splendour'.[18] Repeatedly during his exhibiting career, reviewers acknowledged de Loutherbourg's ability to overpower other landscape artists whose works had been placed in proximity to his own.[19] His capacities as a showman were never in doubt, and references to his 'original' or 'inimitable' 'manner' became a stock-in-trade in exhibition reviews.

But there was only a small step from 'manner' to 'mannerism' and its connotations of artificiality and posturing. By 1785 certain critics had begun to associate de Loutherbourg's style with the allegedly mannered character of French art; though in the opinion of the *Morning Post and Daily Advertiser*, the results were still worthy of praise: 'This Artist has as few faults as the greatest master that ever exhibited in this line of painting, and when we say this, we may be excused for observing that there is rather too much of the lead colour in several of his pictures in the present exhibition. His inclination to the *maniéré* of the French school cannot be imputed to him as a defect.'[20] While the *Morning Post*'s reviewer was obviously ready to tolerate de Loutherbourg's signature 'lead colour' – that is, colour brightened by an intermixture of lead white – as a natural function of his French training, in subsequent years similar judgements took on an increasingly negative tone. It quickly became a habitual practice among exhibition critics to reproach the artist for his use of 'gaudy' and 'glaring' tints; more specifically, his use of exaggerated colours in combination with his lavish application of varnish was charged with arresting the spectator's gaze at the surface of the picture, thus erecting a barrier not only between 'nature' and its representation – no longer imitated but merely approximated – but also between the representation and the viewer. The *Whitehall Evening Post*, for instance, while still favourably impressed with de Loutherbourg's powers of design and composition, found fault with the three Welsh views that he exhibited in 1787: 'Most admirably handled but for one defect – his style of colouring is too gaudy: his grass is too green, his mountains too blue, his water too transparent, and yet these are capital pieces: – they are however varnished as high as a Birmingham tea-board, which takes off very much from the deception'.[21] The reference to Birmingham lacquer ware, and by implication to the more general practice of japanning, soon to be taken up by other critics, condemned de Loutherbourg's pictures by association with tawdry and inexpensive consumer goods.

Not only did his obtrusive, attention-seeking technique make his own works look cheap; reviewers also thought that his example had inspired too many younger landscapists to follow the same misguided path. As the *Morning Herald* observed with dismay in its discussion of the Academy display of 1787, 'Mr. Loutherbourg appears to be forming a school of *japanners* rather than painters; at least so we may infer from the numerous imitations of his manner which have this year been introduced into the academy'.[22] And by diverting the course of landscape art from its proper object, the close imitation of nature, this Frenchman and his British followers threatened to degrade the exhibition arena by attracting 'common', 'ignorant' and 'vulgar' spectators with an array of eye-catching but worthless productions.[23]

There is no single, obvious cause that can easily explain the rapid decline in de Loutherbourg's critical fortunes – though apparently not in his popularity – from around 1786 onwards. In his case (unlike Rigaud's, at more or less the same moment) increased pressure from local practitioners does not seem to have been a factor; competition from the rising generation of British landscape artists would not appear until the 1790s. Instead, de Loutherbourg appears simply to have outstayed his welcome, as the repetitive employment of his well-honed technique came more and more often to be seen as the deployment of a manipulative strategy by an artist long known for his adroit showmanship, and who was to gain a reputation as a charlatan through his ill-fated attempts at faith-healing in 1789.[24]

But more significantly, by the later 1780s, almost two decades after the establishment of the Academy, its critics could justifiably demand to see evidence in the exhibitions of the promised national 'school', in place of a medley of (however attractive) disparate performances.[25] The term 'school', of course, implies at least a modicum of shared features, and in view of Britain's renewed and intensifying rivalry with France from the eighties onwards, it is not surprising that the emerging native school should be defined in opposition to the alleged characteristics of French art.[26] In the Academy's exhibitions of the 1780s and 1790s, de Loutherbourg was one of the most prominent exhibitors in various sub-genres of landscape painting, as well as the most visible product and 'outpost' of the French School, and thus offered himself as an ideal 'anti-type' against which to articulate a peculiarly British kind of landscape painting.

French art had long been condemned, most commonly with reference to luxury goods, as superficially beguiling and 'gaudy', laboriously made yet intrinsically flimsy, alien to 'nature' and devoid of true 'taste'.[27] Thus, when de Loutherbourg's art was repeatedly described in terms of 'glaring' and 'gaudy' colours, 'flimsy . . . labours' and 'mechanical dexterity', the association with Frenchness could be made without having to be spelled out.[28] Significantly, the first attempts to tar his works with the brush of the despised French School went hand in hand with efforts to contrast his putative shortcomings with the strengths of past British masters like Wilson, Barret and Gainsborough. According to the champions of this native tradition, British landscape painters were capable of faithfully imitating the appearances of nature, and possessed the higher ability to stimulate pleasurable and elevating associations in the minds of their viewers. The *Morning Post* found such a capacity singularly lacking in de Loutherbourg's *View of Winandermeer [Windermere]* (RA 1786; fig. 209):

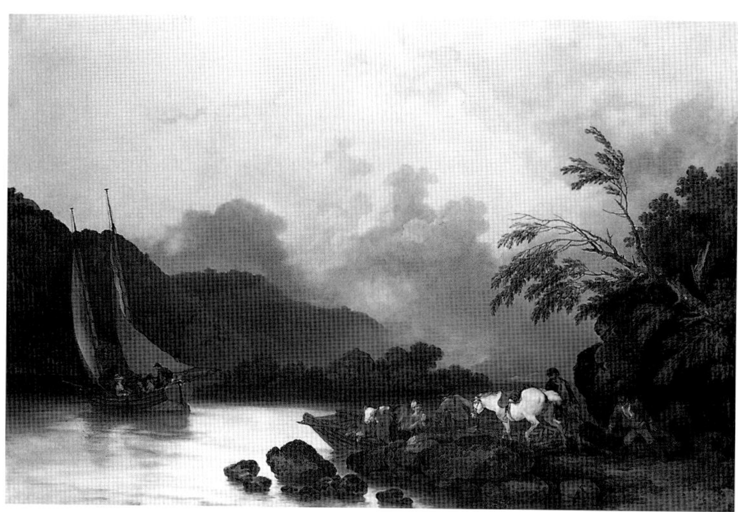

209 Philippe Jacques de Loutherbourg, *View of Windermere near the Ferry – a Sunset* (also known as *Belle Isle, Windermere, in a Calm*), RA 1786. Abbot Hall Art Gallery, Kendal.

> His landscape is replete with an assemblage of incongruous appearances, without any general connecting idea; consequently it contains no mark of character. It is neither joyful nor gloomy, nor grand nor elegant, nor simple nor magnificent; in short it is incapable of impressing any sentiment, which is the only sure criterion of genious [*sic*], and which appears in the works of the first painter of this country, the late Mr. Wilson; and indeed not in an inconsiderable degree by Gainsborough.[29]

A year later, his *View of Snowden* [*sic*], *from Llan Berris Lake* failed to 'convey on canvas an idea of immensity in Landscapes and Water', while 'Mr *Gainsborough's* Lakes were attempts that we shall never see surpassed'.[30]

As Dian Kriz has recently demonstrated, landscape painting took on even greater importance in the formation of a distinctly British cultural identity after the outbreak of open conflict with France, in the wake of the Revolution of 1789. This period saw an intensification of the critical campaign to define a native 'school' of landscape painting in opposition to an alien/French 'anti-type'. This came to be associated in particular with the kind of overtly commercial showiness that had for years been ascribed to de Loutherbourg, and which reviewers opposed to an ideal of 'British' art as 'chaste', self-effacing and 'natural'.[31] Similar reproaches against native artists, most prominently the narrative painter Richard Westall, show that accusations of a 'foreign' manner were not necessarily tied to foreign origin.[32] None the less, de Loutherbourg was singled out as the fountainhead of stylistic excess and held personally responsible for forming the styles of his followers Peter Francis Bourgeois and Julius Caesar Ibbetson: 'Mr Ibbetson would do well to forget that such as man as Mr. Loutherbourg existed', urged Anthony Pasquin, for instance, with reference to the younger artist's *View in Pembrokeshire* in the exhibition of 1796.[33] Throughout the 1790s, and by contrast with the previous decade, the faults with which de Loutherbourg was charged were explicitly tied to his 'Frenchness' and his 'foreignness': 'But yet, Monsieur', wrote the pseudonymous Solomon Gundy in 1792, 'I cannot but despise Your *Clouds of Marble*, and your *Lilac Skies*'.[34] Whereas French 'monsieurs' produced artificial landscapes, the British (implicitly) were masters of nature.

But we still need to remind ourselves that throughout the later eighteenth and early nineteenth centuries there was no consensus on what should constitute the national 'school'. 'English School Discourse'[35] offered no singular argument with a fixed outcome, a national school of definite characteristics, but only the ebb and flow of contesting opinions, which fluctuated in strength at different points in time. Hence while Philippe de Loutherbourg's press was never uniformly good or bad – he still had certain admirers throughout the nineties and beyond – the desire to establish a clear identity for British culture effectively placed his exhibited landscapes beyond the pale, in the province of the alien 'other'. The only exceptions that proved this rule were three scenes of contemporary historical events: the *Cutting out of the French Corvette 'La Chevrette' by English Soldiers, with Portraits of the Officers Engaged, 21st July 1801*, (RA 1802; Bristol City Art Gallery), along with the *Decisive Battle of Alexandria* and the *Landing of the British Troops in the Bay of Aboukir*, both shown three years later (figs 210 and 211). Although not exhibited until four years after the actions they depicted, the patriotic appeal of de Loutherbourg's dramatic rendering of two crucial moments in the Egyptian campaign remained undiminished. None of the reviews made any reference to his French 'manner', and he was widely praised for both composition and execution; but clearly it was primarily the subject matter – 'highly interesting to the feelings of every true Briton' – that made these pendants 'the pride of the present Exhibition'.[36]

Even well before this time, Britain's growing sense of cultural insularity, evident in the Francophobic sentiments expressed by large sections of the contemporary press, had penetrated into the Academy, which in consequence altered its overall policy with regard to foreign artists. Shearer West has recently charted in detail the various manifestations of nationalist bias against, and suspicion of, foreigners, within the Academy from the late 1780s to 1800.[37] Although her particular concern is with the treatment of Italian practitioners, council resolutions that granted, for instance, import licences only to British artists returning from Italy (1793), or which required foreigners to produce evidence of their membership of academies abroad (1796) obviously applied to foreigners across the board.[38] Reynolds's failed championship of the Italian architect Giuseppe Bonomi's application for the professorship of perspective offers only the most visible instance of the Academy's effective closure, by 1790, to the full participation of foreign talent that had characterized its early years.[39] Out of the 107 new Associates elected between 1780 and 1836, only seven were of foreign origin – though six of these were later made full members. (For a breakdown of RA

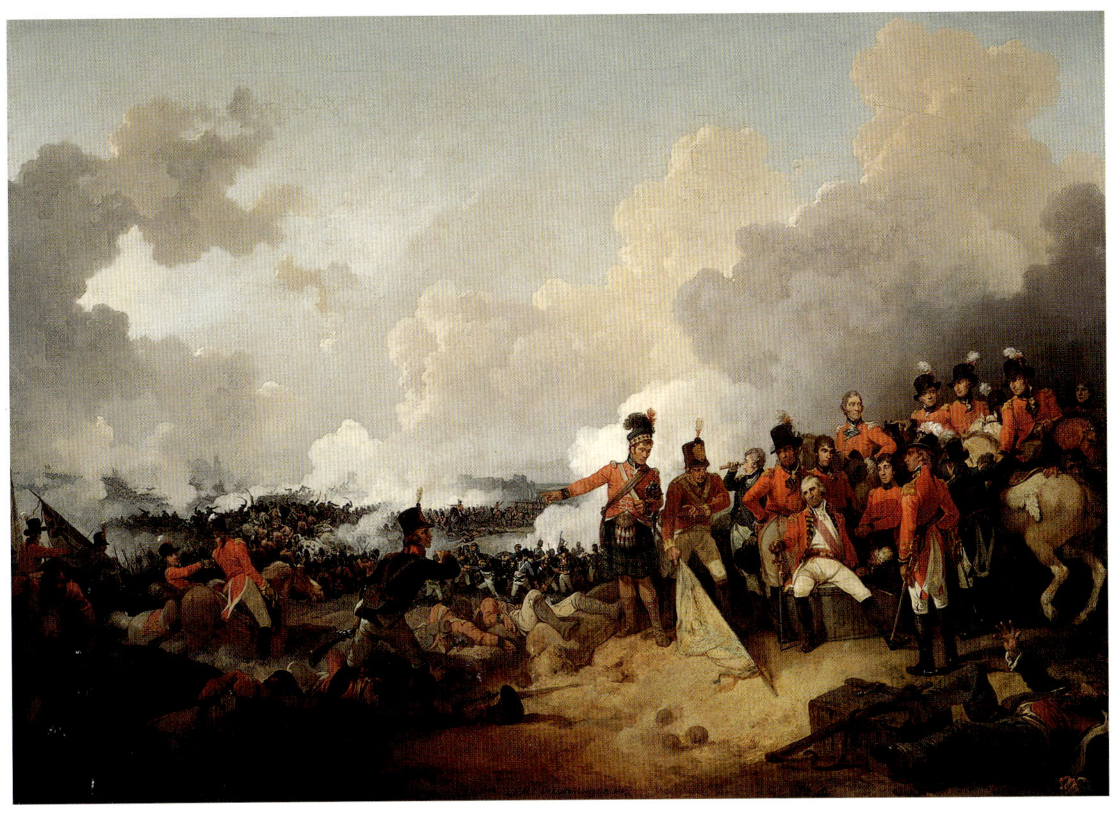

210 Philippe Jacques de Loutherbourg, *Decisive Battle of Alexandria, Fought on 21st March, 1801*, RA 1805. Scottish National Portrait Gallery, Edinburgh.

211 Philippe Jacques de Loutherbourg, *Landing of the British Troops in the Bay of Aboukir . . . on the 8th of March, 1801*, RA 1805. Scottish National Portrait Gallery, Edinburgh.

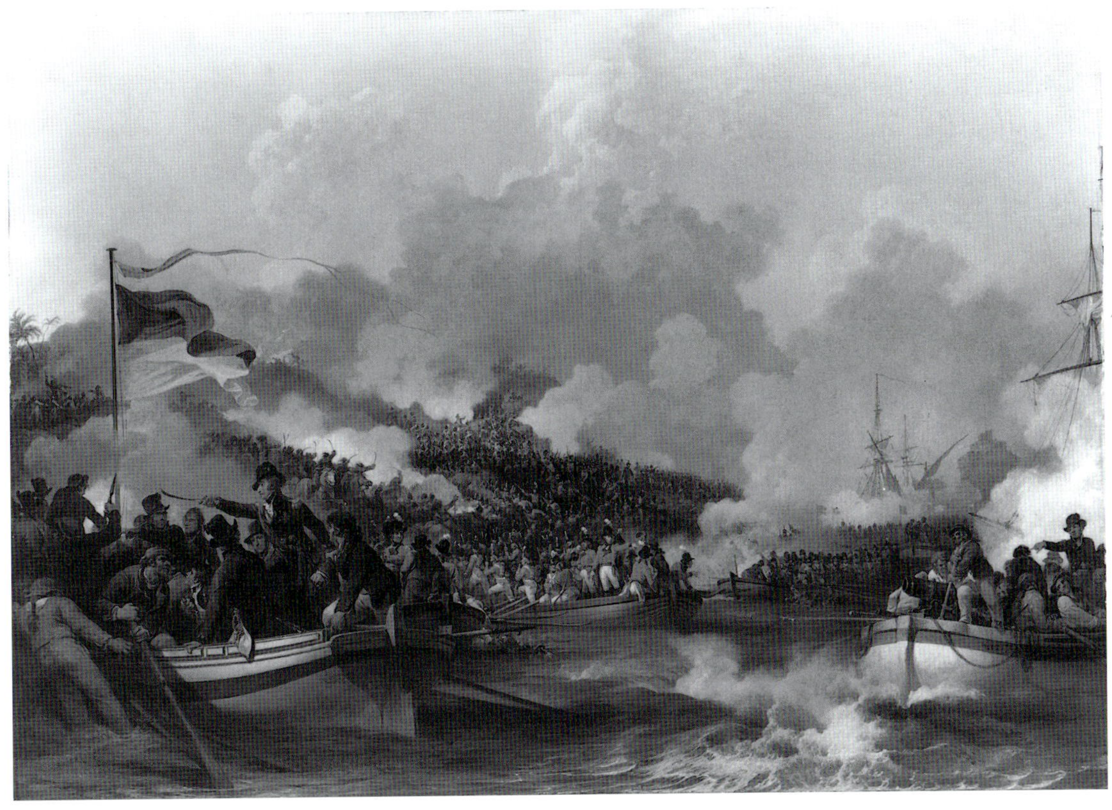

membership 1768–1836, see p. 254, Table 4.) The Bonomi affair gave the first public indication that the larger body of Academicians had begun to see themselves as constituting an exclusively 'English' body, a notion subsequently underlined in a number of overtly xenophobic discussions that Joseph Farington recorded in his diary.[40] It was against this hostile background that a new wave of French artists – *émigrés* seeking refuge in the turbulent aftermath of 1789 – arrived in London and began to make their presence felt at the annual exhibitions.

In the time-honoured spirit of hospitality to political refugees, certain sections of the British press professed themselves quite happy to welcome these victims of Gallic republicanism gone mad. At the exhibition of 1797, the *Morning Post* congratulated one L. de Longastre on his pastel *Portrait of a Lady*, on the grounds that 'We believe that this Gentleman was expatriated for his attachment to the late unfortunate French Monarch, and, as a Professor by necessity, he is entitled to our liberality'.[41] With the exception of this work, none of Longastre's other RA exhibits – four portraits in oil in the Great Room in 1790, and a small number of pastels between 1795 and 1798 – appears to have attracted any critical comment. As 'a Professor by necessity', Longastre was probably one of the many *émigrés* – some belonging to the French aristocracy – who took to the production of pastels, watercolours and miniature portraits as a reasonably 'respectable' way of alleviating periods of economic hardship.[42] Such relatively minor works tended to be shown in the crammed and ill-lit secondary galleries on the ground and first floors of Somerset House, where they attracted little if any attention from either visitors or the press.

But the 'liberality' shown by reviewers to such largely invisible and uncompetitive newcomers almost entirely vanished when the livelihood and reputation of indigenous artists was put at risk – as occurred with the arrival from Paris of Jean-Laurent Mosnier. A fashionable portrait painter, French Academician and *Peintre de la Reine* to Marie-Antoinette from 1766, Mosnier established himself in London in 1790, and immediately secured a number of important commissions. He also quickly became acquainted with Sir Joshua Reynolds – they were neighbours in Leicester Fields during the initial part of Mosnier's residence in London – and it is testament to the period's growing xenophobia that Reynolds's continued spirit of friendly engagement with accomplished foreign practitioners was presented as an undue, even unpatriotic championship of alien interests.[43] One journalist in 1791, for instance, commented that Reynolds's introduction of his '*élève*' Mosnier to the Academicians' annual dinner had justifiably prompted murmurs of discontent; from their standpoint it was bad enough that Sir Joshua had hung 'his favourite's' pictures in the exhibition 'with a *sic jubeo* without seating an artist not of their body to their professional dinner by a similar *sic volo*'.[44]

The fact that a dinner invitation to a celebrated foreign artist should have caused such offence indicates the extent to which Mosnier's presence irritated his British peers, and the extent to which the Royal Academy had distanced itself from usual Continental practice.[45] Honorary membership – which would have automatically entitled an artist to participation in such convivial and celebratory events – had long been a standard feature of academies throughout Europe and was granted to a large number of British artists working abroad.[46] In England's Royal Academy, however, such a status did not exist; indeed the issue was not raised for debate until 1844, and was left unresolved even then.[47]

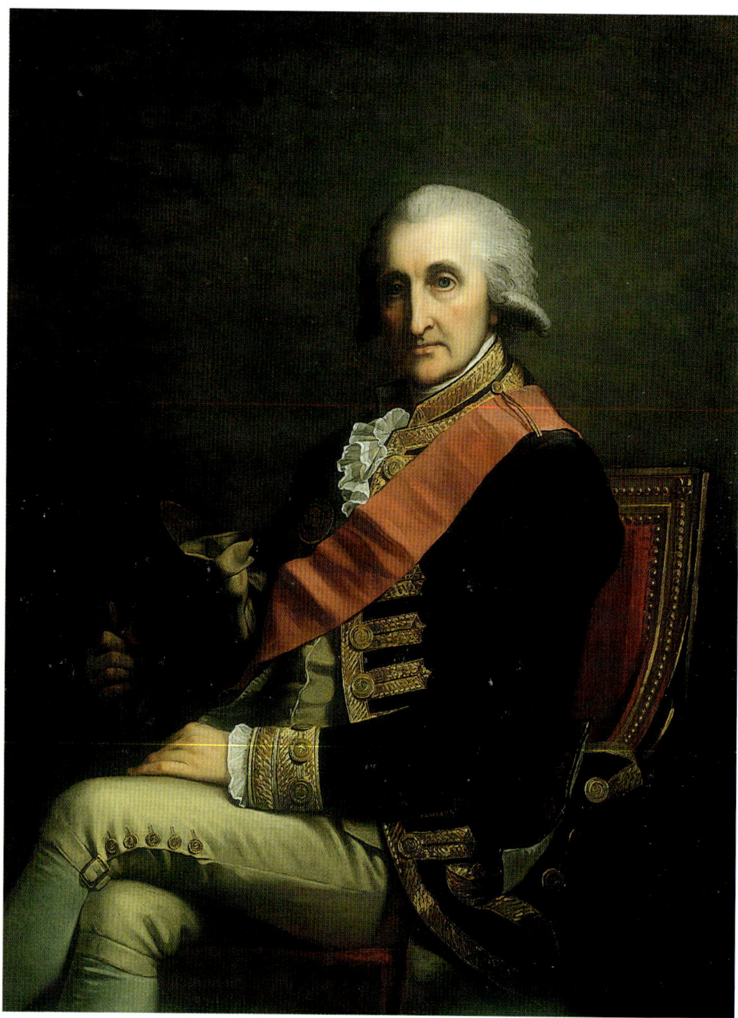

212 Jean-Laurent Mosnier, *Admiral Lord Rodney*, RA 1793. National Maritime Museum, Greenwich.

Although Mosnier certainly made a prolific début at the Academy with no fewer than nine portraits, Reynolds's alleged championship did not stretch to gaining all of them advantageous positions in Somerset House. One, a portrait of Mademoiselle D'Eon, was placed in the Ante-room, while four smaller works were displayed 'in so exalted a situation', one critic complained, 'that it is not possible to judge of their merit or demerit with any degree of certainty, without one of Herschell's telescopes'.[48] Yet even so, the appearance of the 'new French Painter' created considerable apprehension, particularly at the prospect that he might seduce an undiscerning but fashion-bent element within the native patron class. In the *Morning Chronicle* one reviewer warned that, 'This artist will engage much of the public notice. His portraits are finished with the most minute care. He is in truth at the head of an old and exploded style; but still he will have many admirers'.[49] The fact that Mosnier was soon commissioned to depict so celebrated a 'beauty' as Lady Caroline Campbell – her portrait was exhibited in 1792 – appeared to justify such fears. Over the course of his residence in Britain the artist attracted such eminent sitters as the Duchess of Leeds (RA 1792), the admiral-hero Lord Rodney (RA 1793; fig. 212), the actor Kemble as 'Coriolanus' (RA 1793) and the 7th Marquess of Tweeddale (RA 1795), and enjoyed continued prominence at the exhibitions, showing a total of thirty-two oils, all but eight of which found places in the Great Room.

Portraiture, for better or worse, had long been recognized as the main source of employment for British artists, and constituted the one pictorial genre where they fancied themselves superior to their Continental rivals. In response to a previous incursion – when the French court artist Jean-Baptiste Vanloo had set up shop in London between 1737 and 1741 – native practitioners and their defenders had launched an urgent campaign aimed at persuading local patrons not to switch their custom to the polished invader.[50] Between 1791 and 1796, however, when Mosnier exhibited at the Academy, critics did more than admonish a fickle public for its prejudice in favour of a fashionable outsider. Instead they invoked a specific and highly unflattering notion of French art in order to promote and define how the British 'genius' made its superior character manifest in the arena of portraiture.

The *Morning Chronicle* was only one of many newspapers to point to Mosnier's 'minute' finishing as a key characteristic of his art. The ostentatious self-portrait at the easel and *en famille* (fig. 213), which Mosnier showed at his first exhibition in London (and which had previously appeared at the Salon of 1787), was criticized for its 'high finishing, and a polished smoothness', deemed 'incompatible with expression and spirit'.[51] Where Mosnier's talent really showed, the same critic continued, was in the successful imitation of his eldest daughter's black satin robe – implicitly the least important part of a likeness – and successive observers would emphasize the artist's facility at rendering hands, hairstyles and drapery, but not 'heads' or 'faces'.[52] This not only robbed his sitters of their individuality – 'all his *Ladies* are of the same family, they have universally the same features and the same hair' – but it betrayed the intellectual inferiority of an artist unable to distinguish essentials from what was secondary or trivial.[53]

High finish was presented as a 'knack' – more properly employed in the artisanal workshop than the artist's studio – which turned what should have been a representation of 'natural ease and gracefullness' into a stiff and hard linearity, and made sitters look like so many 'figures on the lid of a snuff box'.[54] Recast as an entirely mechanical achievement, as a triumph of the hand over the mind, the much-vaunted precision of French draughtsmanship provided a perfect foil for the broad and 'free' brushwork of native artists. A reviewer for the *St James's Chronicle* in 1791, for instance, lamented that Mosnier's talents in the rendition of chiaroscuro were not 'united . . . [with] a taste and freedom of execution'.[55] Meanwhile other critics invoked 'taste' – or the above-mentioned 'expression and spirit' – as the sign of a higher artistic 'genius', targeting not only Mosnier himself, but that undiscerning minority of press commentators who earnestly cited the pictures of this 'great' master as 'a good lesson to our artists, who are not apt to finish their works so carefully'.[56]

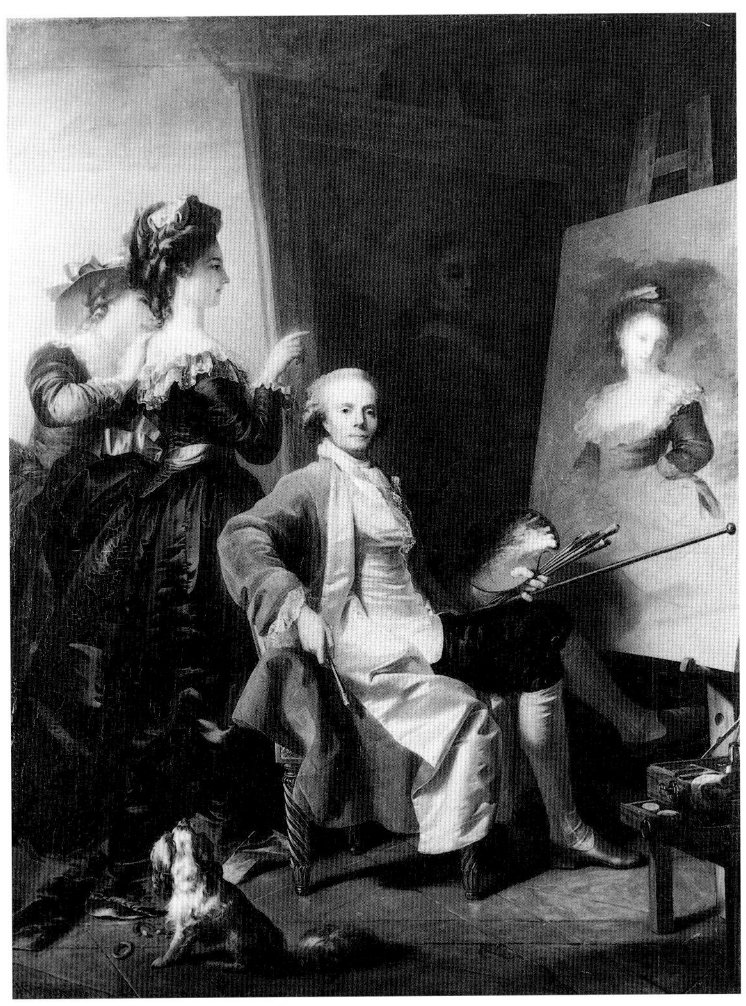

213 Jean-Laurent Mosnier, *Portrait of the Artist in his Studio*, RA 1791. The Hermitage, St Petersburg.

The Frenchman's critics were in no doubt that his flaws belonged to his national school in general, and not to him alone. The pamphleteer Anthony Pasquin was, as ever, exceptionally forthright on this point; in 1794 he condemned Mosnier's *Mrs Bradshaw* in the following terms:

> There is a labour evident throughout the whole of this picture, which is ineffectual; it is highly finished but *hard*, and

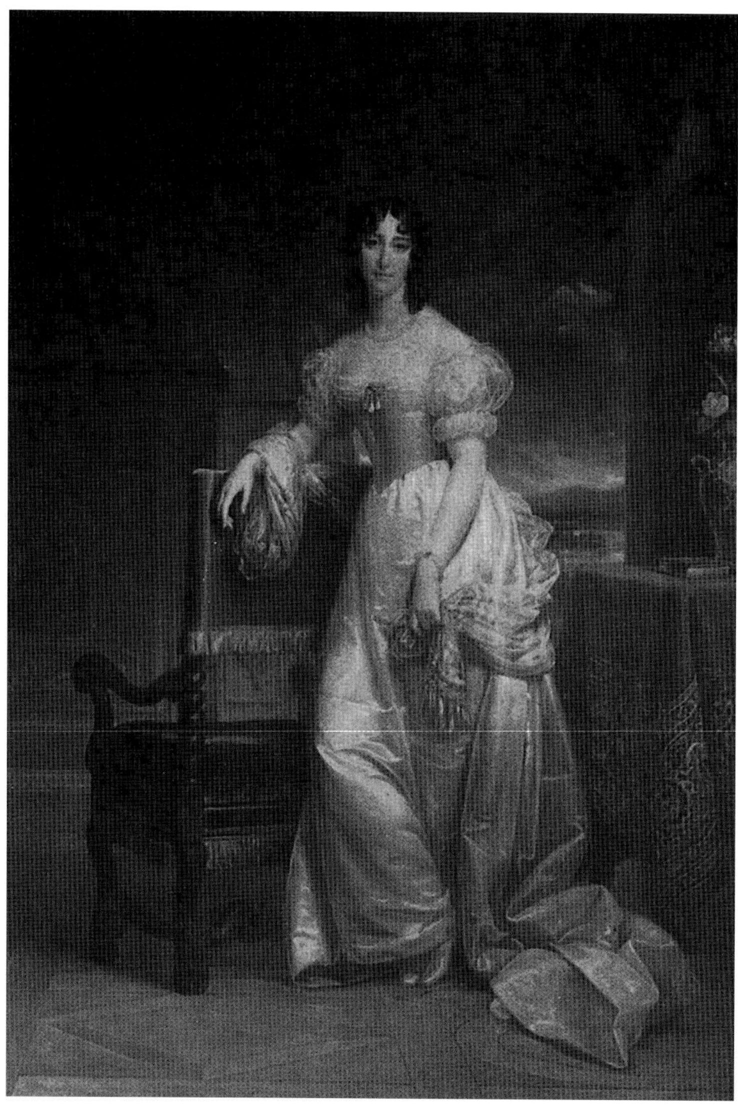

214 François Gérard, *Sarah Sophia, Countess of Jersey*, RA 1830 (destroyed in 1949 in a fire at Osterley House).

> gaudy, but not free; it conveys all the worst characteristics of the *French* school, and does more honour to industry, than the more noble capabilities of the artist; the finishing is superfluously particular.[57]

Two years later Pasquin levelled much the same charges at Mosnier's *Lady Callander and her Son, John Kearney* (fig. 215), dismissing it as tastelessly elaborate, trivial, and typically French.[58]

Attacks such as these were fundamentally political in nature and motivation: to criticize French artists as laborious and mechanical, and their works as evidence of a servile devotion to the minute imitation of nature, was also to criticize the French nation as a people in thrall to tyranny and lacking in both spirit and intelligence. In British portraiture, by contrast, as in Britain itself, one found freedom (of brushwork), 'naturalness' (in colouring), and a concern for true character as opposed to mere appearances.[59] Represented as a truly creative art, portrait painting was also coming to be championed as a channel for the native school's higher genius, and for aspirations hitherto frustrated by the lack of support for history painting. It is worth emphasizing that this 'elevation' was no longer effected, as had been Reynolds's strategy, by making learned references to old master models; both greatness and Britishness were now to be found in a portraitist's style, in the manner rather than the matter of the artist's work.

Five years after Mosnier's departure for new hunting grounds in Hamburg, the Treaty of Amiens in 1802 brought what has been called 'a mass exodus of French exiles from Britain'.[60] Although artists continued to flee the Napoleonic regime from all over Europe, and to migrate to England for a variety of reasons, the Somerset House exhibitions were no longer to feature any new high-profile long-term settlers such as Philippe Jacques de Loutherbourg, or any more illustrious temporary visitors like Mosnier.

When Baron François Gérard's *Sarah Sophia, Countess of Jersey* (fig. 214) was exhibited in 1830, a reviewer noted, and lamented, the rarity of the event: 'It is not often that the London exhibition contains the productions of eminent foreign artists. This portrait would induce us to wish to see such deviations from the common practice more frequently. It is extremely well painted; somewhat colder in colour than our present style, but still a picture of great merit.'[61] Actually, the work of this 'eminent' Frenchman had featured once before, in the exhibition of 1824, when his portrait of a Mrs Wynne Aubrey (unlocated) had been placed in one of the secondary galleries and ignored by the critics. There is no evidence that Gérard visited London either in 1824 or 1830; and since the two portraits are of British sitters, it is likely that both were submitted by their respective patrons rather than by the artist himself. By now well established as one of Europe's most sought-after court and society portraitists, Gérard had no need to advertise his wares in London – though presumably two of his British sitters were happy to bask in their painter's reflected fame.

With the sole exception of the critic for *La Belle Assemblée*, who found the *Countess of Jersey* 'cold and chalky', and condemned the lady's chair as 'vulgar', the picture garnered friendly reviews, entirely different in tone from those with which French exhibitors had had to contend during the 1790s.[62] Indeed, although Gérard's comparatively cool palette and careful finishing were recognized as characteristics of the French, and implicitly of the more recent Davidian school, his work was still widely recommended to other painters in the show as a 'chaste' and 'pure' example of the portraitist's art.[63]

Such serenity in the face of so prominent an 'invader' reflects of course the fact that one isolated exhibit in 1830 by the elderly and distant Gérard – unlike the *resident* Mosnier's prolific contributions during the 1790s – presented no real threat to native artists. Furthermore, the Francophobic climate of the war years had relaxed considerably after nearly fifteen years of peace. But even more importantly, perhaps, by now the British had

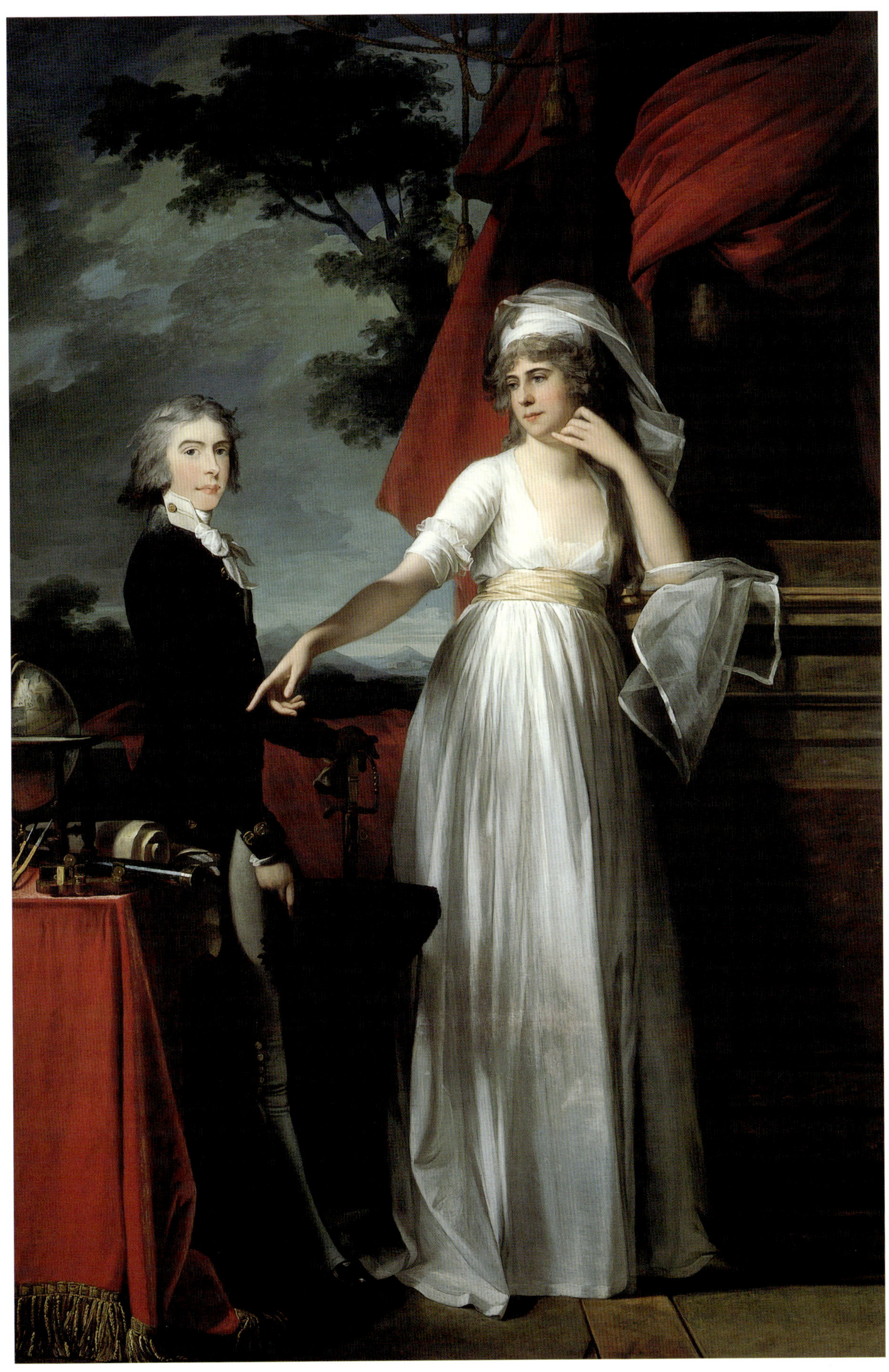

215 Jean-Laurent Mosnier, *Lady Callander and her Son, John Kearney*, RA 1796. Yale Center for British Art, Gift of Lowell Libson and Spink-Leger Pictures.

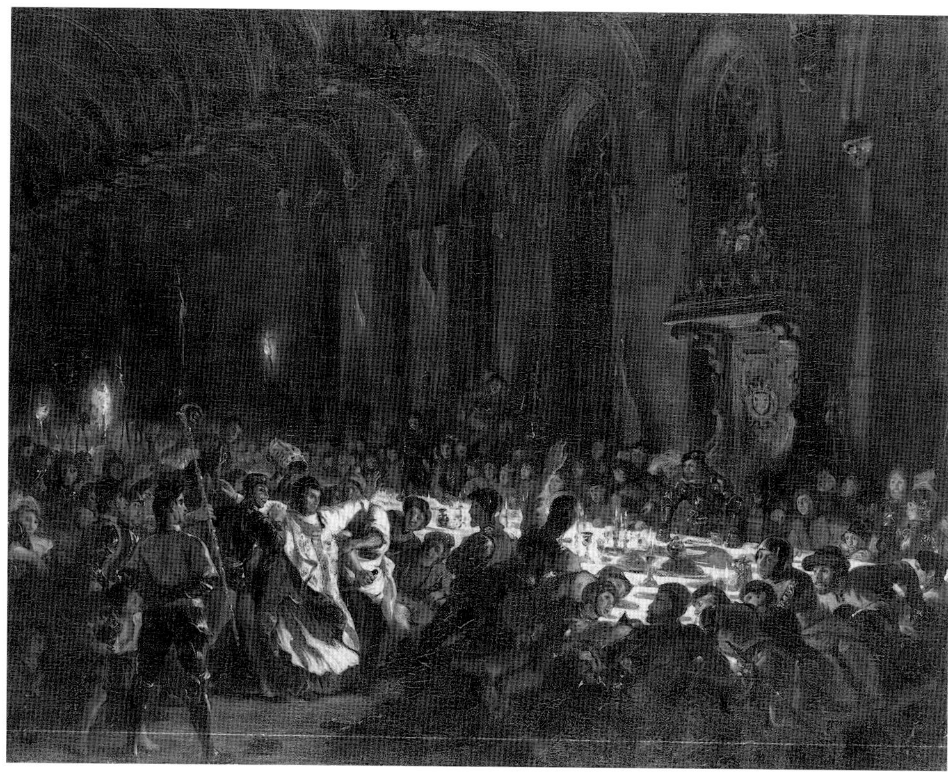

216 Eugène Delacroix, *The Murder of the Bishop of Liège* (exhibited in London as *The Boar of Ardennes*), RA 1830. Musée du Louvre, Paris.

developed far more confidence in the worth of their own artistic productions. In the recently deceased Sir Thomas Lawrence, the country had had at least one artist of uncontested international renown. And even if many were still willing to dispute the claim that the Academy had finally produced a British School truly worthy of the name, few could deny that it had nurtured a considerable 'pool' of talent practising in a variety of genres.[64] The dramatic growth in the number of exhibited works – from some 400-odd in the 1780s to well over a thousand by the late 1790s and to the end of our period – also suggested that the exhibitions had been an enormous success.

As the annual shows expanded in size, it must have become increasingly difficult for any but the most celebrated foreign artists, or at least those who could depend on an illustrious patronage, to get their works good positions at Somerset House. Unlike Gérard, in 1830 the young and largely unknown Eugène Delacroix probably submitted his *Murder of the Bishop of Liège* to the exhibition himself (or perhaps through a dealer as intermediary), where it was shown under the title of the *Boar of Ardennes* (the *nom-de-guerre* of the assassin Guillaume de la Marck; fig. 216).[65] A visit to London five years earlier must have alerted him to the city's commercial possibilities; in 1828 he sent over (without publicly exhibiting) *Greece on the Ruins of Missolonghi* (1826; Bordeaux, Musée des Beaux-Arts) and the *Execution of Doge Marino Falieri* (1826; London, Wallace Collection), presumably in hopes of capitalizing on the current craze for things Byronic.[66] But the pictures failed to sell. He fared no better with his *Boar of Ardennes* – which, despite Delacroix's connections among the British artistic community, and despite the perennial demands by critics for more exhibited examples of historical art, was hung in 1830 in the 'School of Painting', where it received only a small number of brief, if generally positive, reviews.[67]

In contrast, the sculptures that the Italian Antonio Canova exhibited in 1817 and 1823 received overwhelming public and critical attention. By all accounts Canova's brief visit to London in 1815 had been regarded as a highly prestigious mark of recognition by the Royal Academy, which exhorted all of its members to attend a special dinner given in his honour.[68] Two years later, the institution was delighted to display his statues of *Hebe* (see fig. 154) and *Terpsichore* (Cleveland Museum of Art) – a *Bust of Peace* (untraced) was also shown – although they had been submitted late by the diplomat William Richard Hamilton, and in 1823 the Committee of Arrangement included his *Danzatrice* (exhibited version untraced) as the centrepiece of the sculpture gallery as a posthumous mark of respect.[69] Canova was thus treated highly favourably, in spite of the widespread perception, which may or may not have been justified, that he (against his will and in spite of his modest nature) was likely to absorb the most important British patronage.[70]

In their discussions of Canova's Academy exhibits, critics once again sought to distinguish his works from those of native sculptors by contrasting two opposing sets of ostensibly 'national' characteristics. The *Examiner*'s Robert Hunt, for instance, juxtaposed 'the most beautiful Sculptures of modern Art' in the exhibition of 1817, Canova's *Hebe* and *Terpsichore*, and Chantrey's monument to Ellen Jane and Marianne Robinson (see fig. 155), not only to compare their respective merits but, more importantly, to answer the question whether England had finally produced a 'high' art equal to that of (ancient and) modern Italy. Canova's pieces may have been 'exceedingly graceful', Hunt readily conceded, but he implied that their charms were derivative of 'various antiques'; moreover, he had no hesitation in declaring 'our English commoner greater than the Italian nobleman' for possessing greater 'purity and originality', and 'moral feeling' above all.[71] Since 'ideal', poetic sculpture was regarded as the equivalent of historical art in painting, England could thus claim to have produced its own proper 'school', at least as far as sculpture was concerned. Six years later that school appeared to even greater advantage when compared with Canova's *Danzatrice*. Though some commentators thought it lively and graceful, the critic of the *European Magazine* found the sculpture 'foreign and peculiar'.[72] Another reviewer described the piece as graceful and admirable, but 'of that fantastic French [neoclassical] school, to which this celebrated artist belonged'.[73] 'Fancy', but also artificiality, and grace, but combined with a cold technical perfection, were perceived to be on the side of the foreign artist, whilst Edward Hodges Baily's mother and child group, *Affection*, in particular demonstrated native qualities of 'feeling', warmth, originality and 'nature' (see fig. 159).[74]

The treatment of Canova reminds us once again of the complex relationship between the Academy, the exhibitions and their foreign participants. On one level, the involvement in the exhibitions of well-known foreigners – most notably Canova himself – conferred prestige and credibility on the institution and on British art in general. In its earliest days, moreover, the RA had relied on the participation of foreign artists, as both members and exhibitors, in its attempt to raise a native school of elevated art. At this point the Academy's accommodation of foreign talent and its reception in the exhibitions by the supportive press had been largely unproblematic, thanks also in part to the widespread understanding of ambitious art as something that transcended narrow national boundaries. The 'foreignness' – as a negative factor – of Continental artists seems to have become an issue mainly in response to developments well outside the art world, when Britain's rivalry with France reached new peaks of intensity, particularly after 1789. In a period of heightened nationalism Britain's relation to its 'hostile other' came to be understood, perhaps more than ever before, in cultural, as well as military and political terms. Patriotic sentiment found one important outlet in debates about the essential characteristics, and functions, of British visual art. Hence, as I have tried to demonstrate, the presence of foreign exhibitors, especially those connected by origin or training with France, facilitated efforts by contemporary critics to define what 'British' art was or should be, by contrast with that identified with the nation's hated rival. Understandably, too, the issue of 'foreignness' took on a degree of urgency whenever an outsider threatened – or appeared to threaten – the livelihood of native practitioners. A more insular understanding of national identity also affected the Academy, leading to the growing marginalization of foreign talent. A greatly increased number of native practitioners in all genres had at any rate drastically diminished the Academy's and exhibitions' dependence on artists from abroad.

In the period following the Napoleonic wars, a range of significant factors – including the Academy's own policies, a lingering popular suspicion of foreign cultural involvement, a vastly increased pool of native talent, and a growing confidence in Britain's own artistic productions – combined to make London, and its exhibitions, a much harder, and less desirable, place for most foreign artists to be. A British 'school' may finally have come into being, at least in the eyes of certain observers. But if such a school did indeed exist, it had been forged at the cost of an increasing cultural self-centredness, and the isolation of British art from that of its Continental neighbours.

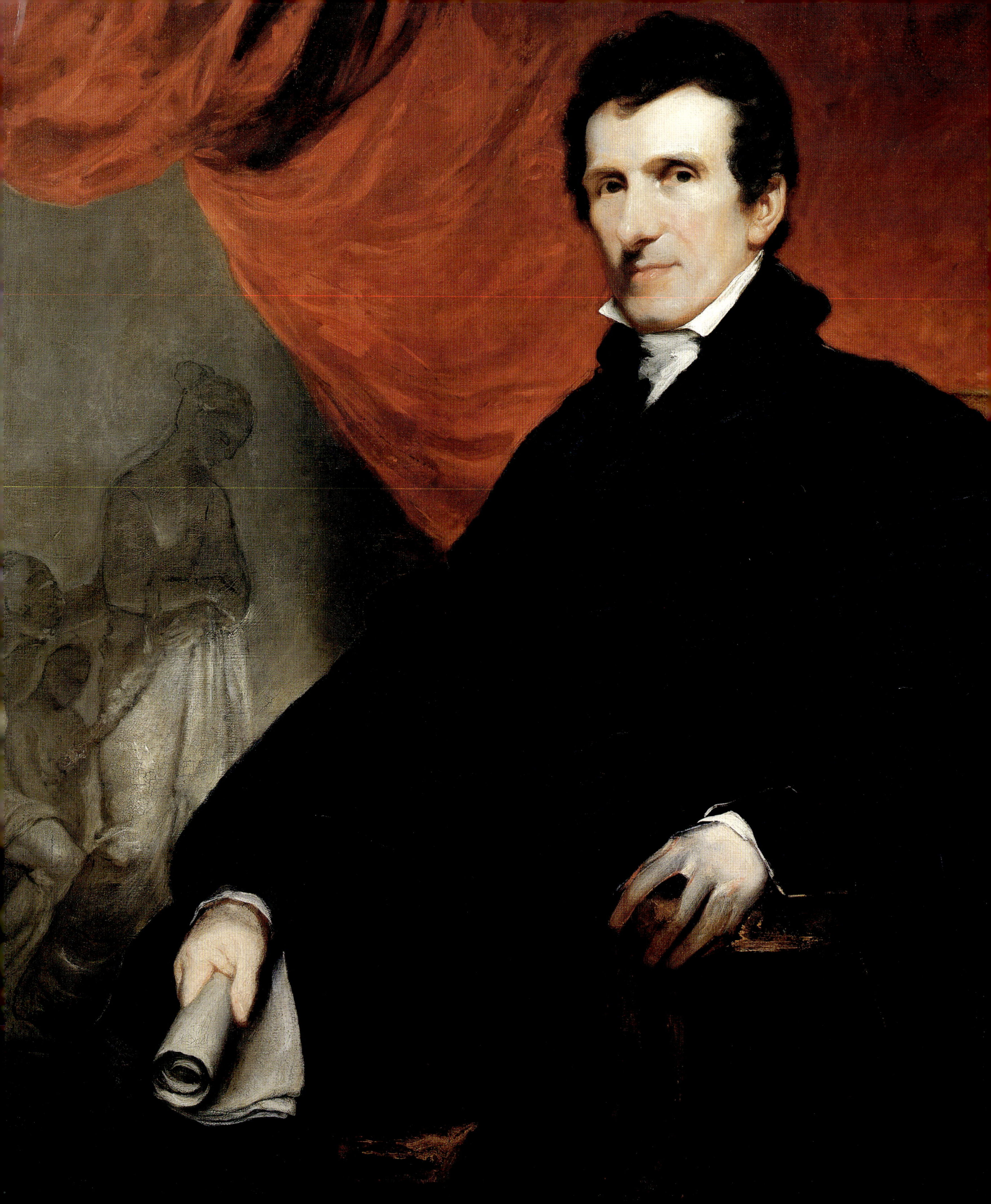

17

Taste and the Multitude: The Somerset House Exhibitions in Continental Eyes

WILLIAM VAUGHAN

'NO JUDICIOUS FRIEND OF THE ARTIST would maintain, that the voice of the public is the voice of true taste, or that a fickle and partial multitude would be likely to encourage the artist to attempt the nobler departments of painting.'[1] This observation by the German artist Johann David Passavant, prompted by a visit to the Royal Academy exhibition in 1831, followed a long line of commentaries on Academy exhibitions by Continental visitors. Though there was nothing exceptional about Passavant's conclusion, his judgement had more purchase than earlier comments of a similar nature because it was issued in an English translation – and at a time (1836) when concern about the effects of unmediated public exhibition on the arts was reaching a crisis point in Britain itself.

From the earliest years, accounts of the Royal Academy exhibitions appeared in print abroad as well as at home. The institution, finally, of an official (or quasi-official) Academy in England attracted curiosity and attention, particularly after Reynolds's *Discourses* began to become known.[2] Yet whereas Sir Joshua's lectures gained general approval for the way in which they provided an accessible exposition of academic theory, the Academy's exhibitions aroused more mixed emotions. Rather than adhering to the ideals promoted by the President, most of the works on display seemed to attend far more closely to the exigencies of the marketplace. In itself this was not an exclusively British phenomenon; concerns about the effects of the market economy on the exhibition and practice of art were expressed in most European countries during the period. But in Britain the consequences were believed to have reached an extreme, and the annual Academy shows tended to be considered in this light.

Prior to around 1815, comments by foreign travellers on the London art world had tended to be rather casual. A marked deepening of interest seems to have occurred during the post-Napoleonic period, however, for a complex variety of reasons. One important factor was a growing fascination with all things British, after the United Kingdom had emerged at the end of her wars with France as the wealthiest, most powerful and most technologically advanced country in Europe. Continental observers viewed this with a mixture of awe and disparagement. Rather like Europeans looking at the U.S.A. after the Second World War, they saw developments in Britain as an indication of what might be about to happen in their own country and were keen to explore these, if only to ensure that some of the more unwelcome effects might be ameliorated or contained.

In this scenario the contemporary visual arts – let alone the Academy exhibitions themselves – played a relatively minor part. There was general recognition that Britain had no traditional strength in this area – yet it was also acknowledged that there had been a startling series of developments from the middle of the eighteenth century, and that these could not be altogether ignored. In particular the question arose about whether this new British art, with its gaudy colours and bold technique, was simply the product of a 'practical' nation with innate bad taste, or whether it could be tied more specifically to the effects created by a modern commercial society. If it was the latter, then what was going on in Britain would have to be taken as a warning to others about what lay in store for them in the future.

The impetus to consider the Academy exhibitions seriously was also stimulated by the knowledge that there was a growing lobby in Britain which supported many of the features that

Jackson, *Antonio Canova*. Detail of fig. 69.

distinguished native art production from that of other European countries. As the French visitor A. J. B. Defauconpret commented in a report on his visit to Somerset House in 1816: 'They defy France and Italy to name two living painters capable of challenging the pre-eminence of the British School'.[3] This bullish talk about British art had grown apace during the Napoleonic period, when it was stimulated by military conflict. However, after the wars the chorus of patriotic sentiment continued and, if anything, increased in volume. The discourse of the visual arts also witnessed a significant change in the nature of the claims being made. As the shortcomings of home-grown historical painting became increasingly evident, the focus shifted to British achievements in genre, portraiture and landscape painting, which were often regarded in a political light. As the right-wing journal the *Morning Chronicle* put it in a review of the 1825 Academy exhibition, 'The impulse that has recently renewed the energies of this empire seems to have contributed a share of its electric animation to the elegant arts'.[4] From a more liberal standpoint, there was support for the idea that British art, with its naturalism and modernity, reflected the spirit of free enquiry and experimentation that was held to be the bedrock of the nation's commercial and political achievement. The exhibition, in this scenario, was to be welcomed as a means of promoting free and open competition – a situation to be contrasted with the control and authoritarianism that reputedly dominated artistic production in most Continental countries.[5]

By 1825, the British could be encouraged in their view by the success of certain groups of progressive artists abroad, particularly in France. The previous year had seen English artists make a much-publicized impact in the Paris Salon, most notably through Constable gaining a gold medal for his *Hay Wain* (RA 1821; London, National Gallery). Prior to this, moreover, there had been enthusiastic reports from visitors to London about the novel and striking effects to be found in both landscape and genre; for example in the enthusiastic account of Wilkie's *Chelsea Pensioners* (see fig. 142) sent back by the painter Walbonne to the fashionable portraitist François Gérard in 1822.[6] The year 1825 saw Eugène Delacroix come to Britain to study her art at first hand – a journey stimulated both by the successes of the 1824 Salon, and by Théodore Géricault's accounts of his trip across the Channel in 1821.

It is noticeable that German commentators, on the whole, expressed a greater level of concern about the character of British art than did the French.[7] This can be seen in the response to the British triumphs in Paris in 1824 by the leading German art magazine of the period, *Kunst-Blatt*. Its reviewer acknowledged that Constable, Bonington, Lawrence and their fellow countrymen had taken a different and opposed path to that of the French,[8] but saw this as a false direction. Having been seduced by the 'charm of the brush',

> The British adhere to a contrary system. From a distance their works appear to possess much truth. But when you come close to them the delusion disappears and you find only vile combinations of colours and coarse handling.[9]

The censorious tone of this commentary is doubtless related to the artistic affiliations then dominant in Germany. This was the period when the revivalist painters the Nazarenes had emerged to be celebrated as the restorers of German art through an ascetic system of painting that stressed neatness and careful craftsmanship, and which was perceived as offering a counterblast both to the poor methods taught at academies, and to the destructive effects of commerce on good taste. The editor of *Kunst-Blatt*, Dr Ludwig Schorn, was an enthusiastic supporter both of the Nazarenes in Rome and of Peter Cornelius and the other painters who were currently employed by Ludwig of Bavaria on the vast mural schemes designed to turn Munich into the art capital of Europe. In 1821 the *Kunst-Blatt* had published Johann David Passavant's seminal review of the Nazarene exhibition in Rome – a discussion that played a key role in establishing these artists as national heroes.[10] Passavant was no ordinary reviewer. Having trained as a painter relatively late in life, after an unhappy career as a businessman, he was at this time immersing himself in art-historical literature, using the new methods developed in Germany from Winckelmann onwards to view contemporary art in a historical perspective. As we shall see, such a viewpoint was to be crucial for the way that he came to assess contemporary British art during his visit to that country in 1831.

But before examining Passavant's account we need to consider several other significant interventions which he was to acknowledge as important factors in the genesis of his own outlook. These opinions were voiced both in periodicals – notably the *Kunst-Blatt* itself – and in a number of tours of England written by German travellers in the years prior to his own journey.

Like other contemporary periodicals devoted to the fine arts, the *Kunst-Blatt* frequently made use of reviews from sister journals to report on exhibitions in other countries. For Britain its habitual source was the *European Magazine*, though on occasion Dr Schorn felt compelled to give some warning to his readers about the bias that would be found there. In 1825, a few months after discussing the previous year's Paris Salon, the *Kunst-Blatt* published a laudatory assessment of the current state of British art taken from the *European Magazine*'s review of the Academy exhibition of 1824. This article rehearsed the by now familiar celebration of the originality of British painting, and of the cultural benefits accruing from a modern entrepreneurial society. In the anonymous English critic's opinion, 'Originality of conception, effective chiaroscuro and an almost consistent delicacy of colouration constitute the particular characteristics of our painting.'[11]

But the redoubtable Dr Schorn would have none of this. In his editorial prefacing the translated review he commented:

> It will not be uninteresting to learn of the judgment of an Englishman on the present state of sculpture and painting in

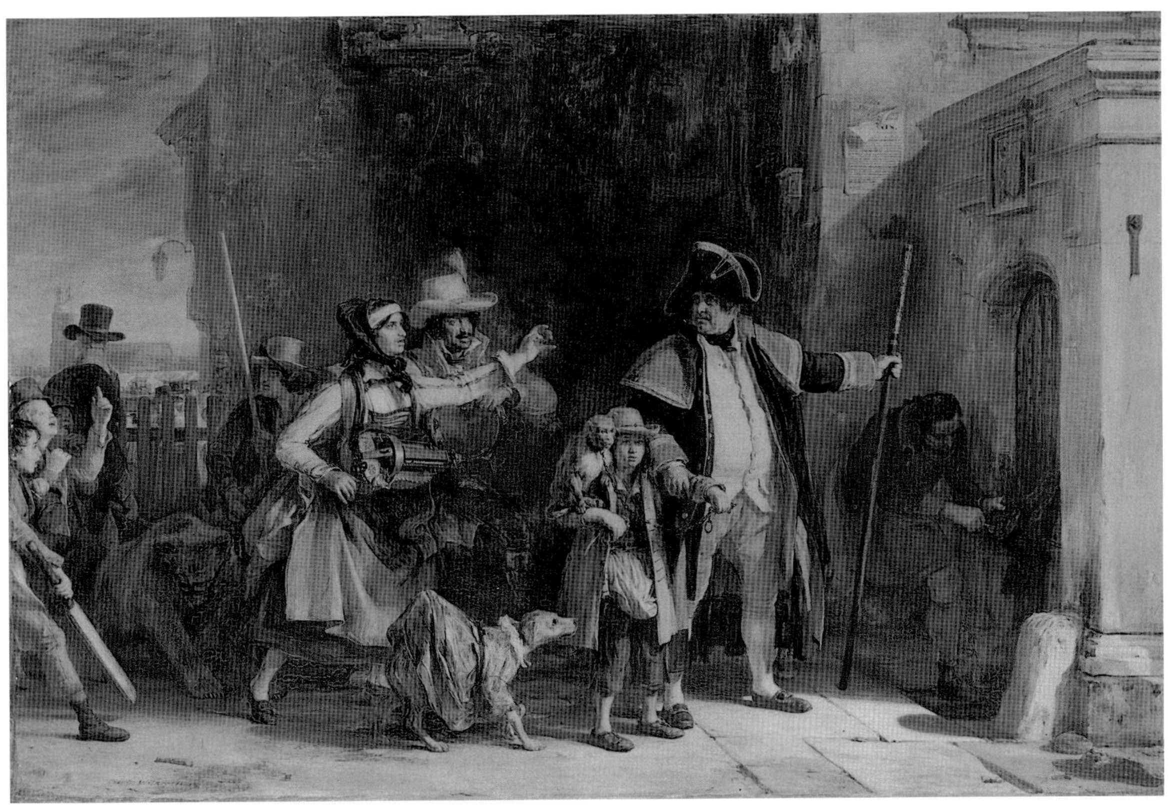

217 David Wilkie, *The Parish Beadle*, RA 1823, oil on wood. Tate, London.

England. However it should be noted that he shares the mistake made by all art critics of his country in ascribing an independence to English art that it does not in fact possess. Further, although he also fails to make a distinction between style and manner – ascribing the first for the most part to works that only merit the second – he does nevertheless give a reasonably accurate view of the condition of the different types of art, as well as of the abilities of the artists and the taste of the public.[12]

Schorn also reminded his readers of an earlier German account of English art – incorporating a review of a Royal Academy exhibition – that the *Kunst-Blatt* had published in 1823, in a series of articles by the poet and literary scholar Johann Valentin Adrian.[13] A great admirer and translator of British literature,[14] Adrian would later write the period's two most widely read German accounts of contemporary Britain, *Bilder aus England* (1827–8) and *Skizzen aus England* (1830–33). Despite the pictorial-sounding titles, these 'pictures' and 'sketches' consist mainly of observations on the life and literature rather than the fine art of the country. But the latter does figure in a number of chapters in both of Adrian's books. His reports on the fine arts in Britain in the *Kunst-Blatt* are essentially the same as the sections that later appeared in *Bilder aus England*. Based on a visit to London in 1823, they paint a picture of British art as being entirely ruled by the marketplace. Adrian comments that art can be seen everywhere – but only in a commercial context – whether in the print-shops on the Strand, in the galleries of celebrated artists like Lawrence and West (where, he notes, the ubiquitous charge of a shilling entrance is made) or in the exhibition halls. 'English art', he concludes, 'is a hired maid-servant [*eine feile Dienerin* – this could also mean a prostitute] of the requirements of the day, of the transient fashion, of vanity'.[15] He also suggests that matters are getting worse – something that might be symbolized by the succession of the fashionable portrait painter Lawrence as President of the Royal Academy to the history painter West. He detects a sign of what is in his eyes the detrimental effect of Lawrence's 'false striving after brilliance and ostentation'[16] on the other exhibitors at the Academy. Here he is saddened to see the much-admired Wilkie also abandoning his former meticulous manner in favour of the 'chasing after effect' of the day, particularly in his portrait of the Duke of York (London, National Portrait Gallery).

> Effect makes this picture also one without purpose, it is just fireworks and theatrical glitter . . . in short this is not the old Wilkie, this is just one more person who seeks to outbid the president in stage-effects.[17]

Only in the *Parish Beadle* (fig. 217) does he find some of the former Wilkie, 'the old droll friend',[18] again full of honest observation and direct painting. Adrian's admiration of Wilkie may remind us that, while he supported the historical, he was no enemy of modernity. Indeed, like most of the German commentators of the time – even those most wedded to Nazarene revivalism – he had a great respect for Hogarth, Wilkie and the whole English tradition of vigorous, realistic and critical painting and engraving. While not a substitute for ideal art, such work was recognized as authentic and important, and perhaps the best that a 'practical' people like the British could be expected to achieve. What worried Adrian was the way in which this robust approach seemed to have become undermined by a more servile attitude in recent years.

In the later *Skizzen aus England* he espouses even more pessimistic views. By 1830 Adrian had become aware of critical voices within the London art world, and in particular that of Benjamin Robert Haydon, who must have bent his ear on one or more occasions. The *Skizzen* include a eulogy in praise of Haydon, both for his historical works and for his contemporary scenes in the Hogarthian mode. In the course of this Adrian launches into a diatribe against the Academy, which, doubtless inspired by Haydon's own rhetoric, he sees as 'A lame old nag that can no longer drag its legs after it. It admits people of genius into its circle to enable it to get some blood easily into its shrivelled veins.'[19] He then goes on to call on the Academy to reform itself, as Parliament has just done.

Given Adrian's forthright language, never mind his characterization of British art as the whore of commerce and the Royal Academy as a knackered old horse, it is perhaps not too surprising to find that his books were not translated into English. More judicious critical voices were, however. By 1833, the year in which the last volume of the *Skizzen* appeared, concern about British art and the role of the Academy had spread beyond the limits of malcontents like Haydon. Concerns were now being expressed by sober artists within the establishment, not least of all Haydon's own pupil Charles Lock Eastlake. Eastlake had recently returned from Rome, where like many other visitors of the 1820s he had been deeply impressed by the art, and the arguments, of the Nazarenes. Amongst the many German artists he had befriended while in Rome was Passavant.[20] During the 1830s such contacts were to be important for ensuring that the critical voices from Germany were taken seriously in Britain.

Passavant published the account of his visit to England and Belgium, *Kunstreise durch England und Belgien*, in 1833.[21] This book – possibly the first published 'artistic tour' of Britain – was not precipitated by an interest in contemporary work. As the author clearly states in his introduction, he went to England to study works by Raphael, in preparation for a monograph on the artist.[22] His decision to go into print first with an account of his journey was motivated largely by monetary considerations. The cost of his year-long trip had brought him into financial difficulties, and he published his *Kunstreise* as a means of recouping his expenses.[23] What made such a publication possible was the central discovery that Passavant had made in the course of his visit: of the fabulous collections of old masters that had been amassed in England as result both of the activities of eighteenth-century aristocratic Grand Tourists, and of dealers acquiring works from impoverished Continental collectors during the Revolutionary and Napoleonic periods.[24]

Not only did Passavant's book alert an international audience to the existence of this rich hoard, but his *Tour of a German Artist in England* – this was the title given to the English translation published in 1836 – also helped make the British themselves more aware of the riches they possessed. For while there had been much anecdotal literature about British collecting,[25] there had been no inventory of the country's holdings of works of art. Passavant's text filled this gap, at least until Gustav Waagen's monumental *Kunstwerke und Künstler in England* appeared a few years later.[26]

Passavant's book was not primarily concerned with British art – still less so with the Royal Academy. However, after spending the first two sections of his text discussing the art collections he had visited in London and then in the rest of England, he did devote the third section in its entirety to a 'General Survey of Art in England'. This survey gained poignancy by its position in the book, coming as it did at the end of a gazetteer of the country's great collections of old masters.

Passavant laid down the reasons why he had decided to take stock of contemporary British art, and the method of his investigation, in the following simple terms:

> As a foreigner, when removed from England, has but few chances of becoming acquainted with the English school of art, I sought every opportunity of extending my acquaintance with English artists, and in the exhibitions then open, was enabled to take a tolerably complete survey of their productions.[27]

The first part of this statement was undoubtedly true. Although British art was known on the Continent through the medium of prints, original paintings were few and far between, making anything like a comprehensive understanding impossible for anyone who had not spent a considerable period of time in England itself. However, Passavant was not simply engaged in an act of reportage. He was also attempting an evaluation, bringing his experience of scholarly art-historical method to bear on the analysis of an unfamiliar art form. His determination to apply such an approach was stimulated by his awareness that the only British treatments of native art production had been of the traditional anecdotal and narrative type. At the time of his arrival in England, the first substantial book on British art since Horace Walpole's *Anecdotes of Painting*, published between 1762 and 1780, had just appeared. This was Allan Cunningham's *Lives of the English Painters, Sculptors and Architects* (1831), which Passavant dismisses as full of errors, and as overly dependent on unreliable and dishonourable anecdotes.[28]

Passavant's objections to Cunningham's *Lives* may have been more than methodologically motivated. For Cunningham evaluated British art essentially in terms of the triumph of naturalism, an interpretation that apologists like James Memes had encouraged during the preceding decades.[29] A champion of Hogarth and Wilkie, Cunningham felt that Reynolds's promotion of the grand manner had been fundamentally misguided; he even went so far as to claim that state patronage of historical art – something that had been demanded on many occasions – would be detrimental to the independent Protestant spirit which in his opinion informed the best of modern British painting.[30] Passavant's views on such matters could hardly have been more different. As a champion of the Nazarenes, he was deeply committed to a negative judgement of untrammelled naturalism as a symptom of modern materialism, and no less to the concept of artistic production being supported by high-minded, disinterested and non-commercial forms of patronage. The Royal Academy exhibition was proof, in his eyes, that the stimulus of the marketplace led only to the production of meretricious and flashy art.

However, it would be wrong to regard Passavant's approach as a simple condemnation of modernity. One of the points on which he and Cunningham were agreed (along with Adrian) was their admiration of Hogarth and Wilkie, who in their different ways both represented independent and critical voices. For Passavant was no advocate of artistic slavishness: quite the reverse. He saw true art as the expression of inner necessity, believing that this motive had guided the Nazarenes when they launched their protest against the Vienna Academy and formed their own breakaway artistic community. Similarly, even if Hogarth had been a deeply commercial artist, Passavant felt that he had nevertheless maintained his integrity through his commitment to social critique. Wilkie, too, he believed, had asserted his autonomy by proclaiming the noble virtues of the Scottish peasant to the denizens of the modern metropolis. But Passavant was convinced – like Adrian before him – that the power of the marketplace in Britain had got out of hand, to the point where art was held in thrall to commercial interests and the indiscriminate demands of the multitude. These forces were no longer counterbalanced, as they had been in the eighteenth century, by the aristocratic public promotion of higher cultural ideals.

Although he mentioned exhibitions in the plural, it was only with the Royal Academy's that Passavant was concerned. As he asserted in the opening part of his survey, this exhibition 'ranks the highest',[31] and presumably he felt that its status made it the best place on which to base his observations. His coverage of the Academy adhered to a well-established format, with a preamble followed by a discussion of examples of history, portraiture, genre and landscape. And while his comments on individual artists and types may not have been particularly novel, what was new was the way he developed his arguments with reference to a sense of historical process, absorbed from his studies of Carl Rumohr and other German scholars.

Like other observers, Passavant felt that historical art in Britain was at a low ebb. Unlike most critics, however, he felt compelled to ask why. The answers he came up with fall under two main headings, the racial and the circumstantial:

> Upon the causes for this utter absence of an historical school in England, it may be expedient to offer a few remarks. For the attainment of the higher branches of art, there appear to be two indispensable requisites: – the one, that in a people capable of cultivating art, there should exist a self-contemplative thoughtfulness, such as can penetrate into the depths of our spiritual being, and is disposed for the abstraction of those higher studies – in a word, a people imbued with a deeply poetical feeling; – the second condition, that a nation thus gifted should have the advantage of liberal and extensive establishments, and thus secure a suitable sphere of action for the nurture and exercise of talent, screened alike from the caprices of private individuals, the varying fashions of a court, and the visionary speculations of artists themselves; – in short that art should not be considered as a thing of a separable nature, but that it should interweave itself with the ties of life, and be employed in adding beauty to its nearest and dearest interests.[32]

In Passavant's opinion, England lacked both these prerequisites. Its people, he claims, are 'more disposed to an active than to a contemplative life',[33] even if they do possess a literary tradition equal to that of any other nation. To explain this Passavant indulges in a bit of special pleading, to the effect that every nation that has sought to develop its language and express itself has been capable of great literature. But 'purer' art forms such as music and the visual arts occur only in those nations that have a particular propensity for speculative thought – in the ancient world the Greeks, in the modern the Italians and the Germans. Thus Passavant rather cattily concludes that

> To determine how far, or in what line the English may proceed in the development of this their now rising school, would be somewhat premature. Enough has already been said to prove that there exist no grounds for anticipating their advancement in the higher walk of art, or even of admitting that the feeling for it is possessed by them.[34]

Nevertheless, Passavant is willing to concede that even if a nation has no innately speculative propensity, it may still produce high art if the right kind of patronage is available. This, he suggests, had been made available in France and Spain, but circumstances in Britain had failed to provide it. Here instead a peculiar kind of commercial patronage had arisen, ostensibly public but in effect private, which made it impossible for anything but the lower forms of art to thrive. When the judgement of art was left in the hands of the populace at large, the most noble cultural ideals were bound to wither on the vine. The exhibitions, in other words, encapsulated all that was wrong with the current state of high art in Britain. According to Passavant, these annual events

> tend to keep the state of art at a low ebb, being almost exclusively favourable to subject and landscape-painting; and works of this kind, with the never-failing tribe of portraits, occupy,

> with very few exceptions, the walls of an English exhibition room . . .[35]

From Passavant's point of view, art exhibitions in Britain were commercial affairs, organized by practitioners whose main interest lay in selling their own works to an audience of equally self-centred buyers. For him the Academy was nothing but a front for the marketplace.

The conditions under which British history painting suffered exercised Passavant in particular. In his brief survey of past production he had already mentioned the tragic case of James Barry, who had painted his great cycle at the Society of Arts for no patron but for the public good, labouring for years without recompense – and was afterwards expelled from the RA. Similarly Passavant noted the position of Benjamin Robert Haydon, by that time no longer exhibiting at the Academy. Even if their German admirer felt obliged to acknowledge that neither of these two great exiles had ever realized his full potential, he felt that both at least had struggled in a noble cause – by stark contrast with William Etty, whose works offered evidence only of the degradation of historical art. Looking at Etty's major exhibition-piece of 1831, his *Judith's Maid Waiting outside the Tent of Holofernes* (now in a ruinous state in the National Gallery of Scotland), Passavant conceded that it was 'A picture of extraordinary effect, and dark but powerful tone'. But he quickly added that all the works of Etty, 'although evincing talent of a high and extraordinary class, yet betray an attempt rather at the eccentric and not infrequently the licentious, than at originality or depth of feeling'.[36]

This insistence on the distinction between 'eccentricity' and 'originality' ties in with Passavant's earlier comment about the dangers of leaving artists on their own to develop their own visionary peculiarities. The origins of his opinions are not difficult to find: much the same sentiments had often been voiced by German art critics of the Napoleonic period, when they rejected the individualistic 'eccentricities' of artists like Caspar David Friedrich and Philipp Otto Runge in favour of the revived communal vision of the Nazarenes – a vision which was supposed to reach to the soul of the entire nation.

The same reasons why Passavant took pride in the recent 'return to order' in German art led him to lament the continued hegemony of commerce in Britain – not just because it fostered an excessive cultural individualism, but also because it made victims of those few artists who were capable of painting in a more sober and reflective manner.

The test case cited by Passavant was that of his old friend Eastlake. The two men had been in Rome together, where Eastlake had tempered his British penchant for effect with a neat and modest manner evidently influenced by the Nazarenes; there in 1827 he had scored a notable success with his *Pilgrims Arriving in Sight of Rome*,[37] a work that combined the British genre tradition with a more sober style of execution. Subsequently, after returning to London, he specialized mainly in Italian peasant scenes and anecdotal religious subjects. Passavant found him the most 'solid' or 'genuine' (*gediegen*) of all British history painters, duly praising his principal contribution to the exhibition of 1831, *A Peasant Woman Fainting from the Bite of a Serpent* (fig. 218). But he felt that Eastlake's paintings suffered from the company they were forced to keep:

> His works, although found on close inspection to be spiritedly coloured, are monotonous in general effect. This may be partly accounted for by the gaudiness of the surrounding pictures in the exhibition, in which the eye is dazzled by the gayest colours, and the most extravagant contrasts of red and white, and which, compared with Eastlake's works, may not unaptly be likened to tinsel next a pearl.[38]

In the inability of most English observers to distinguish a true gem from mere dross, Passavant sees a symptom of the exhibition's destructive effects on taste:

> How strangely the judgement of the English public is perverted by the extravagant style of their artists may be deduced from the criticisms upon Eastlake's productions. His correct drawing is censured as hard; his natural tones as colourless; and the whole is summed up with the invariable exclamation 'See to what the study of the old Italian masters tends'.[39]

But it is in his consideration of landscape that Passavant most fully develops his theme of the corrupting effects of commercial competition on genius. For him the most compelling evidence comes from the art of J. M. W. Turner. 'This artist is decidedly the most talented of all the living landscape painters; but such is his extravagance of effect, and total neglect of form, that the English, although great admirers of his genius, are seldom found willing to purchase his work'.[40] Paradoxically, however, Passavant attributes the aberrant manner responsible for Turner's commercial failure to the deleterious influence of commercial culture. One reason why the painter has run into difficulties, he claims, is because his 'pictures . . . are finished off in the most hurried manner, and only just in time to be admitted to the exhibition'. He further implies that Turner has been seduced by the allure of money, especially in the form of commissions for books and almanacs, which in England offer artists work 'of the most lucrative kind'.[41] Yet Passavant also stresses his great admiration for the talent made manifest in Turner's early pictures, citing the *Dolbadern Castle* that he had seen in the Academy's Diploma collection. But he cannot make head or tail of the artist's exhibits in 1831, 'where everything seems to be lost in coloured blotches until the catalogue informs us that we are to see in one of the pictures the artist Watteau, working according to Fresnoy's rules' (see fig. 125). This then prompts him to exclaim at the end of the passage, 'To what purpose is talent, when unrestrained by rules?'[42] Thus Passavant returns to the main theme of his criticism: that art needs to be 'guided' if it is to become genuinely useful to the community at large, and not disappear into personal idiosyncrasy.

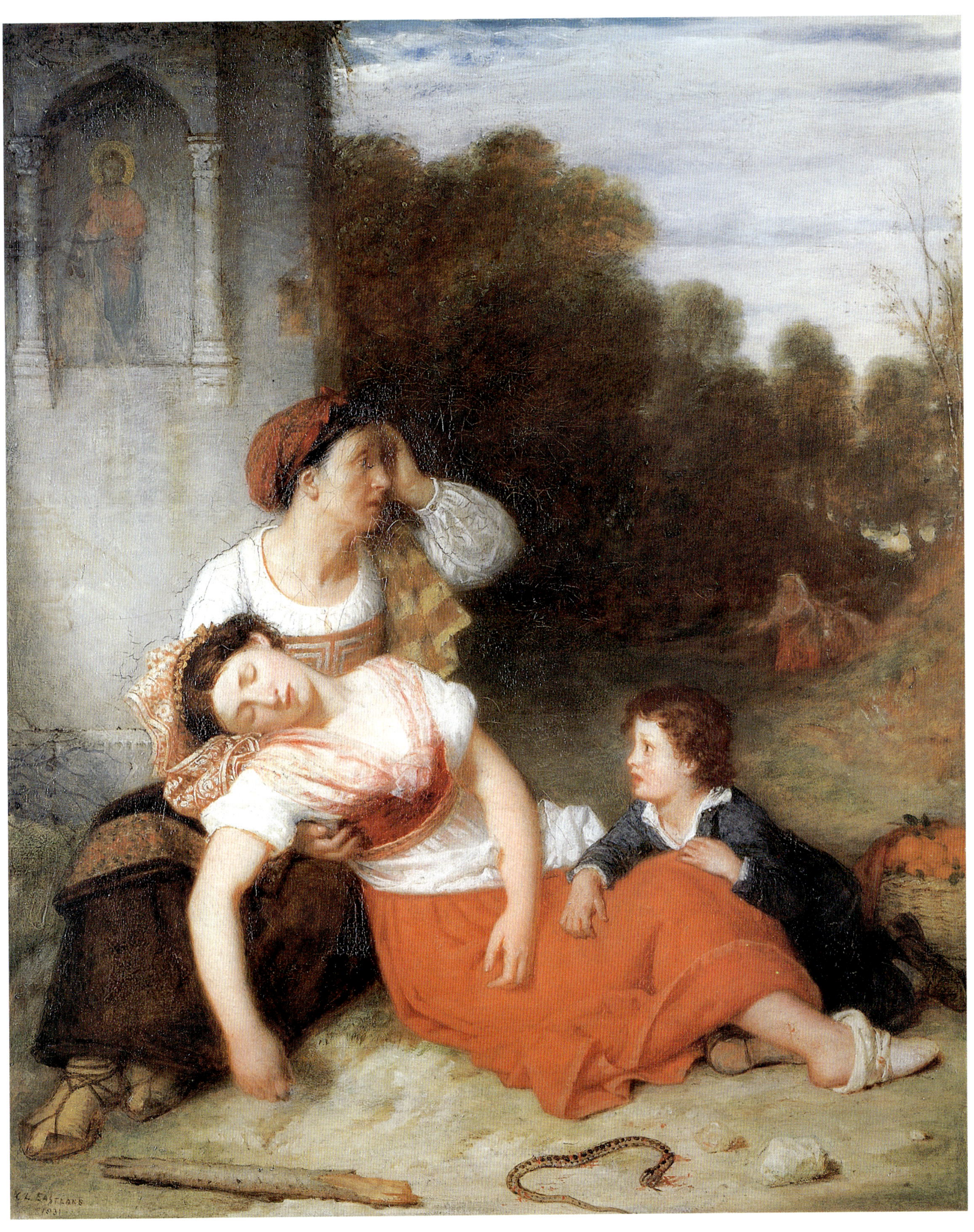

218 Charles Lock Eastlake, *A Peasant Woman Fainting from the Bite of a Serpent*, RA 1831. Courtesy of the Board of Trustees of the Victoria & Albert Museum.

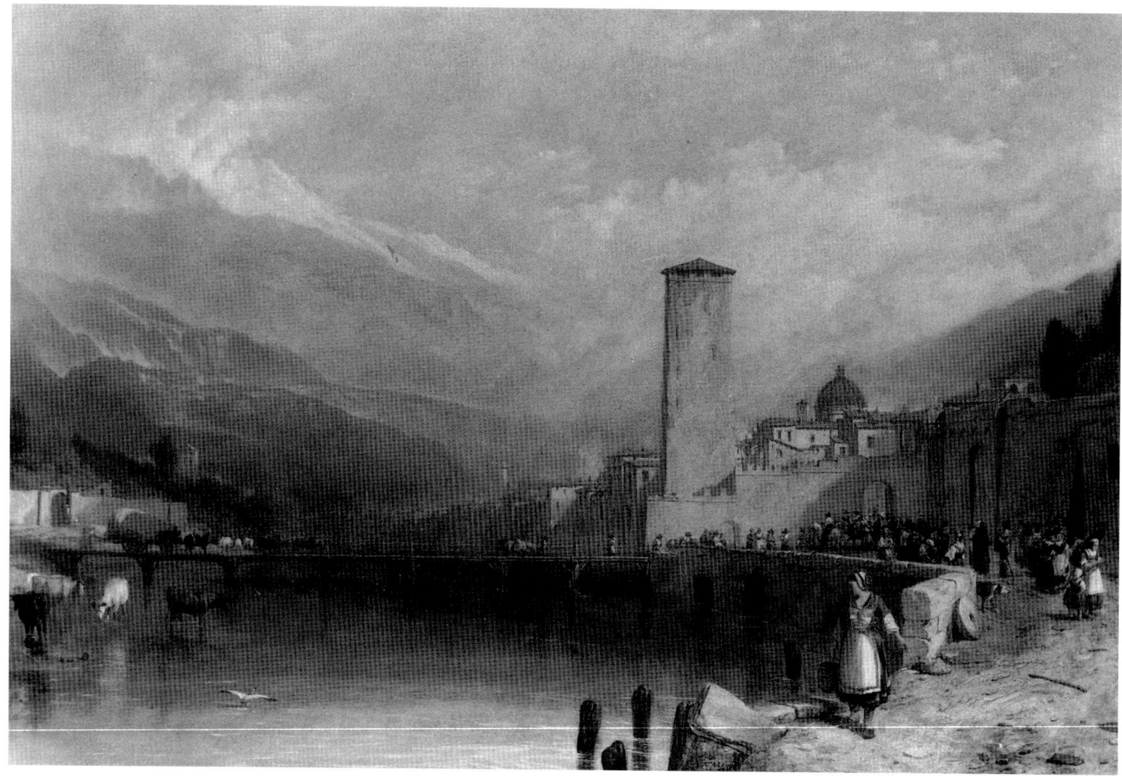

Another landscape artist, however, indicates the right path to follow. Salvation for Passavant comes in this instance in the person of Augustus Wall Callcott (fig. 219), who 'may be considered to hold the same rank in landscape, as Eastlake in historical painting. Beauty of outline, clearness of tone, a correct knowledge of perspective, and a commendable severity of design and execution, distinguish this artist before all other English landscape painters'.[43] Passavant's own 'commendable severity' led him to seek out the same qualities in modern British art.

Views similar to Passavant's were expressed by Gustav Waagen, who was Director of the National Gallery in Berlin when he made his art tour of England in 1835. The principal aim of Waagen's journey was likewise to document the main British art collections, a task he carried out with such thoroughness that his work remains a standard reference for historians today. But one of his secondary interests lay in contemporary British art, which he judged largely according to what he saw on exhibition at Somerset House. This experience he found no less disagreeable than it had been for Passavant in 1831; and Waagen was equally convinced that the works on display were far from measuring up to the best of British art in the previous century. 'The total impression is by no means satisfactory', he writes; 'the great mass of the pictures, compared with those of the older English painters, manifest progressive decline and licence. Individual feeling, drawing, truth of colouring, careful execution are here sought in vain. The whole object is to produce a striking but unmeaning effect, by the harshest contrasts and the most glaring colours.'[44]

Like other Germans, Waagen admired David Wilkie, though regretting that his current work no longer had 'the refinement and decided colour of his earlier pictures'.[45] He was also a friend of Eastlake, and showered fulsome praise on his *Pilgrims Arriving in Sight of Rome*, a version of the painting the artist had exhibited so successfully in Rome in 1827 (fig. 220). Echoing Passavant's opinions, Waagen lauded Eastlake for the correctness of his work, while lamenting that his 'lack of exaggeration . . . appears to most English people as coldness and stiffness'.[46] This last assertion may have been deemed too strong for the British public; in any case it did not appear in the translation of 1838.

By then, however, Waagen's views on British art – and on the detrimental effects of the Academy shows in particular – had became known through a different channel. For he was amongst those who were asked to give evidence on the state of art in Britain before the Parliamentary Select Committee which reported on this subject in 1836.[47]

The functions of the Select Committee were wide-ranging and complex. They have been much discussed in the context of the setting up of the Government Schools of Design, and of the initiation of a state programme for the arts to enhance the quality of design and manufactures.[48] But the Committee was equally interested in the problem of promoting public taste, and for this reason its members were deeply concerned with the role of art exhibitions. They must have listened with interest when Waagen told them of his firm conviction that the Academy's yearly displays, at least as they were currently constituted, posed a real danger to the nation's cultural well-being.

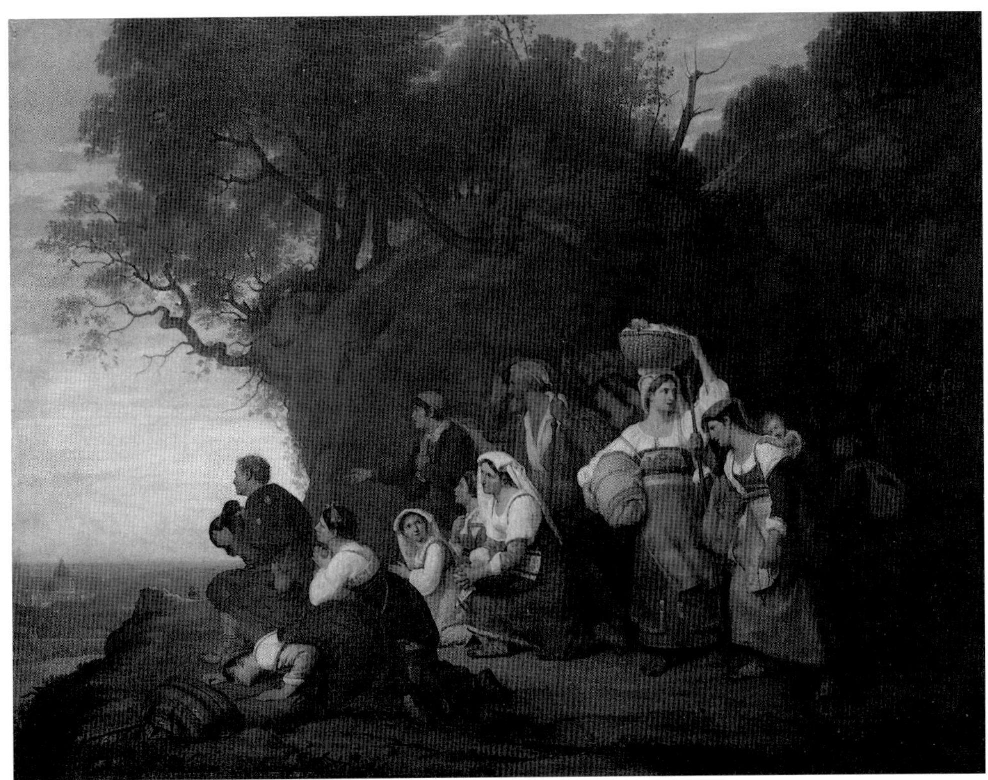

219 Augustus Wall Callcott, *View of Trent in the Tyrol*, RA 1831. Private Collection.

220 Charles Lock Eastlake, *Pilgrims Arriving in Sight of Rome*, RA 1835. Philadelphia Museum of Art.

Giving evidence in July 1835, just days after his visit to Somerset House, Waagen focused his attack on the process of self-selection and the dependence upon commercial success that lay behind exhibitions like the one he had just seen:

> It is in no case right that any man should be judge in his own case, and it is not advisable that a number of artists, who are about to exhibit their own works, should have the sole right to decide what works are to be admitted, and how other and different works of art are to be placed in the exhibition.[49]

'In order to avoid all partiality', Waagen proposed a state-regulated system that would place responsibility for selecting the exhibits into the hands of 'a committee which should be composed of artists and connoisseurs of taste and judgement'.[50] He then went on to recommend that works of 'distinguished merit', as chosen by an informed public, should be assembled over time into a 'national museum of British art', modelled on the Luxembourg Gallery in Paris.

The conjunction of this project with a reform of the Academy's annual exhibition may seem quite puzzling, until we recall that Waagen was giving his testimony at the time when the new National Gallery was under construction in Trafalgar Square, in a building designed to give equal space to the nation's collection of art and the Royal Academy.[51] The RA's opponents felt that this would hold British art up to derision in perpetuity, by setting up a regular confrontation between the eternal verities of the old masters, and the meretricious products of modern commercial culture. Although Waagen was too diplomatic to voice such opinions, except in the most circumspect fashion, there was no holding back the principal witness for the prosecution – Benjamin Robert Haydon. By now the sworn enemy of the Academy, Haydon told the Committee it would be utter folly to allow the Academy to pervert the image of British art in this way. Although he would later become a bitter opponent of German art – which he termed the 'gilt ground inanity of the middle ages'[52] – in the mid-1830s Haydon found common cause with the German critics of the British art system.

On being asked whether he felt that the taste of people could be 'improved or injured' by the practice of exhibition, he replied 'very much injured'. On being asked how, he extrapolated, 'By the glare of colouring, a competition to outshine each other without reference to art. I have known some academicians send their canvas only with a head on it, and wait to finish it till they saw what would be hung by the side of it, and dress up the thing in a week for the public, like an automaton. Think of that, and Titian taking eight years about "Peter Martyr"!'[53] Great masterpieces, in other words, took time.

The Committee then asked for further elaboration: 'You seem to think a national collection should be, as nearly as possible, for the eternal works of art, not for the ephemeral productions of the year?' To which Haydon answered, 'Yes, a species of mausoleum for all that is great and grand in the nation. If we had a thing of that sort, when foreigners come, we should have something to show them: while some of the best known works of art are rotting for want of space (my own *Judgment of Solomon* and *Lazarus*)'. After blowing his own horn, the artist referred to another German visitor to Britain who had recently been critical of the Academy exhibition. This was the Prussian historian and diplomat Friedrich von Raumer, whose remarks were about to appear in his book *England in 1835*;[54] how Haydon got wind of them is far from clear. A friend of Waagen, von Raumer, like so many Continental observers, took much the same dim view of the current state of British art. 'Why is that?' Haydon asked the Select Committee, before providing the answer himself:

> He comes to the Royal Academy, and sees a series of whole-length portraits standing on tiptoe, and he goes away and says they cannot put men on their legs; but if the fine works were gradually purchased and put in a gallery, year after year, in the course of 20 years there would be a fine collection[55]

– and people like von Raumer would be duly impressed. But in the event matters were not to turn out as Haydon had wished. As Thomas Gretton has recently pointed out, the wide-ranging programme of reform envisaged by the Select Committee was only partially implemented, partly because a change from a Liberal to a Conservative government during the compilation of the report led to a clampdown on its more rigorous proposals.[56] After abandoning Somerset House, the Academy survived unscathed, retaining its independence together with the privilege of continued state support when it joined the National Gallery under the same new roof in Trafalgar Square. The Royal Academy exhibition, too, remained much as it had been before. But not quite. For in their new premises the Academicians and their fellow exhibitors did indeed have to run the gauntlet of competition from the country's expanding public collection of significant old masters. Much as Passavant had done in his *Tour*, contemporary critics could now accept the invitation to compare the works on view at the Academy with those that had been amassed by British connoisseurs over the previous century and more before becoming part of the National Gallery. Perhaps this juxtaposition did not lead to the general elevation of taste that both Passavant and Waagen had envisioned and desired; yet its consequences were none the less significant. Indeed by moving from Somerset House into Trafalgar Square, the Royal Academy may have unwittingly planted the seed of that rebellion which would ultimately displace its annual exhibitions from the centre of the British art world. For in the 1840s the young Academy students who were to form the Pre-Raphaelite Brotherhood enjoyed daily access to the National Gallery, where they encountered such key examples of fifteenth-century art as Jan van Eyck's *Arnolfini Wedding* and Giovanni Bellini's portrait of Doge Loredan. Thus inspired with a vision of pre-Academic painting, Dante Gabriel Rossetti, John Everett Millais, William Holman Hunt and their circle embarked on a path of vigorous reform similar to that followed forty years previously, by the Nazarene Brotherhood of St Luke in Vienna.

Tables

Table 1: Foreign exhibitors (251 in total) by country of origin and by medium*

Nationality	Painters	Sculptors (including wax modellers and medallists)	Architects	Engravers and Gem Engravers	Miniature Painters	Honorary Exhibitors in all media	Total
French	61	5	1	1	28	9	105
German	32	1	1	1	6	–	41
Italian	23	9	2	1	3	1	39
Swiss	10	–	–	–	9	–	19
Flemish	13	–	–	–	–	–	13
American	8	–	–	–	2	1	11
Dutch	7	–	–	–	–	–	7
Danish	5	–	–	1	–	–	6
Austrian	3	–	–	–	–	–	3
Russian	2	–	–	–	–	1	3
Swedish	2	–	–	–	–	–	2
Savoyard	1	–	–	–	–	–	1
Spanish	1	–	–	–	–	–	1

*There are at least another 213 artists with names of foreign origin and generally with brief periods of activity at the RA/in Britain/London. (Of those some may, of course, be the British descendants of previous Huguenot and other foreign immigrants.) These artists are often known *only* through their exhibiting activities at the RA and are therefore generally counted among the 'British School' by standard dictionaries such as Thieme-Becker and Bénézit. An example is one L. de Longastre (mentioned in my text), whom press cuttings clearly identify as a French *émigré*. Daphne Foskett's *Miniatures: Dictionary and Guide* (Suffolk, 1987) is more careful and for instance characterizes the obscure 'Duvigneaud' who exhibited miniatures in 1797, according to his then residency, as 'of London'. This does not mean, of course, that Duvigneaud was not a French artist temporarily seeking refuge in London. Of those additional artists of possible foreign origin, 120 are probably French (of whom 50 are miniature painters), 30 Germans, 19 Italians, 12 Netherlandish, 2 Swiss, 2 Swedish, 1 Polish, and 28 of unknown origin.

Table 2: Activities of foreign exhibitors by period

Nationality	Medium	1780–1789	1790–1815	1816–1836
French	Painters	10	22	31
French	Sculptors	1	3	3
French	Architects	–	1	–
French	Engravers	–	1	–
French	Miniature painters	4	15	13
French	Honorary exhibitors	2	5	2
German	Painters	11	15	14
German	Architects	–	1	–
German	Sculptors	–	–	1
German	Engravers	–	1	–
German	Miniature painters	2	2	3
Italian	Painters	6	9	11
Italian	Sculptors	2	4	7
Italian	Architects	2	1	–
Italian	Engravers	1	1	–
Italian	Miniature painters	1	3	–
Italian	Honorary exhibitors	1	–	–
Swiss	Painters	3	7	7
Swiss	Miniature painters	2	4	5
Flemish	Painters	2	4	7
American	Painters	4	5	5
American	Miniature painters	–	1	2
American	Honorary exhibitors	–	1	–
Dutch	Painters	3	3	4
Danish	Painters	3	2	1
Danish	Engravers	–	1	–
Austrian	Painters	1	2	2
Russian	Painters	1	1	–
Russian	Honorary exhibitors	–	1	–
Swedish	Painters	2	2	–
Savoyard	Painters	1	1	–
Spanish	Painters	–	1	–
Total		65	120	118*

*The relatively high number of artists active between 1816 and 1836 appears to contradict my thesis that the participation of foreign artists in the exhibitions declined in importance in the post-war period; however, a large percentage of artists active in that period exhibited only once or at most twice; Baron Gérard or Eugène Delacroix are thus only the most illustrious representatives of a general trend.

Table 3: Foreign Artists: Associate and full RA membership and election to academic office, by period and artist

Artist	Nationality	Academic office
Non-Academician foreign honorary officers		
Joseph Baretti	Italian	Secretary for Foreign Correspondence, 1769–1789
Foreign artists among founder members, 1768: 9 of 34		
Francesco Bartolozzi	Italian	–
Agostino Carlini	Italian	Keeper 1783–90; also made a bust of George III for the RA's entrance hall.
Giovanni Battista Cipriani	Italian	no office, but was commissioned to design the RA's diploma
Francesco Zuccarelli	Italian	–
George Michael Moser	Swiss	Keeper 1768–83; Deputy Librarian 1782
Angelika Kauffmann	Swiss	no office, but commissioned to design four oval, allegorical paintings for the RA's entrance hall
Jeremiah Meyer	German	–
Benjamin West	American*	President 1792–1820 (with the exception of the academic year 1805–6, when James Wyatt was briefly elected President)
Dominique Serres	French	Librarian 1792–93
Additionally elected in 1769: 1 of 2		
Johann Zoffany	German	–

*The 'foreignness' of artists like Benjamin West, who were born as British (colonial) citizens – and even of those born in the USA – is clearly a matter of debate. However, a considerable number of contemporary critics perceived these artists (including, on occasion, West), in terms of their 'foreign' origin and of their (admirable or contemptible) difference in political and social organization.

Information drawn from Sir Walter R. M. Lamb, *The Royal Academy: A Short History of its Foundation and Development*, London, 1951, 119–70.

Table 4: Election of foreign artists to Associate and full membership

Artist	Nationality	ARA	RA	Office
Foreign artists elected 1770–79: 8 of 34				
Simon François Ravenet	French	1770	–	–
Peter Charles Canot	French	1770	–	–
Antonio Zucchi	Italian	1770	–	–
Biagio Rebecca	Italian	1771	–	–
Elias Martin	Swedish	1770	–	–
Nicholas Thomas Dall	Danish	1771	–	–
Jean François Rigaud	b. Turin (Savoy)	1772	1784	Deputy Librarian 1810
John Singleton Copley	American	1776	1779	–
Foreign artists elected 1780–92: 3 of 25				
Philippe Jacques de Loutherbourg	French	1780	1781	–
Henry Fuseli	Swiss	1788	1790	Prof. of Painting 1790–1805, Keeper 1804–25
Joseph Bonomi	Italian	1789	–	–
Foreign artists elected 1793–1803: none of 19				
Foreign artists elected 1804–15: 1 of 25				
Alfred Edward Chalon	Swiss	1812	1816	–
Foreign artists elected 1816–36: 3 of 38				
John James Chalon	Swiss	1827	1841	–
Washington Allston	American	1818	–	–
Gilbert Stuart Newton	American	1828	1832	–

[Foreign artists elected 1837–1951: 17 of 310. The first foreign honorary Academicians were elected in 1869].

Notes

Frequently Cited Sources

Farington, *Diary*	*The Diary of Joseph Farington*, 16 vols and index, I–VII ed. Kenneth Garlick and Angus Macintyre, VIII–XVI ed. Kathryn Cave, index by Evelyn Newby, New Haven and London 1978–98
Reynolds, *Discourses*	Sir Joshua Reynolds, *Discourses on Art*, ed. Robert R. Wark, New Haven and London 1975
Whitley, *Artists and their Friends*	William T. Whitley, *Artists and their Friends in England 1700–1799*, 2 vols, Cambridge 1928
Whitley, *Art in England*	William T. Whitley, *Art in England 1800–1830*, 2 vols, Cambridge 1928, 1930

Introduction

1 I have taken much of my factual information about the *Tribuna* from Oliver Millar, *Zoffany and his Tribuna*, London and New York 1966.

2 *Morning Chronicle, and London Advertiser*, May 1780, in Royal Academy Library, 'Royal Academy Critiques &c', I, 1769–93, fol. 59.

3 *Morning Chronicle, and London Advertiser*, 2 May 1780.

4 Brian O'Doherty, *Inside the White Cube: The Ideology of the Gallery Space*, expanded edn, Berkeley, Los Angeles and London 1999, 16.

5 Ibid., 19.

6 John Hamilton, *Stereography, or, a Complete Body of Perspective*, 2 vols, London 1738, II, 389, quoted in Peter de Bolla, *The Discourse of the Sublime: Readings in History, Aesthetics and the Subject*, Oxford 1989, 194. My thinking about the visual experience of the exhibitions owes a great deal to de Bolla's stimulating book.

7 Hamilton, *Stereography*, II, 393–4, quoted in de Bolla, 195.

8 Marginal comment in British Library copy of John Joshua Kirby, *Dr Brook Taylor's Method of Perspective Made Easy Both in Theory and Practice*, London 1754, 62, quoted in de Bolla, 197.

9 *Repository of Arts, Literature, Fashion, and Manufactures, &c.*, 2nd ser., 13 (June 1822), 350.

10 *Champion*, 441 (16 June 1821).

11 Reynolds, *Discourses* (III, 1770), 43.

12 Anon., review of Richard Payne Knight, *An Analytical Inquiry into the Principles of Taste*, *Edinburgh Review*, 7 (June 1806), 302.

13 *Literary Gazette, and Journal of the Belles Lettres*, 277 (11 May 1822), 296.

14 Andrew Hemingway, 'Art Exhibitions as Leisure-Class Rituals in Early Nineteenth-Century London', in *Towards a Modern Art World*, ed. Brian Allen, New Haven and London 1995, 97. This is the best analysis of late Hanoverian exhibition culture, and I have drawn upon it in a variety of ways.

15 Anon., 'Our Royal-Academical Lounge', *Fraser's Magazine*, 5 (July 1832), 710–11.

16 Ibid., 711–12.

17 Reynolds, *Discourses* (V, 1772), 89–90.

18 *Morning Chronicle*, 17 April 1792. Here I am treading on some of the same territory covered by C. S. Matheson and (especially) by Dian Kriz in their chapters in this volume.

19 James Stephen, *The Memoirs of James Stephen: Written by Himself for the Use of his Children*, ed. Bevington Merle, London 1954, 342, 344; also reported in *Morning Herald*, 3 May 1781, and *Whitehall Evening Post*, 3–4 May 1781; quoted in Karen Stanworth, 'Picturing a Personal History: The Case of Edward Onslow', *Art History*, 16, no. 3 (1993), 413. My summary of this episode is based mainly on Stanworth's excellent article, to which I would like to acknowledge my debt.

20 *London Chronicle*, 1–3 May 1781.

21 Stanworth, 'Personal History', 413–14, 416–17.

22 Here I am referring to the 'Vauxhall Affray', where three gentlemen, one the son of a nobleman, refused to stop staring at the actress Elizabeth Hartley, until they were confronted by Henry Bate, the editor of the *Morning Post*. Insults were traded, a duel was arranged, and a boxing match followed. For a stimulating analysis of this affair and its implications, see Miles Ogborn, *Spaces of Modernity: London's Geographies 1680–1780*, New York 1998, 116–57.

23 This according to the Academy's accounts for 1820, as reported by Hemingway, 'Leisure-Class Rituals', 99.

24 For a more developed consideration of the carnivalesque character of the Academy shows, see Dian Kriz, Chapter 4 in this volume.

25 Unidentified newspaper, 'RA Critiques', I, fol. 15. Dian Kriz has perceptively informed me that the reference to the black implies a connection with the contemporary campaign to abolish the slave trade – a cause which the anonymous critic evidently opposed.

26 *Literary Gazette*, 277 (11 May 1822), 296.

Chapter 1

1 Joseph Baretti, *A Guide through the Royal Academy*, London, Royal Academy n.d., [1780], 3.

2 Ibid., 6.

3 Ibid., 7; John Newman, 'Somerset House

and Other Public Buildings', in *Sir William Chambers, Architect to George III*, ed. John Harris and Michael Snodin, London, Courtauld Gallery 1996, 118.

4 Robin Middleton, 'Chambers, W. "A Treatise on Civil Architecture" London 1759', in Harris and Snodin, *Chambers*, 69.

5 Baretti, *Guide*, 3.

6 Ibid., 15; the relief must be the Triumph of Marcus Aurelius, one of the set of three on the stairs of the Palazzo dei Conservatori.

7 Baretti lists the statues alphabetically, sometimes under names which are now unfamiliar. Together with the whole figures was a collection of busts of the emperors, of detached heads from figures particularly valued for their expressions, and of genre and animal figures. There were also some casts after admired Renaissance sculptures. In 1780 the collection was still not comprehensive: for example, there was no Farnese Hercules. A cast of that colossal figure was acquired in 1793. After much discussion in Council it was finally assembled in 1797 as the centrepiece of the staircase group, in the place of the Medici Vase. This must have involved the flooring over of the small Doric vestibule in the basement – significantly, after Chambers's death.

8 John Harris, *Sir William Chambers, Knight of the Polar Star*, 1970, 18–21; Janine Barrier gives a fuller account of Chambers's friendships with French architects and artists in Paris and Rome in 'Chambers in France and Italy', in Harris and Snodin, *Chambers*, 19–33.

9 Nicholas Savage, 'The "Viceroy" of the Academy: Sir William Chambers and the Royal Protection of the Arts', in Harris and Snodin, *Chambers*, 193–8.

10 Harris 1970, 97, citing BL Add. MSS 41135, 26 r and v.

11 Now Place de la Concorde.

12 On the Monnaies see especially Allan Braham, *The Architecture of the French Enlightenment*, London 1980, 117–20 (fig. 150).

13 Chambers's observations are recorded in watercolour drawings in his 'Paris Album' of that year. See John Harris, 'Sir William Chambers and his Parisian Album', *Architectural History*, 6 (1963), 54–90; also Janine Barrier in Harris and Snodin, *Chambers*, 28–32.

14 The design sources of the Strand block are complex, and include, obviously, the 'gallery' of Old Somerset House, which was believed to be by Inigo Jones. During his campaign to secure the commission for the new Somerset House, Chambers had castigated William Robinson, his predecessor on the project, for not attempting to preserve the gallery, nor the fairly recent additions to the river garden front by William Kent. Baretti, perhaps in consultation with Chambers, cites Antonio Sangallo's Palazzo Farnese in Rome as the source of the 'general idea' of the vestibule.

15 'En 1692, le Roi décida de concéder des appartements à ses académies' (Louis Hautecoeur, *L'Histoire des Chateaux du Louvre et des Tuileries* . . . , Paris 1927, 196). The Académie de Peinture et de Sculpture held two exhibitions in 1699 and 1704 in part of the Grande Galerie of the Louvre. The first exhibition in the Salon itself was in 1725 and the next in 1737. Thereafter *salons* took place annually until 1751, when they became biennial and continued until 1848.

16 Apollo is a tutelary deity of the arts, and presides over the Muses on Parnassus. Hence he was given the task of introducing the iconographic programme of the building, though at the upper levels Minerva, goddess of learning and the useful arts, emerged as the main figure. Apollo was also the personal god of the Emperor Augustus, whom some held to be his son. He was therefore appropriate in an institution such as the Royal Academy, which was Augustan in the sense that its purpose was to promote art in the interest of the state.

17 Baretti, *Guide*, 16.

18 Ibid., 30.

19 Ibid., 31.

20 Johnson was the Academy's Professor of Ancient Literature from 1770 to 1784. Baretti (*Guide*, 31) however attributes the idea of the inscription to 'the learned Physician Sir George Baker, who took it from that famous one over the door of Plato's Library'.

21 Baretti, *Guide*, 31.

22 Ibid.

23 The dimensions are 53 × 43 feet, × 32 feet high.

24 There are indications of close professional attention in Paris to the new buildings in London: 'In November 1777, N. H. Jardin, just back from England, read to the Académie [d'architecture] a memoire in which "M. le Chevalier Chambers" had described the "vast project he is carrying out in London to house public offices as well as the Academies etc". Jardin was then asked to thank M. Chambers in the name of the Académie, and to invite him to provide plans and elevations of "such an essential and considerable building".' Janine Barrier (in Harris and Snodin, *Chambers*, 27), citing 'Procès-verbaux de l'Académie d'architecture'; the reference is to *Procès-Verbaux de l'Académie Royale d'Architecture, 1671–1793*, ed. Henri Lemonnier, 9 vols, Société de l'Art Français, sous les Auspices de l'Institut (Académie des Beaux-Arts, Fondation Debrousse, Paris, 1911–26, VIII (1924), 317). Chambers was the Académie's official English correspondent.

25 Christiane Aulanier, *Le Salon Carré, Histoire du Palais et du Musée du Louvre*, Paris 1950, 18, 75; Saint-Aubin's preparatory drawing is her figure 3.

26 'Une sorte de trappe . . . presque toujours engorgée'; quoted ibid., 35.

27 The Crown had acquired Buckingham House in exchange for Somerset House.

28 Royal Academy Council Minutes, I, 358 (16 April 1784). The portrait of *The Three Eldest Princesses* is in the Royal Collection and has been cut down to 51 × 70in.; Ellis Waterhouse, *Gainsborough*, London 1958, no.135, 59.

29 On Turner's refusal to have *Hannibal Crossing the Alps* hung as number 1 in the show, over the door of the Great Room, see Chapter 2 in this volume.

30 Aulanier, *Salon Carré*, 36–7; she quotes the extremely important correspondence between Amadée van Loo, the Tapissier of the Académie, and the comte d'Angiviller and Maximilien Brébion, respectively the head of the royal Bâtiments and the Louvre house architect, whereby an elaborate and re-usable 'établissement' of steel, planks and wainscoting was developed in 1784–85, to simplify the task of hanging the Salon and to bring order to the arrangement, following developments in London. Its effect was to cover up windows and to establish a horizontal 'line' around the walls, above which the walls were extended upward and outward, again as in London. Its use is visible for the first time in Pietro Martini's print of the 1785 Salon; this is reproduced in Thomas Crow, *Painters and Public Life in Eighteenth-Century Paris*, New Haven and London 1985, 213.

31 In 1792 the Committee of Arrangement consisted of Sandby, Webster and Yenn.

32 The king made up total deficits of £5,116 1s. 11¾d., all incurred between 1769–70 and 1779–80 (Royal Academy Ms. Summary of Income and Expenditure compiled by George Dance and William Tyler, 1795).

33 Royal Academy Council Minutes, I, 141 (26 April 1791).

34 Sir John Soane's lecture diagram, showing the Strand front 'corrected' in accordance with professional orthodoxies, with the three central bays advanced, the columns disengaged, and a pediment instead of the attic storey and Great Room lantern, is discussed and reproduced in Newman, 'Somerset House', in Harris and Snodin, *Chambers*, fig. 63; and see especially 118–20.

35 'Advertisement' prefacing *The Exhibition of the Royal Academy*, London 1780.

36 *St James's Chronicle; or, British Evening Post*, 29 April–2 May 1780.

37 Ibid., 16–18 May 1780.

38 Letter to the Editor, *Morning Post, and Daily Advertiser*, 15 May 1780.

39 *Gazetteer and New Daily Advertiser*, 20 May 1780.

40 *Whitehall Evening Post*, 27–29 April 1780.

41 *Morning Post, and Daily Advertiser*, 2 May 1780.

42 *London Courant, and Westminster Chronicle*, 2 May 1780.

43 *Morning Chronicle, and London Advertiser*, 2 May

1780. A few years later a German visitor to the exhibition described the experience thus: 'There are many steps to be climbed before one reaches the level of the room . . . one is obliged to climb until one is quite breathless – as if [the Academicians] had set up their works to be admired in some higher atmosphere'. G. F. A. Wendeborn, *Der Zustand des Staats, der Religion, der Gelehrsamkeit und der Kunst in Grossbritannien gegen das Ende des achtzehnten Jahrhunderts*, Berlin 1785, 376. I owe this reference and translation to Jonathan Conlin of Gonville and Caius College, Cambridge.

Chapter 2

The authors are grateful to John Murdoch and Martin Myrone for providing material support for this chapter.

1 *Abstract of the Instrument of Institution of the Royal Academy of Arts in London, 10 December 1768*, London 1781, 26.
2 As midsummer approaches, these are of course the windows through which the sun shines. The Great Room is very liable to overheat, partly the effect of solar gain, partly the stack effect of heat rising via the staircase into the Great Room, where it vents naturally through the Diocletian windows.
3 It is significant that there is no mention of storage on Neale's invoice, though there is on Seddon's.
4 Royal Academy Council Minutes, III, 143 (29 April 1802).
5 Ibid., 281 (23 April 1804).
6 See William Sandby, *The History of the Royal Academy*, 2 vols, London 1862, I, 274.
7 Ibid., II, 239–40.
8 C. R. Leslie, *Autobiographical Recollections*, 2 vols, ed. Tom Taylor, London 1860, I, 201–2.
9 Royal Academy Council Minutes, XII, 84 (21 April 1862), quoted from Sidney C. Hutchison, *The History of the Royal Academy 1768–1986*, London 1986, 101.
10 For a discussion of how the numbering system changed when the Academy moved to Somerset House, and of the important implications of this shift, see C. S. Matheson, Chapter 3 in this volume.
11 Although the miniatures were grouped around the fireplace (until 1793, that is), they were always numbered separately in the catalogue, after the listing of the Great Room paintings.
12 Farington, *Diary*, II, 317 (20 March 1795).
13 Ibid., 319 (27 March 1795).
14 Ibid., 324 (8 April 1795).
15 Ibid. (9 April 1795).
16 Ibid., 326 (13 April 1795).
17 Ibid. (15 April 1795).
18 Ibid., 326–7 (17 April 1795).
19 Ibid., 330–1 (24 April 1795).
20 Ibid., IV, 1191 (2 April 1799).
21 *The Diary of Benjamin Robert Haydon*, ed. Willard Bissell Pope, 5 vols, London 1960, I, 61.
22 Edward Edwards, *A Letter to Sir Martin Archer Shee, F.R.S., President of the Royal Academy of Arts, on the Reform of the Royal Academy*, London 1839, 33–4.
23 Royal Academy Council Minutes, VI, 131 (10 April 1820).
24 Farington, *Diary*, III, 826 (20 April 1797).
25 Ibid., 827 (24 April 1797).
26 Ibid., 828–9 (28 April 1797).
27 *Morning Post*, 5 May 1797, quoted from Martin Butlin and Evelyn Joll, *The Paintings of J. M. W. Turner*, 2 vols, London 1984, I, 2. This criticism was reprinted in *A Critical Guide to the Present Exhibition at the Royal Academy*, London 1797, by John Williams, 'whose public appellation is Anthony Pasquin'.
28 Farington, *Diary*, XI, 4107 (10 April 1812).
29 Leslie, *Autobiographical Recollections*, II, 12.

Chapter 3

The first version of this chapter was delivered at the North American Association for the Study of Romanticism conference at Duke University, North Carolina, in 1994 and published in *The Lessons of Romanticism*, ed. Thomas Pfau and Robert Gleckner, Duke University Press, 1998.

1 *A Catalogue of the Pictures, Sculptures, Models, Drawings, Prints &c of the Present Artists. Exhibited in the Great Room of the Society for the Encouragement of Arts, Manufactures and Commerce, on the 21st of April, 1760*, London 1760.
2 The letter, sent in December 1760, was composed by Samuel Johnson. See 'The Papers of the Society of Artists of Great Britain', *The Walpole Society*, 6 (1917–18), 119–21.
3 Giles Waterfield, et al., *Palaces of Art: Art Galleries in Britain, 1790–1990*, Dulwich Picture Gallery, London 1991, 131.
4 Society of Artists of Great Britain, *A Catalogue of the Pictures, Sculptures, Models, Drawings and Prints, &c*, London 1762, iv–v.
5 Advertisement in the *Exhibition of the Royal Academy MDCCLXIX, THE FIRST*, London 1769, n.p.
6 Brandoin and Earlom's print was sold for 10s. 6d., making it a relatively expensive production. See Robert Sayer and John Bennett, *For 1775. Sayer and Bennett's Enlarged Catalogue of New and Valuable Prints*, London 1775 (1970 reprint), 3.
7 In 1771 the Chevalier Manini exhibited two works at the [Royal Incorporated] Society of Artists, *Armida before Geoffredo* from Tasso and *Mount Parnassus* from Bocalini. Bragge (d. 1777–78) is mentioned by Horace Walpole in a letter dated 11 December 1743 as a 'virtuosi' who offered him information on the provenance of a work by Correggio. *Horace Walpole's Correspondence with Sir Horace Mann*, ed. W. S. Lewis, W. H. Smith and G. L. Lam, XVIII, New Haven 1954, 355. For further details concerning Bragge's place within the structures of eighteenth-century connoisseurship, see Iain Pears, *The Discovery of Painting: The Growth of Interest in the Arts in England 1680–1768*, New Haven and London 1988, 92–6.
8 British Museum Satires no. 4768. This print is reproduced in Pears, *Discovery of Painting*, 190, fig. 59.
9 *The Craftsman, or Say's Weekly Journal*, 11 May 1771, 2.
10 Diana Donald, 'Caricatures', in *Reynolds*, ed. Nicholas Penny, Royal Academy of Arts, London 1986, 365.
11 Wilkes was Treasurer of the Foundling Hospital and the nominal 'President' – though apparently for only one meeting – of the group of artists who resolved in November 1759 to begin the practice of exhibiting their works annually. He condemned the king's removal of the Raphael Cartoons from Hampton Court, supported a scheme in the 1770s to decorate St Paul's Cathedral with paintings (scotched by the Bishop of London), and later (in a speech in Parliament on 28 April 1777) agitated for the nation's purchase of Robert Walpole's Houghton pictures. See *The Speeches of John Wilkes*, 2 vols, London 1777, II, 59.
12 *Sayer and Bennett's Enlarged Catalogue*, 7.
13 Diana Donald, *The Age of Caricature: Satirical Prints in the Reign of George III*, New Haven and London 1996, 80.
14 A correspondent to the *Public Advertiser*, 12 April 1775, complains bitterly about the original organization of the catalogue and offers an alternative: 'Many Persons, who visit the annual Exhibitions of the R.A., and other Societies, have found the Mode of classing the Works of the Masters in the printed Catalogue very inconvenient and troublesome, being not at all conformable to the Disposition of them in the Room . . . it is very difficult to find any particular Performance sought for without much Trouble and Patience; and the blending [of] various and distant Numbers upon the Pieces, which succeed each other, creates a confused and disagreeable Process. Now as most People pursue their View in a progressive Course round the Rooms from Left to Right, it is submitted whether the Exhibitions may not be render'd more convenient and agreeable by ordering the Arrangement of the Pieces in the Room and in the Catalogue to go Hand in Hand; that is, after the Pieces are properly placed in the Room, then to Number them progressively. . . . This Method would be more easy and pleasant to the Company, as well as doing Justice to the Artist; for it is the Merit of a Picture that

leads us to enquire who the Painter is – not the Name of a Painter that induces us to engage in a vain Search after his Performance . . .'.

15 Frederick A. Wendeborn, *A View of England Towards the Close of the Eighteenth Century*, 2 vols, trans. by the author, London 1791, II, 198. The first German edition appeared in 1785 (see Chapter 1, n. 43).

16 Anthony Pasquin (pseud. of John Williams), *A Critical Guide to the Exhibition of the Royal Academy for 1796*, London 1796, 18.

17 *The Letters of Samuel Johnson*, ed. Bruce Redford, Princeton 1984, IV, 135.

18 Ibid., 136.

19 Joseph Baretti, *A Guide through the Royal Academy*, London 1780, 31.

20 Wendeborn, *View of England*, II, 197–8.

21 *Morning Post, and Daily Advertiser*, 27 April 1784.

22 On the circumstances that prompted Gainsborough's boycott of the Academy, see John Murdoch, Chapter 1 in this volume.

23 *St James's Chronicle*, 27 April 1784.

24 Quoted in Whitley, *Artists and their Friends*, I, 401.

25 Jürgen Habermas, *The Structural Transformation of the Public Sphere*, trans. T. Burger, London 1992, 5.

26 William Sandby's translation of the inscription is much harder-edged: 'Let none but men of taste presume to enter'; see his *History of the Royal Academy*, 2 vols, London 1862, I, 157. For another alternative and some further information about the source of this motto, see p. 15 above.

27 By 1787 the Prince of Wales had become a problematic candidate for the exemplary role ascribed him by Ramberg's design. The scandals surrounding his behaviour, finances and amours had reached a frenzy the previous year with rumours of his marriage to Mrs Fitzherbert and whispers of her pregnancy. This prompted the publication of numerous satirical prints, to which Ramberg may have been trying to respond.

28 'Old Artist', *Observations on the Present State of the Arts, with the Characters of Living Artists*, London 1790, 20–1.

29 *Gentleman's Magazine*, 57, pt. 1 (June 1787), 542.

30 Reynolds, *Discourses* (IX, 1780), 171.

31 The grouping of the younger princesses is based on John Singleton Copley's portrait (RA 1787) in the Royal Collection.

32 *The Microcosm of London, or, London in Miniature*, I (1808), 10.

33 Ibid.

34 Roger Sales, 'Pierce Egan and the Representation of London', in *Reviewing Romanticism*, ed. P. Martin, New York 1992, 154–69.

35 Pierce Egan, *Life in London; or the Day and Night Scenes of Jerry Hawthorn, esq, and his Elegant Friend Corinthian Tom: accompanied by Bob Logic, the Oxonian, in their Rambles and Sprees through the Metropolis*, London 1821, 334–5, 339, 346.

36 Ibid., 339.

Chapter 4

1 The drawing has been dated *c.*1800 by John Hayes, in *The Art of Thomas Rowlandson*, Alexandria, Virginia 1990, 72.

2 Reynolds, *Discourses* (IX, 1780), 169.

3 Ibid., 171.

4 David Hume's essay, 'Of Refinement in the Arts' (in his *Essays Moral, Political, and Literary, Part II*, orig. pub. London, 1752 under the title 'Of Luxury'), is perhaps the most well known of these writings. For a cogent analysis of the relationship between art, commerce and refinement see David Solkin, *Painting for Money: The Visual Arts and the Public Sphere in Eighteenth-Century England*, New Haven and London 1993.

5 Reynolds, *Discourses* (IX, 1780), 171.

6 John Barrell has analysed the liberal discourse on the fine arts as a masculine discourse in *The Political Theory of Painting from Reynolds to Hazlitt: The Body of the Public*, New Haven and London 1986, esp. 63–8.

7 See Lynda Nead, *The Female Nude: Art, Obscenity and Sexuality*, London 1992, 17–24.

8 [Mauritius Lowe], *The Ear-Wig; or an Old Woman's Remarks on the Present Exhibition of Pictures of the Royal Academy*, London 1781, 19. The figure is shown holding a spear, rather than natural bounty. Given the position of the figure at the top of the gateway, other distinguishing features would not be discernible to viewers in the courtyard.

9 Cesare Ripa, *Iconologia*, ed. Piero Buscaroli, 2 vols (1618), reprinted Turin 1988, II, 294. This popular compendium of allegorical figures circulated widely throughout Europe in the seventeenth and eighteenth centuries. The words on the scroll Reynolds's figure holds are: 'THEORY is the knowledge of what is truly NATURE'.

10 'in atto di scendere dalla sommità d'una scala'; Ripa, *Iconologia*, II, 295.

11 Joseph Baretti's *A Guide through the Royal Academy*, London 1781, published on the occasion of the Academy's relocation to Somerset House, describes Reynolds's *Theory* as 'an elegant and majestic Female' and as a 'noble Specimen of that elegance of taste, strength of imagination, spirit, and brilliancy of colouring, for which he [the artist] has been so often and so justly celebrated (p. 17).

12 John Brewer, '"The Most Polite Age and the Most Vicious": Attitudes towards Culture as a Commodity, 1660–1800', in *The Consumption of Culture 1600–1800: Image, Object, Text*, ed. Ann Bermingham and John Brewer, London 1995, 351–2.

13 Joseph Grego dates the print to *c.*1811 in his *Rowlandson the Caricaturist: a Selection from his Works*, 2 vols, New York 1880, II, 217. This date has been accepted by Hayes, *Rowlandson*, 72, and by M. Dorothy George in the *Catalogue of Prints and Drawings in the British Museum. Division I: Political and Personal Satires*, 11 vols in 12, London 1870–1954, IX, 70–1. The print derives from an undated drawing in the collection of the Yale Center for British Art.

14 Andrew Hemingway, 'Art Exhibitions as Leisure-Class Rituals in Early Nineteenth-Century London', in *Towards a Modern Art World*, ed. Brian Allen, New Haven and London 1995, 95–108.

15 *Morning Post*, 3 May 1785.

16 *World, Fashionable Advertiser*, 8 May 1787.

17 See also Ann Pullan's dissertation on the role of periodicals in the regulation of the female viewer, 'Fashioning a Public for Art: Ideology, Gender and the Fine Arts in the English Periodical *c.*1800–1825', University of Cambridge 1994.

18 *Morning Post and Daily Advertiser*, 15 May 1780.

19 Ibid.

20 Ibid.

21 *Morning Herald*, 9 May 1786 (reprinted in the *Daily Universal Register*, 10 May 1786). For further discussion of this passage, see Gill Perry's chapter in this volume.

22 'Gaudenzio', Letter I to the *St James's Chronicle*, 17–19 April 1777.

23 'Gaudenzio' is undoubtedly an Englishman; women rarely (if ever), and foreigners seldom wrote art criticism in eighteenth-century English newspapers. My argument does not depend upon whether an Italian or English writer produced this review; rather it is concerned with the question of why the persona of a continental writer would be an appropriate one to assume on this occasion.

24 'Gaudenzio', Letter I.

25 'Gaudenzio', Letter II to the *St James's Chronicle*, 24–26 April 1777.

26 For Reynolds's views on fashion and its necessary exclusion from the 'Art of Painting', see *Discourses* (III, 1770), 48–9.

27 For an analysis of writings on this subject by literati in France and England see Sylvana Tomaselli, 'The Enlightenment Debate on Women', *History Workshop Journal*, 20 (Autumn 1984), 101–24.

28 William Alexander, *The History of Women from the Earliest Antiquity, to the Present Time*, 3rd ed, 2 vols, London 1782, I, 151, cited in Tomaselli, 'Enlightenment Debate', 114.

29 For an insightful account of the accomplished woman, see Ann Bermingham, 'The Aesthetics of Ignorance: The Accomplished Woman in the Culture of Connoisseurship', *Oxford Art Journal*, 16, no. 2 (1993), 3–20. Bermingham takes up this topic more fully in her recent book, *Learning to Draw: Studies in the Cultural History of a Polite and Useful Art*, New Haven and London 2000, esp. 183–224.

30 'The Merits of the Fair Sex Considered', *Universal Magazine*, I (October 1765), 546.

31 Andrew Hemingway has analysed much early nineteenth-century art criticism, and observes that whether a critic writes positively or negatively about the exhibition as a space for 'fashionables' is often a political question based upon class interests. See his *Landscape Imagery and Urban Culture in Early Nineteenth-Century Britain*, Cambridge 1992, esp. 109–48.
32 *Morning Chronicle*, 3 May 1802.
33 I discuss the gendering of the critical discourse on painting in Chapter 2 of my book, *The Idea of the English Landscape Painter: Genius as Alibi in the Early Nineteenth Century*, New Haven and London 1997.
34 *Morning Herald*, 6 May 1786.
35 Hannah More, *Strictures on the Modern System of Female Education* (1799), in *The Works of Hannah More*, 7 vols, New York 1836, VI, 201. Many thanks to David Solkin for this reference.
36 Iain Pears, *The Discovery of Painting: The Growth of Interest in the Arts in England 1680–1768*, New Haven and London 1988, 201. I am grateful to Hope Saska for bringing this passage to my attention.
37 Samuel Johnson, *A Dictionary of the English Language* (London 1755); repr., New York 1979, s. v. 'satire' and 'burlesque'.
38 *World, Fashionable Advertiser*, 8 May 1787.
39 Peter Stallybrass and Allon White, *The Politics and Poetics of Transgression*, Ithaca, New York 1986, 22–3.
40 Ronald Paulson, 'The Severed Head: The Impact of French Revolutionary Caricatures on England', in *French Caricature and the French Revolution, 1789–1799*, ed. James Cuno, Chicago 1988, 56. See also Diana Donald's account of the diffusion of aristocratic forms of caricature into prints that circulated widely among the upper and the middling classes in her excellent book, *The Age of Caricature: Satirical Prints in the Age of George III*, New Haven and London 1996, 9–21.
41 Russell was active in the third quarter of the eighteenth century as an artist well known for his pastel portraits and genre scenes. The man depicted may have been John Withers, who was then the senior porter at Somerset House.

Chapter 5

1 *Public Advertiser*, 27 April 1784.
2 For enabling me to write this chapter, I am hugely indebted to the staff at the Paul Mellon Centre for Studies in British Art, and to their remarkable collection of press cuttings for the period 1760–93, assiduously compiled over many years by Claire Lloyd-Jacob.
3 Arthur Aspinall, *Politics and the Press c.1780–1850*, Brighton 1973, 6.
4 *Morning Post, and Daily Advertiser*, 28 April 1784.
5 *Public Advertiser*, 28 April 1784.
6 Ibid.
7 For a recent discussion of the representation of the connoisseur in this period, see John Brewer, *The Pleasures of the Imagination: English Culture in the Eighteenth Century*, London 1997, 252–87.
8 *Morning Post, and Daily Advertiser*, 14 May 1784. For further discussion of de Loutherbourg's critical reception during the 1780s and beyond, see Chapter 16 in this volume, by Anne Puetz.
9 *Public Advertiser*, 27 April 1784.
10 *Morning Chronicle, and London Advertiser*, 27 April 1784.
11 Ibid., 5 May 1784.
12 Charles Taylor, *The Artist's Repository and Drawing Magazine, Exhibiting the Principles of the Polite Arts in their Various Branches*, London 1794, IV (part 2), 31.
13 Anthony Pasquin (pseud. of John Williams), *A Liberal Critique on the Present Exhibition at the Royal Academy. Being an Attempt to Correct the National Taste; to Ascertain the State of the Polite Arts at this Period; and to Rescue Merit from Oppression*, London 1794, 26.
14 *General Advertiser*, 28 April 1785.
15 *Morning Herald, and Daily Advertiser*, 30 April 1784.
16 *St James's Chronicle; or, British Evening-Post*, 27–30 April 1782.
17 See Hannah Barker, *Newspapers, Politics and Public Opinion in Late Eighteenth-Century England*, Oxford 1998.
18 Brewer, *Pleasures of the Imagination*, 3.
19 At the same time, of course, the newspaper exhibition review provided a specifically literary form of representation that must be understood in relation to the discourses of journalism and, more particularly, to the pleasures on offer in the texts that surrounded it on the page. In this respect, one of the pleasures offered by the newspaper exhibition review, as in the case of reports that detailed distant military campaigns, exclusive social events or even barbarous crimes, was surely that of a vicarious involvement with what was being written about, whereby the reader was invited to engage with the Academy exhibition at the level of fantasy and imagination, rather than in an actual social encounter, either remembered or planned. Indeed, the emergence of the newspaper exhibition review must have witnessed the ordinary newspaper reader – particularly those physically distanced from London – regularly enjoying the visual arts on what we might call a virtual basis. Doubtless, many of the readers of eighteenth-century exhibition reviews, just like their counterparts today, would often not have entered the arena these reviews described, and would never have seen even a reproduced version of what was on show. These same readers were already participating in what seems a peculiarly modern mode of artistic appreciation, in which the newspaper review comes to substitute for the event reviewed, and the encounter with the art object is defined by that object's visual absence.
20 Pasquin, *A Liberal Critique*, 24.
21 Ibid., 16.
22 [Robert Baker], *Observations on the Pictures Now on Exhibition at the Royal Academy, Spring Garden, and Mr Christie's*, London 1771, 21.
23 *A Candid Review of the Exhibition (Being the Twelfth) of the Royal Academy*, London 1780, 12.
24 Ibid., 14, 33.
25 The attribution of *The Ear-Wig* to Lowe was first made in William T. Whitley, *Gainsborough*, London 1915, 173.
26 *The Ear-Wig; or An Old Woman's Remarks on the Present Exhibition of Pictures of the Royal Academy*, London 1781, 1.
27 Ibid., 4, 5.
28 Pasquin, *A Liberal Critique*, preface, title page, 8–9, 15.
29 For the French equivalent, see Thomas Crow, *Painters and Public Life in Eighteenth-Century Paris*, New Haven and London 1985, esp. Chapter 7.
30 *The Exhibition; or, There Is None Greater than I, No Not One, by Timothy Tar-Barrel*, London 1793, 30.
31 Ibid.
32 For a discussion of the various machinations that took place behind the scenes of the hanging process, see John Sunderland, Chapter 2 in this volume.
33 *The Bee; or, the Exhibition Exhibited in a New Light*, London 1788.
34 Terry Eagleton, *The Function of Criticism: From the Spectator to Post-Structuralism*, London 1996, 37.
35 Pasquin, *A Liberal Critique*, 29.
36 Taylor, *Artist's Repository*, IV (part 1), 93, 97, 89, 75, 103, 112.
37 Ibid., IV (part 2), 28.
38 *Morning Post, and Daily Advertiser*, 30 May 1794.

Chapter 6

1 Reynolds, *Discourses* (III, 1770), 43.
2 André Félibien, *Seven Conferences on Painting*, trans. Henri Testelin, London 1740, xxvi–xxvii.
3 Reynolds, *Discourses* (IX, 1780), 169–71.
4 See e.g. *Athenaeum*, 11 May 1833, 297 and 10 May 1834, 355; [W. H. Leeds], 'The Somerset House Annual', *Fraser's Magazine*, 12 (July 1835), 49.
5 Sir Joshua Reynolds, letter to Lord Grantham, 20 July 1773, in Jeremy Black and Nicholas Penny, 'Letters from Reynolds to Lord Grantham', *Burlington Magazine*, 124 (1987), 734.
6 BL Add. MSS 41,135, fol. 22 verso.
7 [Mauritius Lowe], *The Ear-Wig: Or An Old Woman's Remarks on the Present Exhibition of Pictures of the Royal Academy*, London 1781, 3.
8 13 June 1783, BL, Egerton MSS 1970, fols. 139–139 verso.

9 *Mirror*, 25 March 1780.
10 BL Add. MSS 47,792, fol. 2. Please note that the spellings have been modernized in this quotation.
11 Ibid., fol. 14.
12 Ibid., fol. 14 verso.
13 Reviews include: *Public Advertiser*, 29 April 1784 and 1 May 1784; *London Chronicle*, 24–27 April 1784; *Whitehall Evening Post*, 27–29 April 1784.
14 This phrase comes from Thomas Crow, *Painters and Public Life in Eighteenth-Century Paris*, New Haven and London 1985, 134–8 and *passim*.
15 This term was coined by James Dallaway, *Anecdotes of the Arts in England*, London 1800, 524.
16 *Literary Gazette, and Journal of the Belles Lettres*, 125 (12 June 1819), 368.
17 Henry Fuseli to Robert Smyth, 17 August 1780, in *The Collected English Letters of Henry Fuseli*, ed. David H. Weinglass, Millwood, London and Nendeln 1982, 20. For a recent study of the confrontation between Fuseli's and Reynolds's versions of *Dido*, see David A. Brenneman, 'Self-Promotion and the Sublime: Fuseli's *Dido at the Funeral Pyre*', *Huntington Library Quarterly*, 62.1 and 2 (2000), 69–87.
18 This was commented upon in the *St James's Chronicle* (28 April–1 May 1781): 'It would be no Disparagement of either of these artists, that I compare their Works, as they have been placed fronting each other in the room'; and by the *Morning Chronicle*, 5 May 1781, which compares Fuseli's picture to 'the same subject on the opposite side of the room'. Other reviews include: *Public Advertiser*, 3 May 1781; *London Courant*, 1 May, 12 May and 28 May 1781; *Morning Herald*, 8 May 1781; also, [Lowe], *The Ear-Wig*, 7, 13.
19 Henry Fuseli to William Roscoe, 22 October 1791, in Weinglass ed., *Letters*, 74.
20 Edward Dayes, *The Works of the Late Edward Dayes*, London 1805, 58–9, 344; [Thomas Bernard], 'The Life of Mr Thomas Procter' in *The Director*, 1 no. 7 (1807), 193–205; J. T. Smith, *Nollekens and his Times*, 2 vols, London 1828, II, 62–6. West's comments are recorded contemporaneously by a student at the Academy, A. J. Oliver, in a letter to Henry Thomson, 10 December 1794, BL Add. MSS 50,066, fol. 14. John Opie's comment occurred in his 'Lecture III. – On Chiaroscuro,' in Ralph Wornum, ed., *Lectures on Painting by the Royal Academicians*, London 1885, 293. Westmacott's lectures were never published in their original form, and the few portions that survive do not deal with Procter (see Mario Busco, *Sir Richard Westmacott: Sculptor*, Cambridge 1994, 28–9). However, his views on Procter were noted in Smith, *Nollekens*, II, 66.
21 Taylor, *Artist's Repository*, IV, part 1 (1785), 110.
22 *European Magazine*, 9 (1786), 311.
23 Unidentified clipping inscribed '1792' in the collection of newspaper cuttings on British art in the Courtauld Institute of Art library.
24 West's unpublished remark is recorded by A. J. Oliver in a letter of 10 December 1794 to Henry Thomson, BL Add. MSS 50,066, fol. 14.
25 [Bernard], 'Procter', 200, 201, 196.
26 [Thomas Bernard], 'Banks's Statue of Achilles', *The Director*, 1 (1807), 65–78. See also Julius Bryant, '"Mourning Achilles": a Missing Sculpture by Thomas Banks', *Burlington Magazine*, 125 (1983), 742–5.
27 *Gentleman's Magazine*, 75, part 2 (September 1805), 794.
28 Farington, *Diary*, VII, 2594 (24 July 1805).

Chapter 7

1 Portraits outnumber other genres in every exhibition and the ratio tends to increase over time. In 1780, 44% of paintings in the Great Room were portraits, in 1799 it had gone down to 36.2% but by 1829 it was back at 46%. These figures are based on Anne Puetz's calculations for the earlier period (provided in correspondence with the author) and on the Select Committee's figures for the later. See fig. 62.
2 Report of the Select Committee appointed to inquire into the best means of extending a knowledge of the Arts, and of the Principles of Design among the People (especially the Manufacturing Population) of the Country; also to inquire into the Constitution, Management and Effects of Institutions connected with the Arts, *Session 1836*, London: House of Commons (1836) IX, part ii Minutes of Evidence, para. 837.
3 Signed by King George III on 10 December 1768. Quoted in Sidney Hutchison, *The History of the Royal Academy 1768–1968*, London 1968, 209.
4 Paul Monod, 'Painters and Party Politics in England 1714–1760', *Eighteenth-Century Studies*, 26, no. 3 (Spring 1993), 369.
5 Report of the Select Committee, *Session 1836*, IX, part ii, para. 1921.
6 For a discussion of the commercial aspects of portrait painting in the period 1780–1840, see David Mannings, 'At the Portrait Painter's: How the Painters of the Eighteenth Century Conducted their Studios and their Sittings', *History Today*, 27 (1977), 279–87; David Mannings, 'Notes on Some Eighteenth-century Portrait Prices in Britain', *British Journal for Eighteenth-Century Studies*, 6 (Autumn 1983), 185–96; Marcia Pointon, *Hanging the Head: Portraiture and Social Formation in Eighteenth-Century England*, New Haven and London 1993, 13–52; Jacob Simon, 'James Northcote's Sitters' Book', *Walpole Society*, 58 (1996), 21–125; Jacob Simon, *The Art of the Picture Frame*, London 1996.
7 Report of the Select Committee, *Session 1836*, IX, part ii. para. 816.
8 George Rennie, ibid., 683, 685.
9 *Morning Chronicle*, 2 May 1781, quoted in Maura Barnett, 'The Contemporary Response to British Art before Ruskin's *Modern Painters*: an Examination of Exhibition Reviews Published in the British Periodical Press and the Journalist Art Critics Who Penned Them, from the Late Eighteenth Century to 1843', Ph.D. thesis, University of Warwick 1993, 158–9.
10 The account of the king's visit in 1787 and Cosway's assertion that he 'had an excellent memory for faces and rarely made a mistake' is contained in Whitley, *Artists and their Friends*, I, 78–80.
11 *La Belle Assemblée*, 1, no. 1 (February–July 1806), 214.
12 *National Register*, 1 (8 May 1808), 302.
13 *Literary Gazette, and Journal of the Belles Lettres*, 485 (6 May 1826), 283.
14 Ibid., 328 (3 May 1823), 284; 432 (30 April 1825), 283.
15 The demands on Wellington's time are recounted in Whitley, *Art in England*, II, 301.
16 *Examiner*, 10 May 1818, 333. Kenneth Garlick, *Sir Thomas Lawrence. A Complete Catalogue of the Oil Paintings*, Oxford 1989, 279–80, cat. no. 805, lists seven separate portraits of the Duke of Wellington by Lawrence.
17 Allen Staley, *Benjamin West: American Painter at the English Court*, Baltimore Museum of Art, Baltimore 1989, 25.
18 A reference to Mrs Nollekens and other butter modellers appears in Amelia Earland, *John Opie and his Circle*, London 1911, 71.
19 Mary Linwood (1756–1845) executed embroidered replicas and displayed them in London, Edinburgh and Dublin. She had permanent exhibition rooms in London from 1798; the quotation is from the Countess of Wilton, cited in the *Dictionary of National Biography*.
20 Appointed 1801; exh. RA 1799–1824.
21 See Richard Altick, *The Shows of London*, Cambridge, Mass. and London 1978, 52–3.
22 *Public Advertiser*, quoted in Whitley, *Artists and their Friends*, I, 392–3.
23 Whitley, *Artists and their Friends*, I, 355–7.
24 Ibid., 357. One suspects that the real figure must have been considerably less than £5,000.
25 The *OED* indicates the origins of 'raree' in a foreign pronunciation of 'rare' and identifies the term with peep-shows, spectacles and itinerant showmen.
26 See for example the detailed account of portraits at Stationers' Hall, *Gentleman's Magazine* 84, no. 2 (November 1814), 417. For an account of the importance of portraits to the history of the Royal College of Surgeons see Ludmilla Jordanova, *Defining Features: Scientific and Medical Portraits 1660–2000*, National Portrait Gallery, London 2000.
27 Known popularly as the Adelaide Gallery, it displayed specimens and models free of charge in the fashionable arcade between the Strand and Adelaide Street; portraits and other works of art hung in a double tier the length of the galleries. See Altick, *Shows*, 377–9.
28 *The Monthly Mirror Reflecting Men and Manners with Strictures on their Epitome, The Stage* (1799–1811).

29 Stephen Gwynn, *Memorials of an Eighteenth-century Painter* (James Northcote), London 1898, 232.
30 Dorinda Evans, *Mather Brown. Early American Artist in England*, Middletown, Conn. 1982, 105.
31 *Annals of the Fine Arts for MDCCCXVI*, I (1817), 91–2; the life-size portrait of Napoleon was exhibited at the Picture Gallery, Frankfurt Place, Plymouth and then, from 23 December 1815 in London. See David Robertson, *Sir Charles Eastlake and the Victorian Art World*, Princeton 1978, 250.
32 Reviewed in preparation in *Gentleman's Magazine*, 84, no. 1 (April 1814), 352.
33 *Catalogue of Painted British Portraits . . . Now Selling . . . [at the Premises of] Horatio Rodd, 17, Air St. Piccadilly*, London 1827, introduction to this the third catalogue.
34 Henry Crabbe Robinson, *Diary, Reminiscences and Correspondence*, ed. T. Sadler, 2 vols, London 1869, II, 163.
35 Ibid., I, 322.
36 *Examiner*, 5 May 1811, 283: 'by Portraits that would not have shamed the pencil of Van Dyck and by Landscapes that even Claude Lorraine could not have seen without delight'.
37 Ibid., 30 June 1816, 412.
38 Ibid., 24 June 1827, 395.
39 Whitley, *Art in England*, I, 201.
40 *European Magazine*, May 1782, 325.
41 *Examiner*, 22 June 1812, 414. Grenville, who was Speaker and subsequently Prime Minister, was portrayed also by Lemuel Francis Abbott, Gainsborough Dupont (*c*.1790) and John Hoppner (*c*.1800). The question of the proper celebration of national heroes had been keenly debated throughout the eighteenth century.
42 Elizabeth Montagu to Matthew Montagu, 1 January 1788, MS MO 3887, Huntington Library, San Marino.
43 *Literary Gazette*, 1010 (28 May 1836), 345, campaigned for Carpenter's election to the RA.
44 See Charlotte Miller, 'Thomas Phillips, RA, FRS, FSA, 1770–1845, Portrait Painter', MA thesis, Courtauld Institute of Art, London 1977.
45 *The Dictionary of Art*, ed. Jane Turner, London and New York 1996, XXIII, 683–4.
46 J. P. Davis exhibited many portraits from 1811 until 1824 when he went to Rome – giving rise to the nickname Pope Davis. He returned in 1826 and continued to exhibit a small number of paintings until his death around 1866. There is no record of his *Lady Wellesley* at Stratfield Saye or in the Heinz Archive at the National Portrait Gallery, London.
47 *Examiner*, 20 May 1827, 311.
48 Whitley, *Art in England*, II, 88.
49 Ibid., 251. In 1833 all but one of the pictures above the line were portraits; see the *Literary Gazette*, 298 (11 May 1833).
50 Quoted in Hutchison, *Royal Academy*, 67.
51 See Chapters 1 and 2 in this volume.
52 *Literary Gazette*, 590 (10 May 1828), 299.
53 Whitley, *Art in England*, II, 100.
54 *A Memoir of Thomas Uwins, R.A. by Mrs Uwins* (1858), 2 vols, East Ardsley 1978, II, 256.
55 *New Monthly Magazine*, 1 June 1820, 716, quoted in Barnett, 'Contemporary Response to British Art', 159, where it is suggested that the author may be William Carey.
56 Regulations prohibited more than one image in a single frame. It was on account of a breach of this regulation that Beechey's work was rejected in 1787; see Whitley, *Artists and their Friends*, II, 84–5.
57 *Annals of the Fine Arts*, 3 (1819), 305.
58 Whitley, *Artists and their Friends*, I, 400–1.
59 See *La Belle Assemblée*, 1 (February–July 1806), 270, on Hoppner's *Sir Arthur Wellesley*: 'As we have not the honour of knowing him, we are incompetent to decide upon [the resemblance] but . . . our principal object is the art . . .'.
60 *Examiner*, 24 (June 1810), 397.
61 *London Chronicle*, 64, no. 4959 (7–9 August 1788), 137.
62 'Painted women' refers to those who use cosmetics.
63 Whitley, *Artists and their Friends*, II, 68–9.
64 William Hazlitt, *The Conversations of James Northcote Esq. R.A.*, London 1949, 12.
65 See, for example, the report in the *Literary Gazette*, 1157 (23 March 1839), 187.
66 Quoted in *Annals of the Fine Arts*, 3 (1819), 264, where the author is cited as 'SHERIDAN', probably indicating Thomas rather than Richard Brinsley Sheridan.
67 *Monthly Magazine*, 1805, quoted in Whitley, *Art in England*, I, 89.
68 Jackson was admired for his still-life painting of boots and his use of boot polish to render his paintings glossy; see *Examiner*, 4 July 1819, 430. On Beechey see *Examiner*, 11 June 1809, 383.
69 *Examiner*, 15 May 1808, 316.
70 Ibid., 11 June 1826, 372.
71 Whitley, *Art in England*, II, 129.
72 Anon., obituary of Thomas Phillips, *Athenaeum*, 913 (26 April 1845), 418.
73 *Examiner*, 24 June 1810, 396.
74 Samuel Lane's *Telford* measures 96½ × 58 in.; Lawrence's *George IV in his Coronation Robes* (probably also RA 1822) measures 114 × 79 in.
75 William Hazlitt, *Morning Chronicle*, 3 May 1814, quoted in Barnett, 'Contemporary Response to British Art', 158–9.

Chapter 8

1 Garrick's *Isabella* was an adaptation of Thomas Southerne's Restoration tragedy *The Fatal Marriage*.
2 John Brewer, *The Pleasures of the Imagination: English Culture in the Eighteenth Century*, London 1997. Chapters 8 and 9 provide a useful discussion of the Georgian theatre.
3 The Academy, however, was indirectly subsidized by the king via the Privy Purse prior to 1780, when increased attendance at its annual exhibitions, now in the expanded quarters of Somerset House, began producing enough revenue to support its activities throughout the year.
4 *Morning Herald*, 26 April 1786. The other two papers were the *Public Advertiser* and the *Morning Post, and Daily Advertiser*.
5 Apart from the larger works listed below, the same critic mentions 'a great number of smaller theatrick pictures'.
6 Interestingly, in 1786 the critic of the *Public Advertiser* (27 April) actually claimed that the exhibition 'is a very respectable one: and what must give pleasure to the lovers of the arts, is, that it abounds less in *portraits* than of former years, and more in works of imagination'. That year one of the most highly praised history paintings exhibited was Benjamin West's *Alexander the Third Rescued by the Intrepidity of Colin Fitzgerald* (Edinburgh, National Gallery of Scotland).
7 Much the same suggestion has been made by William T. Whitley (*Thomas Gainsborough*, London 1915, 179), that the Duke of Dorset had his portrait withdrawn because 'he did not care to appear with such publicity in the company of Baccelli, the Italian dancer whom he had installed as mistress of Knowle'.
8 Accounts vary as to the amount of money paid by the king to Robinson for the letters. See John Ingamells, *Mrs Robinson and her Portraits*, Wallace Collection Monographs, London 1978, 15.
9 An unidentified contemporary source quoted in Elizabeth Einberg, *Gainsborough's Giovanna Baccelli*, Tate Gallery, London 1976, 8.
10 The *Morning Herald*, for example, regularly reviewed her performances and closely followed her career and her personal life. For extracts from reviews from this period see Einberg, *Baccelli*.
11 While the *Westminster Magazine* for May 1782 (cutting in Whitley Papers, British Museum Print Room) identified a 'striking likeness', the *St James's Chronicle* argued that Gainsborough has 'hardly given a likeness' (27–30 April 1782).
12 Whitley, *Gainsborough*, 188. The reviews appeared in the *Morning Herald* and the *Daily Register* of May 1786. One of these extracts is discussed by Dian Kriz in the present volume, p. 60.
13 Kimberly Crouch has discussed some of these issues in 'The Public Life of Actresses: Prostitutes or Ladies?', in *Gender in Eighteenth-Century England: Roles, Representations and Responsibilities*, ed. Helen Barker and Elaine Chalus, London 1997, 58–77.
14 The details of commissions were not always clear and rarely documented, but many of the better known portraits of Jordan which were shown at the Royal Academy were probably

commissioned by the duke. See, for example, Beechey's *Mrs Jordan*, RA 1797 (cat. no. 24 in English Heritage, *Mrs Jordan: The Duchess of Drury Lane*, foreword by Claire Tomalin, London 1995), and Hoppner's *Mrs Jordan as the Comic Muse* (RA 1786; see fig. 84).

15 Taken from a poem of 1783 addressed to Siddons by William Russell:

The nerve of Pleasure on the rock of Pain:
It thrills already in divine excess!

Quoted in Shearer West, 'The Public and Private Roles of Sarah Siddons', in *A Passion for Performance: Sarah Siddons and her Portraitists*, ed. Robyn Asleson, J. Paul Getty Museum, Los Angeles 1999, 18. Most biographies and accounts of Siddons's life report these audience reactions. See especially James Boaden, *Memoirs of Mrs Siddons*, 2 vols, Henry Colburn, London 1827, and *The Reminiscences of Sarah Kemble Siddons 1773–1785*, ed. William Van Lennep, Cambridge, Mass. 1942.

16 Anon., 'Mrs Siddons', *Monthly Mirror*, 6 (September 1798), 166.

17 See West, 'Public and Private Roles', 16.

18 For a discussion of the role of women in the theatre audience see Leo Hughes, *The Drama's Patrons: A Study of the Eighteenth Century London Audience*, Austin, Texas 1971.

19 Like many other eighteenth-century artists, Hamilton was influenced by the theories of Charles LeBrun (1619–90), whose *Lectures on Expression*, first published in 1698, sought to codify the expression of the passions through the representation of facial expressions. Along with the poses of classical sculpture, this was an important source for painters seeking to represent human emotions.

20 The literature on the iconography of this work is exhaustive. Some useful texts include: Robert R. Wark, *Mrs Siddons as the Tragic Muse*, Pasadena, California 1965; *Reynolds*, ed. Nicholas Penny, Royal Academy of Arts, London 1986, cat. no. 151; Martin Postle, *Sir Joshua Reynolds: The Subject Pictures*, Cambridge 1995; Heather McPherson, 'Picturing Tragedy: *Mrs Siddons as the Tragic Muse* Revisited', *Eighteenth-Century Studies*, 33, no. 3 (Spring 2000), 401–30.

21 This term was used by the reviewer of the *Morning Post, and Daily Advertiser*, 5 May 1784, who argued that the painting 'proceeded from the most poetic mind'.

22 Boaden, *Memoirs of Mrs Siddons*, I, 60.

23 William Roberts, *Sir William Beechey RA*, London 1907, 45.

24 The confusion which surrounds the provenance is documented in Penny, *Reynolds*, 324, and Whitley, *Artists and their Friends*, II, 3–13.

25 Robyn Asleson, '"She was Tragedy Personified": Crafting the Siddons Legend in Art and Life', in Asleson, *Passion for Performance*, 77.

26 Reynolds, *Discourses* (XIII, 1786), 238.

27 *An Essay on the Pre-Eminence of Comic Genius: with Observations on Several Characters Mrs Jordan Has Appeared In*, London 1786, 2–3.

28 *Morning Chronicle*, 5 May 1786. Significantly, all the reviews I have located of Brown's picture concentrate on Anne Brunton, to the exclusion of Joseph Holman.

29 The critic of the *Daily Universal Register* described both the Hoppner and the Beach as 'masterly in their kinds', but I have found relatively little detailed discussion of the Beach, and even less of the Brown, in the newspaper reviews.

30 This interpretation is suggested in Claire Tomalin, *Mrs Jordan's Profession: The Story of a Great Actress and a Future King*, London 1995, 70.

31 Denise Sechelski has discussed the importance of the physical body of the actor in the transmission of meaning, 'Garrick's Body and the Labour of Art in Eighteenth-Century Theater', *Eighteenth-Century Studies*, 29, no. 4 (1996), 369–89.

32 Preface to 'Clearly Delineating Our Present Theatrical Performers, by a Feminine Reflection', *Green-Room Mirror*, London 1786.

33 *Annals of the Fine Arts*, 3 (1818), quoted in Andrew Hemingway, *Landscape Imagery amd Urban Culture in Early Nineteenth-century Britain*, Cambridge 1992, 5.

34 Hoppner's *Mrs Jordan as Viola in Twelfth Night* (The Iveagh Bequest, Kenwood) was probably exhibited in the RA of 1796 under the title Portrait of a Lady (no. 81). See English Heritage, *Mrs Jordan*, no. 8.

35 Shearer West has argued that Lawrence's portraits of the actor John Philip Kemble from the 1790s and early 1800s represent the climax of a tendency to use the theatrical portrait as a means of fusing portraiture and history painting. See 'Thomas Lawrence's "Half History" Portraits and the Politics of Theatre', *Art History*, 14, no. 2 (1991), 225–49.

Chapter 9

1 *London Literary Gazette, and Journal of Belles Letters*, 68 (9 May 1818), 299. I am very grateful to Anne Puetz and David Solkin for their assistance in researching the backgrounds of the paintings I discuss, and for helping me to gather reviews of them.

2 Ibid.

3 Ibid.

4 A number of art historians have made this claim, most recently Lionel Lambourne in his *Victorian Painting*, London 1999, 150–67.

5 *Champion*, 8 May 1810.

6 On the subject of the *Champion's* attacks and newspaper reports on the exhibition of landscape at Somerset House see Andrew Hemingway's *Landscape Imagery and Urban Culture in Early Nineteenth-century Britain*, Cambridge 1992, 5–6 and *passim*.

7 In order to accommodate the increased number of entries extra rooms in Somerset House were pressed into service, such as the Ante-room at the entrance of the Great Room, the Library, and eventually, various painting studios.

8 Farington, *Diary*, V, 1757 (13 March 1802).

9 Edward John Nygren, 'The Art of James Ward, R.A.', Ph.D. dissertation, Yale University, 1976, 111.

10 Ibid., 127. *New Monthly Magazine & Universal Register*, 1 July 1815, 551.

11 Whitley, *Artists and their Friends*, II, 106.

12 Ralph Hyde, *Panoramania! The Art and Entertainment of the 'All-Embracing' View*, introduction by Scott Wilcox, Barbican Art Gallery, London 1988, 20–1. See also Scott Wilcox's 'The Panorama and Related Exhibitions in London', M. Litt. dissertation, University of Edinburgh, 1976.

13 Bernard Comment, *The Panorama*, London 1999, 51.

14 *John Constable's Correspondence*, II, ed. R. B. Beckett, Ipswich 1964, 34.

15 Wilcox in Hyde, *Panoramania*, 28.

16 Ibid.

17 Ibid., 46. Panoramas by military officers exhibited by Baker and his successor Burford in Leicester Square include: *Boothia* by Capt. John Ross; *Polar Regions* by Lt Browne; *Lima* by Lt W. Smyth RN; *Benares* and *Delhi* by Capt. Robert Smith RE; *Hong Kong* by Lt F. J. White RE; and *Sabastopol* by Capt. Verschoyle (Hyde, *Panoramania*, 60).

18 On the technical aspects of panoramas see Martin Kemp, *The Science of Art: Optical Themes in Western Art from Brunelleschi to Seurat*, New Haven and London 1990, 212–15.

19 Ann Bermingham, *Learning to Draw: Studies in the Cultural History of a Polite and Useful Art*, New Haven and London 2000, 78–91.

20 For the classic formulation of this argument see John Barrell, 'The Public Prospect and the Private View: The Politics of Taste in Eighteenth-Century Britain', in *The Birth of Pandora and the Division of Knowledge*, London 1992, 41–62. The panorama has also been associated with a new bourgeois way of seeing, with a commanding and extensive viewpoint that was synonymous with a new literal and metaphorical desire to 'see things from a new angle'. This new way of seeing resulted in the democratization of perspective from the single point system used in Baroque illusionism to the multiple points used in the panorama. See Stephen Oettermann, *The Panorama: History of a Mass Medium*, trans. Deborah Lucas Schneider, New York 1997, 20–32.

21 Helmut and Alison Gernsheim, *L. J. M. Daguerre: The History of the Diorama and the Daguerreotype*, London 1956, 17.

22 Hyde, *Panoramania*, 119.

23 On the diorama viewer's passivity see Walter Benjamin, *Charles Baudelaire: Lyric Poet in the Era of High Capitalism*, trans. Harry Zohn and Quintin, London 1973, 69.

24 On de Loutherbourg's staging see Sybil Rosenfeld, *Georgian Scene Painters and Scene Painting*, Cambridge 1981, 19–20, 33–4, 43–4, 61–3, 55, 58–9.

25 Richard D. Altick, *The Shows of London*, Cambridge, Mass. and London 1978, 120. The first programme contained the following five scenes:

1) Aurora; or, the Effects of the Dawn, with a View of London from Greenwich Hill.
2) Noon; the Port of Tangier in Africa, with the distant View of the Rock of Gibraltar and Europa Point.
3) Sunset, a View in Naples.
4) Moonlight, a View in the Mediterranean, the Rising of the Moon contrasted with the Effect of Fire.
5) The Conclusive Scene, a Storm at Sea, and Shipwreck.

In January 1782 a new programme was substituted which included the following scenes:

1) The Sun rising in a Fog, and Italian Seaport.
2) The Cataract of Niagara, in North America.
3) The Setting of the Sun, after a Rainy Day, with a View of the Castle, Town and Cliffs of Dover.
4) The Rising of the Moon, with a Water Spout, exhibiting the Effect of three different Lights, with a View of a Rocky Shore on the Coast of Japan.
5) Satan arraying his Troops on the Banks of the Fiery Lake, with the Raising of Pandemonium, from Milton.

26 Oettermann, *The Panorama*, 71.

27 From the *Journal des Luxus und der Moden* of 1823, quoted ibid., 71.

28 Gainsborough's peep-box and glass slides are today in the Victoria & Albert Museum.

29 Anon. press cutting of 1801 from the Royal Academy of Arts volumes of 'Royal Academy Critiques', vol. II (of III), 1794–1818.

30 Gernsheims, *Daguerre*, 20. The Gernsheims confuse Daguerre's assistant, the painter Charles Arrowsmith (b. 1798) with Charles's older brother John (1790–1873).

31 Quoted in Hyde, *Panoramania*, 34.

32 On this subject see Morton Paley, *The Apocalyptic Sublime*, New Haven and London 1986.

33 *London Weekly Review*, 2 (14 May 1828), 300; *Athenaeum*, 30 (21 May 1828), 473.

34 *Morning Herald*, 5 May 1829, *Literary Gazette*, 9 May 1829, and the *Athenaeum*, 13 May 1829. All quoted in Martin Butlin and Evelyn Joll, *The Paintings of J. M. W. Turner*, 2 vols, New Haven and London 1984, I, 185.

35 On the personal conflicts surrounding the hanging of *Hannibal Crossing the Alps*, see Chapter 2 in this volume, pp. 36–7.

36 C. R. Leslie, Constable's friend and first biographer, reports that Sir George Beaumont believed that autumnal tints were necessary in some part of the landscape. When he asked Constable whether he found it difficult determining where to put a 'brown tree' in the landscape he was painting, the artist replied 'Not in the least, I never put such a thing into a picture'. C. R. Leslie, *Memoirs of the Life of John Constable*, Ithaca, New York 1980, 114.

37 *Mirror of Fashion*, 2 May 1808, n.p.

38 *Monthly Retrospect of the Fine Arts*, 1 June 1807, 484.

39 *Champion*, 8 May 1810, n.p.

Chapter 10

I should like to thank Matthew Hargraves for assistance rendered during the preparation of this chapter.

1 Royal Academy General Assembly Minutes, IV, 99–101 (1809), quoted in Sydney C. Hutchison, *The History of the Royal Academy 1768–1968*, London 1968, 87.

2 George Dunlop Leslie, *The Inner Life of the Royal Academy with an Account of its Schools and Exhibitions Principally in the Reign of Queen Victoria*, London 1914, 138, 142.

3 John Gage, *J. M. W. Turner. 'A Wonderful Range of Mind'*, New Haven and London 1987, 89, citing Farington, *Diary*, XI, 3915–18 (22–25 April 1811); Martin Butlin and Evelyn Joll, *The Paintings of J. M. W. Turner* revised edn, 2 vols, New Haven and London 1984, I, 95, entry to no.131, citing the *Sun*, 16 May 1815. See also Andrew Wilton, *Turner in his Time*, London 1987, 178–86.

4 E. V. Rippingille, quoted in Whitley, *Art in England*, II, 293.

5 Rippingille, quoted in Gage, *Turner*, 92.

6 Leslie, *Royal Academy*, 146.

7 Richard and Samuel Redgrave, *A Century of British Painters* (1866, 2nd edn 1890), Oxford 1981, 264–5; also Anthony Bailey, *Standing in the Sun. A Life of J. M. W. Turner*, London 1997, 178–86.

8 Edwin Landseer, quoted in Bailey, *Standing in the Sun*, 296.

9 Frederick Goodall, R.A., quoted in Butlin and Joll, *Turner*, I, 148.

10 Redgraves, *Century*, 263.

11 Leslie, *Royal Academy*, 145–6.

12 For Stanfield, see Peter van der Merwe and Roger Took, *The Spectacular Career of Clarkson Stanfield 1793–1867 Seaman, Scene Painter, Royal Academician*, Tyne and Wear Council Museums, Gateshead 1979, 111–12, entry to no.174. For Turner, see Butlin and Joll, *Turner*, 200–1, entry to no.349.

13 Quoted in Butlin and Joll, *Turner*, 200–1, entry to no.349.

14 *Spectator*, 11 May 1833; *Arnold's Magazine*, 3 (1833–34); *Athenaeum*, 2 (May 1833), quoted ibid.

15 George Jones, *Memoir*, ed. John Gage in *Collected Correspondence of J. M. W. Turner. With an Early Diary and a Memoir by George Jones*, Oxford 1980, 5.

16 For Turner and Stanfield, see Wilton, *Turner*, 149.

17 For Turner's obliquity, see Redgraves, *Dictionary*; Henry Fuseli, *Lectures on Painting*, London 1820, 185.

18 Charles Robert Leslie *Autobiographical Recollections*, 2 vols, London 1860, I, 202–3.

19 The most likely Turner would have been *Caligula's Palace and Bridge* (Clore Gallery, Tate Britain) which, measuring 54 × 97 in *may* have been in a space large enough to accommodate the *Salisbury* at 59¾ × 74¾ in. This is the opinion, too, of Helen Guiterman, '"The Great Painter": Roberts on Turner', *Turner Studies. His Art and Epoch 1775–1851*, 9, no. 1 (Summer 1989), 9, n. 25.

20 Guiterman, 'Roberts on Turner', 4.

21 *John Constable's Correspondence*, IV ed. R. B. Beckett (*JCC* IV), Ipswich 1966, 368; Constable to David Lucas, 28 February 1832.

22 *John Constable's Correspondence*, VI, ed. R. B. Beckett, (*JCC* VI), Ipswich 1968, 78; Constable to John Fisher, 23 October 1821.

23 *JCC* IV, 370; Constable to David Lucas, 3 March 1832.

24 Ibid.

25 *John Constable's Correspondence*, III, ed. R. B. Beckett (*JCC* III), Ipswich 1965, 67–8, Constable to C. R. Leslie, 24 April 1832. Constable's comment about 'between the doors and the doors' presumably means between the doorway into the Great Room and that opening on to the landing.

26 For these see Judy Crosby Ivy, *Constable and the Critics 1802–1837*, Woodbridge 1991, 158–64.

27 Reynolds, *Discourses* (VIII, 1779), 159.

28 For Canaletto see Michael Liversidge and Jane Farington eds, *Canaletto and England*, Birmingham Museums and Art Gallery 1993, and, for Westminster Bridge, Mark Hallett 'Framing the Modern City: Canaletto's Images of London', ibid., 46–64.

29 *JCC* III, 64; Constable to C. R. Leslie, 4 March 1832.

30 K. Dian Kriz, *The Idea of the English Landscape Painter: Genius as Alibi in the Early Nineteenth Century*, New Haven and London 1997, 44–5.

31 *Monthly British Magazine*, 1 (1830), 475–6.

32 For *Staffa*, see Butlin and Joll, *Turner*, 198–9, entry to no.347.

33 Quoted ibid., 192, entry to no.340.

34 *Library of the Fine Arts*, June 1830, quoted ibid.

35 Ibid., 141–3, entry to no.232.

36 See *Examiner*, 1 July 1827, 104; *New Monthly Magazine*, 3 (September 1827), 375; *Gentleman's Magazine*, 99, part 1 (May 1829), 442; *London Magazine*, 3, 3rd ser. (June 1829), 604, 606–7. Quoted in Ivy, *Constable and the Critics*, 123–4, 133–5.

37 *Metropolitan*, 1 (1831), 68, 70, 114.

38 *Athenaeum*, 240 (2 June 1832), 356.

39 *New Monthly Magazine and Literary Journal*, 34 (1 June 1832), 255.
40 *The Times*, 8 May 1832, in Ivy, *Constable and the Critics*, 159.
41 *Literary Gazette, and Journal of the Belles Lettres, Arts, Sciences, &c.*, 800 (19 May 1832), 314.
42 *Spectator*, 12 May 1832, 450, quoted in Ivy, *Constable and the Critics*, 159. See also van der Merwe and Took, *Stanfield*, 109–10, entry to no.171.
43 *London Magazine*, 1 (May 1820), 695.
44 *Blackwood's Edinburgh Magazine*, 29 (January–June 1831), 214.

Chapter 11

1 For a draft of this letter, see 'The Papers of the Society of Artists of Great Britain', *Walpole Society*, 6 (1917–18), 118–19.
2 Hence the Academy's annual expenditure on Bow Street constables; see my introduction, above, p. 8.
3 Reynolds, *Discourses* (v, 1772), 89.
4 Ibid. (III, 1770), 51.
5 We know that this is where Bigg's larger exhibits were shown in 1792, thanks to the information provided by Thomas Sandby's drawings of the installation of that year. See fig. 25.
6 Unidentified newspaper (1795), in Victoria & Albert Museum Press Cuttings, III, fol. 719. In fact the *Truants Discovered* was engraved by William Ward in 1796.
7 Unidentified newspaper (1805), in Royal Academy of Arts Library, 'Royal Academy Critiques &c', II, fol. 61.
8 By far the best study of this important episode in the history of English taste can be found in Harry Mount's unpublished doctoral thesis, 'The Reception of Dutch Genre Painting in England, 1695–1829', Cambridge University 1991, 2 vols, II, part II. Here I wish to acknowledge numerous debts to Mount's important work.
9 Anon. [Richard Payne Knight], 'The Works of James Barry', *Edinburgh Review*, 16 (August 1810), 299.
10 See John Brewer, *The Pleasures of the Imagination: English Culture in the Eighteenth Century*, London 1997, 252–81.
11 *Memoirs and Recollections of Abraham Raimbach, Esq. Engraver . . . including a Memoir of Sir David Wilkie, R.A.*, ed. M. T. S. Raimbach, London 1843, 155.
12 Allan Cunningham, *The Life of Sir David Wilkie*, 3 vols, London 1843, I, 103.
13 Farington, *Diary*, VII, 2716 (12 April 1806).
14 Cunningham, *Wilkie*, I, 95–6.
15 Ibid., I, 115.
16 *Morning Herald*, 6 May 1806.
17 *Monthly Magazine*, 21 (June 1806), 451.
18 *Public Ledger*, 8 May 1806; also *Star*, 8 May 1806.
19 *Sun*, 3 May 1806; reprinted in *British Mercury*, 7 May 1806.
20 *Public Ledger*, 8 May 1806; also *Star*, 8 May 1806.
21 *Morning Post*, 6 May 1806.
22 *La Belle Assemblée*, 1 (May 1806), 216. The same assessment appeared in *Bell's Weekly Messenger*, 25 May 1806, 167, and was later reprinted with variations in the *Cabinet*, 4 (August 1808), 73.
23 Jon P. Klancher, *The Making of English Reading Audiences, 1790–1832*, Madison, Wisconsin 1987, 62, 68.
24 See Cunningham, *Wilkie*, I, 115–16; also Farington, *Diary*, VII, 2716 (12 April 1806), and VIII, 3009 (8 April 1807).
25 See, for example, *Le Beau Monde*, 1 (June 1807), 452; *Daily Advertiser, Oracle and True Briton*, 22 May 1807; *Bell's Weekly Messenger*, 24 May 1807, 164; and *Morning Post*, 12 May 1807.
26 Cunningham, *Wilkie*, I, 144. According to the *Cabinet*, London 1807, 245, the *Blind Fiddler* was hung between Richard Westall's *Flora* and Turner's *Blacksmith's Shop*; presumably the Westall is the work of 'overpowering brightness' which Cunningham had in mind.
27 *London Chronicle*, 7 May 1807, 434; *General Evening Post*, 5–7 May 1807.
28 *News*, 8 May 1808, 567.
29 Lindsay Errington, *Tribute to Wilkie*, National Gallery of Scotland, Edinburgh 1985, 31.
30 'R. H.' [Robert Hunt], *Examiner*, 21 May 1809, 332.
31 *Repository of Arts*, n.s. 1 (June 1816), 355.
32 'James Weathercock' [pseudonym of Thomas Wainewright], *London Magazine*, 1 (1820), 701.
33 *The Exhibition of the Royal Academy M.DCCCXXII. The Fifty-Fourth*, London 1822, no. 126, 10.
34 *Literary Gazette, and Journal of the Belles Lettres*, 278 (18 May 1822), 314.
35 *European Magazine*, 81 (May 1822), 466.
36 *Literary Speculum*, 2 (1822), 60.
37 *Literary Gazette*, 278 (18 May 1822), 314.
38 I am grateful to Tom Gretton and Charles Ford for pointing this out to me.

Chapter 12

1 *Literary Gazette, and Journal of the Belles Lettres*, 277 (11 May 1822), 297.
2 For the background to this aspect of government patronage see Alison Yarrington, *The Commemoration of the Hero 1800–64: Monuments to the British Victors of the Napoleonic Wars*, New York and London 1988. For the sculptural celebration of Wellington's victories, see Yarrington, *His Achilles Heel? Wellington and Public Art*, The Tenth Wellington Lecture, University of Southampton, Southampton, 1999.
3 *The Exhibition of the Royal Academy, MDCCLXIX. The First*, London 1769. Of course Bacon is listed first because his name came first alphabetically of all the exhibitors; it was only in 1780, with the move to Somerset House, that works came to be catalogued in order of position on the walls or in the rooms. The medallion of the king also signalled loyalty to the Crown.
4 David Irwin, *John Flaxman 1755–1826, Sculptor, Illustrator, Designer*, London 1979, 10.
5 *Abstract of the Constitution and the Laws of the Royal Academy of Arts in London, Established December 10, 1768*, London 1815, 42: 'no . . . models in coloured wax, or any such performance, nor any Work of Art which has been publicly exhibited elsewhere for emolument, shall be admitted into the Exhibition of the Royal Academy'.
6 Alison Yarrington, Ilene D. Lieberman, Alex Potts and Malcolm Baker, 'An Edition of the Ledger of Sir Francis Chantrey, R. A., at the Royal Academy, 1809–41', *Walpole Society*, 56 (1991–92), 192.
7 Ibid., 214–15.
8 In 1812 there were 52 sculptures out of a total display of 940 items; in 1817, 70 out of 1,077, and in 1820, 68 out of 1,072.
9 *Literary Gazette, and Journal of the Belles Lettres*, 390 (10 July 1824), 442. See also *New Monthly Magazine*, 9 (1 June 1818), 442.
10 On Chantrey's manipulation of his 'Englishness', see Alex Potts, 'Chantrey as the National Sculptor of Early Nineteenth-Century England', *Oxford Art Journal*, 4 (November 1981), 17–27, and his catalogue *Sir Francis Chantrey, 1781–1841: Sculptor of the Great*, National Portrait Gallery, London 1981.
11 *Literary Gazette, and Journal of the Belles Lettres*, 388 (26 June 1824), 409: 'The deities, male and female, may be discarded from our monuments; but they must be found in the studio, and forever under the eye of the sculptor, or his works will degenerate into the mere imitation of texture or the form of a fold'.
12 *Blackwood's Edinburgh Magazine*, 14 (1823), 10.
13 See, for example, *La Belle Assemblée*, 3rd ser., 3 (1826), 275–6.
14 Royal Academy, General Assembly Minutes, III, 3 (10 February 1810).
15 John Flaxman, *Lectures on Sculpture*, 2nd edn, London 1838, 17. This first lecture was originally delivered in 1812.
16 St Mary's, Fort St George, Madras. Webbe was Chief Secretary in Madras.
17 *Examiner*, 29 April 1810, 268.
18 In 1810, thirty-five out of the fifty sculptures were busts.
19 See for example *National Register*, 3 (29 April 1810), 271.
20 Royal Academy of Arts, Council Minutes, IV, 287 (18 April 1811). The books recording the meetings of the Committee of Arrangement commence in 1814, and show that generally this committee began its activities in early April. But the sculpture was not arranged until the last few days before the exhibition opened.

21 *Examiner*, 11 August 1811, 518.
22 *National Register*, 6 (13 June 1813), 57: 'In the Model Academy we have remarked and applauded a much better arrangement and disposition of the exhibited pieces'.
23 This annotation appears beside no. 893 in R. E. W. James's copy of the 1813 RA catalogue, according to a typewritten transcript by Hamish Miles.
24 Thirty-five portrait busts out of fifty-two exhibited sculptures in total.
25 Hopper also exhibited a Bacchus (no. 903).
26 The monument was to a J. Pares of Leicester and remains untraced.
27 *National Register*, 6 (13 June 1813), 58.
28 *Examiner*, 23 June 1816, 398.
29 Ibid., 21 May 1815, 328. This approach was occasionally adopted by others; the most extreme example, with sculpture being considered first and at some length, is found in *European Magazine*, 85 (May 1824), 456–60.
30 *National Register*, 6 (2 May 1813), 254.
31 'Les sculptures, placées dans une petite salle au rez-de-chaussée, étaient peu nombreuses, l'exécution de la plupart était fort médiocre', according to A. J. B. Defauconpret, *Six mois à Londres en 1816*, Paris 1817, 125. Here Flaxman, Nollekens and Bacon are singled out for notice at an exhibition that is described as being composed nearly entirely of busts and funerary monuments.
32 *European Magazine*, 81 (July 1822), 63.
33 Ibid.
34 *Literary Gazette, and Journal of the Belles Lettres*, 492 (24 June 1826), 395.
35 Richard Sievier's *Psyche* at the 1824 exhibition was seen to have been placed by the Committee of Arrangement to hide staining in the marble but this hid the finest part of the statue from public view, see *European Magazine*, 85 (May 1824), 460.
36 *Literary Gazette, and Journal of the Belles Lettres*, 283 (22 June 1822), 393.
37 *London Magazine*, 2, n.s. (May–August 1825), 266.
38 Ebeneezer Rhodes, 'Memoir of Chantrey, the Sculptor', in *Peak Scenery or Excursions in Derbyshire: Made Chiefly for the Purpose of Picturesque Observation*, London 1824, 281.
39 Royal Academy Council Minutes, VI, 130 (10 April 1820).
40 Two sources confirm this mode of display: Rhodes, 'Chantrey', and *Literary Gazette, and Journal of the Belles Letters*, 284 (29 June 1822), 409.
41 *Literary Gazette, and Journal of the Belles Lettres*, 284 (29 June 1822), 409.
42 Ibid.
43 At the 1818 exhibition Wyatt's drawing of the elevation of the Temple of the Graces (no. 907) showed the complete setting including the Eagle by Garrard and the two statues of the Duke of Bedford's daughters by Thorvaldsen and Chantrey to either side. The sculpture section of the same exhibition featured Westmacott's model of the high relief of cupids for the external face of the Temple (no. 1111) and Chantrey's statue of Louisa Russell (no. 1116).
44 I argued this excluded and exclusivity of viewing in 1995, in a paper delivered at a symposium on Canova's *Three Graces*, held at the Victoria & Albert Museum. Members of the public were allowed access to the Abbey on Mondays 'under certain regulations'; see *Annals of the Fine Arts*, 5 no. xvii, (1820), p. 415.
45 Thomas Frognall Dibdin, *A Bibliographical Antiquarian and Picturesque Tour in France and Germany*, 2nd edn, 3 vols, London 1829, II, 309.
46 Ibid., 312–16.
47 See Andreas Blühm, *The Colour of Sculpture 1840–1910*, Van Gogh Museum, Amsterdam and Henry Moore Institute, Leeds 1996, 122, illus. 109. This shows the structure, which has a further iron barrier around its outer perimeter to keep the public at bay.
48 'Arrangement of the Elgin Marbles at the British Museum', *Examiner*, 23 June 1816, 399.
49 Ibid.
50 See Marion Spielmann, *British Sculpture and Sculptors of Today*, London 1901, 132.
51 Katherine Eustace, '"Questa Scabrosa Missione": Canova in Paris and London', in *Canova Ideal Heads*, Ashmolean Museum, Oxford 1997, 9–38.
52 Royal Academy Committees of Arrangement Attendance books (unpaginated), 1817. The 1817 Committee consisted of the President, Benjamin West, Owen, Fuseli, Northcote, Beechey, Mulready, Chalon, Phillips and Shee. Westmacott attended on his own on 29 and 30 April and 2 May.
53 Both Flaxman and Westmacott exhibited works under this title taken from church monuments. Flaxman's work shown at the 1809 RA exhibition under this title was considered by the *Gentleman's Magazine* (79, pt I (1809), 473) to render the exhibition room 'attractive' by its presence. This work may have been the plaster model or a variant of the figure from the central panel monument to the Baring Family, St Mary, Micheldever, Hampshire, completed in 1806.
54 Canova's and Chantrey's involvement in the exhibition and their professional connections are discussed in Alison Yarrington, 'Anglo-Italian Attitudes: Chantrey and Canova', in *The Lustrous Trade*, ed. Cinzia Maria Sicca and Alison Yarrington, London and New York 2000, 132–55.
55 See *Literary Gazette, and Journal of the Belles Lettres*, 120 (8 May 1819), 295.
56 Royal Academy, Committees of Arrangement Books, 1819. Seventeen meetings were held between 8 and 28 April.
57 The monument, completed in 1819, is in St Tegai's, Llandegai, Gwynned.
58 *Examiner*, 6 July 1823, 443.
59 Ibid.
60 Ibid.

Chapter 13

1 The problem of identifying which works shown at the Academy employed watercolours intensified with the move to Somerset House, when the catalogues ceased to specify the medium.
2 Architectural perspectives employed watercolour, but they functioned within a different professional context, and they were hung together as a distinct group in the exhibition space and from 1811 were shown in a separate room.
3 See, for instance, *Review of Publications of Art*, 2 (1808), 173.
4 Royal Academy General Assembly Minutes, I, 74 (21 December 1772).
5 For instance, John Downman's parallel practice as a painter allowed him into the Academy as an Associate in 1795.
6 John Russell deposited a pastel as his diploma piece, and in 1802 Benjamin West adjudicated on the candidature of John Raphael Smith by declaring that 'Crayon painting, was painting' (Farington, *Diary*, V, 1927 (1 November 1802)). Ozias Humphrey was allowed to deposit a miniature, *A Bramin in India Telling the Fortune of Some English Ladies* (RA 1788), as his diploma picture.
7 *St James's Chronicle*, 8–10 May 1794; ibid., 21–23 May 1795.
8 *Morning Chronicle*, 30 May 1792; ibid., 21 May 1793.
9 *London Packet*, 10–13 June 1799; *St James's Chronicle*, 20–23 May 1799.
10 Timothy Wilcox, *Francis Towne*, Tate Gallery, London 1997, 163.
11 Felicity Owen and David Blayney Brown, *Collector of Genius. A Life of Sir George Beaumont*, London 1988, 151.
12 Letter to William Gilpin, Bodleian Library, Oxford, MS Eng. misc., C.389, fol. 40–1.
13 Farington, *Diary*, XI, 3953 (21 June 1811).
14 Ibid., VII, 2686 (27 February 1806).
15 William Marshall Craig, *A Course of Lectures on Drawing, Painting, and Engraving, Considered as Branches of Elegant Education*, London 1821, 121.
16 *Le Beau Monde*, I (May 1809), 117–18. The reference to Edridge suggests that the author had inside knowledge of the Academy, since Farington records that the portraitist had been at the centre of a convoluted debate about the status of painting and drawing; see Farington, *Diary*, IX, 3292 and 3310 (9 June and 6 July 1808).
17 Farington, *Diary*, IX, 3299 (18 June 1808).

18 Craig bemoaned the injustice of what he saw as the 'general custom to call every thing drawing that is performed on paper' whilst applying 'the word painting to the very same process when exercised on ivory' (Craig, *Lectures*, 16).
19 Walter Henry Watts, *The Remonstrancer Remonstrated With*, London 1806, 26–7.
20 Martin Archer Shee, *Rhymes on Art; or, the Remonstrance of a Painter*, London 1805, 30–1.
21 Of the eleven who attended the founding meeting on 1 July 1807, Henry Pierce Bone, James Green, Huet Villiers, Andrew Robertson, Walter Henry Watts and William Wood were portraitists.
22 Associated Artists in Water-Colours, Letters, Minutes, Etc., National Art Library, Victoria & Albert Museum, London, 1 July 1807.
23 Farington, *Diary*, IX, 3261 (18 April 1808).
24 Ibid., X, 3715 (23 August 1810).
25 Royal Academy General Assembly Minutes, IV, 21 (30 November 1810).
26 Royal Academy Council Minutes, I, 326 (12 April 1782); ibid., 358 (9 April 1784).
27 *St James's Chronicle*, 17–20 May 1788. The paper also took up Downman's case (22–24 and 24–27 April 1784).
28 *The Bee; or the Exhibition Examined in a New Light*, London 1788, 7. Reynolds's *Infant Hercules* is now in the Hermitage.
29 Farington, *Diary*, VI, 2484–5 (30 December 1804).
30 *Repository of Arts*, 9 (March 1813), 148–9.
31 See, for instance, *Review of Publications of Art*, 2 (1808), 173.
32 *Gazetteer and New Daily Advertiser*, 4 May 1789; *St James's Chronicle*, 22–24 May 1788.
33 *St James's Chronicle*, 24–27 April 1784.
34 *Literary Panorama*, 2 (1807), 621; *Somerset House Gazette*, 1 (6 December 1823), 130.
35 *Morning Post*, 15 May 1806. The poor treatment of miniatures was often commented on. See, for instance, *The Times*, 26 April 1796 and 3 May 1797, for the consequences of their display successively in the Antique Academy and the Library.
36 *Repository of Arts*, 9 (March 1813), 149.
37 Farington, *Diary*, X, 3638–9 (19 April 1810).
38 *Catalogue of the Exhibition of the Royal Academy*, London 1811, 3.
39 Newspaper Cuttings on the Fine Arts, Courtauld Institute Library, London, I, 297.
40 Farington, *Diary*, XI, 4110 (15 April 1812).
41 Courtauld newspaper cuttings, II, 6.
42 *Literary Gazette, and Journal of the Belles Lettres*, 700 (19 May 1830), 402; ibid., 803 (9 June 1832), 362.
43 This view is supported by the fact that the watercolours that Turner and Constable occasionally exhibited at the RA attracted much less critical attention than the works of contemporary specialists shown at the watercolour societies.
44 See, for instance, Jane Bayard, *Works of Splendor and Imagination: The Exhibition Watercolour, 1770–1870*, Yale Center for British Art, New Haven 1981.
45 *Abstract of the Testament of Institution and Laws of the Royal Academy of Arts in London*, London 1797; Royal Academy Council Minutes, II, 133 (23 March 1791); notice to exhibitors from the 1818 catalogue.
46 *Letters and Papers of Andrew Robertson*, ed. Emily Robertson, London 1895, 151.
47 The conventions were developed in the 1780s by Richard Cosway, and John Downman, Henry Edridge, Alfred Edward Chalon and George Richmond successively developed profitable practices based on distinctive variations on the basic format.
48 Henry Edridge's royal portraits were framed and hung at Frogmore House, for instance.
49 The best discussion of the presentation of watercolours is Pippa Mason, 'The Framing and Display of Watercolours', in *Watercolours from Leeds City Art Gallery*, Leeds City Art Gallery, Leeds 1995.
50 Robertson, *Letters*, 177. The catalogues from the Jupp and Anderdon collections are in the Library of the Royal Academy.
51 The one difference is that a narrow slip was often inserted between the frame and the image, as with the framing of prints. This was Turner's preference; he recommended in 1819 that a 'small flat of matted gold' be placed round one of his works should the owner choose to frame it (Mason, 'Display of Watercolours', 33).

Chapter 14

1 I am indebted to Anne Puetz and Greg Smith for drawing my attention to this and other important references to architecture in exhibition reviews of the period, not least because this has revealed the exceptional character of Philo-Architectus's comments and the fact that, unlike other works in the exhibition, architectural drawings were largely unaffected by either market considerations (they were never offered for sale) or any sustained critical reception.
2 Newton's *Sketch of a Design for an Academy of Arts & Sciences: Entrance Elevation* at the Royal Institute of British Architects (RIBA) may be the exhibited drawing; see RIBA, *Catalogue of the Drawings Collection: L–N*, ed. Jill Lever, London 1973, 138, no.[29].7.
3 RA 1836 (no.93): *Comparative Characteristics of Thirteen Selected Styles of Architecture . . .* (Soane Museum); RA 1837 (no.1030): *Comparative Architecture Continued, vide Catalogue of the Exhibition, 1836, No.936, – an Emblematic Sketch* (Soane Museum); RA 1838 (no.1165): *Architecture; its Natural Model – vide Catalogue of Royal Academy Exhibition, 1836, for a Textile* [sic] *Notice* (Soane Museum).
4 On Yenn's drawings, the most important surviving group of which is held at the Royal Academy of Arts, London, see John Harris, *John Yenn, Draughtsman Extraordinary*, exh. cat., RIBA Heinz Gallery, London 1973; and Nicholas Savage, *John Yenn: an 18th-century Pioneer of the Architectural Exhibition Drawing*, exh. cat., Royal Academy of Arts Library, London 1997.
5 *Morning Post, and Daily Advertiser*, 8 May 1776.
6 RA 1775 (no.349): *A Garden Seat to be Executed for a Gentleman in Surrey* (Royal Academy); (no.350): *The Principal Front of a Greenhouse, for a Person of Distinction* (Royal Academy); (no.351): *A Design for a Bridge, in the Manner of the Palladian Bridge in the E[arl] of Pembrokes Garden at Wilton* (Royal Academy).
7 Philo-Architectus's description leaves no doubt that Chambers was exhibiting his celebrated perspective of an unexecuted proposal for a mausoleum for Frederick, Prince of Wales (Soane Museum, 17/7 no.716), designed in Rome in 1751 (see John Harris, *Sir William Chambers, Knight of the Polar Star*, London 1970, 213). The related plan, which was evidently exhibited with it, is in the V&A (see *Catalogues of Architectural Drawings in the Victoria and Albert Museum: Sir William Chambers*, ed. Michael Snodin, London 1996, no.627).
8 Carl Paul Barbier, *William Gilpin: his Drawings, Teaching, and the Theory of the Picturesque*, Oxford 1963, 59.
9 Robert and James Adam, *The Works in Architecture*, 2 vols, London 1773–78, I, pt. 1, p.[3], note A.
10 Out of only 46 architectural designs in the 1780 exhibition, five are described as plans, three as sections, and none as perspectives; in 1795, 1796 and 1797 no plans or sections are recorded at all, while 16 out of a total of 253 architectural designs exhibited in these three years are described as 'views' or in perspective. The removal of architectural drawings to the Library in 1811, where they remained, was probably done mainly to improve the conditions for exhibiting sculpture in the Life Academy.
11 John Soane, *Plans, Elevations and Sections of Buildings Executed in Norfolk, Suffolk, . . .* [&c.]. London 1788, pl.14.
12 RA 1809 (no.773): *East Front of the Grange, Hampshire, the Seat of H. Drummond Esq.*; or RA 1820 (no.917): *The Grange, Hampshire, a Seat of H. Drummond, Esq.*
13 RA 1806 (no.902): *South-east View of the House Now Building at Rose-neath, Dumbartonshire, a Seat of his Grace the Duke of Argyle*; (no.917): *North-east View of a House Now Building at Rose-neath. . . .*
14 Bonomi's wish to distance himself from the pictorialism of his earlier exhibition drawings is evident also in the way be began to use other draughtsmen in the late 1790s, including J. M. W. Turner for the landscape, sky and figures in the Longford Hall perspective. See

Andrew Wilton, *The Life and Work of J. M. W. Turner*, London 1979, 337, no. 329.

15 For Wyatt's employment of John Dixon, and disapproval of a draughtsman in his employ exhibiting designs in his own right, see Farington, *Diary*, I, 146 (21 January 1794), and II, 630 (4 August 1796). For Farington's orchestration of opposition to Malton's candidacy see ibid., II, 395–8, (1–4 November 1795).

16 Having exhibited perspectives in 1784 and 1785 of country houses built by Wyatt, Dixon showed his own designs on seven occasions between 1788 and 1802; see Algernon Graves, *The Royal Academy of Arts: A Complete Dictionary of Contributors and their Work from its Foundation in 1796 to 1904*, 8 vols, London 1905–6, II, 339–40.

17 Florence, Uffizi A 2; reproduced in Wolfgang Lotz, *Studies in Italian Renaissance Architecture*, Cambridge, Mass. 1977, fig. 29.

18 Unusually this drawing was Soane's only exhibit this year (1833). It is significant that the next year he turned away entirely from exhibiting drawings, showing instead his original New State Paper Office proposal and design for completing buildings at Whitehall in the form of two finely detailed plaster models (RA 1834; Soane Museum), a form of representation still virtually unknown in the exhibition at this date. I am indebted to Helen Dorey of the Soane Museum for sharing with me the results of her ongoing research into Soane's Academy exhibits.

19 RA 1781: *A Bridge of Magnificence, Design'd for the Sixth Lecture on Architecture*; (no.462): *View from the Entrance on the Bridge* (no.450). Numerous drawings of Sandby's bridge design survive and it is not known which if any of these were the pair exhibited in 1781. The five-metre-long lecture drawing of the bridge's river elevation in the RIBA (BAL Drawings Collection, 18, Sandby [3].1) seems unlikely to have been allowed the space necessary for its display in the Life Academy and would, in any case, surely have caused press comment on account of being over five times the normal size of an architectural drawing. A more probable candidate for identification as its companion (no. 450) is the perspective reproduced here as fig. 189.

20 *St James's Chronicle*, 15–17 May 1781. The vacuity of the language stands in marked contrast to the perceptiveness of Philo-Architectus's 'Mirror', and highlights the fact that, in spite of this earlier isolated example, there was no critical tradition, or appropriate vocabulary, to draw upon to analyse architectural drawings in an exhibition review.

21 *Public Advertiser*, 4 May 1781.

22 The absence in the exhibition of most of the leading architects of the day – men like John Carr of York, Robert Mylne, Sir Robert Taylor, Robert Adam and Henry Holland – must have been very noticeable.

23 Luke Herrmann, *Paul and Thomas Sandby*. London 1986, 141. According to Horace Walpole, Thomas Sandby drew this watercolour 'by the eye in two days and a half. His brother Paul put in the pictures, and Mr. [Edward] Edwards painted the carpet, chairs and table' (quoted in Whitley, *Artists and their Friends*, II, 395).

24 For Soane's memory of 'the powerful impression the sight of that beautiful work produced on myself and on many of the young Artists of those days', see David Watkin, *Sir John Soane: Enlightenment Thought and the Royal Academy Lectures*, Cambridge 1996, 564.

25 *Morning Post, and Daily Advertiser*, 6 June 1788.

26 Soane, *Plans, Elevations*, 7, n. 12.

27 RA 1798: *Priam's Palace* (RIBA); RA 1799: *Palace of Alcenous*; RA 1800: *Ulysses' Palace. . . .*

Chapter 15

1 See John Gage, 'An Early Exhibition and the Politics of British Printmaking, 1800–1812', *Print Quarterly*, 6, no. 2 (June 1989), 123–38, and Celina Fox, 'The Engravers' Battle for Professional Recognition in Early Nineteenth-Century London', *London Journal*, 2 (1976), 6ff.

2 David Alexander and Richard Godfrey, *Painters and Engraving: The Reproductive Print from Hogarth to Wilkie*, New Haven and London 1980, 1.

3 Timothy Clayton, *The English Print, 1688–1802*, New Haven and London 1997, 202, referring to Robert Strange's claim that the Academy's refusal to grant engravers full academic status was primarily owing to the court party's fury at his refusing a royal commission, aggravated by his Catholic faith and Jacobite sympathies.

4 Raymond Williams, *Keywords: A Vocabulary of Culture and Society*, London 1976, 41.

5 Royal Academy General Assembly Minutes, I, 2 (14 December 1768).

6 Ibid., 16 (25 March 1769).

7 Ibid., 28 (11 December 1769).

8 Ibid., 29.

9 Ibid., 34 (19 March 1770).

10 1785 and 1794.

11 Royal Academy Council Minutes, I, 359 (14 April 1784).

12 Anthony Pasquin (pseudonym of John Williams), writing in the *Observer*, 6 June 1794, from a volume of cuttings and pamphlets by John Williams in the Royal Academy Library; I am grateful to Greg Smith for drawing this to my attention.

13 *Literary Gazette, and Journal of the Belles Lettres*, 803 (9 June 1832), 363; and 593 (31 May 1828), 347.

14 Ibid., 647 (13 June 1829), 394.

15 Farington, *Diary*, XI, 3873 (10 February 1811).

16 The first lithographs to appear in England were *Specimens of Polyautography*, London 1803, published by Phillip André and James Heath.

17 One exception was Richard Westall's *Queen Judith Reciting to Alfred . . . a Print in Imitation of a Drawing* exhibited in 1801 (569). This print was unique in being shown by a Royal Academician, rather than an Associate Engraver, as well as probably the only exhibited example of colour printing and of hand colouring; I am grateful to Greg Smith for drawing my attention to this work, which is now in the Victoria & Albert Museum.

18 Most engravers standing for election as Associates were elected unopposed, but a few – James Mason, (?)James Meadows, Anthony Cardon, Luigi Schiavonetti, John Young, Henry Meyer and John Samuel Agar – were defeated in the ballot and never reapplied.

19 For example John Landseer in 1813 (Royal Academy Council Minutes, II, 42–4ff., 20 April 1813) and Anker Smith in 1814 (ibid., 152–3, 21 April 1814).

20 For example, the Council at first refused to accept Valentine Green's print of "Lord Chatham's monument' on the grounds that it had already been published (see Royal Academy Council Minutes, I, 358, 9 April 1784); they later relented.

21 Royal Academy General Assembly Minutes, III, 97 (30 December 1812).

22 *New Monthly Magazine*, 21 (1827), 381.

23 'The engraver has the advantage of being able by himself to convey his talent in very little time to the whole of Europe', *Observations sur les ouvrages de MM de l'Académie de peinture et de sculpture, exposés au Salon du Louvre . . .*, Paris 1753, 43–4, quoted in Clayton, *English Print*, 200.

24 Anthony Pasquin, *A Critical Guide to the Royal Academy*, London 1796, 30.

25 Ibid.

26 Ibid.

27 *Examiner*, 13 July 1823.

28 *Morning Post*, 18 May 1797.

29 Royal Academy General Assembly Minutes, I, 17 (25 March 1769).

30 Whereas engravers incised lines into metal printing plates by hand, etching utilized the action of acid to do the cutting, and thus involved the etcher only in the simpler process of drawing a needle through a soft, waxy, acid-resistant 'ground'.

31 *Blake: Complete Writings*, ed. Geoffrey Keynes, London 1972, 59.

32 Of the 36 prints by Angelica Kauffmann listed in Andreas Andresen, *Der Deutsche Peintre-Graveur*, 1866, V, 380–98, seven are reproductions after painters such as Correggio, Barocci and Reni.

33 See Farington, *Diary*, IV, 1575 (11 July 1801): Benjamin West 'told me that Val: Green has made designs of subjects which he proposed to engrave & publish by subscription but they are not better than if done by a Child from the streets, so deficient in all necessary knowledge of composition &c. He had given Green prudent advice against exhibiting them.'

34 Royal Academy Council Minutes, IV, 174 (29 December 1809).

35 Royal Academy General Assembly Minutes, III, 95–7 (23 December 1812).

36 In his evidence to the Select Committee, John Pye pointed out that academic honours were given to die-engravers, watch-chasers and enamel painters, whom he regarded as no more (and no less) entitled to such recognition than engravers. See Edward Edwards, *The Administrative Economy of the Fine Arts in England*, London 1840, 159–60.

37 Farington, *Diary*, XII, 4301 (16 February 1813): Smirke reports that William Daniell meant to conceal his intention to produce a series of aquatint prints until after his election as an R.A.: 'we should have been led to elect an engraver an Academician, all was to be secret till then'.

38 See Howard C. Levis, *A Descriptive Bibliography of the Most Important Books in the English Language Relating to the Art and History of Engraving . . .*, London 1912, 95–6.

39 John Landseer, *Lectures on the Art of Engraving Delivered at the Royal Institution of Great Britain*, London, 1807, 180.

40 Ibid., 140.

41 Two pictures sent by 'Mrs Angelica' were returned 'as it did not appear that they were sent by her order' (Royal Academy Council Minutes, II, 5, 8 April 1785); a letter written to the *Morning Post* by 'De Marcy' claimed that this happened twice, and Whitley assumed that this was because Kauffmann's paintings were submitted by a printseller (Whitley, *Artists and their Friends*, II, 38).

42 The arguments are summarized by Edwards, *Administrative Economy of the Fine Arts.*

Chapter 16

I should like to thank David Solkin for his help in shaping a somewhat unwieldy subject to the requirements of this book, and William Vaughan, John Murdoch and Holger Hoock for their helpful comments on an earlier draft.

1 In this chapter, for reasons of simplicity, I shall use the terms 'British' and 'Britain' throughout, although contemporary writers used both 'English' and 'British', often apparently synonymously. For a specifically 'English' nationalism from the 1760s among the supporters of Wilkes, see Linda Colley, *Britons*, New Haven and London 1992, 113–17.

2 Joshua Reynolds, 'Apologia', 1791, quoted by Shearer West, 'Xenophobia and Xenomania' in *Italian Culture in Northern Europe in the Eighteenth Century*, ed. West, Cambridge 1999, 137.

3 Sidney C. Hutchison, *The History of the Royal Academy 1768–1986*, 2nd ed, London 1986, 245.

4 Royal Academy Council Minutes, I, 120 (23 December 1771). Extended to the members of the Academy of St Luke in Rome on 31 December, ibid., 121 and to all members of foreign academies in 1814; see Royal Academy General Assembly Minutes, III, 129 (29 March 1814).

5 Robert Rosenblum, 'Reynolds in an International Milieu', in *Reynolds*, ed. Nicholas Penny, Royal Academy of Arts, London 1986, 45–6, and Janine Barrier, 'Chambers in France and Italy', in *Sir William Chambers: Architect to George III*, ed. John Harris and Michael Snodin, New Haven and London 1996, 19–33.

6 William L. Pressly, ed., 'Facts and Recollections of the XVIIIth Century in a Memoir of John Francis Rigaud, RA by Stephen Francis Dutilh Rigaud [his son]', *Walpole Society*, 50 (1984), 6–7.

7 *St James's Chronicle; or British Evening-Post*, 3–5 May 1781.

8 In 1784 and 1785 the *Morning Post* employed unnamed artists to write RA reviews; Hoppner himself later admitted to having written savage critiques in 1785 of the work exhibited by Benjamin West, Maria and Richard Cosway, and John Singleton Copley. See Whitley, *Artists and their Friends*, II, 39.

9 For numerous examples see Pressly, 'Rigaud', esp. 12, 36–7, 65, 76, 87, 107.

10 See Rüdiger Joppien, *Philippe Jacques de Loutherbourg, RA*, Kenwood, Greater London Council, London 1974, n.p.; and Stephen Daniels, 'Loutherbourg's Chemical Theatre: *Coalbrookdale by Night*', in *Painting and the Politics of Culture*, ed. John Barrell, Oxford 1992, 198.

11 See, for example, *Middlesex Journal*, 1–4 May 1773, and *Morning Chronicle*, 27 April 1774.

12 *Morning Chronicle*, 29 May 1776.

13 See, for example, *Morning Chronicle*, 25 April 1777; *Public Advertiser*, 26 April 1777; and *Morning Post, and Daily Advertiser*, 25 April 1777.

14 *Morning Post, and Daily Advertiser*, 30 April 1785.

15 *Public Advertiser*, 27 April 1784; *General Evening Post*, 26–28 April 1785.

16 On the Academy's early understanding of high art, as expressed by Reynolds, see William Vaughan, 'The Englishness of British Art', *Oxford Art Journal*, 13, no. 2 (1990), 12.

17 See, for instance, *General Evening Post*, 24–27 April 1784, and *Gazetteer and New Daily Advertiser*, 27 April 1784.

18 See, for example, *Morning Chronicle*, 25 April 1777; *General Evening Post*, 26–28 April 1785.

19 For the juxtaposition of Bourgeois's *Morning* with de Loutherbourg's *Evening of a Summer's Day in the South of France*, see *Public Advertiser*, 16 May 1783; for a later example – that of Callcott's *Watering Place* with de Loutherbourg's *The Landstorm, with an Overturned Waggon* in 1809 – see *National Register*, 11 June 1809.

20 *Morning Post, and Daily Advertiser*, 5 May 1785.

21 *Whitehall Evening Post*, 3–5 May 1787.

22 *Morning Herald*, 9 May 1787.

23 *Morning Post, and Daily Advertiser*, 12 May 1786; *Morning Herald*, 9 May 1787 with regard to de Loutherbourg's *View of Grasmeer [sic] in Westmoreland, Evening*: '. . . his flimsy, glaring labors [*sic*], are alone calculated to please the ignorant'. Or the reviewer in an unidentified newspaper on *A View of Coalbrook Dale by Night* (RA 1801; fig. 101): 'The general aspect of this Picture is like the *nocturnal Transparencies* which excite so much vulgar admiration in our *Print Shops*'. Cutting in Royal Academy archives, 'Royal Academy Critiques &c.', II, fol. 35.

24 Morton D. Paley, *The Apocalyptic Sublime*, New Haven and London 1986, 52–3.

25 Vaughan, 'Englishness of British Art', 12.

26 See ibid., 13, on the increasing importance of the issue of rivalry with France to the 'British School' discourse from the 1780s onwards.

27 For an evaluation in the late 1740s of the respective merits of British and French silk designs, for instance, see *Rococo: Art and Design in Hogarth's England*, ed. Michael Snodin, Victoria & Albert Museum, London 1984, 217–18.

28 See for instance, *Morning Herald*, 9 May 1787; *Morning Post*, 6 June 1788.

29 *Morning Post, and Daily Advertiser*, 12 May 1786.

30 *Morning Herald*, 9 May 1787. The *Herald*'s response reminds us of the often partisan nature of journalistic art criticism. The paper was then edited by a ceaseless advocate of Gainsborough's, Sir Henry Bate Dudley, and the art critic of the *World*, who was altogether more supportive of de Loutherbourg, complained that Gainsborough was 'always puffed in the same page Mr Loutherbourg is abused in' (quoted in Whitley, *Artists and their Friends*, I, 366). To make matters even more personal, it appears that by 1787 the artists themselves had fallen out; see W.T. Whitley, *Thomas Gainsborough*, London 1915, 286. I am grateful to William Vaughan for drawing my attention to these relationships.

31 Kay Dian Kriz, *The Idea of the English Landscape Painter: Genius as Alibi in the Early Nineteenth Century*, New Haven and London 1997, 44–5; and for the defence of similar, eye-catching strategies by *British* artists, 56, 110–24.

32 Ibid., 51–3.

33 Anthony Pasquin (pseudonym of John Williams), *A Critical Guide to the Exhibition of the Royal Academy, for 1796*, London 1796, 13. On Pasquin, see Mark Hallett, Chapter 5 in this volume.

34 Sir Solomon Gundy, *For the Year 1792. To the Royal Academicians. Bad Pictures Placed in a Good Light . . .*, London, 1792, 21. Gundy's criticism echoes sentiments previously expressed by 'Peter Pindar' (i.e., John Wolcot), one of the very few commentators unfavourable to de Loutherbourg during the early 1780s. See Kriz, *Idea of the English Landscape Painter*, 110.

35 The term is Morris Eaves's; see *The Counter-*

Arts Conspiracy: Art and Industry in the Age of Blake, Ithaca, New York and London 1992, preface, xvii–xviii & *passim*.

36 *St James's Chronicle*, May 1805, in Royal Academy Library, 'Royal Academy Critiques &c.,' II, fol. 62.

37 West, 'Xenophobia', 116–39.

38 Ibid., 136, and Royal Academy Council Minutes, II, 298 (3 December 1796).

39 West, 'Xenophobia', 136–9.

40 E.g., Farington *Diary*, IV, 1136 (15 January 1799); IV, 1140 (24 January 1799); IV, 1145–6 (24 January 1799), quoted by West, 'Xenophobia', 138. For evidence of the longevity of such feelings, see Farington, *Diary*, X, 3696 (21 July 1810).

41 *Morning Post*, 18 May 1797. The author may have been Anthony Pasquin, who included some reviews that had previously appeared in the *Morning Post* in his pamphlet entitled *The Royal Academy, or, a Touchstone of the Present Exhibition*, London 1797.

42 Baron Roger Portalis, *Henri-Pierre Danloux et son Journal durant l'émigration*, Paris 1910, 154, 220–1, 226. See also Tony Halliday, *Facing the Public: Portraiture in the Aftermath of the French Revolution*, Manchester 1999, 27.

43 Among those contacts was the Swedish portrait painter Carl Fredrik von Breda (exhibited RA 1788–96), who spent some time in Reynolds's studio after his move to England in 1787. For Reynolds's increasingly isolated position, see Richard Wendorf, *Sir Joshua Reynolds: the Painter in Society*, London 1996, 205.

44 The review is from an unidentified paper (possibly the *Morning Herald*) of 8 June 1791, in volume VIII of the Whitley Papers in the Print Room of the British Museum.

45 The lavish attention bestowed on Canova in 1815 – see p. 240, below – was an exception. However, in 1821 a dinner guest was dropped from the list to make space for Théodore Géricault, who was himself omitted from the guest list in favour of someone else in the following year. Royal Academy Council Minutes, VI, 201 (18 April 1821) and 279 (16 April 1822).

46 On honorary membership elsewhere, see for instance William Sandby, *The History of the Royal Academy of Arts*, 2 vols, London 1862, I, 64, and Henri Delaborde, *L'Académie des Beaux-Arts depuis la fondation de l'Institut de France*, Paris 1891, 'Liste alphabétique des associés étrangers de l'Académie des Beaux-Arts' and 'Liste alphabétique des correspondants de l'Académie des Beaux-Arts', [380–5].

47 Sandby, *Royal Academy*, II, 376–80. Honorary foreign membership was finally established in 1868.

48 *Gazetteer, and New Daily Advertiser*, 3 June 1791.

49 *Morning Chronicle*, 2 May 1791.

50 Ronald Paulson, *Hogarth: High Art and Low 1732–1750*, Cambridge 1992, 152–3, 159, 179.

51 *St James's Chronicle*, 12–14 May 1791.

52 For example, *Gazetteer, and New Daily Advertiser*, 3 June 1791; *Public Advertiser*, 17 May 1792.

53 *Morning Chronicle*, 10 May 1792.

54 *Diary: or Woodfall's Register*, 2 May 1793.

55 *St James's Chronicle*, 12–14 May 1791.

56 *Public Advertiser*, 5 May 1791.

57 Anthony Pasquin (pseudonym of John Williams), *A Liberal Critique on the Present Exhibition of the Royal Academy . . .*, London 1794, 22.

58 Pasquin, *A Critical Guide to the Exhibition . . . for 1796*, 17.

59 For the association of the respective British and French aesthetics with political characteristics, see William Vaughan, '"David's Brickdust" and the Rise of the British School', in *Polish and English Responses to French Art and Architecture: Contrasts and Similarities: Papers Delivered at the University of London, University of Warsaw History of Art Conference, January and September 1993*, ed. Francis Ames-Lewis, Birkbeck College, University of London, Department of History of Art 1995, 95–110.

60 Helen Smailes, *A French Painter in Exile: Henri-Pierre Danloux (1753–1809)*, Scottish National Portrait Gallery, Edinburgh 1985, 36.

61 The review is from an unidentified newspaper of 1830 in volume II (1812–52), 239, of the Courtauld Institute Library's four volumes of contemporary press cuttings. There appear to be three other Gérard portraits of Lady Jersey at Versailles, two dated 1819 and one 1825.

62 *La Belle Assemblée*, 3rd ser., 11 (June 1830), 273. For positive reviews, see, for instance, the *Literary Gazette, and Journal of the Belles Lettres*, 696 (22 May 1830), 338, and the titles in the following note.

63 *Olio*, 5 (1830), 301; also *Gentleman's Magazine*, 100, pt. 1 (May 1830), 444.

64 See, for example, Robert Hunt in defence of a varied and 'natural' national school in the *Examiner*, 14 May 1820, 316. The counter-position was taken, for instance, by *Fraser's Magazine*, 12 (July 1835), 62, whose critic denied the existence of a national school in the absence of history painting.

65 The scene is based on the twelfth chapter of Sir Walter Scott's *Quentin Durward*. See Lee Johnson, *The Paintings of Eugène Delacroix: A Critical Catalogue 1816–31*, 2 vols, Oxford 1981, I, 132.

66 Eugène Delacroix, letter to Théophile Silvestre, 31 December 1858, in *Selected Letters*, selected and translated by Jean Stewart Eyre, Spottiswode 1971, 551.

67 *La Belle Assemblée*, 3rd ser., 11 (June 1830), 276; *Gentleman's Magazine*, 100, pt. 1 (May 1830), 447; *Literary Gazette*, 697 (29 May 1830), 353.

68 The dinner was given on 1 December 1815; see Royal Academy Council Minutes, V, 235 (28 December 1815).

69 For *Hebe* and *Terpsichore*, see ibid. 380–1 (12 April 1817); for *Danzatrice*, see Robert Hunt, in the *Examiner*, 11 May 1823, 313. For the prestige conferred on the exhibition and on British sculpture in general through Canova's participation, see Alison Yarrington, Chapter 12 in this volume.

70 Timothy Clifford, 'Canova in Context', in *The Three Graces: Antonio Canova*, ed. Hugh Honour, National Gallery of Scotland, Edinburgh 1995, 11, 13, 16.

71 *Examiner*, 29 June 1817, 414. Alison Yarrington suggests that Chantrey, who had *Hebe* in his studio prior to the exhibition, conceived his exhibit as a deliberate contrast to Canova's work. See Yarrington, 'Anglo-Italian Attitudes: Chantrey and Canova', in *The Lustrous Trade: Material Culture and the History of Sculpture in England and Italy, c.1700–c.1860*, ed. Cinzia Sicca and Alison Yarrington, London and New York 2000, 141–2.

72 *European Magazine*, 83 (June 1823), 535.

73 *La Belle Assemblée*, new ser., 27 (1823), 281.

74 For example, *European Magazine*, 83 (June 1823), 535; Robert Hunt in *Examiner*, 6 July 1823, 443.

Chapter 17

1 Johann David Passavant, *Tour of a German Artist in England*, trans. Elizabeth Rigby, London 1836, 249.

2 Reynolds's first seven Discourses were published in an Italian translation by Giuseppe Baretti in Florence in 1778. French and German editions soon followed.

3 A. J. B. Defauconpret, *Londres et ses habitans ou quinze jours à Londres*, Paris 1817, 120.

4 *Morning Chronicle*, 3–5 May 1825.

5 William Vaughan, 'The Englishness of British Art', *Oxford Art Journal*, 13, no.2 (1990), 15–17. For a more recent exploration of this theme, see Kay Dian Kriz, *The Idea of the English Landscape Painter: Genius as Alibi in the Early Nineteenth Century*, New Haven and London 1997, 33–56.

6 *Lettres addressées au Baron François Gérard . . .* 2nd ed, 2 vols, Paris 1886, I, 231–2.

7 For an analysis of German responses to British art during this period see A. D. Potts, 'British Romantic Art through German Eyes', in *Sind Briten Hier? Relations between British and Continental Art 1680–1800*, Zentralinstitut für Kunstgeschichte in München, Munich 1981, 181–206. Potts's article, which contains useful references to earlier literature, stresses the high reputation of Wilkie and Landseer in Germany. It also covers descriptions of British art by German visitors in the 1840s, a period that lies beyond the scope of this chapter.

8 *Kunst-Blatt*, 6, no.28 (1825), 112.

9 Ibid.

10 Ibid., 2, no.32 (1821), 125–8.

11 Ibid., 6, no.22 (1825), 85.

12 Ibid.

13 Ibid., 4, nos 101–3 (1823), 401–3, 405–6, 409–11.
14 *Allgemeine Deutsche Biographie*, Leipzig 1875, I, 123.
15 *Kunst-Blatt*, 101 (1823), 403.
16 Ibid., 404.
17 Ibid., 102 (1823), 405.
18 Ibid.
19 Johann Valentin Adrian, *Skizzen aus England*, 4 vols, Frankfurt 1830–33, IV (1833), 186.
20 David Robertson, *Sir Charles Eastlake and the Victorian Art World*, Princeton 1978, 11.
21 Johann David Passavant, *Kunstreise durch England und Belgien*, Frankfurt am Main 1833; for the English translation of 1836 (from which the section on Belgium was omitted), see note 1 above. I have used the English version of the book for the quotes in this chapter. Although not completely accurate, it is the form in which the text would have been known to most British readers of the period.
22 Passavant, *Kunstreise*, vii; *Tour*, x.
23 See the biography of Passavant in *Allgemeine Deutsche Biographie*, Leipzig 1887, XXV, 198–201.
24 See Francis Haskell, *Rediscoveries in Art*, London 1977, 25–6.
25 The most celebrated account was that by the dealer William Buchanan. See ibid., 27–9.
26 Gustav F. Waagen, *Kunstwerke und Künstler in England*, 3 vols, Berlin 1837; *Works of Art and Artists in England*, trans. H. E. Lloyd, 3 vols, London 1838.
27 Passavant, *Kunstreise*, 279; *Tour*, 203.
28 Passavant, *Kunstreise*, 346.
29 Vaughan, 'Englishness of British Art', 15–16.
30 Ibid., 17.
31 Passavant, *Tour*, 203.
32 Ibid., 241–2.
33 Ibid., 242.
34 Ibid., 245.
35 Ibid., 250.
36 Ibid., 251.
37 *Italian Scene in the Anno Santo, Pilgrims Arriving in the Sight of Rome and St Peter's: Evening.* Oil on canvas, 32¼ × 41½in., 1827. Duke of Bedford. Painted for the 6th Duke of Bedford. Several subsequent versions.
38 Passavant, *Tour*, 252.
39 Ibid., 253.
40 Ibid., 262.
41 Ibid.
42 Ibid., 264.
43 Ibid., 265.
44 Waagen, *Works of Art*, II, 148.
45 Ibid., 149.
46 Waagen, *Kunstwerke*, I, 120.
47 *Report from the Select Committee on Arts, and their Connexion with Manufactures*, London, House of Commons, Reports from Committees, 1836, IX (568), iv.
48 The standard treatment of this remains Quentin Bell, *The Schools of Design*, London 1963. For a recent discussion of the structure and scope of the Committee's inquiry see Thomas Gretton '"Art Is Cheaper and Goes Lower in France"', in *Art in Bourgeois Society*, ed. Andrew Hemingway and William Vaughan, Cambridge 1998, 84–100.
49 *Report from the Select Committee,* 1836, 14.
50 Ibid., 15.
51 For an account of the Academy's role in the development of this scheme see Gordon Fyfe, 'Auditing the RA: Official Discourse and the Nineteenth-Century Royal Academy', in *Art and the Academy in the Nineteenth Century*, ed. Raphael Cardoso Denis and Colin Trodd, Manchester 2000, 121–41.
52 *The Diary of Benjamin Robert Haydon*, ed. W. B. Pope, 5 vols, Cambridge, Mass., 1963, V, 79.
53 *Report from the Select Committee*, 1836, 93.
54 Friedrich von Raumer, *England in 1835: Being a Series of Letters Written to Friends in Germany, during a Residence in London and Excursions into the Provinces . . . Translated from the German by Sarah Austin [and H. E. Lloyd]*, 3 vols, London 1836.
55 *Report from the Select Committee*, 1836, 96.
56 Gretton, '"Art is Cheaper . . ."', 98.

Photograph Credits

Courtesy of Agnew's, London: 121, 219; © Bildarchiv Preußischer Kulturbesitz, Berlin, Foto: Jörg P. Anders: 13; The Bridgeman Art Library: 23, 209; © The British Museum: 17, 18, 19, 35, 36, 37, 38, 44, 52, 95, 96, 97, 100, 102, 170, 193, 194, 196, 197, 198, 199, 201, 202, 203, 204, 207, 208; Christie's Images Ltd 2001: 215; Courtesy of the Conway Library, Courtauld Institute of Art: 12, 42, 146, 147, 149, 151, 153, 155, 156, 157; © A. C. Cooper (colour) Ltd: 86, 186, 187, 189; Samuel Courtauld Trust © Courtauld Gallery: frontispiece, 5, 16; © Crown Copyright: UK Government Art Collection: 70; Photograph © 1986 The Detroit Institute of Arts: 41, 53; © The Frick Collection, New York: 87, 111, 124; Photo by courtesy of Hazlitt, Gooden and Fox, London: 91; © National Gallery, London: 49, 115, 117, 123; © National Maritime Museum: 75, 212; Courtesy of The Paul Mellon Centre for Studies in British Art: 4, 71; Photographic Survey, Courtauld Institute of Art: 3, 106, 129, 135, 148, 150, 154; © Photo RMN-H. Lewandowski: 20, 216; © PMVP/negative: Ladet: 8; © RSC Collection: 93; Science Museum/Science & Society, London: 101; Sir Geoffrey Shakerley, Photographic Records Ltd.: 119; © Slide Library, Courtauld Institute of Art: 10, 11, 163; Courtesy of Sotheby's, London: 164; Courtesy of Mary Ann Steggles 158; © Tate, London 2001: 54, 66, 88, 103, 107, 113, 114, 120, 122, 125, 126, 132, 217; © Photo: theartarchive/The Garrick Club, London: 83; © Photo V & A Picture Library: 72, 136, 138, 142, 143, 144, 145, 159, 168, 178, 195, 200, 218; Courtesy of the Witt Library, Courtauld Institute of Art: 34, 165, 214

Index

'ART ON THE LINE': THE ROYAL ACADEMY E

A recreation of the historic hang in the Great Room, Cou

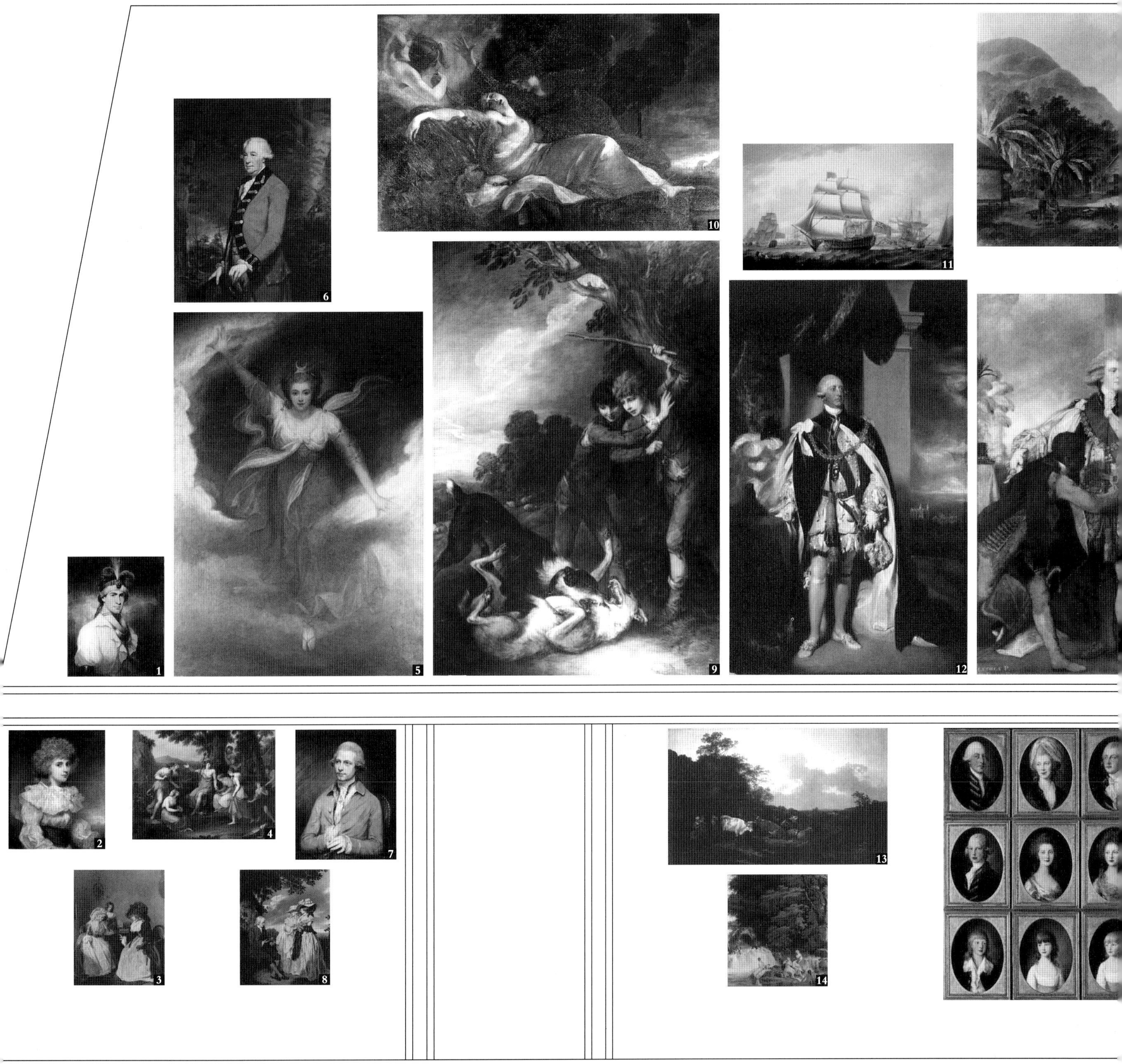

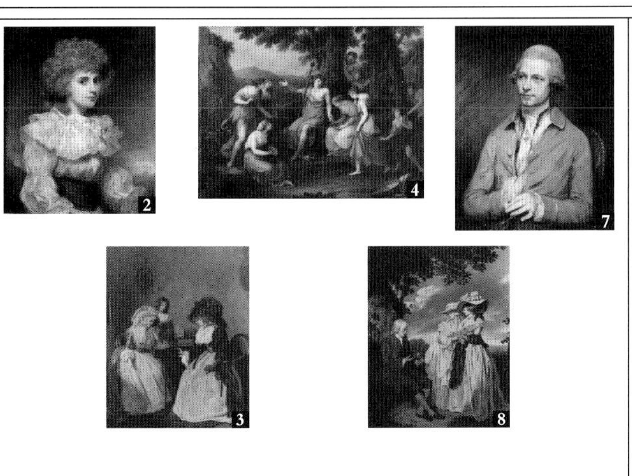

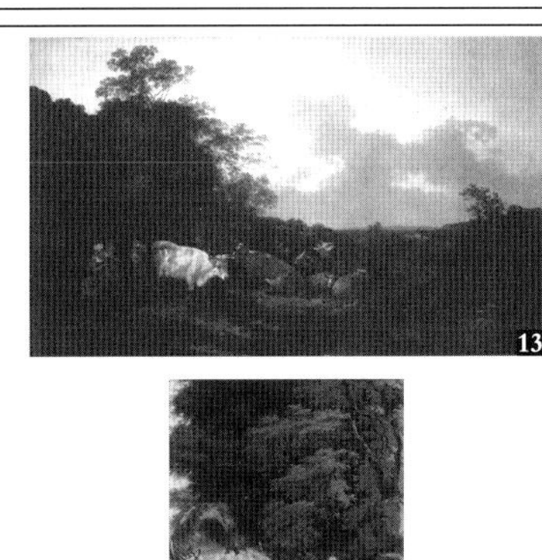

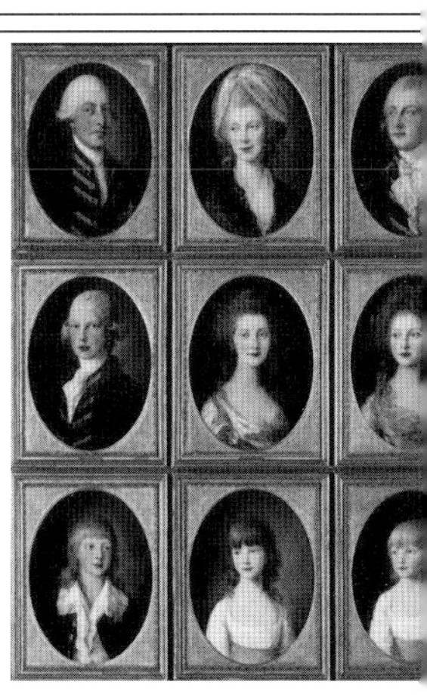

WALL 1 (WEST)

1. Thomas Hardy *William Augustus Bowles as an Indian Chief* (RA 1791)
National Trust (Upton)

2. Sir Joshua Reynolds *Lady Elizabeth Foster* (RA 1788)
Trustees of the Chatsworth Settlement

3. John Raphael Smith *The Widow's Tale* (RA 1788)
Derby Museums and Art Gallery

4. Angelica Kauffmann *Bacchus Teaching the Nymphs to Make Verses* (RA 1788)
Private Collection

5. Maria Cosway *Georgiana, Duchess of Devonshire as Diana* (RA 1782)
Trustees of the Chatsworth Settlement

6. James Northcote *Sir Ralph Milbanke* (RA 1785)
Yale Center for British Art, Paul Mellon Collection

7. Thomas Gainsborough *John Joseph Merlin* (RA 1782)
English Heritage (The Iveagh Bequest, Kenwood)

8. John Raphael Smith *The Moralist* (RA 1786)
Derby Museums and Art Gallery

9. Thomas Gainsborough *Two Shepherd Boys, with Dogs Fighting* (RA 1783)
English Heritage (The Iveagh Bequest, Kenwood)

10. Sir Joshua Reynolds *The Death of Dido* (RA 1781)
Royal Collection © 2001 Her Majesty The Queen

11. Robert Dodd *HMS Victory Sailing from Spithead with a Division from a Grand Fleet* (RA 1792)
National Maritime Museum, Greenwich

12. Sir Thomas Lawrence *George III* (RA 1792)
Herbert Art Gallery and Museum, Coventry Arts and Heritage

13. Philippe-Jacques de Loutherbourg *Landscape with Cattle and Figures* (RA 1782)
Royal Academy of Arts

14. Francis Wheatley *The Salmon Leap at Leixlip*
Yale Center for British Art, Paul Mellon Collecti

15. Thomas Gainsborough *The Royal Family* (RA
Royal Collection © 2001 Her Majesty The Que

16. Sir Joshua Reynolds *George IV as Prince of W*
By kind permission of his Grace the Duke of No

17. John Webber *View of Cracatoa, an Island in the*
Ministry of Defence Art Collection

18. Mather Brown *Sir Francis Buller* (RA 1792)
National Portrait Gallery, London

19. Sir Thomas Lawrence *Queen Charlotte* (RA 1
The National Gallery, London

20. Richard Wilson *View of Tabley, Cheshire, the*
Private Collection

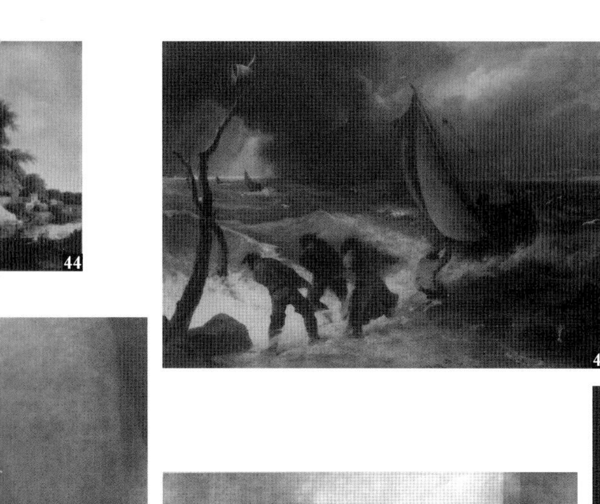
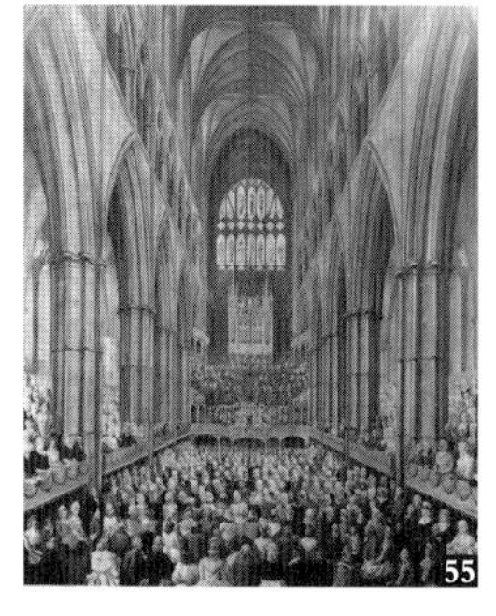
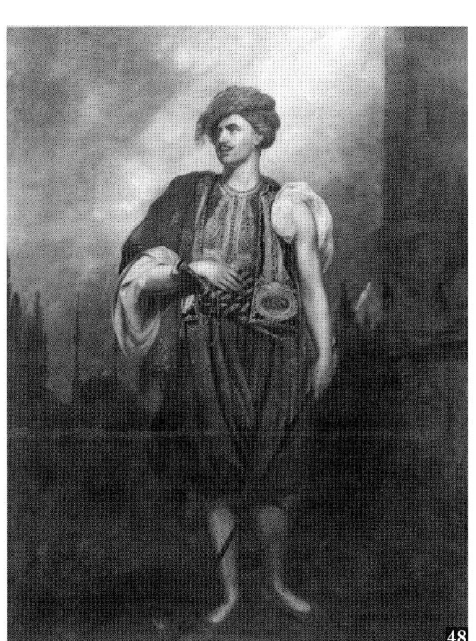
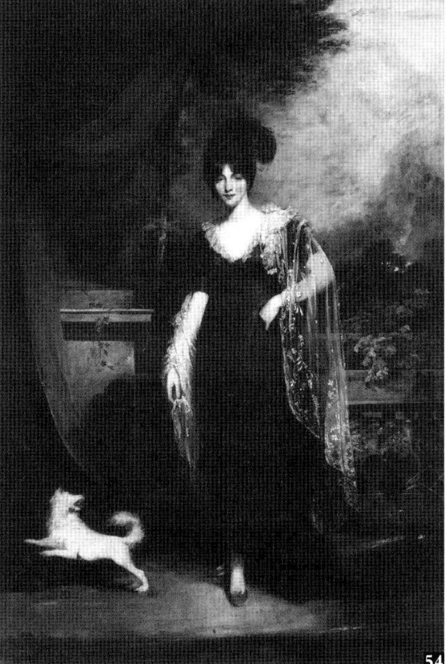
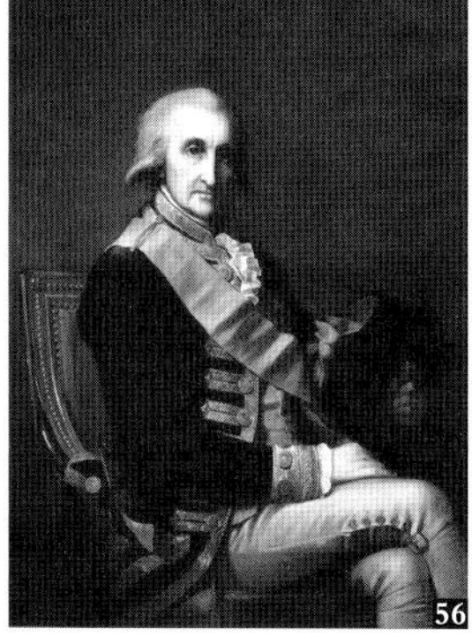
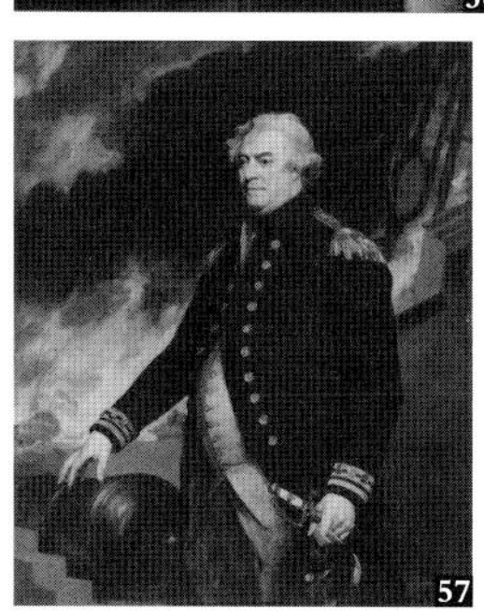
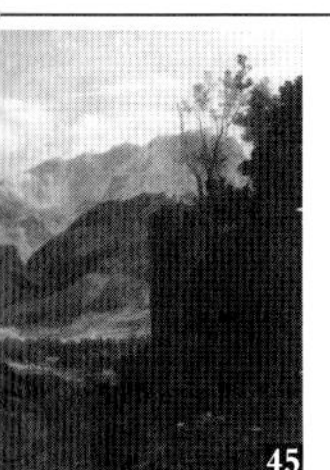
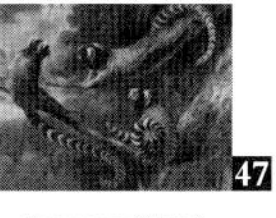
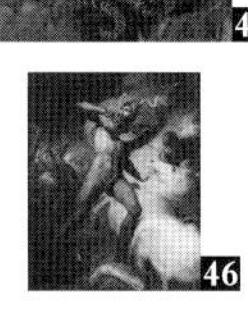
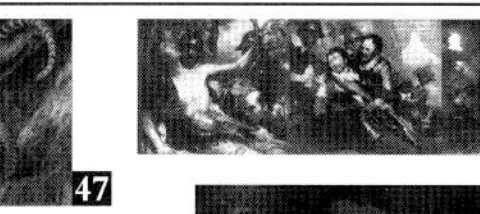
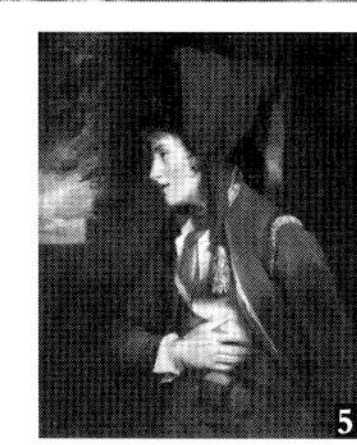
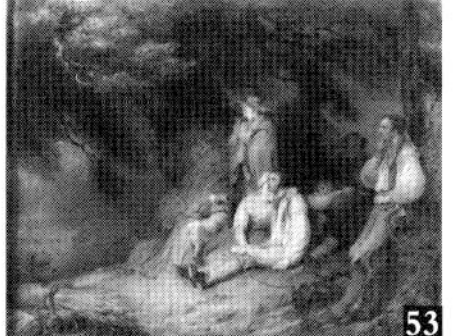
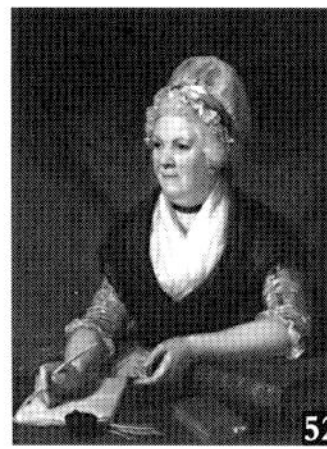
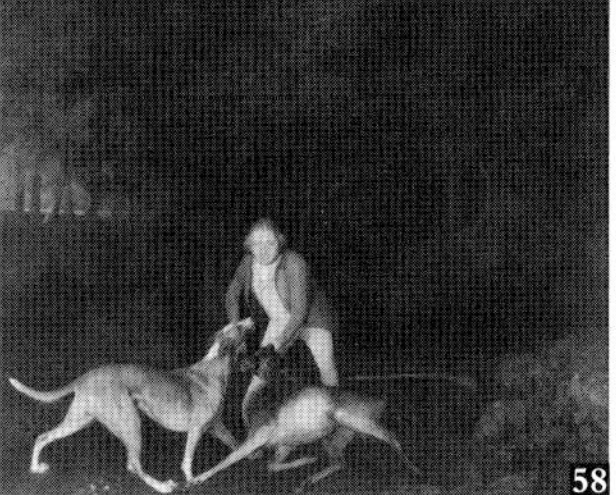
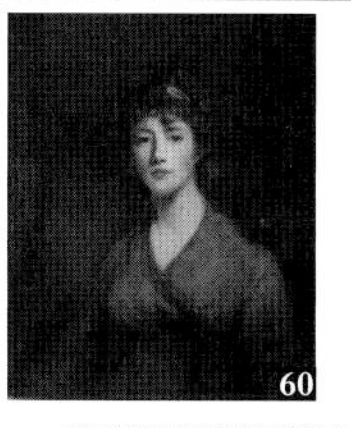
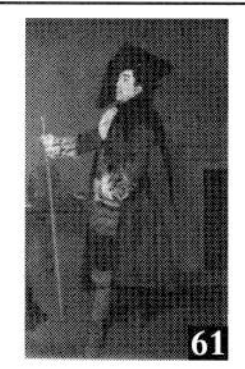
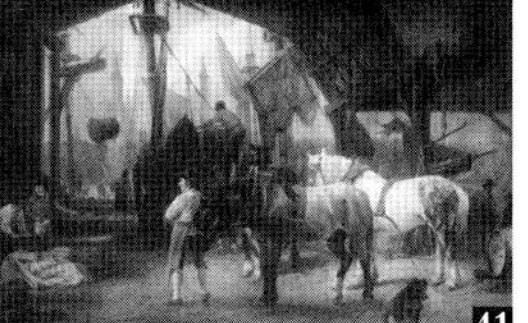

…d on the Jumna (RA 1797)

…ville, Savoy (RA 1803)
…tion

…revious to the Battle of Tooton (RA 1797)

…des (RA 1793)
…tion

…ess (RA 1799)

50. Benjamin West *The Deaths of Epaminondas, Sir Philip Sidney, and the Chevalier Bayard* (RA 1799)
Wakefield Museums and Art Gallery

51. John Hoppner *Mrs Jordan as Viola in 'Twelfth Night'* (RA 1796)
English Heritage (The Iveagh Bequest, Kenwood)

52. Henry Howard *Sarah Trimmer* (RA 1798)
National Portrait Gallery, London

53. Richard Westall *Haymakers in a Storm* (RA 1795)
Private Collection

54. William Owen *Mrs Robinson* (RA 1803)
National Trust (Petworth)

55. Edward Edwards *An Interior View of Westminster Abbey* (RA 1793)
Yale Center for British Art, Paul Mellon Collection

56. Jean-Laurent Mosnier *Admiral Lord George Brydges Rodney, 1st Baron Rodney* (RA 1794)
National Maritime Museum, Greenwich

57. John Singleton Copley *Vice Admiral Adam Duncan, 1st Viscount Duncan* (RA 1798)
Scottish National Portrait Gallery

58. George Stubbs *Freeman, the Earl of Clarendon's Gamekeeper* (RA 1801)
Yale Center for British Art, Paul Mellon Collection

59. George Garrard *A Wharf on the Thames, near London Bridge* (RA 1796)
Private Collection

60. John Hoppner *Elizabeth, Countess of Sutherland* (RA 1799)
The Countess of Sutherland

61. Samuel de Wilde *Joseph Munden as Peregrine Forester in 'Hartford Bridge'* (RA 1795)
Garrick Club

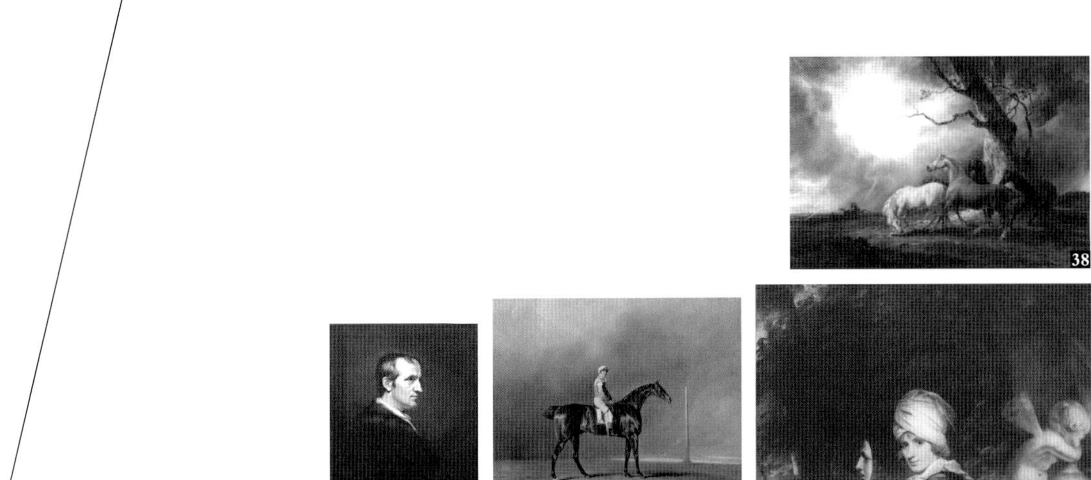

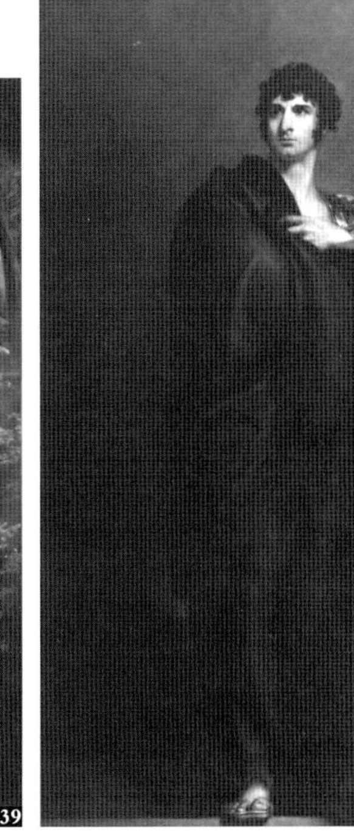

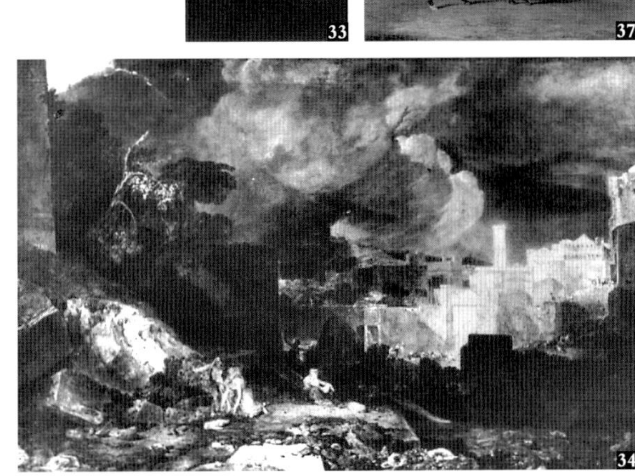

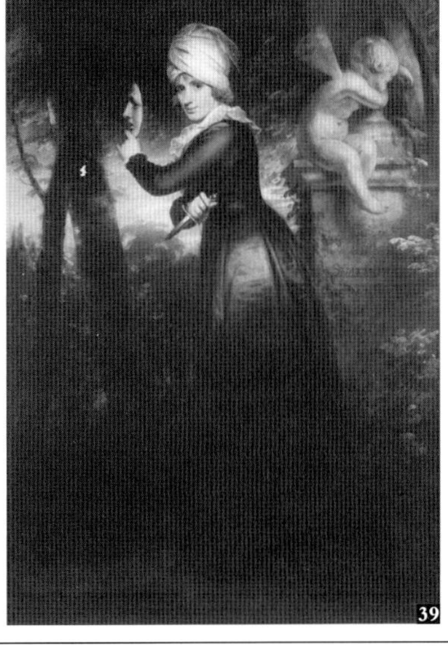

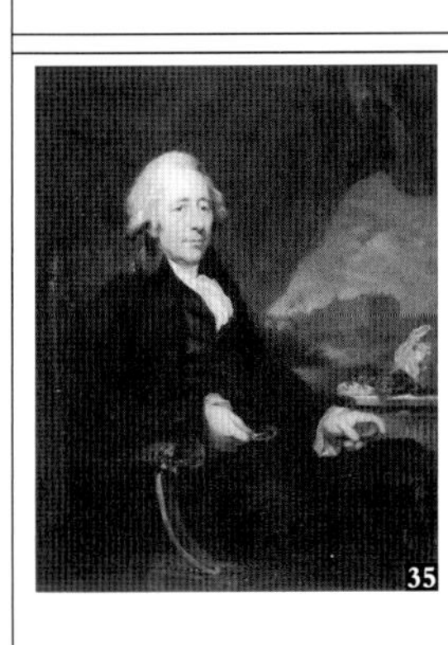

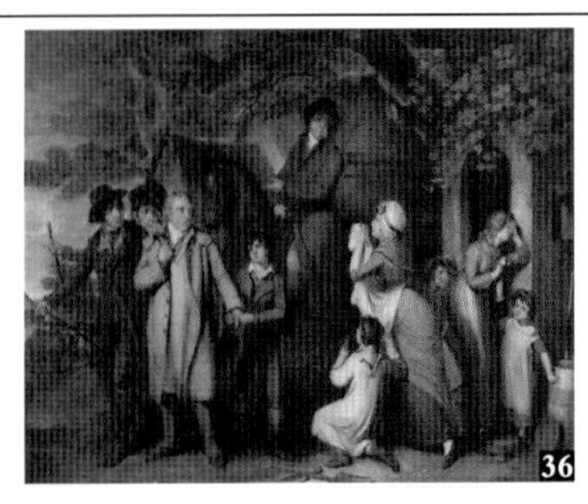

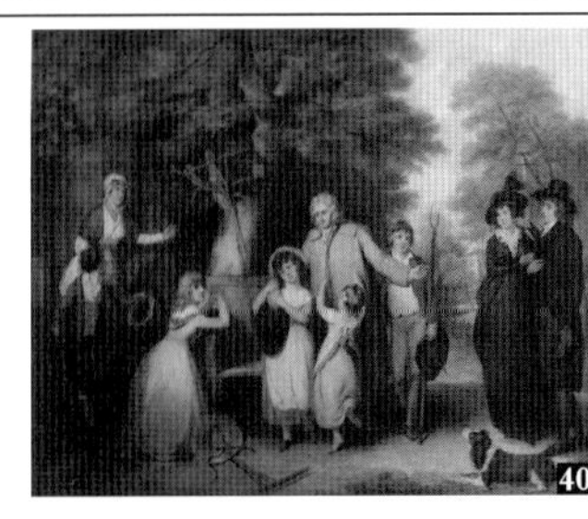

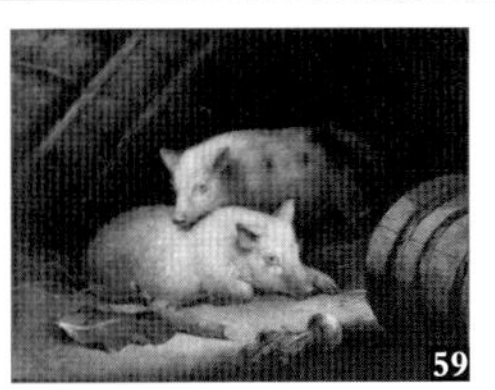

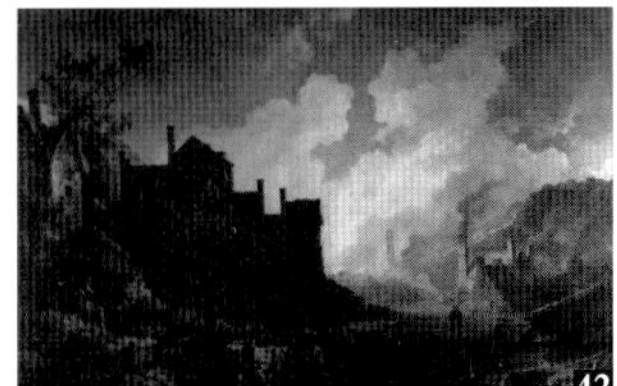

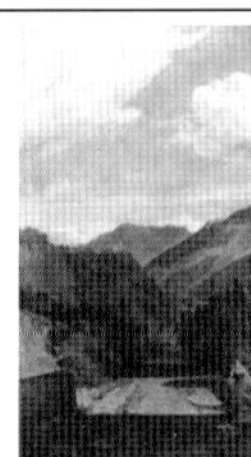

WALL 2 (NORTH)

33. James Northcote *William Godwin* (RA 1803)
National Portrait Gallery, London

34. JMW Turner *The Tenth Plague of Egypt* (RA 1802)
Tate Britain

35. Carl Frederick von Breda *Matthew Boulton* (RA 1793)
Birmingham Museums and Art Gallery

36. William Redmore Bigg *The Rapacious Steward; or Unfortunate Tenant* (RA 1801)
Yale Center for British Art, Paul Mellon Collection

37. Benjamin Marshall *Diamond with Mr. Dennis Fitzpatrick* (RA 1800)
Yale Center for British Art, Paul Mellon Collection

38. Sawrey Gilpin *Horses in a Thunderstorm* (RA 1799)
Royal Academy of Arts

39. Sir William Beechey *Mrs Siddons, with the Emblems of Tragedy* (RA 1794)
National Portrait Gallery, London

40. William Redmore Bigg *The Benevolent Heir Restoring an Old Cottager to his Family* (RA 1797)
Yale Center for British Art, Paul Mellon Collection

41. George Morland *Pigs* (RA 1797)
Birmingham Museums and Art Gallery

42. Philippe-Jacques de Loutherbourg *Coalbrookdale by Night* (RA 1801)
National Museum of Science & Industry

43. Sir Thomas Lawrence *John Philip Kemble as Coriolanus* (RA 1798)
Guildhall Art Gallery, Corporation of London

44. Thomas Daniell *Hindoo Temple at Bindrabu*
Royal Academy of Arts

45. JMW Turner *Chateaux de St Michael, Bonn*
Yale Center for British Art, Paul Mellon Colle

46. Henry Tresham *The Earl of Warwick's Vow*
Manchester City Art Galleries

47. George Garrard *A Marmoset, in Three Attit*
Yale Center for British Art, Paul Mellon Colle

48. Sir William Beechey *Mr Hope in Turkish D*
National Portrait Gallery, London

49. John Hoppner *A Gale of Wind* (RA 1794)
Tate Britain

XHIBITIONS AT SOMERSET HOUSE 1780–1836

rtauld Institute Gallery October 2001 to January 2002

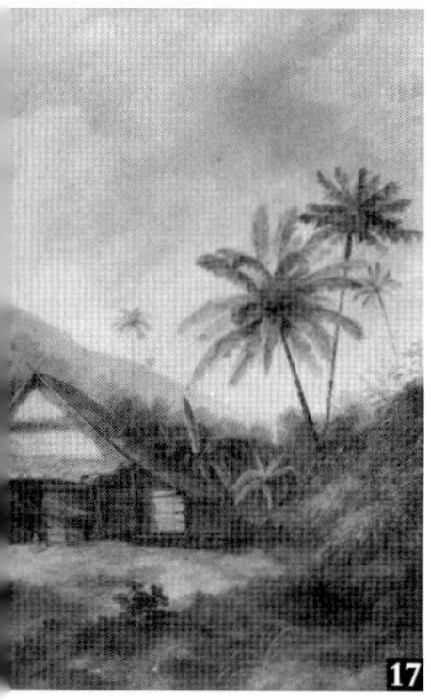

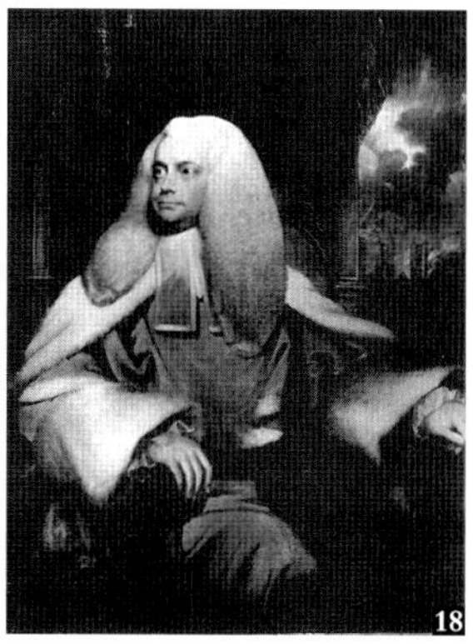

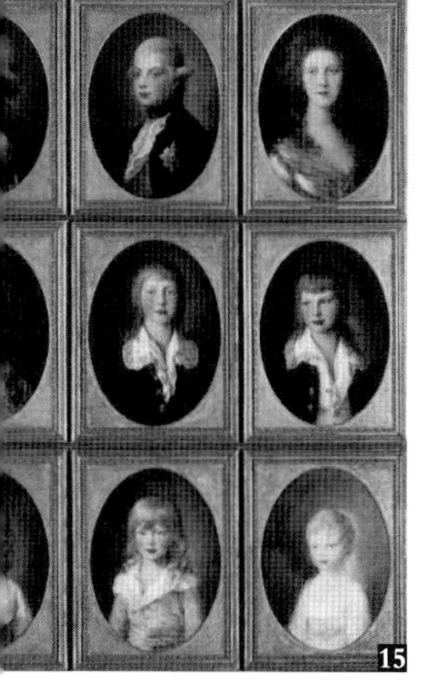

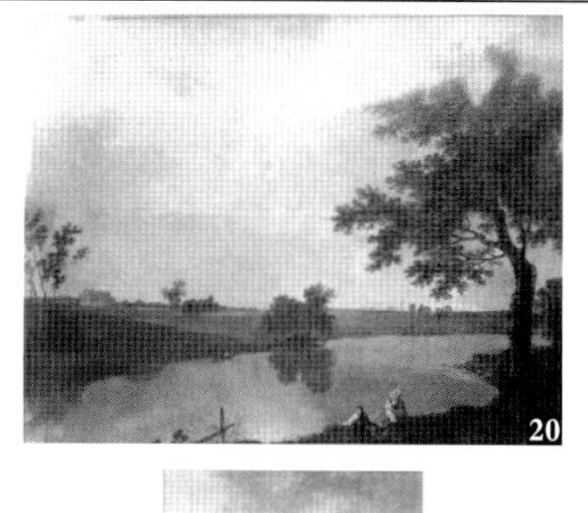

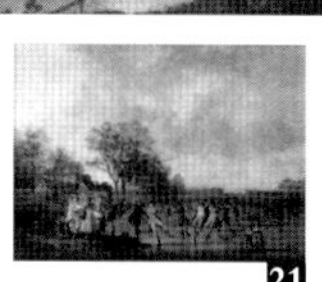

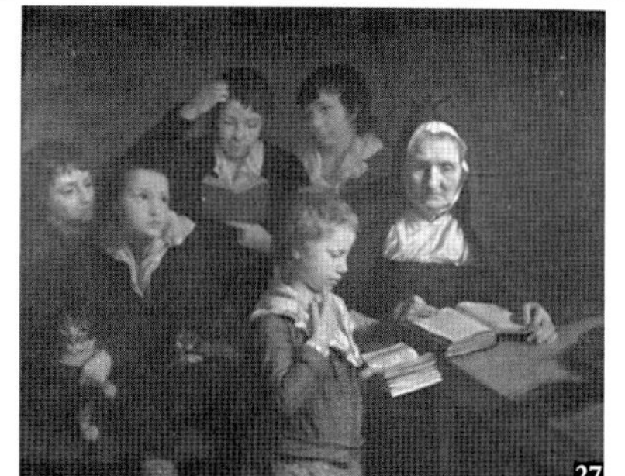

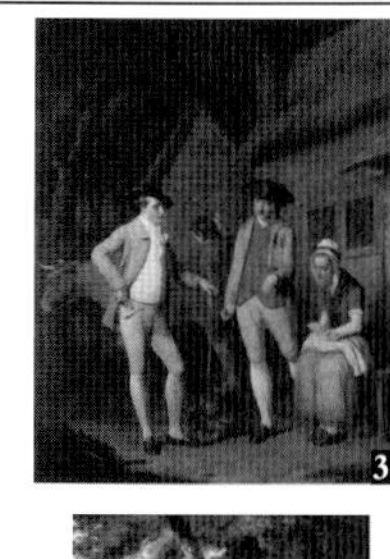

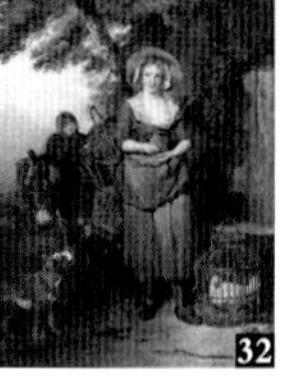

Ireland, with Nymphs Bathing (RA 1784)
on
1783)
n
s (RA 1787)
folk
China Seas (RA 1785)

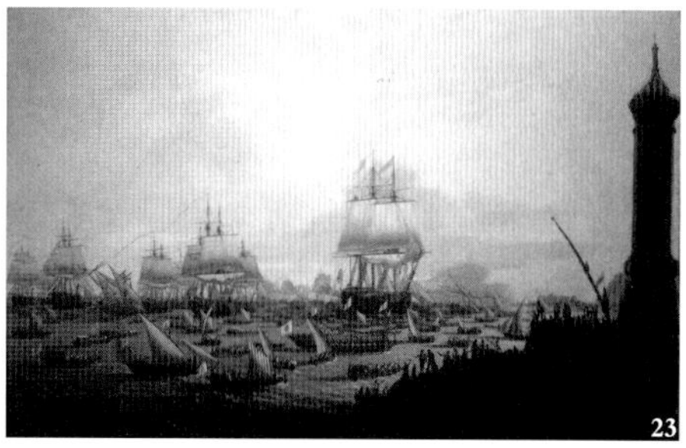

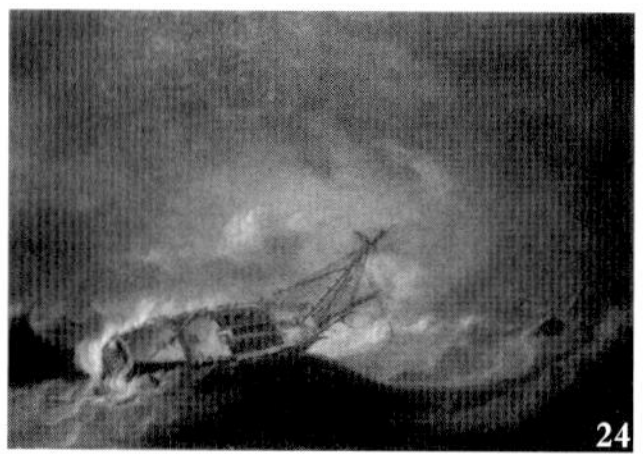

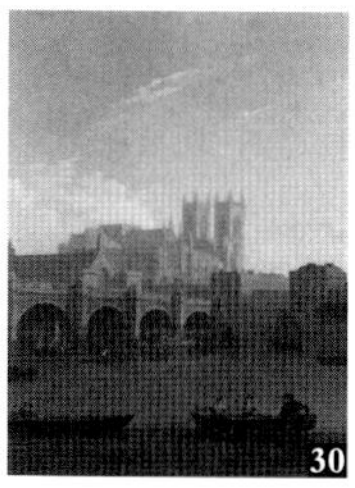

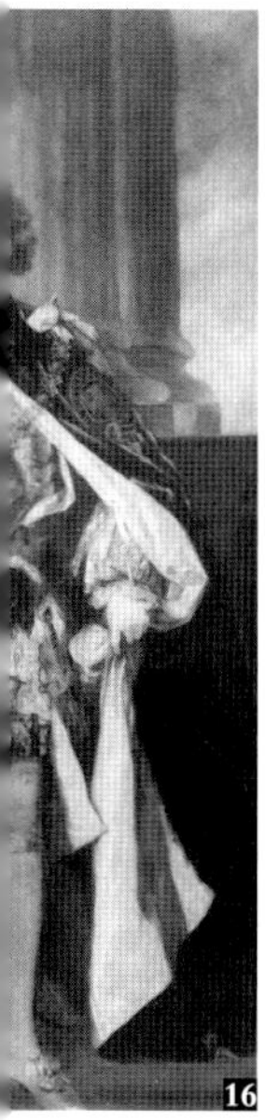

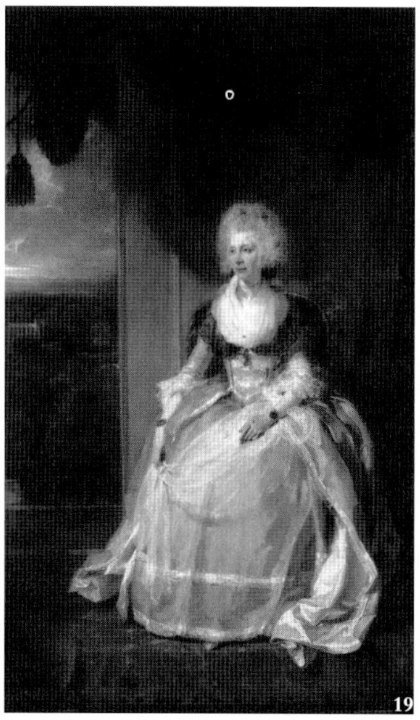

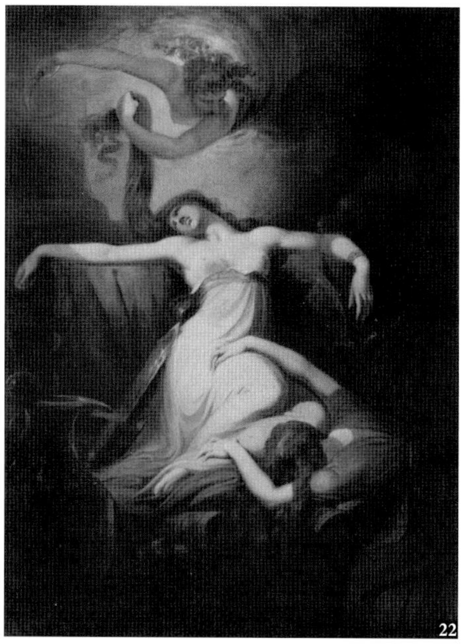

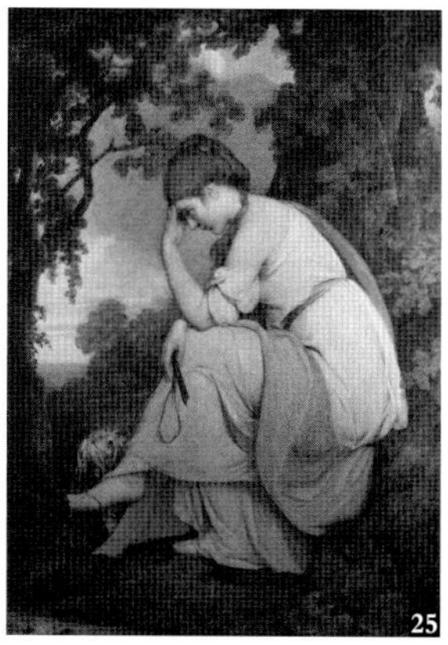

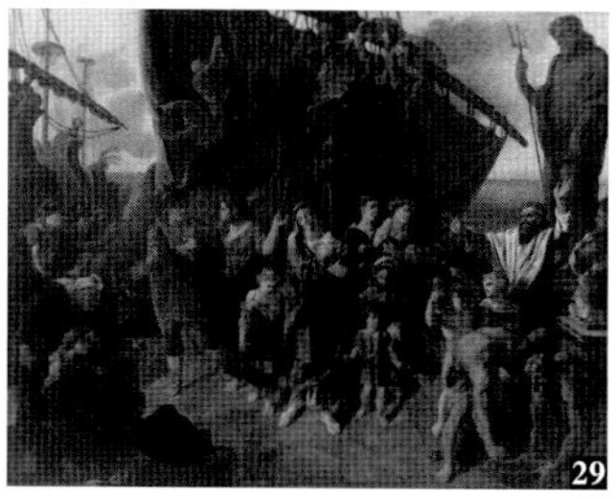

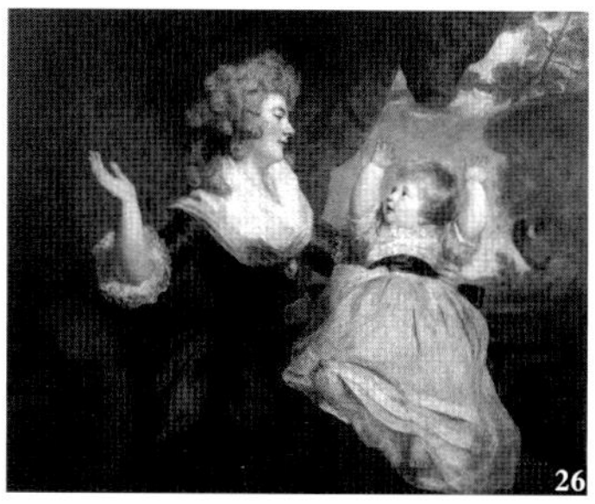

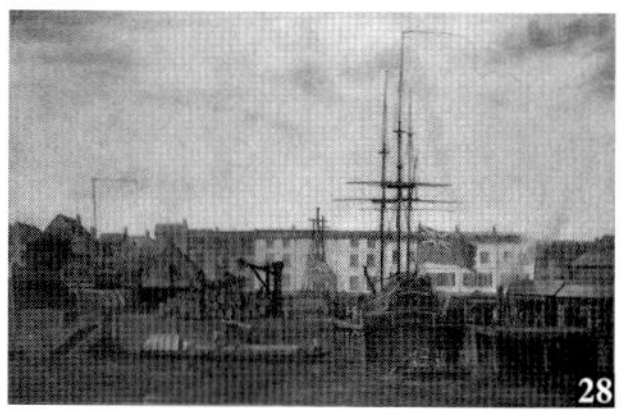

90)

at of Sir John Leicester (RA 1780)

21. Julius Caesar Ibbetson *View in Hyde Park: a Winter Scene* (RA 1786)
Private Collection

22. Henry Fuseli *The Death of Dido* (RA 1781)
Yale Center for British Art, Paul Mellon Collection

23. Dominic Serres *The Arrival of Their Sicilian Majesties at Naples* (RA 1788)
National Maritime Museum, Greenwich

24. Robert Dodd *Loss of HMS Ramillies: on her Beam Ends* (RA 1786)
National Maritime Museum, Greenwich

25. Joseph Wright of Derby *Maria, from Sterne* (RA 1781)
Derby Museums and Art Gallery

26. Sir Joshua Reynolds *Georgiana, Duchess of Devonshire and her Daughter Georgiana* (RA 1786)
Trustees of the Chatsworth Settlement

27. John Opie *A School* (RA 1784)
Loyd Collection

28. Francis Holman *A Dockyard at Wapping* (RA 1784)
Tate Britain

29. Alexander Runciman *Agrippina Landing at Brundisium with the Ashes of Germanicus* (RA 1781)
National Gallery of Scotland

30. Joseph Farington *Westminster Abbey and Westminster Bridge Seen from the South* (RA 1792)
Yale Center for British Art, Paul Mellon Collection

31. Edward Penny *The Widow Custard's Cow and Goods, Redeemed by Johnny Pearmain* (RA 1782)
Yale Center for British Art, Paul Mellon Collection

32. Francis Wheatley *The Return from Market* (RA 1788)
Leeds Museums and Galleries

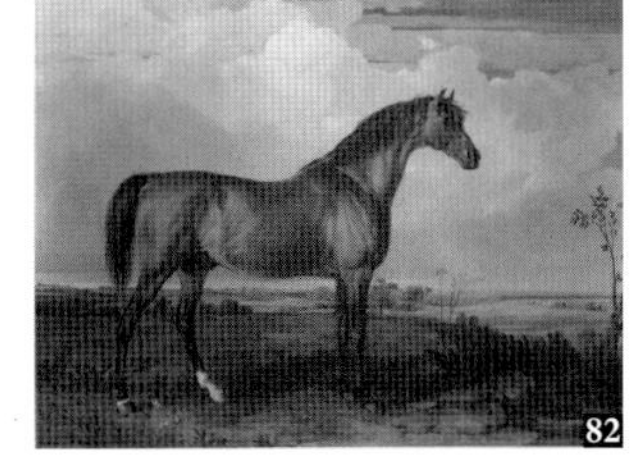

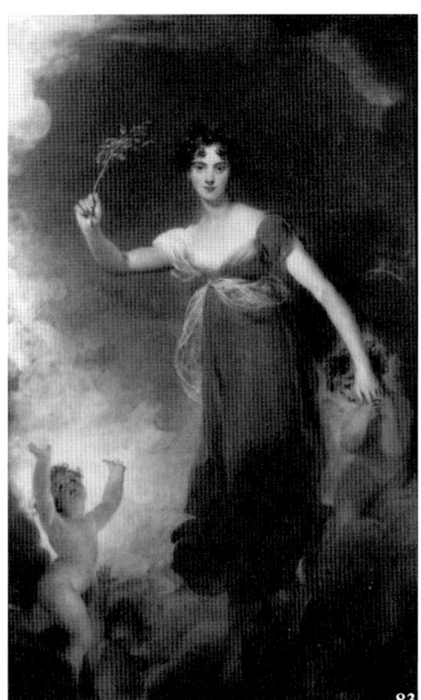

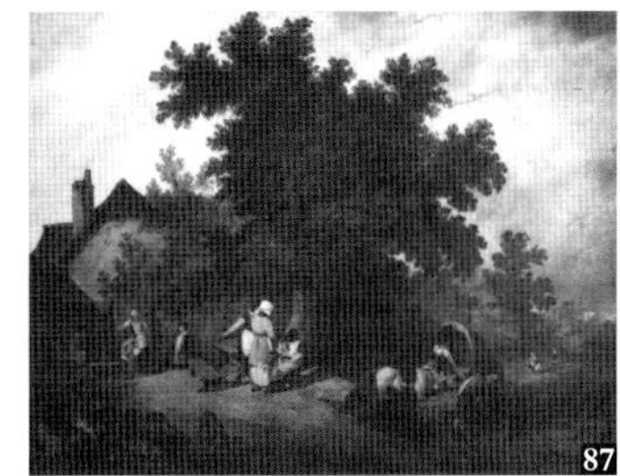

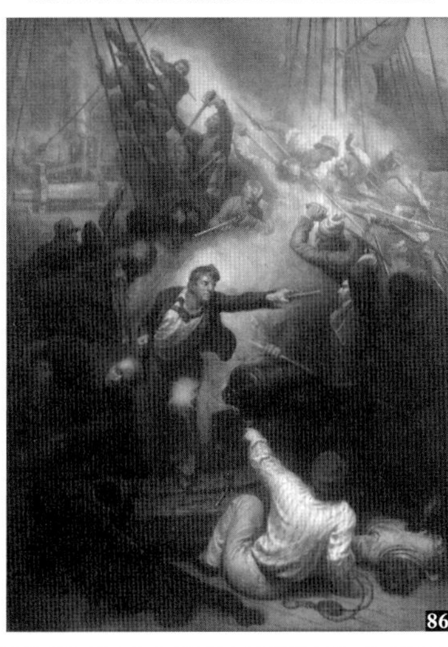

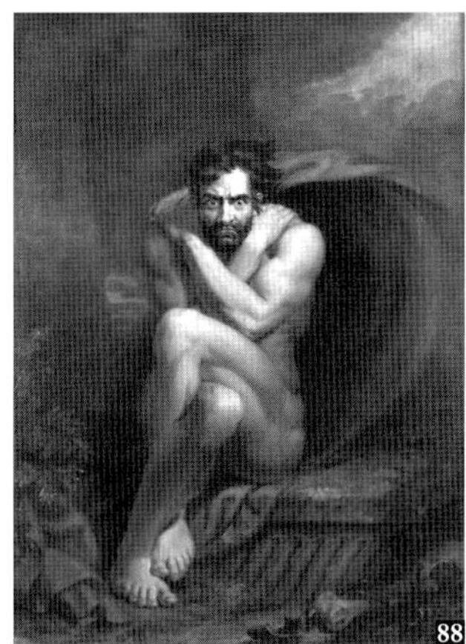

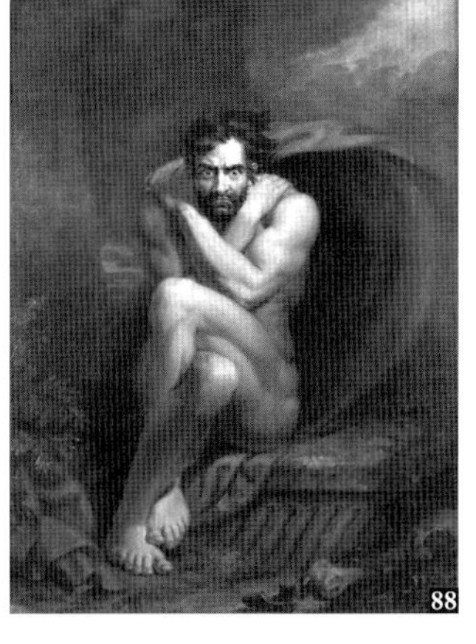

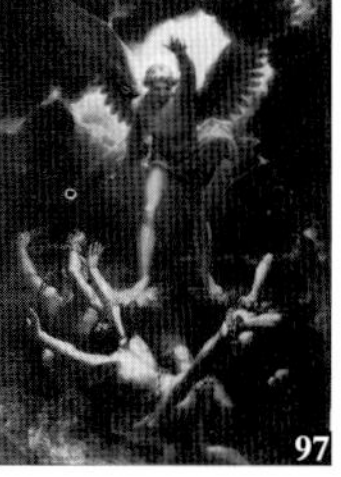

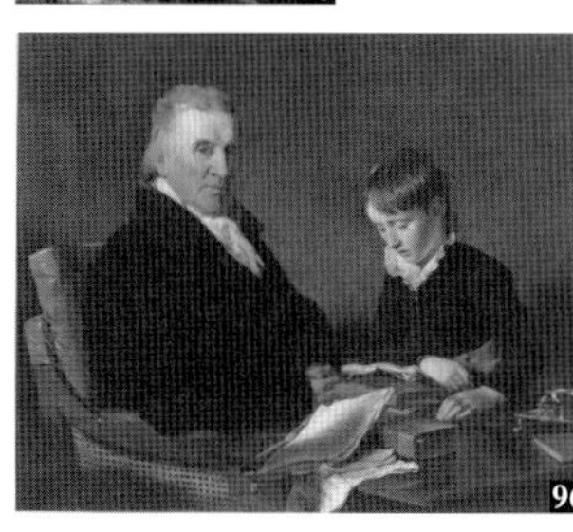

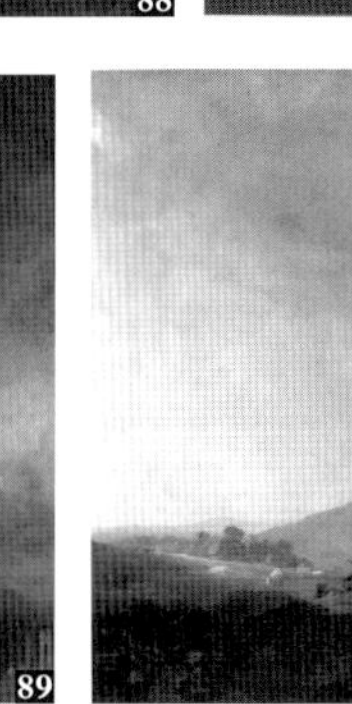

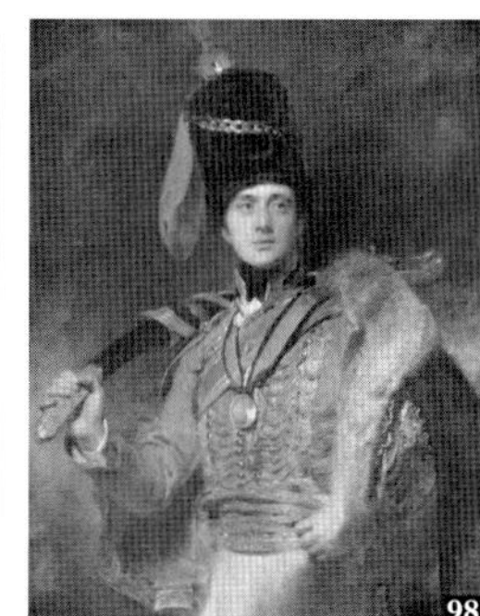

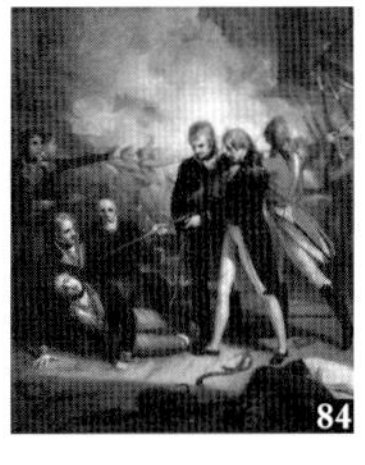

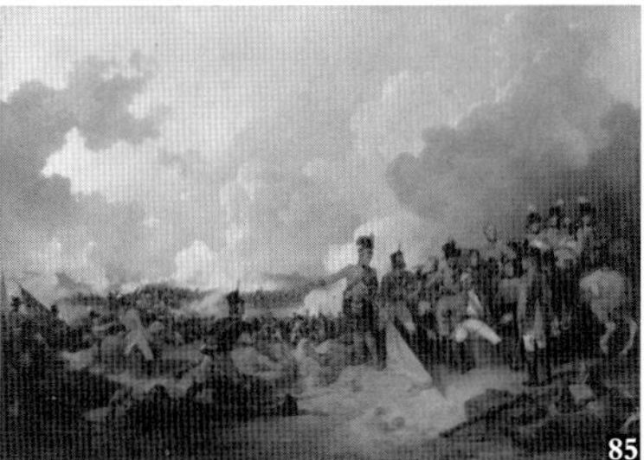

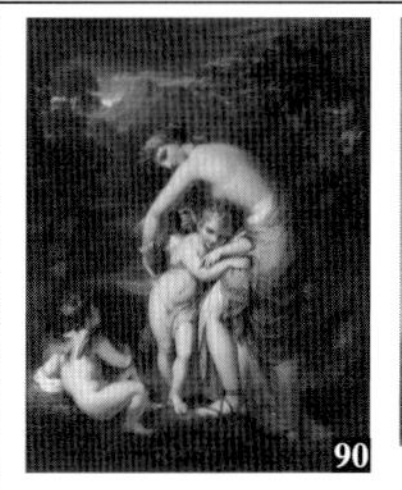

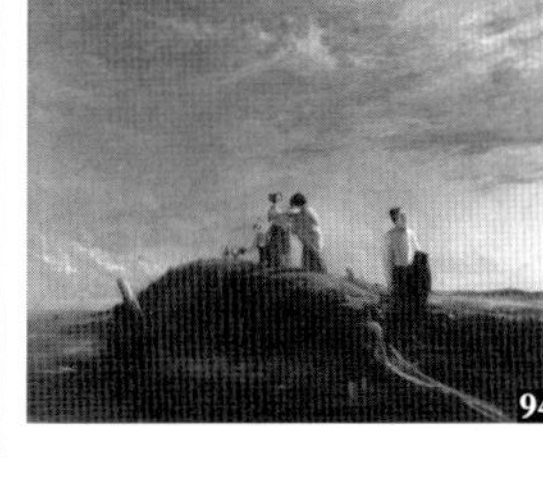

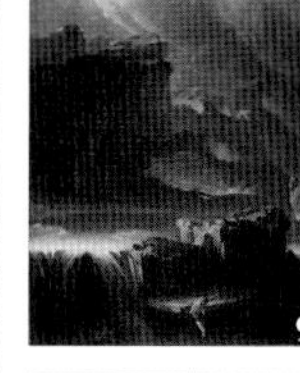

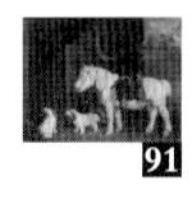

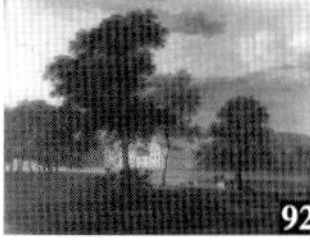

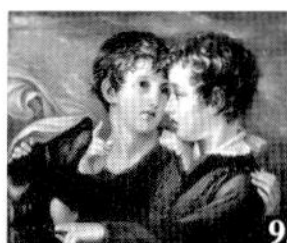

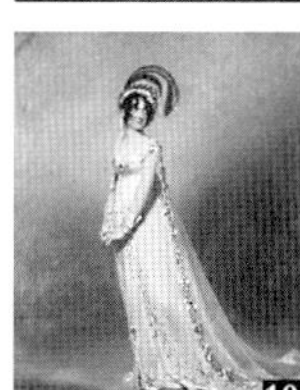

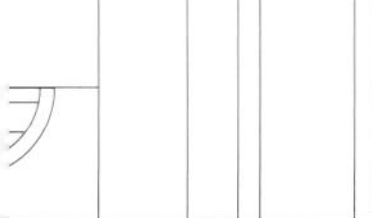

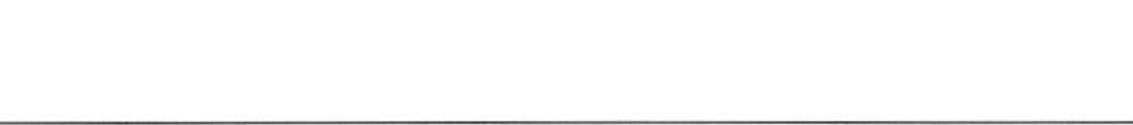

st Earl St Vincent (RA 1805)

otheosis of Nelson' (RA 1807)
n

conore in the Cavern of the Banditti (RA 1804)

, Bihar (RA 1811)
n

n
814)

f the San Nicolas (RA 1807)

85. Philippe-Jacques de Loutherbourg *Decisive Battle of Alexandria* (RA 1805)
Scottish National Portrait Gallery

86. Samuel Drummond *Captain William Rogers Capturing the Jeune Richard* (RA 1808)
National Maritime Museum, Greenwich

87. Sir Augustus Wall Callcott *Morning* (RA 1811)
Royal Academy of Arts

88. George Dawe *The Demoniac* (RA 1811)
Royal Academy of Arts

89. Thomas Phillips *Lord Byron in Albanian Costume* (RA 1814)
Government Art Collection (H.M. Embassy Athens)

90. Henry Howard *Venus and Cupid* (RA 1810)
Yale Center for British Art, Paul Mellon Collection

91. Abraham Cooper *"Scrub": A Shooting Pony and Two Clumber Spaniels* (RA 1815)
National Trust (Stourhead)

92. Philip Hutchins Rogers *West View of Saltram, the Seat of Lord Boringdon* (RA 1813)
National Trust (Saltram)

93. Robert Fagan *Sarah and Geoffrey, the Children of Lord Amherst* (RA 1812)
National Gallery of Ireland

94. William Collins *The Reluctant Departure* (RA 1815)
Birmingham Museums and Art Gallery

95. Sir Augustus Wall Callcott *Cow Boys* (RA 1807)
Herbert Art Gallery and Museum, Coventry Arts and Heritage

96. Ramsay Richard Reinagle *Francis Noel Clarke Mundy and his Grandson, William Mundy* (RA 1810)
Yale Center for British Art, Paul Mellon Collection

97. Henry Howard *The Sixth Trumpet Soundeth* (RA 1804)
Royal Academy of Arts

98. Sir Thomas Lawrence *Lieutenant-General the Hon. Sir Charles Stewart* (RA 1813)
National Portrait Gallery, London

99. John Martin *Sadak in Search of the Waters of Oblivion* (RA 1812)
Southampton City Art Gallery

100. Henry Singleton *Maria Davison as Juliana in 'The Honey Moon'* (RA 1805)
Garrick Club

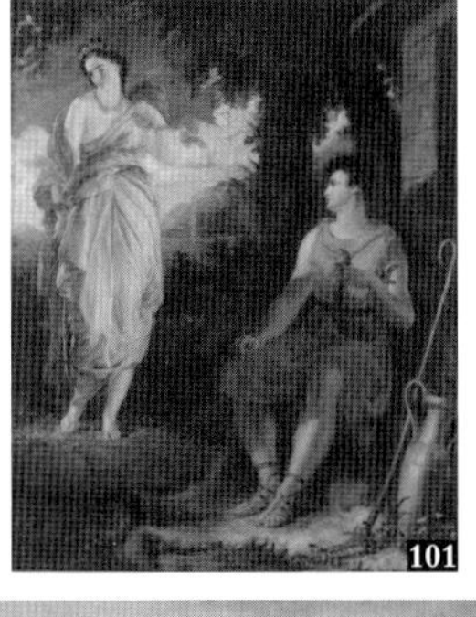
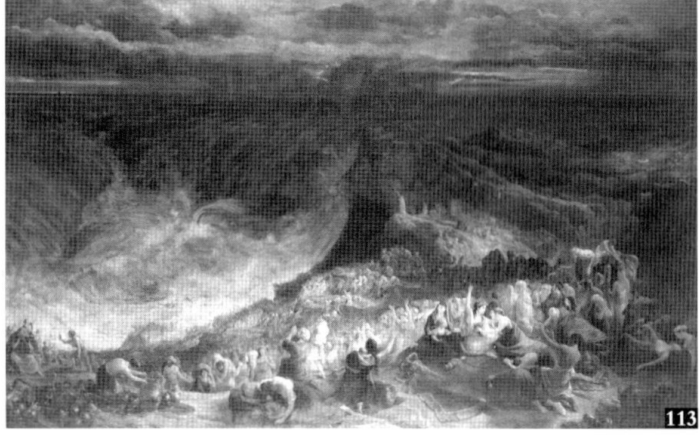
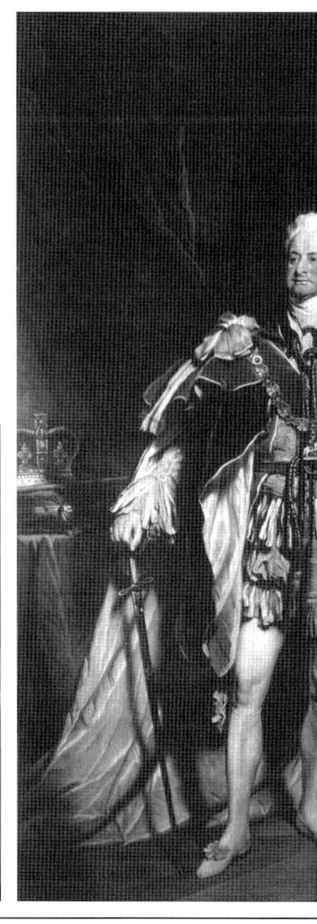
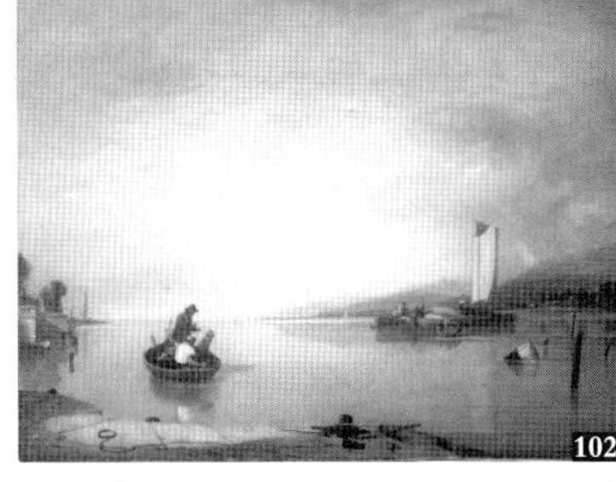
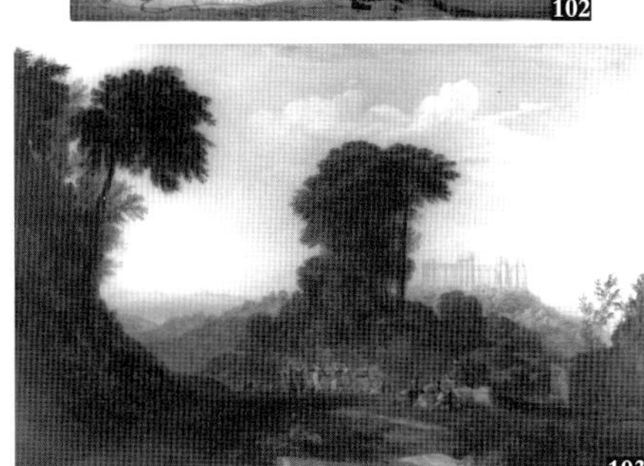
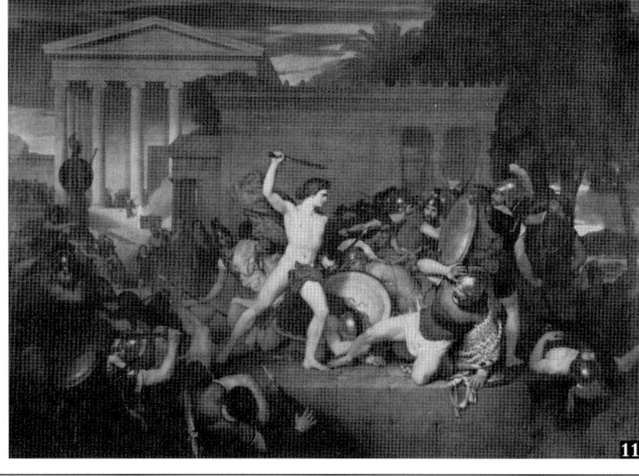
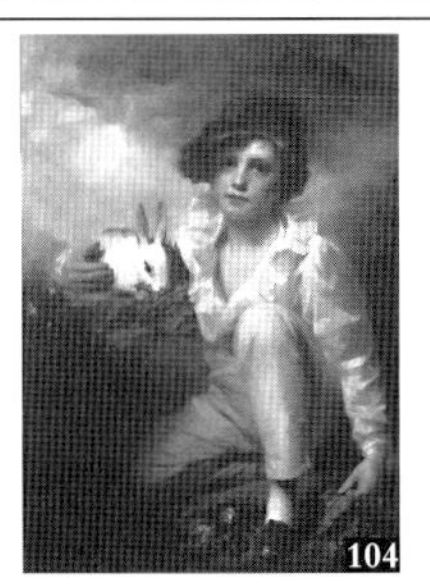
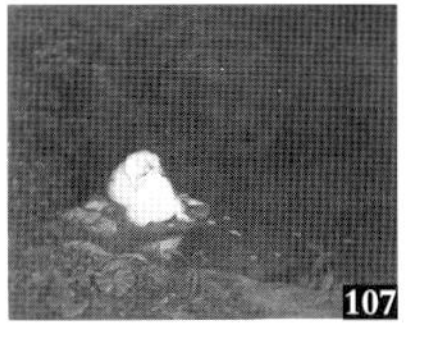
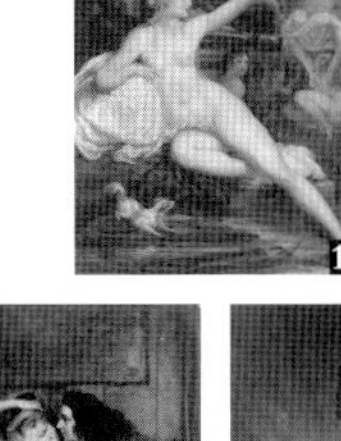
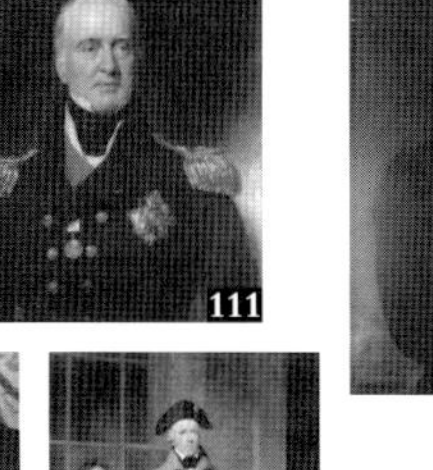
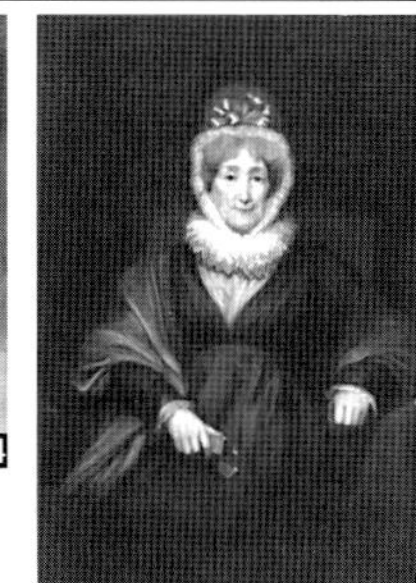
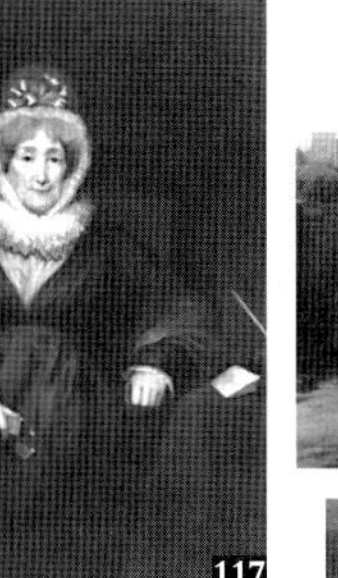
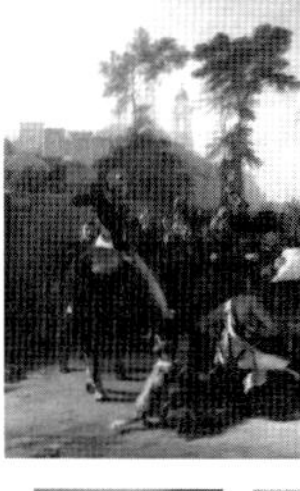
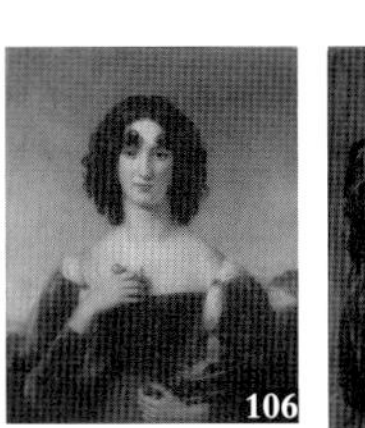
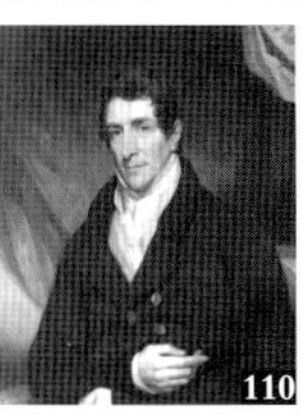
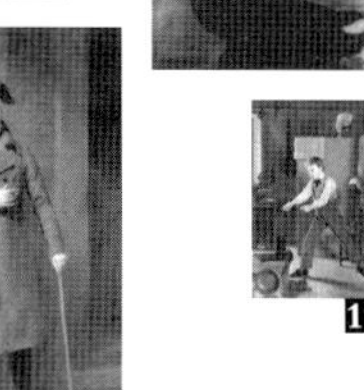
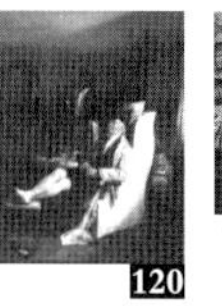
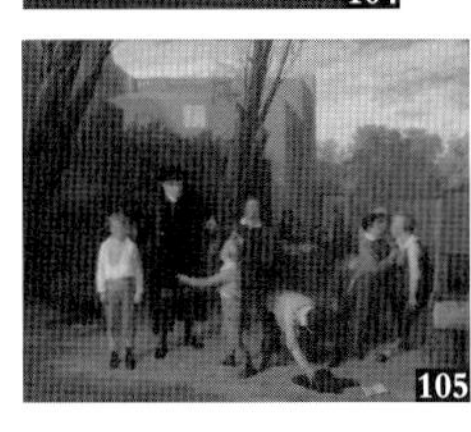

WALL 4 (SOUTH)

101. Benjamin Robert Haydon *Venus and Anchises* (RA 1826)
Yale Center for British Art, Paul Mellon Collection

102. Augustus Wall Callcott *Dead Calm: Fishing Boats off Cowes Castle* (RA 1827)
National Maritime Museum, Greenwich

103. JMW Turner *The Temple of Jupiter Panellenius, in the Island of Aegina* (RA 1816)
Collection of the Duke of Northumberland

104. Henry Raeburn *Boy and Rabbit* (RA 1816)
Royal Academy of Arts

105. William Mulready *The Fight Interrupted* (RA 1816)
Victoria and Albert Museum

106. Henry Howard *The Florentine Girl ('The Artist's Daughter')* (RA 1827)
Tate Britain

107. Francis Danby *Disappointed Love* (RA 1821)
Victoria and Albert Museum

108. James Ward *Diana at the Bath* (RA 1830)
Yale Center for British Art, Paul Mellon Collection

109. Charles Robert Leslie *Uncle Toby and the Widow Wadman from 'Tristram Shandy'* (RA 1831)
Tate Britain

110. John James Halls *Thomas Denman, 1st Baron Denman* (RA 1819)
National Portrait Gallery, London

111. Samuel Lane *Sir Pulteney Malcolm* (RA 1836)
Scottish National Portrait Gallery

112. Sir Charles Lock Eastlake *The Spartan Isadas* (RA 1827)
Trustees of the Chatsworth Settlement

113. Francis Danby *The Delivery of Israel out of Egypt* (RA 1825)
Harris Museum and Art Gallery, Preston

114. Sir George Hayter *Lord Lynedoch* (RA 1824)
Scottish National Portrait Gallery

115. George Clint *Charles Matthews as Monsieur Mallet* (RA 1832)
Garrick Club

116. Thomas Sword Good *Practice ('The Wig*
Private Collection

117. Henry William Pickersgill *Hannah More*
National Portrait Gallery, London

118. Sir Martin Archer Shee *William IV* (RA
Royal Academy of Arts

119. David Wilkie *Chelsea Pensioners*
Victoria and Albert Museum (Apsley House)

120. William Kidd *Indulging* (RA 1832)
National Gallery of Scotland

121. George Richmond *Christ and the Woma*
Tate Britain

122. Samuel Palmer *The Waterfalls at Pistil M*
Tate Britain

123. William Etty *A Family of the Forests ("Th*
York City Art Gallery

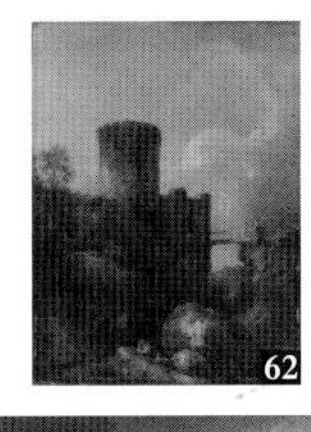

62

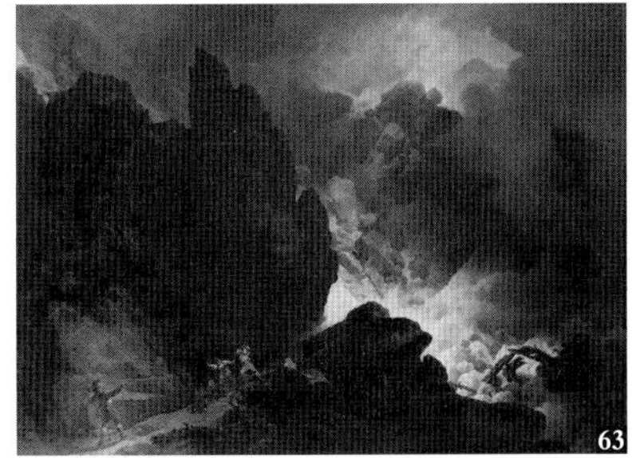

63

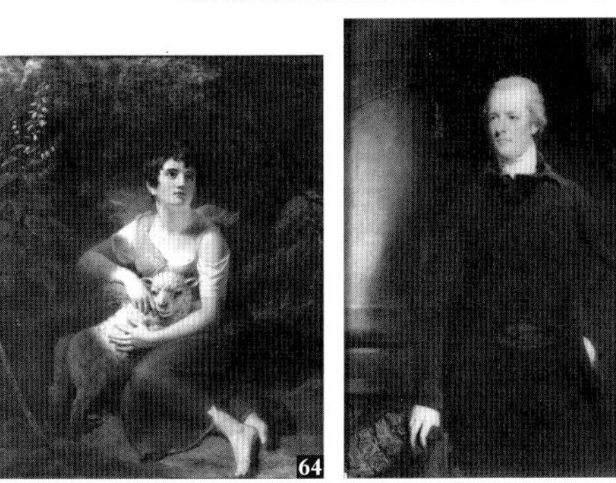

64

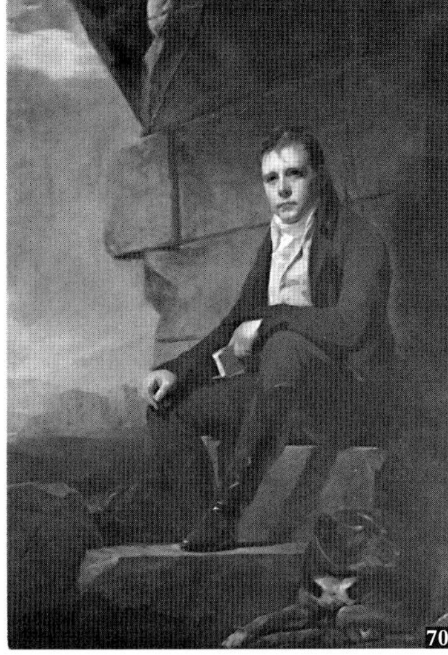

70

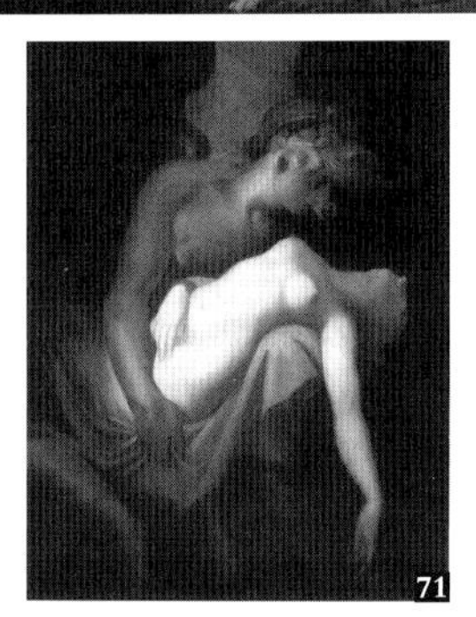

71

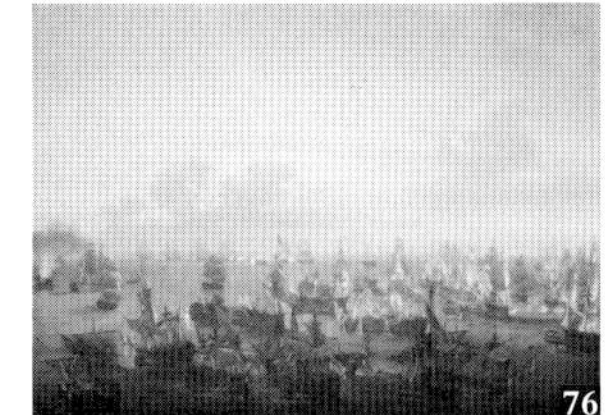

76

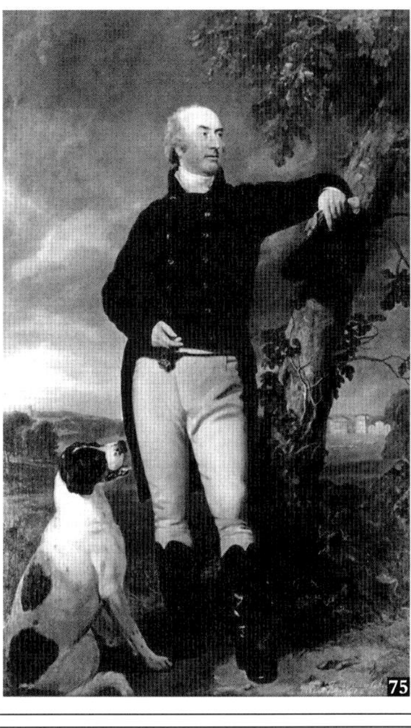

75

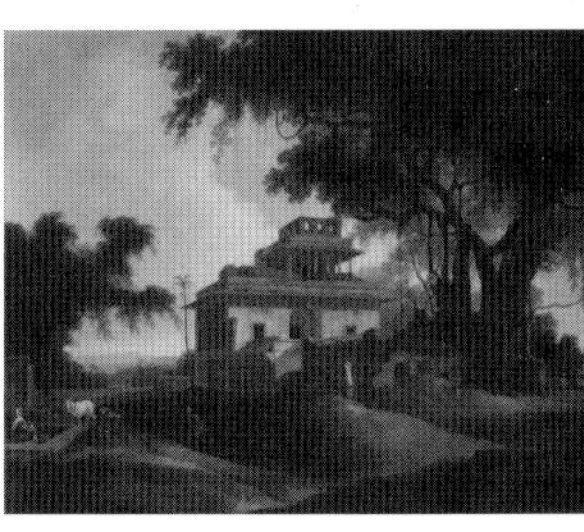

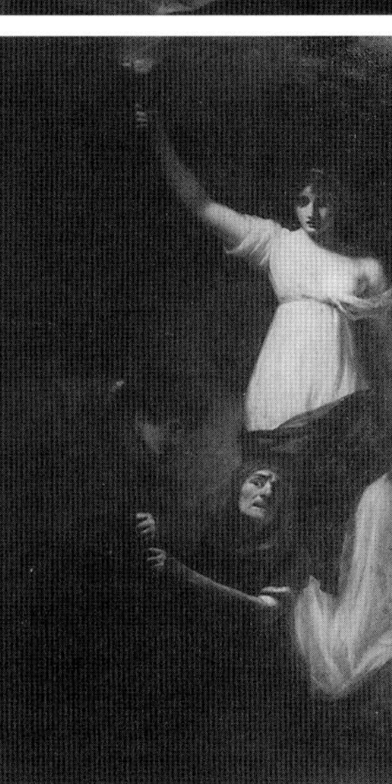

69

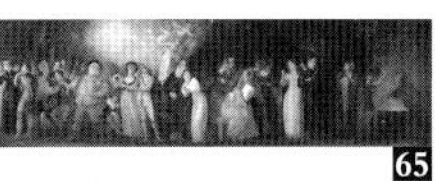

65

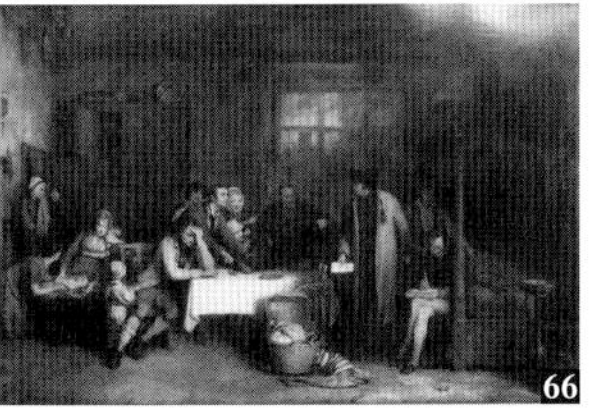

66

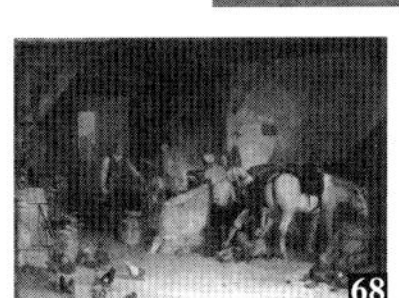

67

68

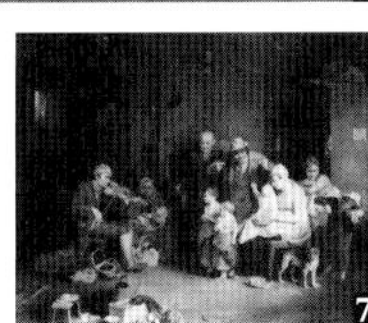

73

72

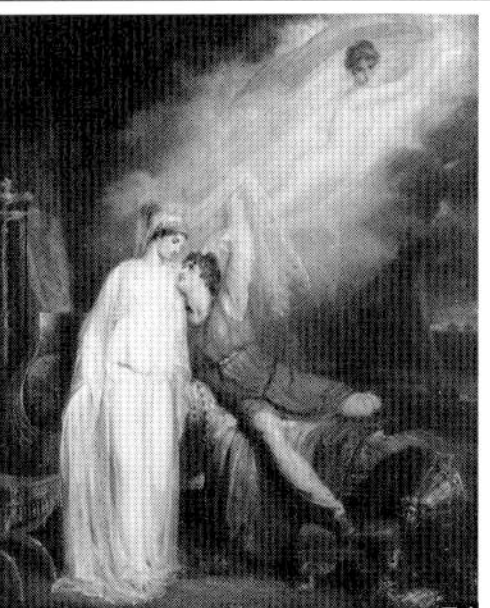

74

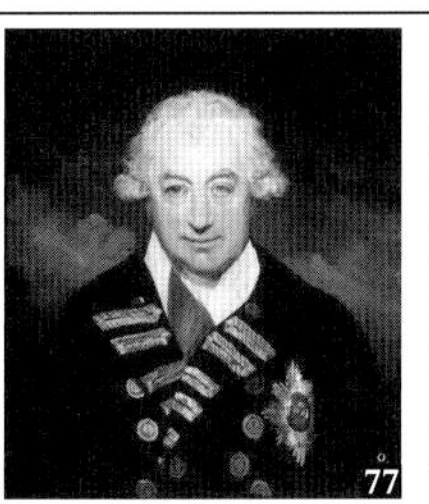

77

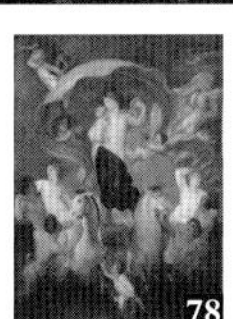

78

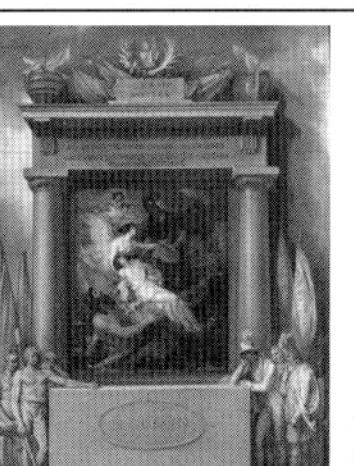

79

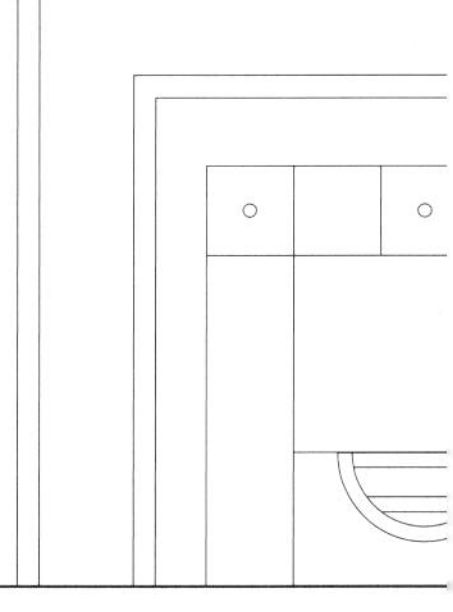

WALL 3 (EAST)

2. Sir George Beaumont *Entrance to Conway Castle* (RA 1810)
ale Center for British Art, Paul Mellon Collection

3. Philippe-Jacques de Loutherbourg *An Avalanche in the Alps* (RA 1804)
ate Britain

4. Samuel Woodforde *A Shepherdess with a Lamb in a Storm* (RA 1812)
ational Trust (Stourhead)

5. Thomas Stothard *Shakespearean Characters* (RA 1813)
ate Britain

6. David Wilkie *Distraining for Rent* (RA 1815)
ational Gallery of Scotland

7. John Constable *The Church Porch, East Bergholt* (RA 1810)
ate Britain

8. JMW Turner *A Country Blacksmith disputing upon the Price of Iron* (RA 1807)
ate Britain

69. John Hoppner *The Rt. Hon. William Pitt* (RA 1806)
Private Collection

70. Henry Raeburn *Sir Walter Scott* (RA 1810)
In the collections of the Duke of Buccleuch and Queensberry KT

71. Henry Fuseli *Amor Reviving Psyche* (RA 1812)
Kunsthaus, Zürich (Donated by Union Bank of Switzerland)

72. JMW Turner *Tabley, the Seat of Sir J. F. Leicester Bart.: Calm Morning* (RA 1809)
Tate Britain

73. David Wilkie *The Blind Fiddler* (RA 1807)
Tate Britain

74. Richard Westall *The Reconciliation of Paris and Helena* (RA 1805)
Tate Britain

75. Ramsay Richard Reinagle *Thomas William Coke, 1st Earl of Leicester, M.P.* (RA 1815)
By kind permission of the Earl of Leicester and Trustees of the Holkham Estate

76. Nicholas Pocock *The Battle of Trafalgar: End of the Action* (RA 1807)
National Maritime Museum, Greenwich

77. Sir William Beechey *Rear-Admiral John Jervis,*
National Maritime Museum, Greenwich

78. Thomas Stothard *Amphitrite* (RA 1812)
Birmingham Museums and Art Gallery

79. Benjamin West *Project for a Monument: 'The A*
Yale Center for British Art, Paul Mellon Collecti

80. John Opie *Gil Blas Taking the Key from Dame*
Maidstone Museum and Bentlif Art Gallery

81. Thomas Daniell *Ruins of the Naurattan, Sasara*
Yale Center for British Art, Paul Mellon Collecti

82. James Ward *Eagle, a Stallion* (RA 1810)
Yale Center for British Art, Paul Mellon Collecti

83. Thomas Lawrence *Lady Leicester as Hope* (RA
Tabley House Collection Trust

84. Richard Westall *Nelson Receiving the Surrender*
National Maritime Museum, Greenwich

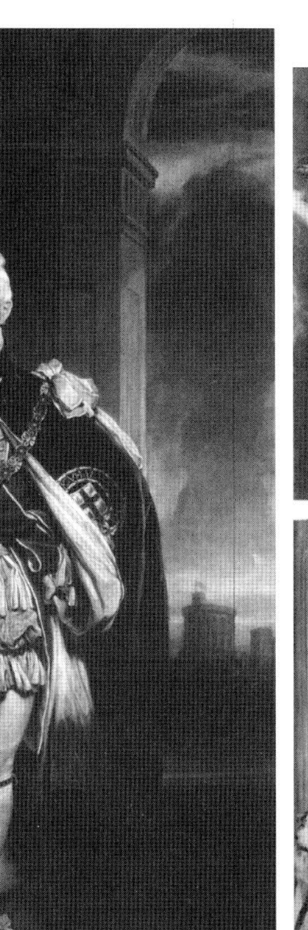
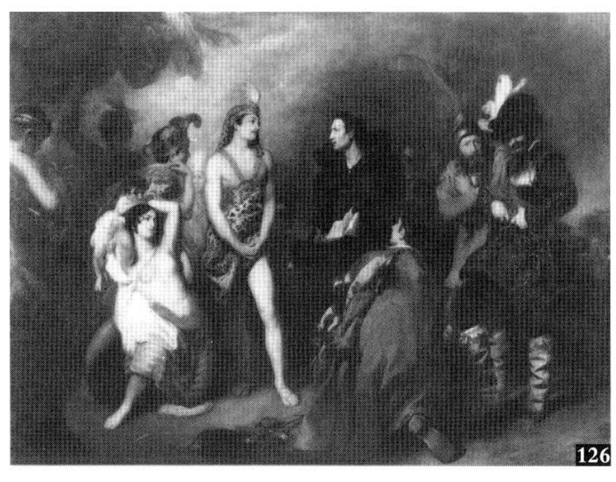
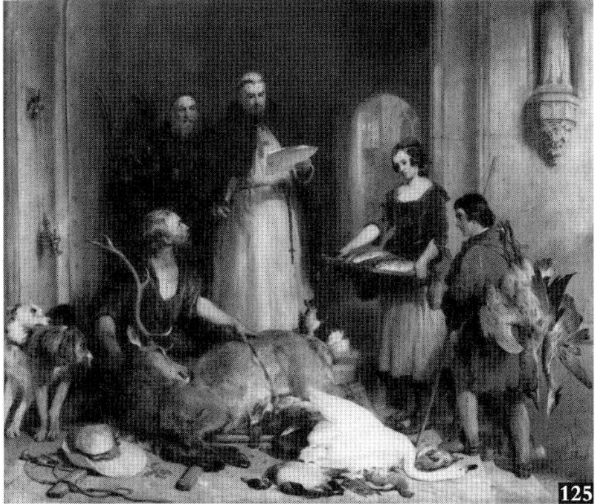
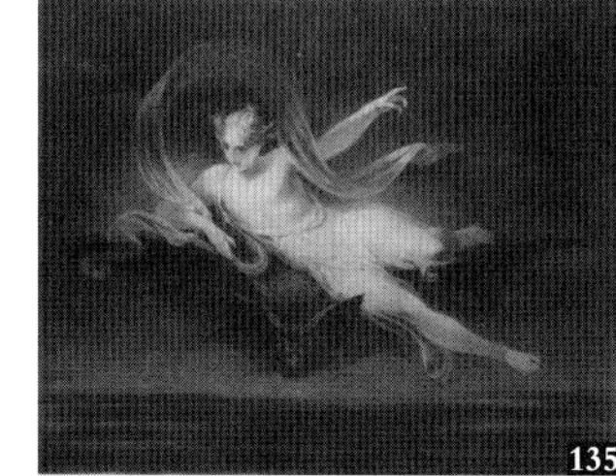
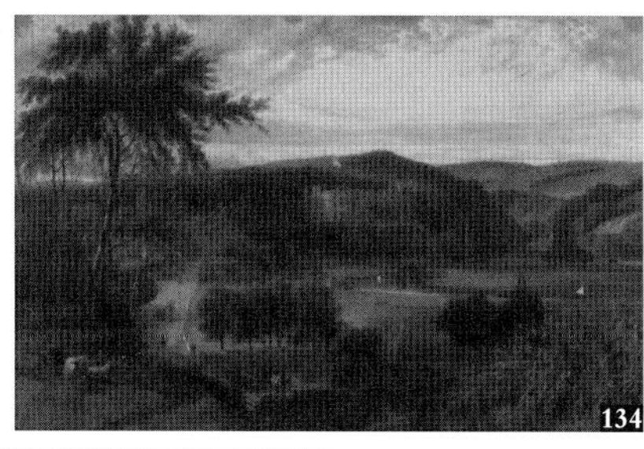
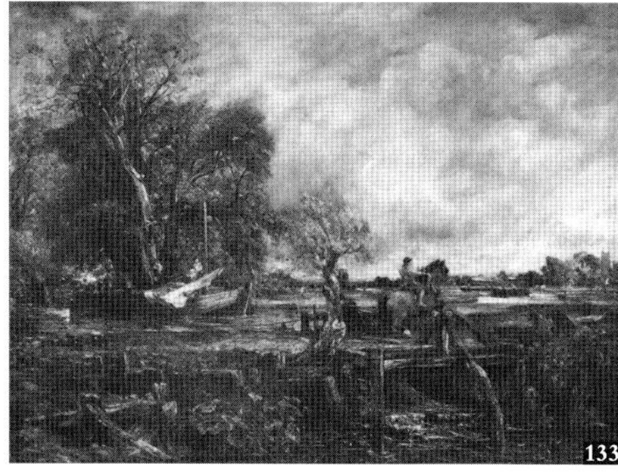
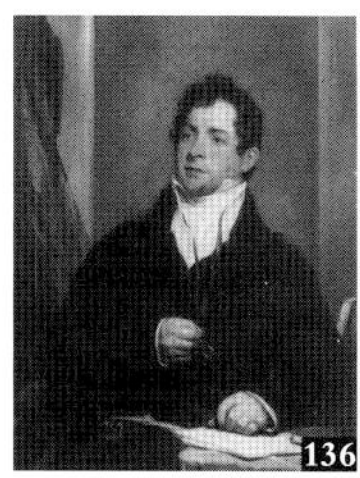
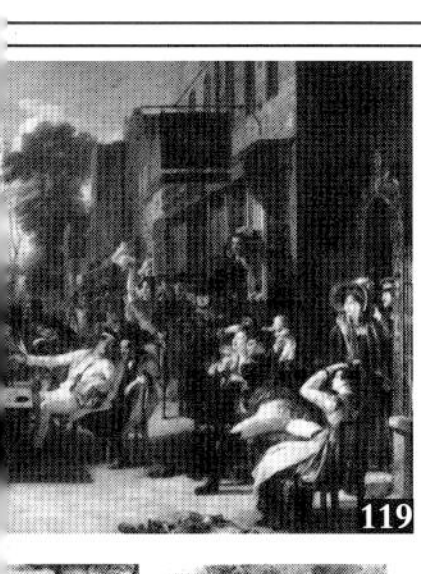
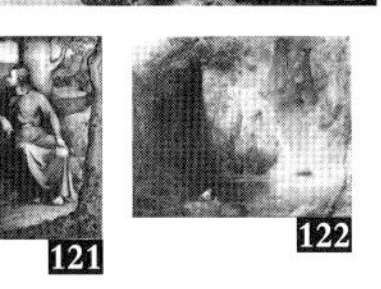
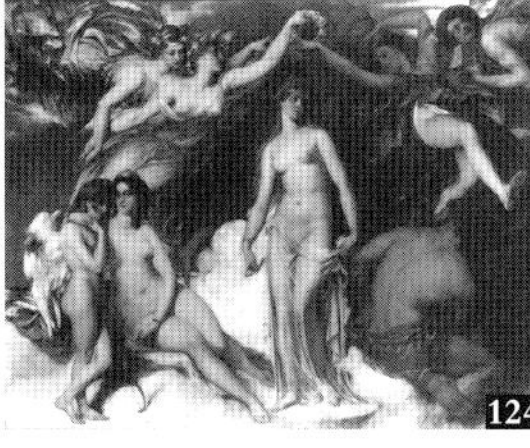
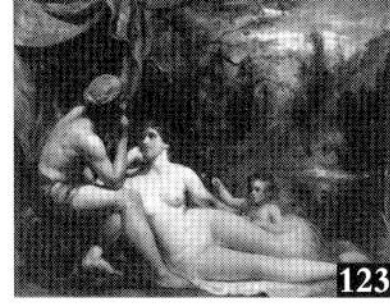
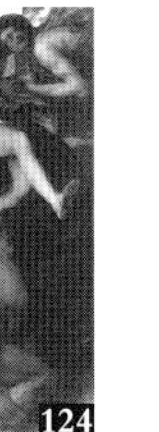
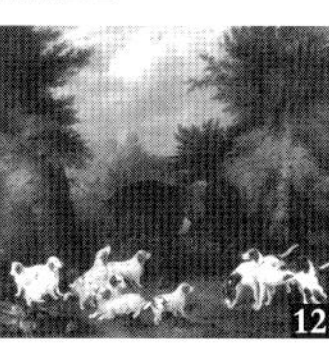
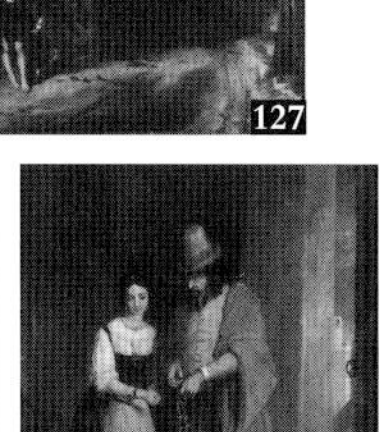
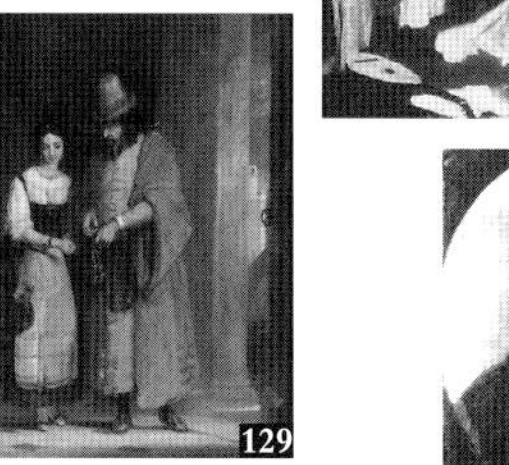
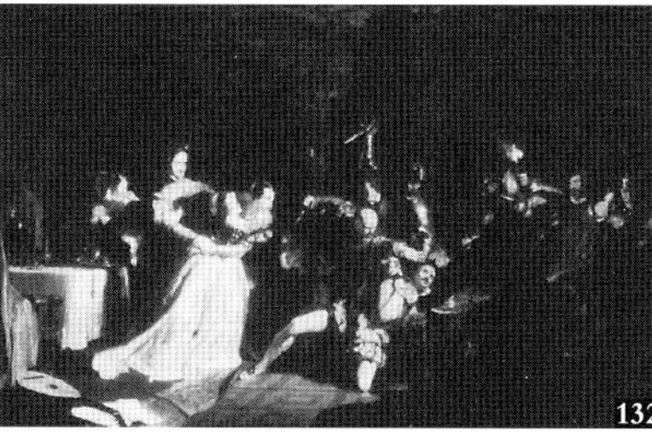
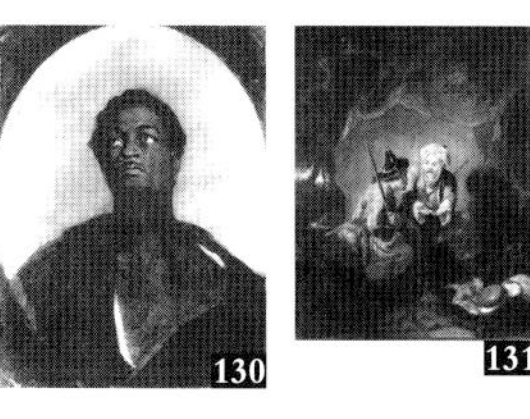
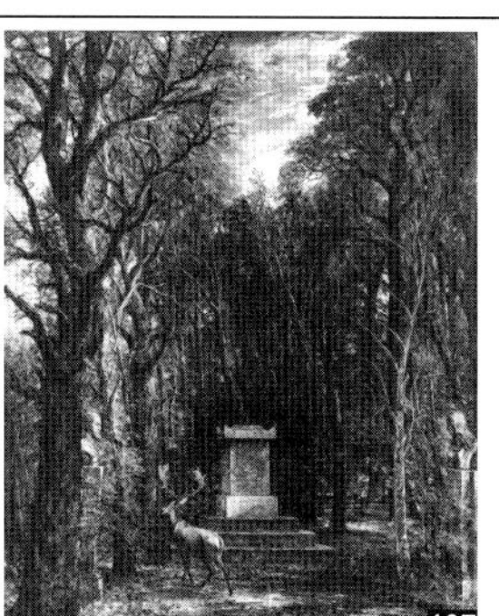

Recreation of the exhibition by Amanda Robinson

·aker's Apprentice') (RA 1823)

RA 1822)

·835)

of Samaria (RA 1828)

vddach, North Wales (RA 1836)

y lived with calm untroubled mind.") (RA 1836)

124. William Etty *Pandora* (RA 1824)
Leeds Museums and Galleries

125. Sir Edwin Landseer *Bolton Abbey in the Olden Time* (RA 1834)
Trustees of the Chatsworth Settlement

126. Henry Perronet Briggs *The First Interview between the Spaniards and Peruvians* (RA 1826)
Tate Britain

127. William Collins *Coming Events ('Rustic Civility')* (RA 1832)
Trustees of the Chatsworth Settlement

128. George Morley *A Favourite Shooting Pony and Dogs* (RA 1835)
By kind permission of his Grace the Duke of Norfolk

129. Gilbert Stuart Newton *Shylock and Jessica from 'The Merchant of Venice'* (RA 1830)
Yale Center for British Art, Paul Mellon Collection

130. John Simpson *Head of a Negro* (RA 1827)
Tate Britain

131. William Allan *Tartar Robbers Dividing the Spoil* (RA 1817)
Tate Britain

132. William Allan *The Murder of David Rizzio* (RA 1833)
National Gallery of Scotland

133. John Constable *The Leaping Horse* (RA 1825)
Royal Academy of Arts

134. William Daniell *Arundel Castle from the Littlehampton Road* (RA 1823)
By kind permission of his Grace the Duke of Norfolk

135. Henry Singleton *Ariel on a Bat's Back* (RA 1819)
Tate Britain

136. Sir Martin Archer Shee *Thomas Moore* (RA 1817)
National Gallery of Ireland

137. John Constable *Cenotaph to the Memory of Sir Joshua Reynolds* (RA 1836)
The National Gallery, London

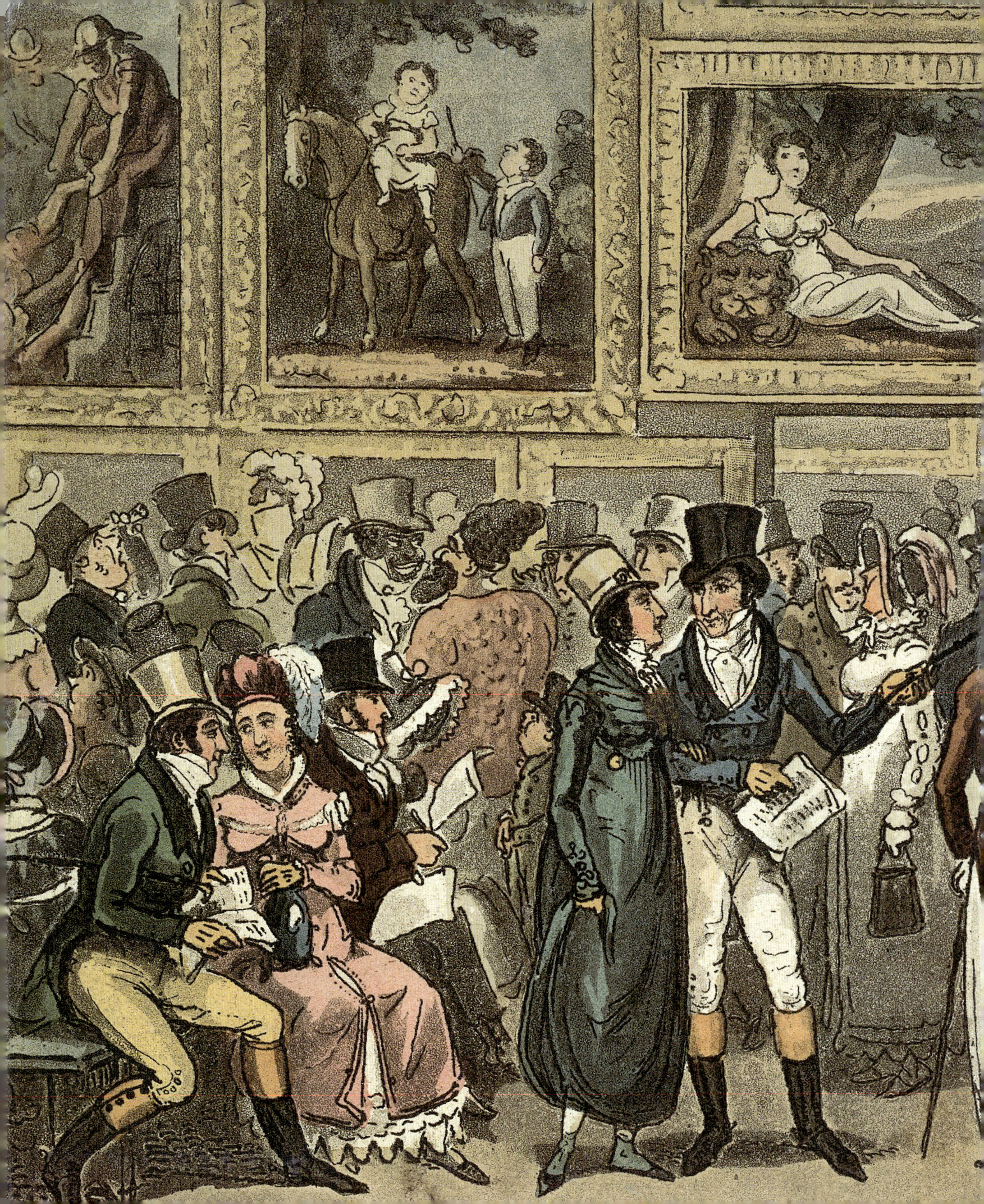